# Political Economy and the Changing Global Order

**Second Edition**

Edited by
Richard Stubbs and
Geoffrey R.D. Underhill

**OXFORD**
UNIVERSITY PRESS

*In Memory of Susan Strange*
*1923–1988*

## OXFORD
### UNIVERSITY PRESS

70 Wynford Drive, Don Mills, Ontario M3C 1J9
www.oupcan.com

Oxford University Press is a department of
the University of Oxford. It furthers the University's
objective of excellence in research, scholarship,
and education by publishing worldwide in

Oxford  New York
Athens  Auckland  Bangkok  Bogotà  Buenos Aires
Calcutta  Cape Town  Chennai  Dar es Salaam  Delhi
Florence  Hong Kong  Istanbul  Karachi  Kuala Lumpur
Madrid  Melbourne  Mexico City  Mumbai  Nairobi
Paris  São Paulo  Singapore  Taipei  Tokyo
Toronto  Warsaw

with associated companies in  Berlin  Ibadan

Oxford is a trade mark of Oxford University Press
in the UK and in certain other countries

Published in Canada
by Oxford University Press

Copyright © Oxford University Press Canada 2000

Cover & Text Design: Brett J. Miller
Cover Image: © Paul Aresu/FPG International LLC

**Canadian Cataloguing in Publication Data**

Main entry under title:

Political economy and the changing global order
2nd ed.

Includes bibliographical references and index.
ISBN 0–19–541464–0

1. International economic relations.
2. Economic history—1990–  .
3. World politics—1989–  .  I. Stubbs, Richard.
II. Underhill, Geoffrey R.D.

HF1359.P65 1999   337   C99–931726–1

1 2 3 4 — 03 02 01 00

This book is printed on permanent (acid-free) paper ∞

Printed in Canada

# Contents

## III  Regional Dynamics

# IV  Responses to Globalization

# Abbreviations

ACCs advanced capitalist countries

AFTA ASEAN Free Trade Area

AFL-CIO American Federation of Labor-Congress of Industrial Organizations (US)

AMF Asian Monetary Fund

AMS aggregate measure of support

AMUE Association for Monetary Union in Europe

ANZCERTA Australia-New Zealand Closer Economic Relations Trade Agreement

APEC Asia-Pacific Economic Co-operation

ARF ASEAN Regional Forum

ASEAN Association of Southeast Asian Nations

ASEM Asia-Europe Meeting process

BIS Bank for International Settlements

CACM Central American Common Market

CAG Competitiveness Advisory Group

CAP Common Agricultural Policy

CCET Centre for Co-operation with the Economies in Transition

CCP Chinese Communist Party

CEFTA Central European Free Trade Agreement

CEO chief executive officer

CET Common External Tariff

CFSP Common Foreign and Security Policy

CIT countries in transition

CITES Convention on International Trade in Endangered Species

CLM-WG Cambodia-Laos-Myanmar Working Group

CNC computerized numerical controller

CNCE National Commission for External Trade

COMESA Common Market for Eastern and Southern Africa

CTM Confederación de Trabajadores de México

DAC Development Assistance Committee

DSB Dispute Settlement Body

EAC East African Co-operation

EAEC East Asian Economic Caucus

EBRD European Bank for Reconstruction and Development

ECA Economic Commission for Africa

EC European Community

EEC European Economic Community

ECOMOG Economic Community of West African States Cease Fire Monitoring Group

ECOWAS Economic Community of West African States

EFTA European Free Trade Association

EMEs emerging market economies

EMU Economic and Monetary Union

EPZs export processing zones

ERT European Round Table of Industrialists

EU European Union

FAO Food and Agriculture Organization

FDI foreign direct investment

FIFA Fédération internationale de football association

FLG Financial Leaders Group

FREPASO Frente Pais Solidario

FTA  free trade agreement

FTAA  Free Trade Area of the Americas

FZLN  Frente Zapatista de Liberacion Naciónal

GATS  General Agreement on Trade in Services

GATT  General Agreement on Tariffs and Trade

GDP  gross domestic product

GMPs  genetically modified products

GNP  gross national product

HST  hegemonic stability theory

ICFTU  International Confederation of Free Trade Unions

IBRD  International Bank for Reconstruction and Development

IFIs  international financial institutions

IGAD  Intergovernmental Authority on Development

ILO  International Labour Organization

IMF  International Monetary Fund

IPC  Intellectual Property Committee

IPE  international political economy

IR  international relations

ITO  International Trade Organization

JHA  Justice and Home Affairs

JICA  Japan International Co-operation Agency

KMP  The Peasant Movement of the Philippines

KRRS  Karnataka State Farmers' Association

LAFTA  Latin American Free Trade Area

LAIA  Latin American Integration Association

LDCs  less-developed countries

LTCM  long-term credit management

MAI  Multilateral Agreement on Investment

MITI  Ministry of International Trade and Industry (Japan)

MERCOSUR  Mercado Común del Sur

MFN  most-favoured nation

MNCs  multinational corporations

MNEs  multinational enterprises

NAFTA  North American Free Trade Agreement

NATO  North Atlantic Treaty Organization

NC  numerical controller

NGOs  non-governmental organizations

NICs  newly industrialized countries

NST  Movemento sem Terra

NTBs  non-tariff barriers

ODA  official development assistance

OECD  Organization for Economic Co-operation and Development

OPEC  Organization of Petroleum Exporting Countries

OSCE  Organization for Security and Co-operation in Europe

PCAs  Partnership and Co-operation Agreements

PGA  People's Global Action against Free trade and the World Trade Organization

PMU  Project Management Unit

PRI  Partido Revolucionario Institucional

RMB  Renminbi

RTZ  Rio Tinto Zinc Mining and Exploration Limited

SAA  South African Airways

SAB  South African Breweries Limited

SADC  Southern African Development Community

SAFTA  South American Free Trade Area

SAPs  structural adjustment policies

SDIs  spatial developmental initiatives

SEA  Single European Act

SEZ  special economic zone

SMP  Single Market Program

SOEs  state-owned enterprises

SPD  Social Democratic Party

SWIFT  Society of Worldwide Interbank Financial Telecommunications

TFAP  Tropical Forestry Action Plan

TNCs  transnational corporations

TRIMs  trade-related investment measures

TRIPs  trade-related intellectual property rights

UCR  Union Civica Radical

UK  United Kingdom

UMNO  United Malays' National Organization

UN  United Nations

UNCTAD  United Nations Conference on Trade and Development

UNICE  Union of Industrial and Employers' Confederations of Europe

UNRISD  United Nations Research Institute for Social Development

UNSNA  United Nations System of National Accounts

US  United States of America

USTR  United States Trade Representative

VERs  voluntary export restraints

WID  Women in Development

WRI  World Resources Institute

WTO  World Trade Organization

# Preface

The first edition of this book was prompted by the need to introduce students to the rapid changes taking place in the global economy in the early 1990s. The pace of change has not abated in the second half of the 1990s. The relatively strong and surprisingly sustained performance of the North American economies, the increasing economic integration of the European Union, and the economic crises in Asia and Russia all attest to the increasing pace and apparent unpredictability of changes to the global economic order. Perhaps the only certainty is that during the first years of the next millennium more change will occur, affecting the lives of millions. The need to understand the major trends in the global economy and to assess how best to analyse these trends is just as compelling as it was five years ago. With this in mind, and urged on by a number of our colleagues who noted the success of the first edition, we decided to put together a new edition of the book.

The contributions to the first edition focused principally on the question, 'How have we arrived where we are in the changing global order?' In other words, how did a dynamic, market-oriented economy emerge in the postwar period? In turn, the second edition asks, 'How will the global order unfold as we move into the next millennium?' Once again we emphasize the linkages between the political and the economic domains, on the one hand, and between the domestic and international dimensions, on the other. We focus on conceptualizing the state and its role in the international political economy, on the increasing importance of non-state actors, and on the growing influence of both public and private forms of transnational governance.

We draw attention to the complex interaction of political authorities and market structures in the global system, identifying the causes of changing economic structures in the political conflicts that take place at the individual, national, regional, and international levels of analysis. The book is organized to reflect both the issue-structure of the international political economy and the global, regional, and state levels at which these issues are debated and contested.

While the second edition of the book has roughly the same format as the first, the content has changed drastically. Only one of the chapters from the first edition, that by Gill, remains relatively intact. Two other chapters, by Whitworth and Bernard, are based on their respective chapters from the first edition but have been revised so substantially as to warrant new titles. The other 30 chapters have been written expressly for this edition. Following the successful approach used in assembling the first edition we asked each contributor, while keeping the student readership in mind, to develop an argument that briefly explores a specific aspect of IPE. Once again we are extremely grateful for the unfailing co-operation of our contributors as we put the collection together. Of course, despite the size of the volume and the number of chapters, we have not been able to cover everything and we are very conscious of the fact that inevitably specialists in one field or another will feel that we have been neglectful.

Many of our colleagues and friends have been a major source of advice, support, and encouragement. We would especially like to thank Philip G. Cerny, William D. Coleman, Daniel Drache, Eric

Helleiner, Richard Higgott, Kim Richard Nossal, Robert O'Brien, Lou Pauly, Tony Porter, Susan Sell, Grace Skogstad, and the late Susan Strange; we are sure to have missed a number. We would also like to thank the anonymous reviewer for Oxford University Press Canada; our many colleagues around the world and their students who, having used the first edition, offered advice on the second edition; and our own students who read many of the chapters for the second edition as they came in and offered their thoughts. Thanks also go to Klarka Zeman and Peter Frise for research assistance and especially to Gerald Bierling and Mara Giannotti for helping to get the manuscript ready for the publishers. At Oxford University Press Canada we would like to acknowledge the work of the staff, particularly Richard Kitowski and Phyllis Wilson and our editor, Richard Tallman.

As with the first edition we hope that this collection contributes as much to scholarship as to teaching in the field of IPE.

Richard Stubbs
Geoffrey Underhill

April 1999

# Part I

# Understanding the Changing Global Order

# Conceptualizing the Changing Global Order

## Geoffrey R.D. Underhill

Political power and wealth creation have been intimately intertwined throughout the history of the modern international system.[1] In a now classic article, Jacob Viner invoked the example of the seventeenth and eighteenth centuries when the view was strongly held that 'wealth and power are each proper ultimate ends of national policy; [and] there is a long run harmony between these ends.'[2] Whether there is harmony or tension between the two in the formation of state policies, political conflict in the international system has continued to focus on these two interrelated elements of power and wealth and on their relative distribution, thereby attracting the attention of international relations scholars. Of course, the historical setting of this conflict has undergone dramatic changes since the decline of the mercantilist system to which Viner was referring. At that time, most European absolutist monarchies saw control over both foreign and domestic economic relations as intimately related to their centralization of power.

The most recent expression of the complex relationship between power and wealth (or more specifically, between the political and economic domains) in international politics is the link between political authority, on the one hand, and the system of production and distribution of wealth referred to as the market economy, on the other. Let us first of all make an important distinction with regard to the 'market'. Historically, markets have always existed in one form or another as economic exchange relationships ('trade') among individuals, enterprises, or communities. However, the general notion of a market as a localized pattern of exchange should be distinguished from the particular form of market economy or system, with its origins in the Industrial Revolution, that we know today.[3]

This market system, characterized by industrial capital, lies at the heart of the phenomenon analysed by the classical political economists (Smith, Ricardo) and by Marx, wherein owners of capital, workers, and intermediaries are all linked in social relationships via a complex pattern of political and market institutions. These generate investment capital for the production of commodities and facilitate the circulation of money for the purchase of goods/services, land, labour, and, of course, money itself. In the mercantilist period and before, there were markets, to be sure, but there was no market system based on capital investment and industrial production; the market did not form the basis of economic and social relationships to the extent it does today. Until the Industrial Revolution and its aftermath, most domestic economies were scarcely integrated either internally or internationally; they consisted of markets that were essentially local, their development spatially limited by technology and the subsistence nature of agriculture.[4]

This market economy began to emerge in the second half of the eighteenth century and went through its 'classical' phase in the mid- to late nineteenth century.[5] National economies integrated internally as well as outwardly with the structures of international commerce. Even the market system has undergone profound transformations since its inception, with the collapse of *laissez-faire* in the 1930s and the construction of the postwar mixed economy system, which in turn underwent significant transformations from the 1970s (see Introduction to

Part II). These transformations in the market system have all been intimately bound up with important changes in the political domain. Not surprisingly, therefore, it has become largely accepted by most scholars in political economy, whether domestic or international, that an intimate and reciprocal connection exists between the control of significant resources in the market economy and the exercise of political power, even in democratic societies; changes in the nature of economic structures are bound up with political and social changes in the society in question. There is, however, considerable debate concerning the substance of this relationship and how to think about it.

The essays in this volume demonstrate why it is important to consider the relationship between the political and economic domains, between economic structures and political interaction, in contemporary international context. This is the central question of the discipline of *international political economy*. This chapter aims to demonstrate how one might meaningfully think about this relationship.

On the whole, and despite a diversity of perspectives, the contributors to this volume generally share three fundamental premises. The first is that the political and economic domains cannot be separated in any meaningful sense. When the two domains are separated in our understanding of the world around us, important errors of analysis and policy are likely to result. This implies that the dynamics of economic and security issues, of government and the market, are intimately bound up with each other in international politics, a premise that contrasts with the assumptions of traditional approaches to the discipline of international relations or, indeed, economics.

The second premise confronts a widely held intellectual orthodoxy in our societies that leaps from the pages of almost every newspaper or popular publication on the economy, as well as from the pages of economics textbooks. Most accounts of economic issues portray the state and the market as operating in contrasting realms, their dynamics conflicting the one with the other. The authors in this volume in their own ways challenge this assumption, insisting that economic structures are not the result of the spontaneous interaction of individual economic agents, even in a market setting where political authorities may refrain from direct intervention in economic decision-making. The structures of the market and of the larger political economy are inherently contestable, and this is demonstrated by the way they have developed over time. If the principal focus of political conflict, at either domestic or international levels, concerns who gets what, when, and how, and setting out the rules and framework of the market in large part determines just this, *then political interaction is the means by which economic structures, in particular the structures of the market, are established and in turn transformed.*

Understanding the global political economy therefore involves overcoming orthodoxy and understanding markets and political authorities as part of the same, integrated ensemble of governance, not as contrasting principles of social organization:

> Political interaction and conflict generate a transformation of market structure, while changes in structure simultaneously alter the competitive constraints upon agents in the political economy. The political conflicts which are the central feature of this process of structural transformation are mediated by the institutions of the state and co-operative international regimes in the global political economy.[6]

Between them, the institutions of the market and the agencies of political authority are generated by competing sociopolitical interests in a particular economic and institutional setting. The strategies of firms in economic competition are shaped by the rules and structures of the market at the same time as these economic agents employ political resources to affect the terms of competition themselves. Political interaction is therefore as central to economic development (or lack thereof) as the process of economic competition itself, and of course asymmetries of power abound.

There is then a two-way or reciprocal relationship between politics and formal political authorities, on the one hand, and economic structures and institutions, on the other, in the changing global order. As will be discussed later, this very much implies a two-way relationship between the *structures* of global markets and the *agents* of political and economic interaction that constitute them. Let us also bear in mind that any particular economic arrangement, whether mercantilism, Communist central planning, or industrial capitalism, is far from neutral in its effects on access to political resources. Only after major political conflict did the structures of the industrial market economy emerge, first in late eighteenth- and early nineteenth-century Britain[7] and eventually along distinctive national lines in Europe and elsewhere. At the same time, the process of developing a market economy resulted in profound social transformations, which in turn altered the distribution of political resources within the societies affected. By the middle of the nineteenth century the market was developing into a pattern of transnational relations, a complex that transcended borders as much as it altered social structures and relations among states.

The same could be said of the construction of the post-World War II economic order and its rapid transformation in recent years. A market is a political device to achieve certain outcomes, conferring relative benefits on some and costs on others in both political and economic terms; it is, in essence, a political institution that plays a crucial role in structuring society and international politics. The changing market structure gives rise to new patterns of economic and political forces.

The rules of the market economy, then, even in the international domain, are created and enforced through the resolution (or lack thereof) of political conflict among competing interests. Referring to the rise of the international market economy, Karl Polanyi put it in the following manner:

> the gearing of markets into a self regulatory system of tremendous power was not a result of the inherent tendency of markets towards excrescence, but rather the effect of highly artificial stimulants administered to the body social in order to meet a situation which was created by the no less artificial phenomenon of the machine.[8]

Looking at the relationship between the political and economic domains with respect to the international system is a complex task. This task is difficult enough in a domestic political setting, but when one takes into account the international setting, one encounters the twin problems of *anarchy* (lack of overarching political authority) and *levels of analysis*. This brings one to the third shared premise of the volume, and another confrontation with orthodoxy: traditional international relations approaches have emphasized a clear distinction between the dynamics of politics at the domestic and international realms, yet the authors here challenge this in important ways.

As the economies of the market system become increasingly internationalized (perhaps a more appropriate term is interpenetrated or *transnationalized*[9]) and thereby increasingly outside the direct control of individual states, the more it becomes necessary to understand the interaction of domestic and international levels of analysis. States remain the principal (and, indeed, the only legal) decision-makers in the anarchic international order, and they continue to respond to essentially domestic political constituencies. But they are far from possessing all the political and economic resources to continue meaningfully to shape the direction of political and economic development in line with national preferences.[10] With the transnationalization of economic decision-making, what were once essentially matters of domestic politics have now spilled over and become contentious in relations among states and other actors in the international system. Indeed, careful research reveals that the distinction between the domestic and international levels of analysis is in a strict sense artificial: sometimes useful for understanding a complex situation, but not necessarily corresponding to a real state of affairs. Human associations, corporations, markets, and governmental institutions all may spill across borders; what one government, actor, or group does will often affect the options and actions of others. We live in an international system characterized by a high degree of interdependence among states and their societies, at least in relative historical terms.

Therefore, the third shared premise of this volume is the intimate connection between domestic and international levels of analysis. The global political economy (and international politics as a whole) cannot meaningfully be packaged into a separate 'international' realm of politics, structured by the principle of anarchy, which generates the behaviour of an arrangement of 'units' (states) in relation to a particular distribution of power.[11] In fact, the international system is much more akin to a 'state-society complex',[12] spanning domestic and international levels of analysis, with the institutions and agencies of the state at its core. 'Levels of analysis' is an analytical tool useful only to denote the different patterns of institutional arrangements (local, domestic, interstate) that can be found in the global system. The international level of analysis, taken on its own, cannot properly be regarded as the source of an explanation: there is only one 'politics', with the state as the primary focus of political conflict in a larger state-society complex. The state manages the constraints of the domestic and international domains through domestic policy-making and intergovernmental bargaining, the one being intimately embedded in the other. This in turn implies that a vast array of different sorts of agents or actors are part of global political processes focused on the institutions of political authority, states in particular.[13]

Another way of putting this is to consider the international domain as reflecting the specific balance of social forces of the most powerful states as this balance becomes projected into the international system. As John Gerard Ruggie has written, 'to say anything sensible about the *content* of international economic orders . . . it is necessary to look at how power and legitimate social purpose become fused to project political authority into the international system.'[14]

So this book is about the relationship between the political and economic domains, between states and markets, and how that relationship plays itself out across borders. In fact, the fundamental problematic of international political economy has been described by two theorists of quite differing perspectives, Robert Gilpin and Immanuel Wallerstein, in roughly similar terms,[15] that is, that our subject is the interaction of a transnational market economy with a system of competitive states (which, for the record, often co-operate on matters related to the maintenance of a transnational economy). The book will attempt to conceptualize (in Part I) and analyse (in Part II) the principal issues around which this interaction takes place. Part III will examine the dynamics of particular regions, while Part IV will review the responses of both state and non-state actors to what has been named, for better or for worse, globalization.

Indeed, the structure of this book, divided into sections on theory, global issues, regional dynamics, and strategies and responses, represents a commitment to highlight the relationship among levels of analysis. To this end, the volume has sought to include the expertise of specialists in comparative and regional political economy where appropriate. The contributors put forward a diversity of views, but they all tend to share the premises referred to above. It is most important to draw the connections among the structure of the economic domain, the (politicized) interests of the social groups and actors that participate in this structure (the *structure-agent* question), and the patterns of political conflict and change that take place within a particular set of domestic and international institutions. These institutions tend to 'load the dice' in political conflict, enhancing the political resources of some states, groups, or actors as opposed to others. The question of institutions is important in the changing global order, as institutions struggle to keep up with rapid, underlying changes in the international system.

## Theoretical Debates in the Literature

One contribution of a volume such as this is to provide the student with a guide to the theoretical debates in the literature of the discipline. Many texts have adopted the 'three models' or 'ideologies' approach, looking at liberal, Marxist, and realist (sometimes called economic nationalist/mercantilist) approaches as competing models of world order. The authors then tend to settle for one or another approach, or aim for some sort of synthesis, or worse, simply despair at their incompatibility. However, this traditional presentation of the debates in the literature yields rather stale and, indeed, rigid categories, given the diversity *within* each and the cross-fertilization *among* them. There is a tendency to reduce theoretical discussion in IPE to competing and mutually exclusive, even irreconcilable, ideologies.

One problem is that there are perspectives beyond these three, such as post-modernist,[16] environmentalist (see chapter by Helleiner), and feminist analyses of the discipline (see chapters by Whitworth and by Marchand). Most importantly, this focus on competing ideological paradigms severs the connection between the material economic interests of actors or groups and the ideas they espouse: for example, while some might benefit from regulation, powerful firms with a strong competitive position in the international economy tend to argue for relatively unregulated or 'liberal' international conditions that allow them to take unimpeded advantage of their market power. Unless this connection between policy preferences (as expressed in ideas) and concrete economic interests is maintained, the debate becomes detached from the real world of political conflict over who gets what, when, and where: Robert Cox has gone so far as to assert that 'Theory is always for someone and for some purpose.'[17]

It is none the less difficult to avoid discussing these three approaches, from which so much contemporary theory derives or against which it reacts. It is, however, possible to escape the traditional procedure of comparing 'incompatible' models with one another, which only leads to the sterile conclusion that there is little agreement and, consequently, very little real progress on what matters most: deepening theoretical understanding. The purpose of this section, then, is to assess critically how *adequately* each deals with the central theoretical *issues* in international political economy, the better to indicate the direction for further progress.

These fundamental theoretical problems or issues have been hinted at above. International political economy is concerned first of all with the relationship between the economic and political domains across territorial boundaries. Second, attention should be drawn to the role of the state as the focus of decision-making in a system of competitive states that is, in turn, interdependent with a transnational market economy: how political agency and economic competition in a certain structural and institutional setting in turn contribute to the dynamics of change. Understanding the role of the state-as-agent must go beyond glib pronouncements on the 'national interest'. How, and in whose interest, the 'national interest' is determined is precisely the problem. To be sure, dominant socio-economic interests with substantial political resources heavily influence the outcome of policies made in the name of the state. But it is crucial to understand that in the context of a transnational market economy, these dominant domestic groups extend across borders, becoming transnational, and thus have relationships with similar interests in other states, usually precisely because of market relationships.

This implies a third theoretical problem that must be addressed: the linkage between the domestic and international domains (or levels of analysis), given that political-economic processes clearly cut across the lines of political decision-making constituted by the institutional structures of the state. Situating the state and economic interests within this vast 'state-society complex'[18] that we call the global order will be a crucial problem for any theoretical approach. This implies focusing on the nature and political consequences of *interdependence* among states and their societies.[19]

Interdependence deserves some brief explanation. It was defined by Nye and Keohane as *mutual* but *unequal* dependence among states and their societies.[20] At one level this implies that what one state in the system does in some way affects the options of at least some of the others.[21] For example, aggressive behaviour by one country might cause others to reassess their security policies, or protectionist trade policies might cause a commensurate reaction. But interdependence means more than this: it also refers to how states and their societies are linked through (among other factors) the interactions and structures of the market, which in turn affects the politics of the state in the domestic and international contexts. Patterns of interdependence affect patterns of conflict and co-operation in the international system, and indeed within domestic societies, by helping to define who gets what, when, and how. Interdependence and transnationalization affect the politics at both levels. The state very often faces political or economic constituencies that are in the traditional sense domestic, but where many of the dominant interests are in important respects transnational economic actors and can, therefore, elude state policy tools to a considerable degree.

Once again, the role of the state is highlighted, making the state perhaps the central theoretical question. Just how one characterizes and assesses the state in IPE is critical, and the discussion of interdependence raises a fourth question, that of which actors are relevant to a discussion of global order. The ties of interdependence that operate through the changing structures of the market underscore the importance of considering how *non-state actors* affect the politics of the state, and how this in turn rebounds on the political economy of the global system.[22] If this is the case, is it relevant to conceive of the state as a unified rational actor making clear choices among rationally determined alternatives, as in much of the traditional literature on international relations? The discussion of interdependence above would imply this to be a somewhat misleading account. Instead, one must consider the state as a *key decision-making institution-as-agent at the core of the state-society complex*. Successful theories of IPE need to account for the relationship between the political power exercised through and on behalf of state authority in international and domestic politics, on the one hand, and constituent interests and agents of the wider social whole in which the institutions of the state are embedded, on the other.

Finally, there will be methodological issues, in particular concerning the role of structure in

theoretical explanations: the structure-agent problem. The theoretical problems outlined above constantly emphasize the *interactive relationships* between elements of the IPE: between domestic and international levels of analysis; between economic issues and political conflict; and between institutional patterns and economic structures, on the one hand, and the politics that takes place within them, on the other. Interactive relationships are developmental (or *dialectical*) processes. Explanations based primarily on an analysis of structure (and structure is a static concept in and of itself), deriving political outcomes from structural patterns, will have difficulty explaining historical change in the IPE. Theory must do more than highlight the patterns (structures) in a system and their consequences: it must explain how agents in interactive relationships, through the medium of political conflict, generate changes in the structures themselves. Theories that focus primarily on structure[23] will tend to suffer from deterministic predictions about the direction of change because they leave out the complex interrelationships, or 'process variables',[24] that govern change.

A similar set of problems arises with respect to rational choice models of analysis. Many perspectives in IPE theory portray actors (usually the state) in international politics as unitary, rational actors maximizing their power, wealth, or some other utility function in a setting characterized by the absence of an overarching political authority (anarchy). However, the idea of a clear choice between defined alternatives tends to break down as it becomes evident that states, as 'decision-makers', are the scene of political conflict that often proves inconclusive. States have legal decision-making power in international and (depending on constitutional arrangements) domestic affairs, and are units in this sense. They are not, however, unified and single-purpose decision-makers, for an array of competing coalitions of social forces are integrated into the policy process of the state itself. State policies are likely to be ambivalent on most issues, and international agreements consist of a complex mixture of co-operative and conflictual behaviour. The rational choice/unitary state device may well be useful for clarifying a complex situation in a set of international negotiations, for example, but it does not necessarily enhance a general theory of international politics. A broader, more fluid notion of the politics of state decision-making in a global context is needed. *Non*-decisions may result from a failure, deliberate or otherwise, to put certain issues on the political agenda. Indeed, powerful interests in society may even succeed in 'capturing' parts of the policy-making machinery of the state: so-called public purpose may come to serve blatantly private ends.

Furthermore, interdependence among states and their societies means that domestic political conflict and intergovernmental politics become intertwined, which further erodes the rational actor perspective. The state emerges as a social entity caught in a web of pressures and constraints at the domestic and international levels, among the most important of which is the transnational market economy. The relationship between the state and the decision-making environment is an interactive one where the rationality of cause and effect is difficult to discern. If one sticks to a methodology based on rational choice by unitary state actors, the resulting understanding of international politics and political economy will be commensurately limited.

## Contrasting Theoretical Approaches: A Critical Examination

This discussion will make much more sense if it is related specifically to the theoretical literature in IPE. Here we will look at how these points apply to the various approaches that have evolved over time. We can evaluate approaches in terms of how well they deal with the theoretical issues we have identified as central concepts in IPE. Based on critical analysis of these competing perspectives, we will develop some broad parameters for an approach to the discipline of IPE. It is not the intention to produce a single, coherent theoretical approach, but rather to suggest directions for further exploration that are likely to prove fruitful. A number of these questions are also discussed, in different ways, in the essays in this collection, particularly in Part I.

The generalizations arrived at in theoretical inquiry, it should be emphasized, are best understood in relation to empirical research into specific issue-areas in IPE ( money, trade, environment) and specific historical circumstances. A concept 'attains precision only when brought into contact with a particular situation which it helps to explain—a contact which also helps develop the meaning of the concept.'[25] Theory cannot meaningfully be understood in a vacuum, devoid of empirical context; 'theoretically informed' empirical analysis has been the aim of most contributions to this volume. If theory does not successfully enhance our understanding of complex 'real-world' phenomena, it risks becoming an exercise in intellectual fantasy.

### The Realist Tradition

The realist tradition in international relations theory has dominated the relatively young discipline in the postwar period, usurping the place liberal idealism held in the interwar years. This longevity is a tribute to the explanatory power of the approach. In its traditional guise realism was not a coherent theory as such, but it provided a flexible tool for understanding the dynamics and content of relations among states, particularly as far as issues of peace and war were concerned. The central feature of the realist 'model' is the competitive dynamic of the system of states where no overarching authority or government exists. The preservation of sovereignty by national communities organized into states and the competition this engenders within an international system in the absence of higher political authority are fundamental facts of international politics, and this can be borne out by historical analysis. In time, the realist tradition evolved into *neo-realism*, to which the work of Kenneth Waltz was central.[26] This was an attempt to take the basic principles of the realist tradition and to construct a coherent explanatory theory of the dynamics of international politics; it did not stand the test of time well. This section will deal first with the traditional approach, and then comment briefly on the neo-realist attempt at more coherent theory.

When it comes to economic issues, the approach adapts itself to include them on the agenda of international politics by relating economic power to issues of national security[27] in a context of competition among states under conditions of anarchy. Economic issues are considered secondary to the preservation of national independence. In this sense, states may sacrifice much in terms of economic rationality to preserve their socio-economic and territorial integrity, but the power necessary for that preservation could not be attained without adequate capacity to generate wealth.

However, traditional realism is a theory of politics that assumes that the political and economic domains are essentially separate. Hans Morgenthau stated this explicitly in his classic *Politics among Nations*:

> Intellectually, the political realist maintains the autonomy of the political sphere, as the economist, the lawyer, the moralist maintain theirs. He thinks in terms of interest defined in terms of power, as the economist thinks in terms of utility; the lawyer the conformity of action with legal rules; the moralist the conformity of action with moral principles. . . . the political realist asks 'How does this policy affect the power of the nation?'[28]

For traditional realists, international politics was largely about the struggle for power and the skill of statesmen at reaching a workable power balance that provided for systemic stability and the successful management of inevitable conflicts of national interest. International politics became for realists a world apart, divorced from the day-to-day interaction of socio-economic groups and institutions common to domestic politics. In making this questionable distinction, many postwar realists seemed to forget that among the most vital political issues in either the domestic or the international domain was the question of material life: who gets what, when, and where. If politics is not about what goes into people's pockets or purses, then it is difficult to imagine the content of political conflict in a domestic or international context. That this

conflict periodically erupts into violence, which in the international system we call war, is no more surprising than social unrest or civil war at the domestic level. States, after all, are institutions through which particular social groups defend (internally and externally) their power and the particular structures of the society they represent.

Realism, then, assumed the primacy of the political over the economic domain, as well as a separation of the domestic and international realms. Political conflict among or within states could influence the economy, and economic factors might well constrain state decision-makers, but as Morgenthau emphasized, the laws and dynamics of each were separate.

This assumption is problematic: careful research demonstrates that the political economy is an integrated whole, embedding normative, economic, legal, and political dynamics together. It makes little sense to speak of the laws of the economic sphere when the outcome of political conflict over time largely contributed to the establishment of these laws in the first place, and the laws of the economic sphere are constantly contested by those socio-economic groups who find them to their relative or even absolute disadvantage; they may even resort to violence to this end. By the same token, the security framework of the international system is established by states to preserve their individual patterns of socio-economic order. The Cold War was as good an illustration of this as any other: two contrasting socio-economic systems confronted each other, organized into security blocs. E.H. Carr, long associated with the realist school but occupying a subtle niche in the lexicon of international relations theory, argued that socio-economic questions were an integral part of the problem of international security.[29]

Another assumption of traditional realism concerned its conceptualization of the state. The approach was quite correct to draw attention to the importance of the state in international politics, but the state was most often seen as a unified actor making rational calculations with a view to maximizing power and security in a world characterized by the absence of overarching authority structures.

But if the state makes calculations of interest defined in terms of power, this assumes that the state has a single-minded capacity to make such calculations in the first place. In the face of stark choices concerning the survival of the state in the international system, such a view may be relatively accurate, but this situation occurs relatively infrequently. Defining the national interest where less desperate issues are involved may not be so clearcut. Even in national security crises there is considerable evidence that states are far from unified in their decision-making processes.[30] A question arises as to how the national interest is generated, particularly where economic choices are concerned. The view of the state as a unified rational actor is not particularly helpful when state decision-making structures are revealed to be fragmented and often poorly co-ordinated and when coalitions of socioeconomic interests, with power and influence over some issues but not others, compete to alter state policies to their own advantage.

We may summarize the points with respect to the key theoretical issues made so far: the realist approach assumes a separation of the economic and political domains, which sharply reduces the scope of its analysis as a comprehensive theory of international relations. Security is regarded as the primary issue-area in international politics,[31] which fits ill with the fundamental assumptions of the discipline of international political economy: we have argued that security has much to do with the very economic question of who gets what, when, and how. Furthermore, the state is portrayed as a unified and autonomous rational actor, an assumption that has been revealed as problematic. In this sense, the importance of non-state actors is usually overlooked and the relationships between the state and non-state actors in state decision-making processes receive little attention (though need not be excluded from analysis).

While the traditional realist approach was a flexible heuristic device permitting much rich historical understanding of the competitive dynamics of the system of states, and for understanding the difficult foreign policy choices facing states on matters of international security, a coherent theory it was not. This perception led to the steady emergence of what came to be called the *neo-realist* or *structural realist* approach, encapsulated in the works of Waltz, who became immensely influential in the period of the 1980s and the American 'new Cold War' policy of the Reagan era. He emphasized the importance of the anarchic *structure* of the international system as a determinant of behaviour and outcomes in international politics. The competitive pressures of a system characterized by anarchy, with states as the basic units, would lead to persistently conflictual interaction and behaviour based on the principle of self-preservation. The distribution of power among the units under conditions of anarchy essentially determined what states could and would do in their quest for self-help and security. These competitive dynamics tended towards self-sufficiency and a low degree of interdependence (a theoretical prediction at extraordinary variance with the available evidence drawn from any one of the last four centuries!) and to the long-term preservation of the system itself, if not necessarily each and every one of the states constituting that system.

Waltz, therefore, was engaged in an attempt at creating a coherent account of systemic dynamics in international politics, and as such it made the dubious assumption that the dynamics of the domestic level were contrary to and indeed of little relevance to the dynamics of international politics. Waltz's theory, logically consistent as it may have been, was embarrassingly short-lived in terms of its perceived ability to explain the ongoing dynamics of the very international politics it claimed to understand so well. When the bipolar power structures of the Cold War world collapsed for reasons almost entirely related to the dynamics of *domestic*-level developments inside the former Soviet Union (under the leadership of Mikhail Gorbachev) and the Berlin Wall separating East from West came down following unsustainable *internal* social unrest across the former Soviet bloc, it was clear that a theory of the international that pointedly ignored the *interaction* of the domestic and system levels of analysis was problematic.

Neo- or structural realism had its IPE counterpart, the theory of hegemonic stability, wherein neo-realist system-level analysis and more liberal notions of the advantages of the market coexist somewhat uneasily.[32] The idea that a hegemon might provide some of the political preconditions for a liberal economic order ('hegemonic stability') was originally put forward by Charles Kindleberger (1973) in relation to the international monetary system,[33] well before Waltz's *Theory of International Politics* (1979). Several authors projected this into Waltz's systemic framework, providing a neo-realist approach to international economic relations. They postulated that an international market economy, institutionalized in international economic 'regimes' characterized by liberal norms and rules,[34] would constitute a *public good* for all nations in the system because a liberal market order ensured the greatest economic benefit for the greatest number. They also recognized that the anarchic international system provides infertile ground for the degree of co-operation necessary to sustain liberal economic regimes. Consequently, a dominant power or 'hegemon' must be able and willing to bear the 'cost' of providing the 'public good' of a liberal market economy and a correspondingly 'strong' liberal international economic regime. In this way, a political framework is provided for the market despite the anarchic nature of international relations. To tie the theory into its neo-realist assumptions, the existence of a liberal economic order is essentially a function of the distribution of power among states in the system, with a hegemonic distribution being the most propitious ground for the emergence of a liberal market system.[35]

As the hegemonic power declines, however, the established liberal order may well come under pressure and indeed unravel entirely as the weakening hegemon becomes less and less willing or able to bear the costs of openness (costs such as keeping its market open to others in times of economic crisis). Furthermore, the economic success of others, made possible by the liberal order maintained by the dominant state, will slowly challenge the hegemon's position and, therefore, undermine the liberal character of international regimes.

The theory of hegemonic stability suffered from the same sorts of inadequacies as its neo-realist

system-level partner. It is empirically inaccurate in the first place in its portrayal of historical developments in the postwar period, and this problem is dealt with at length in the introduction to Part II of this volume. On a more general note, the existence of a dominant power (in what should be a self-evident proposition) tells us little about its motivations, liberal or otherwise. A systemic-level theory says little about the *content* of relations among states because it does not cut across levels of analysis. An understanding of the social and economic foundations of power is crucial to understanding what purposes a dominant country will turn to in the international system. The feature of anarchy and the distribution of power among states are, of course, important in shaping these interactions, but these factors do not 'cause' such interactions in any substantive way. Levels of analysis simply denotes the various *institutional patterns* or layers within which political conflict is organized. Politics is a continuum across various institutional layers that constitute a social whole, the state-society complex, and the state is the most important of these institutions. It is a decision-making forum within and around which the politics of the international system takes place, providing an institutional bridge between the domestic and the international.

If we are to understand how states manage the constraints of the domestic and international domains, we must understand the politics of the state itself, situated as it is between domestic and international society. If the state is a prime decision-maker, this requires some notion of how the economic interests involved in the transnational market economy become articulated in the politics of the state. We need to disaggregate the state to understand its politics, focusing on the preferences and political resources of social groups and, of course, market actors (largely, but not exclusively, firms) to understand how particular material interests are articulated politically. With the disaggregation of the state and an emphasis on social groups and actors, an understanding of the nature and effects of evolving patterns of interdependence on international politics is a crucial concern. The state appears as the most important decision-making forum in the international political economy, but it is far from the only actor of consequence.

## Liberal Approaches

A political strain of liberal international theory, and derived from this an economic strain, can be identified. We shall be more interested in the economic strain, but we must begin with a brief account of political liberalism in international theory.[36] The underlying assumption of political liberalism is the intrinsic value of individuals as the primary actors in the international system. Liberalism is thus permeated with a concern for enhancing the freedom and welfare of individuals; it proposes that humankind can employ reason better to develop a sense of harmony of interest among individuals and groups within the wider community, domestic or international. Thus, liberalism has as a goal the harmonization of conceptions of self-interest *through political action*. Progress towards this goal is 'seen in terms of possibility rather than certainty',[37] and of course the definition of what constitutes the proper goal of such political action (what constitutes 'progress') is inherently contestable.[38] In the international sphere, these goals are realized through the promotion of liberal democracy, through international co-operation, law, and institutions, and through social integration and technological development. It is fairly easy to see how the economic variant fits into this general picture. The maximization of individual economic welfare is a very important aspect of the enhancement of individual freedoms. States can direct their policies towards this goal through co-operation to realize mutually beneficial economic gains for their peoples.

Therefore, if realism is a political theory of relations among states, then economic liberalism, especially in its neo-classical variant,[39] has become a theory of the interaction of individuals in the economic sphere. This involves understanding the structure of comparative advantage and the international division of labour in a market economy as consisting of producers and consumers who exist, somewhat incidentally, in different political systems. Some of these political entities may be closed

to the market, but this is the result of political suppression of the natural propensity of individuals to truck, barter, and trade. Furthermore, if individuals are indeed offered the freedom to interact as economic agents, this is likely to ensure the most beneficial distribution of welfare among individuals of the international system. The task of the state as rational actor is to recognize the advantages of the international market as yielding the greatest good for the greatest number, and to respond by reducing or eliminating 'artificial' political impediments to 'natural' patterns of exchange. What is more, an assumption of the economic liberal approach is that the market will achieve this *automatically*—markets are self-regulating if individuals are left largely to their own economic devices. Many liberals also maintain that the transactions associated with the international market economy will build patterns of interdependence that will increase the incentives for international co-operation among states: in short, policies aimed at enhancing trade may contribute to international peace. Liberalism has a political program for the international system that emphasizes the market, the role of co-operative international institutions, international law, and national self-determination coupled with electoral democracy.

At first glance the liberal theory appears to be in sharp contrast to traditional realism (especially the optimism of liberalism as against the pessimism of the realists). However, from an IPE viewpoint they are often two sides of the same coin with their shared emphasis on the separation of the economic and political domains, each with its own laws and dynamics. Many realists are economic liberals in their understanding of the international economy, but they will be sceptical of the possibility of achieving a liberal system, and especially liberal international institutions, under conditions of international anarchy.[40]

How successful is the liberal approach at addressing the theoretical issues outlined? In the first place, the separation of markets from politics, from their political and institutional setting, misunderstands what a market actually is. It is not a natural phenomenon resulting from spontaneous interactions among individuals; it is instead a complex political institution for producing and distributing material and political resources. As such, it is relatively advantageous for some and rather bad news for others, depending on the historical circumstances of individuals in their socio-economic context. The institutions of the market are as much part of the governance of our societies as are the institutions of the state, and the two are essentially integrated functions in the global system. If markets are properly understood as political institutions, the assumption that they are automatic or 'self-regulating' breaks down—it becomes clear that markets, like any other political arrangement, are contestable and open to manipulation by those who have the power to do so. Indeed, it is extremely difficult to find historical examples of markets that function as most economists assume they do.

Second, it is difficult to understand the behaviour of economic agents, whether individuals or firms, outside their sociopolitical context. Economic agents do not just react to a series of uniform market incentives: markets differ from sector to sector and from country to country; sociocultural institutions and political conflict shape the pattern of market institutions and vice versa; 'economic' issues are intimately interconnected with other aspects of human existence. In sum, it is essentially a cliché to assert that economic agents interact as members of a social whole that is greater than the sum of its parts.

A third point is that the economic liberal perspective is ahistorical (the separation of markets from politics leads to this). There have always been markets in the sense of local exchanges of goods and services, but the market *system* or economy is a relatively recent development.[41] Liberalism therefore fails to account for the history of political conflict that led to the emergence of the institutions of the market and neglects the ongoing political conflict that has altered the institutions of the market over time. The institutions of nineteenth-century *laissez-faire* contrast greatly with those of the postwar mixed economy, and since the 1970s rapid changes have been under way (see introduction to Part II). The changing patterns of market institutions have

altered the distribution of gains and losses, the pattern of political resources, and the political preferences of players in the game.

Fourth, the liberal perspective is an economic reductionist approach. By this we mean that liberal economists ultimately focus on a feature of economic structure, the pattern of comparative advantage among economic agents, as a source of explanation. The complexity and political content of international economic relations are reduced to a reflection of the international division of labour, or market structure, as individual utility maximizers interact within its confines. By separating our understanding of the state from that of the economy, and of the individual from society, there can be no successful theory of politics or of the state, and we cannot understand the ways in which the state and market are integrated parts of the same sociopolitical dynamics.

Yet, as has been emphasized, it is precisely a political theory of the market that is required. Without a theory of political conflict and the state, we cannot understand how the market structure changes over time. Theories based on structure as a pattern or matrix of relationships in a system, an essentially static concept, run the risk of *tautology*.[42] The structure of comparative advantage certainly does shape and constrain the interactions among actors. However, the emergence and transformation of comparative advantage, of the structure itself, requires explanation. Change is an open-ended political process that takes place within a particular structural setting but with the potential to alter structure itself. Structures are politically contestable in the sense that they confer advantages on some and disadvantages on others.[43]

## Radical Approaches

The principal strength of Marxist analysis and most other radical approaches to international political economy is that they focus precisely on the connection between the social and economic structures of the capitalist economic system, on the one hand, and the exercise of political power in the international system, on the other.[44] Within domestic political systems, the capitalist system of production entrenches the dominance of one class over another: the state is the *capitalist* state. As the economy becomes internationalized, this class dominance projects itself into international politics. The political organization of the international system reflects the power relations of the transnational market economy. This manifests itself both in competition among states in the international system and in the co-operative processes represented by international economic regimes. For some traditional Marxists, the spread of capitalism touches off a process of economic and political development in less developed parts of the globe as capitalist firms, often supported by their home states, seek profitable opportunities for investment abroad. Dependency theorists saw the flaw of this approach and pointed instead to the likelihood of core and periphery areas of the global economy remaining distinct despite incorporation into the capitalist world economy. Johann Galtung, for example, developed a structural theory of *imperialism*, hypothesizing that the mutually beneficial political and economic relationships between élites in core and periphery countries would maintain the structural pattern of dependency in the global economy.[45]

There is considerable risk when one attempts to generalize about this diverse range of theories, but most do share some essential characteristics. The approaches tend to be based on an analysis of the sociopolitical *effects* of economic structure and therefore do not adequately deal with the relationship between structure and agency. In this sense, most are reductionist like the liberal approach. This is not surprising; Marx regarded his work as a critique of the classical liberal political economists, and thus he focused on a similar set of intellectual problems. Politics in the domestic and international domains tends to be reduced to a function of the capitalist production structure and the division of society into classes, which is in turn a result of the individual's relationship to the means of production.[46] Yet the theories are weak on explaining just how this relationship between political power and economic structure is articulated; 'there is an essential, missing ingredient—a theory of how structures themselves originate, change, work, and reproduce themselves.'[47] Once again, what is needed is a theory of politics in the wider sense of the word.

Antonio Gramsci, the Italian Marxist of the interwar period, attempted to develop a more political explanation of the relationship between economic structure and political processes at domestic and international levels of analysis. He sought to explain the relative durability and legitimacy of the capitalist system, despite its clear inequalities and historical tendency to periodic major crises such as the Depression of the 1930s. How could such a system be simultaneously oppressive and unstable on the one hand, yet enduring and resilient on the other? Surely it must satisfy enough of the people enough of the time. Gramsci postulated that the political dynamics of the state were important: class domination existed, to be sure, but it was played out in a series of complex political compromises among capitalists, workers, small landholders, and so on. These political compromises at the heart of the state are what rendered the market and capitalist system of production essentially legitimate instruments of governance. In this sense he sought to avoid the problem of economic reductionism and to resolve in important ways the structure-agent problem.

The pioneering Robert Cox sought to project this basic model into theories of the international system.[48] Cox also followed Gramsci by emphasizing the power of ideas and knowledge structures and how they emerged from the material interests of different constituent elements of the capitalist system. Control over ideas is central to legitimizing and maintaining the fundamentally conflictual socio-economic structures of global capitalism. In this way Cox and other *neo-Gramscian* scholars sought to avoid the problem of economic reductionism referred to above, drawing on Gramsci himself as well as Karl Polanyi, Fernand Braudel,[49] and other social theorists, and in the process overcame many of the limitations of liberalism, Marxism, and realism. Thus was the radical tradition adapted to deal more successfully with the structure-agent problem and to understand better the role of the state as political forum and agent in the *structuration* of global economic order. The neo-Gramscian approach provides a flexible analytical tool of considerable promise for our understanding of international political economy across levels of analysis. Patterns of global order are directly related to the balance of social forces of the system, particularly those in the dominant states. While the traditional Marxist preoccupation with class conflict may be overemphasized in the work of many neo-Gramscian scholars, the approach also permits a focus on the fragmented and often conflictual relationships within the capitalist or business class itself, which are so crucial to the nature of global economic order. Indeed, if Marx was correct and capitalist producers do have overwhelming structural power in the establishment of the sociopolitical order, then it is not surprising that the role of the corporate sector is central to the policies of states and of global economic regimes in trade, finance, environment, development, and the like.

## Towards a Theory for IPE

This review of the theoretical literature has been necessarily brief, leaving out many of the subtleties and much of the variety of all the approaches covered. It has also neglected the growing feminist and environmentalist literature, as well as the post-modern theorists who have built on the work of the French historian Michel Foucault, among others. The final task for theorists will be to lay down the building blocks of a successful approach to understanding the discipline of international political economy. The more modest aim here, however, is to highlight the factors that need to be considered by theorists if a successful approach to the discipline is to emerge. Certainly one would not wish to rule out the possibilities for cross-fertilization offered by the various perspectives put forward by the contributors to this book. So far, this introduction has necessarily been more concerned with critique (what *not* to do in IPE theory) than with advancing a coherent alternative. What follows is an attempt to draw out the implications of the critique, with a view to allowing contributors to the volume to address these points in their own individual ways and in relation to their particular topics.

We have highlighted three interrelated theoretical problems in IPE. (1) The relationship of the economic and political domains must be understood—in a contemporary context, this means politics and markets. (2) The levels of analysis problem must be addressed: how do the politics and economic structures of the domestic and international domains relate to each other? (3) As implied by the second problem, there is, as well, the problem of the state: what is it, what is its role, and how is it situated in relation to domestic and international levels of analysis?[50] In turn, these three points imply the importance of what has been identified as the structure-agent problem, and the question of actors: what kinds of actors and what relationships among them need to be accounted for in our conceptual framework for understanding IPE.

Of these theoretical questions or problems, the problem of the state ties them all together: the socio-economic tensions of changing global capitalism highlight the role of state policy-making processes as the site of struggles for influence within advanced capitalist society. The state emerges as the political focus for the process of adjustment and change. In short, the politics of the state mediates between the economic and political domains, among different types of actors, and between the domestic and international levels of analysis, and contains the key to understanding structure and agency. Understanding the state—what it is, what it does, and where it fits into Cox's state-society complex—is in a way *the* problem of international political economy. Most of the theories of international politics and political economy we have reviewed above suffer from one or both of the following difficulties: 'either they derive the state itself—its structure and autonomous character—from other social structures [the economy, the anarchic structure of the international system]; or they tend to reify the state, virtually personifying it, by giving it the character of a conscious, rational agent.'[51] These theories do not see the politics of societies, economies, and, indeed, the international system as coming together in the processes constituted by the integrated state-market itself.

So how do we make sense of the state, and thereby of the levels of analysis problem, the relationship of politics to markets, and ultimately the structure-agent problem? We need a link between the state, economic structure, and broader notions of politics. That link is the *self-interest of agents or actors*, whether they be individuals, formal or informal groups, the corporate economic entities known as firms, or states. The relationship between individual self-interest and the collective needs of the community is precisely the philosophical problem that so inspired Adam Smith to write the classic text in political economy, *The Wealth of Nations*, published in 1776.[52] We must begin developing an understanding of the 'state-society complex', the integrated state-market package, that comprises the international political economy by analysing the structure of economic relations (production and the market) as it becomes increasingly transnationalized and the ways in which the structure constrains, but is integrated with, the broader politics of distributional and other conflicts. In doing so, we begin to come to grips with the material self-interest of political economic agents, and of key social groups, at domestic and international levels of analysis. In turn, we must analyse the effects this transnationalization of structure has on the perceived interests of actors. The state and the social institutions of the market in which it is embedded[53] together constitute the governance of global society.

In this sense, and despite criticisms above of 'structuralism' in international relations theory, structure is part of a successful theory of international political economy. It is what one means by 'structure' in the first place,[54] and how one employs structure in a theory, that is important. Structure is not a causal variable—in and of itself it does not explain outcomes. Structure does inform one of the terms under which the political interactions of particular agents or groups occur at a particular time in history.

It is worth taking a moment to focus on the structure-agent problem in brief. We should remind ourselves that the distinction between structure and agents (either individual or collective/institutional) is essentially abstract and therefore artificial in the first place. It may be perfectly useful in helping us to conceive of the relationship of individual agents to the wider whole around them, but it remains artificial: structure and agency are not different things at all; each makes little sense without the other when we consider concrete reality around us. The individual (or institutional) actor-as-agent no more exists in isolation from its socially constructed reality than structure can emerge and develop without agency. By the same token, structures make little sense in historical analysis unless they are conceived as dynamic: structure conceived as *process*, set in motion by agents, whether individual or collective actors (such as the state), over time. The conflicts of interest among agents in a particular structural setting give structure its real, dynamic qualities. Self-interest, constrained by the peculiarities of historically contingent structure, provides at one and the same time the motive (including normative bases) for agency to move from the potential to the actual, and explains how structure-as-process is in a constant state of flux. The nature of the structure, and the differential power, costs, and/or benefits it confers on those in contrasting structural positions, is the constant subject of dispute among agents interacting in the context of the institutions of governance (formal and informal) of the international political economy, most importantly the state. In this sense we can view the ongoing process of globalization as a structural change (1) generated by the agency of ongoing conflicts of perceived self-interest among social forces through the practices of individual agents; (2) generated by the agency of firms as bearers of competitive relations in the contingent structures of the market; and (3) generated in the institutionalized context of the policy process of states and regimes, in which firms and social forces are expressed in the practices of individuals and are engaged as constituent interests. The state-market condominium emerges as an integrated but evolving mechanism of governance that serves as an institutional nodal point or site for the process of structural change.

The self-interest of agents will be reflected in their policy preferences as a function of their place in a particular structure. Indeed, different economic sectors with contrasting economic structures and dynamics will require specific analysis.[55] A number of different strategies may be open to any one set of actors, but it is not difficult to understand that a national industrial sector with such structural features as relatively small, uncompetitive firms and little integration into the international economy (in other words, essentially dependent on domestic markets and domestically based production units) will have different preferences from a sector dominated by firms with a multinationalized production strategy heavily dependent on international trade for profitability. The former might prefer the protection of national authorities; the latter is likely to prefer more liberal international economic regimes to allow the free movement of goods and capital from one national economy to another.[56] Thus, one set of domestic-international linkages consists of the ties between respective actors in national economies and transnational markets, or the lack thereof.

Next, we must understand how these material economic interests, expressed as policy preferences and representing a diverse range of state and non-state actors, are articulated politically within the political institutions of the global system. By institutions we mean essentially the state, but also intergovernmental bargaining and international institutionalized behaviour (regimes) in a setting characterized by anarchy through which the politics of the state is projected into the international domain. Political articulation, or how interests are organized and institutionalized, is the link between economic structure and the politics (agency) of the state and political economy (both domestic and international domains).

How unified are these coalitions of interests, and how well can they assert themselves? What kind of political resources do they have, given the pattern of state and international institutions and economic structures that act as constraints and opportunities for the agents involved? 'These sets of constraints and opportunities in effect form structured fields of action upon and within which agents

make choices.'[57] It makes a difference whether a particular coalition of interests, with a given set of policy preferences, enjoys not just market but also political power within the state. Unless they are well placed with institutionalized political resources, they are unlikely to have much impact on state policy. Institutions do load the dice; groups that are economically powerful but divided internally may prove impotent.

By the same token, a coalition or group that is powerful within a particular state, but a state with little ability to project its choices into the processes of intergovernmental bargaining and regime formation, will have little impact outside its domestic setting. As the economic structure or market becomes increasingly transnationalized, these coalitions of interests within relatively impotent states may find their choices severely constrained (unless, of course, they have a strong competitive position in the market itself). They often have a lot to lose and may initiate successful state strategies to adjust to the new structural parameters, or they may find themselves facing economic and political decline or elimination. This is a problem not just for groups of economic interests but also for the state, which is accountable to these political constituencies. In today's increasingly global economy, one can perceive a growing tension between the domestic economic constituencies on which the state is ultimately dependent for its power and legitimacy and the increasingly transnational nature of the economy and economic problems that face governments. The transnationalization of economic structures has reduced the economic space controlled by the state and intensified the competition its domestic economic constituency has to bear. This is the crux of the management problems of the contemporary international political economy. It implies a pressing need for co-operative management structures in the anarchic international setting, but the political constituencies and institutions of such co-operation are relatively underdeveloped. Once again the state emerges as the crucial nodal point for political conflict over structure and institutions.

By the same token, the transnationalization of economic structure has not taken place in a political vacuum. This will be emphasized by a considerable number of contributions in this volume. The interests of firms with multinational production strategies and access to international capital markets have found expression in the policies of, in particular, the United States (see the chapter by Sell). This provides some insight into the real underpinnings and impact of American 'hegemony': the interests of transnational capital have been best articulated politically within the US state. They have pressed, whenever the opportunity presented itself, for more market-oriented international economic regimes, often overcoming stiff domestic and international opposition. The structural changes that intergovernmental negotiations have produced in money, finance, and trade in the postwar period furnish much of the substance of the contributions to this volume. The point here is to emphasize the two-way relationship between the domestic and international domains and between markets and politics. The political choices of important actors or groups, well placed politically within the more powerful states of the international system, are projected into the international domain. This leads to a restructuring of the market and institutions of international economic management, and in turn feeds back into the domestic politics of countries in the system. In this way, liberalization and 'marketization' intensify the competitive pressures on domestic firms, which use their political resources to press for policies that will manage the new situation and allow them to survive and prosper. Whether the political strategies they choose to manage economic change are successful or not remains an open question.

One final point is worth restating. The role of politics (agency), as opposed to structure, as a determinant of outcome has constantly been emphasized. This holds whether we refer to the economic structure of markets and production, as stressed by liberals and Marxists, or the structural features of the competitive system of states (the institutional setting of anarchy), as emphasized by the neo-realists. This point highlights the role of process variables over structural variables in IPE theory. Politics constitutes a two-way relationship between structure and agents in a particular institutional setting. Politics shapes structure at the same time as structure shapes and constrains the options of political actors pursuing their preferences. The politics of the state is the principal linkage between the domestic and international levels of analysis. 'The impact of structure lies not in some inherent, self-contained quality, but in the way a given structure at specific historical moments helps one set of opinions prevail over another.'[58] It is not structure in and of itself that is important but the politics that takes place within it. The changing structure of the international economy and the regimes/institutional patterns that mediate it are shaped by the political conflicts occurring at domestic, transnational, and international levels of analysis, and vice versa.[59] There is a two-way relationship between structure and process, domestic and international, mediated by changing institutional patterns.

The exercise of power in the international political economy therefore takes place in a setting characterized by the complex interdependence among states, their societies, and economic structures at domestic and international levels of analysis. This occurs largely through an integrated system of governance operating simultaneously through the mechanisms of the market and the multiple sovereignties of a system of competitive states. Interdependence, as well as anarchy, is an integral part of the international environment within which states attempt to promote their 'sovereign' interests and those of their domestic constituencies. 'Viewing the international system as a web of interdependencies necessitates a focus on the linkages among actors'[60] and political interaction is the substance of these linkages. The outcome is determined by the complex interaction of systemic and domestic structural and process variables. We live in a system of multiple state sovereignties, 'which is interdependent in its structure and dynamics' with the transnational market economy, 'but not reducible to it.'[61]

## Notes

1  I wish to acknowledge with gratitude those who have contributed many helpful comments on earlier drafts and other works that became part of this Introduction: Barry Buzan, Philip G. Cerny, Daniel Drache, Stephen Gill, Eric Helleiner, Richard Higgott, Helen Milner, Tony Porter, Susan Sell, the late Susan Strange, my co-editor, Richard Stubbs, and the many students over the years with whom I have developed these ideas. Of course, I alone am responsible for any failings or shortcomings.

2  Jacob Viner, 'Power versus Plenty as Objectives of Foreign Policy in the Seventeenth and Eighteenth Centuries', *World Politics* 1, 1 (1948–9): 10.

3  Karl Polanyi made this distinction particularly clear in his classic work, *The Great Transformation* (Boston: Beacon Press, 1944).

4  See Hermann Schwartz, *States versus Markets: History, Geography, and the Development of the International Political Economy* (London: Macmillan, 1994), esp. chs 1–2.

5  Fernand Braudel, followed by Immanuel Wallerstein, would dispute this understanding of the emergence of the market economy. Both see the capitalist 'world-economy' as emerging in Europe during the 'long' sixteenth century. See, for example, Immanuel Wallerstein, *The Modern World System: Capitalist Agriculture and the Origins of the European World-Economy in the 16th Century* (New York: Academic Press,1974). However, their conception of capitalism appears to be based on the notion of market exchange and division of labour as opposed to the system of industrial production based on capital investment that emerged with the Industrial Revolution.

6  G.R.D. Underhill, *Industrial Crisis and the Open Economy* (London: Macmillan, 1998), 19.

7  Polanyi, *The Great Transformation*.

8  Ibid., 57.

9  *International* denotes relations among states as units; *transnational* implies a more complex pattern of relationships across borders, the interpenetration of economies and societies, which is not necessarily limited to state-to-state relations in the formal sense of the term.

10  Susan Strange, *The Retreat of the State: The Diffusion of Power in the World Economy* (Cambridge: Cambridge University Press, 1996).

11  See chapters by Waltz (excerpts from Kenneth Waltz, *Theory of International Politics* [Reading, Mass.: Addison-Wesley, 1979]), in Robert O. Keohane, ed., *Neorealism and Its Critics* (New York: Columbia University Press, 1986), esp. ch. 4, 'Political Structures', 81–97.

12  Robert Cox, 'Social Forces, States, and World Orders: Beyond International Relations Theory', ibid., 205.

13  See Richard Higgott, Geoffrey R.D. Underhill, and Andreas Bieler, eds, *Non-State Actors and Authority in the Global System* (London: Routledge, 1999).

14  John Gerard Ruggie, 'International Regimes, Transactions, and Change: Embedded Liberalism in the Postwar Economic Order', in Stephen D. Krasner, ed., *International Regimes* (Ithaca, NY: Cornell University Press, 1983), 198.

15  Robert Gilpin, *The Political Economy of International Relations* (Princeton, NJ: Princeton University Press, 1987), 11; Immanuel Wallerstein, *The Capitalist World-Economy* (Cambridge: Cambridge University Press/Maison des Science de l'Homme, 1979), 273.

16  See Richard Devetak, 'Postmodernism', in Scott Burchill and Andrew Linklater, eds, *Theories of International Relations* (London: Macmillan, 1996), 179–209.

17  Cox, 'Social Forces, States, and World Orders', 207.

18  Ibid., 205.

19  Robert O. Keohane and Joseph Nye, *Power and Interdependence: World Politics in Transition* (Boston: Little, Brown, 1977); Helen Milner, 'The Assumption of Anarchy in International Relations Theory: A Critique', *Review of International Studies* 17, 1 (Jan. 1991): 67–85; Geoffrey R.D. Underhill, 'Industrial Crisis and International Regimes:

France, the EEC, and International Trade in Textiles 1974–1984', *Millennium: Journal of International Studies* 19, 2 (Summer 1990): 185–206.

20  See Keohane and Nye, *Power and Interdependence*, 8–11.

21  This is akin to the concept of 'strategic interdependence' developed by Schelling. See Milner, 'The Assumption of Anarchy'.

22  See Higgott, Underhill, and Bieler, eds, *Non-State Actors*.

23  It depends, of course, on how one conceives of structure. Some see it primarily as a pattern of relationships that *structure* the overall system, and this is roughly the definition adopted here. Others, for example Robert Cox and Fernand Braudel, see structure as a more holistic concept, or *historical structure*, the totality of social, economic, and political relationships and processes in particular historical circumstances.

24  See Peter Gourevitch, 'The Second Image Reversed: The International Sources of Domestic Politics', *International Organization* 32, 4 (Autumn 1978): 900–7.

25  Robert Cox paraphrasing Antonio Gramsci in 'Gramsci, Hegemony, and International Relations: an Essay in Method', *Millennium: Journal of International Studies* 12, 2 (1983): 162.

26  Kenneth Waltz, *Theory of International Politics* (Reading, Mass.: Addison-Wesley, 1979).

27  See Klaus Knorr, 'Economic Interdependence and National Security', in Knorr and Frank N. Trager, eds, *Economic Issues* and *National Security* (Lawrence: University Press of Kansas; Regent's Press/National Security Education Program, 1977), 1–18; also Barry Buzan, *People, States and Fear*, 2nd edn (Boulder, Colo.: Lynne Rienner, 1991), ch. 6.

28  Hans J. Morgenthau, *Politics among Nations: The Struggle for Power and Peace* (New York: Alfred A. Knopf, 1956), 10–11. Not all traditional realists put forward as narrow a view of politics as Morgenthau in this passage. E.H. Carr, *The Twenty Years' Crisis 1919–1939: An Introduction to the Study of International Relations* (London: Macmillan, 1939), has a view of international politics that includes economic issues as relevant to political interaction in the international domain. The classical realist tradition of the Greek Thucydides, the Italian Renaissance writer Machiavelli, and the French Enlightenment philosopher Jean-Jacques Rousseau offers rich perspectives for the study of politics at the international and domestic levels of analysis.

29  For a recent analysis of the work of E.H. Carr, see Charles Jones, *E.H. Carr and International Relations: A Duty to Lie* (Cambridge: Cambridge University Press, 1998).

30  Graham Allison, *Essence of Decision* (Boston: Little, Brown, 1971), called even this into question through his analysis of decision-making in the 1962 Cuban missile crisis.

31  Unless the concept of 'economic security' is elaborated. See Buzan, *People, States and Fear*, ch. 6.

32  Perhaps the clearest explanation of the theory of hegemonic stability can be found in Robert Gilpin, *The Political Economy of International Relations* (Princeton, NJ: Princeton University Press, 1987), 72–92. For a critique, see, among others, Isabelle Grunberg, 'Exploring the "Myth" of Hegemonic Stability', *International Organization* 44, 4 (Autumn 1990); Underhill, 'Industrial Crisis and International Regimes', 186–92.

33  Charles Kindleberger, *The World in Depression 1929–39* (Berkeley: University of California Press, 1973).

34  'International regimes' is a term that refers to the formal and informal aspects of institutionalized co-operation and conflict in international politics. For the classic definition, see Stephen D. Krasner, 'Structural Causes and Regime Consequences: Regimes as Intervening Variables', in Krasner, ed., *International Regimes*, 2. In IPE, we are largely concerned with international *economic* regimes.

35  While the theory of hegemonic stability does have a distinctively realist flavour about it, this emphasis on a unipolar order contradicts the insistence by many traditional realists on the need for a balance of power to maintain a stable order in the international system.

36  The following account of the principal features of liberal political theory in international relations is drawn from Mark Zacher and Richard Mathew,

'Liberal International Theory: Common Threads, Divergent Strands', in Charles Kegley, ed., *Controversies in International Relations Theory: Realism and the Neoliberal Challenge* (New York: St Martin's Press, 1994).

37  Ibid.

38  In important respects the liberal approach does not as such constitute an *explanation* of the international system, of 'why it is the way it is'. Liberalism's explanatory tools cannot be separated from its strongly prescriptive normative principles. The differing conceptions of 'progress' promoted by liberals are bound to be socially embedded in the sense that they are likely to be perceived as more advantageous to the material interests of some social groups/individuals as opposed to others. The ideas of political liberalism are generally associated, for example, with the historical emergence of merchant classes and industrial capital in modern Europe, and have undergone changes with the subsequent emergence of liberal democracies.

39  The neoclassical economists, unlike their classical political economist predecessors such as Adam Smith and David Ricardo, saw the economy as divorced from political dynamics. Adopting a strong pro-market stance, they portrayed the world as one of individual economic agents maximizing their marginal utility in a setting of perfect market conditions. In recent years, radical free-market approaches to liberal economic theory have been referred to as 'neo-liberal' by most scholars, or even as 'hyper-liberal' by authors such as Cox.

40  Robert Gilpin put this quite candidly in *The Political Economy of International Relations*, 25.

41  Polanyi, *The Great Transformation*.

42  In other words, the derivation of causes from a definition or description of the effects and vice versa: the structure of comparative advantage cannot be explained through an analysis of the division of labour because the one derives from the other by definition.

43  See the discussion of the role of structure and political process in Gourevitch, 'The Second Image Reversed', 900–7. See also Philip G. Cerny,

*The Changing Architecture of Politics: Structure, Agency, and the Future of the State* (London: Sage, 1990), esp. 'Epilogue'.

44  For a more detailed discussion of the variety of radical (among other) approaches to international political economy, see Stephen Gill and David Law, *The Global Political Economy* (Baltimore: Johns Hopkins University Press, 1988), ch. 5.

45  Johann Galtung, 'A Structural Theory of Imperialism', *International Journal of Peace Research* 8 (1971): 81–118.

46  Marx himself was ambivalent on this issue and there are two strains 'at war' in his work. One is his analysis of the laws of capitalist economic development, which focuses on the structural contradictions or tensions of the system and its inherently unstable nature, an approach that risks reducing social and political phenomena to effects of structure. The second is his close attention to the historical, political, and social conflicts, dominated by class struggle, that led to the emergence and development of capitalism over time, thus emphasizing the role of agency in structural change.

47  Cerny, *The Changing Architecture of Politics*, 15.

48  For a collection of Cox's work, see R. Cox (with T. Sinclair), *Approaches to World Order* (Cambridge: Cambridge University Press, 1996). His lead was followed by scholars such as Stephen Gill, also in this volume.

49  Polanyi, *The Great Transformation*; Fernand Braudel, *Capitalism and Material Life* (London: Weidenfeld and Nicolson, 1973); Braudel, *The Wheels of Commerce* (London: Collins, 1982). The neo-Gramscian approach, or *transnational historical materialism*, is employed by Bernard, Cox, Gill, and others in this volume. It is developed more systematically elsewhere: see Robert Cox, *Production, Power, and World Order* (New York: Columbia University Press, 1987); Stephen Gill, ed., *Gramsci, Historical Materialism, and International Relations* (Cambridge: Cambridge University Press, 1993).

50  For a comprehensive attempt to deal with these problems in a contemporary context, especially the problem of the state, see Cerny, *The Changing Architecture of Politics*.

51  Ibid., 12.

52  This point is argued cogently by Claudio Napoleoni in *Smith, Ricardo, Marx: Observations on the History of Economic Thought* (Oxford: Basil Blackwell, 1975), esp. 25–31.

53  See John Lie, 'Embedding Polanyi's Market Society', *Sociological Perspectives* 34, 2 (1991): 219–35.

54  For example, the distinction between economic structure in the Marxist or liberal sense of the term as opposed to political structure in the neo-realist literature. See Higgott, Underhill, and Bieler, eds, *Non-State Actors*.

55  The value of a sectoral approach was highlighted by Susan Strange in, for example, 'The Study of Transnational Relations', *International Affairs* 52, 3 (July 1976): 341–5, and re-emphasized by Helen Milner, *Resisting Protectionism: Global Industries and the Politics of International Trade* (Princeton, NJ: Princeton University Press, 1988), esp. 14–17, and by Underhill, 'Industrial Crisis and International Regimes', 188–92.

56  Of course, the preferences of governments are an important variable here. State authorities might be powerful enough to impose preferences and strategies on actors or groups of actors, or at least to constrain sharply the options of some over others.

57  Cerny, *The Changing Architecture of Politics*, 233.

58  Gourevitch, 'The Second Image Reversed', 904.

59  This notion that theory must account for the ways in which structures themselves are produced and transformed is akin to Giddens's notion of structure as process, or *structuration*. See Anthony Giddens, *Central Problems of Social Theory: Action, Structure, and Contradiction in Social Analysis* (London: Macmillan, 1979). These points were raised comprehensively by Cerny (*Changing Architecture*) and have been adopted to an extent by the constructivist variant of international theory. See Alexander Wendt, 'The Agent-Structure Problem in International Relations Theory', *International Organization* 41, 3 (Summer 1987).

60  Milner, 'The Assumption of Anarchy', 84. Milner deals particularly well with the issue of anarchy and interdependence.

61  Theda Skocpol and Ellen Kay Trimberger, 'Revolutions and the World-Historical Development of Capitalism', in Barbara Hockey Kaplan, ed., *Social Change in the Capitalist World Economy* (London: Sage, 1978), 132.

## Suggested Readings

Block, Fred. *Revising State Theory*. Philadelphia: Temple University Press, 1987.

Burchill, Scott, and Andrew Linklater, eds. *Theories of International Relations*. London: Macmillan, 1996.

Buzan, Barry. *People, States and Fear*, 2nd edn. Boulder, Colo.: Lynne Rienner, 1991.

————, Charles Jones, and Richard Little. *The Logic of Anarchy*. New York: Columbia University Press, 1993.

Carr, Edward Hallet. *The Twenty Years' Crisis 1919–1939: An Introduction to the Study of International Relations*. London: Macmillan, 1939.

Cerny, Philip G. *The Changing Architecture of Politics: Structure, Agency and the Future of the State*. London: Sage, 1990.

Cox, Robert. *Production, Power, and World Order*. New York: Columbia University Press, 1987.

———— with T. Sinclair. *Approaches to World Order*. Cambridge: Cambridge University Press, 1996.

Gill, Stephen, ed. *Gramsci, Historical Materialism, and International Relations*. Cambridge: Cambridge University Press, 1993.

Kegley, Charles, ed. *Realism and the Neoliberal Challenge: Controversies in International Relations Theory*. New York: St Martin's Press, 1994.

Morgenthau, Hans J. *Politics Among Nations: The Struggle for Power and Peace*. New York: Alfred A. Knopf, 1956.

Murphy, Craig, and Roger Tooze, eds. *The New International Political Economy*. Boulder, Colo.: Lynne Rienner, 1991.

Polanyi, Karl. *The Great Transformation*. Boston: Beacon Press, 1944.

Rosenau, James N., and Ernst-Otto Czempiel, eds. *Governance Without Government: Order and Change in World Politics*. Cambridge: Cambridge University Press, 1992.

Strange, Susan. *States and Markets*, 2nd edn. Oxford: Basil Blackwell, 1994.

———. *The Retreat of the State*. Cambridge: Cambridge University Press, 1996.

## Chapter 1

# Political Economy and World Order:
## Problems of Power and Knowledge at the Turn of the Millennium

Robert W. Cox

Theory concerning human affairs is not cumulative and progressive. Theory follows history, so that when the structures and problems of one era give place to emerging new structures and new problems there is a challenge for theory to respond. This is most notably the case with regard to world politics. The concepts and categories that became conventional following World War II are now widely contested in the light of recent history.

Established bodies of knowledge have their own inertia. They represent a considerable investment of time and effort—not to be cast away lightly. Furthermore, even while recognizing that the circumstances that validated established knowledge have changed, ingenious thinkers may adapt accustomed mental frameworks to new circumstances and new perceptions of threats to security without basically changing them. Samuel Huntington, for instance, has adapted the mind-set of Cold War military-political knowledge to his new perception of a threatening 'clash of civilizations'.[1]

However, new historical conditions stimulate the development of alternative forms of knowledge that start from different assumptions and follow different paths. We can characterize the present condition of knowledge about world politics and society as part genetic and part teleological: in part an effort to adapt established bodies of knowledge to new events and circumstances by incremental adjustments; and in part an effort to project thinking forward to perceive the nature of the emerging realities and then to reason what different forms of knowledge might be better adapted to understanding and acting in them. The genetic and the teleological

coexist during periods of fundamental change in world order.

Old realities remain. The state may retreat, to use Susan Strange's recent book title,[2] with respect to some of its erstwhile functions, but it assumes new functions. Economic globalization does not bring about the disappearance of the state any more than *Soviet-style socialism* brought about its 'withering away'. States make the framework for globalization, just as Karl Polanyi pointed out that states made the framework for the self-regulating market in the nineteenth century.[3] But states can also become agencies for bringing the global economy under social control. The state remains a site of struggle for those who would challenge the social consequences of globalization. History does not end with globalization of the economy despite illusory pronouncements by some ideologues.[4] History goes on and has the potential to shape new structures of thought and political authority. The opportunity now opens to develop the forms of knowledge conducive to such innovation.

For three decades and more, knowledge in the sphere of world politics has been built predominantly with reference to the Cold War. What is now called neo-realism is a technology of power, a problem-solving form of knowledge applicable to the rivalry of two superpowers.[5] It was generally adequate to that purpose. Its limitation was that anything not pertaining to the superpower struggle could be ignored.

Of course, for the great mass of humankind other considerations were paramount: physical survival in conditions of hunger, disease, violent conflicts, and, at a more spiritual level, the denial of cultural identity. These were subordinated to the global power struggle or, insofar as they became disruptive, linked instrumentally to the interests of the two superpowers. Two competing forms of homogenization—world capitalism and world communism, respectively picturing themselves as the free world and national liberation—were the only games allowed. Once the overarching control of the Cold War was lifted, the underlying but obscured diversity of the human situation became apparent. Neo-realism lost its monopoly of explaining the world and of proposing action.[6]

In searching for an alternative basis of knowledge, it is well to begin with an understanding of how we got where we are, and then to look to the problems that cluster on the threshold of the new millennium.

## Sources of Globalization

During the Great Depression of the 1930s, the state had to become the agent of economic revival and the defender of domestic welfare and employment against disturbances coming from the outside world. Corporatism, the union of the state with productive forces at the national level, became, under various names, the model of economic regulation; and economic nationalism with the 'beggar-my-neighbour' practices it often involved was its counterpart in international economic relations. Following World War II, the Bretton Woods system attempted to strike a balance between the liberal world market and the domestic responsibilities of states. States became accountable to agencies of an international economic order—the International Monetary Fund (IMF), the World Bank, and the General Agreement on Tariffs and Trade (GATT)—in regard to trade liberalization and exchange rate stability and convertibility, and were also granted facilities and time to make adjustments in their national economic practices so as not to have to sacrifice the welfare of domestic groups. This balanced compromise between defence of welfare and a liberal international economic order sustained three decades of growth and social progress; but a crisis

in the postwar order came about during the years 1968–75. From then until the present the balanced compromise shifted towards a subordination of domestic economies to the perceived exigencies of the global economy, with growing disparity between rich and poor and gradual erosion of the social protections introduced during the postwar decades accompanying this shift. States willy-nilly became more effectively accountable to forces inherent in the global economy; and they were constrained to mystify this accountability in the eyes and ears of their own publics through the new vocabulary of globalization, interdependence, and competitiveness.

How and why did this happen? The matter will be long debated. It is, however, possible to recognize this period as a real turning point in the sense of a weakening of old structures and the emergence of new structures. Some key elements of the transformation can be identified.

### The Structural Power of Capital

Inflation, which at a modest level had hitherto been a stimulus to growth, beneficient alike to business and organized labour, now at higher rates and with declining profit margins, became perceived by business as inhibiting investment. Business blamed unions for raising wages and governments for a cycle of excessive spending, borrowing, and taxation. Governments were made to understand that a revival of economic growth depended on business confidence to invest, and that this confidence depended on 'discipline' directed at trade unions and government fiscal management. The investment strike and capital flight are powerful weapons that no government can ignore with impunity.

### The Restructuring of Production

Insofar as government policies helped to restore business confidence, new investment was by and large of a different type. The crisis of the postwar order accelerated the shift from Fordism to post-Fordism—from economies of scale to economies of flexibility. The large integrated plant employing semi-skilled workers for the mass production of standardized goods became an obsolete model of organization. The new model was based on a core-periphery structure of production, with a relatively small core of relatively permanent employees handling finance, research and development, technological organization, and innovation, and a periphery consisting of dependent components of the production process—outsourcing and temporary and part-time workers. Restructuring into the core-periphery model has facilitated the use of a more precariously employed labour force segmented by ethnicity, gender, nationality, religion, or geographical location. It has weakened the power of trade unions and strengthened that of capital within the production process. It has also made business less controllable by any single state authority.

### The Role of Debt

Both governments and corporations have relied increasingly on debt financing rather than on taxation or equity investment. Furthermore, debt has to an increasing extent become *foreign* debt. As the proportion of state revenue going into debt service rises, governments have become more effectively accountable to external bond markets than to their own publics. Their options in exchange rate policy, fiscal policy, and trade policy have become constrained by financial interests linked to the global economy. Corporations are no more autonomous of international finance than governments. Finance has become decoupled from production to become an independent power, an autocrat over the real economy.[7]

And what drives the decision-making of the financial manipulators? The short-range thinking of immediate financial gain, not the long-range thinking of industrial development. The market mentality functions synchronically (i.e., it takes account of relationships at a given point in time); development requires a diachronic mode of thought (i.e., considering planned and foreseen changes over time, the historical dimension).[8] The result of financial power's dominance over the *real* economy was as often as not the destruction of jobs and productive capital.

## The Structures of Globalization

The crisis of the postwar order has expanded the breadth and depth of a global economy that exists alongside and incrementally supersedes the classical international economy.[9] The global economy is the system generated by globalizing production and global finance. Global production is able to make use of the territorial divisions of the international economy, playing off one territorial jurisdiction against another so as to maximize reductions in costs, savings in taxes, avoidance of anti-pollution regulation, control over labour, and guarantees of political stability and favour. Global finance has achieved a virtually unregulated 24-hour-a-day network. The collective decision-making of global finance is centred in world cities rather than states—New York, Tokyo, London, Paris, Frankfurt—and extends by computer terminals to the rest of the world.

The two components of the global economy are in potential contradiction. Global production requires a certain stability in politics and finance in order to expand. Global finance has the upper hand because its power over credit creation determines the future of production; but global finance is in a parlously fragile condition. A concatenation of calamitous circumstances could bring it down—a number of corporate failures combined with government debt defaults or a cessation of lending by leading creditors and international institutions like the IMF. The major crises of the world economy have been debt crises of this kind—the Mexican crises of the 1980s and early 1990s and the Asian and Russian crises of the later 1990s. Up to now governments, even the combined governments of the Group of Seven (G–7), have not been able to devise any effectively secure scheme of regulation for global finance that could counter such a collapse.

There is, in effect, no explicit political or authority structure for the global economy. There is, nevertheless, something that remains to be deciphered, something that could be described by the French word *nébuleuse* or by the notion of 'governance without government'.[10] A transnational process of consensus formation does exist among the official caretakers of the global economy. It generates consensual guidelines, underpinned by an ideology of globalization, that are transmitted into the policy-making channels of national governments and big corporations. Part of this consensus-formation process has taken place through unofficial forums like the Trilateral Commission, the Bilderberg conferences, the annual World Economic Forum at Davos, Switzerland, and the more esoteric Mont Pelerin Society. Part of it goes through official bodies like the Organization for Economic Co-operation and Development (OECD), the Bank for International Settlements, the IMF, and the G–7. These shape the discourse within which policies are defined, the terms and concepts that circumscribe what can be thought and done. They also tighten the transnational networks that link policy-making from country to country.

The structural impact of this centralization of influence over policy can be called the internationalizing of the state. Its common feature is to convert the state into an agency for adjusting national economic practices and policies to the perceived exigencies of the global economy.[11] Power within the state becomes concentrated in those agencies in closest touch with global finance—the offices of presidents and prime ministers, treasuries, central banks. The agencies more closely identified with domestic clients—ministries of industry, labour ministries, etc.—become subordinated.

Different forms of state facilitate this tightening of the global/local relationship in countries occupying different positions in the global system. At one time, the military-bureaucratic form of state seemed to be optimum in countries of peripheral capitalism for the enforcement of monetary discipline. Now, IMF-inspired 'structural adjustment' is pursued by elected presidential regimes (Argentina, Brazil, Mexico, Peru, South Korea) that manage to retain a degree of insulation from popular pressures. The most powerful states encourage this form of political authority as likely to be more stable in the long run than military dictatorships.[12] India, formerly following a more autocentric or self-reliant path, moved towards integration into the global economy. Neo-conservative ideology sustained the

transformation of the state in Britain, the United States, Canada, and Australasia in the direction of globalization. Socialist Party governments in France and Spain adjusted their policies to the new orthodoxy. The states of the former Soviet empire were also swept up into the globalizing trend; and in the Asian crisis of the late 1990s, the countries of Southeast Asia became subject to the dictates of global finance.

In the European Union (EU), there is a struggle between two kinds of capitalism: the 'hyper-liberal' globalizing capitalism of Thatcherism, and a capitalism legitimated by social policy and territorially balanced development.[13] The latter stems from the social democratic tradition and also from an older conservatism that thinks of society as an organic whole rather than in terms of the contractual individualism of so-called neo-conservatism. In Japan, the guiding and planning role of the state retains initiative in managing the country's relationship with the outside world despite pressures, particularly from the United States, to integrate the Japanese economy more fully into the global economy. The late 1990s is a testing time in the evolution of Japanese capitalism.[14] The EU and Japan, and perhaps China, are now the only possible counterweights at the level of states to total globalization.

## The Changing Structure of World Politics

Out of the crisis of the postwar order, a new global political structure emerged. The old Westphalian concept of a system of sovereign states is no longer an adequate way of conceptualizing world politics.[15] Sovereignty is an ever looser concept. The old legal definitions conjuring up visions of ultimate and fully autonomous power are no longer meaningful. Sovereignty has gained meaning as an affirmation of cultural identity and lost meaning as power over the economy.

The affirmation of a growing multitude of 'sovereignties' is accompanied by the phenomenon of macro-regionalism. Three macro-regions redefining themselves are a Europe centred on the EU, an East Asian sphere in which the transnationalizing of the Japanese economy is the predominant phenomenon, and a North American sphere centred on the United States and looking to embrace Latin America. It is unlikely that these macro-regions will become autarkic blocs reminiscent of the world of the Great Depression. Firms based in each of the regions have too much involvement in the economies of the other regions for such exclusiveness to become the rule. Rather, the macro-regions are political-economic frameworks for capital accumulation and for organizing interregional competition for investment and for shares of the world market.[16] They also allow for the development, through internal struggles, of different forms of capitalism.

At the base of the emerging structure of world order are social forces. The old social movements—trade unions and peasant movements—have suffered setbacks under the impact of globalization; but the labour movement, in particular, has a background of experience in organization and ideology that can still be a strength in shaping the future. If it were to confine itself to its traditional clientele of manual industrial workers, while production is being restructured on a world scale so as to diminish this traditional base of power, the labour movement would condemn itself to a steadily weakening influence. Its prospect for revival lies in committing its organizational and ideological mobilizing capability to the task of building a broader coalition of social forces.

New social movements converging around specific sets of issues—environmentalism, feminism, and peace—have grown to a different extent in different parts of the world. More amorphous and vaguer movements—'people power' and democratization—are present wherever political structures are seen to be both repressive and fragile. In the Philippines and subsequently in Indonesia they have overthrown governments but perhaps not fundamentally changed structures of power. Many social movements evoke particular identities—ethnic, nationalist, religious, gender. They exist within states but are transnational in essence. The indigenous peoples' movement affirms rights prior to the existing state system.

The newly affirmed identities have in a measure displaced class as the focus of social struggle; but like class, they derive their force from resentment against exploitation. There is a material basis for their protest that is broader than the particular identities affirmed. Insofar as this common material basis remains obscured, the particular identities now reaffirmed can be manipulated into conflict one with another. The danger of authoritarian populism, of reborn fascism, is particularly great where political structures are crumbling and the material basis of resentment appears to be intractable. Democratization and 'people power' can move to the right as well as to the left.

## Vulnerability of the 'New World Order'

The emerging world order thus appears as a multilevel structure. At the base are social forces. Whether they are self-conscious and articulated into what Gramsci called a historic bloc,[17] or are depoliticized and manipulable, is the key issue in the making of the future. The old state system is resolving itself into a complex of political-economic entities: micro-regions, traditional states, and macro-regions with institutions of greater or lesser functional scope and formal authority. World cities are the keyboards of the global economy. Rival transnational processes of ideological formation aim respectively at hegemony and counterhegemony. Institutions of concertation and co-ordination bridge the major states and macro-regions. Multilateral processes exist for conflict management, peacekeeping, and regulation and service-providing in a variety of functional areas (trade, communications, health, etc.). The whole picture resembles the multilevel order of medieval Europe more than the Westphalian model of a system of sovereign independent states that has heretofore been the paradigm of international relations.[18]

The multilevel image suggests the variety of levels at which intervention becomes possible, indeed necessary, for any strategy aiming at an alternative to globalization. It needs to be complemented by an awareness of the inherent instability of this emerging structure. Instability arises from the dialectical relationship of two principles in the constitution of order: interdependence and territoriality. The interdependence principle is non-territorial in essence, geared to competition in the world market, to global finance unconstrained by territorial boundaries, and to global production. It operates in accordance with the thought processes of what Susan Strange has called the 'business civilization'.[19] The territorial principle is state-based, grounded ultimately in military-political power.

Some authors have envisaged the rise of the interdependence principle as implying a corresponding decline in the territorial principle;[20] but the notion of a reciprocal interactive relationship is closer to reality. The myth of the free market is that it is self-regulating. As Karl Polanyi demonstrated, enforcement of market rules required the existence of military or police power.[21] The fact that this force may rarely have to be applied helps to sustain the myth but does not dispense with the necessity of the force in reserve. Globalization in the late twentieth century also depends on the military-territorial power of an enforcer.

The Gulf War of 1991 revealed the structure and *modus operandi* of the new world order. The conflict began as a challenge from forces based on the territorial principle—Saddam Hussein's project to use regional territorial-military power to secure resources for Iraq's recovery from the Iran-Iraq War and for consolidation of a strong regional territorial power that could control resources (oil) required by the world economy, thereby extracting from the world economy a rent that could be used to further his developmental and military ambitions. Kuwait, Saudi Arabia, and other Persian Gulf states are fully integrated into the interdependent global economy. Indeed, these states are more analogous to large holding companies than to territorial states. The revenues they derive from oil are invested by their rulers through transnational banks into debt and equities around the world. Within the territories of these countries, the workforce is multinational and highly vulnerable.

The United States responded to the perceived Iraqi threat in its role as guarantor and enforcer of the world economic order; and, consistent with

that role, rallied support from other states concerned about the security of the global economy. The United States took on its own the decision to go to war, had it ratified by the United Nations Security Council, and demanded and obtained payment for the war from Germany, Japan, Saudi Arabia, and Kuwait.

The role of enforcer is, however, beset by a contradiction. The US projection of military power on the world scale has become more salient, monopolistic, and unilateral while the relative strength of US productive capacity has declined.[22] This in turn rests on the contradiction that the United States consumes more than its own production can pay for because foreigners are ready to accept a flow of dollars that, by the end of 1987, had turned the United States into the world's biggest debtor nation. As foreigners came to finance the difference between US consumption and the economy's ability to pay, the hegemonic system of the postwar period was becoming transformed into a tributary system.

The new world order is weak at the top. The coming years will likely make this weakness more manifest. A world order is no stronger than the social base upon which it rests. Economic globalization is generating sources of conflict and cleavages that are working their way slowly but surely into the foundations of world politics. The politics of the superstructure—US military power and coalition politics in support of economic globalization—are challenged by emergent social forces and social tensions, which are evident in both poor and rich countries. To understand these social forces it is necessary to reflect on the formation of identities that give meaning and orientation to people and on the forms of knowledge capable of explaining how to cope with the challenges of the future.

## Identities and Knowledge: Confronting the Future

Identity is important politically because it is the focus around which people can become mobilized to act to change their conditions and to pursue social goals. As already noted the two salient forms of identity of the nineteenth and twentieth centuries, nationality and class, while remaining significant banners of mobilization, have been subsumed into a complex of other identities. The nation-state for people in the richer countries has become a less central feature of their identity (with, perhaps, the notable exception of the United States), while in some poorer countries nationalism has become more virulent and aggressive. Social and economic cleavages remain fundamental as economic globalization accentuates polarization between rich and poor in all parts of the world;[23] but these cleavages are less frequently expressed as social class identities and more often as gender, race or ethnicity, religion, organizational affiliation, or a consciousness of historical grievance and humiliation.

The study of civilizations approaches the question of identity in its largest aggregates. There was a good deal of scholarly thinking about civilizations during the first half of the twentieth century.[24] The notion of a plurality of civilizations was put aside during World War II, which was seen as a war to defend *civilization* in the singular. The concept of a plurality of civilizations was all but eliminated during the Cold War. Now thinking about civilizations has begun again, but in a state of considerable confusion.

What is a civilization? Archaeologists who studied the earliest civilizations understood them to have arisen in certain material conditions, those of Bronze Age technology, with the emergence of large urban agglomerations, a division of labour, a class structure, and structures of political authority or states.[25] Those human aggregates were united by a realm of symbols through which their members could communicate, understand each other's intentions and motives, and interpret the world in which they lived. This realm of subjectivity—or rather, intersubjectivity—was expressed through myth, language, and religion, all of which were the same thing until subsequent ages and the rise of the analytical rationalizing spirit put them into separate compartments.

A working definition of civilization could be a fit between a given set of material conditions of existence and a set of intersubjective meanings. There is no single way in which these two objective and subjective aspects of civilization combine. It is not a case of the material base projecting a single form of consciousness in relation to which other forms of consciousness are 'false'. But the form of intersubjectivity has to be able to make sense of the material world; and there are different ways this may be achieved. Thus different civilizations, even on a common material base, may embody different values and pursue different trajectories.

We should not picture civilizations as fixed entities confronting one another in latent or active hostility but rather consider all civilizations as being in the process of transformation both from internal contradictions and from external encounters. This process of change or transformation, together with the problematic of coexistence among civilizations, could be the foundation of a future knowledge of world order. A number of dimensions of civilizational change would form parts of such knowledge: technology and communications; the social relations of production and the values embodied in society; prevailing concepts of time and space that structure how people think about their world; varieties of the sense of the spiritual and their consequences for human behaviour.

The importance of this study of civilizations lies in some basic premises concerning world order. (1) There are alternatives for the human future. We are not all bound by the inexorable expansion of economic globalization determined by competitiveness in the global market leading to a homogenized global society on the model of contemporary America. Civilizations embodying different values and different patterns of social organization are conceivable, for good or for ill. In other words, there is still a problem of moral and social choice. (2) If different civilizations do coexist, then the problem of mutual comprehension becomes paramount for the maintenance of world order. This arises in an epistemological context far different from the game theory notions popular during the Cold War, which assumed a single shared form of rationality.

The key problem in understanding such a plural world is, first, to be able to enter into the mental framework of people who see the world differently from the way 'we' do (whoever 'we' are)—

people who have different perceptions of reality. 'Reality' is historically and socially constructed, and is thus different for different civilizations, not a universal given. (This, it should be said, does not mean adopting other civilizational perspectives or rationalities, only understanding them.) Following from empathetic understanding of others is the need to work towards finding common ground among these different realities as a basis for some degree of universality within a world of differences.

## The Obsolescence of IR and IPE

Perhaps the most important development in the study of international relations in recent decades has been the emergence of international political economy (IPE) as a pendant or complement to a theory of international relations (IR) that was focused primarily on the military and political. In the academic world, this came about as though a single organism had divided itself into two. The result has been separate funding, separate career patterns, distinct sets of journals. It is now the moment to retrace the origins of this divide and to ask whether the onward march of history does not challenge us to think beyond that phase of separation and to envisage a new, more reintegrated form of knowledge.

Initially, IPE made its mark by giving more prominence to the economic foundations of power. But its importance was not limited to expanding the accepted subject-matter of international relations. IPE gradually changed the way of thinking about world order. It put the emphasis on the frameworks or historical structures within which human activity takes place and on the slow processes of change in these frameworks. This made a sharp contrast with a politics of international relations that worked with fixed assumptions about the nature of the state system and an economics that worked with equally fixed assumptions about economic processes. The conventional methods were useful guides to problem-solving under stable conditions. They were not very useful for understanding changes in how people were coming to understand their places in the world and the nature of the problems they

faced. The emerging multiplicity of identities was an indication of the complexity of these changes.

The real achievement of IPE was not to bring in economics but to open up a critical investigation into change in historical structures. The emphasis on economics became merely an important incident in the movement towards a new knowledge about world order. This movement brought in many subjects other than economics in the narrow sense. It encouraged, for example, inquiry into the power implications of gender and the implications of human activity for the biosphere. And it was accompanied by a broadening of the concept of security that included many of the things that IPE had opened onto, including gender and the biosphere.

Most broadly, IPE began to look more at how historical structures—those conditions not of their own choosing within which people make history, as Marx wrote[26]—are reshaped from the bottom up by slow molecular changes in societies. IPE also brought in a spirit of self-criticism, of reflexivity, the importance of becoming aware of how one's own position in time and place and social structures defines one's perspective on history. Having achieved this revolution in thinking, IPE, along with IR in the earlier conventional sense, has become obsolescent, clearing the ground for a more integrated knowledge about processes of world order.

The search for this more integrated form of knowledge goes beyond the IR/IPE duality to challenge other established boundaries. Insofar as we begin to see social relations as the foundation of political authority and the origin of conflict, the conventional separation of comparative politics from international relations makes little sense. Of course, no one can study everything and some people will know more about things that have been bracketed as comparative politics (which in academic convention usually excludes the home country) than about activities in the diplomatic and multilateral sphere. For the purpose of understanding world order or regional developments, it is necessary to draw together knowledge about power relations in society and knowledge about the relations among the entities like states that are shaped by these social power relations. It is also necessary to breach sacrosanct disciplinary boundaries so as to draw on history and sociology and geography—indeed, on all the social sciences and humanities.[27]

## The Political Process and World Order

If we are to assume that power is grounded in human communities, and if we take a 'bottom-up' perspective on world order, then we need to ask about the condition of public affinity or comfort with the political authorities of the entities that formally constitute world order—the states and multilateral institutions and processes. That affinity seems to range from the tenuous to the hostile throughout the world. The sense of identity between people and polity is weak. Confidence in the political classes is at a low ebb.

In some parts of the world, at one extreme, people regard political rulers as predatory tyrants and seek to avoid contact with them as much as possible. But even in those countries accustomed to constitutional government and the rule of law there is widespread public scepticism about political leadership. The political class is held to be both corrupt and incompetent: corrupt in the sense of holding their own careers above any consideration of public interest; and incompetent in being unable to understand and deal effectively with the things that concern the public, such as unemployment, erosion of public services, and social inequities.

In part, also, this lack of confidence may be attributed to the ideological hegemony of globalization. Ideology proclaims the inevitability of globalization with its categorical imperative of global competitiveness. 'There is no alternative', as former British Prime Minister Margaret Thatcher was wont to say. Globalization thus appears as the ultimate form of alienation: something created by people that has come to wield absolute power over them.

Politicians no longer talk about citizens. A citizen is an autonomous individual in his or her aspect of contemplating the public good or envisaging a good future society. Since globalization abolishes choice, there is really no role left for the citizen. Instead, politicians refer to taxpayers, job-seekers, and stakeholders (echoes of corporatism[28]);

and government, emptied of the possibility of alternative choices about future society, becomes reduced to a question of management—a rivalry among would-be managerial teams.[29]

In these conditions, there is ample scope for forces that operate outside of the control of formal public authorities and beyond the scope of conventional political analysis. An invisible or highly obscure process goes on underneath the formal, open, visible political process. This is the *covert world* of politics. Occasional events bring it to public consciousness: the foul-ups of intelligence operations, efforts to trace laundering of illegal funds, actions by terrorist groups, financial corruption and political funding scandals.

A wide range of agencies operates in this covert world: intelligence agencies, mafias, drug cartels, arms traders, money-laundering banks, terrorist organizations, paramilitaries and mercenaries, religious cults, and the sex trade among them. These agencies engage in co-operation as well as conflict. Political science has quite naturally privileged the study of overt politics. The degraded condition of formal politics—the marginalizing of public debate about social values in favour of technical issues of management, and the abdication of citizenship in favour of private and group interests—calls for more systematic attention and critical analysis of the covert world. When we contemplate this duality of the degraded overt world and booming covert world, the obvious central issue becomes whether the public political process can be reinvigorated so as to regain fuller control over political outcomes and to reduce, if not altogether eliminate, the space for covert activity.

Working on the hypothesis that political authority that is built from the bottom up leads to a focus on civil society, which is the positive pendant to the negative weight of the covert world. More and more attention is being given by political scientists to the development of civil society. In many African countries, people have been organizing themselves on a local community basis to struggle for survival in conditions imposed on them by governments and international organizations.[30] In Indonesia, the spread of organized community movements may constitute the potential basis for a new political authority to replace the corrupt and tyrannical shell of power that remains. A latent civil society in the Congo facilitated the collapse of the Mobutu kleptocracy, although it has played no role as yet in the unstable sequel. In Chiapas, the Zapatistas work to transcend their original condition as an ethnically based guerrilla movement to become a force for the revival of Mexican civil society and in the process, by the use of modern electronic communications, to forge transnational links as an element in a global counterhegemonic movement. In Canada, civil society has been activated in protests against the North American Free Trade Agreement (NAFTA), the Asia-Pacific Economic Co-operation forum (APEC), and the proposed Multilateral Investment Agreement (MIA)—all institutional facets of globalization—and the subordination of human rights to corporate trading interests in Canadian foreign policy. In contrast to the covert world, which by and large functionally sustains established power, civil society movements can be seen as a dissident world. Its components express their lack of confidence in formally constituted power by organizing themselves to express and work for an alternative world, the possibility of which hegemonic ideology denies.

So we have three realms of political activity in the world at the turn of the millennium: the hegemonic power of globalization; the covert world that grows parasitically upon it; and the dissident world groping towards the creation of a counterhegemonic challenge.

## The Challenge of the Biosphere

We are now increasingly aware that these three contending sets of forces operate within the overriding constraint of the biosphere. Humanity is only one part of nature and, within nature, humanity is interdependent with other forms of life and life-sustaining substances. A series of events and concerns have driven home the implications of that interdependence: the hole in the ozone layer, global warming, the decline of biodiversity, the decline of fish stocks, people's sensitivities to environmental pollution, and catastrophic weather patterns.

The irruption of non-human nature into human politics arouses awareness that human survival is at stake, if not tomorrow then in a long run that cannot be ignored. In this perspective, biosphere maintenance becomes the ultimate criterion for judging the viability of political action.

But how do we assess the three realms of politics by this criterion?

Globalization confronts a tragic contradiction. Globalization is driven by global competitiveness; and the counterpart to competitiveness is consumer demand. A prevailing model of demand derived from the affluent societies spurs continuing expansion of existing production patterns that are accompanied by pollution and depletion of natural resources. The geography of environmental degradation may shift when some of the more affluent areas clean up and relatively poor areas adopt the methods they have cast off. Some new technologies may be less polluting and less resource-intensive; and there is money to be made in environmental cleansing. But if globalization persists on anything like its present course, it is running head on into a biospheric veto that could become a crisis affecting human survival.

The implications to be drawn from this latent contradiction are (1) that the affluent societies will have to change their patterns of consumption and production to bring them into compatibility with biospheric survival; (2) that this radically altered behaviour in affluent societies should serve as an alternative model for progress in the less affluent; and (3) that the now affluent societies pioneering an alternative social economy should aid the less affluent to develop in this different way. This is a political challenge that seems now to be beyond the possibilities of the political systems of the affluent societies. Former US President George Bush's remark that 'Our lifestyle is not open to negotiation' is indicative of political realism in the short-term perspective of dominant political élites.

When we come to the second realm of forces, the covert world, the biosphere is totally outside its ken. The covert world does not think of long-term diachronic structural change. It is a synchronic world concerned with immediate gains in money and political power. What goes on here perpetuates existing structures of power and practices. It is a major and usually unrecognized block to action favourable to the biosphere.

It is within the third realm of forces, the dissident world of counterhegemonic activists in civil society, that an alternative vision of social economy can be advanced. These are the forces that can lead in re-educating societies towards a different mode of consumption and production. It must be recognized, however, that civil society is a terrain of conflict. Forces contesting globalization and working to construct a counterhegemony are opposed in civil society by exclusionary forces of racism, nationalism, and other manifestations of the extreme right. Civil society is at the heart of the problem of choice for the future.

## Towards a New Form of Social Economy?

Since World War II, the world economy has gone through one major phase of structural change. The mid-1970s witnessed the transition from Keynesianism and Fordism towards neo-liberal globalization. The postwar world sought to construct an economic order that would ground economic behaviour in social responsibility, to give a priority to the goals of full employment and social security,

and—in a modest but avowed way—to narrow the gap between rich and poor countries. Keynesianism and Fordism were the techniques for allowing politics to redress the inequities of the market. These policies and practices reached a crisis point in the mid-1970s. From that point on, they were gradually abandoned in favour of allowing deregulated markets free rein. The consequences we see now are social conflict arising from growing polarization within and among societies between rich and poor, the prospect of financial collapse, and the impending threat of biospheric crisis.

If there is to be a solution, it is unlikely to be a return to postwar practices. It would more likely have to be a new concept of economy that is less depleting and polluting of resources, more oriented towards the basic material needs of people that advanced technology makes possible with a smaller proportion of workers, and much greater emphasis on the more neglected labour-intensive tasks of satisfying social and human needs for health, education, child and elder care, and conviviality. This, of course, implies a radical reorientation of social values, including how different kinds of work are valued. The state will most likely have to become the regulator and legitimator of these new practices; but it seems clear that response by the state will only be triggered by the bottom-up pressure of citizen activism.

## Notes

1  Samuel P. Huntington, *The Clash of Civilizations and the Remaking of World Order* (New York: Simon & Schuster, 1996).

2  Susan Strange, *The Retreat of the State: The Diffusion of Power in the World Economy* (Cambridge: Cambridge University Press, 1996).

3  Karl Polanyi, *The Great Transformation: The Political and Economic Origins of Our Time* (Boston: Beacon Press, 1957).

4  Most notably by Francis Fukuyama, *The End of History and the Last Man* (New York: Avon Books, 1992).

5  On the distinction between problem-solving and critical theory, see Robert W. Cox, 'Social Forces, States, and World Orders: Beyond International

Relations Theory', in Cox with Timothy J. Sinclair, *Approaches to World Order* (Cambridge: Cambridge University Press, 1996).

6  For a discussion of neo-realism, see Robert O. Keohane, ed., *Neorealism and Its Critics* (New York: Columbia University Press, 1986).

7  See Peter Drucker, 'The Changed World Economy', *Foreign Affairs* 64, 4 (Spring 1986): 783. Drucker wrote that 'in the world economy of today, the "real" economy of goods and services and the "symbol" economy of money, credit, and capital are no longer bound tightly to each other; they are, indeed, moving further and further apart.'

8  For a fuller story of financial antics of the 1980s, see Susan Strange, *Casino Capitalism* (Oxford:

Basil Blackwell, 1986); on the 1990s, see Strange, *Mad Money* (Manchester: Manchester University Press, 1998).

9   Bernadette Madeuf and Charles-Albert Michalet, 'A New Approach to International Economics', *International Social Science Journal* 30, 2 (1978).

10  The title of a book edited by James Rosenau and E.-O. Czempiel, *Governance Without Government* (Cambridge: Cambridge University Press, 1992), which deals with many aspects of world order, although not explicitly with global finance. Strange, *Casino Capitalism*, 165–9, argues that effective regulation over finance is unlikely to be achieved through international organization and that only the US government, by intervening in the New York financial market, might be capable of global effectiveness. But, she adds, US governments have behaved unilaterally and irresponsibly in this matter and show no signs of modifying their behaviour. For an instance of how unofficial private regulation functions, see Timothy J. Sinclair, 'Passing Judgment: Credit Rating Processes as Regulatory Mechanisms of Governance in the Emerging World Order', *Review of International Political Economy* 1, 1 (1994).

11  Robert W. Cox, *Production, Power, and World Order: Social Forces in the Making of History* (New York: Columbia University Press, 1987), 253–67.

12  William I. Robinson, *Promoting Polyarchy: Globalization, U.S. Intervention, and Hegemony* (Cambridge: Cambridge University Press, 1996).

13  See, for example, Michel Albert, *Capitalisme contre capitalisme* (Paris: Seuil, 1991).

14  For an analysis of Japanese capitalism, see Shigeto Tsuru, *Japan's Capitalism* (Cambridge: Cambridge University Press, 1993).

15  International relations analysts use the term 'Westphalian' to refer to an interstate system supposed to have come into existence in Europe after the Peace of Wesphalia in 1648.

16  The Asian financial crisis of the late 1990s has enabled US and European firms to buy up Asian assets, thereby securing long-term control over Asian production capacity. Michael Richardson in the *International Herald Tribune*, 20–1 June 1998.

17  Antonio Gramsci, *Selections from the Prison Notebooks*, ed. and trans. Quintin Hoare and Geoffrey Nowell Smith (New York: International Publishers, 1971), 137, 366–77.

18  Hedley Bull, *The Anarchical Society* (New York: Columbia University Press, 1977), projected a 'new medievalism' as a possible form of future world order.

19  Susan Strange, 'The Name of the Game', in Nicholas X. Rizopoulos, ed., *Sea Changes: American Foreign Policy in a World Transformed* (New York: Council on Foreign Relations, 1990).

20  For example, Richard Rosecrance, *The Rise of the Trading State* (New York: Basic Books, 1986).

21  Polanyi, *The Great Transformation*.

22  It is not for me here to review the literature debating the question of US 'decline'. Suffice it to mention two contributions giving opposite views: Paul Kennedy, *The Rise and Fall of the Great Powers* (New York: Random House, 1987); and Joseph S. Nye, Jr, *Bound to Lead: The Changing Nature of American Power* (New York: Basic Books, 1990). There is very little disagreement about the basic facts: the decline of US productivity relative to European and Japanese productivity and the extent of functional illiteracy and non-participation in economically productive work among the US population. The debate is mainly between optimists and pessimists with respect to whether these conditions can be reversed. See Kennedy, '"Fin-de-siècle" America', *New York Review of Books*, 28 June 1990.

23  United Nations Research Institute for Social Development, *States of Disarray: The Social Effects of Globalization* (London: UNRISD, 1995).

24  Two major works widely discussed were Oswald Spengler, *The Decline of the West* (New York: Knopf, 1939); and Arnold J. Toynbee, *A Study of History* (an abridgement of this multi-volume work originally published by D.C. Somervell was published by Oxford University Press, 1946).

25  Gordon Childe, *What Happened in History* (Harmondsworth: Penguin, 1957).

26  Karl Marx, *The 18th Brumaire of Louis Bonaparte* (New York: International Publishers, 1969), 15.

27  Fernand Braudel, 'History and the Social Sciences: The *longue durée*', in Braudel, *On History*,

trans. Sarah Matthews (Chicago: University of Chicago Press, 1980), 25–54.

28 'Corporatism' is the term applied to a variety of political economy forms that link the state with organized industry and labour in the management of the national economy. These include the Italian fascist corporative state, forms of tripartite economic management in advanced capitalist countries during the era of Keynesianism, and state corporatism in authoritarian regimes of less developed countries.

29 See, for example, Jean-Marie Guéhenno, *La fin de la démocratie* (Paris: Flammarion, 1993).

30 Fantu Cheru, *The Silent Revolution in Africa: Debt, Development and Democracy* (London: Zed Books, 1989).

## Suggested Readings

Braudel, Fernand. 'History and the Social Sciences: The *longue durée*', in Braudel, *On History*, trans. Sarah Matthews. Chicago: University of Chicago Press, 1980.

Capra, Fritjof. *The Web of Life*. New York: Doubleday Anchor Books, 1996.

Cox, Robert W. 'Social Forces, States, and World Orders: Beyond International Relations Theory', in Cox with Timothy J. Sinclair, *Approaches to World Order*. Cambridge: Cambridge University Press, 1996.

Guéhenno, Jean-Marie. *La fin de la démocratie*. Paris: Flammarion, 1993.

Helleiner, Eric. 'International Political Economy and the Greens', *New Political Economy* 1, 1 (1996).

Sakamoto, Yoshikazu. 'Civil Society and Democratic World Order', in Stephen Gill and James H. Mittelman, eds, *Innovation and Transformation in International Studies*. Cambridge: Cambridge University Press, 1997.

Strange, Susan. *The Retreat of the State: The Diffusion of Power in the World Economy*. Cambridge: Cambridge University Press, 1996.

United Nations Research Institute for Social Development. *States of Disarray: The Social Effects of Globalization*. London: UNRISD, 1995.

## Web Sites

World Trade Organization: http://www.wto.org

International Monetary Fund: http://www.imf.org

World Bank: http://www.worldbank.org

Organization for Economic Co-operation and Development: http://www.oecd.org

European Union Central: http://www.europa.eu.int

## Chapter 2

# The Agency of Labour in a Changing Global Order

Robert O'Brien

Students of international political economy, whether beginners or veterans, face a difficult issue when trying to understand global order and the sources for change in that order. Numerous candidates for explanation appear. As outlined in the introductory chapter, some approaches emphasize structures such as anarchical competition between states. An alternative approach has outlined how the transformation of the production structure from Fordism to post-Fordism influences the global political economy.[1] Some have suggested that international arrangements in particular issue-areas (regimes) are essential.[2] Others have focused on the agency of multinational corporations.[3] Another strategy has identified the nature of domestic institutions and interest groups as being crucial to the explanation of international change and co-operation.[4] This chapter argues that one of the prime factors in helping us understand the direction of global change is the activity of people organized around their particular role in the process of production. The agency of labour shapes global order.

The division of labour and the manner in which work is organized are central to understanding the structure of the global economy. People play a role in this global economy based on their position in the division of labour. Some people are fortunate enough to be knowledge workers making impressive salaries in the financial markets, some are manufacturing workers engaged in intense competition with their counterparts around the world, and many others are subsistence farmers trying to survive in a system moving towards the increased commercialization of agricultural production. These positions in the process of production lead to different sets of interests and political action among various groups of workers. Their attempts to influence the trajectory of the global economy are a neglected, but significant, factor in understanding the basis and possibilities of global order.

Labour groups play an important role in shaping the global order through four mechanisms. First, they attempt to influence national state policies. A change in their support for international policies can challenge the basis of global order and the plans of other actors. Second, they engage directly with international organizations to influence the rules of the game that govern international economic activity. Third, they attempt to influence the structure of the market by engaging directly with the most powerful market actors—multinational corporations (MNCs). Fourth, they play a significant role in the development of 'new internationalisms' by linking up with other social movements in counterhegemonic projects. The remainder of this chapter will illustrate these points with specific examples.

Before we move on to the substantial analysis, it is necessary to clarify what is meant by labour in this chapter. It refers to a whole range of people acting in their capacity as workers. It includes workers organized in unions and engaged in bargaining with firms and states. In some states such unions may be autonomous, acting on the instructions of their members. In other states the unions may be penetrated by state or party officials and adopt a relatively passive role. Most students of IPE will be familiar with the existence of organized workers in the form of unions. However, these categories of workers only make up a small percentage of the labour force. Labour also refers to the majority of people who can be classified as 'unprotected workers'.[5] These vulnerable people labour in forms of work that receive little union, political party, or state protection from those who hold power. Examples of such workers are people engaged in subsistence agriculture, peasants working for landholders, informal-sector workers forced to scavenge employment on the streets, and workers within the household (usually women and children). Their role in the shaping of global order is significant, even if it is usually neglected.

Although it is a lifestyle far removed from the reality of most of the readers of this volume, we should not forget that the vast majority of the world's population are subsistence farmers or peasants. The constant liberalization of economic activity and changing global order since the end of World War II has implications for these people as well. More importantly, their response to the further encroachment of the liberal system on their lives will have serious implications for the direction of globalization. Here we are faced with what McMichael calls the 'agrarian question'.[6] Put somewhat crudely, the agrarian question concerns the implications of replacing peasant-based agriculture with capitalist agriculture. Although this was a subject of grave concern in Western states in the nineteenth century and attention to peasant affairs was also raised during social revolutions in China, Cuba, and Vietnam in the middle of the twentieth century, the agrarian question has not been posed again until very recently. It has re-emerged in response to the threat that liberalization of agriculture poses to billions of peasants around the world. The rest of this chapter will consider the relationship between workers (protected or unprotected) and other key actors or structures in the global political economy.

## The State

The nature and influence of labour organizations on the state vary widely across the globe. A 1989 survey of 27 countries examining the purposes and forms of trade unionism developed a fivefold typology that classified national union structures as being dominated by a political party (party-ancillary), dominated by the state (state-ancillary), dominating a political party (party-surrogate), dominating a state (state-surrogate), or autonomous.[7] On investigation the three crucial categories were: labour dominated by the state, labour dominated by a political party, and labour organized in autonomous unions. In states in which labour is dominated by the state or a political party (the majority of states) the influence of unions on policy will be limited. The third category—autonomous unions—can be expected to influence state policy, but this, of course, varies according to the state.

Where autonomous unions have influence, they can take a role in shaping global order. Andrew Martin has argued that the degree of compatibility between international economic order and Keynesian welfare states is partially a function of the relative strength of labour in the most powerful states.[8] He suggests that the undermining of the welfare state by international pressures can be attributed to US state policy, which was less influenced by unions than the social democratic or corporatist states of Western Europe. The content of international economic arrangements is seen to reflect the balance of social forces within the strongest states.

We can take this a step further to argue that recent changes in the US political economy, which have alienated worker organizations from the halls of political power, risk undermining the political foundations of an open liberal economic system. Efforts by labour to protect itself in the face of an increasingly competitive economy and a state less committed to economic redistribution may tip the balance against attempts to build liberal international organizations and regulation.

Since the early 1970s US labour has moved from offering strong support for an internationalizing economy to being a growing obstacle to further liberalization and internationalization. This raises doubts about the social base in the US for maintaining leadership in the liberalization process. Although US labour was relatively weak in the US postwar political system, it still participated in the politics of productivity.[9] This arrangement involved subsuming class conflict by ensuring that growth and productivity gains were distributed across the society. It was a method of neutralizing labour opposition by integrating unionized workers into a division of the economic spoils. For its part, US labour supported the extension of US capitalism by marginalizing radical workers' organizations in Latin America, Asia, and Western Europe.[10] However, this co-operation changed as neo-liberal governments in the United States and Britain, accompanied by a business offensive against workers, led to the ejection of labour from the governing coalition.

In response to being shown out the door of the ruling coalition, labour has begun to re-evaluate its political and economic priorities. A good example of this can be seen in labour's response to the negotiation of the North American Free Trade Agreement (NAFTA). Organized labour reacted differently to this liberalizing agreement from how it had to earlier initiatives (e.g., the GATT) in four ways. First, it acknowledged that the unfettered expansion of US-based MNCs was not in the interest of US workers. This was in contrast to previous policies that supported the expansion of American capitalism to other parts of the world. Second, labour rejected the political leadership of the Democratic Party and opposed the initiative of a sitting Democratic President. Third, it sought out other social movement allies, such as environmentalists, to build a broad-based political coalition capable of slowing the neo-liberal agenda. Fourth, labour worked with autonomous unions (rather than those tied to right-wing governments) in other countries. In dealing with Mexico the AFL-CIO was forced to cultivate relations with the emerging independent Mexican unions rather than rely on the Mexican government-sponsored Confederación de Trabajadores de México (CTM) union. The CTM proved adequate for US workers' interests during the Cold War when the fight was against communism, but allies in the fight against transnational exploitation would have to be found in unions controlled by their members. In summary, the US NAFTA debate is likely to prove to have been a watershed in organized labour's acceptance of the dominant brand of liberalism.[11]

US workers are in the process of re-evaluating their interests in relation to American corporations and the US state. They can no longer be counted on to back the expansion of US capitalism without question. Their political support for international agreements is in doubt, making the task of global governance more difficult. Yet, national interests can and do still motivate workers' organizations. In the recent debate about limits to pollution at the Kyoto climate change conference some US unions stood side by side with US corporations in resisting measures that might increase costs of production.

Workers' organizations have also played a crucial role in changing state policy and elements of international order in states where their activities were often curbed. Two excellent examples are in Poland and South Africa. The collapse of the Soviet empire and the end of the Cold War had several important causes, including the exhaustion of the Soviet economic model and intense competition from Western states and economies. However, the activities of workers' organizations (Solidarity in Poland) in the early 1980s opened the first cracks in the Soviet system of control that would eventually lead to a wider disintegration of East European Communist states in 1989.[12] In South Africa, workers' groups, in alliance with other social activists and the African National Congress, waged a long and ultimately successful campaign to overturn the apartheid system of racial oppression. The labour movement was central to 'creating the conditions for transition, in shaping its character and indeed in legitimating the process itself'.[13]

Agricultural workers have also had an influence on state policy in recent years. Perhaps the most dramatic case has been the peasant and indigenous rebellion in the southern Mexican state of Chiapas.[14] Although the rebellion draws on a historical legacy of oppression, it was clearly linked to steps taken by the Mexican government to liberalize agricultural landholdings in the run up to NAFTA. Local concerns were linked to broader developments in IPE. The Zapatista rebels have been quick to exploit modern technology to broadcast their cause worldwide through their own Web page and have begun the task of forging links with similarly minded groups in other parts of the world. The rebellion soon moved from a local protest to challenging the power structures of the Mexican state, its economic policies, and insertion into the global economy. The potential for peasant-based challenges to state policy exists in other developing states as well, including China, India, Indonesia, and the Philippines.

## International Organizations

Craig Murphy has pointed out that the structure of international organizations is linked to changes in economic organization and dependent on political support within and across state boundaries.[15] Labour groups have had a complex relationship with international economic organizations, ranging from support for their objectives to determined opposition. They have been the cause of the creation of at least one major institution, have tried to influence the policies of others, and have firmly resisted the activities of many international economic institutions.

Worker dissatisfaction with the destructive nature of capitalism led to the creation of the oldest element of the United Nations system—the International Labour Organization (ILO), which originated with the League of Nations, a predecessor of the UN. Fearing the mass mobilization of the working class in World War I and operating under the shadow of the Communist victory in the Russian revolution, the victorious allied capitalist states created an international institution to address and pacify the concerns of the workers. As one former ILO official has put it, 'The ILO was Versailles' answer to Bolshevism.'[16] The ILO constitution recognized that peace could only be based on social justice and that the conditions of workers were central to social justice.

A distinctive element of the ILO is that voting rights are split on a 2:1:1 ratio among state, employer, and labour representatives. Recent union activity in the field of international organizations is aimed at extending some element of the tripartite ILO structure so that labour has a voice in a wide range of policy issues. The goal is to force major international organizations to address worker and social issues. We will consider this attempt within the World Trade Organization (WTO) and the International Monetary Fund (IMF).

The WTO is a product of the Uruguay Round negotiations of the General Agreement on Tariffs and Trade (GATT). It established a permanent international trade organization with enhanced regulatory powers and the mandate to spearhead further liberalization initiatives. Many elements of the international labour movement, such as the International Confederation of Free Trade Unions (ICFTU), viewed the establishment of the WTO as one of a series of international regulatory regimes created to protect the interests of capital in the 1980s and 1990s. The task for the labour movement was to try to re-establish protective social regulation at the national, regional, and international levels.[17]

The goal of the international labour movement (as represented by the main international confederations of trade unions) for the WTO is to have core labour standards (a social clause) brought into its purview. The social clause would commit states to respect crucial ILO conventions. These provide for: freedom of association, the right to collective bargaining, abolition of forced labour, prevention of discrimination in employment, and a minimum age for employment. The key to having the conventions as part of the WTO is that for the first time they would become enforceable and not depend on the whims of individual states. In contrast to the ILO's reliance on moral argument, the WTO has the ability to enforce compliance. To achieve this goal of a social clause, groups such as the ICFTU and affiliates including the AFL-CIO have pressured the United States and the European Union into raising the issue of core labour standards at the WTO, arguing that continued support for trade liberalization in developed states requires a minimum floor for workers' rights.

Other elements of the labour movement have opposed both the idea that core labour standards should be part of the WTO and the existence of the WTO itself. For example, the linkage between labour standards and the WTO was rejected in two national conferences of independent Indian unions in March and October 1995. Delegates expressed fears that the social clause initiative was driven by protectionist desires in countries of the developed North. The Indian union suggestion was that rather than working through the WTO, workers should push for a United Nations Labour Rights Convention and the establishment of national labour rights commissions. The issue was not whether all workers should be entitled to basic rights, but whether the WTO was the appropriate institution for such a task. The conclusion among many grassroots Indian activists was that the WTO, along with the IMF and World Bank, was irrevocably tied to exploitative northern interests.

A similar, oppositional stance towards the WTO has been adopted by an alliance of peasant groups reacting against the liberalization of agriculture—the Peoples' Global Action against 'Free' Trade and the World Trade Organization (PGA). The PGA is an instrument for co-ordination that brings together people's movements to oppose trade liberalization. The PGA organizes conferences approximately three months before the biannual ministerial meetings of the World Trade Organization. Conferences are used to update the PGA manifesto and to co-ordinate global and local action against free trade. The conference committee for the February 1998 event included groups such as the Frente Zapatista de Liberacion Naciónal (FZLN) from Mexico, the Karnataka State Farmers' Association (KRRS) from India, the Movemento sem Terra (NST) from Brazil, and the Peasant Movement of the Philippines (KMP). The PGA is committed to non-violent civil disobedience and a confrontational attitude in pursuit of its opposition to free trade. It represents a constituency firmly in opposition to dominant trends in the global political economy.

Another institution of concern to labour groups is the International Monetary Fund. In developing countries its policy guidelines of privatization, deregulation, and liberalization are seen to be the cause of enormous suffering, savage decreases in living standards, and a justification for anti-union campaigns. IMF policies are interpreted as imposing a neo-liberal economic model on the weakest countries and tolerating, if not encouraging, authoritarian forms of industrial relations.

Recently, the IMF has tried to work with labour groups to formulate and implement structural adjustment programs. The IMF director has called on organized labour to help hold governments accountable for financial mismanagement and the content of structural adjustment programs.[18] He believes that labour can be a strategic partner in ensuring that money is properly spent by national governments. The leadership of the ICFTU has responded positively to these overtures, seeing this as an opportunity to influence policy. Other parts of the union movement are much more reluctant to co-operate because they see IMF policies as the cause of exclusion. Potential interaction between the IMF and the ICFTU is limited by widely conflicting goals. The IMF is seeking the help of unions to limit government corruption and contribute to good governance, whereas the unions desire a rethinking of the core assumptions underlying structural adjustment programs.

While the ICFTU and its affiliates are increasingly engaging with international organizations, the possibility of influencing policy will take much longer to develop. Relations with the WTO, IMF, and World Bank face ideological and interest-based opposition. Although the Bretton Woods institutions are re-evaluating their economic management approaches, neo-liberal ideology opposes political interference in the market, such as international labour standards or social dimensions to structural adjustment policies (SAPs). Financial interests oppose curbs on speculation, while employers in most countries and entrenched authoritarian governments resist the introduction of meaningful international labour standards.

## The Market

Unions and groups concerned about labour issues are also trying to change the nature of market behaviour by direct action against corporations. Where state or international regulatory efforts are non-existent or inadequate to protect workers' interests, corporations are targeted for reform. The movement is following a dual strategy that attempts to restore the power of unions through collective bargaining and to restrict the worst abuses of workers' rights through consumer pressure. The first tactic is meant to curb neo-liberal industrial relations by bringing independent unions into a transnational industrial relations system and by limiting the power of dominant market actors. The second tactic is aimed at limiting authoritarian industrial relations by creating a minimum floor for working conditions that will facilitate worker survival and organization.

Since the early 1970s unions have shown an interest in building a system of multinational collective bargaining. Such a step would bring organized labour closer to the social democratic form of industrial relations because it would legitimate its role in the economy. The aim is to establish a form of global industrial relations where unions are able to bargain with multinational companies unhindered by geographic dispersal. International unions are taking a number of initiatives. One step is to put all the collective agreements of a particular firm into a single database so that union negotiators will be aware of arrangements at sister plants. Another initiative is to host world congresses of workers from the same company, such as Nissan.

An additional example of the globalizing of industrial relations is provided by the conflict around the tire company Bridgestone. In 1994 Bridgestone refused to accept a union deal similar to those reached at Goodyear and Michelin. Bridgestone demanded wage and benefit rollbacks, which led to strikes and the hiring of replacement workers. The United Steel Workers of America responded by working with the International Federation of Chemical, Energy, Mine and General Workers to mount a worldwide campaign. This included lobbying and demonstrations in Europe and Japan as well as in North America. The union viewed the US dispute as the first step in Bridgestone's global anti-union strategy.

Caution should be exercised in anticipating the growth of multinational collective bargaining. In its most fertile ground, Western Europe, progress has been extremely slow.[19] Despite high levels of economic integration, geographic proximity, and an overreaching institutional structure in the European Community and European Union, the obstacles are immense. Unions remain weak and dominated by national structures, employer organizations and firms are reluctant to engage in such activity, and the European Union institutions lack the structure and the desire to become active in the industrial relations domain. Given such difficulty in an area of possible economic and political convergence, the possibilities in more diverse arenas appear remote.

A second area of labour activity has been the effort to influence corporate behaviour by introducing, monitoring, and enforcing codes of conduct, which are meant to set basic principles for the behaviour of MNCs (and their subcontractors) with respect to their labour practices and environmental policies. In some cases firms are willing partners in implementing such codes. For example, the Levi Strauss company's code of conduct is reproduced in ICFTU literature as an illustration of a multinational corporation working with the union movement. Levi Strauss is notable not just for its code of conduct banning labour exploitation but for its withdrawal in 1992 from states operating extreme forms of authoritarian industrial relations, such as Burma and China.

Although codes of conduct are becoming more widespread, they remain a relatively neglected aspect of doing business. For example, a 1997 survey of Canadian multinationals revealed that only 20 per cent of Canadian MNCs had such codes.[20] Of the companies with codes, only 14 per cent had an independent mechanism to monitor the implementation and respect of the codes. In such an environment the task of raising the issue of codes of conduct and publicizing abuses falls to labour organizations. Due to their limited and relatively recent implementation, the effectiveness of such codes in curbing labour abuses remains in doubt.

One prominent union strategy is to select a particularly serious abuse of workers' rights, highlight the abuses in the media, and attempt to pressure governments to legislate, consumers to boycott, and corporations to change behaviour. Good examples are the campaigns against child labour and labour conditions in toy factories in East Asia. Another example is the campaign against child labour in the manufacture of footballs.[21] It coincided with an excellent use of tactics in the campaign. Prior to the start of the European Football Championships (EURO '96), the ICFTU revealed that footballs endorsed by the governing football association, FIFA, were made in Pakistan using child labour. This involved co-operation between the ICFTU, Norwegian unions who supplied the camera crew, British unions in the country of the championships, and Pakistani unions in the targeted country. The adverse publicity resulted in FIFA adopting a new code of practice and more attention being given to labour issues around a key social/sporting event.

The pressure from organized labour and consumer groups in developed countries has forced the hands of government and international organizations as well as MNCs. For example, in April 1995 US President Bill Clinton announced a voluntary code of conduct covering business ethics and workers' rights for US companies working abroad. In an attempt to reinvigorate its role in the labour standards issue the ILO has announced its intention to push for a global social label. The proposal is in response to the numerous private initiatives at social labelling. The ILO label would be applied to countries respecting basic rights rather than to firms. One justification for taking such a step is that under ILO auspices such labels would be policed and prevented from becoming protectionist tools.

## Labour and the New Multilateralism

The labour movement is in a process of transition where international labour activity is moving beyond the preserve of international union organizations such as the ICFTU and the international trade secretariats to encompass the activities of grassroots union locals and non-unionized social groups with an interest in labour issues. Capitalizing on the development of what Castells has called the network society,[22] labour activism is now feasible via networks of concerned people rather than reliant on hierarchical, bureaucratic internationals. Aided by the development of new information technology, labour groups are starting to reinvent their practice of internationalism.

Labour groups are beginning to take their place in efforts at building a 'new multilateralism'. This is a form of internationalism that seeks to 'reconstitute civil societies and political authorities on a global scale, building a system of global governance from the bottom up'.[23] In contrast to traditional notions of multilateralism as 'an institutional form that coordinates relations among three or more states on the basis of generalized principles of conduct',[24] the new multilateralism starts with social organizations independent of the state. In terms of policy, the desire is to create sustainable development shielded from the ravages of neo-liberal competition. This shift to transnational civic activity on the part of a wide range of actors has led to discussion about the development of global civil society. Focusing on the activity of environmental, women's, and human rights groups, scholars have pointed to the development of a world civic politics[25] because of the growing importance of transnational advocacy networks.[26] This is a form of politics that includes the state but goes beyond it to influence market behaviour and societal norms.

What is the significance of this transnational social movement activity? Were it to fulfil its potential, such activity could lay the basis for a counter-hegemonic bloc.[27] It could be the core of an alliance of social forces that would work through states and international organizations to change the principles at the heart of international order. These groups are in the process of articulating a vision of the future counter to the dominant views of how society and global order should operate. Rather than stressing the virtues of a market-based civilization,[28] they pose other values such as environmental sustainability, human dignity, equality, and justice. They are engaged in a long process of changing social norms and influencing those who hold the reins of political and economic power. They have the potential to be the source of structural change.

Labour's contact with the new multilateralism is significant for two reasons. First, the collision of old unionism and new social movements is having a transformative effect on workers' organizations. In an attempt to survive the anti-union environment, unions are turning to new members, especially women, who have forced them to take on a new series of issues, such as gender equity and child care. This shift, in turn, has meant that unions are increasingly looking beyond basic issues of pay to broader questions of social and economic organization. Unions are also reaching out to unprotected workers and other social movements to form broader coalitions. This is tipping the balance away from conservative business unionism to an activist social unionism. Social unionism takes a more aggressive and antagonistic approach to corporations and governments that favour business (i.e., profits) over other interests.

Second, organized labour remains a key strategic actor in any process of political economy. Its relatively high degree of institutionalization has benefits, as well as costs. Labour has firmer claims to represent identifiable constituencies than many non-governmental organizations (NGOs) because of its institutionalized structure and mechanisms for accountability (elections and the payment of dues). Unions can also negotiate agreements with governments or corporations knowing that they can usually deliver their members' compliance. This makes labour a serious and important negotiating partner. Finally, through industrial action unions can impose direct costs on those driving the globalization process—corporate and state élites.

Although it will not be easy, organized labour, social organizations with labour interests, and the new social movements may be capable of working together to influence the evolution of global order. Drawing on their distinct strengths and compensating for each other's weaknesses, they offer a challenge to governing corporate and political élites. Their intention is to transform the structure of global order and reorient the principles of political and economic organization. They are not united and they may not succeed, but labour and the new multilateralism will have a significant role to play.

## Conclusion

This chapter has argued that labour is not simply a passive actor at the receiving end of the dictates of global order; rather it is a crucial actor or agent in the creation of that order.[29] Clearly, it is in a subordinate power relationship with government and business élites. However, as a key area of resistance to neo-liberal globalization, labour's struggles and strategy have an impact on market structures, state policies, and the regulatory content of international organizations. Furthermore, by participating in a broad-ranging, multifaceted society based on internationalism or new multilateralism, labour groups are finding allies and increasing their effectiveness in influencing corporate and state policy. Efforts at creating theories to assist our understanding of the changing global order that ignore the agency of labour risk ignoring a crucial source of change in the global political economy.

## Notes

1  Mitchell Bernard, 'Post-Fordism, Transnational Production, and the Changing Global Political Economy', in Richard Stubbs and Geoffrey R.D. Underhill, eds, *Political Economy and the Changing Global Order* (Toronto: McClelland & Stewart, 1994), 216–29.

2  Volker Rittberger, ed., *Regime Theory and International Relations* (Oxford: Clarendon Press, 1993).

3  John Stopford and Susan Strange, *Rival States, Rival Firms* (Cambridge: Cambridge University Press, 1991).

4  Helen Milner, *Interests, Institutions and Information: Domestic Politics and International Relations* (Princeton, NJ: Princeton University Press, 1997).

5  Jeffrey Harrod, *Power, Production and the Unprotected Worker* (New York: Columbia University Press, 1987).

6  Philip McMichael, 'Rethinking Globalization: The Agrarian Question Revisited', *Review of International Political Economy* 4, 4 (Winter 1997): 630–62.

7  Ross Martin, *Trade Unionism: Purpose and Forms* (Oxford: Clarendon Press, 1989).

8   Andrew Martin, 'Labour, the Keynesian Welfare State, and the Changing International Political Economy', in Stubbs and Underhill, eds, *Political Economy and the Changing Global Order*, 60–74.

9   Charles S. Maier, 'The Politics of Productivity: Foundations of American International Economic Policy after World War II', *International Organization* 31 (1977): 607–33.

10  Ronald Radosh, *American Labour and United States Foreign Policy* (New York: Random House, 1969).

11  Mark Rupert, '(Re)Politicizing the Global Economy: Liberal Common Sense and Ideological Struggle in the US NAFTA Debate', *Review of International Political Economy* 2: 658–92.

12  On the legitimacy challenge posed by Solidarity, see Jack Bielasiak and Barbara Hicks, 'Solidarity's Self-Organization: The Crisis of Rationality and Legitimacy in Poland, 1980–81', *East European Politics and Societies* 4, 3 (Fall 1990): 489–512.

13  Glen Adler and Eddie Webster, 'Challenging Transition Theory: The Labour Movement, Radical Reform, and Transition to Democracy in South Africa', *Politics and Society* 23, 1 (Mar. 1995): 75–106.

14  Andrew Reding, 'Chiapas Is Mexico', *World Policy Journal* 11, 1 (Spring 1994): 11–25.

15  Craig Murphy, *International Organization and Industrial Change: Global Governance Since 1850* (Cambridge: Polity Press, 1994).

16  Robert W. Cox, 'ILO: Limited Monarchy', in Robert W. Cox and Harold Jacobson, eds, *The Anatomy of Influence* (New Haven: Yale University Press, 1974), 101.

17  Robert O'Brien, 'Shallow Foundations: Labour and the Selective Regulation of Free Trade', in Gary Cook, ed., *The Economics and Politics of International Trade* (London: Routledge, 1998), 105–24.

18  Michel Camdessus, 'The Impacts of Globalization and Regional Integration on Workers and their Trade Unions', speech delivered to the ICFTU 16th World Congress, Brussels, 26 June 1996.

19  Bernhard Ebbinghaus and Jelle Visser, 'European Labor and Transnational Solidarity: Challenges, Pathways, and Barriers', in Jytte Klausen and Louise A. Tilly, eds, *European Integration in Social and Historical Perspective from 1850 to the Present* (Boulder, Colo.: Rowman & Littlefield, 1997), 195–221.

20  Craig Forcese, *Commerce with Conscience?: Human Rights and Corporate Codes of Conduct* (Montreal: International Centre for Human Rights and Democratic Development, 1997).

21  ICFTU, *No Time to Play: Child Workers in the Global Economy* (Brussels: ICFTU, 1996).

22  Manuel Castells, *The Rise of the Network Society* (Oxford: Basil Blackwell, 1996).

23  Robert W. Cox, 'Introduction', in Cox, ed., *The New Realism: Perspectives on Multilateralism and World Order* (Basingstoke: Macmillan/United Nations University Press, 1997), xxvii.

24  John Gerard Ruggie, 'Multilateralism: The Anatomy of an Institution', in Ruggie, ed., *Multilateralism Matters: The Theory and Praxis of an Institutional Form* (New York: Columbia University Press, 1993), 11.

25  Paul Wapner, 'Politics Beyond the State Environmental Activism and World Civic Politics', *World Politics* (Apr. 1995): 311–40.

26  Margaret Keck and Kathryn Sikkink, *Activists Beyond Borders: Advocacy Networks in International Politics* (Ithaca, NY: Cornell University Press, 1988).

27  On notions of hegemony and counterhegemony in international relations, see Robert W. Cox, 'Gramsci, Hegemony, and International Relations: An Essay in Method', *Millennium* 12 (1983): 162–75.

28  Stephen Gill, 'Globalisation, Market Civilisation and Disciplinary Neoliberalism', *Millennium* 24, 3 (1995).

29  For a similar argument in the US context, see Andrew Herod, 'Labor as an Agent of Globalization and as a Global Agent', in Kevin Cox, ed., *Spaces of Globalization* (New York: Guilford Press, 1997), 167–200.

## Suggested Readings

Compa, Lance, and Tashia Hinchliffe-Darricarrère. 'Enforcing International Labor Rights Through Corporate Codes of Conduct', *Columbia Journal of Transnational Law* 33 (1995): 663–89.

Harrod, Jeffrey. 'Social Forces and International Political Economy: Joining the Two IRs', in Stephen Gill and James H. Mittleman, eds, *Innovation and Transformation in International Studies* (Cambridge: Cambridge University Press, 1997), 105–17.

Herod, Andrew. 'Labor as an Agent of Globalization and as a Global Agent', in Kevin Cox, ed., *Spaces of Globalization* (New York: Guilford Press, 1997), 167–200.

Lambert, Robert, and Donella Caspersz. 'International Labour Standards: Challenging Globalization Ideology?', *Pacific Review* 8 (1995): 569–88.

Lee, Eddy. 'Globalization and Labour Standards: A Review of Issues', *International Labour Review* 135 (1997): 173–89.

McMichael, Philip. 'Rethinking Globalization: The Agrarian Question Revisited', *Review of International Political Economy* 4 (1997): 630–62.

Moody, Kim. *Workers in a Lean World: Unions in the International Economy.* London: Verso, 1997.

Rupert, Mark. *Producing Hegemony: The Politics of Mass Production and American Global Power.* Cambridge: Cambridge University Press, 1995.

Waterman, Peter. *Globalization, Social Movements and the New Internationalisms.* London: Mansell, 1998.

## Web Sites

Labour Links: http://www.labournet.org

International Confederation of Free Trade Unions: http://www.icftu.org

International Labour Organization: http://www.ilo.org

People's Global Action: http://www.agp.org

Zapatista movement: http://www.ezln.org

# Chapter 3

# Knowledge, Politics, and Neo-Liberal Political Economy

## Stephen Gill

Since the middle of the nineteenth century, the development of the international (and now, increasingly, global) political economy has been associated with the dialectical interplay of the rivalries between more integral nation-states, on the one hand, and the forces of globalizing capitalism, on the other. The economic forces and agents associated with capitalism have tended to transcend the territories, sovereignty, and political control of nation-states. In this chapter I focus on the ideas and policies associated with these tendencies, in the context of aspects of nineteenth- and twentieth-century capitalism. The discussion centres on a neo-liberal radical free market political economy, illustrating its ethical, theoretical, and political aspects and some of the elements it shares with neo-realism.

Recent changes in the global political economy have tended to give added weight to the perspectives associated with neo-liberal ideas. The tendency for governments to adopt policies meant to 'liberalize' their domestic structures has been a key feature since the onset of global economic crises in the mid-1970s. This tendency can be related to political efforts to create what Karl Polanyi called a 'market society' on a global basis.

Forms of regulation associated with the post-1945 world order have been increasingly transformed to redefine the relationship between 'public' and 'private' in contemporary capitalism. Thus, the postwar order is in a period of deep crisis and transformation. The consequences of this development are, in my view, inimical to the establishment of a just and sustainable world order. 'Order' is a contestable concept and is conceptualized and understood in different ways from different perspectives. For example, deregulatory policies in advanced industrial societies have favoured private market forces. The former Communist states have moved towards the application of policies to create a market society, in most cases under the direct or indirect tutelage of international agencies imbued with an economic liberal, utilitarian view of the world. In the OECD countries and the Third World, new forms of mercantilism and increasing economic competition between states have led to governments scrambling to attract foreign investment and inflows of foreign capital, partly to finance government operations in a period of fiscal crisis. This point is elaborated later in this chapter.

## Ontology and the Study of Political Economy

Part I of this book is concerned with understanding the changing global order. The emphasis on understanding reflects the fact that realities are not self-evident and that all 'realities' are to a certain extent theorized. In this sense, the 'reality' of global order is constituted partly by the knowledge structures that prevail in the configuration of production, consumption, and exchange structures of the global political economy, as well as in the political structures associated with the concepts of sovereignty and the state. Knowledge structures are integral to understanding and explaining contemporary processes of historical change.

For the purposes of this essay, knowledge in IPE and IR is understood to have ethical, theoretical, and practical dimensions. Knowledge structures help to constitute and give identity to both institutions and 'material' forces (e.g., military or economic power). In other words, the knowledge structures of political economy are a *part of* the object of our analysis. How people understand, interpret, and explain the world is an aspect of that world: knowledge structures do not simply stand outside it. Theories in social science are not the same as those of the pure sciences, in part because of the role of human consciousness and the capacity to choose and act in different ways. Thus, knowledge structures serve to constrain, but not to determine, human action.

Within such knowledge structures, theoretical perspectives serve to define the nature of and the problems within the 'real world' of the political economy. Thus, either explicitly or implicitly, perspectives are central to the formation of policy alternatives facing governments (local, regional, national), international organizations, political parties, transnational corporations, trade unions, and even churches.[1]

Perspectives involve an 'ontology': the constituent elements and forces that configure sociohistorical reality (and thus world order) in different periods. For IR and IPE, ontology lies at the heart of the construction of general theory. General theory or ontology, then, involves assumptions regarding the nature of a lived reality, the way that parts of this reality relate to the whole, and how that reality changes or might change over time. The approach I take assumes that:

1. social reality is transient, that is, that history is ever-changing and thus any ontology is conditional;
2. no single ontology can be developed to explain adequately social reality over widely different periods, although comparisons can be made between periods for explanatory purposes;
3. in a given historical situation, social action occurs within a certain but not fixed structure of necessity, that is, circumstances that *appear* to be those of necessity. These circumstances only appear to be those of necessity but can be transcended because of consciousness and political will (as well as

by natural, or quasi-natural forces such as ecological degradation; even here, these forces entail a human response to their repercussions).

## Neo-Realism, Neo-Liberalism, Hobbes, and Locke

The ontologies developed in the two dominant approaches are applied across societies, space, and time, virtually irrespective of the variations in conditions in different periods. An example is the hegemonic stability theory. Indeed, transhistorical forms of explanation characterize much contemporary thinking in IR and IPE.

An inspiration for many realists and some liberals was Thomas Hobbes, for whom life was 'nasty, brutish [perhaps, 'British'?] and short'. For Hobbes, human nature was selfish: life was a struggle of individual wills in a battle for survival.[2] In the absence of an order-producing force (such as a government with power, authority, and will) human life would be akin to war: a perpetual situation of fear, insecurity, greed, and (damaging forms of) competition. Sovereign individuals therefore needed to pool their wills to constitute a political authority, or *Leviathan*. A political authority with sovereign power was needed to produce order in a situation that would otherwise tend towards anarchy, a 'war of all against all'. In the nineteenth century, John Stuart Mill took this argument further in his *Essay on Liberty*.[3] The paradox of freedom meant that government was based on the surrender of individual autonomy: i.e., some personal freedom had to be sacrificed in order for society to remain free.

John Locke anticipated the position of J.S. Mill in outlining a theory of civil government. The centralization of power in the sovereign should be mediated and constrained by the creation of a vigorous 'private' sphere, comprising relatively autonomous individuals, associations, and institutions in civil society.[4] This private realm, separated from but constraining the formal public sphere of the state, was held to be central not only for personal liberty but for long-term political order and stability. For such an authority to be legitimate, it required the consent of those with the largest stake in society, that is, those with property.[5] Not surprisingly, then, the political influence of Hobbesian and Lockeian possessive individualism has grown with the rise of industrial capitalism.

Locke's ideas and those of Mill have had much less resonance in the study of IR than have those of Hobbes. Indeed, in contemporary IR and IPE, many realist theories have taken the Hobbesian position as representing the essence of the political problem. (Some theorists of 'international regimes', however, reflect Lockeian thinking insofar as regimes imply some degree of institutionalization of conflict and the role of private actors in international political practice.) Nevertheless, most realist theorists take greed, fear, and the need for survival as axiomatic motivations of states. Neo-realists, following Kenneth Waltz in his *Theory of International Politics* (1979), take anarchy as a structural feature, giving less emphasis to human motivations. Realists share the view that the problem of global order is caused by the absence of political authority to constrain the disorderly consequences of the exercise of conflicting wills of states.

Thus the problem of order at the international level is seen as intractable, and any solution must necessarily be temporary, fragile, and conditional. Solutions, insofar as they are equated with lower levels of interstate violence, have been found in particular configurations of power and domination—empires (which integrate several states into a given territorial jurisdiction under a particular sovereign); hegemonies (the dominance of one state over others, which is held to minimize generalized conflicts)—or else through institutions such as the balance of power, diplomacy, and alliances, and more recently in 'international regimes'.

Often, then, IR becomes tautological: the study of recurring patterns of the rise and decline of states, based on cyclical theories of history. History, in this view, has both an essentialist and an existentialist quality. On the one hand, history is seen as a singular, cyclical process: an essence with universal laws. On the other hand, history is seen as a perpetual struggle among states for survival, security, and

power. To invert Antonio Gramsci's famous maxim concerning 'realistic' explanations in political theory,[6] this type of thinking is an example of the extreme optimism of the intellect—that is, one form of explanation suffices to account for changes in IR and political economy from Plato to NATO. It is also an extreme pessimism of the will: human nature is seen as fixed and immutable, and historical change is determined by this unchanging, essential reality.

Such assumptions concerning the nature of political order and international relations have been very pervasive in Western societies, especially in the English-speaking countries. Their main assumptions are related intimately to those of economic liberalism.

## Economic Liberalism and the Construction of 'Market Society'

For economic liberals the idea of politics is equated with the need to develop social institutions (such as state and market) that conform more closely to a possessively individualist model of motivation and the propensity of ostensibly free individuals to pursue their material self-interest.[7] The state should thus provide the 'public goods' of law and order, sound money, regulation of markets, and protection from invasion, acting, as it were, as a benevolent 'nightwatchman' over society in a world of rival states. From this perspective, realist assumptions about interstate rivalry prevail, making terms such as 'international' economics and 'the wealth of nations' part of the lexicon.

The idea of economics is equated with the maximization of production and consumption in a world of scarcity. Neoclassical liberal economics builds models of how resources can be allocated and used efficiently to promote the maximization of utility (or satisfaction/security) of individuals, or of the greatest number of individuals. The maximization of utility, it is usually argued, is equated with the superior social co-ordination, information, and choice supplied through markets. The market promotes greater allocative and dynamic efficiency, partly because it is decentralized and has a superior co-ordinating capacity: information is instantly made available to market participants through various signals, notably prices. Generally, the most competitive markets are deemed by economic liberals to be the most efficient and most likely to contribute to the general welfare.

For liberals, then, the aim of 'political economy' is to create a market society along these lines, and thus to sweep away barriers to the free play of market forces, with the state providing public goods that the market might fail to supply fully. In this way, the private realm of civil society determines politics and the state. In this sense, economic liberalism is not simply a theoretical doctrine. It is also a form of political action that has tended to justify and promote the ascendancy of the capitalist class in the societies where it is practised—that is, in capitalist market societies.

At different moments in history such doctrines have also been central to what can accurately be called political Utopianism, that is, 'experiments' to promote the social transformation of regulated or protected economies towards a self-regulating market society. Diverse examples of this include nineteenth-century *laissez-faire* in conservative Britain, the authoritarian liberalism of the Pinochet military regime in Chile after the 1973 *coup d'état*, market monetarism in New Zealand in the 1980s under a social democratic government (in the early 1990s that nation had the highest crime rates in the developed world), and the IMF and OECD plans for the restructuring of Solidarity-led Poland after the overthrow of communism in 1989. In each case 'strong' government was needed to provide public goods and to enforce the rules of market society.

Economic liberalism, then, is not a doctrine of weak or necessarily minimal government, even though it arose as both a response to and a critique of mercantilist forms of social organization, which emerged between the sixteenth and eighteenth centuries in Europe. Mercantilism was intended to provide both economic and military security for a given territorial unit and to be a means whereby the state could attempt to accumulate wealth and power relative to other states. Economic liberalism is more a doctrine of the primacy of market forces rather than of the state. Nevertheless, even Adam Smith conceded that security from invasion was more important than the pursuit of 'opulence', and he stressed the need for ethical restraints on unfettered market forces.

In the 1980s and 1990s, mercantilist forces and forms of political and economic organization have been thrown on the defensive by the increasing power of neo-liberal forces associated with transnational capital. In other words, instead of the autonomous individuals discussed by neoclassical economics, the primary agents of globalization are large, oligopolistic companies (including institutional investors in the financial markets), as well as major capitalist states responding to changing economic pressures. This can be seen in a variety of developments, such as the European Community's 1992 Single Market Program (although this program also has elements of Jacques Delors's vision of a new form of European social democracy combined with Anglo-American *laissez-faire*), the attempts to create a North American free trade region, and the move towards institutionalizing the transnational structures of finance and production in the GATT Uruguay Round.

All of these political initiatives are premised on giving greater freedom to market forces, including greater mobility to factors of production. The rise of neo-liberalism, in this sense, has gone with a decline in the economic sovereignty of the vast majority of states, with a corresponding reduction in social provisions and welfare, and a shift away from state capitalism towards private, free-market capitalism. At the same time, in a new form of outward-looking, competitive mercantilism, governments are increasingly competing with each other to attract investment and to keep skills and technology within their jurisdictions.

Driving this neo-liberal restructuring is a combination of the globalization of production and finance and the fiscal crisis of the state (federal, local) in a period of much slower growth in the global political economy. The new era of the 'competition state' is driven by new ideologies of competitiveness and techno-nationalism, particularly within the OECD countries.

## Market Society and the Power of Capital

Karl Polanyi's *The Great Transformation* (1944) detailed the attempt in nineteenth-century Britain to create a market society from above and to sweep away the social protection and regulated structure of mercantilism.[8] Crucial to this was a strong state that could institute measures so as to construct 'fictitious commodities'. These were money, land, and labour. These 'commodities' were then exchanged in interdependent 'free' markets. Polanyi saw these as 'fictitious' in the sense that they were nothing other than, respectively, a store of value/medium of exchange, nature itself, and the lived time of human existence. Marx equated the rise of market society with the rule of capital and the bourgeoisie in the emerging liberal states:

> The assertion that free competition is the final form of the development of productive forces, and thus of human freedom, means only that the domination of the middle class is the end of the world's history—of course quite a pleasant thought for yesterday's parvenus![9]

The process of transforming nineteenth-century Britain into something approximating a *laissez-faire* capitalist market society took at least 70 years. It involved the political power of the state to dismantle the forms of social protection and regulation associated with mercantilism. Its introduction accompanied the onset of industrial capitalism in Britain and was consistent with the interests of the rising industrial and financial bourgeoisie. For Polanyi, as for Marx, as well as for sociologists like Durkheim and Weber and philosophers like Nietzsche, each in their own different way, the advent of capitalist market society with its mass production of commodities (and its corollary, 'the masses') was a profoundly revolutionary change. Prior to this moment, no society had been constructed on the principle of the primacy of an economic mechanism.

The development of the market society had many effects, some of which were to raise the productive powers of the society relatively rapidly, in a process that Joseph Schumpeter termed 'creative destruction'. On the one hand, capitalist industrialization was able to generate, following the revolutions of 1848, a mass production economic system. The result was a cornucopia of commodities and the possibility of their consumption on display to all in the exhibitions, trade fairs, shopping arcades, and streets of the big cities of the Victorian era. This display of commodities was central to consolidating the myth of progress that was to give industrial capitalism much of its cultural identity and political *élan*.

On the other hand, the massive restructuring of society meant new forms of servitude for ostensibly free wage labour. Wage labour as a social form required the creation of a new social category of 'unemployment'. Unemployment was central to the innovation of 'functioning' labour markets, insofar as this involved market discipline over the commodity of labour. Discipline was also exercised over capitalists by competition in the marketplace, and by the capital markets, which allocated credit for investment. Competition forced capitalists to innovate consistently in order to cut costs and sustain profits. Labour markets were also designed to promote the mobility of labour, for example, to encourage an internal migration of people from the countryside to work in the factories.

Conditions in the factories were often brutalizing, and included the degradation of not only adult but also child labour. In nineteenth-century Britain, these conditions were described in Engels's *The Condition of the English Working Classes* and in several of the novels of Dickens. In France, such conditions were explored in the novels of Zola and as a negation of humanity in the poetry of Baudelaire, notably in *Les Fleurs du Mal*.

The rise of trade unions and socialist political parties in the capitalist world, exercising a countervailing political will, was the major reason why these conditions were controlled and ameliorated, and the worst excesses outlawed in factory acts and health and safety legislation. Eventually the welfare state emerged in the West. The struggles of workers and women extended the franchise to encompass those who were not property owners (this process was accelerated after the Russian revolution as concessions were made to workers). The property-owning democracy theorized by Locke gradually gave way to a more representative, although still indirect form of democracy in North America and parts of Europe, and the liberal state became, gradually, the liberal democratic state.

## Neo-Liberalism in the 1980s and 1990s

As the processes of global restructuring intensify and as liberal capitalist market society is introduced more extensively into the Third World (and the former Communist states), many of the supposedly nineteenth-century phenomena noted above are replicated as we approach the twenty-first century. In the Third World the desire for gratification through mass consumption in situations of poverty and deprivation is accompanied by massive internal migrations, unsustainable patterns of urbanization, and, at the same time, early nineteenth-century labour conditions, for example, the super-exploitation of female labour in the *maquiladoras* in Mexico[10] and the persistent use of child labour, as in Colombian coalmines.

Throughout the world, the boundaries between 'public' and 'private' are being redrawn, often under pressure from multilateral agencies such as the IMF and the World Bank, to roll back the public sector and dismantle the apparatus of mercantilist protection and to open previously closed economies to the forces of global economic competition. States are increasingly making reforms in a new international competitive struggle for survival in an age of capital scarcity, indebtedness, and economic depression.

An extreme example of this was the draconian 'shock therapy' strategy applied initially in Poland in 1990, and subsequently, albeit in modified form, in Russia following the collapse of the USSR. This therapy was based on experiments carried out in Latin America in the 1970s and 1980s in countries such as Chile. The reforms have strong parallels with the nineteenth-century British attempt to create a market Utopia—or dystopia—from above. However, the post-Communist reformers seek to restore free-market capitalism in a very short period of time. The time frame initially discussed in the Polish case (in late 1989), in consultation with and under the supervision of the IMF, was set at two years for the completion of the process.

The application of shock therapy was intended to liberate the propensity of the populations of the former Communist states to 'barter, truck, and trade'. The proponents of this strategy, that is, political economists of the neoclassical persuasion, often trained in British and North American universities and in the multilateral development banks, take as an essential premise a possessively individualist concept of human nature. Thus, shock therapy would allow for the 'unseen hand' to permit the pursuit of self-interest and lead to growth, provided that an appropriate institutional infrastructure could be created—that is, markets for land, labour, and capital.

A good example of this type of thinking was given in an Oxford lecture in late 1992 by the chief economist of the newly formed European Bank for Reconstruction and Development (EBRD), Professor John Fleming, who was formerly an economist at the Bank of England and the IMF.[11] The EBRD was set up by the major capitalist countries following the collapse of Communist rule in 1989. The EBRD makes loans on the basis of a clearly specified political conditionality. Unlike the IMF and World Bank, loans are only made to those governments committed to constitutional reforms and to the principles of free-market economics, that is, the political and economic institutions of capitalist market society. Politically, the aim is the 'occidentation' (or Westernization) of the former Communist economies: previously, 'all roads led to Moscow'; now, a more complex set of East European exchange and production structures integrated into world capitalism was the objective of reforms.

Fleming argued in the lecture that 'all countries are the same' for the purpose of policy (despite their different histories) and that the problem of economic reform was premised on two historical 'facts': 'the uniformity of human nature' and the 'universality of technology'.[12] Reform was also premised on the creation of strong governments with 'credible' economic policies (i.e., those deemed to be sustainable by operators in global financial, especially currency, markets).

The example Fleming cited of credible government was Sweden's bipartisanship in 'weathering the currency storms' in Europe in September 1992 in order to defend the parity of the krona relative to the Deutschmark. (At one point the Bank of Sweden raised its overnight interbank lending rate to 500 per cent, to stem a hemorrhage of capital flight, and the government was forced to announce draconian cuts in social programs to restore the government's fiscal position.) In other words, accountability of government policy was subordinated to the power of market forces and to mobile capital. Nevertheless, Sweden was forced to abandon its attempts to peg the krona to the D-mark and devalue its currency. The economic and social costs of the policies required to sustain a strong krona—savage cutbacks in public expenditure, reductions in social provision, privatization—proved to be unsustainable politically.

Fleming argued that, while broad coalitions were needed to topple European Communist regimes, stable bipartisanship was lacking in the early 1990s: governments were insufficiently strong, tended to fragment, and thus were 'subversive of credibility'. The problem was compounded by 'excessive proportional representation' in electoral systems, leading to a vacuum in political accountability. The key economic problem was that prices were 'distorted' from world market prices so that markets, especially labour markets, failed to 'clear'. Privatization, involving 'not only the transfer of state assets to private hands but also the organic growth of the private sector', was proceeding slowly and thus microeconomic market discipline was insufficiently strong. This meant that there was a lack of 'proprietorial responsibility' and of 'corporate governance' in the production structure. Macroeconomic discipline was weak, especially in Russia, where there was a threat of hyper-inflation because of the open-ended supply of state credit by the central bank to subsidize inefficient producers, a problem compounded by the collapse in trade between the former Communist state-planned economies.

## What Have Been the Results of These Policies?

In general, the initial results of the policies developed to steer the political changes in the direction of the self-regulating market society in Eastern and Central Europe and in the former USSR—following failed attempts at restructuring by Gorbachev and other leaders during the 1980s—have so far proven to be disastrous, with output plunging, physical capital being liquidated, infrastructure collapsing, and the pauperization of large sections of the population. In eastern Germany—the place where reforms were most likely to succeed, given the resources of the former West Germany—in late 1998, the effective unemployment rate was in excess of 21 per cent and rising, and economic hopelessness was widely associated in the press with the revival of Nazism and violence directed against foreigners, especially those seeking political asylum.

Another example highlights the stark realities of the new market societies of the East. A Western journalist, writing from St Petersburg (formerly Leningrad), described economic and social conditions there in the early 1990s as worse than in the 900-day siege of the city by the Nazis in 1941, with widespread social chaos and a breakdown in law and order of chronic proportions. He described the meaning of the reintroduction of the market—and one adjoining Peace Square Station in the city centre—in the following way:

> It would take a Hogarth, Goya or Hieronymous Bosch to depict this desolate 'market' where some 5000 people were buying and selling. . . . The term market conjures up visions of neat stalls and well-displayed products. There were few stalls and Peace Square was ankle-deep in slush and black mud. Those with little to sell stood in lines hundreds long, holding out ration cards, tins of sprats, cans of the western dried milk issued to St Petersburg's children, a rusty tap or a handful of nails . . . used light bulbs, military decorations, worn fur hats or broken household fittings. . . . traders walked around with placards reading: Money changed, Russian or

foreign. Drunks slumped against the walls. Everything and everyone is for sale.[13]

Lying behind EBRD and IMF policies, eagerly embraced by post-Communist leaderships in the East, then, is the theoretical construct of an abstract individual, involving a utility-maximizing 'rational actor' model of human behaviour (once called 'rational economic man'; its revisionist variant is 'rational economic person'). It should be emphasized here that the application of such policies is charged with a heavy weight of capitalist constitutionalist ideology. Also, as Fleming's remarks about 'occidentation' and roads leading to Moscow reveal, the policy is intended to reconfigure the strategic map of the world by subjecting the economies of the former Communist states to the discipline of market forces and thus to the penetration of the structural power of capital. In this sense, the policies have much in common with the European Union's Single Market Initiative and the thrust of the GATT agreement concluded in 1993. The policies can also be associated with Western strategic aims towards the USSR since the Russian revolution: to demobilize, subdue, and incorporate the enemy.

Hence, based on a narrow conception of human nature and a restricted view of human possibility, economic liberalism has become the dominant perspective and ideology of the contemporary period. Economic liberalism has deep historical roots, and it is the dominant approach to economics in much of the capitalist world, especially in the English-speaking countries, notably the United States and the United Kingdom. It is central to the frameworks of thought that predominate in key international organizations and in many organs of government. Economic liberalism of this type is a doctrine of the survival of the fittest in the marketplace. Those fittest to survive are generally the holders of wealth and power and those who are most mobile and resourceful. These points partly illustrate that *perspectives* in political economy should be considered as *part of* the global political economy, that is, part of the ontological object of analysis for political economists and students of international relations.

Nevertheless, the movement towards a global political economy organized along neo-liberal disciplinary lines in the age of global restructuring is a profoundly disturbing prospect. The logic of unfettered market forces is, after all, to increase global inequality and to produce a Benthamite world where social outcomes reflect, as it were, a kind of *felicific calculus*, in which the greatest happiness of the greatest numbers of consumers (perhaps 800 million people in the wealthiest urban regions of the world) is matched by a similar number who barely survive and a further 800 million who are on the point of starvation.[14]

According to the United Nations, the gap between the richest 20 per cent and the poorest 20 per cent of the world's population, measured in terms of per capita incomes, increased eightfold in the 1980s.[15] The term 'development' conceals the fact that for the bulk of the world's population conditions markedly deteriorated in the 15 years from 1980 to 1995 as population growth outstripped economic growth such that in two-thirds of the countries of the world living standards fell by at least 25 per cent during the 1980s. Less than 25 per cent of the world's population consumed over 80 per cent of the world's annual consumable resources.[16] In Eastern and Central Europe and the former USSR, production is plummeting, social chaos is widening, and increasing numbers of people are being pauperized.

In global macroeconomic terms, the logic of neo-liberal restructuring has led to a situation of both overproduction and underconsumption, that is, there is a persistent shortfall in global aggregate demand, which has intensified since the early 1970s in an era of slower growth, punctuated by recessions of increasing severity. At the same time, the Group of Seven countries have done little to show concern for this problem or to co-ordinate an international package of expansionary measures to prevent the onset of a world economic slump. Almost everywhere unemployment is rising, the public infrastructure decays, and public services are reduced, hitting the weakest members of society the hardest—women, children, and the aged in particular.

## Concluding Postscript: The Crisis of Neo-Liberalism

Since this chapter was written in 1993 for the first edition of this book, a number of the processes discussed above have intensified. Perhaps the most significant have been how the pace of liberalization of the global political economy has accelerated, despite the conditions of relative stagnation in the major OECD economies, and how the democratic accountability of economic forces and policy has been reduced. This is producing political contradictions and a backlash against neo-liberal globalization in much of the world.

By the late 1990s many of the liberalization initiatives referred to in this chapter had been institutionalized. For example, the World Trade Organization emerged from the GATT negotiations finalized in 1993 and the European Union integration process has gone much further, with Economic and Monetary Union (EMU). These processes of institutionalization have been largely configured by neo-liberal constitutionalist principles, what I call 'new constitutionalism'.[17] The key objectives of new constitutionalism are to keep 'politics' out of economic policy-making and, constitutionally and legally, to secure private property rights and investor freedoms (including free capital mobility) on a world scale. This also involves the pursuit of 'sound' macroeconomic policies (that is, low inflation policy) and the imposition of market discipline on the state and on labour. Financial interests are central to the new constitutionalism, so that it is mandated that aspects of economic policy-making should be removed from democratic accountability (for example, making truly independent central banks focus on low inflation as the priority of policy, as opposed to fighting high unemployment). According to the prevailing liberal economic orthodoxy, all of these measures combine to secure 'credibility' in the eyes of private investors and, more importantly, the large institutional investors and hedge funds in the global currency and capital markets. The new liberal market orthodoxy is also formed by the perspectives and interests of dominant state apparatuses in the G–7, the IMF, the Bank for International Settlements, and the World Bank.

Despite the attempt to move towards a long-term strategy that comprehensively incorporates both the Third World and the former Communist countries under G–7 dominance, the developments noted above may be criticized as short-sighted, fallacious, and economistic. Market forces—especially those in the financial markets—are not the product of careful deliberation about the long-term future; indeed, they are often the product of the herd instinct of financial operators and bankers. This aspect of the financial markets—their propensity to manias, panics, and crashes, with attendant problems of capital flight and financial collapse—was reflected in the debt crisis of the 1980s, the Mexican peso crisis of 1994, and the global financial crisis of the late 1990s.[18] The crisis of the late 1990s originated in Thailand in 1997, and it then spread rapidly through East Asia and engulfed Russia in the summer of 1998. This brought economic misery to the vast majority of the populations of these countries and caused large numbers of bankruptcies, especially among small businesses. Indeed, in the second half of 1998 over half of the population of Indonesia had barely enough money to obtain one meal a day.

The financial crisis reached New York in October 1998. The US financial system was almost brought down by the collapse of long-term credit management (LTCM). LTCM illustrates the confluence of ideas, institutions, and material forces that constitute key structural aspects of the global political economy today. LTCM was a private, unregulated hedge fund that operated in secrecy and invested the money of very wealthy people and huge banks. In this sense it was an offshore fund operating in the heart of the US regulatory system. It boasted two Nobel Prize winners in economics (theoreticians who specialized in the complexities of risk management). It was led by key financiers with backgrounds at the Federal Reserve and in the big Wall Street private banks. These people had the financial reputations and credibility with investors and thus raised capital and took on further loans. LTCM employed large numbers of Ph.D.s in mathematics. These younger specialists made the necessary computations, applying the risk management and investment techniques with computerized precision. Its name, LTCM, however, was an oxymoron, since it specialized in exploiting *short-term* differences in asset prices across jurisdictions. It came to grief when Russia effectively defaulted on its bonds. Some observers estimated that LTCM had massively over-leveraged its base capital of approximately $5 billion into $1.25 trillion of investments in a range of financial instruments, including complex derivatives. The motivation for this level of leverage was greed. LTCM was saved by a rescue operation organized by the New York Federal Reserve Bank and a consortium of large, private institutional investors. They pumped liquidity into LTCM and thus propped up the New York system. At the time, new capital was scarce since investors were taking their money out of equity and bond investments and placing it in the last 'safe haven' available to them in a deflationary situation—cash.

The deterioration in global financial conditions that led to the collapse of LTCM was intimately linked to the contradictions that arose because of the application of the new neo-liberal orthodoxy. The austerity policies often needed to satisfy its low inflation/sound money criteria, plus the freedom of capital mobility, have produced conditions that are globally deflationary. This creates what economists call the 'fallacy of composition'. What this means is that if all countries deflate simultaneously, an economic depression is created, either intentionally (in the form of planned recession) or unintentionally. The competitive, interstate rivalry aspect of the new constitutionalism impels political leaders to seek to outbid others in providing for a low-inflation investment climate.

In this type of situation, when conditions deteriorate—especially following financial bubbles (associated with the so-called emerging markets in the 1990s, and also with the boom in North American and Western European stock markets)—investors tend to panic, *en masse*. Yet (elected) political leaders, on the one hand, have not paid sufficient attention to problems of systemic risk in finance. On the other, they have tied their hands in the form of new constitutionalist orthodoxy and thus have little flexibility to deal with changes in financial and macroeconomic conditions. For example, the Maastricht agreements and the EMU in the European Union mandate strict limits on budget deficits when fiscal expansion might help to alleviate a slump.[19] Another example is Japan for most of the 1990s under its Fiscal Stabilization Law.

Now the credibility of the G–7, the IMF, and the panoply of disciplinary neo-liberal policies is at a very low ebb. The general legitimacy of the neo-liberal project is being increasingly called into question by the contradictions associated with some of the forces noted and outlined earlier in this chapter. The politics of the global political economy is likely to be different as we enter the twenty-first century.

## Notes

1  See Stephen Gill and David Law, *The Global Political Economy: Perspectives, Problems and Policies* (Baltimore: Johns Hopkins University Press, 1988), 17–24; Stephen Gill, *American Hegemony and the Trilateral Commission* (Cambridge: Cambridge University Press, 1990); 1–54, 203–31; Stephen Gill, ed., *Gramsci, Historical Materialism and International Relations* (Cambridge: Cambridge University Press, 1993), 21–48.

2  Thomas Hobbes, *Leviathan*, ed. C.B. Macpherson. (Harmondsworth: Penguin, 1986).

3  J.S. Mill, *An Essay on Liberty* (Harmondsworth: Penguin, 1969).

4  John Locke, *Two Treatises on Government*, ed. Peter Laslett (Cambridge: Cambridge University Press, 1965).

5  One way to interpret the subsequent variations in the construction of European and North American liberal capitalist states is in terms of the ways the ideas of Hobbes and Locke and other liberal theorists (such as Tom Paine in the United States) have been applied in practice. That is, there have

been variations in the form of the state in the major capitalist societies in terms the nature of and relations between the state and civil society, with, in general, latecomers to industrialization more Hobbesian (e.g., Japan, Brazil, South Korea) than their precursors (Britain, United States). Of course, most capitalist states have been somewhere along a continuum between the Hobbesian and Lockeian models, with the Hobbesian form predominating in the post-colonial Third World. This line of thinking was first developed by Kees Van Der Pijl in *The Making of an Atlantic Ruling Class* (London: Verso, 1984).

6  Antonio Gramsci, 'Pessimism of the Intellect . . . Optimism of the Will', in *Selections from the Prison Notebooks of Antonio Gramsci*, ed. and trans. Q. Hoare and G. Nowell Smith (New York: International Publishers, 1971), 175. The original of this quotation is a maxim of Romain Rolland.

7  Adam Smith, *An Enquiry into the Nature and Causes of The Wealth of Nations* (Harmondsworth: Penguin Books, 1970); F.A. von Hayek, *The Road to Serfdom* (Chicago: University of Chicago Press, 1944). 'The individual and isolated hunter or fisher who forms the starting point with Smith and Ricardo belongs to the insipid illusions of the eighteenth century. They are Robinson Crusoe stories . . . the anticipation of "civil society", which had been in the course of development since the sixteenth century. . . . In this society the individual appears to be free of the bonds of nature, etc., which in former epochs of history made him part of a definite, limited human conglomeration.' Karl Marx, *Grundrisse*, ed. David McLellan (St Albans: Paladin, 1970), 26–7.

8  K. Polanyi, *The Great Transformation: The Political and Economic Origins of Our Times* (Boston: Beacon Press, 1957).

9  Karl Marx, 'Individual Freedom in Capitalist Society', in Marx, *Grundrisse*, 153.

10  The *maquiladoras* are tax-free manufacturing and export-processing zones contiguous with the US border. They are principally used by North American transnational corporations because labour is cheaper than north of the Rio Grande. Most of the workers are women, who are said to be cheaper to employ, more politically pliant, and more dextrous than men. Mexican migrant workers within Mexico are drawn to this region because wages, even for lower-paid female workers, are higher than those possible for most peasants on the land.

11  John Fleming, 'Economic Reform in Eastern and Central Europe', lecture to Oxford University International Political Economy Society, Brasenose College, 26 Oct. 1992. Fleming is the Warden of Wadham College, Oxford.

12  Of course, to make plausibly such claims about human nature and historical processes across different civilizations and eras would imply a vast knowledge not only of history but also of philosophical anthropology.

13  Jack Chisholm, 'Where Have All the Roubles Gone?', *Financial Times*, Weekend Supplement, 7–8 Mar. 1992.

14  Jeremy Bentham was the key philosopher of utilitarianism. The utility-maximization principle underpins classical liberal and neoclassical analysis of market motivations.

15  United Nations Development Program, *Human Development Report, 1992* (New York: Oxford University Press, 1992), 35, cited in R.W. Cox, 'Globalization, Multilateralism and Democracy', John Holmes Memorial Lecture, delivered at the headquarters of the International Monetary Fund, 19 June 1992.

16  World Bank, *World Development Report, 1989*, cited in J. MacNeill, P. Winsemius, and T. Yakushiji, *Beyond Interdependence: The Meshing of the World's Economy and the World's Ecology* (New York: Oxford University Press for the Trilateral Commission, 1991). The authors add: 'Many governments fail today to enable their people to meet even their most basic needs. Over 1.3 billion lack access to safe drinking water; 880 million adults cannot read or write; 770 million have insufficient food for an active working life; and 800 million live in "absolute poverty", lacking even rudimentary necessities. Each year 14 million children—about 10 per cent of the number born annually—die of hunger' (p. 6).

17  See Stephen Gill, 'European Governance and New Constitutionalism: EMU and Alternatives to

Disciplinary Neo-Liberalism in Europe', *New Political Economy* 3, 1 (Mar. 1998): 5–26; Stephen Gill, 'New Constitutionalism, Democratisation and Global Political Economy', *Pacific Review* 10, 1 (Feb. 1998): 23–38.

18  For a long historical view of this process, recurrent in the history of liberal capitalism, see Charles Kindleberger, *Mania, Panics and Crashes: A History of Financial Crises*, revised edn (New York: Harper Collins, 1989).

19  Stephen Gill, 'An Emu or an Ostrich? EMU and Neo-Liberal Economic Integration: Limits and Alternatives', in Petri Minkkinen and Heikki Patomäki, eds, *The Politics of Economic and Monetary Union* (Helsinki: Finnish Institute for International Affairs; Boston: Kluwer, 1997), 207–31.

## Suggested Readings

See the chapter by Cox in this volume.

Biersteker, Thomas J. 'The "Triumph" of Neoclassical Economics in the Developing World: Policy Convergence and Bases of Governance in the International Economic Order', in James N. Rosenau and Ernst-Otto Czempiel, eds, *Governance Without Government: Order and Change in World Politics* (Cambridge: Cambridge University Press, 1992).

Gill, Stephen, and David Law. *The Global Political Economy: Perspectives, Problems and Policies*. Baltimore: Johns Hopkins University Press, 1988.

Gill, Stephen. *American Hegemony and the Trilateral Commission*. Cambridge: Cambridge University Press, 1990.

Gill, Stephen, ed. *Gramsci, Historical Materialism and International Relations*. Cambridge: Cambridge University Press, 1993.

Martin, Andrew. 'Labour, the Keynesian Welfare State, and the Changing International Political Economy', in Richard Stubbs and Geoffrey R.D. Underhill, eds, *Political Economy and the Changing Global Order* (Toronto: McClelland & Stewart, 1994), 60–74.

## Web Sites

OECD Web site for the Multilateral Agreement on Investment:
http://www.oecd.org/daf/cmis/mai/maindex.htm

European Institute publication page:
http://www.europeaninstitute.org/ei25a1.htm

Research and Analysis Division of the World Trade Organization:
http://www.wto.org/research/research.htm

International Forum on Globalization:
http://www.ifg.org/index.html

## Chapter 4

# New Voices in the Globalization Debate:
## Green Perspectives on the World Economy

Eric Helleiner

At the centre of current debates in IPE is the phenomenon of economic globalization. These debates are often characterized as taking place between the three ideological camps that have dominated the field of IPE since the nineteenth century. On the one side are economic liberals who, like their nineteenth-century counterparts, are the greatest enthusiasts of free trade and integrated global markets. To them, economic globalization promotes greater efficiency and prosperity as well as increased co-operation between countries. On the other side of the debate are representatives of economic nationalism and Marxism. Economic nationalists worry that economic globalization undermines the ability of national communities to determine their own destinies, while Marxists see it as increasing inequality and exploitation in ways that serve only an increasingly powerful and coherent transnational capitalist class.

Characterizing the debate surrounding economic globalization into these three camps highlights three important perspectives on the phenomenon. But this approach is also increasingly too restrictive. By drawing only on the three traditional ideological camps outlined in most IPE texts, it neglects new voices that bring different perspectives to debates about economic globalization. Feminists, who have highlighted the gendered nature of the world economy in a way that economic liberals, nationalists, and Marxists have previously ignored, comprise one set of different voices that has begun to be recognized.[1] A second set of voices that has received less attention to date is made up of the 'greens'. This neglect of the greens is unfortunate, because both as a social movement and as a

political party, they have come to play an increasingly prominent role in debates about the world economy as leading opponents of economic globalization. In this chapter I outline the distinctiveness of their perspective on issues of IPE and globalization, and highlight how this world-view leads them to propose that we must 'think globally, act locally'.[2]

## The Human Economy and the 'Great Economy'

As with any ideological school, there is considerable diversity of thought within green circles. One point that unites all greens, however, is the view that the three traditional IPE perspectives have historically downplayed the fact that the human economy is only one part of, and ultimately dependent on, the biosphere. The biosphere—what Wendell Berry calls the 'Great Economy'—is what sustains all life, human and non-human, and for this reason the greens insist, in Daly and Cobb's words, that 'it is the Great Economy that is of ultimate importance.'[3]

The historical neglect of the importance of the 'Great Economy' by the traditional schools is seen by many greens as a product of the fact that they first achieved prominence in the age of the Industrial Revolution, which brought with it a considerable change in human views towards nature. As long as humans lived primarily in localized agricultural settings, the dependence of the human economy on the ecological setting in which it existed was obvious. In everyday life, this setting provided 'the limits of the possible' for human activity in a very clear way.[4] The rise of the industrial age, however, seemed to enable humans to overcome the limits imposed by nature as new energy sources were unleashed and constraints of space were increasingly transcended. In this context, the human economy no longer appeared to be as deeply reliant on, or vulnerable to, ecological constraints. Indeed, nature began to be seen in economic analyses as something easily conquered and dominated to serve human ends rather than as something to be feared and respected. These views are ones that greens suggest have pervaded much literature in the traditions of economic liberalism, nationalism, and Marxism during the nineteenth and twentieth centuries.

For the greens, this kind of perspective is deeply flawed. They agree that the industrial age marked a sharp break in the relationship of the human economy and the biosphere. But rather than enabling humans to transcend ecological limits, this era is seen as one when humans launched themselves down an environmentally unsustainable path. With its emphasis on rapid economic growth and mass consumption, the industrial age is seen to have encouraged humans to draw excessively on the renewable and non-renewable resources of the world. In addition, industrial societies began to produce waste, pollution, and toxic by-products at levels that could not be absorbed in a sustainable way by the biosphere. On both the 'input' and 'output' sides, then, industrial economies are viewed as having produced an unsustainable relationship between the human economy and the 'Great Economy'. The result, the greens argue, has been increasingly apparent not only in local environmental degradation around the world but also at the global level with the emergence of such world-scale environmental problems as the depletion of the ozone layer, global warming, and the loss of biodiversity.

The greens emphasize that environmental problems have also been encouraged by the large-scale nature of economic life in industrial societies. This is partly because considerable inputs and outputs are required to organize production as well as distribute and trade goods over large distances. It is also because large-scale economic activity often encourages integrated, monoculture-based ecosystems to be introduced by humans in place of

previously more isolated and diverse local systems. This kind of transformation both increases the fragility and vulnerability of ecosystems and often destroys or devalues important indigenous forms of human knowledge about local environmental conditions and practices that have accumulated over generations. Greens also worry that people's sense of ecological awareness and responsibility may be undermined as economic processes are spread out over greater and greater distances. When unsustainable harvesting of resources or dumping of wastes takes place in locations far away, individuals are no longer aware—as they are in more local economies—of the ecological consequences of their consumption behaviour.

These various concerns about the impact of the rise of the industrial age help to explain the greens' worries about economic globalization. To them, economic globalization intensifies many of the negative trends they associate with the industrial age. The phenomenon is seen to be encouraging more economic growth, mass consumption, and large-scale economic activity, plus the global spread of industrial production processes. The greens predict this will only exacerbate the unsustainable extraction of resources and the production of waste and pollution around the planet, as well as contribute to the loss of biodiversity and the increased vulnerability of local ecosystems. Moreover, by increasing the spatial extension of production processes as well as the link between producers and consumers, globalization is further distancing humans from an awareness of the environmental consequences of their behaviour. Inhabitants of rich countries, in particular, are increasingly unaware that their high consumption lifestyles have serious environmental consequences for poor regions of the world both on the input side (e.g., deforestation) and on the output side (e.g., the export of toxic waste and pollution-intensive industry from rich to poor countries).

Economic globalization is also seen to be challenging traditional patterns of human life that had often developed in long-standing and viable relationships with local ecosystems, a development that not only upsets ecological balance in specific locations but also undermines important local knowledge sources. Indeed, as the influence of distant current events and trends within local settings is increased, the greens argue that the significance of lifestyles and world-views deeply embedded in local settings and tradition is increasingly marginalized. To use Vandana Shiva's phrase, the local is increasingly 'globalized' in ways that prioritize decontextualized, short-term temporal perspectives and synchronic cosmologies over conceptions of social life that derive from a more ecological, long-term sense of time that values the future and past just as much as the present.[5]

By calling attention to the importance of the biosphere, the greens have advanced an important critique of the three traditional schools in IPE. In recent years, however, representatives of these schools have increasingly sought to respond to this critique. Both Marxists and economic liberals have produced a considerable volume of writing in the last decade on the relationship between the world's ecology and the human economy. Marxists have argued that environmental problems are closely linked to the dynamics and logic of global capitalism. Economic liberals have adopted a very different perspective, seeking to demonstrate that many of today's environmental problems are caused primarily by imperfectly functioning markets, insufficient regulatory co-operation between governments, and economic pressures created by poverty. To the extent that economic globalization encourages greater use of market prices, interstate co-operation, and prosperity, they have argued that it may prove to be a beneficial phenomenon from an ecological standpoint.

As the traditional schools increasingly incorporate environmental issues into their analyses, it is no longer accurate to say that one of the characteristics of the green world-view that distinguishes it from the traditional schools is its emphasis on the environment-economy relationship. But what does remain distinctive is the greens' approach to the issue. From their perspective, the roots of the world's environmental problems can be found in the kind of economic activity that emerged in the industrial age, which was characterized by a commitment to rapid economic growth, mass consumption, and

large-scale production. The problem with economic globalization, in their view, is that it reinforces this economic paradigm. For this reason, they are very sceptical of the liberal case that economic globalization and environmental sustainability can go hand in hand. At the same time, they are also sceptical of Marxists' belief that the source of environmental problems is capitalism. Since socialist societies have seemed just as inclined to adopt the economic model of 'industrialism' as capitalist societies, this model is seen as the key problem. It is thus important not to make the mistake of seeing all environmentalists as 'greens'. Many people concerned with environmental issues adopt different perspectives from the greens, such as liberal or Marxist ones. The distinctive focus of the greens is on the link between environmental problems and large-scale industrial society.

## The Social Consequences of Large-Scale Political and Economic Life

A second reason not to see the greens and environmentalists as interchangeable is the fact that greens are not just concerned with environmental issues. Alongside their environmental critique of industrial society is an equally important—though often less well known—social critique.

What concerns the greens about social life in the industrial age is its large scale. The greens place a strong emphasis on the desirability of small-scale community life, but not just for the environmental reasons outlined above. In E.F. Schumacher's memorable phrase, they believe that 'small is beautiful' for politico-economic reasons as well.[6] Only in smaller social settings do they believe it is possible to foster a genuine democratic community in which individuals are able to participate actively and in meaningful ways in political decision-making. Smaller-scale community life, they argue, enables potential abuse of political and economic power to be more effectively controlled and can foster a greater respect for the personal dignity, values, and individuality of each member of that community. Similarly, the greens argue that people also have a greater sense of control over their economic life in more localized self-reliant economies both because economic processes are more transparent and more organically embedded in community life and because of their relative insulation from the vagaries of external market trends.

For these various reasons, the greens are sceptical of the large-scale nature of industrial societies. In large political settings, democratic values and individualism have been inevitably undermined as power is concentrated in distant, difficult-to-control state authorities, and people are transformed from active individual 'citizens' into passive mass 'subjects' of the state. The key target of green critiques in this respect has traditionally been the modern nation-state, an institution the greens associate with the industrial age. Green writers have argued that modern nation-states have potential coercive and intensive powers over the populations they rule that are much greater than previous forms of state and that these powers are, and have been, inevitably prone to abuse in ways that people have found hard to prevent. At the same time, they have suggested that a sense of powerlessness and loss of individuality have been key political experiences for many people in modern nation-states because of the 'bigness' of this political community. The result of political life in large-scale nation-states, the greens argue, has been a decline in the prospects for a genuine participatory democracy and a rise of mass ideologies such as nationalism, as well as deference to rule by distant authorities.

In the economic realm, the greens worry about forms of concentrated corporate power found in the large-scale national markets that arose in the industrial age. While small-scale markets are usually quite transparent and efficient, the greens argue that large-scale markets tend to become dominated by giant oligopolistic corporations whose influence becomes extensive in both the economic and political realms. In large-scale economies, individuals experience a sense of alienation as large and anonymous economic forces seem to control their destiny in ways that are hard to understand. This alienation is reinforced as their participation in the economy no longer seems closely tied to meaningful local values and social relationships. Thus, while a greater and

greater division of labour may increase economic efficiency and the overall production of material goods, the greens argue that this does not necessarily translate into a higher 'standard of living' in the fullest sense of that phrase. Indeed, for this reason, the greens—often drawing on Gandhi's economic ideas[7]—are often supporters of a simpler life and are frequently strong critics of the argument that modern large-scale economic development has been a positive experience and is a goal to be pursued.

Since economic globalization is expanding the scale of social life even beyond the scale greens were already uncomfortable with, it is hardly surprising to find them as leading opponents of this trend today. In addition to their environmental concerns, they worry that worldwide economic integration is further curtailing the prospects for genuine local participatory democracy. Not only is globalization fostering dangerous concentrations of power in the form of large multinational corporations and growing influence of international institutions such as the World Trade Organization (WTO) and International Monetary Fund (IMF). Also, the fate of individuals and local communities is now increasingly caught up in the movements and trends of large, difficult-to-understand worldwide market forces. The resulting sense of powerlessness and alienation among peoples of the world is only reinforced, argue the greens, by the fact that these market forces seem so disembedded from the priorities and values of local communities and, indeed, are often contributing to the eradication of the very diversity and autonomy of these communities.

These social concerns about economic globalization provide a distinctive perspective on the phenomenon from those offered by the three traditional schools of thought in IPE. The greens' view is obviously most different from the rosy perspective offered by economic liberals, a perspective that sees global economic integration resulting in greater efficiency, prosperity, and international harmony. From the green standpoint, economic liberals neglect the oligopolistic power in large-scale markets as well as the social dislocation and alienation that such markets produce for individuals and local communities. The kind of harmonious and efficient market society liberals imagine may have been possible in the small-scale markets of Adam Smith's time, but the greens think it does not apply to the large-scale markets of today's global economy.

The greens have a little more in common with Marxists in that both share a concern about the dangers of social alienation and the concentration of corporate power at the global level. But the greens are less inclined to see class struggle and economic exploitation as the central problematics within IPE. To them, individuals derive much of their identity and meaning not primarily from their economic relationships to each other, but rather from the broad social values and experiences of the community of which they are a part. The greens' critique of globalization—like Karl Polanyi's critique of market society in the industrial age[8]—is thus more a 'cultural' one focusing on social dislocation and the undermining of local community life rather than a 'materialist' one emphasizing economic exploitation and inequality. This position also leads the greens to their 'anti-development' stance, something that most Marxists do not share.

The greens also have some grounds for agreement with economic nationalists in that both express a concern about the way globalization can undermine community autonomy and cohesion. But the community that nationalists seek to defend—the nation-state—is one that most greens have traditionally critiqued, while the viability of the small-scale local community to which the greens remain so committed is of little interest to most nationalists. The community values so prized by the greens—local participatory democracy and respect for the dignity and individuality of community members—are also not always central to the nationalist agenda, which is often more concerned with state power and rapid development. The latter commitment of economic nationalists is also at odds with the greens' anti-development position.

In sum, perhaps the most distinctive feature of the green perspective on economic globalization is the focus on the importance of the scale of social life. To liberals, Marxists, and nationalists, the scale of the economy and polity is not a central variable in their analyses of the global political economy.

While these schools debate the respective virtues of states versus markets, the greens ask a different question: what is the scale of the market or state being discussed? For this reason, the greens show a particular interest in and concern with the process of globalization. This phenomenon is, after all, best described as an expansion of the scale of social life or, in Antony Giddens's words, an 'intensification of worldwide social relations which link distant localities in such a way that local happenings are shaped by events occurring many miles away and vice-versa'.[9] For the greens, this feature of globalization is the most worrying.

## Act Locally

The distinctive green perspective on economic globalization also leads to a unique normative project, best captured by the well-known green slogan 'think globally, act locally'. The meaning ascribed by greens to this slogan has often been lost as it has proliferated not just on political buttons and banners but also in corporate strategy sessions. It can, however, be briefly described.

The meaning of the second part of the slogan is more straightforward than that of the first. 'Act locally' is a call to resist the forces of economic globalization by selective 'delinking' from the global economy at the local level and by reinvigorating the kind of locally oriented communities that greens value so highly. The greens are keen, for example, to promote economic activities that draw on local factors of production and cultivate a self-reliant, democratic, and environmentally friendly ethic within a local community context. They also favour initiatives that encourage people to recognize the social and environmental benefits of a simpler lifestyle and to reject the values of modern mass consumerism. In promoting this 'turn to the local', the greens place particular emphasis on the role of local community-based and individual voluntary initiatives, and they are often quite hostile to any ideas involving centralized planning or strong state involvement. Initiatives of this kind that are trumpeted by the greens include: the creation of local producer and consumer co-operatives, community-based micro-credit schemes, local currency networks, and community-supported organic agriculture projects, as well as the activities of such groups as the Green Belt Movement in Kenya, the Chipko movement in India, and the Consumers' Association of Penang.

Many of these local initiatives encourage the growth of the 'informal' sector of economic life—or what Hazel Henderson calls the 'countereconomy'[10]—which does not enter the market and in which the state is also not involved. A parallel is sometimes drawn to the pre-industrial era when vast segments of economic activity had little direct link to the market economy or the state and were encompassed within what Fernand Braudel has labelled the realm of local 'material life'.[11] Although the greens are strong opponents of economic liberalism in the contemporary age, the initiatives they embrace and promote also make considerable use of small-scale markets. The transparency and efficiency of these markets is often celebrated as supportive of their vision of local communities in which power is decentralized and individual freedom and creativity flourish. Moreover, they see this scale of market as more likely to be embedded within local community values and relationships. Indeed, many of the greens' economic proposals are designed to foster this 'embeddedness' of local markets in innovative ways. Local currencies, for example, of which over 300 now exist in Britain, encourage the self-reliance of the communities where they are used by acting as a means of exchange that is essentially inconvertible to non-members of the community. Moreover, they permit trade to be denominated according to alternative theories of value—such as labour time—that may reflect community priorities instead of pure market logic.

The greens' localist agenda thus exists in an uneasy relationship with liberal economic priorities in this age of globalization. The greens see themselves very much as a movement working against the liberal globalization agenda. And they do represent a radical challenge to the liberal agenda at the global level through their rejection of worldwide economic integration and their value system that prioritizes community values and eco-

logical sensibilities, often in quite alternative ways. At the same time, however, the greens' enthusiasm for small-scale markets and voluntary initiatives in a local community context, as well as their often strongly anti-statist stance, can sometimes dovetail with liberal goals of scaling back the role of government and delegating social welfare functions to local civil society groups. As a result, while greens and economic liberals clash strongly in their views on global economic issues, liberals can sometimes find grounds for agreement with the greens at the local level. For example, the micro-credit movement is increasingly being trumpeted by the liberal public international financial institutions as an example of market-friendly and self-reliant social activism. Similarly, some governments with a liberal orientation are beginning to look favourably on local currency networks as a vehicle through which welfare payments and services can be channelled.[12]

For the same reason, many contemporary Marxists are often wary of the greens' 'radical' credentials. On the one hand, the greens are often seen by modern Marxists—particularly those of a Gramscian persuasion—as an important partner in a broad-based counterhegemonic movement against global capitalism because of their attacks on globalization and their calls for a very different set of values in the economy from individualism and consumerism. But the greens' enthusiasm for voluntary community-based initiatives and small-scale markets is often seen as naïve and reminiscent of proposals of 'Utopian socialists' of the nineteenth century. The greens' support for small-scale markets and the 'countereconomy' also sometimes draws on the ideas of Braudel, a scholar whose argument that these two levels of economic life needed to be sharply distinguished from that of large-scale capitalism is viewed as quite heretical by many Marxists.[13]

## Think Globally

The second half of the greens' project—'think globally'—is usually less well understood than the first, in part because it is sometimes used in different ways by different thinkers. At the most general level, it highlights that the greens, for all their decentralist leanings, recognize that the local frame of reference is not adequate. One reason is that they worry about the danger of localism becoming too stagnant, parochial, and perhaps even repressive. The call to 'think globally' is partly designed to encourage people to retain strong links to ideas and groups beyond one's local community to avoid this danger. Particularly encouraged is the acquisition of knowledge about the urgency and seriousness of the global predicament, a knowledge that they hope will prevent complacency at the local level. In this sense, 'thinking globally' is partly meant to reinforce the urgency of the need to 'act locally'.

A second reason is that the greens recognize that localism is inadequate to address existing and large-scale environmental problems at the global level in the short to medium term, despite all its potential environmental benefits over the longer run. Indeed, their decentralist project may make these problems worse by increasing the collective action dynamics and leaving unaddressed existing global disparities of power and wealth that contribute to the problems. Localism, thus, must be combined with some kind of wider global frame of reference for political action. This wider frame is also necessary because the greens' localist agenda can increasingly be thwarted by very powerful global actors and forces—from international financial markets and transnational corporations to the rules of the WTO—that have emerged in this era of globalization. To defend the ability of localist strategies to survive, the greens recognize the necessity to think beyond the local.

The call to 'think globally' is thus partly an attempt to form the basis for the kind of political activity at the global level that the greens recognize to be an unfortunate but necessary part of their political project. It is designed to cultivate a sense of membership within a community of shared fate at the planetary level, challenging traditional concepts of nationalism and state sovereignty that have been so prominent in the modern age. The hope, then, is that those sharing this world-view will be encouraged to engage in a kind of 'world civic politics' involving various political activities at the global level that promote the green agenda.[14]

These activities might include challenging multinational corporations or international financial institutions pursuing agendas detrimental to the environmental goals or the autonomy and priorities of local communities. They might also involve the promotion of alternative international trade and financial networks between like-minded groups that enhance the ability of local communities to pursue local practices that meet green goals. Certain forms of trade and aid flows between groups in the North and South may, for example, redress global inequities that contribute to environmental problems as well as enhance the capacity of local communities in the South to develop more self-reliant and environmentally friendly economic practices.[15]

The greens also often express support for the construction of limited formal political institutions at the global level that can help promote the green agenda. Given their critique of large-scale political institutions, it is not surprising that the greens seek to delegate political power above the local level only when absolutely necessary. One task usually seen as falling in this category is the solving of existing and pressing global-level environmental problems. A second is the containment and regulation of various global economic forces working against green objectives. Since existing global economic institutions such as the World Bank, IMF, and WTO are not seen as serving these goals, the greens would like to see a thorough reform of these institutions, transforming them into bodies that helped to shield local communities from global market forces and transnational corporations.

To the extent that regional supranational bodies or the nation-state can play a similar role, the greens also sometimes support the delegation of powers to them. Herman Daly and John Cobb, for example, argue that the nation-state today is the only political institution capable of regulating and challenging the power of global markets and transnational corporations in a serious way. Thus, they support capital controls and trade protectionist measures that would strengthen the nation-state's economic role and self-reliance in the short term, a project that allies them closely with many economic nationalists.[16] Many greens in Europe advocate such measures at an EU-wide level, as well as a considerable strengthening of common environmental and social standards within the EU, for similar reasons.

'Think globally' also has one further and final meaning that should not be forgotten. Réné Dubos, who is usually credited with originating the slogan 'think globally, act locally', hoped that the first half of this slogan would act as a caution to those engaging in the practice of politics above the local level. Having participated in many international environmental conferences and initiatives, he had become deeply sceptical of the tendency of people in these circles to attempt to solve environmental problems in a globally uniform manner. In his mind, it was vital to recognize the diversity, distinctiveness, and complexity of local environments and peoples. Solutions dreamed up by distant bureaucracies and advocates usually overlooked this reality and the value of local knowledge and local community initiatives. His call to 'think globally' was thus designed to encourage green activists working at the global level to develop a humble awareness of the complex diversity of the world and to favour locally developed initiatives and knowledge over strategies for reform developed by large, distant bureaucracies.[17]

## Conclusion

It is unfortunate that IPE texts and scholarship have been so slow to recognize the greens as an important new school of thought in the field. Not only do they offer a distinctive normative project and framework of analysis within the global political economy, but they are also far from marginal players in contemporary political debates surrounding world economic issues. Within the last few years they have rapidly emerged as among the more vocal critics of economic globalization. In the trade sphere, they were important members of coalitions opposing the North American Free Trade Agreement, the '1992 project' in Europe, and the latest

GATT round.[18] Greens have also been key critics of the Bretton Woods financial institutions[19] as well as of the recent initiative to create a Multilateral Agreement on Investment. In addition, they have played a lead role in organizing 'The Other Economic Summit', which has been shadowing the annual G–7 summit over the last decade. If IPE scholars aim to understand contemporary political debates about the future direction of the global economy, they must broaden their horizons to acknowledge that these debates no longer take place just between representatives of the three traditional schools that have dominated IPE since the nineteenth century.

It is interesting to speculate about the reasons for the emergence and growing popularity of the greens' approach to issues of global political economy at this historical moment. One reason may be that they approach issues of IPE free from certain nineteenth-century assumptions held by the three traditional schools, such as a commitment to large-scale industrial development or a neglect of the environment-economy relationship. Equally important, in this age of globalization, the greens' analysis addresses the central feature of this phenomenon—the expansion of the scale of social life—in a much more direct way than the other schools. And their concerns about it seem to tap into a widespread sense of unease about democratic accountability, environmental degradation, and social upheavals and alienation in the new globalized economy. Furthermore, their promotion of 'global thinking' also resonates well in an age when there is a growing sense of worldwide interconnectedness and global diversity as well as increasingly widespread post-modern scepticism of universalistic political projects. Similarly, the greens' advocacy of localism attracts attention as globalization encourages both a search for local identities and a sense that the nation-state is no longer the most capable or even most appropriate agent of social change and protection. For all these reasons, the rise of the greens is unlikely to be a transient phenomenon and IPE scholars would do well to recognize their contribution to the widening of debate in the field at the end of the twentieth century.

## Notes

1 See, for example, Sandra Whitworth, 'Theory as Exclusion: Gender and IPE', in Richard Stubbs and Geoffrey R.D. Underhill, eds, *Political Economy and the Changing Global Order* (Toronto: McClelland & Stewart, 1994).

2 My task in this chapter is a descriptive and pedagogical one. I am not seeking to endorse the greens' views, nor do I attempt to evaluate the strengths or weaknesses of the perspective. I should also emphasize that, in highlighting the distinctiveness of their views in relation to the three traditional schools, I focus less attention on disagreements and opposing factions that exist among the greens. One further point: I have kept notes to a minimum. Readers seeking more detailed analysis should consult works listed in the notes and suggested readings.

3 Herman Daly and John Cobb, *For the Common Good: Redirecting the Economy Toward Community, the Environment, and a Sustainable Future* (Boston: Beacon Press, 1989).

4 Fernand Braudel, *The Structures of Everyday Life: The Limits of the Possible*, trans. Sian Reynolds (London: Fontana, 1985).

5 Vandana Shiva, 'The Greening of Global Reach', in W. Sachs, ed., *Global Ecology* (London: Zed Books, 1993).

6 E.F. Schumacher, *Small is Beautiful* (New York: Harper and Row, 1989).

7 See, for example, M.K. Gandhi, *Hind Swaraj and Other Writings*, ed. Antony Parel (Cambridge: Cambridge University Press, 1997).

8 The greens often cite favourably Karl Polanyi's *The Great Transformation* (Boston: Beacon Press, 1944).

9 Antony Giddens, *The Consequences of Modernity* (Cambridge: Polity Press, 1990), 64.

10 Hazel Henderson, *The Politics of the Solar Age* (Garden City, NY: Anchor Press, 1981), 9.

11 Braudel, *Structures of Everyday Life.*

12 See, for example, C. Williams, 'The New Barter Economy', *Journal of Public Policy* 16, 1 (1996): 85–101.

13 See Fernand Braudel, *Civilization and Capitalism: 15th–18th Century*, trans. Sian Reynolds (London: Fontana, 1985).

14 Paul Wapner, *Environmental Activism and World Civic Politics* (Albany: State University of New York Press, 1996).

15 See, for example, Michael Barrett Brown, *Fair Trade* (London: Zed Books, 1993).

16 Daly and Cobb, *For the Common Good.*

17 Réné Dubos, *Celebrations of Life* (New York: McGraw-Hill, 1981), 82–3.

18 See, for example, Tim Lang and Colin Hines, *The New Protectionism* (London: Earthscan, 1993), and many of the articles in Earth Island Press, ed., *The Case Against Free Trade: GATT, NAFTA and the Globalization of Corporate Power* (San Franciso: Earth Island Press, 1993).

19 See, for example, Bruce Rich, *Mortgaging the Earth: The World Bank, Environmental Impoverishment and the Crisis of Development* (London: Earthscan, 1994).

## Suggested Readings

Chatterjee, P., and M. Finger. *The Earth Brokers: Power Politics and World Development.* London: Routledge, 1994.

Daly, H. *Beyond Growth: The Economics of Sustainable Development.* Boston: Beacon Press, 1996.

Dobson, A. *Green Political Thought: An Introduction.* London: Unwin Hyman, 1990.

Ekins, P. *The Living Economy.* London: Routledge & Kegan Paul, 1986.

———. *New World Order: Grassroots Movements for Social Change.* London: Routledge, 1992.

Helleiner, E. 'IPE and the Greens', *New Political Economy* 1, 1 (1996): 59–77.

Korten, D. *When Corporations Rule the World.* West Hartford, Conn.: Kumarian, 1995.

Mander, J., and E. Goldsmith, eds. *The Case Against the Global Economy and For a Turn Toward the Local*. San Francisco: Sierra Club, 1996.

Robertson, J. *Future Wealth: New Economics for the 21st Century*. London: Cassell Publishers, 1990.

Sale, K. *Human Scale*. New York: Coward, McCann and Geoghegan, 1980.

Shiva, V. *Monocultures of the Mind*. London: Zed Books, 1993.

Tickner, J. 'An Ecofeminist Perspective on IPE', *International Political Science Review* (1993): 59–69.

## Web Sites

Communications for a Sustainable Future: csf.colorado.edu

Econet: www.igc.org/igc/econet

E.F. Schumacher Society: www.schumachersociety.org

International Institute for Sustainable Development: www.iisd.ca

The Other Economic Summit: pender.ee.upenn.edu/~rabii/toes

Third World Network: www.twnside.org.sg

## Chapter 5

# Explaining the Regional Phenomenon in an Era of Globalization

Helge Hveem

## Background and Argument

Regional integration projects are a growing phenomenon and are paradoxically occurring in tandem with what is loosely called 'globalization'. The two are by no means unconnected. This chapter will conceptualize the connection and suggest causes of regionalization. In so doing it will discuss the implications of these parallel developments for the contrasting regional cultures of capitalism and corporate governance that compete in the context of globalization.

Geopolitics was a major factor behind even the economically motivated regional projects during the early post-World War II period. Later, the factors and forces behind the regional phenomenon become more varied and the causal relationship more complex. As we enter the new millennium, the main factor pushing and shaping regional action is believed by many observers to be globalization, the role of which is usually explained in terms of the rational maximization of utility on the part of the state or corporate actors involved. These observers thus see regional integration as part of the effort of states to cope with a pervasive globalization, and they see the region as a staging post for corporate actors on their way to becoming global participants.

This chapter reformulates this argument to include theories emphasizing ideational and institutional factors. As a result of this reformulation, perceptions about the deepening and spread of globalization processes are revealed as exaggerated. The political, social, and cultural barriers that these processes confront, as well as problems inherent in

the processes themselves, may cause them to halt, recede, or collapse. Although signs of such outcomes were visible long before the financial crisis in East and Southeast Asia in 1997,[1] that crisis left no doubt about them. The crisis led many, including the IMF chief, to ask if another 1929 would soon be upon us. It vindicated Polanyi's analysis of systemic transformation as a 'double movement': as radical economic liberalization dissociates the economy from society, the response is social protest that may turn into radical political change. The present chapter will look more specifically at another Polanyi thesis: that regional collective action is not only a necessary response but the only possible international response to globalization.[2]

From the end of World War II, the 'first generation' of regional projects was to achieve the goals of security and political stability, an example of what may be termed 'doubly embedded regionalization'. First, regional projects had to take the geopolitical and ideological context of the Cold War as a primary ordering principle. Second, they were premised on the 'embedded liberalism' of Bretton Woods: liberalizing international economic transactions (within the Western world) would be done (only) along with social stabilization and state-building. The 'second-generation' regional integration episode started with decolonization in the 1960s and faded out early in the 1970s. It was also strongly premised on the limits of the Cold War. Practically all the regional projects of these two generations of regional action are thus built on the Westphalian state system and were to serve economic growth as well as security motives in their assistance to state-building goals. But embedded liberalism allowed them considerable freedom to impose barriers vis-à-vis non-members.

The advance of globalization processes and the end of the Cold War have changed that context. Not only have they given more weight to regional powers;[3] they have also reordered the relative salience of economic growth and sociopolitical stabilization goals, but with different effects on different parts of the world. While Western nations may have put Westphalia behind them, 'transition' economies are trying to complete state-building processes while integrating with the developed market economies.

The contextual changes have also allowed other motivations and types of agency to come to fruition. These are *trans*national and *trans*-state regional efforts that reflect the emergence of *society* at the regional level; sometimes these regional efforts co-ordinate with the *inter*national state system, but often they are in contrast to it. These efforts are not primarily for *efficiency* in terms of economic growth and globalization, but for political *legitimacy* and identity.

The primary institution of globalization, the self-regulating market, is held to be legitimate because it creates equal opportunities to compete. But individuals, groups, and classes are differently endowed with capabilities to exploit the process. Thus, trends towards greater socio-economic inequity and systemic instability result along with, and sometimes instead of, greater efficiency and growth, while legitimacy is guaranteed through equitable outcomes, not equal opportunity. This gives rise to contentious action by agents who perceive or realize that they lose in the process. To the extent that agents affected associate deepening social crisis with economic globalization, they will turn against it. These agents may accept losing in relative terms. But when they lose in absolute terms as well, peoples and even governments voice protest or may attempt to exit from the process.

A neo-utilitarian perspective assumes that globalization is driving or dominating regional processes. This is one way to explain the 'third-generation' regional projects such as the resurgence of the European single market project—as an attempt to maintain or improve competitiveness in more globalized markets, using regional action to 'ride on' globalization. Yet these theories err by interpreting the apparent dominance of the riding motive as a lasting tendency. This is wrong because it overrepresents rationality and assumes that agents are driven by utilitarian motives only or mostly, neglecting the possibility that humankind is driven by ideas or norms rather than utility considerations. It also risks ignoring that agents are subject to bounded rationality and that individual rationality may create collective irrationality. Cognitive, reflectivist, and social constructivist conceptions should thus complement utilitarian theories.

The regional phenomenon may be a rational strategy by governments to maximize their utility, but there are also collective action problems. Governments certainly are no longer able to act individually with authority the way they used to be. The key problem at the end of the 1990s has become one of disputed authority and of insufficient governance. Neither global markets nor national government suffice, nor do they provide the necessary normative basis for legitimacy. This, it is argued, creates a wider opening for the regional project and makes a global convergence of different forms of capitalism unlikely.

## Conceptualizing the Phenomenon

Regional projects differ considerably with respect to how they relate to globalization. A regional project may represent globalization or attempt to ride on it, to regulate it, or to resist it. The next section discusses under which conditions each of these outcomes is likely to happen. However, there is relatively little consensus over definitions in the literature, so theorizing must start by clarifying concepts.[4]

Globalization is often defined too broadly and imprecisely. One implication of this is that people tend towards determinism, to perceive globalization as inevitable, as destiny.[5] In the economic sphere globalization consists in the setting up of production organizations under a global strategy, in world capital markets, and/or in globally competitive markets for goods and services with a distinctly global reach, and in convergence of economic policies. It is assumed to advance through technological innovations, cultural assimilation, and adoption of the ideology of liberalization and deregulation worldwide. That advance normally also presupposes negotiation of multilateral institutions with some (but a limited) degree of worldwide authority and legitimacy. The fall of the Berlin Wall led to an exponential growth in the number of McDonald's restaurants in previously closed economies, to convergence of consumer expectations. But convergence of policies and implementation of common rules and principles, although advancing, were not close to representing a de facto globalized world system except in the important case of capital markets. National and regional variation in economic-political culture remained important when the crisis of the financial system broke out in 1997 (see Chapter 9 by Story in this volume).

To understand the relationship between globalization and the regional phenomenon it is equally necessary to define the latter precisely and properly. To start with, there are at least three ways to define a 'region': by geographical spatial indicators, by the existence of networks or structures of transaction and communication, and by way of cognitive maps and collective identities. Delimitation by geography is a long tradition that characterizes many or most utilitarian theorists. The 'social networks' tradition is still indebted to Deutsch's classical study of the North Atlantic area.[6] As we shall see below, this variant is paralleled, but not necessarily copied, by contemporary regional networks in Asia and Africa. Finally, representing the third class of definitions, 'cognitive regions' are a possibility.[7] In this case the 'region' exists in the minds of people but is not necessarily an objective, institutionalized community. All three classes of definition are relevant to the phenomenon, because regional projects are multifaceted.

## Regionalism and Regionalization

The distinction between regionalism and regionalization helps draw out these definitional points.[8] *Regionalism* is the body of *ideas* promoting an identified geographical or social space as the regional project. Or it is the presence or the conscious construction of an identity that represents *one specific* region. It is usually associated with a policy program (goals to be achieved) and strategy (means and mechanisms by which goals should be reached), and it normally leads to institution-building. Regionalism ties agents to one specific regional project that is clearly limited spatially or socially, but not limited in time. A historical example of a truly regionalist project is the European Coal and Steel Community. Its founders, motivated by the need to build a security community among previous enemies by means of economic co-operation, built top-down political integration prior to the existence of important economic transactions.

*Regionalization*, on the other hand, refers to the *process* that actually builds concrete patterns of transaction within an identified regional space. It may be caused by regionalism. But as mentioned above it may also emerge irrespective of whether there is a regionalist project or not. For those agents who are not directed by regionalism, the boundaries of the 'region' are rather pragmatically defined and regional action is temporary. As an example, a number of Finnish and Norwegian firms set up affiliates in Sweden in the 1960s and 1970s not primarily motivated by Nordic identity, but as a stepping-stone to an even wider regional level and then to the global level.

Conceptualizing regionalism, finally, is further complicated by what is referred to as the '*new regionalism*'.[9] It reflects a tendency to emphasize subregions within nation-states and to give priority to building a network of transactions and collaboration across national boundaries between such subregions, an example being the Rhine border region. This tendency is a reaction, perhaps a postmodernist one, to globalization or to the regional projects of the state system, or to both. It appears to be strong in Europe, but may also be found in the Chinese diaspora and in some regions of Africa.

## Internationalization and Transnationalization

In order to account for these two phenomena—the example of the Nordic firms and the 'new regionalism'—the distinction between internationalization and transnationalization may help. They roughly correspond to top-down and bottom-up agency. *Internationalization* is a process initiated and managed by public authorities. It opens up national political economies to transactions abroad. The defining criterion is that it is state-managed, at least *de jure*. Transactions are seen as *inter*action between sovereign political entities.

*Transnationalization* results in the same outcome—an opening up of economic transactions. But private, non-state agents initiate and manage this process. It *trans*cends national boundaries as a flow not of diplomatic exchanges, but of spontaneous individual or group behaviour. At least in principle it is not dependent on the state system for initiation and management. Rather, it relies on the strategy, resources, and management of transnational corporations (TNCs) or transnational NGOs, networks, and communities. These sources of action are of increasing importance in the 1990s. In particular, transnational NGOs have grown exponentially over the last years. Their action may favour regionalization as much as globalization.

We should think of these categories as ideal types. In reality, the processes of internationalization and transnationalization are often related, one conditioning the other, sometimes even initiating it. Transnationalization thus depends entirely on internationalization in those cases where foreign investments are barred or restricted and the state is needed to remove barriers. In other cases internationalization is a policy that results from prior transnationalization: economic interdependence that results from a growing trade or investment exchange is one example; the opening up of national financial markets after the emergence of offshore finance markets is another. The example of the Nordic firms reflects both processes: on the one hand their foreign investments were reflecting a transnationalization strategy, but at the same time it was facilitated, to some extent even stimulated, by the conscious internationalization conducted by the states of the national economies in the Western European region.[10]

Since options are affected by changing contexts, agents may also choose a flexible approach. They may keep options open, in other words, *hedge*.[11] If or when the regional effort becomes institutionalized, or particular contextual factors demand that a definite choice is made, however, flexibility is reduced and the effort tends towards choosing one particular option. Hedging was not possible during the Cold War, and it may not be possible against the will of hegemonic authority even after it has ended. It is therefore possible only under particular conditions and as a temporary strategy.

## Explaining the Contemporary Regional Phenomenon

The third generation of regional projects was to a large extent a number of responses to global competitive pressures, thus representing regionalization. Yet there is a close relationship between this regionalization process and the more state-led process of regionalism through the negotiation of formal regional trade agreements. States have responded to the pressures of corporate actors for more transnationalization on a regional basis, providing them with the framework they needed through further internationalization.

Third-generation projects emerged for two reasons. First, they were spearheaded in the mid-1980s by the then European Community, where significant institutional development and political leadership contributed to reinforcement of the European project. A number of regional projects around and after 1990 were demanded by private transnationalizing agents as a response to the European initiative for a single market and monetary union.[12] Second, the wave of projects was also greatly accelerated by the end of the Cold War and the breakup of the Soviet Union, for these events reduced the impact of global political factors.[13]

The projects of the 1990s are mostly free trade arrangements. Few aimed at the rather mercantilist type of customs unions of the 1960s that led neoclassical economic theorists to see regional trade projects as 'trade diversion' rather than 'trade creation', and many of them to take a principled stand against regionalization. Some of the third-generation projects did, however, have elements of neomercantilism, or they were so perceived by third parties.

As the third generation of regional projects matures and, as a result of destabilizing financial crises, globalization starts to fragment into contradictory tendencies, the regional phenomenon also becomes more complex and thus more complicated to explain. The outcome looks like the result of a convergence of several factors and an alliance of agents with rather different motives. What we witness is that transnationalization becomes relatively less associated with globalization and is more likely to result in regionalization. There are also compelling reasons for believing that internationalization will become relatively more influenced by regionalism and thus more opposed to globalization. The reasons why this is likely are found in growing problems with the efficacy of patterns of governance and with legitimacy and identity in the face of globalization.

### Transnationalization and Regionalization

Received wisdom is that transnational capital represents the most consistent protagonist of globalization and of a multilateral system.[14] If the agents of capital accept regional projects, it is only as a means to further globalization. This type of motive is true for large investment banks and funds, but it is not necessarily true for transnational corporations investing with a long-term stake in production and services. Such corporations may rather take a pragmatic view on the choice between globalization and regionalization. Many of them have indeed been actively pushing regionalization, a fact indicated by the increase in intraregional as compared to interregional transactions, both in investments and in trade, over the last decades. If these agents follow a sequential strategy, regional action is a transition to a global market arrangement and typically pursuing the riding on or hedge options. But corporate management differs in style along broad national and regional divisions,[15] partly because business-society relations continue to differ widely,[16] and significant political and cultural barriers to global strategies continue to exist in many sectors. Managers are mostly pragmatic and often bow to cultural particularism. There is, therefore, no compelling logical reason why corporate managers should always prefer global over regional arrangements—granted, of course, that they do have a choice and are not strictly bound by obligations to global multilateral institutions. For small and medium-sized firms, the regional option is often simply the only option consistent with the resources they have at their disposal to reach out to external markets.

In West Africa *trans-state regionalism* illustrates a contradiction between transnationalization and internationalization. In this case the state border is not a barrier but a major source of profit for economic agents. A relatively undeveloped, non-diversified economy offers few alternative sources of accumulation. Here, small firms, artisans, and traders represent agency in favour of regional economic circuits across borders but in opposition to tariff-hostile globalization. Transnational flows of goods and individuals are stimulated, not discouraged, by the discrepancies between neighbouring tariff and trade systems: goods from low-tariff jurisdictions are smuggled where weak states cannot ensure enforcement, and regional integration results. Extra-regional sources of transnationalization are present as investors and traders, but their accumulation is mainly related to traditional colonial-type investments in raw materials extraction and trade, where they are still dominant. The continent receives only a small fraction of global direct investment flows despite its radical shift to a more welcoming policy.[17] Africa internationalizes because of global pressures and processes, but it is not transnationalized by them. The phenomenon referred to as trans-state regionalism transcends the state, but is not necessarily opposing it. Rather, this type of regionalism is opposing internationalization (the tearing down of tariffs and other formal barriers) because the latter destroys an important source of income from intraregional transactions.

If private agents have been taking the initiative in most of the third-generation cases, political actors often have picked up the process and institutionalized the initiatives. Governments endorsed regional projects partly for fear of a deadlock in the Uruguay Round negotiations or for fear of a 'fortress Europe', or for both reasons. In one case, that of Central America, governments initiated a very ambitious institutionalization project, no doubt modelled on the EU, and SADCC changed to the Southern African Development Community (SADC) by strengthening (although almost from scratch) its central institutions. A scramble for regional support contributed to the North American Free Trade Agreement (NAFTA) and to Mercado Común del Sur (MERCOSUR), the customs union comprised of Argentina, Paraguay, Uruguay, and Brazil, as well as to reinvigoration of several second-generation projects such as the Association of Southeast Asian Nations (ASEAN). At the same time the end of the Cold War and the coming of globalized markets coincided with a paradigmatic shift in large parts of the South. State-centred economic policy and 'delinking' from the North were replaced by an acceptance of and invitation to market-based policies. This coincidence of trends led to less contentious behaviour within the Lomé agreement between the EU and African-Caribbean-Pacific or ACP countries, to the integration of Mexico with the United States and Canada in NAFTA, and to the setting up of the Asia-Pacific Economic Co-operation forum (APEC).

## Internationalization and Regionalization

When and how does internationalization turn into regionalization as more than just a temporary stage, as more than simply an exercise in riding on globalization? And under what conditions do transnationalization and internationalization converge to initiate, defend, or strengthen regionalism? The answer may be found by introducing a simple analytical scheme that addresses the agency-structure issue.

It was argued above that second-generation regionalization was shaped more by structure than by agency, whereas agency has had greater influence on the third-generation and contemporary regional projects. Our understanding of the motivations for action may begin with the perceived utility and

efficacy of action; this corresponds to March and Olsen's 'logic of expected consequences', wherein agents ask which institutional solutions offer maximum profit, growth, welfare, and security. But to link action only to a logic of consequences is to ignore the role of identity and of rules and institutions—or 'the logic of appropriateness'—in shaping behaviour.[18] The latter represent important motivating factors, and it is quite possible they will eventually dominate the regional phenomenon.

Structural factors include: *level of development; market structure* and *industrial organization* (oligopoly, oligopsony, i.e., oligarchy of purchasers, corporate structures where there is little incentive to co-operate); and power balances and the existence (or not) of *hegemony* (the presence of a dominant power is, for example, a potential boost for a weakly institutionalized project). If there is radical change in any one or several of these structural factors, this may affect the relationship between globalization and regional action quite strongly. The effect may be seen in the structure of authority, in perceptions about problems of governance, and in preferences with respect to how they should be resolved. This raises the issue of how economic efficiency relates to legitimacy in the context of regional projects.

## Efficiency, Efficacy, and Legitimacy

Explanations focusing on the legitimacy issue in relation to regionalization mainly take domestic political institutions and processes into account, such as the character of state institutions, civil society's strength, and state-civil society relations.[19] While efficiency in terms of security or growth is a major concern in the initiating stage of regional integration, legitimation becomes more important after the momentum of it has been established. There are two ways of legitimizing: by rules and by results. The core of the globalization ideology is the self-regulating market, which, its advocates claim, offers both economic efficiency and legitimacy. If all agents enjoy the same competitive conditions (rules), then they see the arrangement as legitimate.

Liberal democracy and market economy are considered by many to be twins. Even if this were so, it is also true that democracy consists of more than market rules and property rights. Democracy may also be associated with popular resistance to the inequalities that the market generates. Both Polanyi and Hirsch have, from somewhat different perspectives, argued that the advance of the market economy and democracy since the Industrial Revolution has occurred together, but that both *cannot* coexist with an increasingly uneven distribution of welfare.[20] This incompatibility, according to Polanyi, led to totalitarian political regimes and eventually to war in the 1930s. While a precise repetition of events is unlikely, some trends *are* repeated in the 1990s. The self-regulating market is advancing, democratization of national polities is a global trend, yet inequality in the distribution of welfare between and within nation-states and regions is, with some few exceptions, increasing. The self-regulating market may certainly produce more efficient allocation of resources. But if there is insufficient redistribution of the result, and there is at the same time democratization, the discrepancy becomes not only more transparent, it is also contested. And when the self-regulating market produces systemic instability, such as has happened in the financial system, democratic governance is threatened.[21] The authority of the system loses legitimacy; it is challenged and may eventually break down.

But why and how would such a process lead to regionalization of the *regionalist* kind? Postmodernist critics notwithstanding, the nation-state is the level of authority still most vested with collective identity (perhaps less so in the EU, where the link between the regional project and identity is most advanced). From the point of view of most citizens the nation-state is also, but probably to a lesser extent, the level of authority most vested with legitimacy. The problem of the nation-state in the era of globalization is that it is found to be less effective than it once was in delivering security, welfare, and a secure sense of identity. Evans is right in pointing out that the 'eclipse of the state' thesis is grossly exaggerated and that there are good reasons to argue that states are still viable.[22] Still, if legitimacy and

collective identity combine, they represent a strong challenge to the logic of efficiency if or when the former two collide with the latter. Therefore, the authority of global markets, being based on equal opportunity, is challenged if or when globalization is associated with marginalization. At that point, legitimacy of institutions tends to be associated with welfare creation and distributional outcomes. Legitimizing becomes result-based, not rules-based. Thus, *the comparative advantage of the regional project is that it may be more effective in governing globalization than the nation-state, while potentially offering more legitimacy and collective identity than globalization itself.*

When the regional project attempts to *regulate* or *resist* globalization, it is often a response to problems related to legitimizing the distributive implications of the latter. The response also results from several agents with coinciding but sometimes even different motives combining in alliance across nation-states. As a result, authority relationships in regional action are both more complex and more unpredictable in third-generation projects than was previously the case. Rather than searching through contrasting theories such as functionalist, neo-functionalist/federalist, or intergovernmentalist approaches, we should look for combinations of theories focusing on the efficacy (in terms of governance), legitimacy, and identity triangle as causes of behaviour.

## Identity and Regionalization

Great powers may ride effectively on globalization, but even they may experience problems in doing so. If states attempt to regulate bilaterally, which was the US trend in the 1980s, this tends to increase the level of conflict.[23] If they attempt to do it on a global level, the number of participants and thus collective action problems become too large. There will still be efforts to sustain global multilateral institutions. But even the United States has been active in developing regional projects on its own doorstep, demonstrating that a regional institution may thus be an optimal solution to collective action problems.

The recent financial crisis appears to have reduced the viability of projects in Southeast Asia, including ASEAN itself. But the longer-term effects of the East Asian and Southeast Asian crisis will not necessarily sustain the current trend of embedding the crisis-torn nations firmly into the globalization path. In 1997 leaders in the region floated the idea of creating a regional fund for handling short-term stabilization problems. The idea was put on ice due to strong opposition from the United States and the IMF. They apparently saw the idea as a potential threat not only to global multilateral rules, but to US power.[24] There have been, however, initiatives to warm it up, partly as a response to widespread criticism of the IMF's role in the Asian crisis.

There are basically three reasons why Asian regionalism may grow. First, several of the countries in the East Asian region have a legacy of opposing tight links with global trends in culture and the political economy. Although references to an 'Asian identity' are wrong and to a 'Southeast Asian' identity mostly exaggerated, there are indications of a growing awareness of the latter. It may be partly security-driven, as the recent expansion of ASEAN membership may indicate. This tentative and still unsettled expression of identity represents a defence of a policy of emphasizing sovereignty over globalization. Second, the suggested regional financial fund is also an illustration of a new tendency. Japan's problems with its own domestic finance system and continued political and cultural strains between Japan and several of the regional states make the odds for such ideas to materialize not particularly high. But while old political animosities remain, mere pragmatism may come to dominate them. If the global financial system is not reformed and stabilized rapidly and the Asian depression continues, the opportunity costs of failing to develop a regional alternative may be high. The countries of the region have become economically so interdependent over the past decade of rapidly growing intraregional investments and trade that they may simply have to let economic reality prevail over history.[25]

The third reason to expect an Asian way as a path distinct from globalization is what may be referred to, with perhaps a bit of exaggeration, as the 'nationalist' or 'ethnic' factor. One such element is the growing linkage between diaspora and mainland Chinese, which appears to lead to capital invested abroad being repatriated to the region as a response to the crisis.

### *Regional Action as Global Governance*

In the final analysis, therefore, the region may be preferred for reasons having to do with a need for authority and the lack of appropriate global governance. True, this applies to subregions as well; in several parts of the world they are preferred as a response to the perceived weakening of the nation-state. But it also applies to the phenomenon dealt with here—the international region.

Rationalist accounts of regional action refer to it as an element of 'layered governance'. A liberal institutionalist variant thus views regionalization as a *delegation of power* from a liberal global order. Because of the complexity and variety of issues that this order has to deal with, some governance tasks have to be referred to a lower level of governance. This perspective is represented both by those who emphasize the interstate system[26] and by those who argue that international society is of growing importance.[27]

While these perspectives may have some value, they miss the vital need for agency—for somebody to have the *idea* or a pressing *interest* in choosing the regional level of governance before other solutions. To the extent that these perspectives have agency in mind, top-down initiatives are generally emphasized over bottom-up ones. In neo-functionalist and, in particular, intergovernmentalist accounts, the agent is a state bureaucrat or national politician, respectively.

But as indicated above, private agency and bottom-up initiative are highly potent sources of regional action. For firms under the pressure of globalization, the regional level may represent collateral in helping to sustain particular capitalist cultures. Regional institutions may contribute to competitiveness by helping to fund research and development and to organize industrial policy supports in several ways,[28] even to protect firms with long-term investments and high-asset exposure against the volatility of the financial system.

If the 'layered governance' perspective is valid, it is because it helps us view regionalization as part of transnational and international *alliance-building*. Besides being a means of organizing collective action to support competitiveness or represent a sense of identity, regional action may also be a means to achieve national domestic political reordering and convergence towards the dominant regional culture. Domestic interest groups thus may build alliances at the regional level in order to strengthen their own relative power at the expense of other domestic groups. Business groups in several of the democratic-corporatist Western European countries that applied for membership in the EU at the beginning of the 1990s thus lobbied domestically for membership, *inter alia*, to weaken domestic corporatist structures and procedures. Mexican industrial élites also appear to have wanted NAFTA as a means to deregulate and liberalize the domestic economy, including agriculture.[29] Regional decision-making, therefore, may be used to level the playing field nationally. But it is also true that in several countries with a strong social democratic and corporatist tradition, such as Norway and Sweden, regional institutions were defined by leading proponents of this tradition as an optimal level of governance by which global capital may be regulated.[30]

Environmentalists, on the other hand, may use the regional level to pressure business to adopt more environment-friendly policies and practices. Even labour may pursue this strategy. Liberalizing regional projects may be perceived as a zero-sum game by labour if they are facilitating the free movement of capital. Again, NAFTA illustrates both tendencies from the perspective of US interest groups: environmentalists found it legitimate only after having the environmental side agreement passed, whereas US labour opposed it because it was feared business would transfer jobs abroad. But the 'Eurostrike' in 1997 illustrates that national labour unions may use the regional level to their own advantage. Workers in a Renault plant in Belgium mobilized unions all over the EU because they could point to Renault's decision to close the Belgian plant as a breach of EU policy that the interests of the totality of the corporation's workforce at the regional level be taken into account.[31] The plant, however, was subsequently closed.

Operating at a global level may mean considerable transaction costs for even the most efficient firms. There are several reasons why a bilateral arrangement of market transactions may be more cost-efficient than multilateral options, particularly global ones.[32] If a large number of bilateral arrangements were to be initiated, implemented, and controlled, however, this would represent a large cost factor for a corporation. But since markets are concentrated for most actors, a limited number of such deals are sufficient to cope with most transactions, a fact that made this option so attractive in the 1980s. A regional solution is the optimal way of reducing transaction costs, and at the same time this provides a regime that is also more legitimate than bilateralism.

## Conclusion

There will still be strong agency in favour of globalization, chiefly by internationalizing governments whose countries stand to gain from it, from transnationalizing big corporations and financiers—and from neo-liberal economists. The need for conflict resolution, standardization, and other aspects of coordination among regional projects will also represent a strong globalizing argument.

The argument developed above is that three main sources of agency will make regional projects more than just episodes or steps towards an inevitable globalization. The first is that, despite years of globalizing efforts, considerable political and cultural diversity still exists among the various national and regional capitalisms. Second, there are strong and apparently growing tendencies for top-down internationalizing and bottom-up transnationalizing forces to work in parallel or even converge over a policy that favours regional action. The third source of regional action is the apparent or likely trend towards emphasizing collective identity and legitimacy in addition to, sometimes even before, efficiency. The declining efficacy of nation-states to organize action that links efficiency (growth and security) with identity and legitimacy combines with pressures from globalizing tendencies, in particular destabilizing and marginalizing patterns, to open up greater room for regional projects as alternative governance structures.

This means that neo-utilitarian theories are necessary, but insufficient, for understanding the regional phenomenon and that they need to be modified and supplemented by alternative accounts drawing on reflectivist and social constructivist perspectives. If security is the utilitarian motive that leads agency and it calls for a regional project, the motivation of economic efficiency may be subordinated to it. And if security is defined broadly,[33] there are even stronger reasons to argue that security may join with collective identity and legitimacy to construct a strong basis for regionalism.

## Notes

1  Susan Strange, *Casino Capitalism* (Oxford: Basil Blackwell, 1986).

2  Karl Polanyi, *The Great Transformation* (Boston: Beacon Press, 1957; (first published 1944); Polanyi, 'Universal Capitalism or Regional Planning', *London Quarterly of World Affairs* (Jan. 1945).

3  Peter J. Katzenstein, 'Regionalism in Comparative Perspective', *Cooperation and Conflict* 31, 2 (1996): 123–59.

4  This section is based on critical reading of several different sources of insight, including Louise Fawcett and Andrew Hurrell, eds, *Regionalism in World Politics: Regional Organization and International Order* (Oxford: Oxford University Press, 1995); Peter Katzenstein and Takashi Shiraishi, eds, *Network Power: Japan and Asia* (Ithaca, NY: Cornell University Press, 1997); Jeffrey A. Frankel and Miles Kahler, eds, *Regionalism and Rivalry: Japan and the United States in Pacific Asia* (Chicago: University of Chicago Press, 1993); Andrew Gamble and Anthony Payne, eds, *Regionalism and World Order* (London: Macmillan, 1996).

5  For a broad definition, see Philip Cerny, 'Globalization and the Changing Logic of Collective Action', *International Organization* 49, 4 (Autumn 1995): 595–626. See also Charles Oman, *Les défis politiques de la globalisation et de la régionalisation* (Paris: OECD Development Centre, 1996).

6  Karl W. Deutsch et al., *Political Community and the North Atlantic Area* (Princeton, NJ: Princeton University Press, 1957).

7  Emmanuel Adler, 'Imagined (Security) Communities', paper presented at the annual meeting of the American Political Science Association, New York, 1–4 Sept. 1994.

8  A. Hurrell, 'Regionalism in Theoretical Perspective', in Fawcett and Hurrell, eds, *Regionalism in World Politics*, 39, introduces a similar distinction, but with another content; in his vocabulary 'regionalism' corresponds to the definition proposed here, whereas 'regionalization' refers to the 'growth of societal integration within a region and to the often undirected processes of social and economic interaction'. Haggard, in Frankel and Kahler, eds, *Regionalism and Rivalry*, makes a similar distinction.

9  See Bjørn Hettne and Andras Inotai, *The New Regionalism* (Helsinki: WIDER, 1994); Brian Keating and John Loughlin, eds, *The Political Economy of Regionalism* (London: Frank Cass, 1997).

10  In fact, the formation of the European Free Trade Association (EFTA), which in its formative years included the United Kingdom, Switzerland, and Austria as well as the five Nordic countries (Finland becoming member only a few years later) had its greatest impact in stimulating trade *within* the Nordic region, as opposed to between the Nordics and the EFTA. See Jan Fagerberg, 'Technology,

Trade Structure, and European Integration: An Examination of Intra-Nordic, Nordic-EC, and Intra-EC Trade 1961–1987', in Fagerberg and Lars Lundberg, eds, *European Economic Integration: A Nordic Perspective* (Aldershot: Avebury, 1993).

11  Davis B. Bobrow and Robert T. Kudrle, 'Regionalism as Accelerator, Brake, Ratchet and Hedge: FDI and Competition Policies', paper presented at the Third Pan-European Conference of the ECPR Standing Group on International Relations, organized jointly with the International Studies Association, Vienna, 16–20 Sept. 1998.

12  Gerard Lafay and Deniz Unal-Kesenci, 'Les trois pôles géographiques des échanges internationaux', *Économie prospective internationale* 45, 1 (1991); Alice Landau, 'Multilatéralisme et régionalisme dans les relations économiques internationales', in Daniel Bach, ed., *Regionalisation in Africa: Integration and Disintegration* (London: J. Currey and Indiana University Press, 1999).

13  Peter Katzenstein, 'Asian Regionalism in Comparative Perspective', in Katzenstein and Shiraishi, eds, *Network Power*.

14  Helen Milner, *Resisting Protectionism* (Princeton, NJ.: Princeton University Press, 1988).

15  Louis Pauly and Simon Reich, 'Enduring MNC Differences Despite Globalization', *International Organization* 51, 1 (Winter 1997): 1–30.

16  David Soskice, 'Divergent Production Regimes', in Herbert Kitschelt et al., *Continuity and Change in Contemporary Capitalism* (Cambridge: Cambridge University Press, 1998).

17  *World Investment Report* (Geneva: United Nations, various years).

18  James G. March and Johan P. Olsen, 'The Institutional Dynamics of International Political Orders', ARENA Working Paper no. 5, Apr. 1998, to be published in *International Organization*.

19  Katzenstein, 'Regionalism in Comparative Perspective'.

20  Polanyi, *The Great Transformation*; Fred Hirsch, *Social Limits to Growth* (London: Routledge & Kegan Paul, 1977).

21  Eric Helleiner, 'Democratic Governance in an Era of Global Finance', in Max Cameron and Maureen Molot, eds, *Democracy and Foreign Policy* (Ottawa: Carleton University Press, 1995).

22  Peter Evans, 'The Eclipse of the State? Reflections on Stateness in an Era of Globalization', *World Politics* 50 (Oct. 1997): 62–87.

23  M. Bernard and J. Ravenhill, 'Beyond Product Cycles and Flying Geese: Regionalization, Hierarchy, and the Industrialization of East Asia', *World Politics* 47 (1994): 171–209.

24  Paul Krugman, interview on CNBC, reported on Internet in *Dow Jones Newswires*, 28 Aug. 1998.

25  Richard Higgott, 'Globalisation, Regionalism and Identity in East Asia', in Peter Dicken et al., eds, *The Logics of Globalisation in the Asia Pacific* (London: Routledge, 1998).

26  Beth V. Yarbrough and Robert M. Yarbrough, 'Regionalism and Layered Governance', *Journal of International Affairs* 48, 1 (1994): 95–118.

27  James N. Rosenau, 'Governance in the Twenty-First Century', *Global Governance* 1, 1 (Winter 1995): 13–43.

28  Razeen Sally, *States and Firms: Multinational Enterprises in Institutional Competition* (London: Routledge, 1995); Lynn Mytelka, 'Regional Cooperation and the New Logic of International Cooperation', in Mytelka, ed., *South-South Cooperation in Global Perspective* (Paris: OECD, 1993).

29  José Luis Calva, *La Disputa por la Terra* (Mexico City: Fontamara, 1992).

30  Jacob Gustavsson, 'The Politics of Foreign Policy Change', doctoral dissertation (University of Lund, 1998).

31  *The European*, 13–19 Mar. 1997.

32  Lisa Martin, 'Interests, Power, and Multilateralism', *International Organization* 46, 4 (Autumn 1992): 765–92.

33  Barry Buzan, Jaap de Wilde, and Ole Weaver, *Security: A New Framework for Analysis* (Boulder, Colo.: Lynne Rienner, 1998).

## Suggested Readings

Coleman, W.D., and G.R.D. Underhill, eds. *Regionalism and Global Economic Integration: Europe, Asia, and the Americas*. London: Routledge, 1998.

Fawcett, Louise, and Andrew Hurrell, eds. *Regionalism in World Politics: Regional Organization and International Order*. Oxford: Oxford University Press, 1995.

Fernandez Jilberto, A.E., and André Momenen, eds. *Regionalization and Globalization in the Modern World Economy: Perspectives on Third World and Transitional Economies*. London: Routledge, 1998.

Lavergne, Real, ed. *Regional Integration and Co-operation in West Africa: A Multidimensional Perspective*. Trenton, NJ: Africa World Press, 1997.

Tussie, Diana, ed. *Developing Countries and International Trade Negotiations*. London: Macmillan, 1999.

## Web Sites

Asia-Pacific Economic Co-operation:
http://www.apecsec.org.sg/

Agriculture and Agrifood Canada, Trade Agreements:
http://www.agr.ca/itpd-dpci/ta5.html

European Access: http://www.europeanaccess.co.uk/

European Commission:
http://europa.eu.int/index_eu.htm

Chapter 6

# World Order, Non-State Actors, and the Global Casino:
## The Retreat of the State?

Susan Strange[*]

This is not a book about world order as narrowly understood by the old-fashioned international relations realists. For them, world order meant only the absence of war between states, especially rich and powerful states. Their solution was some kind of balance of power, or balance of terror, among the potential contestants.

Rather, its purpose is both more limited and more in tune with the times. For, as I and others have argued, the competition between states is no longer for territory but for shares in the world market for goods and services. In this chapter I start with the observation that we have arrived in a global financial casino, and world order is dominated by this. I try to assemble the theoretical ingredients to explain these changes. Karl Polanyi, in his insistence that markets do not evolve organically but are instead the creations of vested interests exercising political power, is the inspiration. I lay the groundwork for understanding how order might be restored to the global system for the creation, allocation, and trading of credit in particular, and how this relates to the competition among states.

This book is very much an exercise in developing the study of international political economy. The contributors share a consensus that the political and economic domains cannot be conceptually separated any more than the domestic arrangements defining the role of markets and authorities in determining who-gets-what at the end of the day can be separated from the transnational ones. I share that consensus, and since the international financial and market system is so dynamic and has been changed over the past decades both by markets and by states and other authorities, it may be

useful to examine the theoretical implications of these changes. This is what this chapter aims to do, putting forward arguments derived from my last book, *Mad Money*, and also from the theoretical chapters of *The Retreat of the State*. This seems worth doing because some of the contributions to the original Stubbs-Underhill volume rather assumed that the international financial and economic systems were static, remaining unchanged from year to year. Yet change there was, and it brought new costs and benefits, as well as new risks and opportunities, to the players in the system. Understanding the sources of change, therefore, is a necessary foundation to any understanding of the who-gets-what in the overall system.

One of these sources is to be found in the technologies of international finance. Technological change is briefly mentioned in my contribution to the first edition of this volume (pp. 104–5), drawing heavily on the analysis in Chapter 2 of *Rival States, Rival Firms*. But it does not explore either what those changes were or why they happened and what the consequences and theoretical implications are. That will be my purpose in the following pages.

*Mad Money* was written as a sequel to *Casino Capitalism*. Its purpose was to record and, if possible, explain what has changed in the system since the mid-1980s and what is still much the same. Heavy emphasis—indeed a whole chapter—is devoted to the technological changes in financial markets. In combination with the push for liberalization from the United States and its compliant International Monetary Fund, the technological changes—cheaper and faster computers plus

cheaper and faster communications with satel-
lites—enhanced the profitability of financial services firms and consequently brought in many new
players to compete for valuable market shares. One
theoretically important observation based on this
development runs contrary to the conventional
wisdom of liberal economics. Liberal economists
stubbornly held to a belief in the benefits of competition for consumers; the more competition, the
lower the prices and the higher the quality of goods
or services. In financial services, this did not
happen. Increased competition among banks and
non-banks never led to lower prices. It led to the
competitors taking bigger risks with other people's
money and now, dangerously, sometimes with
their own.

   This development has important implications
for the system. Seventy years ago Frank Knight drew
the important distinction between actuarial risks,
which could be calculated and allowed for, and
business risks, which were totally unpredictable
because all entrepreneurs believed in their own
innocence and that they had the key to material success and fame.[1] Their fond conviction did not affect
the system so long as they looked to others for the
capital necessary to launch their enterprises. But
once the erstwhile lenders began to invest their own
money they became, by any definition, capitalists
rather than intermediating bankers.

   There is little in conventional theory to help us
come to terms with such developments. These
sorts of changes in world order were initiated by a
variety of players in the system, but they have
affected us all. The accelerating global casino owes
as much to state policies and technology as to private actors and international institutions. How they
come together in the process of change that we call
globalization is what we need to understand. I shall
argue that it is no good looking to theories of international relations. Nor is it any good looking for
help from neo-liberal economics in understanding
globalization, even though its followers have often
been the most enthusiastic supporters of globalization—defined as removing barriers of all kinds to
the free transnational movement of capital, goods,
services, and (sometimes) people.

## Theory? What Theory?

I am not generally regarded—nor would I wish to
be—as a theorist in international relations. Instead,
I devoted much time to analysing the global financial system and how it emerged. But during 1998,
I was buying and reading recent books on IR
theory.[2] I found them not only dull reading for the
most part, but also largely irrelevant to the dominant political issues of the day. They are irrelevant
because they take as the central problematic of the
world system the resolution of conflict between
states. (The maximization of interstate co-operation
on common problems is sometimes added, but
usually takes second place to the old issues of peace
and war between states claiming territorial sovereignty.) In my view, this is an obsolete—or at least,
obsolescing—problematic. Violent conflict, of
course, is not an obsolete problematic. On the contrary, it is very much a central problem of contemporary human society.[3] But conflict between major
states is no longer the critical problematic of world
politics. Rather, it is violent conflict within states,
usually over who is to control the levers of power
given to recognized governments. That is why so
much IR theory is irrelevant and uninteresting.

   The reason why there has been this very fundamental change in international relations has not
yet been generally recognized. Indeed, it is not even
universally recognized that there has been such a
change. Witness the agonizing—in the United
States especially—over the testing of nuclear
devices by the Indian and Pakistani governments in
the summer of 1998. There was much alarmist talk
of a regional arms race that would lead to open conflict between the two countries. The fact that the
United States itself and the Soviet Union had
nuclear weapons and indeed engaged in an arms
race for nearly 40 years without going to war was
conveniently overlooked. In American political circles, new—i.e., Asian—countries could not be
trusted to behave so prudently. That was the
implicit assumption behind the Non-Proliferation
Treaty. Yet the puzzling thing was not that either
state should seek to acquire nuclear capability for
its greater security. It was why, despite continued

and worsening mutual provocation arising from the Kashmir situation, neither government had come near to open conflict with the other. It looked as though both thought—in disregard of the hothead extremists on either side—that there were more important objectives for national policy than the territorial matter of who controlled Kashmir.

The assumption that states had lost interest in the acquisition of more territory was argued by John Stopford and myself in *Rival States, Rival Firms*. This had to do with the changing nature of the competition between states for wealth and power. In the old so-called Westphalian system of interstate relations, wealth and power could be acquired by war and the conquest of more territory. Military strength and better military technology were the necessary conditions for the successful acquisition of other people's land. By the second half of the twentieth century, these assumptions no longer held. As John Mueller argued, making war to acquire more territory had gone out of fashion.[4] Neither of the new 'winners' in the competition between states—Germany and Japan—either had or coveted military strength and capability. None of the Asian tigers following Japan's example had sought to acquire more territory as a means to greater wealth. One of them—Singapore—had minimal territory and was essentially a city-state.

Stopford and I offered a theoretical explanation for this sea-change. Our book was generally ignored by writers on international relations, who regarded it as a mere exercise in development economics and business management having no relevance to their own work. Not surprising, really. For our theoretical hypothesis was that the reason for the changing competition between states was to be found in technology. Here lay the answer to Mueller's puzzle: why had war 'gone out of fashion'? We argued that in manufacturing industries (and, indeed, in agriculture and mineral exploitation, as in the service sector) there had been, first, an observable acceleration in the rate of technological change; second, this change almost always involved the enterprise, whatever it was, in the substitution of capital for labour; and third, this substitution was expensive. The net result of this general technological acceleration was

that the enterprise incurred higher capital costs, but at the same time—because of the continued acceleration of technological innovation—had less time in which to amortise its investments with the profits gained by its innovative strategies. In the business literature, this proposed theory of economic change could be seen as a development of Vernon's rather primitive product-cycle theory of interfirm competition.[5]

Our theory was based on the observation of structural changes in the world market economy, notably in finance—the mobility of capital—and technology—the mobility of knowledge. It was also consistent with more recent theoretical explanations of the rising trend in the world market economy to a shift of manufacturing capacity from the early industrialized economies to the newly industrialized ones. Similarly, it buttressed theories offered for the 'hollowing-out' of American, European, and Japanese economies and the popularity of 'downsizing' (a euphemism for sacking workers in home-based plants or offices) as a corporate strategy for maintaining profitability and market share.[6]

The analysis was taken a stage further in *The Retreat of the State*. This book appeared at a time when there was increasing comment on the disappearing distinction between international relations or politics and domestic politics.[7] Historians had always been well aware of this, but teachers of international relations, going back to the international lawyers of the interwar years, had always fiercely maintained that the study of interstate relations was a distinct and separate discipline from the general field of politics. Hence the establishment at the London School of Economics as early as the 1930s of a Department of International Relations independent of the Department of Government. The declaration of academic independence was understandable enough, but the theoretical basis for it was, and always had been, weak.

*The Retreat of the State* posed much the most direct challenge to this basic proposition of IR theorists. In two theoretical chapters, it argued, first, that the concepts of power used in the IR literature were superficial and inadequate. Second, it argued that the concept of politics accepted by most political scientists was far too limited. Politics was not just what politicians, or governments, did. Politics entered into every kind of social relations, including the social relations of firms, both internally and in social relations with other firms and with governments. This notion harked back to a proposition developed in *Rival States, Rival Firms*, which was that two additional dimensions of diplomacy need to be added to research agendas. One was the diplomacy between firms. The other was the diplomacy—increasingly necessary and crucial—between the firm and foreign (or indeed, home) governments. We developed a triangle diagram[8] showing that each of the three dimensions of diplomacy interacted with the other two. Firms, therefore, had to be treated as political actors and the consequences of their actions analysed in the 'who-gets-what' framework of international political economy. Non-state actors, especially firms, were central to any explanation of world order, an order increasingly dominated by global finance. This accords with much recent literature in international business and business history, which has confirmed the view that the unit of analysis to be researched and analysed is not 'the multinational enterprise' or the sector of the world market economy, but rather the individual firm.

What *The Retreat of the State* was saying was not just that the powers and responsibilities of state governments were being eroded, but why this was so. It was due, I argued, to the structural forces in a predominantly market economy set free, not by blind chance, but by the conscious decisions of governments, more especially of the government of the United States. This was what Ronen Palan was getting at when he coined the term 'the second structuralists' and applied it to myself, to Stephen Gill (see Gill in this volume), and to some of the post-modernist and feminist theorists.[9]

The role of governments in assisting and promoting globalization is responsible for some current confusions and disagreements about globalization and the changing role and power of states. Some of those who deny that the state is in retreat see that states themselves have taken decisions that augment the power of markets over governments. They are right. But the fact that a person or an institution

decides to limit or constrain its own freedom of action does not alter the fact that, as a result, it loses power—in short, retreats. A woman who voluntarily accepts a marriage arrangement that limits her independence and a debtor who accepts a tough repayment agreement that constrains his current spending are everyday examples of self-inflicted retreat from autonomy. Like the state today, they have decided that survival as an individual may require adapting to new circumstances and new forces of change; and adapting may require a limitation of autonomy as the price of survival.

I shall return to this common-sense insight into the realities of power relationships later. It forms an essential part of an IPE framework for the understanding of globalization. Meanwhile, let us ask the next question. If international relations theory has so little to offer as explanation for the causes and consequences of globalization, what about liberal economic theory?

It is unfortunate that the contributions of liberal economists to understanding globalization have been so overrated by some political scientists engaged in international studies.[10] These writers have perceived the greater attention paid by government policy-makers and corporate strategists to the pronouncements of liberal economists. They have praised the rigour, the parsimony, the internally consistent logic of liberal economics and seen it as an example to be followed. They have observed the confidence with which liberal economists have forecast future trends and events—even though these forecasts have as often proved wrong as right. The 1970s fashion in America (and elsewhere) for the collection and analysis of quantitative data reflected this copycat mentality. If economists used quantitative data as the basis for their forecasts, perhaps writers on world politics could also predict wars, or international co-operation, through the use of comparable quantitative data sets. In the event, the results were either banal or inconclusive. Envious emulation of liberal economists has produced little of enduring value.

The reasons for this can be briefly stated, for they are to be found in the basic presumption of liberal economics that the subject is a science, comparable to the natural sciences in being governed by certain universally acknowledged laws that are unaffected by the beliefs or perceptions of the human observer. Such a claim, however, could only be sustained by making certain basic and fundamental premises about the functioning of an economic system. It is these premises that are the Achilles' heel of liberal economic thinking, for none of them conform to the realities of life in the real world of political economy.

One of the most fundamental false premises has been noted by George Soros, the famous financial buccaneer, drawing on the work of Karl Popper.[11] From his personal observation of financial markets, Soros argues that, far from the human observer and the object of study being unconnected, in practice a reflexive principle is always at work, so that the object of study—a financial market or a whole political economy—affects the perceptions of the observer, and conversely, the perceptions of the observer can move the market.

Perhaps the most important—and influential—of the premises of liberal economics has been that economic decisions are governed by reason, not whim or prejudice or emotions like pride, jealousy, or spite. A second key premise is that these rational choices are made according to relatively stable and observable preferences—preferences, for example, for maximum profit and minimum costs and risks. Borrowed or adapted by rational choice theorists in international studies, this premise has translated into the assumption that governments, too, make rational choices according to a predetermined set of preferences. The premise is supported by the (limited) logic of game theory. But it is flawed by the reality that governments' choices in practice seek both more power and more wealth, and have to satisfy the demands of both domestic politics and foreign policy. There is, therefore, no stable and observable set of preferences governing national policy-making.

From its earliest beginnings a hundred years ago, 'economic science' conceded that markets could be perfect but were more often imperfect.[12] More recently, the useful distinction has been made between managed markets and contested markets,

where some buyers or sellers challenge the way the managed market is being run. Ideology—the presumption that markets know best and that state intervention always has negative effects—has, however, produced an important blind spot for liberal economists. While they have shown much indignant concern over the interference of governments in markets—through protectionism, subsidies, preferential treatment of national champions, and so forth—they have turned a blind eye to the private management of markets by combinations of buyers or sellers. Their interest in cartels, for instance, has been minimal. Yet private protectionism of vested interests can have just as distorting effects as state protectionism. There is much discussion of 'market failure'—but the failures of markets to function according to the laws of economics are habitually attributed to interventions by governments, seldom to intervention by firms.

The other blind spot has been over the benign intervention of the state that has provided the security from violence and the political and legal framework necessary to the smooth functioning of any market. Liberal economists, in the United States especially, have taken this benign intervention for granted, as if it were an immutable fact of life. They ignore the fact that such a framework sustains a market only for as long as the limits of political jurisdiction and of the market more or less coincide. Once the market becomes global but the jurisdiction by and large does not, this disjunction raises the difficult question whether the market itself can provide the necessary framework of governance or whether some other political agent has to do it.

This question is the essential problematic for theories of globalization. But we have seen the failure of both IR theory and liberal economic theory to address it. IR theory has had a different problematic—the relations between states, not the relation of authority over markets. Liberal economics has based its theorizing on assumptions that (as we have seen) do not accord with the realities of the global financial structure governing the creation and management of credit for a market economy or with the transnational structures of production and trade that run parallel to the financial structure.

What about insights from other social sciences? For brevity, I will take just two examples. Both are contemporary historians, but both ignore or do not recognize the key role of credit and finance in the working of a market economy. David Landes has written an interesting comparative study of the economic performance over past centuries of states and civilizations, focusing on their ability to adopt or innovate new technologies.[13] Western Europe, for a variety of cultural and political reasons, led other cultures and civilizations. Its greater technological capabilities, military and economic, enabled Europeans to extend their political domination over other continents. The detail is often illuminating. But what is missing is the means by which innovators—whether in the public or private domains—found the necessary credit to develop and market their innovations. As every inventor knows only too well, it is not enough to invent a better mousetrap. The problem is to find the people with access to credit who will finance its production.

The other historian, Francis Fukuyama, focuses on the role of what he calls 'social capital' in smoothing the path to economic growth.[14] The trust necessary to any market economy—trust between buyers and sellers, creditors and debtors, managers and employees—cannot be provided by law or decree, nor by the unaided market. It is the product of social capital built over time. The book examines a range of cases taken from history, from China to Italy, and makes a distinction between low-trust societies—France, for instance—and high-trust societies—the Japanese *keiretsu* and its member enterprises. But, like Landes, Fukuyama pays little or no attention to the role of authority in either kind of society in managing financial markets and institutions.

This prevailing neglect is not new. If we go back to the classical writers on political economy, to Adam Smith in Scotland or the physiocrats in France, we look in vain for clear guidance on how much intervention is necessary, and in what form. David Ricardo came nearest, with the publication in 1809 of *The High Price of Bullion*. But this was more concerned with the international system of payments than with the regulation of banking. Having experienced the oversupply of paper money in the Napoleonic wars and its consequences for prices and the economy generally, Ricardo looked for means to limit the issue of paper money and thus to prevent an outflow of gold: 'He developed a rigorous theory of the quantity of money, applied it to the international mechanism, showed that inflation and depreciation caused an outflow of gold and proposed that the Bank of England should gradually reduce the amount of notes in circulation until the price of gold had been brought down to its previous level.'[15]

It was his influence on politicians that produced for Britain a system of statutory controls over the propensity of governments to create credit for their own purposes. The Bank Charter Act of 1844—for which there is no comparable statute in US law—kept the value of sterling in terms of gold stable for 70 years, until World War I. As I have argued before, the so-called 'gold standard' of the nineteenth century was really a gold-sterling standard maintaining stable money not only for Britain but for transactions in a world economy dominated by British trade and British investment carried on in sterling as the reserve currency. What Ricardo overlooked, though, was that banks as well as governments could create credit; and this power could also cause problems for the wider economy.

And banks did create credit. In the aftermath of the American Civil War overlending by a major British bank, Overend Gurney, meant it found itself unable to meet its obligations and either had to be rescued by the Bank of England or allowed to fail with possibly serious repercussions in the wider financial market. The dilemma was analysed, not by John Stuart Mill or any of the academic economists but by Walter Bagehot, long-time editor of *The Economist*. Significantly, Bagehot's seminal work on the City of London gets no mention in the economics literature. His comment on the causes of trouble at Overend Gurney were sharp and derisive. Not even a child, he said, would have been so foolish as to make the sort of loans it had made. Bad management by bankers was the weak point in the system in the 1860s, just as it was 130 years later.[16]

Both Landes and Fukuyama are quite right to highlight neglected factors in the competition between states for market shares. The generation and handling of innovative technology need to be included. And so does the contribution of social capital to national performance. Yet while useful, neither contribution is sufficient. The role of finance and the organization of credit are hardly mentioned by either writer.

## Conclusion

This chapter has highlighted the crucial weaknesses of two schools of thought—traditional international relations and liberal economics. Both lead in their own way to important misunderstandings about the nature of our world order, the subject of this book.

This analysis has attempted to fill in some of the missing ingredients. Without these missing ingredients we cannot begin to understand how we arrived at the global casino, nor can we grasp the dangers with which it presents us. Without understanding the role played by private and other non-state actors; the ways in which states have voluntarily ceded their powers to firms; the ways in which technology has been exploited to change the structures of the political economy—without these factors we cannot face squarely the dilemmas we must confront. We must properly understand where we are coming from if we wish to make better where we are going to.

## Notes

*Susan Strange died in October 1998, and this volume is dedicated to her memory and to her contribution to international political economy. In many respects, she invented the contemporary manifestation of the discipline, as a recent obituary acknowledged. The introductory section to this chapter is the last piece she wrote. She asked that the introduction be combined with a paper she had written for the Third Pan-European Conference on International Relations in Vienna, Austria (16–20 September 1998). The paper forms the body of the chapter and was published posthumously as a working paper of the Centre for the Study of Globalisation and Regionalisation, University of Warwick (No. 18, December 1998) As editors, we sincerely hope we have produced a chapter in keeping with her wishes and intentions.

1    Frank Knight, *Risk, Uncertainty, and Profit* (Boston: Houghton Mifflin, 1921).

2    Hugh C. Dyer and Leon Mangasarian, eds, *The Study of International Relations: The State of the Art* (New York: St Martins Press, 1989); Steve Smith, ed., *International Relations: British and American Perspectives* (Oxford: Basil Blackwell, 1985); Steve Smith, Ken Booth, and Marysia Zalewski, eds, *International Theory: Positivism and Beyond* (Cambridge: Cambridge University Press, 1996); T. Knutsen, *A History of International Relations Theory* (Manchester: Manchester University Press, 1992); C. Brown, *International Relations*

*Theory: New Normative Approaches* (Hemel Hempstead: Harvester, 1992); S. Guzzini, *Realism in International Relations and International Political Economy* (London: Routledge, 1998).

3    Fred Riggs, ed., special issue of *International Political Science Review* 19, 3 (July 1998) on inter-ethnic relations.

4    J. Mueller, *Retreat from Doomsday: The Obsolescence of Major War* (New York: Basic Books, 1989).

5    Raymond Vernon, *Sovereignty at Bay: The Multinational Spread of US Enterprise* (New York: Basic Books, 1971). Vernon's product cycle model was based on the assumption that firms were rent-seeking. If they could find a way to exploit even a temporary monopolistic advantage by being the first to exploit a product innovation, there was profit to be made from it.

6    Jeremy Rifkin, *The End of Work: The Decline of the Global Labour Force and the Dawn of the Post-market Era* (New York: G.P. Putnam's Sons, 1993); J.H. Dunning, *The Globalization of Business: The Challenge of the 1990s* (London: Routledge, 1993); De Anne Julius with Richard Brown, *Global Companies and Public Policy: The Growing Challenge of Foreign Direct Investment* (New York: Oxford University Press for American Express, 1993).

7    Robert Keohane and Helen Milner, *Internationalization and Domestic Politics* (Cambridge:

Cambridge University Press, 1996); James Rosenau, *Along the Domestic-Foreign Frontier: Exploring Governance in a Turbulent World* (Cambridge: Cambridge University Press, 1997).

8  John Stopford and Susan Strange, *Rival States, Rival Firms* (Cambridge: Cambridge University Press, 1991), 22.

9  Ronen Palan, 'The Second Structuralist Theories of International Relations: A Research Note', *International Studies Notes* 17, 3 (1992). The 'first structuralists' were the Waltzian realists who interpreted change in international relations in terms of the shifts in state power between states. The 'second structuralists' are international political economists who interpret change in world politics in terms of shifts in structural power over outcomes in world society and economy.

10  For instance, see Robert Keohane, *After Hegemony: Cooperation and Discord in the World Economy* (Princeton, NJ: Princeton University Press, 1984).

11  George Soros, *The Alchemy of Finance: Reading the Mind of the Market* (New York: Simon and Schuster, 1987).

12  A perfect market exists when no single buyer or seller is able to determine prices and when all buyers and sellers have equal access to full information. It becomes imperfect when these conditions do not apply.

13  David Landes, *The Wealth and Poverty of Nations: Why Some Are So Rich and Some So Poor* (New York: W.W. Norton, 1998).

14  Francis Fukuyama, *Trust: Social Values and the Creation of Prosperity* (New York: Penguin, 1995).

15  Eric Roll, *A History of Economic Thought* (New York: Prentice-Hall, 1939), 192.

16  David Laascelles's survey of opinion in the City in 1997 and 1998 came to that conclusion. Bad management was the most feared of the 'banana skins' on which the financial system might slip and fall. *EMU—A Fairy Tale* (London: Centre for the Study of Financial Innovation, 1997).

## Suggested Readings: Selected Works of Susan Strange

'International Economics and International Relations: A Case of Mutual Neglect', *International Affairs* 46, 2 (Apr. 1970): 304–15.

*Sterling and British Policy*. Oxford: Oxford University Press, 1971.

'The Dollar Crisis 1971', *International Affairs* 48, 2 (Apr. 1972): 191–215.

*International Monetary Relations*. Oxford: Oxford University Press, 1976.

'The Management of Surplus Capacity: Or How Does Theory Stand Up to Protectionism 1970s style?', *International Organization* 33, 2 (Summer 1979): 303–35.

'Cave! Hic Dragones: A Critique of Regime Analysis', *International Organization* 36, 2 (Spring 1982): 479–97.

*Paths to International Political Economy*. London: Allen and Unwin, 1984.

'Protectionism and World Politics', *International Organization* 39, 2 (Spring 1985): 233–59.

'Interpretations of a Decade', in L. Tsoukalis, ed., *The Political Economy of International Money: In Search of a New Order* (London: Sage, 1985), 1–44.

*Casino Capitalism*. Oxford: Basil Blackwell, 1986.

'The Persistent Myth of Lost Hegemony', *International Organization* 41, 4 (Autumn 1987): 551–74.

*States and Markets*. Oxford: Basil Blackwell, 1988.

'The Future of the American Empire', *Journal of International Affairs* 42, 1 (Fall 1988): 1–17.

'Finance, Information, and Power', *Review of International Studies* 16, 3 ( July 1990): 259–74.

'Big Business and the State', *Millennium: Journal of International Studies* 20, 2 (Summer 1991): 245–50.

*Rival States, Rival Firms: Competition for World Market Shares*, with John Stopford. Cambridge: Cambridge University Press, 1991.

'From Bretton Woods to the Casino Economy', in S. Corbridge, N. Thrift, and R. Martin, *Money, Power and Space* (Oxford: Basil Blackwell, 1994).

'Who Governs? Networks of Power in World Society', *Hitotsubashi Journal of Law and Politics* (Special Issue 1994): 5–17.

'Wake Up Krasner! The World has Changed', *Review of International Political Economy* 1, 2 (1994): 209–19.

'The Defective State', *Daedelus* 24, 2 (Spring 1995): 55–74.

*The Retreat of the State: The Diffusion of Power in the World Economy*. Cambridge: Cambridge University Press, 1996.

'"Who are EU?" Ambiguities in the Concept of Competitiveness', *Journal of Common Market Studies* 36, 1 (March 1998): 101–14.

*Mad Money*. Manchester: Manchester University Press, 1998.

## Web Sites

Bank for International Settlements: www.bis.org

The Group of Thirty, consultative group on international economic and monetary affairs: www.group30.org

BISA—International Political Economy Group: snipe.ukc.ac.uk/international/bisa.dir/ipeg.dir/ipeg.html

## Chapter 7

# Theory and Exclusion:
## Gender, Masculinity, and International Political Economy

### Sandra Whitworth

In women's studies, a good piece of conventional wisdom holds that it is simply not enough to 'add women and stir'. In political science, women are just now being added, and the field has hardly begun to stir.

—Nannerl Keohane[1]

Stop the whining and just get on with it.

—Susan Strange[2]

Once one views international relations through the lens of sex and biology, it never again looks the same. It is very difficult to watch Muslims and Serbs in Bosnia, Hutus and Tutsis in Rwanda, or militias from Liberia and Sierra Leone to Georgia and Afghanistan divide themselves up into what seem like indistinguishable male-bonded groups in order to systematically slaughter one another, and not think of the chimps at Gombe.

—Francis Fukuyama[3]

If masculine privilege is so all-pervasive and absolute, we must ask . . . why it is that men live substantially shorter lives than women, kill themselves at rates vastly higher than women, absorb close to 100 percent of the fatal casualties of society's productive labour, and direct the majority of their violence against 'their own' ranks. . . . They surely deserve more sustained, non-dogmatic attention than . . . every feminist theorist I have encountered grants them.

—Adam Jones[4]

Several years ago, when a previous version of this chapter was written for the first edition of the volume at hand, it was appropriate to note that Nannerl Keohane's statement was perhaps even more true of the discipline of international relations (IR) than it was political science. In the years since the 'new women's movement' emerged in the late 1960s, progress had been made by at least some feminist academics in incorporating analyses of women and gender relations into traditional areas of academic study, but the same could not be said of a feminist international relations theory. Indeed, of the little work that had been done on women and international relations to that point, one shared observation was that IR, of all the social science disciplines, had been one of the most resistant to incorporating feminist analyses of women and gender relations.[5]

My argument then focused on the extent to which, despite how much contemporary work within international political economy (IPE) converged with the kinds of questions feminists have raised, there was a disturbing silence on the part of IPE scholars when it came to questions of gender.[6] Like mainstream IR before it, IPE had rarely acknowledged, much less analysed, how female subordinations are created and sustained both nationally and internationally.[7] This absence is important because many IPE scholars have taken it as part of their project to explore the social and political complex as a whole rather than its separate parts.[8] This is not merely an empirical claim, but a political one as well. As Craig Murphy and Roger Tooze note, many authors within the 'new' IPE 'are more concerned with the involvement in the global political economy of people who are often ignored because they are considered less powerful.'[9] By this view, I argued, the continued invisibility of women and gender within IPE could no longer be sustained.

Today, the terrain is in some ways dramatically different, and in other ways it remains very much the same. Most feminist contributions to IR and IPE go far beyond the simple liberal notion of 'adding women in' to which Keohane referred, and it is certainly true that the field has finally begun to stir—though, as the quotations above indicate, not always in ways we may have anticipated. On the one hand, there has been a virtual explosion of literature within the realms of gender and IR and of gender and IPE in both journals and monographs, with institutional acknowledgement in the form of a new journal, *International Feminist Journal of Politics*, debuting in 1999 as well as the continued success of the 'feminist theory and gender studies' section at the International Studies Association, which draws some of the largest audiences throughout that professional association's annual meetings.

On the other hand, feminist interventions have elicited a range of responses from the rest of our field. Some have tried to interject attention to women or to gender, and while too often this remains a token and largely unintegrated effort, this is sometimes more of an effort than was previously visible. At the same time, however, others, such as Susan Strange in her call to feminists to 'stop whining' and Francis Fukuyama in his use of chimp behaviour to illustrate his agreement with '*the* feminist view'[10] that a world run by women would be less aggressive, competitive, and violent, have offered up baffling accounts of feminism that only serve to underline the extent to which this literature remains almost entirely unread and unheard by too many scholars within both IR and IPE.[11]

Others seem to take more seriously the feminist IR literature—insofar as they actually read it—but see in that literature a threat to traditional sites of power and so reproduce the backlash we have witnessed over the past decade against a whole host of social justice issues, including affirmative action, human rights for gays and lesbians, anti-racist activism, pay equity, and, of course, feminism. In each, the form of the argument is the same, with

'new' issues consistently depicted as redirecting attention or resources away from more traditional concerns or groups. In IR we have seen this most recently in Adam Jones's celebrated[12] lament that feminist attention to women within IR has detracted attention away from the usually more important concerns facing men.

This chapter will attempt, first, to situate the emergence of the feminist IR literature within the field of IR and will note the ways in which many of the questions raised by feminists have paralleled those raised by international political economists. It will then argue, following recent work by V. Spike Peterson, that the contemporary structural crisis of capitalism and, in conjunction with that crisis, the feminist and critical analyses made of it constitute in part a crisis of masculinity.[13] Seen in this light, Peterson argues, reactions of continued silence, as well as those seeking to reassert and reprivilege traditional understandings of naturalized forms of masculinism, are responses to the 'deeply disturbing' attempts to 'disrupt' what is understood to be natural. As Peterson writes:

> Gender is conventionally invisible because the *longue durée* of masculinism obscures the power required to institutionalise, internalise and reproduce gender hierarchy and its associated oppressions. In this sense, gender is hard to see because it is so taken for granted. But gender also resists visibility and critique due to its pervasiveness and our personal investments: it is not only 'out there' structuring activities and institutions, and 'in our heads' structuring discourse and ideologies; it is also 'in here'—in our hearts and bodies— structuring our intimate desires, our sexuality, our self-esteem and our dreams. As a consequence, our investments in gendered selves fuel heroic and self-sacrificing as well as despotic and self-serving actions.[14]

## International Relations and Feminism

One of the reasons that feminist issues have been raised only quite recently within the study of international relations has to do with the very different concerns of IR and feminism. International relations is a subfield of political science, and is much younger than its parent discipline. A product of the twentieth century, mainstream IR was born in the interwar period and located primarily in the United States.[15] It was created in large part to serve the needs of government, specifically the American government, in training diplomatic and government personnel and answering the 'What should we do?' questions about important diplomatic and strategic issues of the time. More than most other social science disciplines, mainstream IR has had an intimate relationship with government, both through the funding of IR research institutes and in the regular exchange of academic and government personnel. As Stanley Hoffmann notes, IR academics and researchers operate 'not merely in the corridors but also in the kitchens of power'.[16]

Informed by this goal of serving government, scholars of mainstream international relations have taken as their central concerns the causes of war and the conditions of peace, order, and security.[17] Such inquiry appears to be antithetical to the study of women. The 'high politics' of international security policy is, as J. Ann Tickner writes, 'a man's world, a world of power and conflict in which warfare is a privileged activity' and from which women traditionally have been excluded.[18]

Much of international relations theorizing, moreover, posits a separation between inside and outside, community and anarchy. It is argued that while one may appropriately raise questions of ethics and politics when examining relations within civil society, such questions are irrelevant outside, in the society of nations, where it is appropriate to ask only how rational states may enhance their power within an anarchic system.[19] Apparently absent from the particular substantive concerns of IR, in fact or by definition, the suggestion that women or gender relations should be examined in international relations is often met with, at best, incredulity or, at worst, hostility.

In contrast to the field of international relations, contemporary feminism has its roots in a social movement: the women's liberation movement. It represents a protest against prevailing gender-based power structures and against accepted societal norms and values concerning women and men. Feminists have expressed this protest in a variety of ways, with some demanding that women be allowed to join the spheres in which only men, historically, have been permitted and others demanding more dramatic and fundamental social change. Whatever its different prescriptions, however, feminism is a politics of protest directed at transforming the historically unequal power relationships between women and men.[20] As a politics of protest, feminism clearly follows a different path from that of IR. It is concerned with those 'inside' questions often defined as irrelevant to the study of international relations. That IR and feminism may be antithetical, then, does not follow merely from their apparently different substantive concerns, but more importantly from their normative and political predispositions: mainstream IR has been aimed primarily at maintaining the (international) status quo while feminism aims at precisely the opposite. It is little wonder that studies of women and international relations do not proliferate.

## Feminism and IPE: Affinities?

From the preceding sketch, it should be clear that many of the issues raised by feminists about IR have previously or are currently being raised by specialists in IPE. While the political motivations often are quite different, political economists share a dissatisfaction with mainstream IR's emphasis on, among other things, questions of 'high politics', its lack of theorizing about the relationship between domestic and international politics, the inappropriate and usually untenable separation of 'politics' and 'economics', and the failure to assess co-operation and interdependence to the same degree that it has anarchy.[21]

International political economists have approached their critique of IR in a variety of ways. Some have sought to enlarge the number of relevant actors through adding firms, international organizations, and sometimes even social movements to the usual consideration of state behaviour and consequences of state action. Others have focused instead on the addition of new issues, arguing that trade and monetary concerns are as important in their own right as military and strategic ones. Still others examine new forms of behaviour, whether examples of co-operation or the intersubjectively shared norms associated with regimes and rule-governed activities within international relations.[22]

More recently, some IPE work has moved well beyond simply 'adding in' actors and issues to a far more profound ontological and epistemological challenge to the discipline.[23] As Stephen Gill observes, 'we may be in the throes of an ontological change or shift: a redefinition of understandings and experiences that form basic components of lived reality. This includes mental frameworks—for example, the way that we think about social institutions and forms of political authority.'[24] Such an account suggests that critical and Gramscian IPE is beginning to address how, as Mark Laffey writes, 'social subjects understand themselves and their relations to social structures, structures which are in turn constituted in and by social practices informed by intersubjective understandings.'[25] Not only does such a move create more 'spaces' for a discussion of women or gender within IR and IPE, but feminist approaches in all of their guises are centrally involved in a project that reveals both the complexities and deep-seatedness of some of our most fundamental and naturalized 'mental frameworks'.[26]

## Feminists Examine IR

Feminist analysts share with IPE scholars many of their epistemological strategies.[27] Like liberal political economists, for example, numerous feminists have sought to introduce women as a new actor or issue within IR and IPE. This work seeks to document the underrepresentation of women in traditional areas of international relations activities, or conversely, to show how women do participate in international relations. For example, much of the early work on women and development was written from this perspective and aimed at demonstrating how women were involved in the development process and the manner in which this involvement

had been ignored previously by development researchers and practitioners. Ester Boserup's pioneering book, *Woman's Role in Economic Development*,[28] documented women's economic contributions in the Third World, and from Boserup's own and later work we now know that women constitute 60 to 80 per cent of the agricultural workforce in Africa and Asia and more than 40 per cent in Latin America.[29] Development planners ignored these facts because they assumed that women in the developing world were involved primarily in household chores and tasks. As such, the policies that they produced tended to bypass women workers, fundamentally misunderstanding the economic processes they were supposedly analysing and thereby exacerbating women's inequality rather than alleviating it.[30] By showing women's true role in developing societies, Boserup and her colleagues created the basis for Women in Development (WID) programs and departments in almost all major international development agencies. The WID agenda has been to take women into account in the formulation and implementation of development policies around the world.

While the collection of information about women's roles in development and other issue-areas of relevance to IPE is useful and important, a number of criticisms of this approach have emerged. These parallel the criticisms made of liberal political economy more generally and suggest that the collection of empirical information about women is made at the expense of any assessment of the structural features of relations of inequality between women and men.[31] Implicit in a liberal analysis, the critics argue, is the assumption that the inclusion of women into areas previously denied them will eliminate gender inequalities. By contrast, feminists who attempt to introduce analyses of class or patriarchy argue that inequalities are a defining characteristic of the very structures in which women might participate, and as such their participation alone will not change this fundamental fact.

Theorists who have focused on patriarchy, described variously as standpoint theorists or radical feminists, suggest that the relations of inequality observed within both the study and practice of international relations reflect the simple fact that both of these represent the viewpoint of men over that of women.[32] These feminists argue that women have a unique perspective, different from that of men, and that this perspective should be given a voice within many of the decisions associated with international relations. By this view, women tend to be more nurturing and pacifistic than men and thus should be brought into international relations not on equity grounds but to allow women's more peaceful views some influence. Accordingly, a feminist reformulation of notions such as power, security, and national interest—in which, from a 'feminine' perspective, 'power' is defined as empowerment and 'security' as including development and ecological concerns—is an important first step towards a better understanding of women and international relations.

Other authors focused instead on the dynamic of class and gender oppression. They (and others) argue that analyses presuming a single 'feminine' perspective essentialize and universalize the category of 'woman' (and 'man') at the expense of other forms of domination.[33] Analyses like those of Maria Mies or Gita Sen and Caren Grown have assessed the impact of the changing international division of labour on women and the ways in which women's subordination is sustained under different historical modes of production, with forms of domination associated with class relations taking advantage of, and building on, pre-existing relations of domination between women and men.[34] For example, with the introduction of private property during the colonial period, women tended to suffer more than men because they lost completely their access to traditional land-use rights.[35] Likewise, as production shifts to the export sector during the forms of structural adjustment we are witnessing today, it is again women who are moving into these poorly paid positions with little or no opportunities to improve wages or benefits and the prospect of only short-term, limited employment.[36] The point here, of course, is that class and gender oppression work together rather than separately.

These demonstrations of the way sex and class oppression are linked improve yet again on the previous analyses outlined above, but they, too, have been subject to criticism. Primarily, the concern is that analyses of gender must examine as well how racist ideologies and practices figure into these issues. Many feminists argue also that gender oppression is sustained as much by the ideas surrounding certain practices, the self-understandings reproduced through institutional as well as individual action, as by those practices themselves. Informed by these kinds of concerns, feminists from a variety of perspectives have sought to explore how gender—understood as the prevailing assumptions concerning women and men, their roles in family and society, even what it means to be a man or woman, masculine or feminine—affects and is affected by the practices of international relations. As Chandra Talpade Mohanty writes:

> The idea I am interested in invoking here is not 'the work that women do' or even the occupations that we/they happen to be concentrated in, but rather the ideological construction of jobs and tasks in terms of notions of appropriate femininity, domesticity, (hetero)sexuality, and racial and cultural stereotypes.[37]

Cynthia Enloe provides one of the most sustained accounts of the ways in which gender figures within IPE. She examines a whole series of issues, including tourism, foreign domestic servants, and export processing zones, and the manner in which particular 'packages of expectations' associated with masculine and feminine behaviour are used to sustain and legitimize certain practices within IR. She notes, for example, the manner in which developing countries are increasingly relying on tourism as a source of foreign exchange, and the profoundly gendered nature of the tourism industry. As Enloe writes: 'On the oceans and in the skies: the international business travellers are men, the service workers are women.'[38] This includes not only flight attendants and chambermaids, but the burgeoning market for prostitutes within the sex tourism industry.

Enloe's project is not simply to recount the places in which women find themselves, however, but rather to provide some insight into 'how' this has happened. How particular material conditions join together with existing assumptions and ideas about women and men is made clear in the following passage:

> To succeed, sex tourism requires Third World women to be economically desperate enough to enter prostitution; having done so it is made difficult to leave. The other side of the equation requires men from affluent societies to imagine certain women, usually women of colour, to be more available and submissive than the women in their own countries. Finally, the industry depends on an alliance between local governments in search of foreign currency and local and foreign businessmen willing to invest in sexualized travel.[39]

Understood in this way, not only are the activities of women placed within the realm of international relations, but they are understood in specific ways because of the particular material conditions and ideas associated with their activities: in this case, women's economic desperation is joined with the eroticization of racist stereotypes. The entire scenario works only if all of these factors are considered together and not separately.

Developing countries' search for foreign exchange also leads Enloe to examine multinational corporations and export processing zones (EPZs). She outlines in detail the various practices used, first, to recruit young women into the assembly lines of EPZs, and then the ways in which their continued docility is ensured until that time that they are pushed out of such employment.[40] This is achieved not only through assumptions around women's 'cheaper' labour (both real and imagined), through which MNCs are enticed in the first place, but more importantly by sustaining a vision of the female worker as a member of a large family, a family ruled by fathers and brothers/supervisors and managers. These women, moreover, because of prevailing social attitudes about the role of young women, are employable for only a few short years,

after which time they may return to their family homes in rural areas or turn to prostitution in the larger urban centres in which they find themselves.

Finally, Enloe draws a series of links between the adoption of IMF austerity measures and the capacity of women to respond to those measures. She argues that a government's ability to maintain its legitimacy depends at least in part on the capacity of families to tolerate those measures, specifically on the capacity of women to stretch their budgets, to continue to feed, clothe, and care for their families. This may include severe domestic financial management as well as travelling abroad as foreign domestic servants, often with the requirement that a significant proportion of their salaries be repatriated back to the home country. As Enloe argues, IMF austerity measures depend on these women and the choices they are forced to make:

> Thus the politics of international debt is not simply something that has an impact on women in indebted countries. The politics of international debt won't work in their current form unless mothers and wives are willing to behave in ways that enable nervous regimes to adopt cost-cutting measures without forfeiting their political legitimacy.[41]

A dynamic is set up around ideas about what women will and will not do, the actual material conditions of their lives, and the policies produced by international organizations and foreign governments. This dynamic both sustains and is dependent on assumptions about what are considered the appropriate roles and qualities of women, and women of particular races, in specific times and places.

When women do travel abroad to work as foreign domestic servants, they often face unregulated and unsupervised workplace environments with less than subsistence wages, in countries where labour and citizenship rights are differentially applied, and in some instances they are subject to sexual and physical assault. Yet, assumptions about work, familial relations, and race are again used to justify lower pay and different rights from those of other workers. The terms of work are shaped in part by the fact that foreign domestic servants are employed in the 'home' and perform work (child-rearing, house cleaning, cooking, and so on) that is not normally recognized as such. Ideologies about 'family' join with assumptions around race, and as Abigail Bakan and Daiva Stasiulus note, 'racialized images of womanhood play an important role in justifying to employers why non-white women of colour are "naturally" suited for childcare and housework.'[42]

The point here, of course, is that pressures to work as a foreign domestic servant derive in part from the pressures of the global capitalist system, the structural adjustment policies imposed by international financial institutions, and the historical legacy of imperialism and colonialism in many developing countries. Those pressures not only depend on women acting in a certain way, as Enloe describes, but, once having decided to work as a foreign domestic servant, a woman is involved in a complex of issues that includes assumptions about femininity, citizenship, and the transformation of a 'family home' into a workplace, and all of these are informed by gendered and racialized attitudes.[43] Or, as Jan Jindy Pettman more bluntly states: 'Domestic service has long been the site for "close encounters" between colonising and coloniser women.'[44]

International organizations more generally are also involved in promoting and sustaining assumptions around gender relations. Marilyn Waring has documented in considerable detail the ways in which women and women's work are made almost completely invisible within the United Nations System of National Accounts (UNSNA). This invisibility is important, she argues, because national governments and international agencies decide what is important, both politically and economically, based in part on the various measures found within the UNSNA; for example, when aid donors use the UNSNA to decide which countries are the most 'needy' and which projects are the most important; when governments determine economic policy priorities based on UNSNA figures; and when multinational corporations decide where, whether, and

how to invest internationally based on what is recorded in the UNSNA.[45] More importantly, Waring notes, the *meanings* associated with women's work are fundamentally affected: women, by virtue of their absence in standard measures of 'work', are understood not to be involved in productive activities, despite the fact that they may be collecting food and fuel and caring for children and home from well before dawn to well after dusk. This has an impact on those women's lives, for the absence of women and women's work from these figures, and from the meaning of work at all, makes it very convenient to ignore their interests, concerns, and demands and, as Enloe has noted, to 'cheapen' the various forms of work that women are involved in.

Chandra Talpade Mohanty develops the notion of the meanings attached to women's work in specific locales even further. In her analysis of the lacemakers of Narsapur and electronics workers in Silicon Valley, she notes how gender and race and caste-based ideologies inform understandings of work, workers, and leisure-time activities. Seclusion and purdah, she notes, are a sign of higher status, and lacemaking in Narsapur came to be associated with higher-caste women but was linked also to the assumption that these women were just sitting in the house. As Mohanty writes, 'The caste-based ideology of seclusion and purdah was essential to the extraction of surplus value.'[46] But she goes further:

> Ideologies of seclusion and the domestication of women are clearly sexual, drawing as they do on masculine and feminine notions of protectionism and property. They are also heterosexual ideologies, based on the normative definition of women as wives, sisters, and mothers—always in relation to conjugal marriage and the 'family.'[47]

This same dynamic is at work, she argues, in Silicon Valley where the work done by Third World women is described as 'easy as a recipe', tedious, and a 'supplementary activity for women whose main tasks were mothering and housework'.[48] 'There is a clear connection between low wages and the definition of the job as supplementary', Mohanty writes, 'and the fact that the lifestyles of people of color are defined as different and cheaper.'[49]

In addition to analysing the assumptions about women and work, some feminist analyses explore also the ways in which particular assumptions about men are embedded within the practices associated with work. This is well illustrated by the efforts of international organizations such as the ILO to promote protective legislation for women during pregnancy.[50] Such legislation is usually aimed at prohibiting heavy lifting during pregnancy or removing women from workplaces in which they might be exposed to substances hazardous to their pregnancy, such as lead or benzene. Such protection is, of course, laudable in many respects. As Zillah Eisenstein notes, pregnancy is engendered; women do, or may, bear children. This fact already structures their choices within the labour force, and protective legislation that recognizes pregnancy may protect some women from further discrimination based on it.[51] But at the same time, a number of tensions emerge, one of which is that protective legislation that removes women from reproductive health hazards leaves men subject to those same hazards.

As early as 1860, the reproductive effects on men exposed to lead were documented with indications that their wives had a very high incidence of spontaneous abortion. More recently, lead and other substances have been linked to low sperm counts, childhood cancers, heart defects, genetic damage to sperm, and chromosonal aberrations.[52] With the assumption that only women play an important enough role in reproduction to require protection, it becomes clear that men's role in reproduction does not entitle them to any sort of special consideration—they become, in effect, invisible. In short, women are recognized not as workers, but only insofar as they are childbearers, and men are ignored insofar as they *are* involved in reproduction. Men are in both a privileged and invisible position through this sort of protective legislation: privileged because it is normally men with whom women are compared, and invisible because they do not exist outside of this category, that of the 'normal' worker.

## Conclusions

The above examples illustrate briefly the ways in which quite traditional IPE issues, such as debt management, export processing zones, divisions of labour, and protective labour legislation are informed by assumptions around gender. More specifically, what they illustrate is how 'ideas about the "naturalness" of forms of gender inequality are integral to understanding how the international economy functions.'[53] It is this naturalness that V. Spike Peterson argues is being challenged, both by feminist analyses and by the very structural transformations of the global political economy that many of those feminists seek to analyse. Thus, not only are IR and IPE experiencing a renewed 'theoretical effervescence',[54] as was discussed above, but dramatic changes within the so-called 'real world' have produced a crisis in both our thinking and practices around international relations. The end of the Cold War, economic realignments, and many of the other issues raised by the authors in this volume suggest that, at the very least, the ways in which gender relations are maintained and constructed will be made clear, for it is in periods of crisis that prevailing notions become threatened. As Peterson writes:

> gender is hard to see and critique because it orders 'everything' and disrupting that order feels threatening—not only at the 'level' of institutions and global relations but also in relation to the most intimate and deeply etched beliefs/experiences of personal (but relentlessly gendered) identity. Yet, however much we are uncomfortable with challenges to gender ordering, we are in the midst of them. Failure to acknowledge and address these challenges both impairs our understanding of the world(s) we live in and sustains relations of domination.[55]

## Notes

1  Nannerl O. Keohane, 'Speaking from Silence: Women and the Science of Politics', in E. Langland and W. Cove, eds, *A Feminist Perspective in the Academy* (Chicago: University of Chicago Press, 1981), 87.

2  Susan Strange, Presidential Address to the International Studies Association, 1995. Though these comments were deleted from the published version of her address, Strange's remarks are reported in Craig Murphy, 'Seeing Women, Recognizing Gender, Recasting International Relations', *International Organization* 50, 3 (Summer 1996): 532.

3  Francis Fukuyama, 'Women and the Evolution of World Politics', *Foreign Affairs* (Sept.-Oct. 1998): 33.

4  Adam Jones, 'Does "Gender" Make the World Go Round? Feminist Critiques of International Relations', *Review of International Studies* 22, 4 (Oct. 1996): 423–4.

5  Fred Halliday, 'Hidden from International Relations: Women and the International Arena', *Millennium* 17, 3 (Winter 1988): 419. See also other essays in this special edition of *Millennium*.

6  This argument is made about critical international relations theory in my 'Gender in the Inter-Paradigm Debate', *Millennium* 18, 2 (Summer 1989): 265–72.

7  Paraphrased from Nancy Fraser, 'What's Critical About Critical Theory? The Case of Habermas and Gender', in S. Benhabib and D. Cornell, eds, *Feminism and Critique* (Minneapolis: University of Minnesota Press, 1987), 31.

8  Robert W. Cox, 'Social Forces, States and World Order: Beyond International Relations Theory', in R.O. Keohane, ed., *Neorealism and Its Critics* (New York: Columbia University Press, 1986), 208.

9  Craig N. Murphy and Roger Tooze, 'Introduction', in Murphy and Tooze, eds, *The New International Political Economy* (Boulder, Colo.: Lynne Rienner, 1991), 6.

10  Fukuyama, 'Women and the Evolution of World Politics', 27; emphasis added.

11  As Murphy pointed out, much of the work that Strange described as 'whining' was in fact doing the very empirical research that Strange seemed to be calling for. See also J. Ann Tickner, 'You Just Don't Understand: Troubled Engagements Between Feminists and IR Theorists', *International Studies Quarterly* 41, 4 (Dec. 1997): 611–32, and the dialogue that followed with interventions by Robert O. Keohane, 'Beyond Dichotomy: Conversations Between International Relations and Feminist Theory', Marianne H. Marchand, 'Different Communities/Different Realities/Different Encounters: A Reply to J. Ann Tickner', and J. Ann Tickner, 'Continuing the Conversation . . .', *International Studies Quarterly* 42, 1 (Mar. 1998): 193–210.

12  Jones's essay won the British International Studies Association graduate student essay prize for 1996. It is worth noting that Jones's general point is a good one; that is, that analyses concerned with gender need to address prevailing assumptions of both men and women and the effects that those assumptions have. It is a point made by numerous feminist scholars. As Jan Jindy Pettman writes, IR ensures that 'most men and all women are erased from view.' Jan Jindy Pettman, *Worlding Women: A Feminist International Politics* (New York: Routledge, 1996), viii; see also selections from my own *Feminism and International Relations* (Basingstoke: Macmillan, 1994), esp. ch. 5.

13  V. Spike Peterson, 'Whose Crisis? Early and Postmodern Masculinism', in Stephen Gill and James H. Mittleman, eds, *Innovation and Transformation in International Studies* (Cambridge: Cambridge University Press, 1997), 185–201.

14  Ibid., 199.

15  See Stanley Hoffmann, 'An American Social Science: International Relations', *Daedalus* 106, 3 (1977): 41–60.

16  Ibid., 49, 58.

17  K.J. Holsti, *The Dividing Discipline: Hegemony and Diversity in International Theory* (Boston: Allen and Unwin, 1985), ch. 1.

18   J. Ann Tickner, 'Hans Morgenthau's Principles of Political Realism: A Feminist Reformulation', *Millennium* 17, 3 (Winter 1988): 429.

19   R.B.J. Walker, 'Sovereignty, Security and the Challenge of World Politics', *Alternatives* 15, 1 (1990): 3–28.

20   Chris Weedon, *Feminist Practice and Poststructuralist Theory* (Oxford: Basil Blackwell, 1987), 1; see also Rosalind Delmar, 'What is Feminism?', in Juliet Mitchell and Ann Oakley, eds, *What Is Feminism?* (New York: Pantheon Books, 1986), 8. Alison M. Jaggar, *Feminist Politics and Human Nature* (Sussex: Harvester Press, 1983), provides an excellent account of some of the different approaches to feminism.

21   For general explorations of this theme, see George T. Crane and Abla Amawi, *The Theoretical Evolution of International Political Economy* (New York: Oxford University Press, 1991), esp. 3–33; Stephen Gill and David Law, *The Global Political Economy: Perspectives, Problems and Policies* (Baltimore: Johns Hopkins University Press, 1988), 3–24.

22   Ibid.

23   See especially Murphy and Tooze, eds, *The New International Political Economy*; Cox, 'Social Forces, States and World Order'.

24   Stephen Gill, 'Transformation and Innovation in the Study of World Order', in Gill and Mittleman, eds, *Innovation and Transformation in International Studies*, 7.

25   Mark Laffey, 'Ideology and the Limits of Gramscian Theory in International Relations', paper presented to the annual meeting of the International Studies Association, 1–4 Apr. 1998, 2 and *passim*.

26   See also Anne Sisson Runyan and V. Spike Peterson, 'The Radical Future of Realism: Feminist Subversions of IR Theory', *Alternatives* 16 (1991).

27   For recent reviews of feminist scholarship within international relations, see Jacqui True, 'Feminism', in Scott Burchill and Andrew Linklater, *Theories of International Relations* (New York: St Martin's Press, 1996), 210–51; Jill Steans, *Gender and International Relations: An Introduction* (New Brunswick, NJ: Rutgers University Press, 1998).

28   Ester Boserup, *Women's Role in Economic Development* (London: George Allen and Unwin, 1970).

29   Asoka Bandarage, 'Women in Development: Liberalism, Marxism and Marxist-Feminism', *Development and Change* 15 (1984): 497.

30   Ibid. See also Barbara Rogers, *The Domestication of Women: Discrimination in Developing Countries* (New York: St Martin's Press, 1979).

31   In terms of women and development, this critique is made by Lourdes Beneria and Gita Sen, 'Accumulation, Reproduction, and Women's Role in Economic Development: Boserup Revisited', *Signs* 7, 2 (1981): 279–98.

32   See, for example, Tickner, 'Hans Morgenthau's Principles of Political Realism'.

33   Lynne Segal, *Is the Future Female?* (London: Virago Press, 1987).

34   Maria Mies, *Patriarchy and Accumulation on a World Scale: Women in the International Division of Labour* (London: Zed Books, 1986); Gita Sen and Carea Grown, *Development, Crises and Alternative Visions: Third World Women's Perspectives* (New York: Monthly Review Press, 1986). This section draws on Abigail Bakan, 'Whither Woman's Place? A Reconsideration of Units of Analysis in International Political Economy', paper presented at the annual meetings of the Canadian Political Science Association, Victoria, BC, May 1990.

35   Sen and Grown, *Development, Crises and Alternative Visions*, 30–1.

36   Ibid., 37.

37   Chandra Talpade Mohanty, 'Women Workers and Capitalist Scripts: Ideologies of Domination, Common Interests, and the Politics of Solidarity', in M. Jacqui Alexander and Mohanty, eds, *Feminist Genealogies, Colonial Legacies, Democratic Futures* (New York: Routledge, 1997), 6.

38   Cynthia Enloe, *Bananas, Beaches and Bases: Making Feminist Sense of International Politics* (London: Pandora, 1989), 33.

39   Ibid., 36–7.

40   Ibid., ch. 7.

41   Ibid., 185.

42   Abigail B. Bakan and Daiva Stasiulis, 'Foreign Domestic Worker Policy in Canada and the Social Boundaries of Modern Citizenship', in Bakan and

Stasiulis, eds, *Not One of the Family: Foreign Domestic Workers in Canada* (Toronto:.University of Toronto Press, 1997), 12 and *passim*.

43  Ibid., 40–3 and *passim*.

44  Pettman, *Worlding Women*, 189.

45  Marilyn Waring, *If Women Counted: A New Feminist Economics* (San Francisco: Harper, 1988), 2; Marilyn Waring, *Three Masquerades: Essays on Equality, Work and Human Rights* (Toronto: University of Toronto Press, 1997), ch. 2.

46  Mohanty, 'Women Workers and Capitalist Scripts', 13.

47  Ibid.

48  Ibid., 15–16.

49  Ibid., 17. See also Eileen Boris and Elisabeth Prügl, *Homeworkers in Global Perspective* (New York: Routledge, 1996).

50  This is drawn from my *Feminism and International Relations*, ch. 5.

51  Zillah Eisenstein, *The Female Body and the Law* (Berkeley: University of California Press, 1988), 204–6.

52  Michael J. Wright, 'Reproductive Hazards and "Protective" Discrimination', *Feminist Studies* 5, 2 (Summer 1979): 303. See also Carolyn Bell, 'Implementing Safety and Health Regulations for Women in the Workplace', ibid., 296; Sandra Blakeslee, 'Fathers linked to child defects', *Globe and Mail*, 1 Jan. 1991, A1.

53  Jill Krause, 'The International Dimension of Gender Inequality and Feminist Politics: A "New Direction" for International Political Economy?', in John Macmillan and Andrew Linklater, eds, *Boundaries in Question: New Directions in International Relations* (London: Pinter, 1995), 130.

54  Yosef Lapid, 'The Third Debate: On the Prospects of International Theory in a Post-Positivist Era', *International Studies Quarterly* 33 (1989): 238.

55  Peterson, 'Whose Crisis?', 199.

## Suggested Readings

Alexander, M. Jacqui, and Chandra Talpade Mohanty. *Feminist Genealogies, Colonial Legacies, Democratic Futures*. New York: Routledge, 1997.

Kofman, Eleonore, and Gillian Youngs. *Globalization: Theory and Practice*. London: Pinter, 1996.

Peterson, V. Spike, and Anne Sisson Runyan. *Global Gender Issues, 2nd edn*. Boulder, Colo.: Westview Press, 1999.

Pettman, Jan Jindy. *Worlding Women: A Feminist International Politics*. London: Routledge, 1996.

Steans, Jill. *Gender and International Relations*. New Brunswick, NJ: Rutgers University Press, 1998.

Waring, Marilyn. *Three Masquerades: Essays on Equality, Work and Human Rights*. Toronto: University of Toronto Press, 1997.

Whitworth, Sandra. *Feminism and International Relations*. Basingstoke: Macmillan, 1994.

## Web Sites

International Labour Organization Site for Women and Gender Issues:
http://www.ilo.org/public/english/140femme/index.htm

Gender, Science and Technology:
www.ifias.ca/GSD/GSDinfo.html

Women in Development Network:
http/www.focusintl.com/widnet.htm

# Part II

## Global

## Issues

# Introduction

# Global Issues in Historical Perspective

## Geoffrey R.D. Underhill

World War II was one of the most important punctuation marks in human history in terms of both economic and security matters, to say nothing of its effects on human life. While the war itself was experienced in different ways in various parts of the globe, it was the first genuinely global conflict. In dramatic and asymmetrical ways it altered the balance of power and the distribution of wealth among territories of the globe, undermining the dominance of Europe. The United States and Canada, along with Australia and New Zealand, were almost alone among developed nations to emerge unscathed by the destruction, but the war had served its purpose for them as history's most successful industrial development policy.

While one would not wish to underestimate the continuities between the interwar and postwar worlds, to a considerable extent there was an opportunity to begin afresh, combined with a strong sense that this time things *had* to be done better. The interwar period had been a disaster in terms of international economic management, and there was a determination not to repeat the perceived mistakes. If the war was not a 'full stop' as punctuation marks go, it came close.

This, of course, makes the postwar period a fascinating laboratory in international political economy. Through careful historical analysis it is possible to chart the emergence and transformation of an order, to identify causal factors, and to determine the distribution of costs and benefits, all from a relatively clear starting point.

Although today one is inclined to think in terms of a *global* order, until the collapse of the Soviet bloc in 1989 there were in fact *two* orders

organized into separate security blocs. The politics of security in the Cold War evolved around the protection of and competition between these two distinct forms of political economy. We are concerned here with the so-called 'Western' order, as opposed to the centrally planned economies of the Soviet bloc. This Western order was dominated by the advanced market economies. In reality it was not much of a 'bloc'; there was a wide variety of national patterns of development, economic policies, and economic structures among the states in the system, including the developing world. National economic strategies ranged from the relatively *laissez-faire* approach of the Americans to the more interventionist approach of Japan and several Western European states.

There remains no doubt, however, that the greatest beneficiary of the events of the war was the United States. Its economy emerged as the most competitive and advanced and as the principal source of capital for economic development elsewhere. Seldom, in historical terms, has a country been as dominant, at least economically, as the United States in 1945. The USSR emerged from the war as a military colossus, but it was an economic cripple devastated by invasion and occupation, having paid the heaviest cost of all the wartime allies.[1]

Therefore, any historical account of the postwar international political economy must explain the role of America in fashioning and transforming the global economic order (see chapter by Moon in this volume). None the less, several myths have established themselves in the literature on postwar international economic relations: myths about the character of the order itself and about ways of explaining its emergence. These myths are encapsulated in hegemonic stability theory (HST): that the United States used its dominant position to the benign purpose of leading other countries towards the benefits of a liberal world order. As American decline set in from the 1970s, this liberal order has become frayed and more difficult to maintain.[2] If it is fairly evident that the US played a central role in planning and implementing the postwar world, what precisely was that role and how do we understand it?

I will argue here that liberalization cannot be explained in the state-centric terms of the realist school and HST. To explain the long gestation of our current liberal world economy, one must turn to the underlying socio-economic dimensions of the political economy and the deep sociopolitical dynamics of structural change in global markets.[3] The theory turns out to be a refuge for apologists who share a clear view that US power is by definition benign and who therefore seek to square the undoubted liberal idealism of much US policy throughout the postwar period with the considerable vagaries of the actual content of policy since the 1970s in particular.[4]

This argument can be developed by exposing three important and interrelated myths. The first is that the US was a *consistent* sponsor of liberalization and that it got its way through its hegemonic position in the postwar order. In reality, the era of liberalization did not correspond to the putative period of hegemony, and the US was as inconsistent as the rest in promoting it. Progress towards liberalization has in fact accelerated during the period of relative American decline. The second myth is that the role of the United States in the politics of the world economy is essentially reducible to the role of the US 'state-as-actor'. The role of social coalitions or private corporate actors in domestic and international policy processes, across the global political economy, must also be taken into account; decisions and compromises made by private economic agents *interacting* with political authorities and agencies have driven changes in market structure. Finally, there is the myth that the US hegemon necessarily acted in an enlightened fashion, leading

often recalcitrant horses to the waters of liberalization and gently persuading them of the benefits for all concerned of a long drink. This in turn implies that the decline of the United States is largely responsible for many of the difficulties encountered in the last two decades, leading the Americans to behave in a more self-serving manner. However, US leadership on liberalization, when it occurred, was quite naturally self-interested, as were the very deviations from liberal multilateralism that the US has sponsored in a fairly regular fashion since imposing unilateral restrictions on agricultural trade and textile imports in the mid-1950s.

To summarize, the American state was often ambivalent about liberalization. Sometimes it experienced difficulties in persuading sceptical domestic interests of the bounties of international competition to the extent of violating its international commitments. Sometimes domestic firms sought radical freedom from government guidance at home and abroad and this met determined international resistance, for the pursuit of liberalization might destabilize relations with important allies. Liberalization did occur, but for reasons only partially related to American state power and purpose, and the liberalization of trade followed a different path from the liberalization of the financial system. This process of liberalization has greatly intensified competition among producers, which in turn has enhanced the political and economic instability associated with ongoing market-led adjustment. Whether political systems can withstand these pressures over time is an open question, especially where the spate of financial and monetary crises are concerned.

This essay, in tandem with much of the rest of the volume, is therefore quite deliberately revisionist. The main focus is on the global regimes for money, finance, and trade, as these constitute the framework of the international political economy. The aim is not to cover all the details or issues, but to provide the reader with a broad background for understanding the subsequent contributions to this volume. I will deal first with the financial and monetary system, demonstrating that early postwar US dominance of the international monetary system did not lead to a liberalized system of global finance; globalization came later and for reasons linked less to state power and more to the interests of New York and London financiers, among others. The second section will focus on trade and will demonstrate once again that the development of liberal trade regimes corresponded not to US dominance but to relative decline, and was linked less to exertions of state power than to structural developments in the global economy that first came to fruition within the United States and spread to Europe and Asia.

## Money, Payments, and Finance in Historical Perspective

The planning began as Anglo-American wartime collaboration, with substantial input from the Canadian government,[5] in what came to be known as the Bretton Woods process.[6] Bretton Woods was about the monetary and payments system and the financial order, and agreement was reached in 1944. Money and finance were seen as crucial because the monetary regime provides a backdrop for the settlement of trade accounts and other transactions across state boundaries. A parallel series of conferences on the trade regime culminated in the Havana Charter of 1948, which will be dealt with later.

The monetary and financial system would, then, largely determine the overall nature of the global economic order. Control over the circulation of money (or lack thereof) was considered to shape the possibilities in other issue-areas. At stake was the very nature of the economic order. How market-oriented should it be? What kind of role should state authorities have? How could the pitfalls of pre-war *laissez-faire* and the eruption of economic nationalism that characterized the breakdown of the pre-war market system be avoided? The answers to these and other questions would largely determine the relative distribution of benefits, and costs, in the postwar era.

In the end the answers were not always clear, and sometimes the answers initially provided were altered as the system evolved. Right from the start there was considerable conflict within the US administration over the proper role of the market

versus public institutions, and conflict existed as well between the government and the business community, and even within the business community, over the appropriate extent of openness and market orientation of the international system under negotiation.[7] The Treasury Department, which handled the Bretton Woods monetary negotiations, strongly supported a monetary and financial order based on the involvement of public multilateral institutions in managing exchange rates, payments systems, capital flows, and domestic adjustment to disequilibrium in the system. In short, the aim was 'to drive the usurious money lenders from the temple of international finance'.[8] The British delegation, headed by John Maynard Keynes, was no less emphatic in this regard. This was not just a matter of self-interest with regard to a war-weary British economy. It was considered that volatile short-term capital flows had contributed substantially to the interwar period of economic disaster.

Public multilateral institutions—the International Monetary Fund (IMF) in the short term and the World Bank in the long term—were therefore to provide a cushion to help states adjust to balance-of-payments and economic development problems. The system, while it placed greater constraints on countries in deficit as opposed to surplus economies, was to permit them to square the maintenance of a stable (fixed-rate) monetary exchange mechanism and payments system with the goals of domestic economic development. As this was the dawn of the era of postwar welfare states, domestic sociopolitical stability was perceived, quite rightly, as a crucial ingredient of international co-operation on monetary and trade issues. Unless states, within certain agreed limits, could pursue their own socio-economic aspirations in keeping with internal democratic (or otherwise) debate, the pressures of international economic interdependence would have an adverse effect on the prospects for co-operation anyway.

The agreement signed at Bretton Woods provided for *a fixed but flexible* system of exchange rates. Adjustment to imbalances that might emerge was to be eased through the right to draw foreign exchange on fairly liberal terms (at least initially) from the IMF. Longer-term economic development and reconstruction would be financed by the World Bank, officially known as the International Bank for Reconstruction and Development (IBRD). States agreed that controls on the short-term flows of capital across borders were a necessary and desirable part of the system. A stable monetary and payments system compatible with domestic policy goals was furthermore seen as a necessary precondition for the successful liberalization of trade, judged by most to be desirable. Keynes had long maintained that an open trading system, with the constant adjustment to a changing international division of labour which that implied, would soon collapse in the presence of volatile short-term capital flows that could skew the exchange rate and adjustment process and undermine the aspirations of domestic populations. Liberal trade and the integrity of the fixed exchange rate system would be facilitated by a relatively closed financial system.[9]

Someone had to pay for the resources the system required. As the only major creditor country, the United States, not surprisingly, was somewhat ambivalent about providing the funds to finance everyone else's adjustment to the consequences of the war. Indeed, conservative congressmen, powerful elements of the American business community, and officials in the Department of State, for example, combined forces to push through alterations to the plan in the negotiations and in the implementation process.[10] This reduced the resources of the IMF to nowhere near the level required for the scale of payments problems linked with wartime devastation and the extraordinary competitive edge of American industry. Yet, somehow, if the global economy was to be resurrected in a way that would ensure continued co-operation, money had to be introduced to the system to facilitate the process of international exchange upon which recovery depended. If the IMF could not provide it, *someone* would have to, and the only available candidate was the US Treasury. Furthermore, American industry needed the overseas customers to maintain the levels of economic activity wartime production had hitherto provided, while Europe and the Far East

needed capital goods for reconstruction to regenerate their domestic economies. There was a common interest to be exploited.

The more rapidly Europe recovered, the more glaring the imbalances became between the US and the rest as recovery sucked in imports that no one could pay for, at least in the short term.[11] When the payments crisis of the winter of 1946–7 erupted, wartime controls had to be extended, limiting trade to an elaborate system of barter. The likelihood of a liberal system of trade and convertible currencies seemed distant indeed.

As Britain's balance of payments collapsed under the pressure, an opportunity to accelerate liberalization presented itself, which the new officials of the Truman administration did not miss. In 1945, Britain had approached America for a loan, and the terms obliged Britain to make sterling convertible and help promote a liberal trade regime.[12] Probably neither side fully appreciated the desperate nature of the payments crises. The view from the United States was often rather shortsighted: American business saw opportunities in a more liberal system, and some US officials were convinced that recovery would be facilitated by a greater role for the market. The British reluctantly agreed to the main American conditions. In return, the Americans would provide $3.75 billion, which the UK hoped to use to restore monetary reserves.

Implemented in 1947, the move was an abject failure. Intended to accelerate the introduction of the Bretton Woods agreement by reducing the transition period, the effect was to kill the accord altogether. Within about six months the British Treasury's reserves were as exhausted as Mother Hubbard's cupboard, exchange and currency controls were reimposed, and yet Britain had probably the healthiest of the European economies.

It was clear by then that the problems of postwar reconstruction were greater than anticipated. More money (or 'liquidity', as it is referred to by economists) was required in the system if a virtuous circle of international trade and payments was to be established in the world economy. The resources of the World Bank were dwarfed by the problem, as were those of the IMF. The inappropriate conditions of the American loan made the US case for the free market look increasingly self-interested. Further attempts by the erstwhile US hegemon to use aid as a lever would be met with the increasing resolve of Europeans to pursue their own particular national economic strategies as a *prerequisite* to eventual liberalization. Not surprisingly, exertions of raw American power had provided infertile ground for multilateral co-operation. The European Payments Union, set up in 1950 and lasting to 1958, remained a poor substitute for US-led global multilateralism and reflected European determination to go their own way.[13] The dream of a relatively open monetary, payments, and financial order dominated by the Bretton Woods institutions appeared dead. Unlike the apocryphal death of Mark Twain, the death of Bretton Woods was far from exaggerated. Transitional arrangements would persist; the IMF was sidelined, the World Bank marginalized, eventually to become a long-term lender to the emerging ex-colonies and other less-developed countries (LDCs). Virtually all currencies were subject to exchange controls and seldom were directly convertible into dollars, and trade remained heavily protected.

Direct US provision of liquidity was substituted for the role the Fund was supposed to play through what came to be called the Marshall Plan (officially, the European Recovery Program), certainly among the most brilliant developments in US postwar diplomacy. It was a plan of aid to European economies that they would administer themselves in co-operation with each other under specified conditions. The aid would fill the payments gap with billions of liquid dollars. The idealism of the American move was obvious, but this should not entirely cloak the shrewd self-interest of US policymakers. The Marshall Plan aid, at approximately $18 billion,[14] essentially *gave* Europeans the resources they needed to purchase the American capital and agricultural goods required for reconstruction. Occupied Japan benefited from equivalent largesse after the outbreak of the Korean War. The resulting exports to Europe helped to compensate for the substantial reduction in economic activity in the US economy, which it was feared would follow the turning off of wartime production. It was

hoped, in vain, that the aid program would provide leverage over the Europeans as well—aid recipients were banned from drawing on the IMF.[15] Marshall Plan aid, furthermore, was extensively supplemented by Korean War rearmament. Rearmament, including US assistance, accelerated the supply of dollar liquidity and stimulated economies, especially that of West Germany, and had the same function as Marshall Plan aid for US allies in Asia.[16]

The problem was to persuade Congress that US generosity was as good for America as fiscal conservatives saw it to be for thankless (and state-interventionist) Europeans, including the British with their reviled imperial preference system of trade discrimination. The growing perceived Soviet threat to Western European security was instrumental in helping the US administration to extract the funding. Marshall Plan aid became America's first Cold War policy; Korean War rearmament the second. When eventually, in 1958, European countries were sufficiently recovered to allow the relatively free convertibility of their national currencies with the dollar, what had emerged was a 'key currency system' or 'dollar standard'.[17]

There were some apparent similarities with the original Bretton Woods plan, such as the fixed-price convertibility of the dollar into gold and the pegging of other currencies in terms of the dollar and the right of countries to control capital flows. Despite this, the international monetary and payments system built on this new key currency foundation was not regulated by the Bretton Woods institutions but by the American Treasury and the Federal Reserve.[18] The growing pool of dollars in foreign hands, not the meagre resources of the IMF, oiled the wheels of international commerce, and so the international monetary system hinged on confidence in the US dollar. As the economist Robert Triffin pointed out at the time,[19] this posed a dilemma that would eventually lead to instability and the collapse of the system. The world economy needed an ample supply of dollar liquidity to ensure growth and trade, yet the more dollars there were the more shaky would be the ability of the United States to honour its pledge to convert unlimited amounts of dollars to gold on demand at the fixed price of $35 an ounce. The payments system and exchange rate mechanism were therefore at the mercy of unilateral US willingness and capacity to manage the dollar in keeping with the needs of a stable international system: some combination of maintaining the international trade competitiveness of the American industrial and service sectors and controlling the capital outflows linked to private overseas investment and government expenditure.

America had become the world's banker, largely replacing the multilateral institutions of the agreements, with all the privileges and responsibilities that entailed. The system of fixed exchange rates would collapse if these privileges and responsibilities were not exercised with caution. However, it is a cliché to assert that US domestic pressures, as opposed to the exigencies of international co-operation, were always likely to overshadow the dollar system.

The post-convertibility world of the 1960s was not, then, the Bretton Woods system at all, nor was it as stable as the notion of benign hegemonic stability implies. There was a persistent element of crisis as the American keeper of the key currency responded more to its domestic preferences than to the imperatives of international stability.[20] First, the US commitment to the Cold War led to military and other government expenditures overseas, which swelled the dollar holdings of foreigners, many of whom cashed them in for gold at the official rate, depleting the Treasury's gold stocks. Second, European and Asian economies recovered and came to compete with the United States on more equal terms. Slowly, the seemingly invincible US trade surplus began to dwindle. Finally, the international activities of American corporations completed the picture. Through foreign direct investment in dollars, American firms contributed to the outflow, and the administration was understandably reticent to curtail this activity.[21] These firms eventually began even to raise capital (in dollars) overseas as their bankers followed them in their international exploits. Dollar-based capital markets emerged in the City of London, which allowed the private sector to expand the supply of dollars once again through the credit multiplier of bank lending. It was

all unregulated by US monetary or supervisory authorities, with the British turning a blind eye in the hope of rejuvenating the City through offshore banking.[22]

Ultimately, a lack of trade competitiveness and accelerating financial outflows meant that the foreign holdings of dollar IOUs severely overshadowed US gold stocks. No one really believed the dollar was worth what the system maintained it was, either in terms of gold or other currencies. Speculation began sporadically in the early and mid-1960s, reaching a fever pitch in 1968 and again in 1971.

The problem was what to do about it. Numerous stopgap measures were negotiated multilaterally,[23] but the fundamental problem was one of American adjustment to declining competitiveness and financial outflows. The Vietnam War, with its domestic inflationary pressures and vast overseas military expenditures, distorted the US economy while boosting the development of Asian economies, which eventually emerged as important competitors for US industry. However, as the US controlled unilaterally the key to the system, the dollar, there was little others could do to compel American adjustment. The United States was equally unwilling to restrain the overseas activities of its multinational firms and financial institutions or to reduce overseas military expenditures. Eventually, short-term capital flows overwhelmed the financial capacity of governments to maintain the pegged system, precipitating its collapse.

Characteristically, the American government chose a unilateral approach to the problem, an approach hardly the stuff of benign hegemony. In August 1971 the Nixon administration sought to free itself from the constraints of the exchange rate mechanism, breaking the link with gold and allowing the dollar to float. Despite attempts to resurrect the pegged system with greater flexibility, by 1973 most countries had to accept a floating currency. The onset of economic crisis and greater international economic disorder associated with the OPEC oil price rise made international co-operation to reform the system difficult.

The vast pool of Eurodollars on international capital markets had given rise to short-term capital flows that swamped governments and central banks in their attempts to maintain currency parities. As private firms began to enjoy the unrestricted transnational financial game, they increased the pressure on their governments to ease restrictions on business activity, especially financial institutions, and to deregulate domestic markets. Thus, in the 1970s financial deregulation was added to the emergence of a floating dollar. This trend accelerated in the 1980s and lay behind the global integration of financial markets, building on the offshore Euromarkets.[24]

The problems of the pegged system were more closely linked to the policy of dollars on the loose and US failure to adjust internally than to the pressures of the fixed rates. None the less, the touted *object* of the deregulation of the exchange rate mechanism was to regain the national policy-making autonomy restricted by the obligations of a fixed-rate system. Contrary to expectations, the collapse of fixed exchange rates, combined with the increased volume and volatility of private financial flows, effectively jeopardized the capacity of governments to pursue the independent policy goals so cherished in the postwar period while maintaining the ties of economic interdependence that were so costly to break. By abandoning fixed exchange rates, international monetary governance was left increasingly to market forces to the detriment of state capacity to manage the domestic macroeconomy in line with domestic preferences and imperatives. Governments would henceforth find it more difficult to pursue social and economic policies at variance with the preferences of market players.

A further result of the state retreat from international monetary management was to accelerate the growth of the capital markets that had undermined the fixed-rate system in the first place.[25] American capital controls were removed in the late 1960s, and in 1979 the UK government followed. Most other major Western countries and many LDCs have since conformed under pressure from private lobbies and other states. Similar pressures from financial sectors have led to comprehensive programs of domestic financial deregulation and a corresponding cross-border integration of capital

markets in a process of globalization. This liberalization of capital flows and global financial integration have removed many of the last vestiges of domestic policy-making autonomy, completing the transformation of the postwar global order (see chapters by Pauly, Story, and Webb in this volume) in a way that had little to do with US decline or otherwise. This more 'marketized' financial order, in combination with the liberalization of trade, permits owners of capital to seek their preferred investment climate among a variety of economies in terms of lower inflation, more advantageous interest rates, less restrictive rules on wage rates, hiring practices, and other aspects of government regulation.

In this sense, financial market integration meant that major investors were no longer restricted to opportunities in their respective home countries or equally restrictive conditions elsewhere. Deregulation and liberalization have produced a dynamic conferring greater freedoms on private corporate actors in the international political economy. That is what the creation of a more liberal, or 'marketized', economic order is all about, and this represents both a dramatic reversal of the intentions of the postwar planners and a dramatic reversal in the balance of public and private in domestic and international economic management. This financial globalization was caused by the unplanned emergence of the dollar standard, the incompatible objectives of states in international monetary relations, the rise of the Euromarkets, and consistent private lobbying for financial liberalization. The policies of democratic states must increasingly conform to the exigencies of the international market order, making international constraints difficult to square with the demands of many domestic sociopolitical constituencies. The consistent outbreaks of financial crises, as in Latin America and Asia, have not helped matters, particularly for fragile emerging market economies.

## Trade Issues and the Postwar Order

The postwar monetary system provided the backdrop for the international trade regime. The development of the trading order was also a long and difficult story that conforms little to traditional accounts of the role of the United States and the causes of liberalization.

Negotiations took place during and after the war, culminating in the Havana conference of 1948. While most parties agreed that protectionism had been a negative aspect of interwar economic relations, there was a lack of agreement on the timing, extent of, and preconditions necessary for liberalization. Given the extraordinary international competitiveness of the America economy and the US worry about a possible postwar slump following the winding down of war production, it is not surprising that the Americans tended to see access to foreign markets through multilateral trade liberalization as a prerequisite for full employment and future growth. The much more vulnerable British and Europeans saw things rather differently. Their delicate balance-of-payments positions, their need for substantial imports of capital goods and food, and their crippled manufacturing capacity linked to wartime devastation meant that they tended to see a move towards reconstruction and full employment as a necessary precondition of trade liberalization.[26]

In the end, however, all revealed themselves ambivalent about the liberalization of trade. US trade policy historically had been characterized by high tariffs, and the Americans continued to be cautious for a number of reasons: most of the firms in the American economy were domestically oriented, with no desire to see their markets threatened by foreign competition; those firms that were export-oriented were far from convinced that other countries would play the liberalization game fairly and allow highly competitive US producers into domestic markets (the classic argument of protectionists in liberal clothing); and the US government was ambivalent because it had to strike a balance between these different perceptions of national self-interest. Furthermore, the US Congress was jealous of its trade policy-making prerogatives and was suspicious by nature of international institutions that might diminish this constitutional right in any way. None the less, the administration consistently maintained that reciprocity and non-discrimination in trade relations would form a foundation for

mutual benefits from international trade in a climate of ongoing liberalization.[27]

European countries and less-developed countries (Latin America and the emerging ex-colonies) were likewise sceptical about liberalization, but for different reasons. In the British case, there was an understandable loyalty to the countries of the imperial preference system that had stood by Britain in the dark days of the war prior to Soviet and American entry into the conflict. Europeans generally were aware that their devastated economies could not cope with liberalization. The potential effects of a liberal international trade regime on employment and domestic social stability, in view of the legacy of the interwar depression, were ominous. Europeans were also toying with the idea of a comprehensive system of regional economic integration, which the US encouraged in its own way. The LDCs were worried about the effects of trade liberalization on their development prospects.

All agreed on the need for some sort of stable system of multilateral rules and norms to reduce to a minimum the arbitrariness and unpredictability of national practices. What was needed, then, was a compromise. The underlying principles promoted by the Americans (reciprocity and non-discrimination) were readily enough adopted, but there were various opt-outs and caveats in the Havana Charter and a transition period of uncertain length, with a view to permitting adjustment prior to the cold shower of trade competition through liberalization. Once again, states sought to ensure that the international order would be largely compatible with domestically formulated social and economic policy objectives and sufficient national decision-making autonomy.

The resulting International Trade Organization (ITO) was therefore a compromise for the long-term achievement of non-discriminatory and liberalized international trading relations, preserving the right of states to opt out, for example, when in balance-of-payments difficulties. It also provided for a dispute settlement mechanism with the legal powers to question national trade policies should they be deemed in violation of the principles and rules underpinning the ITO. Its principles encapsulated the broad agreement that full employment was to be fully compatible with the emergence of the new rules of international trade. The Charter also incorporated a 1947 interim agreement that provided a procedural and policy framework for negotiations to liberalize access to national markets, an agreement called the General Agreement on Tariffs and Trade (GATT, now the World Trade Organization or WTO).

The ITO was never ratified by the American Congress, and therefore the trade pillar of the Bretton Woods order was abandoned from the start. The defection of the US business community was crucial to this failure. Some appear to have favoured continued US protectionism through tariffs; others felt the Charter did little to promote access to foreign markets for American firms, with too many opt-outs and caveats to the accord and not enough firm commitment to the systematic removal of barriers, especially those posed by the British imperial preference system.[28] The US Congress continued to provide a brake on attempts to proceed to a more liberal order.[29] The Americans and their partners turned to the interim GATT of 1947, which contained the essential rules of the failed ITO. The GATT remained provisional, an executive agreement stripped of most ITO institutional substance, but it did provide a set of rules and a sufficient basis for intergovernmental co-operation.[30]

The GATT has since developed its rules and become more intrusive on sovereignty (see chapter by Winham in this volume). With limited progress in the 1950s and early 1960s, economic recovery and reconstruction in Europe and elsewhere provided a firm foundation for substantial agreement. The United States provided crucial leadership in this regard by launching the Kennedy Round of negotiations (1963–7), seeking to benefit from a perceived competitive edge in international competition and to tie the emerging European Union (EU) into the global trade regime. Major tariff cuts resulted, and the efforts were continued in more difficult economic circumstances in the Tokyo Round (1974–9).[31] These two rounds of tariff cuts brought tariffs on manufactured goods to near-negligible levels and set out the major lines of conflict for the Uruguay Round, in particular the EU-US dispute over agriculture, the (somewhat waning) demands from LDCs for preferential treatment, and the 'back-door protectionism' of non-tariff barriers. The Uruguay Round success cemented these developments and extended, gingerly, liberalization and rule-making to agriculture, trade in services, intellectual property issues, and foreign investment protection (see Sell in this volume).

It should be clear that the US failed to persuade others of the bounties of liberalization until relatively late in the day, and the erstwhile liberal champion itself had been ambivalent about thoroughgoing trade liberalization for compelling domestic reasons. Substantive moves towards liberalization were not under way until American dominance was declining in the late 1960s. Despite American decline, the process continues. Furthermore, the drive for liberalization was never the policy of self-denial by the hegemon—it was more an off-on instrument of national policy in a limited but growing range of producer and service sectors than an enlightened blueprint for global economic order and prosperity. When liberalization began in earnest, it was a longer and more arduous process involving complex domestic and international compromises for all parties concerned. Raw assertions of state power were never successful in the construction of a liberal trade order.[32] Only when domestic conditions were simultaneously right in the EU, the United States, and Japan could the regime move towards substantive liberalization and the development of the dispute-settling role originally foreseen in the Havana Charter.

It should also be emphasized that the process of trade liberalization was not simply a matter of state policies and decision-making, though these helped. Private-sector actors played a key role in accepting and indeed promoting policies aimed at a more liberal trading order, and the process was underpinned by the emergence of transnational economic structures.[33] Governments were often only the legal surrogates for private coalitions of liberal or protectionist interests. While the 1947 rules of the trading order were crucial foundations, strategic decisions by private firms (often despite state protectionism) led to the web of international economic interdependence upon which liberalization was built. As prosperity grew and domestic firms became more oriented towards international trade and investment, the domestic support for liberalization strengthened.[34]

For all the progress, protectionist pressures have not disappeared by any means. In fact, the adjustment process associated with tariff cuts and other forms of liberalization has consistently forced many industrial sectors in industrialized economies on the defensive, leading to the implementation of various 'new protectionist' non-tariff barriers (NTBs) such as voluntary export restraints (VERs) and 'orderly marketing arrangements'.[35] The US has been as guilty as any on this score, often leading the pack, pushed by narrow sectional interests with power in the Congress; in the late 1990s, the US steel industry was once again pushing for protectionist measures against imports from a range of competing producers as recessionary conditions hit manufacturing in the wake of the Asian financial crisis. Furthermore, LDCs have historically seen their fundamental economic weakness as a handicap in accepting a liberal order, though there has been much change in this regard, especially in Latin America (see chapter by Phillips in this volume).

On the whole, however, the perceived costs of a return to a closed system are now seen to be high, not least because a substantial coalition of the private interests across a range of countries participating in the policy process identifies continued profitability with improved access to foreign markets. Many even have multinational production strategies and substantial networks of intra-firm trade, moving intermediary as well as finished goods across borders to benefit from the most advantageous mix of factor and input costs available. For example, it was estimated as far back as the 1980s that some 60 per cent of US imports derived not from traditional cross-border trading between national producers but from intra-firm and intra-industry trade carried out by transnational corporations (TNCs) within their own company structure.[36] The integrated production strategies of TNCs have had an important impact on trade balances, often displacing domestic production to overseas locations where it is reimported as foreign value-added products.

While the rise of highly competitive newly industrialized countries (the first of which was Japan in the 1950s) and the rise of regional integration projects (see Hveem in this volume) such as the European Union, the Canada-US/North American Free Trade Agreement, and MERCOSUR have complicated the multilateral picture, the worst fears of free-traders have yet to materialize. Defensive regional blocs currently seem unlikely,[37] new forms of protectionism have not led to a repudiation of the GATT/WTO, and efforts at liberalization continue with a trade round proposed for the dawn of the millennium. This will build on the Uruguay Round of negotiations successfully concluded in December 1993, which established the WTO and greatly expanded the liberalization agenda. As in the past, the trade regime continues to be a mixture of liberal principles combined with protectionist reflexes. Conflict will be ongoing as states with different patterns of competitive advantage and different policy mixes confront each other on old and new issues, but few contemplate a return to the pre-GATT era.

## Conclusion

This introduction has highlighted a number of interrelated points about the postwar order. Although this has been a story of liberalization, probably more far-reaching than many postwar planners thought possible, the explanation provided here has contrasted with much of the IPE literature. In particular, while American leadership was important at crucial junctures, the evolution of the system cannot be explained by the exercise of US power alone.

In the first place, the period of greatest American dominance was the most illiberal. US attempts to apply leverage of various kinds failed to persuade the Europeans and Japanese in turn to accept the American vision. The period of relative US decline, in contrast, has seen dramatic developments with respect to liberalization in trade, but especially in the monetary and financial order. Like most countries, the United States has remained ambivalent about the liberalization of trade, pursuing tariff cuts and the elimination of discrimination in a self-interested fashion and displaying reticence to remove barriers, even easy readiness to erect new ones, when domestic sectors appeared threatened.

Perhaps most importantly, the achievement of a liberal order in trade and finance is as much a market phenomenon as it is a matter for state decision-making. The transnationalization of American and other firms created its own policy dynamic over time, with states and market actors integrated in ongoing dialogue for the governance of the global economy. The growing patterns of interdependence, while far from eliminating conflicts of interest in the system, fostered a constituency of economic agents dependent on transactions across borders. The GATT/WTO provided a relatively orderly framework in which states could negotiate openness where support was forthcoming, while they responded with at least equal vigour to more vulnerable constituencies (such as farmers) seeking continued protection. The underlying social and economic interest bases behind state policies were more important variables than the power of individual states.

This introduction has sought to allay other myths as well. It has been argued, for example, that the Bretton Woods plan was not implemented. The short-lived fixed-rate system after convertibility in 1958 was, in contrast, a key currency system—the dollar standard. This afforded the United States considerable control over the international monetary system: the world's currency system was manipulated through US monetary policy, and this was perhaps the principal source of American influence in international economic relations. The move to floating currencies has not necessarily diminished this power because US policy can manipulate the value of the dollar, the world's main fiduciary asset. Only the rise of the competing Euro, the fruit of European Monetary Union, is likely to change the situation, and that over some time.[38]

What this essay has left out is addressed in the upcoming chapters, but two final questions invite reflection. In the first place, the successful pursuit of liberalization has elevated the liberal creed to the level of a doctrine. The case for the ongoing liberalization of economic relations has ben accepted rather uncritically, either *faut de mieux* or because of its perceived benefits. The liberal case is fairly clear: a market-oriented order leads to a more efficient allocation of resources and therefore provides the key to future economic growth and prosperity. The logical conclusion of this is the effective removal of public authorities from the economic domain and the removal of embedded barriers to market transactions, including the protective social policies and other restrictive practices that have accompanied the success of many postwar economies.

Yet this creed should be questioned for a number of important reasons related to what the postwar planners were trying to do in the first place and to the increasing frequency of financial crisis in the contemporary global economy. They were trying to find an alternative to *laissez-faire*, which had proved so problematic in the interwar period, leading to the Great Depression. The market proved unsustainable as the principal arbiter of economic decision-making and led to an outbreak of economic nationalism that greatly exacerbated the crisis at the time. For all the failures of postwar multilateral co-operation, one is pushed to conclude that John Maynard Keynes and Harry Dexter White, respectively the British and American negotiators at Bretton Woods, addressed these problems with a considerable degree of wisdom, a commodity often in shorter supply than base self-interest in international relations. They realized that political authority would lose its legitimacy where the market ran rampant, leading to a general and very undesirable failure of international co-operation altogether. A proper role for public authority is a prerequisite for a sustainable economic order.[39]

There is little in contemporary experience that would lead one to question these lessons, and yet an incautious liberal creed has come to dominate much thinking on these matters. It should be observed, however, that as liberalization has proceeded, especially in the domain of finance, economic growth has become more problematic and economic cycles more volatile. The golden age of postwar growth occurred *prior to* the dramatic liberalization of trade and finance in the 1970s and 1980s. Furthermore, some of the main postwar success stories, such as Japan, France, and Germany, and more recent successes like Korea (despite its considerable difficulties in the late 1990s) are not necessarily the most liberal. One would not wish to imply simple cause and effect here, but despite anticipated howls of protest from many economists there is at least reason to pause for reflection on these issues.

Second, it is not clear that continued liberalization of the global economic order is politically sustainable, at least not unless approached with considerable caution. The removal of trade barriers intensifies competition and requires constant industrial restructuring and rapid economic change. The market is probably the most efficient tool of social engineering, but its results can be unpredictable, wasteful, and unsettling. The liberalization of the financial order is more disquieting.[40] The excessive freedom and volatility of capital markets and financial flows threaten investment, payments equilibrium, and the ability of national communities to attain their collective aspirations. The Asian crisis has threatened some of the most noteworthy successes in the developing world and might yet push Russia (with its nuclear weapons!) into a political maelstrom. The new financial order has forced deflationary strategies on many unwilling governments, much like the nineteenth-century classical gold standard.

Of course, one would not wish to call into question the institutionalization of international co-operation that has developed in the postwar era, whatever the policy pursued. Yet might one conclude that *multilateral rules* to attenuate conflict and foster some sense of fairness across levels of development are almost certainly more important than liberalization *per se*? If co-operation can indeed bring sustained benefits, then its participants must find the *outcome*, not just the promise, legitimate in one way or another.

## Notes

The author would like to thank Peter Burnham, Susan Strange, and the many students over the years who have contributed to this essay.

1  See estimates of Soviet military and economic resources by American intelligence in Walter Lafeber, *America, Russia, and the Cold War 1945–1984*, 5th edn (New York: Alfred A. Knopf/Newberry Award Records, 1985), 26–7, 49–50.

2  Robert Gilpin, *The Political Economy of International Relations* (Princeton, NJ: Princeton University Press, 1987). Gilpin is an eminent exponent of the HST.

3  For two approaches that address these underlying dimensions in different ways, see Herman Schwartz, *States versus Markets: History, Geography, and the Development of the International Political Economy* (New York: St Martin's Press, 1994), esp. chs 3, 8, 9, 10, a remarkable and underrated study; and Robert W. Cox, *Production, Power, and World Order* (New York: Columbia University Press, 1987).

4  For a critical analysis of the motivations behind HST, see Isabelle Grunberg, 'Exploring the Myth of Hegemonic Stability', *International Organization* 44, 4 (Autumn,1990): 431–78.

5  See Thomas Keating, *Canada and World Order: The Multilateralist Tradition in Canadian Foreign Policy* (Toronto: McClelland & Stewart, 1993), esp. chs 1–2.

6  For detailed accounts of the negotiations and aftermath, see Richard Gardner, *Sterling-Dollar Diplomacy in Current Perspective* (New York: Columbia University Press, 1981); Armand van Dormael, *Bretton Woods: Birth of a Monetary System* (London: Macmillan, 1978).

7  See Gardner, *Sterling-Dollar Diplomacy*; Fred Block, *The Origins of International Economic Disorder* (Berkeley: University of California Press, 1977), esp. chs 1–5; and the very important work by Marcello de Cecco: 'Origins of the Post-war Payments System', *Cambridge Journal of Economics* 3 (1979): 49–61; de Cecco, 'International Financial Markets and US Domestic Policy since

1945', *International Affairs* 52, 3 (July 1986): 381–99.

8   Henry Morgenthau, US Treasury Secretary, as quoted in Gardner, *Sterling-Dollar Diplomacy*, 76.

9   See Eric Helleiner, *States and the Re-emergence of Global Finance: From Bretton Woods to the 1990s* (Ithaca, NY: Cornell University Press, 1994).

10  Block, *International Economic Disorder*, ch. 3; de Cecco, 'Origins of the Post-war Payments System'; de Cecco, 'International Financial Markets'.

11  See Alan S. Milward, *The Reconstruction of Western Europe 1945–1951* (London: University Paperbacks/Methuen, 1984), ch. 1 and Conclusion.

12  See Block, *International Economic Disorder*, ch. 3; Peter Burnham, *The Political Economy of Postwar Reconstruction* (London: Macmillan, 1990), ch. 3 (esp. p. 51, quotation from Will Clayton, US State Department: 'if you succeed in doing away with Empire preference . . . it may well be that we can afford to pay a couple of billion dollars for it.').

13  See Burnham, *Postwar Reconstruction*, ch. 5; William Diebold, *Trade and Payments in Western Europe* (Washington: Council on Foreign Relations, 1952).

14  There is considerable controversy over the eventual size of the aid package. The original budgetary request in the congressional legislation was for $17 billion (Block, *International Economic Disorder*, 87), but it seems accurate to say that the total was over $20 billion. See Fred Hirsch and Peter Oppenheimer, 'The Trial of Managed Money: Currency, Credit, and Prices 1920–1970', in C.M. Cipolla, ed., *The Fontana Economic History of Europe* (Glasgow: Collins/Fontana, 1976), 626.

15  Block, *International Economic Disorder*, 111–12.

16  See Richard Stubbs, 'War and Economic Development: Export-oriented Industrialization in East and South-east Asia', *Comparative Politics* (1999).

17  The term 'dollar standard' is borrowed from Richard Gardner. Let us also be reminded that while convertibility was an aspect of liberalization, the global financial order remained segmented along national lines. Globalization would have to wait.

18  See de Cecco, 'Origins of the Post-war Payments System'; de Cecco, 'International Financial Markets'.

19  Robert Triffin, *Gold and the Dollar Crisis: The Future of Convertibility* (New Haven: Yale University Press, 1961).

20  See Susan Strange, *International Monetary Relations*, vol. 2 of Andrew Shonfield, ed., *International Economic Relations of the Western World 1959–1971* (Oxford: Oxford University Press, 1976).

21  Block, *International Economic Disorder*, chs 6–7, provides a good analysis of the growth and management of the American payments deficit.

22  See Michel Aglietta, 'The Creation of International Liquidity', and David T. Llewelyn, 'The Role of International Banking', in Loukas Tsoukalis, ed., *The Political Economy of International Money* (London: Sage, 1985).

23  See Strange, *International Monetary Relations*.

24  The 'Euromarkets' were financial markets dealing mainly in dollars but outside the United States itself. The City of London came to be the centre of the 'Eurodollar' market by the mid-1960s, operating primarily through US banks with branches in London, Paris, or Frankfurt.

25  See G.R.D. Underhill, ed., *The New World Order in International Finance* (London: Macmillan, 1997), esp. ch. 1.

26  See Gardner, *Sterling-Dollar Diplomacy*, chs 6, 8, 14, 17.

27  Certainly it seems fair to say that the US government was more concerned with discriminatory trade practices than liberalization *per se*. See Gerard and Victoria Curzon, 'The Management of Trade Relations in the GATT', in Andrew G. Shonfield, V. Curzon, et al., *Politics and Trade*, vol. 1 of Shonfield, ed., *International Economic Relations of the Western World 1959–1971*, vol. 1, (Oxford: Oxford University Press, 1976), 143–67.

28  See Gardner, *Sterling-Dollar Diplomacy*, 372–80. These criticisms were levelled at the Charter despite the admission of the US government that 'if we want to be honest with ourselves, we will find that many of the sins that we freely criticize other countries for practising have their counterpart in the United States.' Quote from Will Clayton, Asst. Sec. of State for Economic Affairs, ibid., 378.

29  Curzon, 'Management of Trade Relations', 148.

30 Ibid., 146. The US Congress remained distinctly cool towards the GATT for many years; in fact, it was not until 1968 that the US government felt bold enough to request from Congress permanent authorization for the US financial contribution to the GATT secretariat (Gardner, *Sterling-Dollar Diplomacy*, xxv–xxvi). Furthermore, the US unilaterally exempted agriculture from the GATT provisions in 1955 and initiated such discriminatory practices as voluntary export restraints on cotton textile exports from Japan as early as 1956.

31 See Gilbert Winham, *International Trade and the Tokyo Round Negotiations* (Princeton, NJ: Princeton University Press, 1986).

32 See Shonfield, Curzon, et al., *Politics and Trade*, 39, 48–9.

33 See G.R.D. Underhill, *Industrial Crisis and the Open Economy* (London: Macmillan, 1998), where this argument is taken up in detail.

34 See Helen Milner, *Resisting Protectionism: Global Industries and the Politics of International Trade* (Princeton, NJ: Princeton University Press, 1988).

35 For an in depth study of VERs in the textile case, see Underhill, *Industrial Crisis and the Open Economy*.

36 Gilpin, *The Political Economy of International Relations*, 254.

37 See W.D. Coleman and G.R.D. Underhill, eds, *Regionalism and Global Economic Integration* (London: Routledge, 1998).

38 See Fred Bergsten, 'The Dollar and the Euro', in *Foreign Affairs* 76, 4 (July-Aug. 1997): 83–95.

39 A careful reading of Adam Smith reveals that he was clearly aware of this. It is a pity that most of his latter-day followers are not.

40 See Susan Strange, *Mad Money* (Manchester: Manchester University Press, 1998).

## Suggested Readings

Block, Fred. *The Origins of International Economic Disorder*. Berkeley: University of California Press, 1977.

Burnham, Peter. *The Political Economy of Post-war Reconstruction*. London: Macmillan, 1990.

Gardner, Richard. *Sterling-Dollar Diplomacy in Current Perspective*. New York: Columbia University Press, 1981.

Milward, Alan S. *The Reconstruction of Western Europe 1945–1951*. London: Methuen, 1984.

Schwartz, Herman M. *States versus Markets: History, Geography, and the Development of the International Political Economy*. New York: St Martin's Press, 1994.

Shonfield, Andrew G., Victoria Curzon, et al. *Politics and Trade*, vol. 1 of Shonfield, ed., *International Economic Relations of the Western World 1959–1971*. Oxford: Oxford University Press, 1976.

Spero, Joan. *The Politics of International Economic Relations*, 5th edn. New York: St Martin's Press, 1997.

Stopford, John, and Susan Strange. *Rival States, Rival Firms*. Cambridge: Cambridge University Press, 1991.

Strange, Susan. *International Monetary Relations*, vol. 2 of Andrew G. Shonfield, ed., *International Economic Relations of the Western World 1959–1971*. Oxford: Oxford University Press, 1976.

———. *Mad Money*. Manchester: Manchester University Press, 1998.

Tsoukalis, Loukas, ed. *The Political Economy of International Money*. London: Sage, 1985.

Underhill, Geoffrey R.D. *Industrial Crisis and the Open Economy*. London: Macmillan, 1998.

———, ed. *The New World Order in International Finance*. London: Macmillan, 1997.

## Chapter 8

# Capital Mobility and the New Global Order

### Louis W. Pauly

During the last quarter of the twentieth century, short-term capital flows across the borders of advanced industrial countries expanded at a staggering pace. Even more striking than the rising volumes tracked in every magazine or journal article on the subject was the underlying normative shift witnessed during that period of time. Indeed, the relative ease with which such flows could occur represented a distinct reversal of the dominant set of national policy preferences evident during the years immediately following World War II. By some measures, the scale of international capital movements was only recovering levels evident in the pre-World War I period. But in light of the turbulent decades stretching from 1914 until the end of the Cold War, the explosive growth, global reach, and speed of contemporary capital movements came widely to be seen as the harbinger of a new era. Promising to some and threatening to others, 'global finance' became a short-hand term for evoking the increasingly borderless world of advanced capitalism.

The causes and consequences of the accelerating movement of short-term financial claims across national borders have become important topics for interdisciplinary research. Much economic analysis begins with the assertion that freer international capital flows enhance efficiency, supplement domestic savings, and promote growth. Political and sociological research, conversely, often concentrates on the disruptive effects of such flows as well as on the difficulty of managing financial crises that now routinely span geographic and functional boundaries. Capital flight from many emerging markets in the late 1990s brought such concerns very much to the fore, not least because its

magnitude and ferocity seemed to challenge the normative consensus that had so recently been achieved among advanced countries.

A wide range of policy debates nevertheless remained framed by the assumption that the international mobility of short-term capital facilitates longer-term foreign direct investment and expanding trade in goods and services. It is increasingly understood, however, that the economic expansion associated with such developments comes with new risks for governments, societies, and individuals. In this light, academic and popular commentators draw connections between the principle of international capital mobility and such diverse phenomena as the retrenchment of national welfare states, the bold experiment in monetary union in Western Europe, political and social crises in East Asia, wrenching systemic transformations in Russia and its neighbouring states, and the abandonment of long-standing development models in Latin America and Africa.

Two sets of concerns lie behind these debates. The first highlights the challenge of simultaneously harnessing the power of open markets to accelerate economic development and growth while limiting the political constraints and social costs associated with that openness. The underlying dilemma is one of political legitimacy. The second brings to the fore the difficulty of limiting the possibility of financial market failures (or managing them effectively when they occur) when the power of private actors is enhanced and the authority to regulate them is dispersed. In each case, the political tensions are obvious. They are also not fully resolvable, given the deeper structure of the international political economy at the dawn of the twenty-first century. In such a world, the logic of markets suggests globalism, while the logic of politics remains deeply marked by nationalism.

A short chapter cannot adequately explore such themes or survey the burgeoning research programs currently focusing on them. It can, however, provide an orientation to the underlying political challenges presented to the international system by the evolution of integrated financial markets. This essay therefore begins by placing international capital mobility into conceptual and historical context. It then examines the problem of designing effective systems for crisis management in a world where regulatory power is ever more widely dispersed. Finally, it explores the related but more fundamental dilemma of grounding that power in stable political foundations when the logic of markets suggests globalism but the logic of politics remains local. In the necessarily incomplete resolution of that dilemma, the concluding section of the chapter identifies the new frontier for certain international institutions.[1]

## International Capital Mobility in Context

The cause of freer trade won renewed rhetorical support after the cataclysm once known as the Great War. Rhetoric was translated into successful policy, however, only after an even greater catastrophe ended in 1945. The interdependent international economic order deliberately to be built by the victorious allies (minus the Soviet Union and China) through the expansion of trade was to be underpinned by a system of stable exchange rates. Codified in 1944, the Bretton Woods system was designed to avoid both the perceived rigidities of the nineteenth-century gold standard and the undisciplined currency manipulations commonly deemed to have contributed to the depth and duration of the Great Depression.

During the decades following World War II, the explicit policy preference for freer trade came ever more widely to be supplemented by official efforts to reduce impediments to foreign direct investment. The vast postwar expansion in trade (in both goods and services) and in cross-border investment in plant and equipment had far-reaching effects, many of which are explored in other chapters in this book. The subject of concern in this chapter, which essentially boils down to currency convertibility in the current and/or capital accounts of national payments balances, cannot be separated from that broader policy movement towards more liberal trade and investment regimes.

Production, trade, and investment must be financed. If resulting financial claims are freely convertible across national currencies, liquid balances in governmental, corporate, or personal accounts can be used for a broad range of purposes. In advanced economies, in fact, a historical tendency exists for purely financial operations to grow at a rate far exceeding tangible business requirements. Much of this growth reflects speculation, which can either stabilize or destabilize other economic variables. In practical terms, it has proven impossible to draw a clear and unassailable dividing line between the use of convertible financial claims, on the one hand, prudently to hedge business risks and, on the other, purely to gamble. To many observers, therefore, the economic history of the latter decades of the twentieth century has been decisively marked by cross-border markets for short-term capital taking on a life of their own entirely disconnected from real political economies where goods, services, and new technologies are produced. The truth is more complex.

When national economies are open to trade, investment, and their accommodating financing, their interest rates, exchange rates, and internal prices (including the price of labour) become interdependent. This implies certain policy trade-offs. Those trade-offs define the conceptual terrain of open-economy macroeconomics. In the 1960s, two economists began modelling that terrain in a highly suggestive manner.[2]

The Mundell-Fleming model eventually demonstrated that governments and central banks overseeing open economies could not simultaneously give priority to maintaining the independence of their internal monetary policies, stabilizing their exchange rates, and permitting unrestricted inward and outward capital flows. Since interest rates, inflation rates, and exchange rates influenced one another, only two of those goals—at most—could be achieved. If priority is given to open capital markets and stable exchange rates, domestic interest rates will reflect external developments. When the autonomy of national monetary policy and exchange rate stability are clearly preferred, capital movements must be limited. Finally, if capital mobility and monetary autonomy are defined as top policy objectives, exchange rates must be allowed to adjust.

When fiscal policy—the taxing and spending activities of governments—is brought into the model, the standard economic analysis is also straightforward. If exchange rates are flexible and capital is perfectly mobile, changes in monetary policy become the only effective tool for influencing national economic performance and changes in fiscal policy cease to have any effect. Alternatively, if exchange rates are fixed or capital movements are controlled, fiscal policy becomes effective and monetary policy ineffective. Such trade-offs are forced by systematic and predictable changes in underlying spending, saving, and investing behaviour inside interdependent national economies.

In other words, the more open an economy becomes to inward and outward capital flows, the more difficult it is for governments to maintain stable exchange rates *and* monetary policies targeted to advance exclusively national priorities. If unilateral monetary actions are nevertheless taken—say, money supplies are constricted to dampen domestic inflation—exchange rates will immediately come under pressure. If governments wish their fiscal policies to retain their capacity to reinforce the line of monetary policy, they will have to find ways to dissipate that pressure. In practice, if they are committed to exchange rate stability, this means they will have to find ways to moderate the flow of capital inward or outward. A high level of external indebtedness, that is, a level of national savings and inward investment too low to accommodate national aspirations for growth and development, will complicate that search.

Refinements and modifications of this basic model have filled academic journals and textbooks

during the past 30 years, but its central message remains clear. The space for effective economic stabilization policies at the national level—in other words, the space for monetary and fiscal policies to work at all or to work in complementary directions—is defined by the choice of exchange rate regime and the degree of capital market openness.

In reality, perfect capital mobility or freely floating exchange rates have never existed at the systemic level, but they have sometimes been approached. Monetary autonomy has usually been highly prized by national governments, but some have given it up in order to promote the cause of exchange rate stability and to preserve the net benefits perceived to accrue from capital mobility. Economic and Monetary Union in Europe, for example, rested on such a deliberate policy choice. Conversely, the absence of similar momentum in North America in the late 1990s indicated different priorities: the willingness to preserve a degree of monetary independence at the cost of exchange rate instability. Similarly, the world's financial leaders—the United States, Germany, and Japan—proved willing since the 1970s to sacrifice exchange rate stability among themselves whenever their monetary independence has been threatened by inward or outward capital movements. Rarely, however, were any of them completely indifferent to the external value of their currencies. The basic political reasons are not hard to locate.

Not by accident but by virtue of the design of an increasingly integrated international economy in the post-World War II era, industrial sectors engaged in trade and international investment now have significant political influence. Periodic impulses to stabilize exchange rates between the largest economies arise out of the continuing challenge of maintaining both domestic and international political coalitions of sufficient strength to sustain the postwar experiment. That experiment, which essentially boils down to the progressive opening of national markets, has been embraced by more states in the wake of the end of the Cold War. Although short-term fluctuations in exchange rates do not necessarily compromise the maintenance of supportive coalitions across now interdependent states, longer-term misalignments between major currencies—differences between where real exchange rates should be to promote payments equilibria and where they actually are at any particular moment—threaten to do exactly that.

When trade and investment across borders are unhindered, exchange rates should track underlying changes in the purchasing power of national currencies. Nominal exchange rates might fluctuate, but real (price-level adjusted) exchange rates should be stable. In fact, such stability has often proved elusive. A high degree of international capital mobility may be one reason. When it exists, changes in nominal exchange rates reflect not just underlying trade and investment flows and not just events in now interconnected financial asset markets around the world, but also collective expectations of likely future events in those markets. Volumes of economic research focus on this issue, but the hypothesis that financial asset prices therefore can and do sometimes move wildly, even irrationally, has never been convincingly dismissed. Not coincidentally, it comes as no surprise that exchange rates can overreact to changes in underlying real economies. In light of the fact that the local prices of goods and services can be sticky, however, unpredictable and unstable exchange rates can in principle hurt the real economy by encouraging a misallocation of resources. By complicating the continuous process of economic and social adjustment to openness, and by reinforcing perceptions of unfairness, such a misallocation can erode the domestic political foundations of the great postwar experiment itself. Ebbs and flows in the popularity of economic nationalists around the world are not simply reflections of good speeches.

## The International Politics of Financial Integration

In the real world, is it reasonable to assert that the Mundell-Fleming trade-off reflects an intentional choice? Do governments actually still have the freedom to choose between capital mobility, exchange rate stability, and monetary autonomy? Or are their choices constrained in very practical ways?

Today, there is a widespread sense that one of those policy options—capital mobility—is no longer subject to choice. Most observers acknowledge the increasing openness of financial channels across advanced industrial countries and, especially during the last decade of the twentieth century, across much of the emerging industrial world. Even if 'perfect' capital mobility does not exist, national markets in foreign exchange, money market instruments, bank claims, bonds, and stocks are much more open now than they were when the Bretton Woods system effectively came to an end in the early 1970s. Markets once clearly separated along functional and national lines are much more interdependent. On present trend, certain truly integrated markets—where some financial assets are fully substitutable or where similar assets in different geographic locations trade at identical prices—are no longer hard to imagine. As implied above, however, such developments come at the end of a long line of policy decisions.

Throughout the post-World War II period, albeit at different paces and with occasional backsliding, the United States, Canada, and a number of European states deliberately reduced direct controls and taxes on financial transactions, loosened long-standing regulatory restrictions on financial intermediaries, permitted the expansion of lightly regulated 'offshore' financial markets (the misnamed Euromarkets), and oversaw the introduction of new technologies that sped up capital movements and stimulated the development of innovative financial products. In the 1970s, Japan cautiously joined the trend. Throughout the 1980s, many developing countries followed. And in the 1990s, Russia, many of its former satellite states, and China began to build internal markets for private capital and, at varying speeds, to open them up to external participants.

As capital market liberalization proceeded apace, scholars proposed explanations at various levels of analysis.[3] Some studies emphasized a competitive, system-level dynamic as states are drawn to the economic stimulus, the jobs, and the raw power promised by expanding national capital markets.[4] Others stressed the conjoined role of liberal ideology and the overwhelming influence of dominant class interests.[5] In a complementary fashion, economic analyses tended to stress the pressures towards openness that arose from technological change and financial innovation. More disaggregated studies, however, tended to argue that expanded financial openness was rooted in unique patterns of domestic politics and in the consequences of earlier neo-liberal policy decisions that inclined away from state-directed solutions to resource allocation problems and towards private market solutions.[6] In truth, there was enough evidence to support and to cast doubt on any single mono-causal theory. By the turn of the century, a widespread consensus existed on the need for a dynamic model of policy change and market deepening.

Less consensus existed, however, on the consequences of increasing international capital mobility. In the wake of severe payments crises in many developing countries during the 1980s, and even more clearly in the aftermath of episodes of massive capital flight from prominent Asian and Central European countries in the 1990s, some analysts diagnosed a widening gap between the emergent economic structure and established political institutions incapable of managing that emergence.[7] The connection between this gap and periodic financial panics around the world seemed obvious. This led some to the view that the scale and durability of international capital movements were now constitutive of a new regime in world politics, a regime that made it increasingly difficult for states to diverge from norms of appropriate policy behaviour set in dominant national economies.

Relatively open financial markets were not, in fact, new in world politics. Conditions approximating today's global finance existed before 1914 among the most advanced economies and their dependencies. The extremities of war and economic depression succeeded in disrupting a system of economic adjustment that accommodated, even necessitated, international capital flows. The system, which dated back to the 1870s, rested on a rough consensus among the principal trading nations. At the centre of that consensus lay a

version of the gold standard, backed by the wealth and power of Great Britain. In theory, if not always in practice, the behavioural norms embedded in the system prescribed relatively passive domestic policy responses to external economic changes. British statecraft, and British politics, provided the key to actual practice. The situation changed completely in 1914.

Among other shifts in the tectonic plates of world politics, the tumultuous era that began with World War I witnessed the rise of the modern democratic nation-state, whose citizens expected it to ensure their military security and, increasingly, their economic security. Following the catastrophe of the Great Depression, those national expectations defined the terrain upon which the post-World War II intergovernmental consensus on monetary issues was constructed and, more fundamentally, upon which that consensus evolved in subsequent years. The contemporary reconstruction of global capital markets is intimately linked to the disruption of that consensus in the 1970s and the dawn of a new era of flexible exchange rates. As the twentieth century came to a close, however, it was not yet evident that the expectations of citizens concerning the responsibilities of democratic nation-states had substantively changed. Much rhetoric to the contrary notwithstanding, national welfare states continued to exist. Their financing, however, now confronted the reality of open capital markets. Although, again, such markets were not unprecedented in modern history, it *was* unprecedented to combine the policy preferences supporting them with the acceptance of political responsibility by states for the broadly defined security of their citizens.

Often abstracting from the fact that governments can let their exchange rates float, as the twentieth century came to a close economic commentators, prominent bankers, and conservative politicians frequently underscored the internal 'discipline' on autonomous state action implied by international capital mobility. If that discipline implied cutting back the welfare states of the post-World War II era, they asserted, then so be it. Many of their opponents on the left may have disliked such a conclusion, but they intuitively understood its logic. Indeed, a mounting body of popular literature written by both conservatives and radicals in the 1990s envisaged the consolidation of a new global order, the borderless order of advanced capitalism.

Whether they embraced it or loathed it, such a vision tended to be evoked in the language of inevitability. Enjoining governments to yield to signals emanating from the 'global market', this language implied that a profound shift in policy-making authority was necessarily taking place, a shift away from the national level. Proponents typically extolled the surrender of the retrograde idea of 'sovereignty' to the rational economic logic of markets beyond national control. Opponents might not have liked such a conclusion, but their own research bolstered the notion that transnational coalitions beyond the nation-state increasingly exercised determinative influence over a widening range of economic policies.

Sovereignty has, in fact, always been a contested concept. But conflating it with the notion of policy autonomy is needlessly confusing. A turning away from deeper financial integration by individual states or by the collectivity of states remained entirely conceivable, indeed, some did turn away as severe debt crises confronted them in the 1980s and 1990s. In this sense, states remained as 'sovereign' as they had ever been. In practical terms, however, there was no doubt late in the twentieth century that most states confronted tighter economic constraints—or clearer policy trade-offs—as a consequence of a freer potential flow of capital across their borders. This is the flip side of the opportunities for accelerated growth (beyond that capable of being financed by domestic savings) that can be presented by that same flow of capital. Again, the phenomenon itself is not new. What is new is the widespread perception that all states, all societies, and all social groups are now affected. In light of the historical record, such a perception is ironic. Most importantly, it blurs important distinctions between and within states. Underneath the overt discourse on sovereignty and efficient capital markets, there lay a covert discourse on power, legitimacy, and hierarchy.

If effective governing authority has been usurped by global capital markets, or if such authority has surreptitiously been devolved to those markets by states themselves, surely questions are raised about the process by which such a shift has taken place and about the obligation of citizens to comply. There remains today only one place where such questions can be directed and satisfactorily addressed. And whether we conceive of it as an arena, a structure, or a set of institutions, that place is called the state.

Exchange rate regimes tell us a great deal about the internal choices states make when they seek to harness the benefits of economic openness without incurring unacceptable costs. Again, the sum of those choices during the past few decades underlies contemporary international capital markets. But those markets were not actually built by economic happenstance. They reflect a political project that was shaped mainly by the domestic priorities and external strategies of leading states. Open capital markets increase the range of external policy choices for those states. Within them, such markets expand opportunities for firms and individuals with the wherewithal to take advantage of them. Through those markets, in turn, the priorities and normative preferences of those states, those firms, and those individuals are projected onto other states.

Nevertheless, sweeping general conclusions in this regard are unsatisfying. Even if it is shrinking, room remains for national variation in response to the opportunities and constraints presented by open capital markets. By their nature, moreover, private capital markets obfuscate distributive issues. Indeed, this is arguably the principal reason why their existence correlates so closely with democratic governing systems. Some will win, some will lose, dominant market participants will increasingly define standards for others, but the political blame for such outcomes will be diffused. As the twentieth century came to a close, however, a series of financial crises reminded everyone that those markets could not and did not manage themselves. Throughout the preceding five decades, it was precisely in such a context that certain new kinds of international institutions were designed.

## International Institutions and the New Financial Order

Early in the period between the two great wars of the twentieth century, leading states tried with an increasing sense of urgency to build institutional foundations for a global economy. During the 1920s, a general consensus had been achieved at the level of principle. A bulwark of peace lay within reach if that consensus, which today would be labelled classically liberal and which hinged on a workable gold standard and more open capital markets, could be put into practice. That dream proved to be a disastrous illusion with the stock market crash of 1929 and the onset of the Great Depression.

Following World War II, as we have seen, leading states combined a solid military alliance with a modified set of liberal economic principles. As the international economic system set in train evolved, these states never made stark and irrevocable decisions to favour financial openness above all other economic objectives, but they did adjust a widening range of internal policies to promote and accommodate potentially more mobile international capital flows. In this light, they also shaped or reshaped the mandates of international organizations like the International Monetary Fund (IMF), the World Bank, the Bank for International Settlements (BIS), the Organization for Economic Co-operation and Development (OECD), and less formal networks like the Group of Seven.

As implied above, the Bretton Woods system depended on a rule-based form of international co-operation, specifically on an interstate legal agreement to collaborate through one particular multilateral organization—the IMF. The original Articles of Agreement of the IMF specified certain rules to guide the exchange rate policies of members and gave the organization the power both to sanction justified changes in exchange rates and to provide temporary financing in cases where such changes were not required. Governments did not formally have to co-ordinate their internal monetary and fiscal policies in order to keep their exchange rates stable. The discipline of exchange rate rules, it was hoped, would automatically promote necessary adjustments in internal policies.

In practice, the rules of the game were often honoured in the breach and the IMF was frequently marginalized. When the system worked, it actually depended on a low degree of international capital mobility and on the willingness of the United States to keep its import markets open and its domestic price level stable, thereby providing to its trading partners an adequate supply of liquidity at a reliable price. In any event, technical innovation and policy liberalization in leading currency markets, as well as the financial implications of rapidly rising foreign direct investment, combined to make it ever more difficult to control short-term capital movements. At the same time, inflationary macroeconomic policies in the United States eventually rendered the country an unreliable monetary anchor.

Since the 1970s, efforts to stabilize key exchange rates by way of concerted action or negotiated policy co-ordination have been episodic. In general, the major powers have relied on the assumption that exchange rates would stabilize in the long run if anti-inflationary macroeconomic policies were pursued independently. In short, they are convinced that internal self-discipline, now modestly reinforced by formal surveillance procedures within international organizations like the IMF and the OECD, would have salubrious external effects.[8] Such a shared consensus was logically required if the new priority actually accorded to international capital mobility was not to prove politically disruptive.

To be sure, many states continued to rely on various measures to influence the inflow or outflow of short-term capital. (In Latin America in the 1980s and East Asia during the 1990s, those countries that did not at least moderate the term-structure of their foreign liabilities came to grief when financial panics led to a herd-like withdrawal of external credit.) In the wake of disruptive bouts of capital flight in a number of countries, for example, such measures would sometimes be acquiesced in by other states and by the IMF. But that approval, whether formal or tacit, was almost always now conditional on an understanding that new capital controls would be temporary. After the late 1970s, in short, capital decontrol came ever more clearly to define a normative objective of international economic policy among the leading states and, increasingly, among others who saw no feasible alternative on the horizon.

After 1989, that policy line informed a widening of the scope of the Capital Movements Code devised by the OECD, whose membership was also expanding beyond the advanced industrial countries. This paralleled continuing work on crafting new rules to govern longer-term investment, in both the OECD and the World Trade Organization, and on clarifying and promoting best financial supervisory practices through the BIS and other organizations. In the late 1990s, the same basic objective was behind a hotly debated effort by leading states to expand the formal legal jurisdiction of the IMF beyond the current account of national payments balances and into the capital account.[9]

The reluctance of states unambiguously to embrace the capital mobility norm, their handling of periodic emergencies in international capital markets in an ad hoc manner, and their preference not clearly to designate an international organizational overseer for truly integrated capital markets all suggest deeper concerns. Continuing controversies on these points revolve around traditional issues of power and authority. The legitimacy of a new order tending in the direction of global financial integration remains in question. More fundamentally, the struggle suggests that the architects of such an order cannot easily calibrate emergent market facts with persistent political realities. In short, they cannot lodge ultimate political authority over global finance at the level where it logically belongs. Like subnational governments in a confederation trying to establish a fully integrated national market while retaining all substantive economic powers themselves, contemporary states have a problem.

One does not need to be an extremist to sense the dimensions of the problem. One only needs to observe market and governmental reactions to the financial crises that characterize any order reliant on private markets. Such markets may be 'efficient' in

the long run, but they have always been prone to 'manias, crashes, and panics' in the short run.[10] Since 1945, prompted by periodic emergencies, advanced industrial states regularly engaged in efforts to manage that proclivity. In a global financial order, crises with potentially devastating systemic effects can begin in all but the poorest countries. From Mexico in 1982 and 1995 to Russia, East Asia, and Latin America in the late 1990s, many national disasters threatened to become catastrophes for the international experiment in financial integration. But who was truly responsible for the necessary bailouts and for their sometimes perverse effects? Who would actually be held responsible if the panicked reaction to financial turbulence in one country threatened to bring down large commercial and investment banks and bank-managed investment funds around the world? 'No one', a number of practitioners and analysts now say, for the authority to manage global finance has dispersed into the supranational ether. I disagree. Despite the obfuscation of accountability always implied in private market regimes, the actual crises of the late twentieth century continued to suggest that national governments would be blamed and that they would respond.

The desire to avoid such an end-game in the new world of international capital mobility provides the driving force behind the latest round of multilateral and regional efforts to clarify, strengthen, and rationalize the mandates of international financial institutions. The same dynamic reinforces internal pressures within many states to move towards 'independent' central banks. In the best case, technocratic agencies promise to promote common standards of financial regulation and supervision around the world, design functional programs for crisis avoidance and crisis management, and provide mechanisms for states to collaborate with one another for mutual benefit. In the worst case, such agencies can take on the role of scapegoats, thus serving as a buffer in the political crises that would inevitably follow any systemic financial catastrophe.

What technocratic agencies cannot fundamentally address, however, are basic questions of social justice necessarily implied in any system where the mobility of capital is not matched by the mobility of people. This is another way of saying that the governments of states cannot shift ultimate regulatory power, or legitimate political authority, to the level of governance suggested by the term 'global finance'. Perhaps they do not yet need to do so, because the term exaggerates the reality of international financial integration at the dawn of a new century. But surely the vast majority of their citizens do not yet want them to do so. Only in Western Europe, within the restricted context of a regional economic experiment still shaped by the legacy of the most catastrophic war in world history, was a shift in power and authority beyond the national level in sight. Elsewhere, intensifying interdependence remained the order of the day as the citizens of still-national states sought the benefits of international capital mobility without paying the ultimate political costs implied by true integration.

Futurists now commonly speculate on the ultimate destination. Cosmopolitan liberals predict the inevitable rise of global governing systems. Populist radicals, unable to envisage such systems being democratic, fear the same. Pessimistic realists expect the re-emergence of controls on a broad scale if cycles of competitive currency depreciation re-emerge or if capital mobility does not work to the benefit of the many instead of just the few. The rest of us are left to contemplate a dilemma created by the conflicting logics of global economics and local politics that cannot not be resolved but could, with a bit of skill and a bit of luck, continue to be managed.

## Notes

1  The chapter draws on and develops themes from *Who Elected the Bankers?*, cited below. Support from the Social Sciences and Humanities Research Council of Canada is gratefully acknowledged.

2  Peter Kenen, *The International Economy*, 3rd edn (Cambridge: Cambridge University Press, 1994), ch. 15.

3  For recent overviews, see Benjamin J. Cohen, 'Phoenix Risen: The Resurrection of Global Finance', *World Politics* 48, 2 (1996); David M. Andrews and Thomas D. Willett, 'Financial Interdependence and the State: International Monetary Relations at Century's End', *International Organization* 51, 3 (1997).

4  See, for example, Philip G. Cerny, 'The Deregulation and Reregulation of Financial Markets in a More Open World', in Cerny, ed., *Finance and World Politics: Markets, Regimes and States in the Post-Hegemonic Era* (Aldershot, UK: Elgar, 1993); David M. Andrews, 'Capital Mobility and State Autonomy: Toward a Structural Theory of International Monetary Relations', *International Studies Quarterly* 38 (1994).

5  See, for example, Stephen Gill, 'Globalisation, Market Civilisation and Disciplinary Neo-liberalism', *Millennium* 24, 3 (Winter 1995).

6  See, for example, Andrew Sobel, *Domestic Choices, International Markets* (Ann Arbor: University of Michigan Press, 1994); Geoffrey Garrett, 'Capital Mobility, Trade, and the Domestic Politics of Economic Policy', *International Organization* 49 (1995).

7  See Louis W. Pauly, 'Capital Mobility, State Autonomy, and Political Legitimacy', *Journal of International Affairs* 48, 2 (1995); Geoffrey Underhill, 'Keeping Governments out of Politics: Transnational Securities Markets, Regulatory Cooperation, and Political Legitimacy', *Review of International Studies* 21, 3 (1995).

8  A system that would force such discipline by way of pegged (fixed, but adjustable when underlying conditions warranted) exchange rates was widely viewed as infeasible. Indeed, at the end of the 1990s, the mainstream view suggested that individual states faced an ever starker choice between allowing their currencies to float or fixing their exchange rates irrevocably. See Barry Eichengreen,

*International Monetary Arrangements for the 21st Century* (Washington: Brookings Institution, 1994).

9   See Stanley Fischer et al., 'Should the IMF Pursue Capital-Account Convertibility?', *Essays in Inter-*

*national Finance* no. 207, Princeton University, Department of Economics, International Finance Section, May 1998.

10   Charles P. Kindleberger, *Manias, Crashes and Panics* (New York: Basic Books, 1978).

## Suggested Readings

Cohen, Benjamin J. *The Geography of Money*. Ithaca, NY: Cornell University Press, 1998.

Eichengreen, Barry. *Globalizing Capital*. Princeton, NJ: Princeton University Press, 1996.

Germain, Randall C. *The International Organization of Credit*. Cambridge: Cambridge University Press, 1997.

Helleiner, Eric. *States and the Reemergence of Global Finance*. Ithaca, NY: Cornell University Press, 1994.

Henning, C. Randall. *Currencies and Politics in the United States, Germany, and Japan*. Washington: Institute for International Economics, 1994.

James, Harold. *International Monetary Cooperation Since Bretton Woods*. New York: Oxford University Press, 1996.

Kirshner, Jonathan. *Currency and Coercion*. Princeton, NJ: Princeton University Press, 1995.

Maxfield, Sylvia. *Governing Capital*. Ithaca, NY: Cornell University Press, 1990.

McNamara, Kathleen. *The Currency of Ideas*. Ithaca, NY: Cornell University Press, 1998.

Murphy, Craig N. *International Organization and Industrial Change*. New York: Oxford University Press, 1994.

Pauly, Louis W. *Who Elected the Bankers?* Ithaca, NY: Cornell University Press, 1997.

Porter, Tony. *States, Markets and Regimes in Global Finance*. New York: St Martin's Press, 1993.

Sobel, Andrew. *State Institutions, Private Incentives, Global Capital*. Ann Arbor: University of Michigan Press, 1998.

Strange, Susan. *Mad Money*. Manchester: Manchester University Press, 1998.

## Web Sites

Bank of International Settlements: http://www.bis.org

International Monetary Fund's Searchable Publications Site: http://www.imf.org/pubind.htm

Organization for Economic Co-operation and Development: http://www.oecd.org

World Trade Organization: http://www.wto.org

## Chapter 9

# The Emerging World Financial Order and Different Forms of Capitalism

## Jonathan Story

Two views compete in the market for ideas on how to interpret the emerging world financial order. Economic optimists hold that financial markets have leaped free from government control and envisage a radiant future of 'convergence' where the world economy is at long last launched upon a voyage to integration. 'Within a generation', gasps *The Economist*, 'several [advanced industrial economies] are likely to be dwarfed by newly emerging economic giants.'[1] State-centric democrats and regulators have a more negative interpretation. Their main contention is that the imperfections in world markets derive from the distribution of corporate, state, and market power. World capitalism, they conclude, is in charge, and the populations of even advanced industrial states and regions are at the mercy of 'autonomised and globally uncontrollable, because global, forces'.[2]

Both views exaggerate. If capitalism were uncontrollable, determinism would reign and the future would be predictable. Neither is the case. Quite the contrary, the argument in this chapter is that global financial markets are the result of competing corporate and, above all, *divergent state policies and structures*, which provide significantly different sets of incentives for market participants. The dominant 'globalization vision' of the 1990s is stamped 'made in the USA', and has a 'One World' vision supposedly driving towards shared prosperity, democracy, and better living conditions for all. However, it failed to allow for capitalist diversity, complex interactions, and for '*la longue durée*'. The 1990s version of a One World vision was an impatient program in a hurry.

States are embedded in markets, alongside corporations, and both are also members of the world system or society of states. Abstractly, relations among states, corporations, and markets may be presented in triangular form: state-state, state-firm, and firm-firm.[3] Over time, political systems secrete divergent structures and performances that, in an increasingly interdependent world, become a main cause of turbulence in world markets and politics. Contrasting financial systems lie at the heart of the divergent forms of corporate governance that underpin differing forms of capitalism in world markets. States are participants in, and not separate from, the financial markets they have jointly contributed to create.

## From Different Systems to Global Capitalism

Sometime in the course of the 1970s, the world embarked on four simultaneous, interactive but non-synchronized processes of transformation involving world markets, the norms of state governance, the way that corporations were managed, and the state system itself. After World War II, none in the Bretton Woods discussions (see introduction to this section) wanted to return to orthodox gold standard economics. Both world wars demonstrated that governments could organize national production and consumption on a grand scale, and the interwar years of financial instability stood as a reminder of the dangers of attempts to return to the market-driven ways of the past. Not least, the Soviet Union continued to wage war on capitalism.

The central idea of the Bretton Woods accords of 1944 was that governments were inherently mercantilist in their promotion of domestic industries, their channelling of credit, and their protectionist tendencies. National economic expansion to meet citizens' demands for higher living standards was a government responsibility, for which an extensive array of policy instruments was available. But governments were also beholden to co-operate with the Bretton Woods institutions and, among themselves, to regulate jointly the markets of the world. Optimally, the visionaries of the postwar world economy looked forward to enlightened governance of peoples by officials of international organizations, rather than by the well-heeled denizens of world financial markets. Short-term capital movements were to be kept figuratively under lock and key, and currencies were to be fixed at a rate of $35 to an ounce of gold.

This postwar government-centred design for the world economy, inspired by the ideals of liberal internationalism but implemented within the bounds of the Western containment policy, proved an unprecedented success. Fifty years on, the rising tide of wealth had lifted most boats. Continuous expansion brought extraordinary improvement in living conditions as child death rates tumbled, along with malnutrition and illiteracy, for between 3 and 4 billion people.[4] At the same time, however, the gaps in income between the richest 20 per cent and poorest 20 per cent of countries widened from a ratio of 30:1 in 1960 to 60:1 in the 1990s, with the gap between the richest 20 per cent of the world population and the poorest 20 per cent widening to 150:1 in terms of the three broad categories mentioned above.

Growing inequalities among peoples was only one major imbalance in the world economy. Another was government spending in rich countries, which jumped from an average among advanced industrialized countries of about 28 per cent of GDP in 1960 to 43 per cent in 1980. Ten years later, spending was up to 45 per cent, and the upward creep continued into the 1990s. The main source of the spending boom was an explosion in public transfers and subsidies, in good times as in

bad. Elected politicians learned that re-election was best secured by having governments issue 'securities' (bonds) to cover expenditures rather than raise taxes. Financial institutions discovered the virtues of trading this abundant volume of paper in a liquid world market, thus boosting global capital markets enormously. The share of the world financial market that was liquid and tradeable grew at the expense of the market being under governments' control, i.e., the domestic money supply. 'Bretton Woods' was undermined by fiscal excess; governments often wail at the consequences but they were willing participants in this process.

Imbalances also derived from interstate disagreements about sharing the burden of adjustment to competition in world markets. These disagreements became more salient once the industrialized countries moved in the late 1950s to a partial liberalization of capital movements. Dollar and sterling balances began to build up abroad, but both Washington and London considered that international imbalances were due to trade discrimination in the EU and Japan and that continued growth in the world economy required easy money and expansionary public finances. In August 1971, US President Richard Nixon announced an end to the dollar's convertibility into gold, thereby terminating the US economy's role as anchor of the world financial system. Within two years, the major currencies had abandoned fixed exchange rates.

The two surges in world oil prices followed, as did the recycling of funds that could not be consumed by oil-producing states onto the world dollar markets, located in London and New York. Commercial banks lent dollars to oil-importing states, especially in Central and Eastern Europe, Africa, and Latin America. Real interest rates on the international markets stayed around zero, so borrowers flocked there and banks fell over each other to lend. This was the period when Portugal, Spain, and Greece showed the way to what became a political contagion of transition towards representative forms of government around the globe. Meanwhile, the end of the cheap oil era accelerated the rise of the two champion export economies, Germany and Japan, confirmed the dollar as emperor on world financial markets, and kept the moribund Soviet economy alive for a further couple of decades.

The decade of the 1970s saw a sharpening of the 'struggle for market share'[5] among advanced industrial states. During the mid-century boom, they had all adopted the formalized idiom of Keynesian economics to explain their policies. But their very different reactions to the oil crises of the 1970s revealed the peculiarities of their domestic structures.[6] The opposite ends of the spectrum in policy were allotted to the United States as a paragon of liberal markets and to Japan as the successful practitioner of a mercantilist strategy characterized by extensive intervention by state institutions in the market. France, Germany, and Italy were somewhere in between, with the UK tilting the US way. This more jaundiced view of Western economic policies pointed to differences in internal structures as the source of conflicts in international relations between states.

In October 1979, the mood in the United States and Europe turned in favour of price stability, and the US Federal Reserve engineered a worldwide rise in interest rates. Debtors were figuratively strangled by the high interest rates, and in 1982 the markets responded to the debt crises in Latin America by 'securitization' of commercial bank debts. Bank debts were converted to bonds. The 1982 switch to securities opened the prolonged boom on world capital markets. The exponential development of wholesale capital markets was driven by the growth of government and corporate bond markets, as the United States and European states vied for world savings and the world's corporations raised capital by issuing shares. New York and Chicago set the pace in breaking down the inherited barriers to efficient financial markets and were followed by London, Paris, and Amsterdam, with Frankfurt and Tokyo in the rear. Poorer indebted countries were squeezed until their figurative pips squeaked. Global daily trade in foreign exchange markets shot up from $15 billion in 1973 to $1,200 billion in 1995, or 60 to 100 times the average turnover of trade in physical goods.[7]

US President Ronald Reagan and British Prime Minister Margaret Thatcher set themselves the goal of strengthening the role of the market as the main co-ordinating device for the world polity. The crusade to roll back the state gathered force in the 1980s, while corporations felt their way towards operating as transnationals and the leading financial centres competed to end capital controls. The collapse of the Soviet empire transformed the world system of states.

In the pivotal year of 1990, freeing of short-term capital flows in Europe and German unity marked the end of the Cold War structure that had simultaneously contained communism and capitalism. With savings able to go in search of the highest remuneration, the assumptions informing the Bretton Woods accords, whereby governments should manage their national economies, were undermined because unregulated markets were not to be trusted. In addition, the resolution of the 1980s Latin American debt crisis under a plan advanced by US Treasury Secretary Brady enabled mid-income indebted countries to restructure their debt to commercial banks through officially supported debt reduction programs tied to broad policies of liberalization, stabilization, and privatization. Brady's debt relief plan spurred Mexico to negotiate NAFTA with the United States and Canada, while Brazil and Argentina formed the MERCOSUR customs union with Uruguay and Paraguay. This enabled one Latin American government after another to embark on policies of trade liberalization and privatization, combined with domestic institutional reforms and the introduction of more welcoming foreign direct investment (FDI) regimes. The formula was then applied to Poland, with success, and to Russia, with a redounding failure. A global financial system was emerging rapidly, dominated by short-term capital flows and promoted by widespread economic liberalization policies.

The Soviet collapse converted the world into Western corporations' metaphorical oyster. Its most immediate effect was to precipitate upwards of 3 billion people from the former Soviet Union, Central and Eastern Europe, China, and India onto a *world* labour market. If current demographic trends continue, these 3 billion people will increase to 6 billion by 2025. The average cost of labour around the world fell correspondingly. The implication for high-wage countries was that their relative wage was bid down at home as immigration rose or as companies disinvested and moved to cheaper wage locations. With local governments strapped for cash and eager to attract investment, Western corporations accelerated the adoption of global strategies, such as integrated production and marketing strategies intended to reconcile the contradictory exigencies of competition in world markets, and the need to be responsive to local conditions. In the late 1980s investment flowing to developing countries had been 15–18 per cent of the total recorded, but in the 1990s flows to developing countries leapt to 30–40 per cent. The overwhelming proportion of FDI went to the countries of the Asia-Pacific, notably to China. New technologies facilitated the process as corporations learned to integrate their component manufacturing processes and flexible manufacturing enabled distinct markets to be serviced at low cost.

Developing countries were eager to tap global capital markets to finance their balance of payments or to accelerate the build-up of their productive capacity. This entailed reforming their financial systems to meet investors' demands for liquidity or for transparent information about local opportunities. The set of principles equated with such policy shifts came to constitute the new model of economic development, loosely referred to as the 'Washington consensus', in favour of market liberalization, privatization, and stabilization.

Private capital in the 1990s flowed in unprecedented volumes to 'emerging markets'. The ranks of net suppliers of funds to the markets widened from the initial list of the US and the UK on capital account to the financial surplus from oil-producing states, and to Germany and Japan as chronic trade surplus countries. Central banks, financial institutions, and corporations, all in varying form protected from bankruptcy, placed their surpluses and took their bets in the world casino.[8] The rich from Latin America and Africa, and nomenklatura from the Communist Party states, joined the party. World foreign exchange, government and corporate bonds, and equities formed a seamless web to span the whole risk-and-return spectrum.

Whether or not governments of developing countries were far advanced in reform, the markets often would form a favourable view of their declared intentions and rush to buy assets in the local currency. They could choose between direct investment, buying a long-term stake in a company, and participating in company earnings through capital gains or dividends. The frequent result was a local boom fuelled by cheap credit, a surge in real estate prices, an appreciation of the exchange rate, and a widening deficit on external accounts. If the investment climate turned sour, fleet-footed financial institutions could sell and move into alternative investments in sunnier climes. But in Mexico in December 1994, and again in East Asia in 1997–8, they left behind devalued currencies, governments in disrepute, bankruptcies, and rising unemployment.

The world financial markets had, in effect, become judge and jury of the world economy. Nothing escaped their attention. National economic performances were judged in the foreign exchange markets. Government policies were assessed through the bond markets. Corporate returns were measured through the world's integrated corporate bond and equity markets. Their verdict was recorded in the risk-assessment agencies of the major financial capitals that consigned credit ratings on currencies, bonds, or shares. A rise in the credit ratings of, say, Moody's or Standard and Poor's would lower the cost of capital, while a negative verdict would raise the cost of capital for firms as for governments. Some governments, currencies, or firms were treated with more respect than others, for most of the time, but if governments did not respond to the markets' policy prescriptions, the markets' sanction was to withdraw confidence. They could not impose policies on sovereigns who refused to comply, but they could make the cost of non-compliance very high.

## National Financial Systems, Corporate Governance, and Models of Capitalism

Thus far we have reviewed how the global financial order emerged in the postwar period. We can now turn to consider how different models of capitalism

## Figure 1: Market Competition, Corporate Strategy, and National Structures

| | | |
|---|---|---|
| **HIGH** | **Anglo-American Shareholder System**<br>large, listed firms<br>oligopolistic competition<br>diversification<br>trade, foreign investment<br>larger, limited government<br>extensive regulation | **German-Japanese Corporate System**<br>large conglomerates<br>corporate cross-shareholding<br>diversification<br>trade, foreign investment<br>distinct government structures<br>'self'-regulation pervasive |
| CORPORATE CONCENTRATION | **The Bretton Woods Ideal**<br>small, family firms<br>price competition<br>specialization<br>international trade<br>minimal government | **French State Capitalism**<br>state allocates capital<br>lobbying skills<br>state/family enterprises<br>'cohesion' policies<br>pervasive government |
| **LOW** | | |

CONCENTRATION OF OWNERSHIP

LOW ◄──────────────────────────────► HIGH

are structured and how they interact with one another in world markets. As institutionalist economists point out, how the markets are structured, what values are embedded in the prevailing rules, and which organizations develop within the range of prevailing incentives make all the difference to outcomes.[9] Economic policy within and between states is thus about different conceptions of politics and distinct patterns of policy process. Different models involve different patterns of corporate governance, underpinned by contrasting financial market systems. The muddle at the heart of the Washington consensus was that no final choice was made by market participants about which of the many capitalist models on offer should meet with their approval. A variety of capitalist models were on display after the end of the Cold War that developing countries were invited to learn from.

Corporate strategy is understood here as the link between the external capital market, populated by shareholders and financial institutions, and the internal allocation of corporate resources.[10] Given the nature of oligopolistic competition among few corporations in a particular sector and the variety of states in world markets, such differing conditions provide diverse incentives affecting the strategies of firms.[11] The corporate population of different states may therefore be presented along two dimensions, as illustrated in Figure 1: one dimension is the concentration of ownership, whether dispersed among a wide public or concentrated in the hands of a few institutions; the other is the degree of corporate concentration in terms of assets, sales, and numbers employed.

This matrix provides four models: the implicit model of the Bretton Woods institutions, and three distinct types: the Anglo-American shareholder system; the German or Japanese system of cross-shareholding; and the French statist model, which has many variants around the world.[12] In effect, the Bretton Woods institutions assume that mercantilism is the norm, and that countries and companies may be induced towards an ideal of open markets and thus avoid the worst of self-centred behaviour. We shall use the matrix here to portray different corporate governance and financial market systems and to stylize the dynamics of changing regimes prevailing in states as homes or as hosts to global corporations. States have three options with regard to foreign investment: they may favour direct investment, be hostile to it, or prefer to sponsor international partnerships. As a fifth variant, which straddles the boundaries between our stylized types, we sketch some features of non-Japanese East Asian business systems.

## The Bretton Woods Ideal Model

The starting point must be the implicit model of an ideal state that has informed much of the activities of the Bretton Woods institutions. According to this model, minimum government is a vital complement to an open economy composed of small family farms and firms that compete sharply on price. Their survival depends on specialization and on predictable business conditions. These are best secured by effective government policing of local markets to prevent abuses and by binding agreements on international free trade. A firm from a 'Bretton Woods ideal' country is content with exporting until foreign governments threaten to impose duties or quotas, at which point the exporter decides to invest abroad to ensure continued market access. The government gets into the business of making the country an attractive target for foreign corporate investments through such policies as light taxation and support for education.

## The Anglo-American Shareholder System

In the US and the UK, managerial hierarchies ran large, publicly quoted and diversified corporations and predominated over shareholder interests until the sweeping changes in the tightly linked financial markets of New York, Chicago, and London in the 1970s and 1980s. The revival of shareholder capitalism in both countries drew on a legal tradition, which regards companies as private entities set up

by investors for their own benefit, who in turn hire managers to conduct business. Managers keep constant track of input costs, such as labour, raw materials, and capital, and seek the most efficient use of state-of-the-art technologies or organizational practices to produce goods or services that provide value for the consumer at attractive prices.

Corporate financing is provided by short-term funds from commercial banks, but the major source of external funds for firms is the capital market. Shares of corporations are held by the public, either directly or through institutional investors such as pension funds, and are actively traded. This Anglo-American system gives priority to the shareholder in the payment of dividends even when profits are down. If shareholders sell, then the corporation is vulnerable to takeover as predators bid to buy shares, sometimes with advice from investment banks, at a premium to the market. This market for corporate assets facilitates corporate mergers and restructurings,[13] and is legitimated on the grounds of providing the most efficient set of incentives for all participants in the market to maximize wealth.

Hence, both the US and UK governments have sought a shareholder-driven corporate economy, underpinned by a 'shareholder democracy', whereby the voting public participates in the performance of corporations and in the rewards. Supporters also argue that free markets are the most compatible with political democracy as a system of limited government. Free financial markets allocate savings to the most efficient, not politically determined investments. Labour market legislation in particular has to be supportive, so that labour forces may be shrunk or shifted in task or location with the minimum of friction. The model also assumes (crucially) that the government will not prove a light touch for corporate lobbies seeking to avoid restructuring or takeover through access to the public purse as a less demanding source of funds.

Government's major tasks are to provide the regulatory and legal structure within which open capital markets may function and to supply a safety net for the unemployed, the infirm, and the old. Consumer and shareholder interests are assumed to be paramount. Managers and workers must sweat to earn their keep. Domestic markets are deliberately kept open to foreign competitors and to inward investors. Government policy is predicated less on giving political advantage to national producers than on satisfying the demands of national shareholders and consumers. What the nationality of the shareholders may be is less important than the performance of the corporation. Its performance is best assured by diversifying the locations of its businesses to avoid downturns in any single national market. Both US and UK corporations have worldwide reach.

## The German-Japanese Cross-Shareholding System

The German and Japanese cross-shareholding systems have significant institutional differences, but also share important similarities. Both countries were late industrializers and promoted universal banks taking deposits and investing shares in order to accelerate industrial growth. Both fostered the development of large corporate conglomerates in private hands and sought to reduce trade and financial dependency on foreign sources. Managers were placed in the driving seats of corporate Germany and Japan, along with bureaucracies and political parties, and their powers were legitimated by appeals to corporate or national loyalties[14] or through mechanisms to promote worker participation.[15] Labour policy and capital markets were designed to achieve a cohesive national polity and to overcome the wounds of the wars, rather than as a means to create an 'efficient' economy.

Financial markets in both economies were highly regulated to ensure monetary stability and to protect depositors from bank failure. In both the German and Japanese financial systems of corporate control, the internal market to allocate resources *within* corporations took precedence over the demands of the external capital market. The portion of shares floating freely on the market is small, so that stock markets may be thin and volatile as investors (including foreigners) move in and out of shares. Thus, many of the market disciplinary

functions performed by impersonal capital markets on companies must be generated by the *insider* élites of corporations and financial institutions— the managers. Their attention is therefore focused on the battlefield in product markets rather than on their share performance.

This is possible because, in both Germany and Japan, large, diversified corporations also protect themselves against takeover threats in the share markets by dispersing shares among each other and among financial institutions. Shareholders thereby enjoy institutional representation on the boards of the companies whose shares they hold and whose boards they share. In Germany, employees are also represented, and act against hostile takeovers as additional allies with roots in the labour markets. To avoid pressure from external creditors, the best condition for corporations with high fixed costs is to achieve self-financing by building market share. The bank-industrial crossholding system complements close domestic supplier-customer relationships, with dependability and co-operation often dominating price as transactions criteria.

Such a bank-industrial crossholding system, because of its very 'insider' characteristics, curtails foreign market access and ownership, while requiring open markets for exports and for corporate assets in other countries. The home market is the launch pad for the conquest of foreign markets, and the domestic market may be protected by all manner of corporate practices. The financial system as a whole must be prepared to deal with the consequences of large trade surpluses, which flow from joint corporate interest in market shares. Domestic inflationary pressures have to be kept down through rapid recycling of funds earned from exports. This entails building up portfolio investments in other markets around the world, revaluations of the currency, and foreign direct investments to avoid the high costs of domestic production. This is national mercantilism's Achilles' heel. Corporations become detached from banks as their external sources of funds on world markets grow, while regulatory segmentation within the financial system breaks down as financial institutions compete across boundaries for new clients.

## The State-led Financial Market System

France is the reference point for the model of top-down development through a state-led financial market system.[16] In terms of precedence, though, the title should arguably be awarded to Italy or Turkey. Typically, the state-led model of industrialization featured as some 'third way' between US capitalism and the Soviet system, and appealed to countries whose agriculture was backward, where small business predominated, and where larger corporations were few and often foreign-owned. In France, the Ministry of Finance regulated the capital market directly. Surplus funds of deposit-taking institutions were taken up by public-sector institutions that lent them to specific industries, such as housing, agriculture, nuclear energy, and regional investments.

Over time, the French state-led financial system promoted a queue. Organizations with close contacts and claims on the loyalties of public officials, such as state-controlled economic enterprises and large private firms, got served first. The regular cycle of local, regional, and national elections thus also became a series of contests between competing producer coalitions for a silver key to public finance. The whole edifice ground to a near halt when, in 1981, the new Mitterrand administration extended the public sector just as the external debt exploded and domestic savings shrank. France's financial market reforms of 1984–8 were introduced to promote Paris as an international centre and, above all, to lower the cost of government financing.

The legitimacy of the state officials in the system derives from a claim to act in the public interest, but patronage, too, flows through state officials. Institutions whose resources they deploy directly or indirectly expand their stakes in business enterprises, extending further the field open to public patronage in the pursuit of private promotion. Corporate cross-shareholdings centre on state entities, and top management positions in these firms thereby remain part of the career circuit for élite state officials in what is in effect a political market for corporate control. The stench of corruption and the odour of incompetence creep under the doors and float through the windows of the most exquisitely perfumed salons, and the ruling oligarchy's legitimacy becomes more, not less, difficult to defend.

Such a system is unsustainable. State-led capitalism by definition seeks to allocate national resources for national purposes. Foreign investors seek entry and bring necessary access to technologies, management skills, and foreign markets. Inward investors then compete with national producers on their home markets, and this prompts national producers to retaliate by entering international markets through both trade and investment. But as markets open to foreign competition, government officials find themselves immersed in an ocean of corporate details, about which they know next to nothing. The state finds itself torn between its old role and its new task of championing freer trade. As state capitalism's corporations internationalize, so its domestic purposes and methods must undergo fundamental revision. In the longer term, national corporations join their foreign corporate brothers and sisters as citizens on the world market stage.

## East Asian Business

East Asian countries rode on the coattails of the US and Japanese economies and remained aggressively pro-business and anti-Communist. They developed state capitalisms and relatively closed financial systems characterized by networks of cross-shareholdings among banks and producers. Accumulation proceeded apace, as they followed Japan up the value-added chain of production and exports.

East Asia's boom was further stimulated by the dollar's devaluation against the yen in the 10 years following the September 1985 G–5 Plaza Accord on exchange rates. With their currencies tied to a low dollar and foreign investment pouring in from Japan, Taiwan, Singapore, and Hong Kong, as well as from the United States and the European Union, East Asian exports grew at 20 per cent per annum. East Asian shares in world manufacturing exports shot up, along with growth rates and living standards. Not surprisingly, the East Asian 'growth model' attracted widespread interest around the world in the 1990s among the many countries exiting from import substitution. As the World Bank argued (with some support from the Development Bank of Japan):

> the body of East Asian evidence points to the dominant contribution of stable and competitive economic policies to the unleashing of private entrepreneurship. More often than not, the key to the policymaking process was the positive role of governments in charting a development course, creating a longer-term vision shared among key participants, and fashioning an institutional framework for nonideological and effective policy implementation.[17]

The model was Taiwan and its state élite,[18] not servants of the electorate so much as masters of the market, subordinating their private passions to the public interest.

The World Bank's story of the Asian miracle envisaged Japan and the overseas Chinese business community as the spearhead of Asia-Pacific's economic emancipation. In effect, Chinese business communities are family-based and patrimonial networks, where ownership is not divorced from management, the leadership style is autocratic, and relationships are personal.[19] As mainland China opened up to global economic trends, the overseas Chinese became its major source of inward investment and of foreign exchange earned through exports. By 2010 the East Asian region was expected to account for 34 per cent of the world's total output, with Western Europe and the United States at around 25 per cent each.[20] If South Asia were added, the figure came to 40 per cent. By 2020, the rest of the world, excluding the United States, the EU, and Japan, would equal 67 per cent of the world economy.

The conclusion was obvious: US and EU prosperity would come to depend rapidly on the prosperity of these regions. China and Japan would become alternative centres of power, once China had managed to implement further market reforms to sustain its rapid expansion and when Japan had decided finally to implement the liberalization measures announced in 1986 by Haruo Mayekawa, then governor of the Bank of Japan. Major changes in the global structure of wealth and power would occur within the coming two decades.

The forecasts understated Japan's growing difficulties and failed to accommodate the impact of China's emergence (see Chapter 33, by Breslin). In 1993, China devalued the yuan and entered into direct competition with exports from the Asia-Pacific. Then, in 1995, the US Federal Reserve allowed the dollar to rise against the yen to help the hard-pressed Mexican economy. East Asian exports slowed as their currencies rose against the yen. Savings flooded out of Japan and low-growth EU in search of higher returns in the small East Asian economies at the top of their 10-year boom. Boom abruptly turned to bust as the Asian crisis began and global financial market investors turned on their erstwhile darlings. Currencies and living standards plummeted, while the region's massive production potential, built up in previous decades, was thrust onto US or EU markets in a desperate bid to export or die.

Japan's deficiencies were the main cause of the meltdown in the Asia-Pacific economy in 1997–8. The Japanese economy had reached the end of its mercantilist trail: Japan's trade surplus meant that it effectively had to pay its overseas clients in the United States and in Asia for the products they bought because they could not buy enough yen through sales into Japanese markets. The world was thus treated to the phenomenon of the world's prime creditor facing bankruptcy. Blaming the problems of the world financial system on the 'crony capitalists' of Korea—the giant of Asia's developing countries—and on Southeast Asia's four mini-economies expressed the frustrations of losses incurred and also proved contagious. Once the critical language of 'crony capitalism' was in place, it did not take a genius to apply it generously, for instance, to Boris Yeltsin's Russia. Further, the decline in Asian demand for commodity imports reduced the revenues of commodity exporters in the Persian Gulf, Africa, the Americas, and Asia. Currencies duly adjusted, far too rapidly for comfort, risking further contagion and crisis in the financial markets of the West.

In retrospect, the difficulties affecting the countries of the Asia-Pacific in the late 1990s were a result of their previous successes. Japan had provided an example or model for many. The United States imported the region's goods, underwrote its security and trade, and exported American 'can-do' attitudes. Governments came to base their legitimacy on growth, meaning the expansion of capacity and the race for market share. This transformed their societies, created aspirations, extended interdependence between highly diverse societies, inflicted severe environmental damage, and prompted demands for political development. What the late 1990s revealed was that the old patterns of economic growth—overdependence on the US markets, a still narrow range of export products, and an emphasis on the simple expansion of capacity—was no longer sustainable. While Japan edged painfully towards opening its mind and economy, Asia-Pacific countries, notably Indonesia, moved further along the path to embrace representative government on which adaptable market societies depend.

## Conclusion

It is easy enough to see what happened when world history turned on its hinges in the years between 1989 and 1992. Fortified by 'One World' thinking and supported by global institutions (the IMF, the World Bank, the GATT), the US administration steered financial markets towards a prolonged roller-coaster of boom overall, and bust here and there. The idea was to persuade poorer countries to open to trade and to capital flows in return for an opening of Western markets to their products and for an encouragement of corporations to go global. Worldwide liberalization was to be accompanied by promotion of democracy, and with democracy would come a great era of peace.

The centre of the world economy was expected to slip inexorably to the Asia-Pacific. The implicit watchword of US foreign economic policy was 'no more Japans'. This went for China, too. Countries with national systems of corporate mercantilism

were seen as a major source of disequilibrium in the world economy. Hence the US-supported global institutions' proposals for governments to adopt what in retrospect appears overly hasty full currency convertibility and financial market liberalization. Participation in world business meant universal acceptance of adjustment to markets. But here lay the root of the world travails: governments had radically different views on bankruptcies, some emphasizing the importance of market clearance, but most more concerned to retain political support by their espousal of the too-big-to-fail principle. It was the Chinese diaspora's anticipation of President Suharto's inability to retain political support for adjustment, rather than for continued growth, that prompted them to move money offshore and to contribute thereby to the dramatic impoverishment of Indonesia.

In retrospect, it is clear that the year 1999 marks the end of the world's transition out of the Cold War structures to the new structure likely to shape the first half of the twenty-first century. In January, 11 countries in the EU had their bond markets, swollen by decades of government deficits, converted into Euros. National currencies, still circulating for retail purposes, were fixed at an unalterable price to the Euro. European corporations and governments could now finance their needs by recourse to a capital market the size of the US and in the knowledge that currency relationships were fixed. By 2002, retail payments are to be made in Euros. Given that the EU is a major world trader, the Euro will also develop as the other major trading currency, along with the dollar, and the world's second reserve currency for central banks.

There had been much speculation prior to 1999 about which type of financial system and corporate governance structure—French, German, or Anglo-American—the EU would move towards. There had been three scenarios:

- The continental states would move rapidly to an Anglo-American type of corporate finance, given the stimulation from large, liquid capital markets populated by financial institutions searching for corporate winners.

Shareholders and consumers would become the two kings of corporate strategy, to which managers would have to defer in a highly competitive US-type market.

- The continental states would not change corporate governance structures, predicated on the existence of national cross-shareholdings and on the search for market shares over profits. Governments would still consider trade surpluses to be virtuous and national labour market structures would remain much as before. The only change would be the greater facility afforded corporations in raising funds on the Euro-capital market.
- Some middle ground would be achieved: corporate managers would have plenty of incentive to raise capital to finance the intensive investments required to supply a market of 350 million people. Financial institutions would demand much higher returns for

shareholders than in national capital markets; but the traditions acquired of shareholder patience, existing national labour laws, and taxation differences would provide the basis for an EU-wide social-liberal compromise.

Which way will the EU go? All three imply major changes as the European economy restructures out of its national inheritances. The most probable path is that the different capitalisms in the EU will retain their distinctiveness, but that that distinctiveness will be notably different from inherited forms. The same can be said for the many variants of world capitalism. World financial markets will continue to absorb and transmit through the markets the many forms of capitalism that simultaneously evolve over time, interact, and compete. Politics and finance are inseparable twins in the future, as in the past, of the world's long march to integration.

## Notes

1  'The Global Economy: War of the Worlds', *The Economist*, 1 Oct. 1994.

2  Paul Hirst and Grahame Thompson, *Globalisation in Question* (London: Basil Blackwell, 1996).

3  John Stopford and Susan Strange, *Rival States, Rival Firms* (Cambridge: Cambridge University Press, 1991).

4  Figures from UN Development Program, *Human Development Reports* (annual), 1990–7.

5  Helmut Schmidt, 'The Struggle for the World Product', *Foreign Affairs* 52 (Apr. 1974).

6  See Peter Katzenstein, ed., *Between Power and Plenty: Foreign Economic Policies of Advanced International States* (Madison: University of Wisconsin Press, 1978).

7  Bank for International Settlements, *66th Annual Report 1995–96* (Basel: BIS, 1996), 95.

8  Susan Strange, *Casino Capitalism* (Oxford: Basil Blackwell, 1986); Strange, *Mad Money* (Manchester: Manchester University Press, 1998).

9  Douglas C. North, *Institutions, Institutional Change and Economic Performance: Political Economy of*

*Institutions and Decisions* (Cambridge: Cambridge University Press, 1991), 109.

10  See Michael Porter, 'Capital Disadvantage: America's Failing Capital Investment System', *Harvard Business Review* (Sept.-Oct. 1992).

11  C.K. Prahalad and Yves Doz, *The Multinational Mission: Balancing Local Demands and Global Vision* (New York: Free Press, 1987).

12  See Jonathan Story and Ingo Walter, *Political Economy of Financial Integration in Europe: The Battle of the Systems* (Manchester: Manchester University Press, 1998).

13  T.N. Rybczynski, 'Corporate Restructuring', *National Westminster Bank Review* (Aug. 1989).

14  James C. Abegglen and George Stalk, *Kaisha, the Japanese Corporation* (New York: Basic Books, 1985).

15  Wolfgang Streeck, 'German Capitalism: Does It Exist? Can It Survive?', in Colin Crouch and Wolfgang Streeck, eds, *Political Economy of Modern Capitalism: Mapping Convergence and Diversity* (London: Sage, 1997).

16  John Zysman, *Governments, Markets and Growth: Financial Systems and Politics of Industrial Change* (Oxford: Martin Robertson, 1983).

17  Danny M. Leipziger and Vinod Thomas, *The Lessons of East Asia: An Overview of Country Experience* (Washington: The World Bank, 1993).

18  See Robert Wade, *Governing the Market: Economic Theory and the Role of the Government in East Asian Industrialization* (Princeton, NJ: Princeton University Press, 1990).

19  S. Gordon Redding, *The Spirit of Chinese Capitalism* (Berlin: de Gruyter, 1993).

20  The story is elaborated in the OECD study, *The World in 2020: Towards a New Global Age* (Paris: OECD, Nov. 1997).

## Suggested Readings

Story, Jonathan. *The Frontiers of Fortune.* London: Pitman's, 1999.

Story, Jonathan, and Ingo Walter. *Political Economy of Financial Integration in Europe: The Battle of the Systems.* Manchester and Cambridge, Mass.: Manchester University Press/MIT Press, 1998.

Zysman, John. *Governments, Markets and Growth: Financial Systems and Policies of Industrial Change.* Oxford: Martin Robertson, 1983.

## Web Sites

Corporate Governance: http://www.corpgov.net/

Federal Reserve Board: http://federalreserve.gov/

Ministry of International Trade and Industry, Japan: http://www.miti.go.ip/index-e.html

Organization for Economic Co-operation and Development: http://www.oecd.org/

## Chapter 10

# The Group of Seven and Political Management of the Global Economy

## Michael C. Webb

### Introduction

The globalization of financial markets, begun with the emergence of the Euromarkets in the 1960s, accelerated during the 1980s and 1990s. Short-term financial capital now moves with great speed across national borders among the advanced capitalist countries (ACCs) and increasing numbers of so-called emerging market economies (EMEs). These flows generate international economic instability and pose serious problems for traditional tools of national economic policy, as well as for the achievement of broader political goals such as democratic accountability and government legitimacy. As cross-border economic links have grown, international co-operation has been widely seen as a mechanism for responding to these problems. This chapter examines the response of the Group of Seven (G–7) to the macroeconomic policy problems associated with financial globalization, assessing the character and effectiveness of G–7 policy co-ordination and the implications of G–7 action for the broader political goals of liberal and social democracy.

Broadly speaking, political action is essential both for promoting the growth of international markets and for coping with negative consequences of that growth, especially regarding social equity and stability.[1] Postwar international trade and monetary regimes were designed to promote a kind of international liberalization embedded in a prior concern for domestic economic and social stability.[2] The Bretton Woods system did so by matching trade liberalization with measures to shelter national macroeconomic stabilization policies from international market pressures. These measures included capital controls, balance-of-payments lending through the IMF, and co-ordinated intervention in foreign exchange markets to maintain fixed exchange rates in the face of differences in macroeconomic policies in different countries.

The growth of international capital mobility undermined the Bretton Woods compromise. International capital markets now react very quickly to differences in macroeconomic policies between countries, and especially to monetary policies. For example, a loosening of monetary policy in one country would cause an immediate capital outflow, as investors search for higher interest rates and lower inflation abroad. This would trigger an immediate depreciation of the national currency, a problem exacerbated by the tendency of foreign exchange markets to 'overshoot' appropriate levels. Open financial markets also can impart a deflationary bias to all countries' macroeconomic policies. If each central bank sets interest rates independently, those that set interest rates at relatively low levels will experience capital flight and currency depreciation. These may force them to raise interest rates to defend the currency, regardless of whether higher interest rates are appropriate in light of domestic conditions. The result can be to force interest rates in all countries up to the level of the country most determined to fight inflation, thereby slowing growth and raising unemployment for all. The risk of capital flight can also force governments to pursue restrictive fiscal policies even in the face of weak domestic demand and high unemployment. Finally, international capital mobility can create or exacerbate international financial crises, as investors' herd instincts drive excessive capital flows both into and out of particular countries or regions.

The G–7 has responded to the problems created by international capital mobility primarily by supporting the expansion and efficient functioning of international financial markets. Ideological convergence around orthodox norms for macroeconomic policy has been matched by convergence in economic performance around low inflation rates and shrinking budget deficits. But these have been accompanied by slow growth, serious economic instability, and growing economic inequality. Various possibilities for G–7 co-operation to ensure that the benefits of international trade and investment flow are distributed more widely have been proposed and considered. All involve some reassertion of political authority over markets. Macroeconomic policy co-ordination could reduce international payments imbalances and international economic instability, and in more ambitious forms could tackle slow growth and high unemployment through a co-ordinated pro-growth strategy, sometimes called global Keynesianism. Alternatively, the G–7 could co-operate to restore national macroeconomic policy-making autonomy, either by creating a more stable exchange rate system or by re-establishing government controls over destabilizing foreign exchange speculation. As we shall see, the G–7 has generally rejected these forms of political management in favour of further market liberalization, macroeconomic orthodoxy, and reforms to enhance international financial transparency. Ideology, the sheer technical difficulty of effective action in the face of open international capital markets, and traditional political differences have all contributed to this unbalanced approach to political management of the global economy.

But international policy co-ordination is not just a technical exercise for promoting international adjustment; it is also central to the resolution of broader political questions. The development of a more globally integrated economy has undermined the ways in which the problems of governmental legitimacy and democratic accountability were addressed domestically by individual ACCs, and has

posed them as international problems that need to be addressed at a level above that of the sovereign state. Liberal democratic theory assumed a territorial state in which there was a direct correspondence between the citizens affected by a government's decisions and the citizens who exercised democratic control over that government by virtue of the vote. Economic globalization undermines that correspondence. Governments must now be responsive to non-citizens (e.g., foreign currency traders), which makes them less able to respond to the democratically expressed preferences of their own citizens.[3]

The legitimacy of democratic capitalist governments has also rested in part on their economic performance. A key role of the capitalist state since the Great Depression has been to redistribute some of the fruits of economic development to those who do not share in the benefits distributed by the market, through such means as progressive taxation, social welfare programs, and full employment policies. Financial globalization makes it difficult for most governments to promote economic growth and reduce inequality with conventional Keynesian tools. But as Louis Pauly points out, 'citizens in democratic societies continue to hold the government of their own state, alone, responsible for widening economic prosperity.'[4] The inability of governments to meet these expectations undermines governmental legitimacy and contributes to the anti-government malaise affecting many ACCs in the 1990s.

I return to these arguments about democratic accountability and governmental legitimacy in the conclusions. The next two sections of this chapter examine the G–7 performance in managing the global economy in the 1990s in two key areas—monetary and fiscal policy co-ordination, and managing exchange rates and short-term capital flows.

## Monetary and Fiscal Policy Co-ordination

International capital mobility first became a serious problem for macroeconomic policy-making in the mid-1960s, with the emergence of the Eurodollar market in London. Governments tried to reduce capital flows that threatened fixed exchange rates and macroeconomic policy-making autonomy by tightening capital controls, but by the early 1970s it was apparent that this strategy could not succeed without controls so strict that they would interfere with desirable trade financing and foreign direct investment. Instead, most governments chose to let their exchange rates fluctuate, hoping that flexible exchange rates would adjust gradually to accommodate differences in macroeconomic policies in different countries. This faith in the automatic equilibrating tendencies of private markets underestimated how volatile flexible exchange rates would be in the new context of open capital markets. The 1970s, therefore, were characterized by severe exchange rate volatility and substantial international payments imbalances, as well as slow growth and rising unemployment in many ACCs.

Macroeconomic policy co-ordination as a response to these problems first became an important issue at the G–7 level in the late 1970s, when the United States persuaded Germany and Japan to reflate their economies as part of the 'locomotive strategy' for pulling the world economy out of the stagflation caused by the OPEC oil shock (the key deal was reached at the Bonn summit of 1978). Policy co-ordination lapsed in the early 1980s as the United States and other conservative G–7 governments focused on fighting inflation. But Reaganomics (tight monetary policy combined with huge budget deficits created by military spending and tax cuts) generated huge imbalances, most notably an overvalued dollar and a growing US trade deficit. Consequently, in 1985 the United States joined with other G–5 countries in co-ordinated intervention (announced in the September 1985 Plaza Accord) to bring the dollar down. By 1987 the United States had persuaded the reluctant Japanese and German governments to reflate in return for American commitments to reduce its budget deficit and to co-operate in stabilizing currencies. The key bargain was struck in the Louvre Accord of February 1987, though it was not until the October 1987 stock market crash that co-ordinated reflation began in earnest. But Japanese and West German reflation had the perverse impact of making it easier

for the United States to avoid serious efforts to reduce its budget deficit.

Capital continued to become more mobile during the 1980s, as private international market linkages flourished and official barriers between the financial capital markets of the industrialized countries were largely eliminated. Foreign exchange markets experienced spectacular growth, to the point that daily foreign exchange trading (estimated at $1.26 trillion in April 1995) now greatly exceeds the combined foreign exchange reserves of the industrialized countries (approximately $700 billion in 1995). These markets impose stricter constraints on national policy-making autonomy than those imposed by the Bretton Woods system's fixed exchange rate rules, and they have been extremely unstable.

International macroeconomic problems in the 1990s have stimulated discussion of two broad alternatives. The first would bring government policies more into conformity with market preferences, while the second favours active macroeconomic policy co-ordination to address world economic problems. The G–7 moved clearly in the first of these directions in the 1990s. The rhetorical tide turned strongly against discretionary macroeconomic management. G–7 communiqués rejected counter-cyclical Keynesian demand management in favour of price stability and reducing budget deficits. Central bankers meeting at the G–7 conferences reinforced each others' determination to keep interest rates up to prevent the emergence of inflationary pressures, while finance ministers encouraged their counterparts' efforts to cut spending and shrink deficits. Ideological convergence was accompanied by actual convergence of monetary and fiscal policies. Inflation rates fell sharply, and fiscal deficits shrank even in the face of lingering recession and high unemployment in most G–7 countries.

Nevertheless, orthodox rhetoric and international market constraints did not prevent the G–7 from occasionally attempting to co-ordinate macroeconomic policies. In particular, American efforts in the G–7 made Japanese policy less restrictive in the early 1990s, though not enough so to avoid prolonged stagnation or to meet American demands.

The German government rejected similar American calls for lower interest rates (high post-reunification interest rates were slowing European and world growth), both because it put a higher priority on containing inflation and because it no longer trusted Washington to fulfil any commitments it might make. There were some calls in the mid-1990s for a co-ordinated G–7 growth strategy to combat slow growth and high unemployment, but the G–7 explicitly rejected a Keynesian macroeconomic response to these problems. Macroeconomic policy, it argued, should emphasize price stability and fiscal consolidation. High unemployment should be addressed by deregulation to make labour markets more flexible.[5]

Despite the consistent rejection of the idea of co-ordinated macroeconomic stimulus, global demand stimulus was in fact generated by the United States. The US economy grew faster than its G–7 counterparts in part because the US Federal Reserve was more tolerant of inflation and kept interest rates low even when growth was strong. Rapid US growth generated strong demand for imports, which helped offset the global deflationary impact of Japanese recession and Bundesbank-led deflation in continental Europe. Americans had become 'the consumers of last resort in a world of excess savings'.[6]

The international financial crises of 1997–8 forced a reluctant G–7 to consider more seriously the option of co-ordinated reflation to avoid a global recession, to discourage EMEs from tightening controls on international capital flows, and to contain a situation that threatened the stability of Western financial institutions. The United States relaxed its own monetary policy (despite rapid domestic economic growth) out of concern that higher US rates would worsen Asian economic problems, and called for co-ordinated interest rate cuts and fiscal stimulus by the G–7. The Japanese government did move slowly to introduce fiscal stimulus (having already cut interest rates to near zero), but the Bundesbank in Germany rejected the idea of monetary stimulus. The Bundesbank's president declared that with domestic demand reviving there was no reason for Europe to lower interest rates just to help troubled EMEs. Many European financial leaders shared this view, taking great satisfaction from the fact that the imminent introduction of the single currency seemed to have sheltered EU financial markets from global turmoil. Thus, the G–7 was unable to adopt any co-ordinated macroeconomic policy measures at meetings in September-October 1998, at the height of international concern.

Overall, there has been little active macroeconomic policy co-ordination among the G–7 countries in the 1990s. The G–7 and conservative commentators have argued that there is no alternative to orthodox policies, pointing to the stagflation of the 1970s as evidence of the unworkability of traditional monetary and fiscal tools for stimulating growth and employment. International market constraints are undoubtedly tighter than in earlier periods; nevertheless, the global stimulative impact of US macroeconomic policy choices shows that demand stimulus can still be effective. Constant invocations of international market pressures are part of a strategy to persuade publics of the inevitability of macroeconomic austerity, not a description of objective reality. Political dynamics are the key to the weaknesses of G–7 action. Effective policy co-ordination in a context of capital mobility must involve monetary and fiscal policies, yet these have always been among the most difficult policies to co-ordinate internationally. Taxing, spending, and control of the money supply have long been thought of as core elements of national sovereignty. Different national preferences also pose a substantial obstacle to policy co-ordination. Recent finance ministers' communiqués often paper over unresolved differences in policy priorities by repeating 'the three-word formula "sustained non-inflationary growth". "Sustained" is the code word for Japanese resistance to further stimulus to reduce Japan's current account surpluses; "non-inflationary" is the code word for German resistance to cutting interest rates; and "growth" is the objective pushed by the Americans.'[7]

Macroeconomic policy co-ordination was also blocked by the domestic paralysis of fiscal policy in the three leading countries. Budget battles between

Congress and the administration impeded deficit reduction and blocked the implementation of American commitments regarding fiscal restraint before the mid-1990s, making foreign governments (especially Germany) unwilling to co-ordinate policies with the United States. The pressure of reunification-induced deficits and the Maastricht criteria undermined fiscal flexibility in Germany, while weak political leadership and bureaucratic opposition to deficit spending impeded fiscal policy adjustments in Japan. Active monetary policy co-ordination was impeded by the growing consensus in favour of price stability as the only target for monetary policy, and by the determination of many central banks to assert their independence from political authorities. The Bundesbank's stand on these issues was particularly strong as it tried to ensure that the introduction of a single currency in Europe was not accompanied by any reduction in anti-inflationary zeal.

The weakness of G–7 policy co-ordination also reflects the preoccupation of Germany, France, and Italy with monetary, fiscal, and exchange rate co-ordination within the EU. Potential participants in EMU have been motivated in part by the desire to create a zone of relative stability in Europe that would provide some insulation from instability emanating from the United States and Japan. The governments of these European countries have not lost interest in political management of markets, but they have chosen to pursue it through their regional institutions rather than at the G–7 level. But the orientation of political management of macroeconomic issues in the EU to date has been deflationary, and this has contributed to the poor performance of the European and global economies in the 1990s.

## Managing Exchange Rates and Capital Flows

During the Bretton Woods era, international short-term capital flows were modest and generally subject to governmental restrictions. Co-ordinated foreign exchange market intervention and modest levels of balance-of-payments lending (e.g., from the IMF and surplus-country central banks to deficit countries) were sufficient to maintain fixed exchange rates because private capital flows were relatively small. The abandonment of fixed exchange rates in 1971–3 did not mean the abandonment of efforts to stabilize exchange rates and international financial markets, but the subsequent growth of private international finance—and of foreign exchange trading in particular—means that the task of managing short-term finance and exchange rates is much more difficult today.

Foreign exchange market volatility in the 1990s has generated the same two broad policy approaches as characterized debates about macroeconomic policy co-ordination: bringing government policies more into conformity with market preferences (combined with measures to make markets more efficient) in the hope that this will make markets more stable; and collaborative measures to influence and control international markets directly. The G–7 has generally favoured the first approach, although recent international financial crises have triggered discussion of more direct market interventions.

The G–7 finance ministers have repeatedly claimed that 'the pursuit of sound domestic monetary and fiscal policies' is the key to achieving greater exchange rate stability, especially by reducing inflation rate differentials and fiscal deficits.[8] This view demonstrates a strong faith in the efficiency of private international markets as arbiters of key international economic relationships, but the faith is misplaced. Exchange rate volatility and misalignment have persisted even though G–7 macroeconomic policies have converged around orthodox norms.

Exchange rate volatility has led the G–7 countries to co-ordinate intervention in foreign exchange markets on a number of occasions in the 1990s, as in earlier decades. Their efforts often did have the desired impact, because traders pay attention to the signals that such action sends regarding government intentions.[9] But intervention often came too late to prevent major misalignments, and was sometimes undertaken as a one-shot effort that was not sustained over enough time to have a lasting impact. The G–7 also stepped aside from even attempting to deal with exchange rates among the EU countries, as these countries embarked on a regional attempt to manage international market pressures by first stabilizing exchange rates and then creating a single currency.

Concern about exchange rate volatility has generated interest in proposals for a less flexible exchange rate system. One widely discussed proposal is to establish target zones for exchange rates and defend them by actively co-ordinating foreign exchange market intervention and monetary policies.[10] The G–7 made a half-hearted move in this direction with the 1987 Louvre Accord, but the attempt soon failed because intervention was not consistent enough, because monetary policies were not co-ordinated closely enough in support of the ranges, and because the G–7 countries undermined the credibility of co-ordinated market intervention by publicly criticizing each other. These obstacles to successful exchange rate stabilization are political, not technical. Nevertheless, most G–7 finance ministries have become convinced that mechanisms such as target zones simply cannot work because the volume of private foreign exchange trading so far exceeds the foreign exchange reserves of central banks.

This belief in government powerlessness is exaggerated. The 1992–3 European exchange rate crises, which had a major impact on official thinking, demonstrated that massive speculative flows can overwhelm large-scale co-ordinated intervention. But part of the problem in 1992 was that two currencies under attack, the pound and lira, were clearly overvalued, yet their governments refused to negotiate devaluations. And while the daily volume of foreign exchange trading is enormous, the net volume of open speculative positions is much smaller.[11] Some central banks hold enormous foreign currency reserves, yet are unwilling to commit more than a tiny share to the defence of their currencies (e.g., Japan in 1998).

Another way to deal with market-driven exchange rate instability would be to re-establish some controls on short-term capital flows, reducing the speculative pressures that generate exchange

rate volatility. Attention has focused on James Tobin's idea for a small tax on foreign exchange transactions to discourage unwanted currency speculation without blocking more desirable capital movements, such as foreign direct investment or trade financing.[12]

Despite interest from some G–7 heads of government,[13] the Tobin tax met very strong opposition in the international financial community and from G–7 finance ministers. The latter bluntly dismissed the idea, arguing that the tax could easily be evaded and would prevent countries from capturing welfare gains from international capital flows.[14] A Tobin tax would be easy to avoid unless it was imposed in every major trading centre, an unlikely scenario given opposition from the United Kingdom, the United States, and offshore financial centres. But the idea that free mobility for financial capital brings great benefits is not supported by empirical evidence. Indeed, it is increasingly being challenged by economists, including even some traditional advocates of free trade.[15] The G–7 also has not seriously considered another possibility for dampening speculation, that of imposing reserve requirements on financial institutions' speculative holdings of foreign currencies. These points suggest that the G–7 approach is driven more by ideology than by a careful assessment of costs, benefits, and practicalities.

While the G–7 countries have themselves suffered some ill effects from foreign exchange speculation, the worst effects have been borne by emerging market countries such as Mexico in 1994–5, numerous East Asian countries in 1997–8, and Russia and Brazil in 1998. In many of these cases, international financial liberalization combined with weakly developed or corrupt domestic financial systems to cause major economic crises when investors lost confidence and capital took flight to safe havens such as the United States. But in other cases (such as Brazil), governments had been pursuing policies favoured by international investors and the IMF, yet were still sideswiped by the general collapse of investor confidence in emerging markets. These problems indicate a clear need for stricter political management of short-term capital markets.

However, the G–7 response (at the 1995 Halifax summit and again in 1997–8) once again emphasized the solution of bringing government policies more in line with market preferences rather than directly taming international financial markets. Countries in crisis were encouraged to further liberalize capital flows in conjunction with market-oriented domestic restructuring.[16] In order to reduce the likelihood of such crises in the future, the G–7 called for the development of an 'early warning system' in the IMF, and for IMF measures to increase the transparency of national government policies. The G–7 finance ministers claimed that 'well-informed and well-functioning financial markets are the best line of defence against financial crises',[17] despite overwhelming evidence that market players simply fail to respond to information that runs counter to the instincts of the herd.

Stricter IMF supervision, increased data publication, and more liberal capital markets will expose emerging market economies more fully to the disciplining effects of private international markets and are therefore best seen as measures to regulate governments, not markets. The G–7 has called for enhanced co-operation among national and international financial regulators to improve prudential supervision of private financial institutions, but this is intended to protect the health of the financial sector itself, not to mitigate the impact of short-term capital flows and exchange rate volatility on the real economy.

The severity of the crises in 1998 revealed the inadequacies of the G–7 approach. Increased transparency and market liberalization had not prevented crises, little progress had been made in strengthening prudential regulation, and increases in IMF funding had not been sufficient to meet increasing demand for ever-larger emergency bailout packages for EMEs. In August 1998, both Malaysia and Russia adopted strict controls to prevent or reduce harmful capital flight, and other EMEs examined less drastic measures, such as those that Chile and China had used to insulate themselves from short-term financial market volatility. These developments indicated that if the G–7 and the IMF were unwilling to support systemic efforts to limit speculative short-term capital flows, many EMEs would do so themselves. In response, some G–7 countries (France, Japan, and Canada) and the IMF reluctantly acknowledged that controls on short-term capital flows could be appropriate for countries with weakly developed financial systems and for countries experiencing an international financial crisis. The United States, however, continued to insist on capital market liberalization and denied that speculative financial flows had played a significant role in emerging market crises. As noted earlier, US leaders called for co-ordinated interest rate cuts and fiscal stimulus by the G–7 countries to stimulate global demand and pull EMEs out of depression, thereby discouraging them from implementing unilateral capital controls.

Thus, even though attitudes to capital controls had altered slightly by the fall of 1998, the G–7 continued to reject political management of short-term international finance. The reasons included the G–7's (and especially the US's) deep ideological commitment to the free flow of capital, opposition from the transnational financial industry, and the technical difficulty of devising controls that would dampen financial speculation without interfering with trade-related capital flows and foreign direct investment. The G–7 continued to place faith in better informed and more efficient markets as the way to prevent future emerging market crises, but the strain that increasing demands for bailouts placed on the IMF and World Bank showed that this strategy cannot succeed indefinitely.

## Conclusions

The G–7 is often decried as a failure because it has done so little to tackle problems such as slow growth, high unemployment, and exchange rate volatility in the 1990s. Bergsten and Henning criticize what they call the G–7's 'new consensus on inaction', with G–7 countries claiming to be powerless in the face of capital mobility and tacitly accepting a 'nonaggression pact' whereby each refrains from criticizing the other's policies in return for freedom from foreign criticism of its own policies.[18] But from a perspective that celebrates the global spread of market principles, the G–7 might well be considered a success. The new consensus favours action to reduce government management of private market economies and to submit governments more clearly to the discipline of private market pressures. It explicitly eschews interventionist and Keynesian responses to such problems as high unemployment and currency instability in favour of liberalization and re-regulation to make markets work more efficiently.

Assessed in light of actual global economic problems, however, the G–7 has been a failure in the 1990s. It has rarely engaged in active macroeconomic policy co-ordination to eliminate international imbalances; it has done little jointly to promote global growth in a context of slow growth and high unemployment; it has not co-operated effectively to stabilize exchange rates; and it has rejected international financial re-regulation as a means to reduce harmful currency speculation. The economic performance of most G–7 countries has been weak in the face of this inaction; growth rates have been low, unemployment rates have been high (except in the United States, where unemployment is low but real wages for many workers have fallen), and there has been a regressive redistribution of global income and wealth.

What accounts for the weakness of active political management of the global economy at the G–7 level? Neo-liberal theory claims that active political management of the economy is not viable in a context of open international markets. But this claim ignores evidence that collective political action can have positive effects. In the area of exchange rates, more active co-ordinated intervention is possible and could have a stabilizing impact. Some limits on speculative capital movements are also possible, although the difficulties of implementing highly effective restrictions should not be underestimated. The ability of the United States to stimulate global demand and the modest reflationary impact that international pressure has had on

Japanese macroeconomic policy both suggest that active macroeconomic policy co-ordination to stimulate growth and correct international imbalances is possible.

The obstacles to political management of the global economy therefore are political, not technical. Capital mobility has made macroeconomic management more difficult, but not impossible. The neo-liberal ideology that dominates G–7 discussions is itself one of the key obstacles to action, as it suggests that there is no alternative to orthodox macroeconomic policies and neo-liberal, market-oriented restructuring.[19] The recent replacement of right-of-centre governments with nominally leftist governments in Britain, France, and Germany could challenge the dominance of neo-liberal ideology at the G–7 level, though the international policy stances of the first two of these governments have not been notably less orthodox and market-oriented than those of their predecessors. But effective interference with international capital markets generally must be co-ordinated, given the severe international market pressures that face any government unilaterally diverging from neo-liberal norms. To date the United States has blocked co-ordinated efforts to manage short-term capital flows and G–7 exchange rates directly, while its proposals for co-ordinated macroeconomic expansion have been rejected by Germany and other G–7 governments that favour more conservative monetary or fiscal policies. Another obstacle to effective political management of the global economy is the commitment to EMU of three European G–7 countries (France, Italy, and Germany), with the UK possibly to follow. This commitment, on the face of it, has reduced their interest in inter-regional policy co-ordination, in part because of the success of regional co-ordination in stabilizing exchange rates and insulating continental Europe from recent international financial crises.

The 1990s also marked a decline in the success of American efforts to get foreign governments to alter their macroeconomic policies in line with American preferences. While the United States had been able to persuade West Germany and Japan to reflate their economies in the late 1980s, it met greater resistance in the 1990s. From a broader perspective, however, the United States has been remarkably successful in promoting its ideological vision of a market-oriented society with modest government intervention. The G–7's adoption of this view has been sweeping. Even the difficulties the US government has experienced in persuading foreign governments to reflate is linked to this American success, since open capital markets make it more difficult for governments to adopt the stimulative macroeconomic policies the United States often favours.

Finally, one should note that the very convergence of national macroeconomic policies around orthodox norms meant that payments imbalances among the G–7 countries generally were less serious in the 1990s than in the previous decade. Many of the problems facing G–7 countries in the 1990s are common national problems rather than international problems, and thus they generate less immediate need for international policy co-ordination. One possible exception to this generalization is the problem facing Japan in 1998 (as this chapter was being written); if its recession deepens, its trade surplus with the United States will grow and the deflationary impact on the rest of East Asia will increase. Dramatic crises such as a collapse in world stock market values or the liquidation of overseas investments by Japanese financial institutions seeking to cover losses due to bad domestic loans could trigger a co-ordinated G–7 response.

Even though the potential for policy co-ordination remains, in the 1990s the G–7 has favoured only one aspect of what Karl Polanyi called the double movement of history. The G–7 has acted to promote the expansion of markets across national borders, but has done little to protect societies from the negative consequences of that expansion. This is perhaps most obvious in the case of exchange rates, where the G–7 has done nothing to tame the costly instability and economic distortion generated by private foreign exchange trading. Continued inaction in this area will pose a serious threat to the maintenance of a liberal global economy, as more and more societies are disrupted

by speculative excesses. Over the next few years, the losses that Western banks and hedge funds have experienced as a result of reckless EME crises are likely to lead to less reckless investment practices and to modestly stricter prudential regulation of these activities. These changes may dampen short-term instability, but will do nothing to temper the deflationary pressures facing EMEs and the world economy. Similarly, without Japanese and European contributions to global demand stimulus, the problem of the growing US trade deficit will worsen, bringing with it threats of further instability and American protectionism.

We also need to consider the implications of the pattern of G–7 (in)activity for the problems of governmental legitimacy and democratic accountability. G–7 activities have seriously undermined democratic accountability in macroeconomic policy-making. The trend has been to insulate meetings of G–7 finance ministers and central bank governors from democratic influences by, for example, separating that process from the meetings of the G–7 (now G–8) heads of state or government. As demonstrated by debates surrounding the 1995 Halifax summit, top political leaders are more sympathetic to interventionist measures such as the Tobin tax than are finance ministries and central banks, and the latter want to control the process to prevent serious consideration of less market-friendly possibilities.

Government legitimacy has also been undermined by the generally weak economic performance of most G–7 countries in the 1990s. The poor electoral performance of incumbent governments and growing popular alienation from the political process in many G–7 countries are indicators of a legitimacy problem. But instead of trying to enhance legitimacy by direct interventions to improve economic performance in areas of greatest popular concern (for example, by stimulating demand and growth), the G–7 has tried to make subordination to international market pressures legitimate. G–7 communiqués continually repeat the idea that there is no alternative to orthodox, market-oriented policies, and demonstrate an inordinately strong faith in freer international markets as the solution to most international economic problems. These claims do not correspond to the lived experiences of many people in the ACCs, for whom financial globalization has meant increased economic insecurity and growing inequality. Thus, just as the recent proliferation of international financial crises suggests that the G–7 approach is not economically viable in the long run, popular alienation suggests that it also lacks long-run political viability.

## Notes

1  Karl Polanyi, *The Great Transformation: The Political and Economic Origins of Our Time* (Boston: Beacon Press, 1944, 1957).

2  John Gerard Ruggie, 'International Regimes, Transactions, and Change: Embedded Liberalism in the Postwar Economic Order', in Stephen D. Krasner, ed., *International Regimes* (Ithaca, NY: Cornell University Press, 1983).

3  David Held, 'Democracy, the Nation-State, and the Global System', in Held, ed., *Political Theory Today* (Stanford, Calif.: Stanford University Press, 1991), 197–235.

4  Louis W. Pauly, *Who Elected the Bankers? Surveillance and Control in the World Economy* (Ithaca, NY: Cornell University Press, 1997), 16.

5  Group of Seven, 'Strengthening G7 Cooperation to Promote Employment and Noninflationary Growth' (Finance Ministers' Report to the Tokyo Summit), 1993.

6  Rosanne Cahn, economist with Credit Swisse First Boston, quoted in *Wall Street Journal*, 11 Aug. 1998, A1, A6.

7  William E. Whyman, 'We Can't Go On Meeting Like This: Revitalizing the G–7 Process', *Washington Quarterly* 18, 3 (Summer 1995): 159–60.

8  Group of Seven, 'The Halifax Summit Review of International Financial Institutions: Background Document', 15–17 June 1995.

9  Kathryn M. Dominguez and Jeffrey A. Frankel, *Does Foreign Exchange Intervention Work?*

(Washington: Institute for International Economics, Sept. 1993); C. Fred Bergsten and C. Randall Henning, *Global Economic Leadership and the Group of Seven* (Washington: Institute for International Economics, 1996), ch. 6.

10  For a prominent American proposal, see Bergsten and Henning, *Global Economic Leadership and the Group of Seven*.

11  Ibid., 112–13.

12  See the special issue of *The Economic Journal* 105 (Jan. 1995), for articles by advocates and critics of the Tobin tax and other similar measures.

13  Nicholas Bayne, 'The G7 Summit and the Reform of Global Institutions', *Government and Opposition* 30, 4 (Autumn 1995): 502–4.

14  Group of Seven, 'The Halifax Summit Review'.

15  J. Bhagwati, 'The Capital Myth: The Difference between Trade in Widgets and Dollars', *Foreign Affairs* 77, 3 (May-June 1998).

16  See Group of Seven, 'Halifax Summit Communiqué', 16 June 1995; Group of Seven, 'Statement of G7 Finance Ministers and Central Bank Governors', 21 Feb. 1998.

17  Group of Seven, 'The Halifax Summit Review'.

18  Bergsten and Henning, *Global Economic Leadership and the Group of Seven*, ch. 5.

19  Ibid.; Paul Hirst and Grahame Thompson, *Globalization in Question: The International Economy and the Possibilities of Governance* (Cambridge: Polity Press, 1996).

## Suggested Readings

Bergsten, C. Fred, and C. Randall Henning. *Global Economic Leadership and the Group of Seven*. Washington: Institute for International Economics, 1996.

Block, Fred L. 'Controlling Global Finance', *World Policy Journal* 13, 3 (Fall 1996).

Cohen, Benjamin J. 'Phoenix Risen: The Resurrection of Global Finance', *World Politics* 48, 2 (Jan. 1996).

Dombrowski, Peter. 'Haute Finance and High Theory: Recent Scholarship on Global Financial Relations', *Mershon International Studies Review* 42, 1 (May 1998).

Germain, Randall D. *The International Organization of Credit: States and Global Finance in the World-Economy*. Cambridge: Cambridge University Press, 1997.

Gill, Stephen. 'Global Finance, Monetary Policy and Cooperation among the Group of Seven, 1944–92', in Philip G. Cerny, ed., *Finance and World Politics: Markets, Regimes and States in the Post-Hegemonic Era*. Aldershot: Edward Elgar, 1993.

Hirst, Paul, and Grahame Thompson. *Globalization in Question: The International Economy and the Possibilities of Governance*. Cambridge: Polity Press, 1996.

Webb, Michael C. *The Political Economy of Policy Coordination: International Adjustment Since 1945*. Ithaca, NY: Cornell University Press, 1995.

Whyman, William E. 'We Can't Go On Meeting Like This: Revitalizing the G–7 Process', *Washington Quarterly* 18, 3 (Summer 1995).

## Web Sites

University of Toronto G–8 Information Centre: http://www.g7.utoronto.ca/

G–8 Research Group: http://www.g8online.org

# Post-Fordism and Global Restructuring

## Mitchell Bernard

Globalization is now a fashionable preoccupation of the field of international political economy (IPE). Recent debates have focused on a perilous and false dichotomy centred on state sovereignty. Neo-liberal boosters of globalization have framed it as something inevitable and natural, characterized by the inexorable reduction of the role of the state in relation to both domestic and international markets. In response, some analysts have reaffirmed the continued role of the state, coming to the conclusion that globalization is a myth.[1] The debate over the impact of globalization on the diminution of state power has centred on the vast increase in the size, flow, and speed of foreign direct investment, trade, and currency as well as credit flows. This coincides with the traditional issue-areas of IPE: trade and money/finance.

While globalization has indeed involved a new stage of capital accumulation on a global scale, it has also involved a related restructuring of the workplace and a reconfiguration of the production process more generally. The relationship between production and globalization has been largely depicted in two ways. One is that of national 'models' of capitalism, whereby national competitiveness and firm competitiveness are somehow conflated so that the interests of the latter are self-evidently universalized across national social formations. The second involves 'bringing the firm back in' to make the transnational corporation an 'actor' in the international political economy, challenging the orthodox contention of the centrality of states as, at a minimum, the dominant actors of IPE.[2]

This chapter presents a different perspective by focusing on production and its relationship to global restructuring. By production I refer to the particular modes of organization of the productive forces, the social relations of production that constitute the institutionalization of power relations between different classes, and the ideology or ideologies that are shared or contested and that determine what meaning will be ascribed to work, and by whom. In so doing I make three basic claims. The first is that understanding the changing nature of power in the global political economy requires an inquiry into where power actually lies. Examining changes in production not only helps to explain changes in the balance of power between states, or the spatial reconfiguration of certain economic activity, as in the often discussed shift from the Atlantic to the Pacific, but also allows us to capture the class nature of those changes. In other words, serious consideration of production offers a way of actually grounding notions of the global and locating concepts of globalization in actual places and in relation to the struggles and accommodations over the generation and distribution of surplus. A second claim is that the study of production provides an antidote to the proclivity to look for essentialized national-level models by allowing for a greater appreciation of *how* structures of production are historically constituted by local configurations of power in the context of a legacy of distinct institutions and ideologies. Third, by understanding production in a *political* manner it is possible to grasp that globalization is neither a neutral process happening at a 'global' level with the inevitable force of gravity, nor is it merely about transnational corporations (TNCs) escaping from the nation-state and thereby posing a challenge to national sovereignty.

Rather, it involves a reconfiguration of power at all levels and the production of new spaces, such as the re-emergence in importance of 'macro-regions'. In this way it affords us an appreciation that globalization is not a homogenizing process exogenously imposed from the top down, nor are the global, macro-regional, and local, distinct social spheres.

This chapter will trace the restructuring of production by focusing on the rise of flexible manufacturing in Japan and its diffusion, its implications, and ultimately its contradictions and limitations. To accomplish this it is necessary to trace the evolution of production in Japan from the synthesis of indigenous conditions and American practices in the immediate postwar period through its institutionalization and diffusion in the 1970s, to the profound pressures for its restructuring in the late 1990s. In particular, this chapter examines the impact Japanese production practices have had at three levels of political economy: its relationship to transnationalized production and the global political economy, with specific reference to its partial regionalization in East Asia; its impact on the balance of social forces and the role of the state in, and across, individual countries; and its implications for the organization of work. However, before discussing the changes in Japanese capitalism and their global implications, it is necessary to clarify the different ways that post-Fordism has been theorized.

## Post-Fordism and Political Economy

Post-Fordism has come to be associated with some of the structural changes to the organization of production and, in particular, its social relations. There have been at least three ways of interpreting just what it comprises. Liberal approaches have been more concerned with restructuring the 'firm' and understanding flexibility as a managerial strategy. Post-Fordism has been portrayed as a means to enhance competitiveness and profitability.[3] A second approach is more sociological. In the late 1980s, with the erosion of the material basis of corporatism in Northern Europe, Japan's flexible capitalism was portrayed as a new, more economically robust alternative to Anglo-American neo-liberalism that appeared to be internationally competitive *and* to allow for a large degree of worker empowerment and social solidarity. It was in both its flexible nature and its inclusiveness that it was said to 'transcend' Fordism.[4] A third approach, which is more consistent with the approach taken here, understands post-Fordism in a deeper, more political sense. The continuous search for marginal improvements in costs through the marriage of information technology, specific organizational forms such as subcontracting networks, and the constant stress on readjusting the production system, and in particular the labour process, for the purposes of value maximization are understood as a response to the contradictions inherent in the political bargains of the mid-twentieth century. To this extent it remains an interpretation of the restructuring of work. But this restructuring is crucially accompanied by the reorganization of the state, a reconfiguration of state-society relations, and the transnationalization of finance. In short, this view sees post-Fordist accumulation as the productive basis of a reorganization of social power.[5]

To the extent that post-Fordism indeed represents a new mode of organizing production, it must be emphasized that its diffusion is limited both geographically and sectorally. It exists in relation to other forms of production, in particular the expansion of coercive low-wage labour-intensive production in the world's poorest countries, the existence of a range of small-scale producers as well as proletarianized farmers who produce much of the food that allows for the social reproduction of industry. Technologically, many of the key innovations of post-Fordism were developed in the United States. However, its most important innovations were not technological but organizational and political. They tended initially to be geographically concentrated in Japan and sectorally concentrated in a range of interrelated component- and assembly-intensive sectors such as automobiles, electronics, and display technologies. Japan became the centre of innovation and East Asia the centre of production in these sectors.

These developments have profound implications for political economy and its conceptualization.

The geographic concentration of innovation and production in East Asia came to rest on a configuration of social forces and matrix of institutions reflecting the social power within and across countries of the region. They also intensified both geo-economic rivalry between the region and North America and Europe, on one hand, and conflict within individual countries, on the other, as East Asian production contributed to pressures that precipitated attempts by the state and specific fractions of capital to bring about social change and domestic restructuring. Post-Fordism is also linked to, though not synonymous with, the process of globalization, whereby the transnational organization of production transcends orthodox exchange-centred notions of global political economy while affirming the locally mediated nature of political economy arrangements.

The competitive pressures exerted by new forms of production, coupled with the trend towards globalization, have implications for the configuration of social power within and across countries, for the role of the state, and for the reorganization of the workplace. The impact has varied depending on the specificity of state-society relations, class power, and the ideational context of each country. Yet there are clear limits to these changes as they produce their own tensions and contradictions. Nowhere is this more clearly illustrated than in how the 1980s debates about the way in which new forms of production might provide the material basis for global Japanese leadership have given way, in the late 1990s, to those concerned with the sustainability of those very institutions and relationships of production.

## From Fordism to Post-Fordism

Fordism originated in the United States in the early part of the twentieth century and gradually gained universal acceptance as *the* paradigm of efficient production. There was nothing 'natural' about its emergence. Rather, it is best seen as the outcome of political struggles over several decades marking the rise of a variant of industrial capitalism out of the

particularities of America's political economy. It came to feature large-scale vertically integrated corporations engaged in mass production for undifferentiated product markets. Aggregate demand to facilitate economies of scale was maintained through minimalist state welfare policies, and labour relations were stabilized through a legalistic collective bargaining process that linked wage hikes to increases in labour productivity. Industry-based unions safeguarded elaborate job classification schemes but were not integrated into work-related managerial decision-making. Fordism reached its apogee in its post-World War II 'golden age' and can be considered the social and productive basis of post-World War II American hegemony.[6]

Though American state élites, capitalists, and mainstream labour leaders promoted Fordism internationally as a universally applicable model, there was no reason to assume that Fordism, either as a structure of workplace rule or as a mode of social regulation, would be replicated in non-American conditions.[7] Fordist production was modified incrementally by Japanese corporations attempting to apply advanced American techniques to their particular postwar circumstances. There were six major changes to Fordism emanating from specific features of the Japanese political economy of the time. First, and the precursor to all subsequent changes, was the crushing of independent trade unions as a political force with an alternative vision of society and workplace organization.[8] In their stead, forces favouring co-operation with capital came to control the national union movement, while pro-management company-based unions acted as unofficial administrative arms of management in virtually all unionized workplaces from the 1950s onward. Management created a core of permanent, male, multi-skilled workers with lifetime employment and wages determined by an amalgam of seniority and managerially defined 'merit'. Workers were mobilized into small work groups to meet corporate productivity goals. Reform of training and shop-floor procedures ensured that workers in these groups possessed the necessary skills to solve routine problems, monitor process and quality, and carry out basic maintenance and repair of equipment. They were supplemented by untrained, temporary, and part-time employees, mostly female, who were pressured to leave the labour force upon marriage, allowed to return after child-rearing, and their participation was subject to the vagaries of the business cycle. This gendered division of labour also rested on a broader social base where bureaucratic, corporate, and labour élites all agreed that women bore a primary obligation to 'manage' the family, that the family would remain the predominate institution of social welfare, and that corporations, rather than the state, would be the key providers in a universal but hierarchical system of 'public' welfare.

Second, import barriers and restrictions on foreign investment permitted Japanese companies to experiment with production techniques at a time when the economies of scale, levels of productivity, and technological sophistication of US producers could have overwhelmed many industries. Third, widespread availability of imported technology created an environment where attempts to replicate, absorb, and improve imported know-how led corporate managers to focus on the production process. Innovation often came through application and modification tailored to local conditions. Fourth, the demand for a wide range of products in a relatively small domestic market helped concentrate attention on the need for small-batch production and quick changeover of product lines. Intense competition between producers and widespread copying of products, along with informal price-fixing, encouraged competition on the basis of product differentiation rather than price. Fifth, in the early postwar period, shortages of capital, a large number of former military suppliers with excess capacity, and a tradition of inter-firm and inter-industry collaboration led to the building of long-term supply and subcontracting networks, in contrast to the vertically integrated American corporation. Sixth, the multitude of small and medium-sized manufacturers producing a wide range of products ensured demand for affordable multi-purpose equipment.[9] This was in direct contrast to the costly specialized production machinery predominant in the United States.

These changes were institutionalized over time, but their impact on the global political economy was most profound after the oil shock of 1973. The hyper-inflation that accompanied the precipitous rise in the price of oil was compounded by the American abrogation of the Bretton Woods system of fixed exchange rates, the saturation of markets for most standardized consumer durables, and the rise of import-substitution manufacturing, particularly in the large countries of Latin America. This crisis of overproduction exerted pressure on companies in all advanced capitalist countries to reduce costs. Nowhere was this truer than for Japanese companies dependent on export markets and imported energy. As a result, many Japanese firms began to recognize the coherence and potential benefits of applying these new practices, most advanced in the auto industry, across a range of assembly- and engineering-intensive sectors. At the same time, the application of microprocessors to production equipment enhanced flexibility and facilitated inter-firm communication.

Much attention has been focused on trying to isolate *the* key aspect of Japanese production, be it just-in-time assembly or 'flexible' production by small and medium firms. However, post-Fordist production is better understood not as a practice or set of strategies in a managerial 'tool kit', but in terms of the three dimensions of production outlined above. In many ways Japanese manufacturing came to be associated with post-Fordism because of the seeming fit between the structures of production forged in Japan during the postwar period and the needs of capital to reduce costs by increasing flexibility, introducing new technology, and intensifying pressure on labour. Once microelectronics was introduced as the key technology in both product and process development, for example, large-scale assemblers could no longer profitably internalize increasingly complex technology involved in the production of a wide range of components. The network of suppliers, established in the 1950s, proved ideally suited for this and from their ranks emerged the world's most sophisticated electronics parts makers.

Results of these changes were dramatic and global. The machine tool industry, for example, had been revolutionized when the numerical controller (NC), developed in the United States in the 1950s, was displaced by a computerized numerical controller (CNC). The NC was too large and costly for small and mid-sized producers. The breakthroughs that gave rise to CNC technology resulted from co-operative, inter-industry development in Japan among a machine manufacturer named Fanuc, an electronics company, and a maker of precision bearings. Japan became the world's leading producer and exporter of machine tools, accounting in 1975 for 15 per cent and by 1981 for 45 per cent of world production of CNC lathes. Fanuc came to dominate the global supply of controllers, and the small and mid-sized Japanese users of machine tools came to dominate global markets in a range of industries from eyeglass frames to measuring equipment.

This new approach spread throughout Japanese manufacturing via the vertical and horizontal networks that were solidified in the 1950s. In industries such as textile-related sectors, wholesalers and large producers controlled both the production inputs and markets for finished outputs of small rural-based family producers and regional production co-operatives. To reduce costs they diffused new technologies while transferring risk 'downward' to small-scale producers. As was the case with subcontractors in other industries, these producers were in turn pressured to reduce their costs. With labour shortages removing the option of lowering wages, small-scale producers displayed great interest in labour-displacing automation. State and quasi-public institutions such as technology-leasing companies and subnational prefectural research centres also helped to diffuse these new technologies and arrange financing. This resulted in Japan being the only country in the world where small producers became significant users of robots and CNC machine tools.

This constellation of innovations and social and institutional changes transformed manufacturing. It did so in a way that influenced the location and nature of power in the world—not just the geographic location of power between states but the social location of power between classes, domestically and globally. Japanese corporations came to dominate a range of key industries such as automobiles, consumer electronics, and precision machining. They also came to dominate related component and material industries. These developments contributed to interstate friction between Japan and the United States and European Community and to the pattern of industrialization in the capitalist parts of East Asia. They became one important factor behind attempts to dismantle the institutionalized inter-class bargains put in place under Fordism in America and other variants of the 'politics of productivity' in other advanced capitalist countries. Changes in production led to the increased centrality of Japan and other parts of East Asia in the global political economy, but they also led to reassertion of the power of capital in all capitalist democracies.

## Post-Fordism and Globalization

Japanese production had a major impact on the emergence of what we now think of as globalization. It is, however, inextricably related to the global diffusion of production that commenced under the auspices of postwar American hegemony with the establishment of 'offshore' low-wage assembly in the 1950s. Transnational production was initially the product of increasing rivalry among American manufacturers and retailers for their home market in sectors such as apparel and consumer electronics and was later intensified when Japanese exports in these very sectors became more and more competitive. East Asia became the centre of most of this manufacturing activity, in good part because the US government actively encouraged US investment in front-line anti-Communist countries in the region. A regional pattern of production emerged in the 1960s where small-scale firms in Taiwan and Hong Kong and large-scale vertically integrated conglomerates (*chaebol*) in Korea became enmeshed in global production networks linked backward to Japanese supplies of components, machinery, and materials and forward to markets for end-use products in the United States and, to a lesser extent, Europe. The so-called newly industrialized countries (NICs) achieved export success in the very industries in which Japanese companies had achieved world dominance.

The physical proximity of East Asian producers to Japan and long-term personal relations within and across industries, dating back to the Japanese colonial empire in the case of Taiwan and Korea, provided opportunities for the diffusion of some of the new intra-firm processes and know-how not readily available outside the region. While it would be misleading to refer to this as a regional replication of the Japanese structure of production, these producers did become incorporated in a regional extension of Japan's political economy, but one featuring social relations of production that emerged from local political conditions.[10] Thus the small-scale Taiwanese family firms, which were prominent exporters of conventional machine tools despite limited access to capital and technology, when faced with a precipitous decline in their export sales due to digitalization, came to rely on Fanuc. Fanuc, which not only possessed virtually worldwide control of the key input for digitalization, the control device, established a local support base to custom-design products for local producers in central Taiwan and dispatched technicians to instruct machine-tool makers on how to best use new equipment.

The deeper and geographically more extensive regionalization of Japanese manufacturing across Southeast Asia in the late 1980s, in response to precipitous currency appreciation and increased trade friction, spread Japanese production to countries with only a small, dependent class of indigenous industrial capitalists. Japanese companies were able to orchestrate a more truly regional organization of manufacturing that built on the transplantation of domestic networks of key suppliers and subcontractors in a low-wage setting with state regulation of labour and minimal environmental scrutiny. Domestic suppliers of low-cost inputs and local joint-venture partners politically connected to the state were incorporated into these expanding networks. This regionalization became another important way for Japanese manufacturing capital to manage heightened geo-economic conflict, cost squeezes, and some of Japan's domestic contradictions. However, regionalized production helped create and extend a region characterized not merely by seemingly apolitical Japan-centred networks of firms, but also by a hierarchy of social relations of production built on a region-wide alliance of state élites and class fractions who politically regulated industrialization, not through formal regional institutions but through control of the workplace. Japanese production in Southeast Asia helped foster a decade-long boom that both spawned a new stratum of urban middle class and precipitously turned cities like Bangkok into major platforms for assembly-intensive production for re-export. It also contributed to the need for large-scale infrastructure projects, the escalating cost of land, and a speculative frenzy by the 'new rich' that proved to be so central in the crisis at the end of the 1990s.[11]

Japanese production was thus based on two pillars, its reconfiguration at home and its global diffusion, in particular, its regionalization. This, in turn, precipitated two responses, greater macroregionalism and greater inter-capitalist rivalry. It prompted responses from élites in North America and Western Europe to expand the economic space that could be considered part of the home market, thereby intensifying macro-regionalism. It also precipitated responses where concentrations of production skills and electronic technology increasingly led industrial capitalists from outside of East Asia to locate certain kinds of production there. This trend has been strengthened by the growing incorporation of production units in coastal China with global production.

## Post-Fordism, Restructuring, and Social Power

Production practices forged in the crucible of Japan's postwar political economy were widely diffused domestically because of a series of events that engendered a sense of crisis in Japanese society two decades later. There appeared to be a fit between technological change, industrial structure, and the social relations of production, on the one hand, and a solution to the crisis facing Japanese capital, on the other. Similarly, Japanese industrial corporations were able to build upon a historical legacy in East Asia to regionalize elements of Japan's political economy as part of a 'spatial fix'. Just as Japanese managers sought to absorb American production techniques after World War II, so, too, did Japanese practices precipitate responses in other countries from rival firms, state élites, and various social forces. This in itself is neither novel nor surprising, as capitalism has always spread in part by the compulsion to emulate what are perceived to be 'best' production practices. This is precisely what Marx and Engels contemplated when they observed that the rapid change in production brought about by capitalism in the mid-nineteenth century 'compels all nations, on pain of extinction, to adopt the bourgeois mode of production.'[12]

The sociopolitical bargains that buttressed Fordism in the other advanced capitalist countries, even though they acquired specific national forms, imposed costs that corporate élites came to perceive as being onerous in the changed circumstances of the 1970s. This was particularly so in the United States and the United Kingdom. These costs peaked with the high rates of taxation, inflation, and wages of the late 1970s. Furthermore, the Fordist bargains rested politically on industry and finance remaining anchored domestically and subject to continuing state regulation. However, in response to the crisis of overproduction and the decreasing ability of American industrial corporations to control global prices as reflected in the so-called 'Japanese challenge', a coalition of neo-liberal politicians, bureaucratic élites, internationally oriented firms, and financial institutions, within and across states, sought to reduce the size of the state and change its scope and purpose. A revivified neo-liberal ideology helped constitute this coalition. Over time, one aspect of this new ideology came to be the exhortation from state officials, politicians of virtually all stripes, and, of course, business élites that nations and firms were 'teams' competing in a struggle against foreign competition. The coalition thus attempted to garner support by presenting the

interests of capital and those of subordinate classes as one. It also tried to tap into deep-seated middle-class feelings that taxes were too high and government too large and intrusive. The solution proffered was cast in the form of 'common-sense' propositions such that reduction in the size of the state, an anti-inflationary bias, the promotion of national competitiveness through liberalization, and the inevitability and desirability of globalization were not part of a 'political' project but merely 'natural' solutions to self-evident problems.

Lean production, as it came to be called in North America, appeared to offer cost-cutting solutions to North American business. Books like *The Machine That Changed the World*, written by business consultants, argued for American manufacturers to behave more like their Japanese counterparts.[13] Some American 'Japan experts' made the case for the state to promote industrial competitiveness through industrial policy, arguing that this was the central lesson to be learned from postwar Japan.[14] From the late 1980s through the early 1990s, countless attempts were made to adopt elements of Japanese-style production in other advanced capitalist countries, from just-in-time delivery and zero-inventory introduced by retailers to the adoption of small group production teams and quality control circles in factories.[15] These attempts changed certain workplace practices but were ultimately constrained by the historically constituted contexts into which they were introduced. Whereas learning from Japan injected an element of flexibility into inter- and intra-firm responses to capitalist competition, the more important element of flexibilization, the need to make the labour force more flexible, could only partially draw on Japanese practices. Permanent workers could be pressured to increase output, make shop-floor decisions, and work longer hours, but non-Japanese capitalists could not count on in-house unions, politically quiescent female employees, or leverage over subcontractors to absorb costs, social dislocation, and internalize new technologies. In the United States, flexibility was achieved through the flexibilization of labour markets whereby wages have become compressed, and a late 1990s employment boom has masked the continuing trend towards low-wage, low-productivity, and part-time employment.[16] Even in Germany, where export-oriented industries with high skill levels are characterized by legally mandated firm-level negotiations of any changes in employment, hitherto competitive firms are experiencing pressures from Japanese and American competitors to remove many features of the 'social partnership'.[17]

These attempts to reduce costs, of course, placed pressure on organized labour. East Asian competition increased offshore production and sourcing. It contributed to an inexorable decline in manufacturing employment and high levels of unemployment, especially among blue-collar workers, that undermined Fordist labour relations and the role of industrial unions. Where labour had no tradition of participating in managerial decisions and had a weak social base, such as in the United States and Canada, its influence weakened dramatically as unions were reduced to making an endless series of concessions. Where labour was more integrated through various corporatist arrangements, into workplace decision-making as in Germany or into national-level wage-fixing as in Australia, unions became a 'partner' in restructuring, but in a different manner than was the case in Japan.[18] Indeed, many trade unionists, social democrats as well as the 'moderates' in the first Clinton administration, came to the conclusion that post-Fordist flexible accumulation created a demand for skilled labour, the supply of which, though internalized by Japanese companies, needed to be met proactively through a tripartite promotion of training to enhance national competitiveness.[19]

Because new technologies and new forms of production involve organizational, spatial, and political change, they also directly alter social power over work. How the content of work will evolve also depends on configurations of power and related matrices of institutions. The mass production associated with Henry Ford involved the use of specialized tools, a separation of execution from conception, and a fragmentation of the labour process so as to replace skilled artisans with de-skilled proletarians. This led many to conclude that

capitalist industry would inexorably result in ever greater levels of de-skilling. One reason the Japanese workplace achieved so much attention in the 1980s was because of the 'discovery' that under different kinds of political and institutional arrangements, this trend could be reversed. Some observers concluded that the combination of greater worker participation in shop-floor decisions, as well as the introduction of computerization, could reverse skill erosion and lead to a re-skilling of labour and a more holistic incorporation of workers into the production process.[20] However, the introduction of new technologies has affected skills, the pattern of participation, and power over the production process in more complex and less uniform ways than boosters of flexible specialization acknowledge. Flexible practices and computerization have the potential to break down rigid job classifications and allow for greater decentralization of shop-floor decision-making. But this has often resulted in a significant intensification of work in assembly-line contexts where workers are expected to complete a greater number of tasks. New practices also affect different workers in different ways, as in exacerbating the divisions between a smaller number of 'core' employees and semi-skilled employees hired on an increasingly casual basis.

Finally, new ideas concerning shop-floor organization and the introduction of programmable equipment have given some employers the impetus to design labour out of the production process as much as possible. However the workplace ramifications of the introduction of these new forms of production might vary, a common trend across particular national contexts has been that the productivity gains accruing from these changes, where they exist, have largely been appropriated by an increasingly well-compensated managerial élite, a small cadre of high-tech experts who are in worldwide demand, and, most importantly, shareholders, increasingly through the intermediation of institutional investors. The historic bargains of the mid-twentieth century have increasingly been broken, or at least attenuated, incorporating fewer and fewer workers. This will likely create the basis for political contestation in the coming years over issues of the extent to which and how the gains from flexible work should be redistributed to workers.

## Lean Production in Lean Times: The Transformation of Flexible Production in Japan?

It was possible through the early 1990s to argue that Japan has been spared the kind of restructuring taking place in other advanced capitalist countries. Japan, after all, had been the locus of manufacturing breakthroughs. Japanese production had also underpinned the industrial transformation of East Asia and increasing regionalization had alleviated the pressures that had precipitated restructuring elsewhere. In addition, for so-called 'core' male workers in large industrial companies, the Japanese deflation of the 1990s has translated neither into large-scale job losses nor to a complete severing of the tie between productivity gains and wage increases.[21] None the less, there are visible changes in the organization of Japanese production. It is important to remember that change in production entails more than the standard concern for the continued job security of Japan's most privileged male workers. In addition, one caveat needs to be made when discussing changes to Japanese production. Descriptions of 'massive changes' to Japan's industrial structure put forward by the foreign business press and neo-liberals, both inside and outside Japan, often feature a blurred admixture of description and prescription, i.e., Japan is now acquiring Anglo-American-style employment practices *and,* in any event, it should! As argued more generally above, any change in Japan, as elsewhere, will be built on historically specific conditions and will not merely involve impending convergence with practices elsewhere.

Several components of Japan's post-Fordism either were based on conditions that are being removed or have generated their own internal contradictions. One obvious example is how production process innovations, such as the just-in-time delivery system that relied on timely components delivery, have generated unsustainable traffic congestion and local pollution due to the army of trucks required to ensure punctual deliveries. In a supreme irony, just as business consultants were recommending zero inventories in North America and Europe, Toyota was experimenting with more integrated production in its newly opened Tahara plant in Kyushu to deal with problems precipitated by the zero-inventory practice.

More importantly, basic conditions upon which Japanese flexible production was predicated —easy credit availability for small businesses and continued profitability of domestic sales—have been undermined by the deflationary conditions of the 1990s. While vertical production networks are not likely to disappear, the rate of bankruptcy among smaller subcontractors is removing one of the key sources via which Japanese capital has been able to transfer risk and social dislocation. In addition, large Japanese companies, which engaged in a white-collar recruitment frenzy during the 1980s boom in order to co-ordinate and control overseas production and bubble-induced domestic demand, have reduced entry-level recruitment, begun pressuring long-serving employees into early retirement or acceptance of secondments to regionally based affiliates at reduced pay, and increased pressure on staff to 'perform'.[22]

The result has been a discernible increase in unemployment and underemployment, most notably among young people and women. This includes the increased casualization of labour, as evidenced by the recent legal sanctioning of temporary employment service companies. Japan's official unemployment rate, which tends significantly to understate labour reserves, was higher in 1998 than at any time since postwar statistics were first kept in 1953. Even quasi-ornamental 'office ladies', young women who perform secretarial duties and serve tea in large corporations, are being phased out and replaced by part-timers. In 1997 full-time women's employment decreased by 130,000, while part-time work rose by 220,000.[23]

These changes have produced neither the beginnings of the renewal of organized labour as an independent social force nor any momentum for a politics that problematizes the unbridled power of capital. The historically contingent forms of flexibility that have given Japanese corporations control over labour have been employed to 'deal' with the changed conditions of the 1990s. Japanese capital has been able to maintain its commitment to 'Japanese-style labour practices' and to reject firmly the harsh downsizing witnessed in North America precisely because corporate power in Japanese society is largely unchallenged. This has given business groups the space to restructure employment while appearing as defenders of culturally based consensual labour practices and societal cohesion. The implosion of the Japanese left and the privatization of the public-sector unions over the past decade have removed the traditional organizational forms through which oppositional voices could be articulated.

## Notes

1   For a statement of this position, see Linda Weiss, 'Globalization and the Myth of the Powerless State', *New Left Review* 225 (Sept.-Oct. 1997): 3–27.

2   See John Stopford and Susan Strange, *Rival States, Rival Firms: Competition for World Market Shares* (Cambridge: Cambridge University Press, 1991).

3   This approach is most notable in so-called 'business school' literature. A good example is Daniel Ross et al., *The Machine That Changed the World* (New York: Rawson Associates, 1990).

4   For an example, see M. Kenney and R. Florida, 'Beyond Mass Production: Production and the Labour Process in Japan', *Politics and Society* 16, 1 (1988): 121–58.

5   Kim Moody, *Workers in a Lean World* (London: Verso, 1997), 85–113.

6   See Mark Rupert, *Producing Hegemony: The Politics of Mass Production and American Global Power* (Cambridge: Cambridge University Press, 1995).

7   On American efforts to promote Fordism in Japan, see William Tsutsui, *Manufacturing Ideology: Scientific Management in Twentieth-Century Japan* (Princeton, NJ: Princeton University Press, 1998).

8   See John Price, *Japan Works: Power and Paradox in Postwar Industrial Relations* (Ithaca, NY: ILR Press/Cornell University Press, 1997), esp. chs 2–4.

9   David Friedman, *The Misunderstood Miracle* (Ithaca, NY: Cornell University Press, 1988).

10   On the regionalization of Japanese production, see M. Bernard and J. Ravenhill, 'Beyond Product Cycles and Flying Geese: Regionalization, Hierarchy and the Industrialization of East Asia', *World Politics* 47 (1995): 171–209.

11   See M. Bernard, 'East Asia's Tumbling Dominoes: Financial Crises and the Myth of the Regional Model', in C. Leys and L. Panitch, eds, *Global Capitalism Versus Democracy: The Socialist Register 1999* (London: Merlin Press, 1999), 178–208.

12   K. Marx and F. Engels, *The Communist Manifesto* (Northbrook, Ill.: AHM Publishing, 1955), 14.

13   Ross et al., *The Machine That Changed the World*.

14   There is a vast literature by scholars extracting 'lessons' from Japan. For the classic statement of the proposition, see Chalmers Johnson, *MITI and the Japanese Miracle: The Growth of Industrial Policy, 1925–1975* (Tokyo: Tuttle, 1982).

15   See T. Elgar and C. Smith, eds, *Global Japanization? The Transnational Transformation of the Labour Process* (London: Routledge, 1994).

16   M. Yates, *Longer Hours, Fewer Jobs: Employment and Unemployment in the United States* (New York: Monthly Review Press, 1994).

17   B. Mahnkopf, 'Between the Devil and the Deep Blue Sea: The "German Model" Under the Pressure of Globalisation', in C. Leys and L. Panitch, eds, *Global Capitalism Versus Democracy: Socialist Register 1999* (London: Merlin Press, 1999), 142–77.

18   For an exploration of the Australian case, see John Wiseman, 'A Kinder Road to Hell? Labour and the Politics of Progressive Competitiveness in Australia', in L. Panitch, ed., *Are There Alternatives? Socialist Register 1996* (London: Merlin Press, 1996), 93–117.

19   For an excellent treatment of the debate on training and employment creation, see Gregory Albo, 'Competitive Austerity and the Impasse of Capitalist Employment Policy', in R. Miliband and

L. Panitch, eds, *Between Globalism and National-ism: Socialist Register 1994* (London: Merlin Press, 1994), 144–70.

20   For an influential representation of this view for-mulated before the advent of microcomputing, see M. Piore and C. Sabel, *The Second Industrial Divide* (New York: Basic Books, 1984). They came to the conclusion that microelectronics and flex-ible production had the potential to eliminate the historic antagonism between capital and workers.

21   Y. Higuchi, 'Trends in Japanese Labour Markets', in M. Sako and H. Sato, eds, *Japanese Labour and Management in Transition* (London: Routledge, 1997).

22   For an example of this process in the Japanese auto industry in the early 1990s, see Nampō Hajime, 'Jidosha Sangyo no Risutora no Genjō', *Rodo Undo Kenkyu* 317 (Mar. 1996): 10–13. On white-collar recruitment, see S. Hori, 'Fixing Japan's White-collar Economy: A Personal View', *Harvard Business Review* 71, 6 (Nov.-Dec. 1993): 157–72.

23   *Far Eastern Economic Review*, 16 Apr. 1998, 61.

## Suggested Readings

Cox, Robert W. *Production, Power, and World Order: Social Forces in the Making of History*. New York: Columbia University Press, 1987.

Elger, Tony, and Chris Smith, eds. *Global Japanization? The Transnational Transformation of the Labour Process*. London: Routledge, 1994.

Gordon, Andrew. *The Wages of Affluence: Labor and Management in Postwar Japan*. Cambridge, Mass.: Harvard University Press, 1998.

Harvey, David. *The Condition of Postmodernity*. Oxford: Basil Blackwell, 1990.

Koike, Kazuo. 'The Internationalization of the Japan-ese Firm', in J. Banno, ed., *The Political Economy of Japanese Society*, vol. 2. Oxford: Oxford Uni-versity Press, 1997.

McMichael, Philip. *Development and Social Change: A Global Perspective*. London: Pine Forge Press, 1996.

Moody, Kim. *Workers in a Lean World*. London: Verso, 1997.

Rupert, Mark. *Producing Hegemony: The Politics of Mass Production and American Global Power*. Cam-bridge: Cambridge University Press, 1995.

## Web Sites

[Japan] National Confederation of Trade Unions (Zenroreu): http://www.iijnet.or.jp/cprounion/aa_e/index_e.html

LabourStart http://www.labourstart.org

Labor Notes http://www.labornotes.org

## Chapter 12

# The Uruguay Round and the World Economy

Gilbert R. Winham

## Introduction

The European Union/United States bipolar structure of the contemporary international trade policy regime was established in the late 1950s with the restoration of European currency convertibility and the formation of the European Economic Community (EEC, or Common Market) by the Treaty of Rome (1958). Since that time, there have been three large multilateral trade negotiations under the auspices of the General Agreement on Tariffs and Trade (GATT). All were begun as a result of pressure by the United States.

The Kennedy Round of 1963–7 was the first post-EEC multilateral negotiation held in the GATT. The round was initiated by the Kennedy administration in response to the creation of the EEC and the fear that American products would be shut out of an integrated European market.[1] The second negotiation was the Tokyo Round of 1973–9. It was established in the wake of the US decision in 1971 to abandon the Bretton Woods link between the dollar and gold, which created a crisis in the postwar system of fixed exchange rates.[2] As part of this decision, the United States applied a surcharge on imports and demanded international action to address its first trade deficit in the twentieth century.

Both the Kennedy and Tokyo Rounds were induced by large-scale policy change in leading countries. By comparison, there was no comparable challenge to the multilateral trade system by a leading actor in the run-up to the Uruguay Round. Instead, the early 1980s, when the Uruguay Round was conceived, were a period of recession that affected all countries, and this contributed to wide-spread uncertainty about the performance of the world economy. In these circumstances, the factors that led to the Uruguay Round negotiation are less evident than were those that precipitated the Kennedy or Tokyo Rounds.

The objectives of the Uruguay Round have been summarized by the delegates to that negotiation. For example, consider the statement of the US delegate to a GATT preparatory session in 1985. As recorded in the minutes: 'The representative of the *United States* . . . accepted certainly what the representative of India had said that the real objective [of a new negotiation] was to re-establish confidence in the multilateral system.'[3] But what had caused countries to lose confidence in the system in the first place? In short, what events propelled countries to commence an undertaking as far-reaching as the Uruguay Round eventually became?[4] This chapter argues that the Uruguay Round was initiated because countries recognized the early 1980s were a turning point for the world economy and that fundamental changes were occurring that would call into question the traditional GATT structure. This recognition led the United States to take the lead in calling for a new negotiation, but other countries, especially Japan, the small developed countries, and some developing countries, also supported the US initiative.[5] These countries were motivated by diverse concerns, but they shared a common goal to preserve the multilateral trading system and to make it more responsive to the economic problems they faced in their domestic economies.[6]

The purpose here is to examine the economic circumstances that led countries to negotiate the Uruguay Round. Attention will be focused on factors such as the slowing of the world economy, which affected many countries, as well as developments in sectors like agriculture and services, which had a differential impact on countries. The conclusion will briefly examine other factors related to national policies that are claimed to have precipitated the negotiation.

## Slowing of the World Economy

The Uruguay Round was initiated at a GATT ministerial meeting in Punta del Este, Uruguay, in September 1986. In the discussions leading to this meeting, GATT parties had been concerned about the slowing of the world economy, which became evident in the 1970s. Since the end of the Korean War in 1953, the international economy enjoyed a period of prosperity that was hitherto unknown in the twentieth century. For example, in a study of 32 countries (including 15 developing countries), Angus Maddison found that the average annual compound growth rate for the period 1950–73 was 5.1 per cent, approximately double the rates of two earlier periods in the century (see Table 1).[7] For developing countries, the rate was even higher, at 5.3 per cent for the period. Growth rates of trade were also exceptionally high in the 1950–73 period, and arguably contributed strongly to general economic growth. Underlying both trade and economic growth were annual increases in productivity (GDP/person hour), which in OECD countries rose to 4.5 per cent for the period, up from an average of 1.9 per cent in the first half of the century.[8]

The period 1950–73, which Maddison has referred to as a 'golden age', can be explained by reference to the postwar international economic system and to the domestic and international policies pursued by the major countries. The system was stable and explicitly promoted development, as evidenced by steady flows of capital, including foreign aid, to developing countries. Domestic policies in developed countries were directed towards an expansion of demand and employment. Capital investment was everywhere emphasized, and where it occurred overseas in the form of foreign investment it promoted technology transfer and accelerated economic development.[9]

The 1970s presented a different picture. Maddison's figures show the growth in world production and exports dropping to 3.4 and 4.5 per cent respectively in the period 1973–87, down from 5.1 and 7.7 per cent in the 1950–73 period (see Table 1). Data compiled by the GATT itself confirm Maddison's generalizations, but present an even starker picture of declining economic performance as the 1960s gave way to the 1970s (see Figure 1). The GATT figures show that world production and world exports grew yearly at 6 per cent and 8.5 per cent over the period 1963–73, but fell to 2.5 per cent and 3.5 per cent from 1974 to 1985, the period immediately preceding the Uruguay Round negotiation. These figures reflect especially the serious impact of the recession of the early 1980s on international trade. The conclusion to be drawn is that by the mid-1980s the world economy was going from bad to worse. Again, this conclusion was clearly supported in GATT documentation (see Figure 2).

The event that triggered the end of the boom period was the oil price crisis of late 1973, but problems with inflation had created a drag on

## Table 1: World Real GDP Growth and Export Growth, 1900–1987 (per cent)

|         | 1900–13 | 1913–50 | 1950–73 | 1973–87 |
|---------|---------|---------|---------|---------|
| GDP     | 2.8     | 2.1     | 5.1     | 3.4     |
| Exports | 4.3     | 0.6     | 7.7     | 4.5     |

NOTE: Annual average of gross domestic product (GDP) growth at constant prices; annual average compound growth rate in export volume.

SOURCE: Angus Maddison, *The World Economy in the 20th Century* (Paris: OECD Development Centre, 1989), Tables 3.3, 6.1.

## Figure 1: Volume of World Merchandise Production and Exports, 1968–1985 (annual percentage change)

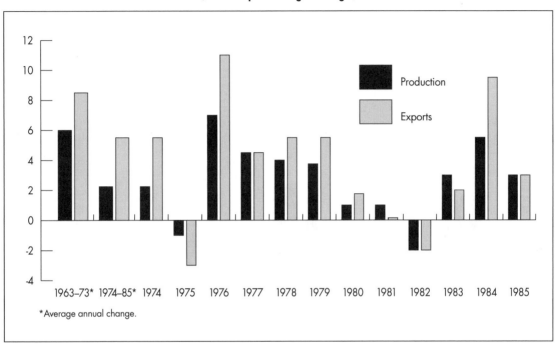

*Average annual change.

SOURCE: Graph compiled from data in GATT, *International Trade 81–82, 83–84, 85–86, 86–87.*

growth that began two years earlier. Inflation was contained in the 1960s, but it commenced after the breakup of the Bretton Woods monetary system in 1971 and then accelerated rapidly with the shock of increasing oil prices. The oil shock had an immediate effect on production and trade in OECD countries, but other less dramatic factors had even greater impact. Productivity growth, which had been at historic high levels, began to slip, and the average annual growth rate of 4.5 per cent for the period 1950–73 fell to 2.2 per cent for the 1973–86 period.[10] A further factor was domestic economic policy, which gradually shifted from maintaining high demand to fighting inflation. The focus on inflation—with attendant high interest rates—forced countries to accept a slowdown of growth and an associated rise in the level of unemployment.[11]

World production recovered sharply in 1976, but then trended downward for the next six years

to conclude in the recession of 1982. Trade performance was equally dismal. The combination of high interest rates, a further oil price escalation, and reduced trade and investment flows brought many developing countries to the brink of fiscal collapse and focused attention on emergency programs for debt restructuring and relief. In sum, by the early 1980s it appeared to many that the world economy was performing poorly for developed countries and contributing to crisis and dislocation in developing countries. This situation created an incentive for governments to re-examine international trade policy.

## Increasing Role of International Trade

Apart from a general concern over the world economy, some countries had specific concerns arising from their trading experience that led them to

## Figure 2: Growth of World Output and Merchandise Trade, 1960–1987
### (annual average percentage change in volume)

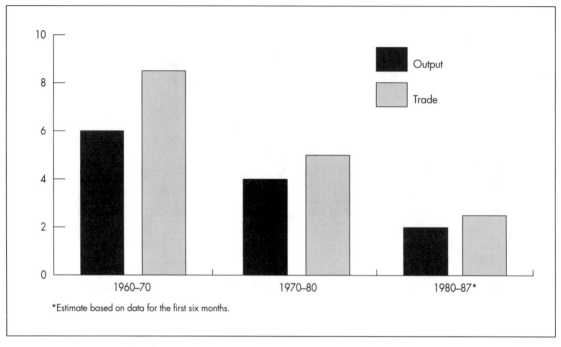

*Estimate based on data for the first six months.

SOURCE: GATT, *International Trade 86–87, 7.*

support a new round of trade negotiations. One such concern was the increasing interdependence between national economies in the world economy. For countries like Switzerland and Austria, this phenomenon had been a factor in economic policy throughout the postwar period, and it led those countries to pursue liberal trade policies.[12]

The increase of interdependence (as indicated by trade/GNP ratios) in smaller industrialized countries can be seen in Table 2. As shown in the table, the international trade regime was relatively open at the turn of the century. Depression and war reduced that openness by mid-century, but the period from the 1950s to the mid-1980s saw considerable growth in the reliance on trade in the five countries surveyed. By 1986, total trade accounted for more than half of national GDP in the five countries, reflecting a high degree of integration into the international economy. This created a strong incen-

tive for those countries to promote liberalizing policies in the GATT and elsewhere.

The effect on smaller industrialized states of increasing interdependence can be seen in Canada's decision to initiate free trade with the United States. Following the recession of the early 1980s, a government commission surveyed Canada's future economic prospects.[13] The commission concluded that Canada's market was too small to stimulate efficient production by itself and that an increase in productivity—on which the standard of living was based—could only be achieved through freer trade. In the language of the day, the commission evaluated the role of an industrial policy and stated that 'a key component of Canada's industrial policy should be a commitment to freer trade.'[14] This commitment led the Canadian government to support freer trade bilaterally with the United States, and multilaterally in the Uruguay Round.

## Table 2: Ratio of Merchandise Exports to GDP for Five Small/Medium Countries (per cent)

|  | 1900 | 1950 | 1986 | 1986 (Total Trade/GDP) |
|---|---|---|---|---|
| Austria |  | 12.6 | 24.0 | 52.6 |
| Canada | 18.3 | 17.5 | 24.8 | 54.3 |
| Norway | 31.8 | 26.9 | 45.3 | 89.0 |
| Sweden | 17.4 | 17.8 | 28.6 | 61.1 |
| Switzerland | 30.5 | 20.0 | 27.7 | 58.1 |

SOURCES: Maddison, *The World Economy*, Table D–6; GATT, *International Trade 87–88*, II (Geneva: GATT, 1988), Table AE2.

Increasing interdependence and rising trade-to-GDP ratios also influenced large as well as smaller industrialized countries. In Europe, the importance of exports grew rapidly. Even in economies where trade volumes were historically low relative to the domestic market, trade dependence increased rapidly after 1950. For example, the export/GDP ratio of Japan more than doubled (4.7 to 10.8 per cent) from 1950 to 1986, while that of the United States went from 3.6 to 5.2 per cent.[15] In the latter country, exports constituted over 20 per cent of industrial output.[16] These figures led many Americans to conclude by the 1980s that 'The United States has become heavily dependent on the world economy.'[17]

The evidence of increasing trade dependence encouraged officials in the United States as well as in other countries to pursue the option of a new trade negotiation. A rising trade dependence meant that national economies were becoming increasingly externalized and therefore were more vulnerable to the actions of other governments. Negotiating new international trade rules was a means to promote market access and economic security in the external economy, which is similar to the role governments have often performed in domestic economies.

## Agriculture

The decline of agriculture was a central concern for those countries that sought a new trade negotiation. By the 1980s, agriculture had long since fallen to a small proportion of industrialized country economies, but it continued to be a major component of

the economies of developing countries. However, its share of the domestic economy in both developing and industrial countries has been declining in recent decades (Table 3). In international trade, agriculture represented almost half of world merchandise trade in 1950, but its share had declined to about 14 per cent by the mid-1980s. This decline was relative and not absolute, and is explained by the failure of agriculture to keep up to the very rapid rates of growth in trade in manufactures in the postwar period. The natural decline of agricultural trade was compounded by an increase of protectionism among major importers, particularly the European Community, as exporters brought increasing pressure on domestic producers in a slow-growing market.

The effect of slow growth in agricultural trade was especially felt in certain countries. For example, in an agricultural exporter like Argentina, exports as a percentage of GDP grew only from 8.4 per cent in 1950 to 8.7 per cent in 1986, while in Australia the percentage actually fell, from 22.0 to 13.5 per cent.[18] Both countries thus failed to benefit from a major source of growth enjoyed by many countries in the postwar period. The continuing decline of agricultural trade motivated agricultural exporters, from Argentina to the United States, to try again to liberalize agricultural trade in the Uruguay Round.

Attempts had been made to liberalize trade in agriculture in the Kennedy and Tokyo Rounds, but they failed mainly because of the unwillingness of the European Economic Community to modify the

**Table 3: Share of Agriculture in Gross Domestic Product and Labour Force in Developing Areas and Industrial Countries, 1965 and 1985 (per cent)**

|  | Gross Domestic Product | | Labour Force | |
|---|---|---|---|---|
|  | 1965 | 1985 | 1965 | 1985 |
| Developing areas | 29 | 20 | 70 | 62 |
| Industrial countries | 5 | 3 | 14 | 7 |

NOTE: World Bank estimates.

SOURCE: GATT, *International Trade 87–88*, I, 29.

protection afforded by its Common Agricultural Policy. By the 1980s, liberalization of agriculture had for many countries become a litmus test of the ability to achieve any reform of the multilateral trade system. For example, the representative of New Zealand to the GATT in 1985 emphasized that agricultural trade rules were overdue for reform:

> The longer a gross imbalance against agriculture in the international trading system remained the greater was the threat to the credibility of an international trading system committed to non-discriminatory treatment and maximizing opportunities for trade. Agriculture was a sector of key importance for developed and developing countries alike. It had assumed the touchstone of commitment to the new round proposal.[19]

The statement of New Zealand, echoed by many other countries, made it clear that the liberalization of agricultural trade had become a *sine qua non* of any new multilateral negotiation.

## Developing Countries

Developing countries were instrumental in building momentum towards a new trade negotiation. This was not obvious, because a group of developing countries led by India and Brazil conducted a vigorous campaign of opposition to the inclusion of some issues, like services, on the negotiating agenda.[20] The reality, however, was that a changing

world economy made developing countries important to the international trade system, and, in turn, reform of the system was important to developing countries.

Developing countries were important in two respects. On the one hand, some were assuming a much larger role in the international trade system by the 1980s than had been the case previously. By 1985, China, Hong Kong, South Korea, and Saudi Arabia were included among the world's top 20 exporters and importers, while Brazil and Taiwan joined the list as exporters and Singapore joined as an importer.[21] The composition of developing country trade was increasingly industrialized, and by 1987 manufactures accounted for nearly half of developing country exports, up by 20 per cent from 1980.[22] Developing countries were also increasingly becoming a market for developed countries, and by 1987 they took approximately one-third of merchandise exports from Japan, one-fourth of exports from North America, and one-eighth of exports from Western Europe.[23] These circumstances motivated developed countries to seek a new negotiation to incorporate developing countries more firmly into GATT rules.

On the other hand, developing countries had their own reasons to seek a new negotiation. The recession and debt crisis devastated many developing country economies and resulted in sharply increased debt repayments with consequent falling imports, which constituted the real cost of the debt crisis (see Figure 3). The experience of the 1980s led developing country governments to recognize

## Figure 3: Merchandise Trade of 15 Heavily Indebted Countries, 1980–1987 ($ billions)

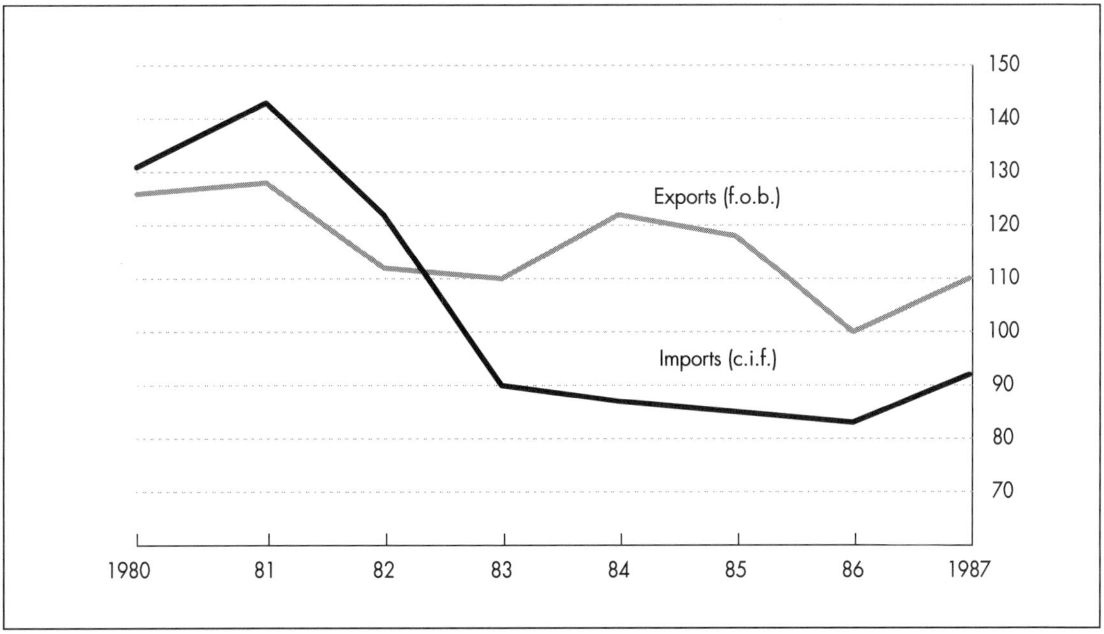

SOURCE: GATT, *International Trade 87–88*, I, 18.

the stake they had in expanded exports and in an open trade system more generally. For example, consider the following extract from the GATT discussions in 1985: 'The representative of *Brazil* said that . . . . [h]is country was interested in promoting economic growth on the basis of an economy open to foreign trade, and needed to generate trade surpluses in a very large magnitude for the servicing of the external debt which consumed only in interest payments around 40 per cent of export earnings.'[24] The position of Brazil was echoed by numerous other developing countries in the preparatory meetings for the Uruguay Round.

## Services

The Uruguay Round was distinctive for the introduction of new issues into GATT negotiations, namely, trade in services, investment, and intellectual property. In the run-up to the Punta del Este Declaration, the focus was mainly on services. The

role of services in the international economy is by now well known, but in the early 1980s the situation was much more opaque. Services such as transport costs and insurance were generally categorized as 'invisibles' and were treated inconsistently in the current account statistics of different nations. GATT statistics focused on merchandise trade, not on services. However, governments were well aware of the increasing importance of services at the domestic level, and by the mid-1980s this information was being published by the GATT.[25]

The issue of services divided the developed and developing countries during the pre-negotiation phase of the Uruguay Round. As seen in Table 4, in the 30 years from 1950 to 1980, all countries showed a decline in the workforce in agriculture and a corresponding increase of labour in industry and services. However, the decline of agriculture and the movement into services were much greater in developed as opposed to developing countries. It was recognized that unless trade in services was

## Table 4: World Labour Force by Sector of Activity, 1950–1980 (per cent)

|  | Developed Countries | Developing Countries |
|---|---|---|
| Agriculture |  |  |
| 1950 | 39 | 82 |
| 1960 | 29 | 77 |
| 1970 | 19 | 72 |
| 1980 | 13 | 67 |
| Industry |  |  |
| 1950 | 29 | 7 |
| 1960 | 33 | 9 |
| 1970 | 36 | 11 |
| 1980 | 35 | 14 |
| Services |  |  |
| 1950 | 32 | 11 |
| 1960 | 38 | 14 |
| 1970 | 45 | 17 |
| 1980 | 52 | 19 |

SOURCE: Adapted from *GATT, International Trade 88–89*, I (Geneva: GATT, 1989), 25.

expanded, there would be little prospect that trade would continue to promote the growth of developed countries in the future, as it had done in the past.[26] A further issue was that some services (e.g., insurance, financial services) were linked to merchandise trade, and that failure to liberalize the former would restrict growth of the latter. Finally, although trade data show that trade in services is only about one-fifth of total world exports, statistics from the 1980s showed trade in services growing at 7.5 per cent on average against an average of 5.5 per cent for merchandise for the decade.[27] The unavoidable conclusion from these data was that liberalization of trade in services was necessary to maintain the GATT as a relevant instrument of international trade policy for developed countries.

The United States took the lead in pushing for the inclusion of trade in services in a new GATT negotiation. 'In today's world', stated a US representative at a preliminary meeting, 'the services sectors are the engine of growth of the world economy and are a major contribution to technological improvement and competitiveness for goods and services.'[28] This policy reflected US economic interests, for it had a higher share of services in the domestic economy than other OECD countries.[29] However, the US lead was quickly followed by the smaller industrialized countries, as indicated in a statement from a Swedish representative: 'the Nordic countries . . . consider that one of the important objectives of a new trade round should be the creation of a system that was capable of handling not only the trade policy problems of today but also those of tomorrow.'[30] Thus, the attraction of adding services to the GATT agenda was that this promised to keep the trade policy agenda consistent with the changes already occurring—or about to occur—in actual trade relations between countries.

The United States attempted to convince the European Community in the early 1980s to support a new negotiation centring on trade in services, but it made little headway until the GATT ministerial meeting at Punta del Este in 1986. The EC delegation was sensitive to the opposition to services among some influential developing countries and attempted to find a middle ground. However, what convinced the Europeans was the recognition that Western Europe accounted for over half of the world trade in services by the mid-1980s.[31] Moreover, services were likely to be as much a growth area for Europe as for the United States in the future. The economic interests of the EU clearly supported a GATT negotiation on services.

## Conclusion

There was widespread agreement at the start of the Uruguay Round that the objective of the negotiation was to restore confidence in the GATT multilateral trade system. This chapter has argued that the reason governments felt a need to revitalize the system was the mismatch between the GATT system and the direction the world economy was taking by the early 1980s. The GATT contract was established to expand trade. However, it was questionable whether this purpose was being served, given (1) the slowdown of the international economy in the 1970s and early 1980s, (2) the inability of the GATT to tackle protectionism in agriculture or textiles, and (3) the development of the service economy.

Incentives other than developments in the world economy also encouraged countries to negotiate the Uruguay Round. One was the threat to multilateralism posed by regional trade agreements, especially the expansion of the European Union and the initiation of a bilateral trade agreement between Canada and the United States. Another was the widespread use of voluntary restraint agreements, or other similar mechanisms,

designed to circumvent the fundamental most-favoured-nation and national treatment requirements of the GATT. Yet a third incentive was the use of unilateral trade sanctions by the United States, inspired partly by the struggle of the US Congress to take control of trade policy from the executive.[32] All these actions were indicative of a world trade system that was not working well, and they likely did encourage countries to enter a negotiation to improve that system. However, the principal incentive to negotiate was that the world economy was becoming a different entity than the one the GATT was created for, and trading countries faced a choice of either revitalizing multilateral trade rules or risking their loss altogether.

International negotiations proceed more on the basis of fear than opportunity, and often a sense of apprehension or threat is the catalyst that initiates the process. In the Kennedy and Tokyo Rounds, that catalyst was provided by the actions of large trading actors, which created in their trading partners an incentive to negotiate. In the Uruguay Round, the threat was more diffuse, and it originated with systemic changes in the world economy that were not under the control of any one or several countries. The threat took time to comprehend, and as a result it took some six years for the GATT to complete pre-negotiations and to initiate formally a new negotiation. It was clear by the mid-1980s that the direction the world economy was taking and the concern this created for the relevance of the trade system were the reasons why governments felt a new negotiation was needed.

## Notes

1 Ernest H. Preeg, *Traders in a Brave New World: The Uruguay Round and the Future of the International System* (Chicago: University of Chicago Press, 1995), 28.

2 GATT, *International Trade 85–86* (Geneva: GATT, 1986), 26. See also Gilbert R. Winham, *International Trade and the Tokyo Round Negotiation* (Princeton, NJ: Princeton University Press, 1986).

3 Senior Officials' Group, Record of Discussions: Note by the Secretariat (GATT doc., SR.SOG/2,

Nov. 1985), 17. This observation is supported by the chief negotiator for the European Union: 'Its [the Uruguay Round] aim was quite simply to carry out a complete overhaul of the multilateral trading system, whilst at the same time broadening and deepening its scope'. Hugo Paemen and Alexandra Bensch, *From the GATT to the WTO: The European Community in the Uruguay Round* (Leuven: Leuven University Press, 1995), 89.

4  The impact of the Uruguay Round has been described in the following terms: 'The agreements, if taken at their face value, show promise of reshaping trade relationships throughout the world.' Raymond Vernon, 'The World Trade Organization: A New Stage in International Trade and Development', *Harvard International Law Journal* 36, 2 (Spring 1995): 329–40.

5  A former Australian head of delegation to the Uruguay Round has observed: 'When the United States started advocating a new trade round, its first supporters were Japan, the smaller industrialized countries and some of the Latin Americans, mainly the agricultural exporters. The European Community was ambivalent.' Alan Oxley, *The Challenge of Free Trade* (New York: St Martin's Press, 1990), 97.

6  Odell has examined market conditions as an explanation for international economic negotiations, which is analogous to the argument presented here. See John Odell, 'Understanding International Trade Policies: An Emerging Synthesis', *World Politics* 43, 1 (Oct. 1990): 139–67.

7  Angus Maddison, *The World Economy in the 20th Century* (Paris: OECD Development Centre, 1989), 36, 67.

8  Ibid., 88.

9  Sylvia Ostry, *The Post-Cold War Trading System: Who's on First?* (Chicago: University of Chicago Press, 1997), esp. ch. 5, 'The East Asian Challenge'.

10  Maddison, *The World Economy*, 88.

11  Paul Krugman, *The Age of Diminished Expectations: U.S. Economic Policy in the 1990s* (Cambridge, Mass.: MIT Press, 1992), ch. 3.

12  See Peter J. Katzenstein, *Small States in World Markets: Industrial Policy in Europe* (Ithaca, NY: Cornell University Press, 1985).

13  *Report of the Royal Commission on the Economic Union and Development Prospects for Canada* (Macdonald Report) (Ottawa: Minister of Supply and Services, 1985).

14  Ibid., I, 263.

15  Maddison, *The World Economy*, 27.

16  C. Fred Bergsten, 'The United States and the World Economy', *The Annals* 460 (Mar. 1982): 12.

17  Ibid.

18  Maddison, *The World Economy*, Table D–6, 143.

19  Senior Officials' Group, *Record of Discussion*, (GATT doc.SR.SOG/4, 22 Nov. 1985), 8.

20  See Gilbert R. Winham, 'Explanations of Developing Country Behaviour in the Uruguay Round', *World Competition* 21, 3 (Mar. 1998): 109–34.

21  *International Trade 85–86*, Table 1.9.

22  GATT, *International Trade 87–88*, II (Geneva: GATT, 1988), 39.

23  Ibid.

24  Senior Officials' Group, Record of Discussions (GATT doc. SR.SOG/10, 22 Nov. 1985), 13.

25  See 'Services in the Domestic and Global Economy', GATT, *International Trade 88–89*, I (Geneva: GATT, 1989), 23–43.

26  See William E. Brock, 'A Simple Plan for Negotiating on Trade in Services', *The World Economy* 5, 3 (Nov. 1982), 229–40. See also Paemen and Bensch, *From the GATT to the WTO*, 17: 'For societies keen to retain the privileges of wealth, the limits to the development of the North-North trade in goods provide justification enough for launching a new initiative to conquer new markets. When it comes to expanding markets, the services sector appears to be promising.'

27  GATT, *International Trade 90–91* (Geneva: GATT, 1991), 1.

28  Senior Officials' Group, Record of Discussions (GATT doc. SR.SOG/9, 22 Nov. 1985), 1.

29  In 1987, the United States had 68 per cent of the GDP in services, 30 per cent in industry, and 2 per cent in agriculture.

30  Senior Officials' Group, Record of Discussions (GATT doc. SR.SOG/9, 22 Nov. 1985), 6.

31  GATT, *International Trade 88–89*, I, 31, Table 22. Western Europe had 58 per cent of services trade (exports plus imports), followed by Asia with 18 per cent and North America with 14 per cent.

32  See Patrick Low, *Trading Free: The GATT and US Trade Policy* (New York: Twentieth Century Fund Press, 1993). Low suggests unilateral actions alarmed US trade partners, including the EU, and may have created an incentive to negotiate.

## Suggested Readings

Cox, Robert W. *The New Realism: Perspectives on Multilateralism and World Order.* Houndmills, Basingstoke: Macmillan, 1997.

Cox, Robert W., and Bjorn Hettne, eds. *International Political Economy: Understanding Global Disorder.* Halifax: Fernwood Publishing, 1995.

Jackson, John Howard. *The Uruguay Round, World Trade Organization and the Problem of Regulating International Economic Behaviour.* Ottawa: Centre for Trade Policy and Law, 1995.

Preeg, Ernest H. *Traders in a Brave New World: The Uruguay Round and the Future of the International System.* Chicago: University of Chicago Press, 1995.

Paemen, Hugo, and Alexandra Bensch. *From the GATT to the WTO: The European Community in the Uruguay Round.* Leuven: Leuven University Press, 1995.

Thomas, Jeffrey S. *The New Rules of Global Trade: A Guide to the World Trade Organization.* Scarborough, Ont.: Carswell, 1997.

## Web Sites

World Trade Organization: http://www.wto.org

International Monetary Fund: http://www.imf.org

World Bank: http://www.worldbank.org

*Chapter 13*

# Big Business and the New Trade Agreements:
## The Future of the WTO?

*Susan K. Sell*

The Uruguay Round of the General Agreement on Tariffs and Trade (GATT) negotiations ushered in a new era in multilateral trade policy by dramatically expanding the scope of disciplines covered and strengthening the dispute resolution mechanisms.[1] For the first time, the multilateral agreements explicitly incorporate intellectual property, investment, and services (e.g., banking, insurance). This chapter examines the role and variable success of the private sector in making the rules of international commerce that determine winners and losers in the global political economy. In each of these cases the driving forces behind these new agreements—trade-related intellectual property rights (TRIPs), trade-related investment measures (TRIMs), the General Agreement on Trade in Services (GATS), and the financial services agreement—were US private-sector actors. These private-sector actors represented the most globally competitive industries and the strongest transnational corporate players. The new agreements enshrined in the World Trade Organization (WTO) were the culmination of decades-long efforts of these private-sector actors to get states to classify these issues as trade-related and assign them pride of place in multilateral negotiations. A traditional state-centric approach simply cannot capture the complex process that led to these agreements; they were developed at multiple levels in multiple venues and involved firm-to-firm negotiations, firm-to-state negotiations, and state-to-state negotiations. These agreements would not exist without the private-sector efforts. The Uruguay Round process and the establishment of these agreements reveal a more complex picture of sources of authority in the global political economy.

Following Susan Strange, this chapter addresses these questions: 'Who, or what, is responsible for change?' and 'Who or what exercises authority—the power to alter outcomes and redefine options for others—in the world economy?'[2] In the new WTO agreements did private authority prevail? To what extent did the private sector achieve its objectives?

If, by 'authoritative', we mean that parties regard agreements as binding and that the agreements alter outcomes for others, the TRIPs and financial services agreements are the clearest examples of the exercise of private authority, the GATS agreement presents a more mixed picture, and the TRIMs agreement is a failure from the private-sector perspective. Placing the new agreements on a spectrum, we find the TRIPs and the financial services agreements are the most authoritative, the GATS is in the middle, and the TRIMs agreement is the least authoritative. The US private sector actively pushed for all these agreements, so the variation in outcomes suggests that private authority is not trumping in all areas. Decisive factors leading to the TRIPs and financial services agreements were transnational private-sector mobilization of an OECD consensus and the lack of sustained opposition. By contrast, in the weaker agreements, the GATS and TRIMs, there was no transnational private-sector mobilization, no OECD consensus, and sustained opposition. The TRIMs agreement was further stymied by two additional factors—substantial host country bargaining power and splits between the US private sector and the American government on matters of national security.

The new WTO agreements are a product of structured agency. Changes in the structure of the global political economy have brought forth a newly powerful group of private-sector players. Changes in technology and markets have empowered a new set of actors who are pushing for greater liberalization in investment and services and greater protection of intellectual property. While the GATT traditionally focused on trade in goods, the importance of services and investment in the global political economy has dramatically increased. Services trade is one of the most dynamic areas of the global economy, growing at an average annual rate of 8.3 per cent.[3] Throughout the 1980s services trade grew faster than trade in goods. By 1993 global services trade amounted to US $930 billion, equalling 22 per cent of global trade (goods plus services).[4] Similarly in investment, between 1985 and 1995 the annual global flow of foreign direct investment (FDI) rose from $60 billion to $315 billion; in 1993 sales by foreign affiliates were estimated at $6 trillion, well above the total world trade in goods and services ($4.7 trillion).[5]

The GATT's success in cutting tariffs and reducing border impediments over successive negotiating rounds has led negotiators to address inside-the-border, or structural, impediments and non-tariff measures that distort free trade. These measures implicate domestic regulatory policy, fundamentally challenging states' policy-making discretion. Issues such as market access, rights of establishment for foreign enterprises, trade-related investment measures (e.g., performance requirements), and the protection of intellectual property rights reach much deeper into state policies than previous GATT issues.

The United States pushed hardest for the inclusion of investment, services, intellectual property protection, and a revamped dispute settlement mechanism. The US interest in these new issues originated from private-sector pressure. Particularly in services and intellectual property protection, the US government responded to a sustained, decades-long effort of private-sector actors to link these issues to trade. These actors succeeded in getting recognition for this linkage in amendments to US trade laws in the 1970s and 1980s, and the United States Trade Representative (USTR, an agency

particularly susceptible to private-sector pressure) pursued their goals by invoking Section 301, Super 301, and Special 301 of the US trade laws and engaging in what has come to be known as 'aggressive unilateralism'.

This chapter first discusses the process leading to the TRIPs agreement. It then provides a comparative overview of the GATS, the financial services agreement, and the TRIMs, and briefly discusses the significance of the new dispute settlement mechanism. The chapter concludes by looking ahead at the future evolution of the WTO.

## Intellectual Property Protection: TRIPs[6]

As technological prowess increasingly has become diffused throughout the global economy, the capacity of others inexpensively to reproduce expensively produced goods has grown. As technological capability has dispersed more widely, certain types of technology have become relatively easy and inexpensive to appropriate. Computer software, pharmaceuticals, and digital audio recordings are just three of the more glaring examples. American-based firms have comparative advantage in these products, but felt they faced losing that advantage without government help in prompting other countries to protect US-held intellectual property. First, acting primarily through industry associations, they urged the government to pressure foreign governments to adopt and enforce more stringent protection. They sought and won changes in US domestic laws—most notably Sections 301 and 337 of the US trade laws.

A handful of US-based transnational corporations spearheaded the effort to secure a multilateral instrument codifying their interest in stricter intellectual property protection and to build an OECD consensus. Twelve US transnational corporations[7] bypassed their industry associations and formed an ad hoc lobby group—the US-based Intellectual Property Committee (IPC)—in March 1986. The IPC lobbied the US government to support and promote a multilateral instrument through GATT. Transnationally, the IPC member executives directly engaged their European and Japanese counterparts to press for a TRIPs agreement in the GATT. In the summer of 1986 the IPC met with the Confederation of British Industries, the Bundesverband der Deutschen Industrie in Germany, the French Patronat, the Union of Industrial and Employers' Confederations of Europe (UNICE), and the Japan Federation of Economic Organizations (Keidanren). The IPC stressed that intellectual property was too important to leave to governments and argued that industry needed to decide on the best course of action and then tell governments what to do. The IPC succeeded in forging an industry consensus with its Japanese and European counterparts, who pledged to present these views to their respective governments in time for the launching of the Uruguay Round. UNICE and Keidanren successfully advanced their cause to their governments in the short time remaining; by the launching of the Round in September 1986, the United States, Japan, and Europe were united behind the inclusion of an intellectual property code in the GATT.

Industry representatives met in October and November 1986 and began work on a consensus document to present to their respective governments and the GATT secretariat. By June 1988 this trilateral group released its 'Basic Framework of GATT Provisions on Intellectual Property'. The IPC, UNICE, and Keidanren then went home to sell this trilateral approach to other companies and industries. The US government requested 100–150 copies of the June 1988 proposal and sent it out as reflecting its views.[8] By 1994, the IPC had achieved its goal in the TRIPs accord of the concluded trade round. According to Jacques Gorlin, adviser to the IPC and primary US author of the 'Basic Framework' document, the IPC got 95 per cent of what it wanted.[9]

The transnational leadership of the IPC was decisive in the achievement of the TRIPs accord. The transnational private-sector coalition seeking to globalize its preferred conception of intellectual property policy needs the GATT to further and legitimize its goals, monitor compliance, and enforce policy. The 1994 TRIPs accord codifies a trade-based conception that requires signatory states to enact implementing domestic legislation, adopt enforcement measures, provide intellectual property

owners with a 20-year monopoly right, and face the threat of trade sanctions if they fail to comply with the TRIPs provisions. The agreement closely mirrors the expressed wishes of the IPC. It is based on a conception of intellectual property rights that privileges property creation over diffusion. In two departures from GATT precedent the TRIPs accord obliges governments 'to take positive action to protect intellectual property rights'[10] *and applies to the private rights of individual rights holders* and not to goods.[11] Further, the dramatic expansion of the scope of intellectual property rights embodied in the TRIPs accord reduces the options available to future industrializers. Industrialized countries built much of their economic prowess on appropriating others' intellectual property; with the TRIPs accord this option is foreclosed for less-developed countries. It raises the price of information and technology by extending monopoly privileges of rights holders and requires states to play a much greater role in defending them. While the long-term redistributive implications of TRIPs are not yet fully understood, the short-term impact of the agreement undoubtedly will be a significant transfer of resources from developing country consumers and firms to industrialized country firms.[12] In short, it represents a decisive triumph for established private-sector interests.

Initially, developing countries resisted the inclusion of intellectual property in the negotiations, but by April 1989 they had dropped their opposition. Having faced escalating US aggressive unilateralism, they hoped that co-operation on TRIPs would ease this pressure. Further, they were willing to go along with TRIPs in exchange for concessions on issues of greater short- to medium-term salience, such as agriculture and the phasing out of the Multifibre Arrangements. The transnational private-sector mobilization of an OECD consensus and the collapse of developing countries' opposition were decisive factors in the TRIPs outcome.

## General Agreement on Trade in Services

The spectacular growth of global trade in services and intensified competition in large markets have sharpened concerns over differences in domestic regulatory policy. The goal of the activist private-sector service providers is expanded market access and the elimination of domestic regulations and administrative practices that interfere with free and open trade. Unlike trade in goods, services trade often requires an established office in host countries through international direct investment; many services depend on the proximity of the provider and consumer. Accounting for 60 per cent of world consumption, services make up only 20 per cent of world trade;[13] this discrepancy highlights the pervasiveness of domestic impediments facing foreign service providers.

The private sector in the United States sought to achieve significant liberalization of foreign services markets. Beginning in the 1970s, the US financial services sector, including the insurance industry, pushed for inclusion of services under the GATT umbrella. This industry lobbied the US government and led a decades-long campaign to promote a multilateral services agreement to remove barriers to market access. Like the intellectual property lobby, private-sector services activists convinced the US government to incorporate services in revisions to its trade laws, and the United States pursued Section 301 actions against Europe and Japan for barriers to services trade. US private-sector lobbyists found a receptive home government preoccupied with its burgeoning trade deficits in the mid-1980s. The services industries pointed to growing surpluses in services sectors and claimed that services were part of the solution to the trade problem. The US government, and particularly the USTR and Treasury, came to champion their cause. Over time, this cross-industry group marshalled additional support from other services sectors and formed a Coalition of Service Industries to promote its concerns in the GATT deliberations. Its primary target was the highly regulated service markets in Japan and East and Southeast Asia. Initially, developing countries, led by India and Brazil, protested the inclusion of services in the Uruguay Round. However, negotiators reached a compromise to negotiate a separate services agreement.

To the extent that a GATS exists at all, the private sector won an important victory by obtaining multilateral recognition that services trade merits multilateral treatment. However, the private sector was largely disappointed with the results of the actual agreement. First, the US private-sector lobbyists favoured, yet failed to achieve, an ambitiously liberalizing agreement, which met with opposition from both developing countries and the Europeans.

Second, the GATS agreement is weak and involves significant derogations from the GATT treatment of trade in goods. For example, the GATT principles of most-favoured nation (MFN) status and national treatment—the twin pillars of non-discrimination—are both compromised in the GATS. GATS signatories are free to include a list of sectors in an annex, for which MFN will not apply. This is referred to as the 'negative list' approach, identifying those sectors for which the general obligation does *not* apply. The MFN exemption annex arose out of concerns of service providers based in relatively open markets that competitors based in sheltered markets would be able to free-ride on the agreements.[14] In a perfect world, US service providers preferred extensive market access; short of that their fallback position was to reserve the right to deny insufficiently open countries MFN treatment. Since the GATS agreement failed to open foreign markets to their satisfaction, US private-sector interests sought to maintain negotiating leverage by invoking sectoral (or mirror-image) reciprocity—withholding MFN privileges from those competitors in restricted markets.

Third, the national treatment commitment is also watered down through a 'positive list' approach in which national treatment applies only to those sectors listed in a member's schedule of commitments.[15] As Low and Subramanian point out, 'national treatment has been transformed from a principle into negotiating currency under GATS.'[16] Thus, the GATS agreement only partly reflects the goals of the private sector; it is 'second best', and is a substantially weaker agreement than the TRIPs. Rather than achieving substantial liberalization, the GATS amounts essentially to a standstill on existing restrictions in various services sectors—there was no significant rolling back of barriers to services trade.[17] The Coalition of Service Industries has argued that standstill commitments do not constitute liberalization and thus fall well short of their preferred outcome. By binding themselves to general obligations only in services sectors they chose to list, states retained considerable discretion in regulatory policy governing services trade and investment. The USTR adviser to the US TRIMs delegation concluded that the GATS is a 'convoluted agreement with limited practical protection for globally active firms'.[18] However, given the fact that it took over 20 years to liberalize trade in goods, the weakness of this agreement is hardly surprising.

## Financial Services Agreement

Throughout the course of the GATS negotiations, negotiators realized that sectors such as telecommunications and financial services were proving to be exceptionally difficult. Therefore, participants agreed to negotiate these as separate agreements after the conclusion of the Uruguay Round. The telecommunications agreement was concluded in February 1997; while it codified significant liberalizations, some glaring discrepancies still remain. For example, while the United States imposes no limitations on foreign ownership of its basic telecommunication service market, the Japanese limit such investment to 20 per cent.[19] The financial services agreements proved quite contentious; indeed, frustrated by the lack of progress at the end of 1995 the US delegation, prompted by its domestic industry, walked out.

Two significant developments occurred between 1995 and December 1997 that turned the tide in favour of a strong multilateral agreement on financial services. First was the changing role of the EU, and second, the Asian currency crisis. I will discuss each of these in turn.

In 1995 the EU 'rallied other WTO members' and they negotiated an interim agreement without the United States.[20] Between 1995 and 1997 the European Union assumed leadership within the deliberations and worked hard to secure improvements in member states' commitments. While the United States had initially pushed hardest for a

financial services agreement, by 1995 the EU was eager for an agreement and worked hard to improve WTO members' offers and to get the United States back on board. The European Commission, national governments, and the private sector sought to engage the US private sector in continuing the dialogue. In Davos, Switzerland, in early 1996, transnational private-sector mobilization began in earnest. US and European service providers discussed the prospects for a financial services agreement. US, UK, and European financial services industry representatives met at the office of British Invisibles (an association to promote UK-based financial services firms); these representatives formed the 'Financial Leaders Group' to present a unified business view of objectives in the financial services deliberations. The FLG largely reflected UK and US views, but substantially broadened its base of support and made significant progress in identifying common ground.

Back in 1995 the United States was particularly frustrated with the lack of market access commitments from East and Southeast Asian countries. However, the currency crisis that erupted in Asia in July 1997 provided an unexpected boost to open Asian financial services markets that were recalcitrant targets of Uruguay Round talks. Market-opening measures were urged to inspire 'investor confidence', and the crisis spurred a conclusion to the financial services negotiations. US negotiators were sufficiently satisfied with the improved market-opening commitments and withdrew broad MFN exemptions based on reciprocity. Negotiators reached an eleventh-hour agreement in Geneva on 13 December 1997. American private-sector representatives of Citicorp, Goldman Sachs, Merrill Lynch, and the insurance industry set up command posts near the WTO headquarters and conferred with American negotiators throughout this last round of talks.[21] As Jeffrey Shafer, the vice-chairman of Salomon Brothers International, said, the agreement 'will go some way to lock in a trend that was already in effect in the world toward liberalization. . . . It's like an insurance policy for the structure of the world.'[22]

## Trade-Related Investment Measures

Of the four agreements reviewed here, the TRIMs are undoubtedly the weakest. Again, US private-sector activists spearheaded this effort, but in this instance they were stymied by a complex array of factors. First, developing countries' opposition to the inclusion of investment issues led negotiators to address TRIMs on a separate track. Countries such as India and Brazil, with their large and relatively protected markets, possess considerable negotiating leverage vis-à-vis foreign investors seeking to do business there. Second, fundamental disagreements among OECD members meant that the ultimate provisions were likely to be weak. The negotiating committee was committed to producing an agreement to which all nations could unanimously subscribe, so that only the 'most egregious of practices in clear violation of existing GATT articles'[23] were ultimately included. And third, the US private-sector activists found themselves at odds with the US government on security issues.

The American private sector lobbied on investment issues through the US Council for International Business (the American affiliate of the International Chamber of Commerce), the Coalition of Services Industries, and the Securities Industry Association.[24] Broadly, those pushing for a TRIMs agreement sought non-discrimination, especially regarding rights of establishment, national treatment, and the elimination of trade-distorting investment measures (e.g., requirements mandating local content and export performance). The overriding concern was to open the Japanese and East and Southeast Asian markets to foreign investment, given Europe's comparative openness and liberalization in key Latin American markets. At the outset of the negotiations, the US produced an ambitious agenda to create a GATT for investment. Faced with stiff opposition from developing countries, 'who sought to preserve their sovereignty over investment policies, the US conceded—for the sake of keeping TRIPs and services on the agenda—to a narrow mandate for the TRIMs negotiations.'[25]

Furthermore, many OECD states were reluctant to lock in liberalizing reforms under a multilateral instrument on investment. As Low and Subramanian suggest, 'doubts linger about how monopolistic MNE [multinational enterprise] behavior might become in some circumstances, and worries about sovereign control of resources also continue to cut political ice.'[26] The TRIMs agreement protects only the 'trade flows of investor-enterprises',[27] and affirms two GATT disciplines—national treatment and the prohibition of quantitative restrictions—for investment policies that directly affect trade flows. Signatories must notify the WTO secretariat of performance requirements, such as local content and trade-balancing policies, that are in violation of these GATT disciplines. Members are then bound to eliminate such measures within the grace periods (ranging from two to seven years depending on the country's level of development). Rather than representing a strong instrument for investment liberalization, in legal terms the TRIMs agreement is 'retrograde, since it recognize[s] that countries were in violation of their GATT obligations, and then [gives] them time . . . within which to establish conformity.'[28] Significantly, the TRIMs agreement neither guarantees rights of establishment nor full national treatment for foreign investors. In addition, much to the dismay of the private-sector activists, export performance requirements were left untouched. Countries such as India have successfully reserved the right to require export performance of investors seeking entry into their large sheltered markets. Host country market power is an important factor militating against a strong investment agreement; as Walter points out, 'with respect to East Asia, seen as the hardest nut to crack on the investment issue, the US business community will take what it can get.'[29]

The business community was deeply disappointed in the TRIMs negotiations; its initial enthusiasm waned as the process unfolded. It soon became apparent that the best they could hope for in the multilateral context was a 'lowest common denominator'[30] approach, which is exactly what they got. Given the failure of the WTO effort, the private sector quickly shifted its attention to the OECD, and the OECD launched negotiations on a Multilateral Agreement on Investment (MAI) in September 1995. Investment enthusiasts hoped that a high-standard OECD agreement would provide the eventual impetus for a meaningful multilateral agreement and inspire a 'race to the top' among non-members trying to attract FDI. The US private sector sought, first and foremost, the right of establishment and an investor-state dispute settlement arrangement rather than the limited WTO state-state dispute settlement mechanism.

However, like the TRIMs negotiations, the MAI negotiations revealed deep and intractable differences even among allegedly 'like-minded' states. While the UK, Germany, the Netherlands, and Japan have been generally supportive of US aims, other OECD countries (France, Canada, Australia, New Zealand, and new members such as Mexico, South Korea, Poland, and the Czech Republic) have not. Furthermore, the US government has opposed certain US business interests in the name of national security. The government has defended its right to uphold the Helms-Burton Act prohibiting investment in Cuba and the Iran-Libya Sanctions Act. In addition, it appears that a new set of lobbyists has wrested control of the agenda from the business lobby; a transnational coalition of labour and environmental groups has become increasingly vocal, active, and effective.[31] The deadline for a final agreement has been consistently postponed because of fundamental disagreements among the negotiating countries. As well, since non-OECD members are significant as both host and home nations to FDI, critics point out that an OECD-only code would be virtually meaningless.[32] At the end of 1998 negotiators finally shelved the MAI effort.

## Dispute Settlement Mechanisms in the WTO

One of the chief aims of the US private sector in the Uruguay Round was to strengthen GATT dispute settlement procedures. The weakness of the GATT dispute settlement mechanism was an important factor motivating the US pursuit of aggressive unilateralism via Section 301. Under the old GATT system, losing defendants were able to veto decisions they found to be unacceptable. Furthermore, disputes could drag on for years and parties were free to engage in 'forum shopping'. The American private sector sought quicker and more binding decisions, and in the WTO dispute settlement mechanism they won an important victory. Negotiators agreed to the establishment of a 'Dispute Settlement Body' (DSB) to oversee the dispute resolution process, effectively ending the forum shopping option. The WTO establishes strict timetables for processing disputes and makes all decisions binding unless the DSB votes unanimously to overrule them.[33] This eliminates the ability of losers to block decisions. A new institution, the WTO's Appellate Body, is charged with hearing appeals. Its decisions are binding unless the DSB unanimously votes to overrule it. Therefore, 'the winning party may veto any attempt by other nations to reject a particular decision.'[34] Under the dispute settlement mechanisms cross-retaliation is now possible, so that, for example, infractions in intellectual property or services can lead to sanctions on goods. The WTO is also empowered to monitor compliance to make sure that defendants carry out their obligations within a reasonable period of time. If the defendants fail to comply, the WTO will authorize the complainant to impose retaliatory trade sanctions if requested to do so. Thus, the new dispute settlement procedures represent significant improvement from the private-sector perspective. Of course, the viability of the dispute settlement mechanism remains an open question. Will powerful states abide by rulings they dislike?

Two further issues may prove to be problematic. One is the question of who should have standing, and the second is the degree to which unilateral action would still be possible under the new arrangements. The private sector remains dissatisfied with the WTO dispute settlement mechanisms insofar as only states have standing. Private-sector activists have sought formal standing whereby firms could bring complaints to the WTO. They have pointed to NAFTA, which gives private actors direct access in specific issue-areas, as a preferable model. A number of commentators support this idea.[35] Yet, environmental, labour, and consumer NGOs have also pressed for direct access in the MAI deliberations and reject the idea of giving corporations standing in MAI dispute settlement. This indicates a burgeoning movement for the incorporation of social, as opposed to purely commercial, interests in multilateral trade institutions. In Gramscian terms this may represent the emergence of a 'counterhegemony' seeking to balance broader social goals with strictly commercial agendas.

Further, article 23 of the dispute settlement procedures 'stipulates that states shall not make any unilateral determinations that treaty violations have occurred' and are barred from imposing sanctions unless they are approved by the DSB.[36] This provision was important to member states whose support of the US Uruguay Round agenda was powerfully motivated by their desire to constrain US unilateralism. Does article 23 bar the United States from employing Section 301 actions? The US private sector, backed by the government, argues that 301 is not incompatible with the WTO, while the Europeans and Japanese maintain that the WTO now makes 301 illegal. Insofar as US trading partners assented to the new dispute settlement mechanisms in large part to end aggressive unilateralism, the controversy over article 23 is likely to intensify. The Americans can be expected to continue to pursue Section 301 actions in areas not covered by WTO disciplines. However, if they try to pursue aggressive unilateralism in areas covered by the WTO, they will be met with opposition.

## Looking Ahead

Returning to the questions raised at the outset, this chapter has argued that the US private sector has been the driving force behind the incorporation of these new issues and the strengthening of the dispute settlement procedures in the multilateral trading system. The more binding the measures, the more they redefine options for others. Evaluating the exercise of private authority in this context, the TRIPs accord and financial services agreement provide the strongest evidence that private authority prevailed and private-sector activists achieved their

objectives. The GATS presents a mixed picture: the private sector achieved some of its aims, but the final agreement fell well short of its liberalizing intentions by reserving a broad scope for state discretion. The TRIMs agreement is the weakest; the private sector failed to achieve its objectives and the weakness of the agreement does little in terms of redefining options for others. The dispute settlement mechanisms certainly do redefine options, but, depending on the outcome of the article 23 controversy, these may undermine the private-sector activists' ability to invoke unilateral action to open markets.

Private-sector success in TRIPs was largely due to transnational private-sector mobilization, led by the IPC, to produce an OECD consensus on specific negotiating proposals. The eventual collapse of developing countries' opposition to the inclusion of intellectual property further facilitated the IPC's goals. Developing countries were willing to accept the OECD intellectual property agenda in exchange for concessions on agriculture and the Multifibre Arrangements. Similarly in financial services, transnational private-sector mobilization—this time led by British and European service providers—and the weakening of developing country opposition, reflected in the improved market access commitments of the Asian states, led to private-sector triumph. By contrast, both the GATS and TRIMs deliberations revealed sharp differences among OECD countries in addition to differences between the OECD and developing countries. Furthermore, the private-sector strategy in the latter two cases appeared to be limited to 'indirect lobbying',[37] whereby private-sector actors lobbied their home governments, rather than transnational mobilization. In the investment area, host country market power and differences between the US private sector and the US government on national security issues further reduced the prospects that the private sector would achieve its goals.

Overall, the evidence presented in this chapter should inspire caution about wholeheartedly embracing the globalization thesis—that somehow commercial interests are triumphing over social interests. Instead, it has revealed the patchy and uneven triumph of private authority. Investigating each sector and each issue reveals different outcomes; sweeping generalizations are less helpful as one moves closer to the ground.

The evolution of the multilateral trading system is a dynamic process, and the agreements now enshrined in the WTO will be subject to re-evaluation and political contestation. There is a long way to go on services and TRIMs, which will be revisited in the year 2000. Whether the WTO moves further in the direction of championing private-sector interests will undoubtedly depend on the outcome of the emerging tension between commercial and social agendas.

## Notes

1   I wish to thank Duncan Matthews, Chris May, Jay Smith, and Andrew Walter for invaluable comments on an earlier draft, and Stephen Woolcock for providing me with helpful information on financial services.

2   Susan Strange, *The Retreat of the State: The Diffusion of Power in the World Economy* (Cambridge: Cambridge University Press, 1996), 184.

3   Bernard Hoekman, 'Assessing the General Agreement on Trade in Services', in Will Martin and L. Alan Winters, eds, *The Uruguay Round and the Developing Economies* (Washington: World Bank, 1995), 329.

4   Bernard M. Hoekman and Michel M. Kostecki, *The Political Economy of the World Trading System: From GATT to WTO* (Oxford: Oxford University Press, 1995), 127.

5   Andrew Walter, 'Globalization and Corporate Power: Who Is Setting the Rules on International Direct Investment?', paper prepared for conference on Non-State Actors and Authority in the Global System, 31 Oct.–1 Nov. 1997, Warwick University (UK), 1.

6   For an expanded discussion, see Susan K. Sell, 'Multinational Corporations as Agents of Change: The Globalization of Intellectual Property Rights', in A. Claire Cutler, Virginia Haufler, and Tony Porter, eds, *Private Authority and International Affairs* (Albany: State University of New York Press, 1999).

7   In 1986, the IPC represented: Bristol-Myers Squibb; Digital Equipment Corporation; FMC; General Electric; Hewlett-Packard; IBM; Johnson & Johnson; Merck; Pfizer; Procter & Gamble; Rockwell International; and Time-Warner.

8   Author's interview with Jacques Gorlin, adviser to the IPC, 22 Jan. 1996, Washington.

9   Ibid.

10  Hoekman and Kostecki, *The Political Economy of the World Trading System*, 156.

11  Michael Reiterer, 'Trade-Related Intellectual Property Rights', in *The New World Trading System: Readings* (Paris: OECD, 1994), 199–200.

12  Dani Rodrik, 'Comments on Maskus and Eby-Konan', in A. Deardorff and R. Stern, eds, *Analytic and Negotiating Issues in the Global Trading System* (Ann Arbor: University of Michigan Press, 1994), 449.

13  DeAnne Julius, 'International Direct Investment: Strengthening the Policy Regime', in Peter Kenen, ed., *Managing the World Economy: Fifty Years After Bretton Woods* (Washington: Institute for International Economics, 1994), 277.

14  Hoekman and Kostecki, *The Political Economy of the World Trading System*, 132.

15  Ibid., 131.

16  Patrick Low and Arvind Subramanian, 'TRIMs in the Uruguay Round: An Unfinished Business?', in Martin and Winters, eds, *The Uruguay Round*, 423.

17  See Walter, 'Globalization and Corporate Power'; Hoekman and Kostecki, *The Political Economy of the World Trading System*.

18  Daniel M. Price, 'Investment Rules and High Technology: Towards a Multilateral Agreement on Investment', in *Market Access After the Uruguay Round: Investment, Competition and Technology Perspectives* (Paris: OECD, 1996), 182.

19  Walter, 'Globalization and Corporate Power', 27.

20  The following discussion of the EU role is based on Stephen Woolcock, 'Liberalisation of Financial

Services', *European Policy Forum*, London (Oct. 1997).

21  'Accord is Reached to Lower Barriers in Global Finance', *New York Times*, 13 Dec. 1997, A1, B2.

22  'Nations Reach Agreement on Financial Services Pact', *Washington Post*, 13 Dec. 1997, A17.

23  Edward M. Graham, 'Investment and the New Multilateral Context', in *Market Access After the Uruguay Round*, 50.

24  Walter, 'Globalization and Corporate Power', 17.

25  Low and Subramanian, 'TRIMs in the Uruguay Round', 416.

26  Ibid., 421.

27  Price, 'Investment Rules', 182.

28  Low and Subramanian, 'TRIMs in the Uruguay Round', 418.

29  Walter, 'Globalization and Corporate Power', 19.

30  The following discussion is based on ibid., 28, 38.

31  For example, Ralph Nader's consumer group, Public Citizen, and environmental lobby groups including the Sierra Club and Friends of the Earth have launched a vigorous anti-MAI campaign.

32  See, for example, Edward Graham, 'Should There Be Multilateral Rules on FDI?', in John H. Dunning, ed., *Governments, Globalization, and International Business* (Oxford: Oxford University Press, 1997), 503.

33  G. Richard Shell, 'Trade Legalism and International Relations Theory: An Analysis of the World Trade Organization', *Duke Law Journal* 44, 5 (Mar. 1995): 846.

34  Ibid., 850.

35  See, for example, Julius, 'International Direct Investment', 282–3; Graham, 'Should There Be Multilateral Rules on FDI?', 482, 501.

36  Shell, 'Trade Legalism', 852–3.

37  Walter, 'Globalization and Corporate Power', 8.

## Suggested Readings

Cutler, A. Claire, Virginia Haufler, and Tony Porter, eds. *Private Authority and International Affairs*. Albany: State University of New York Press, 1999.

Dunning, John H., ed. *Governments, Globalization, and International Business*. Oxford: Oxford University Press, 1997.

Hoekman, Bernard M., and Michel M. Kostecki. *The Political Economy of the World Trading System: From GATT to WTO*. Oxford: Oxford University Press, 1995.

Kenen, Peter B., ed. *Managing the World Economy: Fifty Years After Bretton Woods*. Washington: Institute for International Economics, 1994.

*Market Access After the Uruguay Round: Investment, Competition and Technology Perspectives*. Paris: OECD, 1996.

Martin, Will, and L. Alan Winters, eds. *The Uruguay Round and the Developing Economies*. Washington: World Bank, 1995.

*The New World Trading System: Readings*. Paris: OECD, 1994.

Shell, G. Richard. 'Trade Legalism and International Relations Theory: An Analysis of the World Trade Organization', *Duke Law Journal* 44, 5 (Mar. 1995): 829–927.

Strange, Susan. *The Retreat of the State: The Diffusion of Power in the World Economy*. Cambridge: Cambridge University Press, 1996.

Whalley, John, and Colleen Hamilton. *The Trading System After the Uruguay Round*. Washington: Institute for International Economics, 1996.

## Web Site

World Trade Organization: http://www.wto.org

## Chapter 14

# Trade Blocs: The Beauty or the Beast in the Theory?

*Daniel Drache*

## Introduction

Élites everywhere are adopting trade-enhancing measures to promote interdependence on an unprecedented scale.[1] Their primary objective is to construct a policy-making environment that will accommodate the many structural changes initiated by the global economy. This is problematic because not only are nation-states themselves much weakened by the globalization of markets and the internationalization of their responsibilities, but trade blocs themselves are enormously fragile.[2] Something important is missing with respect to state strategy and corporate response. No contemporary trade regime has found an effective way to neutralize the asymmetry of power among members, nor has such a regime put in place comprehensive programs to foot the bill for a costly adjustment process. Finally, neither in Europe nor in North America has a trade bloc been able to ensure that access is enhanced for all and is not diminished by non-tariff barriers for small and medium-sized countries.[3]

The linked issues of access: how to enhance it; asymmetry: how to neutralize it; and adjustment: how to plan and pay for the resulting job loss and economic restructuring from these new arrangements—hold the key to whether the wheels of integration keep turning. If a trade bloc expects to succeed, it needs a strong set of non-market regulatory institutions to counter market imperfections and failure. Larger markets operating with less regulation create even larger problems of continuous adjustment. If the prospects of increased welfare make a trade bloc tick, a commercially driven arrangement will flourish and endure. But, should

it fail to live up to expectations and prove unable to deliver higher levels of work, welfare, and well-being, it will misfire and ultimately decline as the benefits from increased integration fail to materialize to the degree hoped for. Without these non-market regulatory forms in place, trade blocs such as the North American Free Trade Agreement (NAFTA) and the European Union (EU) are more likely to become victims of crisis rather than viable alternatives to it.

If trade blocs are no longer simply about a country's trade balance and jobs, then, what are they about? The first part of the chapter scrutinizes the powerful vision behind the formation of a free trade area, focusing principally on NAFTA and the EU single market. Both are regulatory and investment-driven projects committed to removing the remaining restrictions and regulations impeding the free movement of capital, but often in unequal or unbalanced proportions. The European Union has an articulated political superstructure, a bureaucratic apparatus, and an influential role assigned to the European Court of Justice. By comparison, NAFTA's regulatory framework is small and underdeveloped with a minimum number of intergovernmental dispute settlement mechanisms. There is no corresponding mode of political regulation.[4] Each of these two regional trade blocs is bound together in a different manner. The question is, are these trade regimes sustainable in their present form? Or, if they are to achieve their goal of economic and political integration, will they need to be substantially modified?

The second part examines the convergence proposition. Economists use convergence as an important measure to gauge whether states have successfully built a level playing field, particularly in the area of state practice, which is often portrayed as the last bastion of the most restrictive trade practices. The argument advanced by free trade policy experts is that when states accept the discipline of markets the hoped-for result is greater transparency in state practice.[5] Empirically, this claim needs to be scrutinized for its accuracy as well as tested against current trends.

The final part of the chapter examines the way the EU and NAFTA face very different choices. The question it addresses is, if economic integration is to go forward, what different scenarios are on offer for each bloc?

## What Is a Trade Bloc?

NAFTA and the EU are prototypical economic projects reflecting opposite ends of the economic integration process. The institutional forms, the interests of capital and labour, the political parties involved, the market actors, and political cultures are strikingly dissimilar. Fifteen European countries building a common future with a supranational authority having a wide range of administrative, legal, and fiscal instruments working towards monetary union is radically different from a hemispheric arrangement between three countries as economically diverse and distinct as Canada, the United States, and Mexico.[6] None the less, what these mega-projects have in common is a vision of markets as the driving force of well-being and wealth-creation. While their goals and objectives are very different, these agreements go beyond promoting trade and dismantling tariffs to promote capital movements and foreign investment, to facilitate the transfer of technology between large-scale enterprises, to influence the location of future production facilities and in the process redraw the line between the state and the market.

The trade blocs issue has emerged in the 1990s because it touches on the most sensitive economic and political questions at the turn of the millennium: the future of the nation-state as we know it. Trade agreements challenge national regimes for tax, social and employment standards, and state aids. Countries have to cede control over many of the key levers of national economic management such as monetary and labour policy in return for the benefits from increased specialization.[7] Thus, the stakes are high.

While comprehensive economic integration is the goal of every trade bloc, it is never easy to attain because the enhancement of national economic interest (power) is the more immediate objective that convinces countries to enter a comprehensive trade agreement. If governments can overcome

## Table 1: Regional Free Trade Agreements: Share of World Trade, 1994

| | |
|---|---|
| EU | 22.8 |
| Euromed | 2.3 |
| NAFTA | 7.9 |
| MERCOSUR | 0.3 |
| FTAA | 2.6* |
| AFTA | 1.3 |
| Aust.-NZ | 0.1 |
| APEC | 23.7* |
| Total | 61.0 |

*Excluding subregionals.

SOURCE: F. Bergsten, 'Globalizing Free Trade', *Foreign Affairs* 75, 3 (May-June): 105–20.

## Figure 1: The Beauty of It All: Is Economic Integration the Right Environment for All Countries?

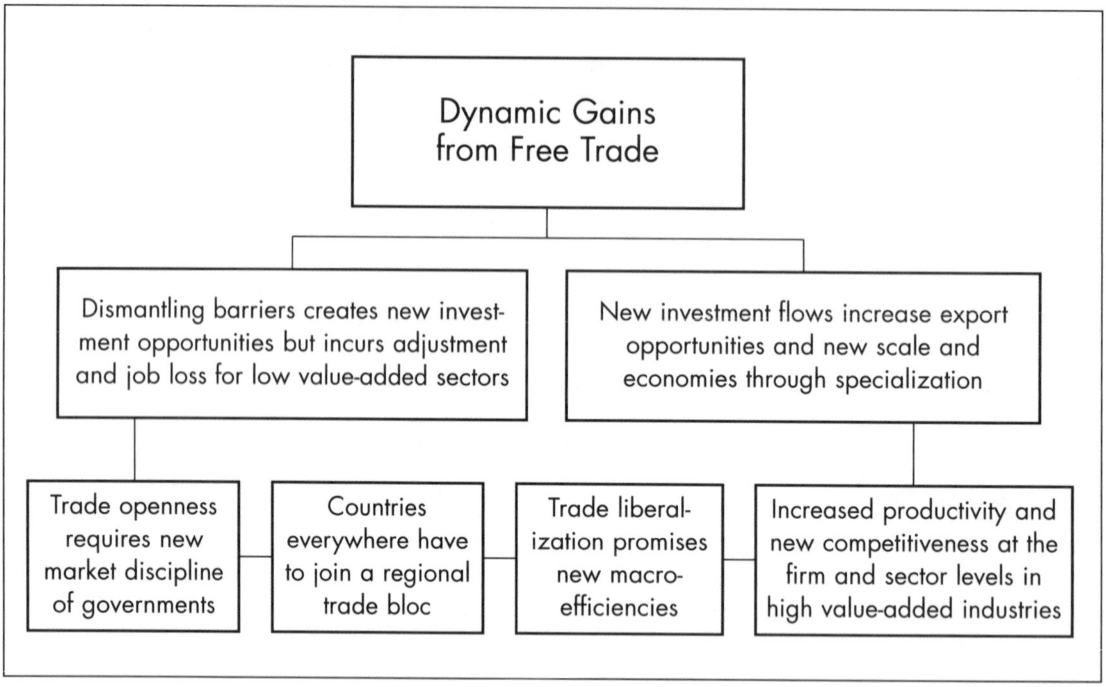

```
                    ┌─────────────────────┐
                    │   Dynamic Gains     │
                    │   from Free Trade   │
                    └─────────────────────┘
```

| Dismantling barriers creates new investment opportunities but incurs adjustment and job loss for low value-added sectors | New investment flows increase export opportunities and new scale and economies through specialization |
|---|---|

| Trade openness requires new market discipline of governments | Countries everywhere have to join a regional trade bloc | Trade liberalization promises new macro-efficiencies | Increased productivity and new competitiveness at the firm and sector levels in high value-added industries |
|---|---|---|---|

their narrow self-interest in preserving their policy sovereignty, these trade alliances, which already account for over 60 per cent of the world's trade (see Table 1),[8] will become a major presence in the world economy.

As countries rush to open their borders, is the vision of global markets as self-organizing entities that make every country a winner borne out by experience? The answer to this question is anything but simple.

Mainstream thinking presents these new trading arrangements (see Figure 1) as an association of nation-states created to reduce barriers to the movement of people, goods, services, and investment capital. This gives smaller regional economies access to larger markets so that they can develop economies of scale and hence generate welfare and efficiency gains through an enhanced export performance.[9] For large economies, a trade bloc means something quite different. It provides secure and enhanced market access for its mass production

industries and its corporations. This is because a trade bloc is a powerful enabling device that requires small countries to open their economies regardless of the costs. On the financial front, it hands the dominant member(s) of the bloc a new investment frontier for its capital-rich financial sector. Balancing these competing interests requires that a trade bloc have an institutional capacity to resolve trade disputes and policy differences between member states, a favourable international climate, and much fortuity. Optimally, a trade bloc functions best when countries are growing quickly and are committed to full employment; they become a high-risk exercise when unemployment is on the rise and economic growth weak.

## The Devil Is in the Details: Two Opposing Views

The chances of a trade bloc's survival depend on six basic characteristics working to sustain it:[10]

1. Member states should have roughly equivalent levels of per capita GNP and consumption norms should be of the same order. If not, blocs will face difficulties because the producers in the poorer country or countries will be seen as swamping the consumer markets of the high-income economy with cheap goods.

2. The members should share a common geographic, regionally based economy. Trade blocs rely on pre-existing geographically linked communication and transportation systems as a way of stimulating intra-industry specialization and enhancing national and transnational economies of scale.[11]

3. Compatible trading practices and norms should exist. Countries must share a commitment to suppressing non-tariff barriers and other state-designed policies, including subsidies, adopting a rules-based rather than a result-oriented approach to trade. In practice, it has proved very difficult to dismantle non-tariff barriers.

4. A political commitment to the regional organization of trade must exist. This entails adopting norms or practices that frequently go beyond internationally agreed norms established by the World Trade Organization.

5. The stability of a trade bloc derives much of its cohesiveness from using a world currency as its own. Monetary and fiscal policy will increasingly be set for all by the central bank of the bloc's dominant member. In a world of linked financial markets, losing control over monetary policy is one of the radically new costs of belonging to a trade bloc.

6. A real potential should exist for growth through economic integration. Countries have to have industries and firms capable of winning new market share inside a trading bloc.

Even on these standard conditions, a regional trade pact may or may not be beneficial, but the above definition also needs serious modification.

The defining characteristic of trade agreements is that they are also highly politicized investment-driven initiatives to accelerate regional economic integration around a core group of states. This requires a high level of state and market co-ordination to bring this new market relationship into existence. In all, they are based on six principles:

1. Trade blocs are legally intrusive, covering most areas of public decision-making and private-sector activity. Public wealth-creation takes a distant second place to maximizing the investment opportunity and gain for large private-sector actors.

2. Regional trade rules affect highly sensitive areas of public policy of member states, including the environment, culture, innovation, labour market regulation, social policy, and the like. Governments find it increasingly difficult to take policy initiatives not shared by other members of the trade bloc, particularly in these policy domains or in the realm of expansionary policies.[12]

3. Each signatory has prescribed rights, responsibilities, and settlement and enforcement obligations set out in a trade constitution. These are not easy to alter or amend.

4. Power asymmetry is routinely legitimized because the dominant member of the bloc controls key levers of fiscal and monetary policy of the other members through the power of its own financial institutions.

5. Benefits are to be distributed by market forces and not by legislated agreement and proactive interventionism on the part of members, whatever historical practice may have been.

6. Public accountability through an elected legislature is reduced because many crucial decisions are not subject to public review, yielding a major democratic and accountability 'deficit'. The entire agreement is subject to legal review and arbitration by non-elected judges and tribunals. Increasingly, the functioning of democratic institutions is weakened by the transfer of

## Table 2: The Institutional Capacity of NAFTA and the EU

| | EU Provisions and Policy Instruments | NAFTA Provisions and Policy Instruments |
|---|---|---|
| Asymmetry | Addressed through structural funds; European Investment Bank; structural adjustment programs. Interest rate set by new European Central Bank. A modest but significant redistribution capacity. As the EU has expanded the asymmetry between members has increased sharply. | No policy instruments. No redistribution mechanism. Interest policy set unilaterally by Federal Reserve. Disputes panel—a low level judicial review. US able to appeal decisions through its own trade law system. Little evidence of a level playing field. |
| Adjustment | The amount of resources is comparatively small for such a large number of states but the EU has gone further than any other trade bloc in this area. Principal policy mechanisms are competition policy; industrial strategy; science/ technology policy; regional funds. Adjustment is monitored and can be proactive. | No co-ordinated response and left to individual member states. Canada and Mexico subject to US trade law rules and rulings. With structurally weaker economies, adjustment is a major policy challenge for Canada and Mexico. |
| Access | Brussels has responsibility to enforce access. Main instruments: competition directorate; regional directorate; industrial policy; technology and science policy, plus national industrial strategy of member states, plus resource to European Court. | Low-level tripartite dispute panel. Many rulings appealable. Individual firms and industries have to pay full costs. US Congress not limited by any proactive provisions in NAFTA. Canada and Mexico subject to US trade law, US Congress, and US lobbyists. |

responsibility for key areas of public policy-making to an élite-based judiciary.

If enhancing the efficiency of markets *tout court* was the single driving force behind greater co-operation and integration,[13] deep integration organized around market-enhancing policies would have happened long ago. But this is not the case. For much of the recent period, integration has been driven largely by non-market and indeed *non-liberal* objectives in the cases of both Europe and North America.

## The Previous Model of Economic Integration

In the aftermath of World War II European integration was largely security-driven, sharing little with a crude market model of integration. The immediate issue was German rearmament. An appropriate forum was needed to bring Germany back into Europe and offset its power. The Schuman Plan of 1950 contained the nucleus of the idea. It brought together under common rules the traditional industries of war production and coal and steel of the six member states. European co-operation was far more than an economic deal to enhance private-sector actors: the ulterior purpose of this economic arrangement, in Robert Schuman's words, was to make war between France and Germany not only 'unthinkable, but materially impossible'. The Schuman Plan mandated the authorities to develop a wide-angled view of the social side of economic adjustment. It provided broad social criteria to limit the purely market side of this arrangement to promote trade liberalization.

It was a relatively small step for all governments to render trade liberalization policies compatible with a mixture of social policy, industrial strategy, and macroeconomic planning initiatives. Trade had to share the front burner with full employment needs of countries everywhere. Member states relied on a variety of industrial policies to address the adjustment costs of greater openness. With rapidly expanding domestic economies, displaced workers from uncompetitive sectors could expect to find alternative employment in the competitive side of the economy. In a Western European setting, integration was seen as something compatible with national sovereignty, particularly in countries with social democratic governments to provide a range of income support programs for those who lost their jobs.

What made trade liberalization an easy policy pill to swallow was that core countries with powerful export sectors were well placed to capture increased market share. Less advantaged members developed industrial strategies to restructure and take advantage of the new export opportunities. The rapid expansion of commerce proved job-friendly. Workers shared in the productivity gains as real wages rose for more than two decades.[14]

One of the cherished myths of free traders is that industrial policy is synonymous with creeping protectionism. This does not square with the empirical reality that economic integration received its greatest push from the golden decades of Keynesian state management of the economy. Jeffery Schott, an ardent supporter of trade liberalization, calculates that the greatest period of intra-European trade was in the heyday of Keynesian practices. In 1963, intra-European trade was less important than exports to the rest of the world. By 1979, trade within the community was 20 per cent higher than to the rest of the world. Intra-European trade grew sharply in the 1980s *before* many of the measures of the Single European Act were implemented. Between 1985 and 1989, trade increased by more than 100 per cent, rising from $337 billion to $678 billion. Again, the acceleration was due to the recovery from the 1982 economic crisis rather than from any strengthening of Community trade ties.

Despite this evidence, liberal economists insist that under all conditions integration promoted a virtuous model of development. At best, this was a half-truth and at worst a dangerous illusion.[15] In fact, economic integration succeeded because markets were only partially liberalized. The Community opted for a balanced agriculture policy and a political compromise to stabilize this sector, and the public sector was largely kept off the table. This permitted public enterprise to remain a critical tool of industrial and social policy throughout the Community during the sixties, seventies, and eighties. Integration went forward because countries had developed extensive social programs and policies that enhanced the long-term viability of the welfare state and social democracy.[16]

North American co-operation followed a noticeably different model and growth trajectory from its European counterpart. Successive governments saw little advantage in formalizing Canada-US relations in a trade pact. The principal worry was that the north-south pull of markets would overpower the east-west economic union achieved by Canada's developmental strategy of nation-building. The postwar St Laurent-Pearson-Trudeau governments opted for a strategy of co-operation rather than formalized integration, and US direct investment rose dramatically. American business interests dominated a continentally oriented Canadian economic élite who did not see any reason to distinguish themselves from their rich and more powerful US counterparts. Less obvious was that much of integration was driven by Canadian tax laws shaped to encourage US investment in the Canadian manufacturing sector.

But North American integration was never as frictionless as it seemed. By the seventies, Canada-US relations became increasingly troubled.[17] The rise of Canadian nationalist movements in the seventies questioned the high levels of foreign ownership, especially in the energy and cultural sectors. What the larger public wanted was a model of Canada-US relations based on co-operation without domination or full-scale deep integration. For Canada, social policy also acted as a brake on economic integration.[18] Integration remained gradual and ad hoc, encompassing limited spheres of public policy. Canadians did not want to lose the benefits of nationalized health care and a system of social security nets tied to the highly regional nature of the Canadian economy. All these programs distinguished Canada from its southern neighbour, which followed a dramatically different system of state-market relations.

In this sense, NAFTA represented a 'great U-turn' for Canada and, indeed, for Mexico. NAFTA brought together fundamentally different sorts of trade partners, in stark contrast to the European case. 'It is the first free trade area in which a developing country has granted investors of the industrialized world the optimal status of national treatment.'[19]

## Trade Liberalization and the Public Policy Agenda

A trade bloc implies accelerating the pace of economic change, institutional machinery to ensure markets remain open, that access is in fact broadened, and that positive trade, investment, and production environments are created. Mainstream economists have little to say about the institutional side of trade blocs[20] or about neutralizing asymmetry, enhancing access, or paying for the costs of adjustment. For Bhagwati, the beauty of the free trade beast is that 'free trade for all' is a radical step in the right direction:

> If one applies the logic of efficiency to the allocation of activity among all trading nations, and not merely within one's own nation-state, it is easy enough to see that it yields the prescription of free trade everywhere—that alone would ensure that goods and services would be produced where it could be done most cheaply. The notion that prices reflect true social costs is crucial to this conclusion, just as it is to the case for free trade for one nation alone.[21]

With objectives and outcomes less closely linked than any time previously, the putative benefits from free trade and open markets frequently fail to materialize (see Figure 2), yielding instead investment shortfalls, technology lags, job loss, and plant closures, and reinforcing the low-skill, low-wage performers. Low value-added strategies of traditional industries and intense competition on polarized labour markets place a premium on falling wages. State policies pay little attention to transforming a static comparative advantage into a dynamic one. State power to shape national markets is reduced even though, historically, high performance economies emerged as a result of state management of the adjustment process. States made large-scale investments in R&D and had an effective competition policy to prevent anti-competitive practices by major firms, many of which were and are located in the export side of the economy.

For many countries asymmetrical gains from free trade have proved to be a chilling experience. In the areas of macroeconomic policy, intra-bloc trade, work and employment conditions, interest-rate volatility, and employment enhancement, a trade bloc regime does indeed dramatically limit member states in precisely the way Bhagwati predicted. But in other ways, the scenario does not fit his vision at all. The reason is that efficient outcomes do not rely on the price mechanism working in an unimpeded way. The fact is that on both sides of the Atlantic it has proven next to impossible to separate a country's external trade from its national economy and make it *independent* of its national self-interest.[22] Why should this be?

## Power Asymmetry: The Core Challenge

Even though trade agreements promote far-reaching co-operation between governments, they leave untouched the asymmetry between member states. Smaller countries need the dominant partner's markets more than the dominant country needs theirs. The juridical framework permanently embeds this inequality in the structure of each agreement, but in very different ways in each case.

## Figure 2: The Beast in the Theory: The Harsh but frequent Reality of Open Markets

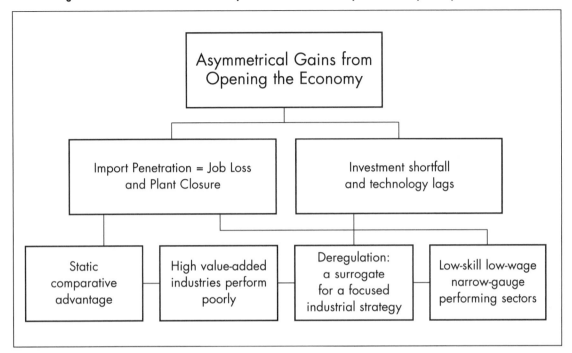

### NAFTA

There is little evidence that being part of NAFTA has levelled power asymmetries among the United States, Canada, and Mexico. Commercial law in the area of unfair practices and the use of subsidies remains national. Canadian and Mexican firms lose claims in front of the trade panels because US exporters are able to manipulate the complexities of the US commercial regulatory system in their favour.[23] There has also been a dramatic growth in the unilateral exercise of US trade power. Cross-border disputes have increased in many areas that were thought to have been conflict-proof with the signing of NAFTA. These include the continuation of the 'voluntary' export restraints that hurt Canadian lumber producers despite rulings against the United States[24] and roadblocks by US officials in North Dakota preventing Canadian hog exports from entering the US,[25] again, despite rulings in

favour of Canada. Contrary to popular perceptions, NAFTA established no new procedures, practices, or norms with respect to US trade law. Canadian and Mexican exports can be targeted as before, and adjustment in policy terms is largely on the Canadian and Mexican side.

The heart of the problem is low US administrative standards; US trade laws 'are biased in favour of the home plaintiff.' Tests for trade injury favour US industries—the subsidies of the US plaintiff are never investigated—and trade disputes are regularly used by 'US industries to obtain protection or shelter from foreign competition'.[26]

Rugman and Anderson argue that US administrative practice is so ad hoc and arbitrary that there is no level playing field. Despite NAFTA, foreign firms still have fewer legal rights under US trade law than do the domestic parties to a case. Thus, Washington has imposed tough new rules on its partners with respect to the formation of public policy while the final interpretation rests with the US Congress, lobby groups, and US trade tribunals with respect to Canadian and Mexican litigants.

Under NAFTA there is no impartial third-party review of non-compliance by governments to any of its provisions. Washington is entitled to review all Canadian and Mexican legislation to see whether the 'offending legislation' (a) impinges on NAFTA's investment provisions and (b) whether any proposed legislation, particularly with respect to government policy, directly or indirectly fails to extend full protection to US investors. On the other hand, NAFTA creates no new significant norms in American practice, policy, or outlook. The US implementing legislation makes this perfectly plain. Wherever there is a conflict between the provisions of NAFTA and US law, US law will prevail. Even the side deals with respect to human rights or other kinds of labour violations carry no penalty to enforce US multinationals to adopt any of the tribunal rulings.

The dilemma facing Ottawa and Mexico is that, even when a dispute settlement panel upholds Mexico's or Canada's side, it does not mean that the exporters have won a victory. American producers can press for a new investigation under US trade law. While binational panels were *supposed* to deliver binding decisions, clearly, this is not so. Even though *three* panels have ruled that Canadian wheat is not subsidized according to existing practices, US farmers continue to demand another anti-dumping investigation. For Mexico, there have been only a handful of cases, perhaps because many Mexican firms do not have the resources to finance a panel dispute and because the entire process takes at least a year, if not longer. The consequence is that the new legal and political norms eliminate to a significant degree the discretionary authority of Canadian and Mexican authorities to favour local firms, communities, regional authorities, and industries, while preserving crucial US trade restrictions.

### The European Union

This kind of crude exercise of market power has no parallel in the EU. Members are bound by the decisions of the European Court, reducing big-power influence. But in a multitude of other ways, the EU's democratic deficit, as well as the de facto power of the governors' of the central banks of member states to set the Community's framework monetary policy, underlines just how much asymmetry continues to haunt European integration.

The EU has created a market of over 300 million people, but is now struggling to come to terms with a new regulatory, financial, and institutional order. Much is still unclear about its operation and the setting of monetary policy. For instance, it is by no means certain how much discretion constituent members will have over fiscal policy. Nor is there an agreement on the need for coherent and consistent policies defining the trade-off between lower unemployment and flexible inflation targets. Even with the approach of monetary union, there is great urgency as to how the EU is going to restructure its 10 steel industries, six automotive sectors, a dozen textile clusters, and the dozens of shipbuilding firms that currently operate in various regions of the Community. To address this problem in the past, Brussels introduced various regional industrial and competitive policies, but none have been adequate to the task for which they were designed.[27] This is why all European countries continue to rely on state aids as a key component of governance rather than subscribe to the vision of a borderless world.

### Labour Standards: A New Global Dynamic?

On both sides of the Atlantic, the process of building larger markets has already dramatically altered employment and wage standards. The spatial reorganization of industries has set the stage for a reorientation of wages and working time. Wages and consumption—historically linked for four decades—no longer are so linked. Since 1980, real wages in most European jurisdictions (including the powerfully organized German trade union movement) have lagged behind productivity growth.[28] In 1997, German wages grew by 1.5 per cent while productivity surged by 3.7 per cent. The trend in Germany is no different from that in other countries, as the workforce in the high-wage sector is cut. Since 1990 job growth on the industrial side of the economy has been negative in five out of seven years. European economies face intense pressures to modify their social market practices as European Monetary Union takes hold.

In Canada and the United States, this same decoupling explains the dramatic disappearance of middle-income earners from the employment pyramid. Proportionately, there are fewer blue-collar workers earning a 'family income' and many more single-parent, most often female, workers being paid poor wages. The labour market has a growing element of casual and part-time employment, and wages and employment levels have again begun to operate as a mechanism of adjustment.

In these emerging trade blocs, new macroeconomic objectives have arisen. Integration means that inflation and relative price movements more than ever determine a country's external position and market share. Competitive labour markets are relied on to adjust employment and wage levels are expected to reflect international competitive conditions,[29] simultaneously eroding union power at the bargaining table. With wages being put back in competition and subject to new global competitive pressures, a free trade zone becomes the chosen instrument to redefine the terms and conditions of the existing capital-labour compromise.[30]

Unions have always understood that global trade wars bid down the price of labour because companies are forced to produce more with less of everything. This was not a problem so long as a country's exports and imports were only a small part of its gross domestic product. Once they are a major element and the economy is wide open, the effect is seismic. Wages will stagnate and the purchasing power of families can only become more unequal across society unless government intervenes to correct growing inequality. So far, most governments have cut social safety nets and reduced the redistributive nature of many of their policies.

## Employment Enhancement vs Trade Efficiency

As can be seen in Table 3, the current environment for trade blocs has not been kind for new job creation. In many sectors, new employment opportunities have failed to materialize. While there is much debate about assessing the employment effect, total job loss due to trade-related and rigid Canadian monetary targets has been huge. The figures are dramatic. Over the last 30 years, the number and quality of manufacturing jobs have shrunk in Canada and the United States. Less than 15 per cent of workers find gainful employment in the manufacturing sector. No amount of export-led growth is likely to reverse this long-term historic trend.

The fact is that, on both sides of the Atlantic, new computer-based technologies now enable employers in the old Fordist industries to become leaner and more productive. Lean production practices pose an irreconcilable dilemma for labour. On one hand, new competitive pressures generated by

### Table 3: Employment and Adjustment in Canada in the Pre- and Post-NAFTA Eras (000s)

| Sector | 1988 | 1993 | Jan. 1997 |
|---|---|---|---|
| Food | 208 | 180 | 175 |
| Clothing | 121 | 85 | 85 |
| Primary metals | 103 | 80 | 80 |
| Fabricated metal products | 174 | 135 | 155 |
| Machinery (non-electrical) | 85 | 65 | 91 |
| Electrical and electrical prod. | 157 | 116 | 117 |
| Transportation equip. (auto and aerospace) | 224 | 197 | 223 |

SOURCE: A. Jackson, *Impacts of the Free Trade Agreement (FTA) and the North American Free Trade Agreement (NAFTA) on Canadian Labour Markets and Labour and Social Standards* (Ottawa: Canadian Labour Congress, 1997).

free trade zones require industries to shed labour in order to boost market share in foreign markets. On the other hand, trade becomes job-destructive, particularly in the mass production industries and in the new technologically intensive sectors, when high-tech and high value-added industries are forced to compete head to head. This is so because the rules of the game have changed most for corporate giants. Cost control is their principal strategy and cutting costs requires smaller payrolls.[31] What governments are loath to admit is that increasing exports today is no longer an employment-creating strategy in the way it once was in the boom times of the fifties and sixties.

## Conclusion

The contemporary preoccupation with building mega-sized regionally based trading blocs is a new twist on a well-worn idea. Countries everywhere want association rather than isolation. The contemporary vision behind European and North American integration to promote closer ties among member states is bold in the extreme, and extends to MER-COSUR, APEC, and others. Both are comprehensive agreements to foster far-reaching interdependency among members. For this reason these trade blocs appear to be benign. But they are not. They lead to the weakening of national authority at a time when national governments need more autonomy and more resources to develop economies buffeted by financial instability and never-ending adjustment. The rise of unemployment in parallel with accelerating integration in almost all industrial countries raises serious questions about social stability and the long-term viability of these kinds of initiatives. Furthermore, few countries want their economic future and well-being to be decided by the dominant partner in a regional trade bloc. Finding ways to address the asymmetry issue in NAFTA and the EU will either secure their future or push them to the brink of collapse. It remains unclear for the moment whether monetary union will have the institutional and political will to revisit the fundamentals of economic liberalism with its rigid zero-inflation targets and low growth/high unemployment.

Compared to NAFTA, the EU has more policy instruments to push the integration process in a different direction and find counterweights to increased capital mobility. Brussels has the power to restructure and shape EU industries on a national and community-wide level.[32] Yet, this sort of macroeconomic approach does not go to the heart of the matter. If integration is to go forward, it has to be based on addressing the social dimension of European integration, including an institutional mechanism to redistribute the welfare gains from the most successful sectors to the least successful regions. If this is not done, there is no incentive for countries to remain part of a bloc if their industries do not benefit to the degree promised and opportunities for creating employment fail to materialize. Redistribution of benefits has to be the top priority in the coming decade.

By contrast, NAFTA's future is uncertain. It has not delivered secure market access to weaker players. At present, NAFTA is an economic integration project driven by the strategic investment needs of US corporations. Mexico and Canada at some point will have to find ways to delimit this investment agreement and focus it on the problem of trade disputes. If this is not possible, there may be strong pressure to renegotiate its terms.

In Canada, public support for this narrowly conceived integration initiative remains well below 40 per cent and pressure by social movements to re-negotiate or abrogate NAFTA continues. Ottawa had serious reservations about the recently failed Multilateral Agreement on Investment. It is important to note, here, that the conceptual inspiration and model for the MAI was Chapter 11 of NAFTA. In Mexico, the Zapatista uprising crystallized the opposition to this trade project. NAFTA is closely identified with the ruling PRI (Partido Revolucionario Institucional) and as Mexico contemplates the end of this political dynasty, it is an open question of whether NAFTA will continue to receive support in a post-PRI Mexico.

With objectives and outcomes less linked than ever before, many now realize that the model of economic integration embodied in NAFTA is a poor substitute for more broadly based initiatives to promote hemispheric co-operation. In a world economy where goods of all kinds and description appear to move effortlessly across borders, regional integration must proceed by addressing the social dimension of markets as well as the environmental dangers of unregulated competition. The future of trade blocs depends on creating new social, labour, and environmental standards, not lowering them as is so often the case at present.

Following the outbreak of financial crisis in 1997, no country wants to be burned at the stake of international competition. Economic integration objectives are always a high-risk activity when markets are being empowered, when state practice is being transformed, when inequality is on the rise, and when economic growth risks are slowing. All of these factors are currently present, and in these dangerous times, when stability and certainty are in short supply, trade blocs can only face an uncertain and risky future with their narrow economic agendas and limited regulatory frameworks.

## Notes

1   Parts of this paper draw on material that has been previously published.
2   Robert Boyer and Daniel Drache, *States Against Markets: The Limits of Globalization* (London: Routledge, 1996).
3   Daniel Drache, 'The Post-National State', in Alain-G. Gagnon and James Bickerton, eds, *Canadian Politics*, 2nd edn (Peterborough, Ont.: Broadview Press, 1994), 549–66.
4   Stephen Clarkson, 'Fearful Asymmetries: The Challenge of Analyzing Continental Systems in a Globalizing World', *Canadian-American Public Policy no. 35* (Sept. 1998).
5   Jagdish Bhagwati, *Protectionism* (Boston: MIT Press, 1988).
6   The European Commission symbolizes these differences and is vested with powers derived from written treaties and Commission directives, including the enforcement of rules. There is no parallel in NAFTA, but given the way it is crafted, the US Congress is the legal and political authority of last resort. See Alan Rugman and Andrew Anderson, 'NAFTA and the Dispute Settlement Mechanisms: A Transaction Costs Approach', *The World Economy* (Nov. 1998): 935–50.
7   Jeffrey A. Frankel, *Regional Trading Blocs in the World Economic System* (Washington: Institute for International Economics, 1997).
8   The other major regional trading arrangements are: Australia-New Zealand Closer Economic Relations Trade Agreement (ANZCERTA); European Free Trade Area (EFTA); Association of Southeast Asian Nations (ASEAN); Central American Common Market (CACM); Latin American Free Trade Area/Latin American Integration Association (LAFTA/LAIA); Andean Community; Economics Community of West African States (ECOWAS); Preferential Trade Area for Eastern and Southern Africa (PTA), and Mercado Commùn del Sur (MERCOSUR). Significantly, there were 37 interregional trade agreements among Western and Central European countries by the 1990s but only four between Western Europe and developing countries of Asia and Africa. Between North America and North Africa there are five such arrangements. It is correct to conclude that regional pacts are principally among the core economies of the world.
9   Gary Clyde Hufbauer and Jeffrey J. Schott, *North American Free Trade Issues and Recommendations* (Washington: Institute for International Economics, 1992).
10  Jeffrey Schott, 'Trading Blocs and the World Trading System', *The World Economy* 14, 1 (Mar. 1991): 1–17.
11  Alfred Tovias, 'A Survey of the Theory of Economic Integration', *Journal of European Integration* 15, 1 (1992): 20.
12  A. Jackson, *Impacts of the Free Trade Agreement (FTA) and the North American Free Trade Agreement (NAFTA) on Canadian Labour Markets and Labour and Social Standards* (Ottawa: Canadian Labour Congress, 1997).
13  William Wallace, *The Transformation of Western Europe* (London: RIIA, Pinter Publishers, 1990).

14  Daniel Drache and H.J. Glasbeek, *The Changing Workplace: Reshaping Canada's Industrial Relations System* (Toronto: James Lorimer, 1993).

15  Susan Strange, *States and Markets* (New York: Basil Blackwell, 1988).

16  Gosta Esping-Andersen, *The Three Worlds of Welfare Capitalism* (Princeton, NJ: Princeton University Press, 1992).

17  Christina McCall and Stephen Clarkson, *Trudeau and Our Times*, vol. 2 (Toronto: McClelland & Stewart, 1994).

18  Daniel Drache and Andrew Ranachan, *Warm Heart, Cold Country: Fiscal and Social Policy Reform in Canada* (Ottawa: Caledon Institute, 1995).

19  I. Morales, 'The Mexican Crisis and the Weakness of the NAFTA Consensus', *Annals of the American Academy of Political and Social Science* 550 (Mar. 1997): 130–52.

20  Hufbauer and Schott, *North American Free Trade Issues and Recommendations*.

21  Bhagwati, *Protectionism*.

22  Ibid., 25.

23  Morales, 'The Mexican Crisis'.

24  *Globe and Mail*, 30 Mar. 1998.

25  Ibid., 2 Oct. 1998.

26  Rugman and Anderson, 'NAFTA and the Dispute Settlement Mechanisms', 936.

27  Gary Hufbauer, ed., *Europe 1992: An American Perspective* (Washington: Brookings Institution, 1990); Alberta M. Sbragia, ed., *Euro-Politics Institutions and Policymaking in the 'New' European Community* (Washington: Brookings Institution, 1992).

28  Dani Rodrik, *Has Globalization Gone Too Far?* (Washington: Institute for International Economics, 1997).

29  OECD, *The OECD Job Strategy: Facts, Analysis and Strategies* (Paris: OECD, 1994).

30  Robert Boyer, *New Directions in Management Practices and Work Organisation* (Paris: OECD, 1994); Michel Albert, *Capitalisme Contre Capitalisme* (Paris: Seuil, 1991).

31  United Nations, *World Investment Report 1992: Transnational Corporations as Engines of Growth* (New York: UN, 1992).

32  If sufficient agreement existed within its ranks, the European Community could produce an integrated package designed to promote macroeconomic co-ordination and to address the mayhem of the money markets. The Commission has enough resources to support growth-promoting infrastructure projects such as road, rail, telecommunications, and energy networks, but over the last 20 years these powers have remained underutilized.

## Suggested Readings

Boyer, Robert, and Daniel Drache. *States Against Markets: The Limits of Globalization.* London: Routledge, 1996.

Fortin, Pierre. 'The Great Canadian Slump', *Canadian Journal of Economics* 29, 4 (Nov. 1996): 761–87.

Frankel, Jeffrey A. *Regional Trading Blocs in the World Economic System.* Washington: Institute for International Economics, 1997.

Jackson, A. *Impacts of the Free Trade Agreement (FTA) and the North American Free Trade Agreement (NAFTA) on Canadian Labour Markets and Labour and Social Standards.* Ottawa: Canadian Labour Congress, 1997.

Morales, I. 'The Mexican Crisis and the Weakness of the NAFTA Consensus', *Annals of the American Academy of Political and Social Science* 550 (Mar. 1997): 130–52.

Rodrik, Dani. *Has Globalization Gone Too Far?* Washington: Institute for International Economics, 1997.

Rugman, Alan, and Andrew Anderson. 'NAFTA and the Dispute Settlement Mechanisms: A Transaction Costs Approach', *The World Economy* (Nov. 1997): 935–50.

## Web Sites

Canadian Centre for Policy Alternatives:
http://www.policyalternatives.ca/

Canadian Council on Social Development:
http://www.ccsd.ca/recent.html

Financial Times: http:/www.ft.com/

Human Resources Development Canada:
http:/www.hrdcdrhc.gc.ca/common/home.shtml

Statistics Canada—The Daily:
http:/www.statcan.ca/Daily/English/today/
daily.htm

United States Trade Representative: www.ustr.gov

Chapter 15

# Network Power

Ronald J. Deibert

For the past several centuries, societies around the planet have been experiencing rapid and fundamental technological changes.[1] The most recent and possibly the most profound has been those associated with the movement and processing of information—a development that has its origins in such late nineteenth-century innovations as the photograph and telegraph, and continues today in the ongoing integration of planetary digital-electronic telecommunications. Although it has been a pronounced weakness among theorists of technology to describe these changes in deterministic terms, we should not underestimate their implications either. Communication technologies are unique because they are implicated in all spheres of society, from knowledge and culture to production and security. Changes in modes of communication can consequently have fundamental effects on the character of societies. The question is, of course, what, precisely, are those implications? More specifically, how will the development of digital-electronic telecommunications—what I call the *hypermedia environment*—affect world order?

One tradition of scholarship that could provide a useful starting point falls under the rubric of 'medium theory'—an approach developed by communication theorists such as Harold Innis, Marshall McLuhan, and Walter Ong. At the core of medium theory is the argument that the media of communications available to human beings have an important independent effect on what is communicated and how. Modes of communication each have a certain 'logic' or 'nature' that makes certain types of communication—and by extension, certain social and political projects—easier or more difficult.

Because communications are so vital to human existence, it follows that a large-scale change in the mode of communication will have substantial effects on factors such as the distribution of power within society, the nature and character of cognition, and the values and beliefs that animate a particular population.

In this chapter, I will first summarize some of the important modifications I make to medium theory in order to rectify its shortcomings and then apply it to the question of world order transformation. Of these modifications, the most important is the elaboration of a Darwinian analogy to help conceptualize the way changing modes of communication, or *communications environments*, reinforce and constrain social forces, collective images, and ideas. Changes in communications environments 'favour' certain social forces and ideas by means of a functional bias towards some and not others, much like natural environments favour different species by selecting for certain physical or behavioural characteristics. To demonstrate the way this theoretical lens can illuminate some of the key transformations at work in the world today, in the second half of the chapter I outline key changes to the global political economy that are being unleashed in the hypermedia environment and how these, in turn, are altering the nature of politics into the twenty-first century.

## Medium Theory and Media as Environments

That we live in a time of profound changes in communication technologies is beyond dispute. The evidence is everywhere: from the 21″ ViewSonic digital computer monitor that displays this very text in one window in front of me, to the T1 connection that links me to the Internet. With a few simple keystrokes, I could send this text to any one of millions of people located around the world in less than a few seconds. Indeed, in a separate window opened next to my text is a RealVideo broadcast of 'BBC World News', with a live report of the after-effects of a tsunami in Papua New Guinea. As an illustration of the contrast, sitting like a museum piece on the floor under the desk are the remnants of a buzzer that was used to alert the previous occupant of my office of an incoming phone call over a shared line. Anecdotes such as these are common. Less well known, however, are the implications for society and politics of these changes. How will world politics change as a result of these new communication technologies?

One tradition of scholarship that has focused on the relationship between changing communication technologies and society is medium theory. At the heart of medium theory is the argument that changes in modes of communication—such as the shift from primary orality to writing or the shift from print to electronic communications—have an important effect on the trajectory of social evolution and the values and beliefs of societies. Medium theory traces these effects to the unique properties of different modes of communication—to the way information is stored, transmitted, and distributed through different media at different times in human history. It argues that media are not simply neutral vessels for conveying information between two environments but are, rather, environments in and of themselves.

Medium theory has received less attention than one might expect given recent developments in communication technologies—a neglect that is probably at least indirectly related to the way it was introduced to a wider audience by its two main practitioners: Harold Adams Innis (the 'father' of medium theory) and Marshall McLuhan ('the oracle of the electronic age').[2] Both theorists had a notoriously dense and complex writing style—a limitation that both invited misinterpretation and discouraged further investigation. In addition,

medium theory has suffered criticism in the past for lapses into technological determinism and monocausal reductionism. This is the type of thinking that attempts to reduce the sources of complex social forces or ideas to a single 'master' variable.

Elsewhere I have made a number of modifications to medium theory designed to resurrect the core propositions of this approach while shedding those elements that have come to be seen through criticism as misguided or overstated.[3] The majority of these modifications are attempts to 'get back to the roots' of this approach, so to speak—to unearth what I see as the historical materialist grounds out of which medium theory developed.[4] At the core of these modifications is the drawing out of one of the more prominent metaphors in medium theory analysis: *media as environments*.

In classical Darwinian theories of evolution, environmental changes strongly condition the differential survival and reproduction of species.[5] Although species are vitally dependent on their environment, the environment itself cannot be said to engage in the selection process by *acting* on species; rather, innovations and genetic mutations produce a variety of physical characteristics that, in turn, are selected according to their 'fitness' or match with the environment. Not to be confused with nineteenth-century social Darwinist views of progressive development, evolution from this perspective assumes no inherent direction or purpose but is a contingent, open-ended historical process.

Similarly, a large-scale change in the mode of communication (environment) will 'favour' certain social forces and ideas (species) by means of a functional bias towards some and not others, just as natural environments determine which species prosper by 'selecting' for certain physical characteristics. In other words, the properties of a communications environment—the unique ways in which information can be stored, transmitted, and distributed in that environment—favour the interests of some social forces and ideas over others. These social forces and ideas tend to flourish or thrive— they are empowered by the technologies of communication at their disposal—while others are placed at a significant disadvantage and tend to wither. Unintended consequences loom large from this perspective. In other words, social forces that initially gave support to and drove the early development of a new technology of communication may find themselves at a disadvantage once the full properties of that environment take root. Likewise, social forces and ideas that were marginalized in one communications environment may find a 'niche' and thrive once that environment changes.

While it could be misleading to stretch it too far, this Darwinist evolutionary analogy is particularly useful because it moves away from the technological determinist view of technologies 'generating' specific social forces and ideas. It affirms that the actual genesis of social forces and ideas ultimately reflects a multiplicity of factors that cannot be reduced to a single overarching 'master' variable. Instead, it argues that the *existing stock* of social forces and ideas will flourish or wither depending on their 'fitness' or match with the new communications environment. From this perspective, a new mode of communication is not an 'agent' but rather a passive, structural feature of the technological landscape in which human beings interact. It imposes certain constraints or limitations on the nature and type of possible human communications, while facilitating other types, but it does not impose thought or behaviour in any crude one-to-one fashion. It is an environment. And like natural environments, when the communications environment changes some species will be favoured while others will be disadvantaged, *not* because of an active intervention on the part of the environment itself but rather because the functional properties of the environment either reinforce or constrain the characteristics and interests of the species within it.

Viewing changing technologies of communication through this medium theory lens can help to illuminate some of the effects of the development of digital-electronic telecommunications today. Beginning in the United States and other major industrialized countries and rippling out across the planet in waves, a series of social transformations is occurring related to the new matrix of constraints and opportunities presented by the hypermedia environment. The following section takes a closer look at some of the more significant of these through the medium theory lens.

## Global Political Economy in the Hypermedia Environment

Perhaps the most profound of these changes have occurred in the global economy, and in particular in the nature and organization of production and finance. Like other aspects of social organization, *production* in the modern world order has generally been framed within the state territorial system. In other words, the production of goods and services, and the organization of economics, has been primarily a 'national' affair and has been undertaken in a 'national' context. Because of the state survivalist *mentalité* into which state leaders were acculturated, economic production has been primarily shaped and driven by a desire for self-sufficiency and autonomy. As Thomson remarks, 'historically, state control of the economy was not meant to be functional to society but to the state's war-making capabilities.'[6] Indeed, this framework still persists: the overwhelming amount of economic transactions is internal to states rather than between them; corporations behave differently according to their national locales; and state élites still justify economic policies in terms of 'national competitiveness'. In the hypermedia environment, however, new constraints and opportunities have emerged that have facilitated not only corporate restructuring along several important dimensions, but an explosive diffusion of production processes across territorial boundaries as well.

Hypermedia have facilitated transnational production processes in several ways. The first, and most obvious, is by providing the infrastructure for what Hepworth calls 'multilocational flexibility'—the ability to disaggregate and disperse various aspects of the production process in different national or regional locations. Corporations value multilocational flexibility primarily because it permits the possibility of crossing political boundaries to evade government regulations or to search for cheap or specially skilled labour, low taxes, and other favourable regulatory climates.

One manifestation of multilocational flexibility is the segmentation of different components of the production chain of individual firms into multiple national locations, not only to neutralize swings in currency differentials among national economies, but also to take advantage of 'niche' regulatory climates or labour pools around the world that favour specific processes (e.g., marketing, management, 'back-room' data processing, and/or research and development).

The hypermedia environment not only favours the transnationalization of production internal to individual firms; it also facilitates it *among multiple firms*. By making it easier to co-ordinate strategic alliances, joint ventures, and joint production arrangements among separate firms regardless of the geographical distance that separates them, this new environment provides a way for individual firms to spread out the risks and costs of research and development, and thus permits an entry into foreign markets that might otherwise be precluded by tariffs or other regulatory restrictions. Although examples of these types of collaborative arrangements can be found prior to hypermedia, they have flourished since its development, becoming a much more dominant feature of the global production landscape. Through teleconferencing systems, faxes, and computer networks (in particular, electronic mail), transnational collaborative arrangements can be as closely co-ordinated as if they were in the same building. Today, it is not uncommon for design teams located thousands of miles from each other to work on the same design in real-time over desktop computer networks. These types of collaborative ventures have also transformed the nature of subcontracting and traditional supplier-client relationships, with suppliers being drawn more closely into the research and design of their clients' products. Inventories can be adjusted electronically in what has been referred to as 'just-in-time' delivery of parts and products. These electronic connections link companies from all parts of the production chain both domestically and internationally into a rapid-response/mutual adjustment system that often begins the moment the bar code is scanned at the retail register when the product is purchased.

Transnational production is also flourishing in the hypermedia environment because of the flexibility of digital technologies, which facilitates rapid and sophisticated shifts in production processes to meet the distinct characteristics of local markets. Whereas in the past, achieving returns to scale involved labour-intensive, mass-produced manufacturing of finished products, today computer-aided design and knowledge-intensive manufacturing allow niche goods and services to be developed without compromising economic efficiency. Even with mass products distributed to a global market, advertising campaigns can easily be altered to match multiple national and regional consumer targets. With computer-assisted consumer profiles and other market-surveillance mechanisms, firms can then maintain a constant watch over disparate localities around the globe, enabling diversified responses to local conditions, as well as rapid adjustments in advertising campaigns to influence parochial consumer tastes.

While globalization is generally associated with massive, multibillion-dollar transnational enterprises, smaller firms are flourishing in the hypermedia environment as well. On the Internet, for example, individuals or small firms with low initial investment can market products to a rapidly increasing global audience through the mere posts of Web-site advertisements. Everything from floral arrangements to pizzas and from computer software to legal consultation is now marketed on the Internet in what has been referred to as a kind of 'cyberspace bazaar'.[7] To date, the full potential of the market has been limited by security concerns over electronic transactions, a barrier that will likely dissipate with advances in encryption and newly emerging digital currencies. But as the Internet continues its exponential growth around the world, and as more private companies and individuals establish a presence on the World Wide Web, a significant portion of the production, marketing, and sale of goods and services will become detached from 'place', existing only in the non-territorial 'space' of globally linked computer networks.

The result of this functional convergence has meant a rapid increase in the extent of transnational production processes around the world. While it is certainly overstating it to suggest we live in a 'borderless' world with 'placeless' corporations, the extent of the changes in the direction of transnationalization are significant and growing. For example, for advanced economies of the 'triad' states—the United States, Japan, and European Union members—from a third to as much as one-half of the trade crossing their borders now consists of internal transfers within the same enterprise.[8] It is estimated that 80–90 per cent of all transborder data flows are generated by such intra-firm transactions.[9] Another indication of the transnationalization of production is the rise in traded services—a particularly difficult feature to gauge accurately, though one that by most accounts is assuming more importance, especially with the commercialization of the Internet. A conservative estimate places service exports at about $700 billion per year worldwide, constituting about 25 to 30 per cent of world trade.[10] Another indication is the growth in foreign direct investment (FDI)—a reasonably accurate data source, though one that unfortunately excludes most non-equity relationships and activities, the very ones that are now assuming such great importance. Worldwide outflows of FDI have increased nearly 29 per cent a year on average since 1983, three times the growth rate of world exports.[11] According to the 1996 UNCTAD *World Investment Report*, total FDI flows into developed and developing countries surged by 40 per cent in 1995, to reach US$315 billion—a trend the report notes is largely attributable to an estimated 39,000 TNCs with about 270,000 foreign affiliates that now have a combined FDI stock of over US$2.7 trillion.[12]

While production processes are fast diffusing across territorial boundaries, another major transformation is occurring in the area of global capital markets, which has been deeply infused with information technologies throughout the sector from everyday banking activities to the movement of finances around the world. Of course, the movement of money across states' borders is nothing new. In the late nineteenth century, for example, capital accumulation in Great Britain resulted in large investments in the United States and elsewhere.[13]

But these financial flows reduced significantly during and after World War I, and remained subsidiary to trade and government aid for some time thereafter. Right up until the 1950s and 1960s, 'international finance served to lubricate trade flows and to finance the operations of transnational firms and governments in a relatively controlled system.'[14] The subsidiary role of finance to production throughout this period was a product of both technological constraints and deliberate policy initiatives designed to keep finance the 'servant' of production, as outlined, for example, by John Maynard Keynes at Bretton Woods.[15] In the last several decades, however, a more liberal regime of internationally mobile capital has emerged, and this regime, when coupled with the hypermedia environment, has erupted into a 24-hour force-field of complex global financial flows.

Of course, the technology alone did not *generate* global capital markets. Normative shifts, regulatory measures, and policy changes were crucial. Of these, perhaps the most important was the collapse of Bretton Woods, the rise of the Eurodollar market, the liberalization of domestic capital controls, and other changes associated with the so-called Reagan-Thatcher neo-liberal movement. What the technology did do, however, was to provide an explosive boost to a process already set in motion. In fact, finance capital and communications technologies have had a mutually reinforcing, symbiotic relationship dating back to the telegraph, with each move towards globalization spurring on the development of more cost-effective, speedy communications, which in turn have led to escalating globalization processes. The result is that global financial services have developed the most advanced hypermedia networks in the world, and are today at the forefront of computing and telecommunications innovations—a place traditionally occupied by military research and development.

The fit between finances and hypermedia is not difficult to understand when one considers the important relationship, as the old adage goes, between 'time and money'. Consider that in the United States alone, on an average day, America's 14,000 banks transfer about $2.1 trillion over their local data networks to settle account balances. The cost for a bank of financing a deficit, even if it is only for overnight, translates into strong incentives to develop networks—both national and transnational—that are efficient and quick.[16] The US-based Bank of America, for example, carries out trades in over 100 foreign currencies for a volume of $60 billion per day.[17] One recent study revealed that a major investment in hypermedia systems gave one major US bank a 10-second advantage over competitors—a powerful advantage that meant gains on the order of *billions* of dollars.[18] The ultimate goal, according to banking technology experts, is 'just-in-time' cash, or what has been called a 'disappearing float'—a real-time clearance of balances that would be inconceivable without hypermedia.

The consequence of the 'time is money' imperative for the financial sector has been an explosion of hypermedia applications, as new innovations in information technology saturate the industry—each new product and service providing yet more information with more speed and more computing power than before. Stock exchanges now no longer require a physical trading floor as electronically linked exchanges, such as NASDAQ and Globex, operate globally in a 24-hour marketplace. Numerous World Wide Web pages provide niche information on a myriad of financial services and investment information from around the world.[19] Complex artificial-intelligence software systems are then developed by securities firms to handle vast, complex stock portfolios that react instantaneously to slight shifts in the market. On-line services, such as Reuters, Telerate, and Quotron in the United States and Extel and Datastream in Europe compete with each other and with global television networks, such as the Cable News Network's Financial Network and Asian Business News, to provide the most up-to-date information on international trading activities. Financial institutions, such as Nomura Securities and Prudential-Bache, are the driving force behind major telecommunications developments around the world, for example, teleports and fibreoptic installations. Leased lines, 'virtual private networks', intranets, and specialized electronic transfer services, like the Society of Worldwide Interbank Financial Telecommunications (or SWIFT), then provide the ever-intensifying, real-time links among these institutions.

Like the tightening of a knot, each advanced application of hypermedia in the financial sector furthers and deepens the global integration of capital markets in a planetary web of complex speculative financial flows. In ways that are similar to the overlapping layers of transnational production, the players in the 'casino capitalism' market represent a complex montage of both massive global enterprises and small entrepreneurs with a planetary reach afforded by hypermedia. The 'big' players—financial institutions like Citicorp, Chase Manhattan, Merrill Lynch, Salomon Brothers, Barclays, National Westminster, Warburg, and Nomura—have offices around the world and dominate trading: typically, the top 20 institutions in a market account for between 40 and 60 per cent of worldwide transactions.[20] Because of the way the hypermedia environment links the globe into a 24-hour market, companies like Salomon Brothers, which can trade up to $2 trillion US in stocks, bonds, and commodities in a single year, is 'always open, everywhere'.[21] Stocks, bonds, and other instruments of debt are continuously traded, bounding from exchange to exchange in response to slight shifts in the market—often without human intervention as computer programs handle portfolios for traders. In the words of Thrift and Leyshon, 'we might conceive of the international financial system as an electronically networked, constantly circulating, nomadic "state", operating 24 hours a day around the world.'[22]

The entire *volume* of capital speeding through hypermedia currents is thus truly staggering, and at times seems almost incomprehensibly large compared to more readily identifiable figures. CS First Boston, a leading global bond trader based in New York, trades more money each year than the entire GNP of the United States.[23] To give some indication of the way in which this 'casino capital' has been decoupled from the so-called 'real' economy (which historically it has been assumed to follow), international trade now amounts to about $2 trillion per year. Today foreign exchange transactions alone—

carried out over computers linked in near-real time—amount to about $1 trillion *per day*.[24]

In response to this massive, global 24-hour circuit of capital, new spaces and flows are arising, and centres and 'hubs' have emerged that may provide a glimpse of the evolving architecture of the postmodern world order. Large cities, such as New York, London, Tokyo, Singapore, and Hong Kong, are assuming more of an importance as 'command centres' in the global 'finanscape'—what an *Economist* survey referred to as 'Capitals of capital'.[25] They act not so much as national cities as they do *world cites*—interfacial nodes in the global hypermedia environment.

Also assuming more importance are the many offshore micro-states, which 'have been transformed by exploiting niches in the circuits of fictitious capital'.[26] Roberts notes that 'these offshore financial centres are sites that dramatically evince the contrary and complex melding of offshore and onshore, of national and international, and of local and global.'[27] For example, because of its strategic time-zone location and lax regulations, the tiny Cayman Islands 'houses' 546 banks from all around the world, of which only 69 maintain any kind of physical presence.[28] The quintessential offshore market is the Eurodollar or Eurocurrency market, which Martin calls 'stateless' money.[29] The prefix 'Euro', as Roberts points out, is a misleading vestige of an earlier time; today, the Eurocurrency market involves a dynamic new geography of flows 'stretching from Panama to Switzerland and on to Singapore and beyond'.[30] Confusing matters even more, regulations designed to offer more competitive financial environments have created extraterritorial 'offshore' markets onshore, *within* state boundaries, such as those that exist in New York, California, and Japan.[31] Developments such as these, where, in Castells's terms, a 'space of flows' seems to dominate and transcend a 'space of places', strain our traditional ways of seeing the world that were constructed and reaffirmed under the modern world order paradigm.[32] They signal not only an 'unbundling' of our practices, but of our conceptual baggage as well.

Together, these transformations in the nature of production and finance have spawned a vast planetary network—a pulsating conglomeration that circulates information and services around the world. Its dense mass covers a swath in the middle of the planet, linked by major nodes centred in Tokyo, Beijing, Singapore, Taiwan, Hong Kong, Vancouver, Los Angeles, Toronto, Chicago, New York, Washington, London, Paris, and Berlin. It is here that the networked epistemic communities—the virtual élite—are located and the operating codes for the rest of the system generated. 'Soft power' has become the catch-phrase for the type of knowledge created by this élite, which in practice translates into domination of film, video, newspaper, and other media underpinned by the structural power of capital. From this central mass, networked tentacles stretch out into southern and northern regions, drawing in raw materials, consumer merchandise, and processed data. Pulsating stratospherically above and around this networked mass is the 24-hour circuit of 'casino capital', shifting astronomical sums in a swarm of electrical impulses.

In the hypermedia environment, these changes in production and finance illustrate that power is increasingly no longer exercised by the control of space or territory but by the control of the pace and flow of information: *network power*. The volume and speed of capital mobility create a 'structural' pressure that systematically circumscribes the macroeconomic policy options available to states—a power large enough to warrant, according to Webb, its inclusion as a 'third-image' attribute of the international structure.[33] Hence, governments at all levels—local, state, and regional—now engage in competitive deregulatory and re-regulatory 'locational tournaments' designed to attract flows of global investment.[34] Although institutional lags and cultural traditions mean that individual state policies differ to some extent, states have increasingly moulded their policies according to the interests of global market forces. And each deregulatory wave only drives the process further, augmenting transborder capital mobility, increasing the potency of network power, and creating demands for yet more accommodating policies.

Accompanying these deregulatory moves have been the creation and emergence of multiple and overlapping layers of authority designed to co-ordinate states' economic policies. Almost all states now find themselves enmeshed in an ever-widening network of informal and formal international institutions, regimes, organizations, and regional trading blocs that have emerged in response to changes in the global economy. Examples of these layers of global governance are numerous, ranging from more informal bodies, like the Trilateral Commission or the G–8 economic summits, to more formal bodies, such as the World Trade Organization, to regional bodies and agreements, such as the European Union, the North American Free Trade Agreement, and the Asia-Pacific Economic Co-operation forum, to more specialized, functional bodies, such as the World Bank, the International Monetary Fund, and the Bank for International Settlements. While it is true that states voluntarily entered into and created such agreements, they establish institutional precedents and routines that cannot easily be reversed.

## Conclusions

Like a massive uprooting in the wake of an earthquake, the hypermedia environment is profoundly altering the landscape of world politics. The pyrotechnics of the virtual global economy now subsume the planet in a dense web of commercial interactions, having erupted out of the major post-industrial states. As with past changes in economic structures, the formation of this planetary network is largely setting the conditions under which other social and political activities take place, though not entirely. Indeed, this networked organism would constitute a planetary Empire of Hyper-Capitalism were it not for equally profound transformations occurring in another dimension of the hypermedia environment: the rise of a global civil society. Through the cracks and the margins, global civil society networks have surged forth, forming alliances, disseminating information, publicizing injustice, canvassing for change, and pressuring governments, corporations, and populations. Although they lack the type of structural power of hypermedia markets, they are able to

exert influence, on the borders and in the margins, over specific issue-areas. Their increasing successes in this respect, as in the Internet-based opposition to the Multilateral Agreement on Investments, suggest a potentially viable avenue for counterhegemonic activities against the unbridled reign of global market forces. Together, these new formations on the world political landscape represent new spheres of authority employing new types of power: the control over the flow, tempo, and presentation of information.

Whereas determinations of world order in the Westphalian system were largely contested by states, today they are being hammered out as well by a constellation of non-state actors who see territorial boundaries as mere inconveniences to their larger aims. To be sure, states have not disappeared in the hypermedia environment, nor should we expect them to anytime soon. To the contrary, states have proliferated in the twentieth century from around 50 at mid-century to nearly 200 today. And despite liberalization and deregulation, their interventions in social and economic processes are formidable and continue to grow. What has changed, however, is that states have been, in effect, turned *inside out*—locked in and interpenetrated by social forces and technologies now partially beyond their control. It is as if they are now digitally embalmed in an electronic web of their own spinning. Indeed, the vast majority of post-industrialized states—Canada, the United States, France, Germany, Great Britain, Japan, and others—now behave more like a single, multi-headed organism than a collection of sovereign independent units. With states no longer monopolizing legitimate authority, the right to rule has dispersed to a much wider domain of actors, and states have become mere links in a wider chain of political structures. *Post*-modern world order is a quasi-feudal, multicentric system comprised of multiple state and non-state authorities.

We are only now beginning to experience some of the many ramifications of this transformation: the swift circuits of capital, the total planetary surveillance, the rise of virtual communities, the spread of global consumer culture, and the reactionary reversions to it in the resurgence of religious and other primordial identities. Of these, however, surely one that looms the largest centres on a fundamental inversion taking place: whereas once questions of 'the good life' were more or less confined to the domestic sphere and there was no 'international theory' to speak of, today such questions have become inherently global. As we enter the twenty-first century, the unit of 'the good life' has become the planet as a whole. From now on, it is world domestic politics. Although the first eruptions out of the hypermedia environment set the material conditions for this change in a hyper-liberal direction, other social forces are just now beginning to emerge: in civil society networks, in articulations of global justice, and in the formation of global governing arrangements that are more than simply vehicles for capitalism. It is out of this mix of interests and values that a planetary polity is now being shaped.

## Notes

1  Parts of this paper are drawn from Ronald J. Deibert, *Parchment, Printing, and Hypermedia: Communication in World Order Transformation* (New York: Columbia University Press, 1997).

2  For Innis, see *Empire and Communications* (Oxford: Oxford University Press, 1950) and *The Bias of Communication* (Toronto: University of Toronto Press, 1951). For McLuhan, see especially *The Gutenburg Galaxy* (Toronto: University of Toronto Press, 1962) and *Understanding Media: The Extensions of Man* (New York: McGraw-Hill, 1964).

3  Deibert, *Parchment, Printing, and Hypermedia*.

4  This tradition includes thinkers such as Harold Innis, Lewis Mumford, and Fernand Braudel—in short, those who recognized the irreducible connections between material context and social *episteme*.

5  For an exposition of Darwinian theories of evolution, see Daniel Dennett, *Darwin's Dangerous Idea: Evolution and the Meanings of Life* (New York: Simon and Schuster, 1995).

6  Janice Thomson, 'State Sovereignty in International Relations', *International Studies Quarterly* 39 (June 1995): 221.

7  For the reference to the 'cyberspace bazaar', see Adam Bryant, 'Am I Bid Six? Click to Bid Six', *New York Times*, 13 May 1996.

8  Harvey, S. James, Jr, and Murray Weidenbaum, *When Businesses Cross International Borders* (London: Praeger, 1993), 3.

9  Mark Hepworth, *Geography of the Information Economy* (London: Bellhaven Press, 1989), 95. As Susan Strange puts it, 'More and more, the goods passing from one country to another are not in any sense of the word actually "sold" or "bought". They are only moved by order of corporate managers between different branches of the same TNCs.' Susan Strange, *The Retreat of the State: The Diffusion of Power in the World Economy* (New York: Cambridge University Press, 1996), 47.

10  See William J. Drake and Kalypso Nicolaidis, 'Ideas, Interests, and Institutionalization: "Trade in Services" and the Uruguay Round', *International Organization* 46 (Winter 1992): 37.

11  James and Weidenbaum, *When Businesses Cross International Borders*, 52. These flows tailed off slightly in the first two years of the 1990s due to worldwide recession, but have recently begun to pick up pace again. UNCTAD, *World Investment Report*, 1996.

12  See UNCTAD, *World Investment Report*, 1996.

13  Robert Gilpin, *The Political Economy of International Relations* (Princeton, NJ: Princeton University Press, 1987), 308–9.

14  Stephen Gill, 'Economic Globalization and the Internationalization of Authority: Limits and Contradictions', *Geoforum* 23, 3 (1992): 273.

15  Ibid. See also Eric Helleiner, *States and the Reemergence of Global Finance: From Bretton Woods to the 1990s* (Ithaca, NY: Cornell University Press, 1994).

16  See Joel Kurtzman, *The Death of Money* (New York: Simon and Schuster, 1993), 170–1.

17  See Stephen Black, 'A Sobering Look at Cyberspace', *Ridgeway Viewpoints* 96–3 (June 1996). Black cites the following Web site as the source for this information: http://www.bankamerica.com/batoday/bacfacts.html

18  As cited in Richard O'Brien, *Global Financial Integration: The End of Geography* (London: Pinter, 1992), 9.

19  See Andrew Allentuck, 'Financial Services That Delight, Amaze', *Globe and Mail*, 14 Nov. 1995.

20  Ron Martin, 'Stateless Monies', in Stuart Corbridge, Nigel Thrift, and Ron Martin, eds, *Money, Power, and Space* (Oxford: Basil Blackwell, 1994), 261.

21  Kurtzman, *The Death of Money*, 109.

22  Nigel Thrift and Andrew Leyshon, 'A Phantom State?', *Political Geography* 13, 4 (July 1994): 311.

23  Kurtzman, *The Death of Money*, 77.

24  John Gerard Ruggie, 'Territoriality and Beyond: Problematizing Modernity in International Relations', *International Organization* 47 (Winter 1993): 141.

25  See 'Financial Centres: A Survey', *The Economist*, 27 June 1992. See also Nigel Thrift, 'On the Social and Cultural Determinants of International Financial Centres: The Case of the City of London', in Corbridge et al., *Money, Power, and Space*, 327–55; Manuel Castells, *The Informational City: Information Technology, Economic Restructuring,* *and the Urban-Regional Process* (Oxford: Basil Blackwell, 1989). The term 'finanscape' is from Arjun Appadurai, 'Disjuncture and Difference in the Global Cultural Economy', *Theory, Culture & Society* 7 (1990): 295–310.

26  Susan Roberts, 'Fictitious Capital, Fictitious Spaces: The Geography of Offshore Financial Flows', in Corbridge et al., *Money, Power, and Space*, 92.

27  Ibid.

28  Ibid.

29  Martin, 'Stateless Monies', 259.

30  Roberts, 'Fictitious Capital, Fictitious Spaces', 94.

31  Ibid., 100.

32  Castells, *The Informational City*.

33  Michael Webb, 'International Economic Structures', *International Organization* 45 (1991): 309–42. See also David Andrews, 'Capital Mobility and State Autonomy', *International Studies Quarterly* 38 (1994), for a comprehensive overview.

34  'Locational tournaments' is a term I borrow from Lynn K. Mytelka.

## Suggested Readings

Castells, Manuel. *The Information Age: Economy, Society, and Culture*. Oxford: Basil Blackwell, 1997.

Corbridge, Stuart, Nigel Thrift, and Ron Martin, eds. *Money, Power, and Space*. Oxford: Basil Blackwell, 1994.

Deibert, Ronald J. *Parchment, Printing, and Hypermedia: Communication in World Order Transformation*. New York: Columbia University Press, 1997.

Innis, Harold. *Empire and Communications*. Oxford: Oxford University Press, 1950.

Spiro, Peter J. 'New Global Communities: Non-governmental Organizations in International Decision-Making Institutions', *Washington Quarterly* 18, 1 (1994).

Strange, Susan. *The Retreat of the State: The Diffusion of Power in the World Economy*. Cambridge: Cambridge University Press, 1996.

## Web Sites

Economics Resources:
http://www.clark.net/pub/lschank/web/econ.html

Electronic Money Links: http://www.ex.ac.uk/~RDavies/arian/emoney.html

IPEnet: http://csf.colorado.edu/ipe/

NGO-Related Resource Site: http://www.xs4all.nl/~laraguy/ngo.html

WebActive: http://www.webactive.com/

## Chapter 16

# The Global Economy and Environmental Change in Africa

## Jennifer Clapp

Africa's environmental crisis has reached severe proportions. Of this there is little doubt.[1] Africa's forests, which account for about 30 per cent of the world's tropical forests, have been destroyed at an average rate of nearly 1 per cent per year over the past decade, resulting in a vast amount of biodiversity loss. The continent's already fragile soils have become more so with large tracts of land turning to unproductive desert. Africa also increasingly faces unsafe exposure to environmental hazards such as agro-chemicals and toxic wastes. These environmental problems have contributed to a continuation of poverty, declining land productivity, and poor health of humans and animal and plant species on the continent. Both local and global forces have contributed to this crisis. But while there has been a large amount of research on domestic factors contributing to Africa's environmental predicament, surprisingly little attention has been paid to global factors that impact on Africa's natural environment. The purpose of this chapter is to highlight those external factors.

Most mainstream accounts of environmental degradation in Africa, particularly those emanating from powerful policy circles, emphasize the local dimensions of Africa's environmental problems by focusing almost exclusively on the mutually reinforcing relationships between poverty, population growth, and environmental degradation.[2] This is not surprising, as the African continent contains 27 of the 41 poorest countries in the world and has the world's highest population growth rate. The latter, at 3 per cent per year, has been higher than the 2 per cent average rate of economic growth per

annum on the continent over the past decade.[3] The World Bank's 1994 report, *Adjustment in Africa*, typifies this poverty-population-environment analysis:

> the poor are both victims and the agents of damage to the environment. Because the poor—especially poor women—tend to have access only to the more environmentally fragile resources, they often suffer high productivity declines because of soil degradation or the loss of tree cover. And because they are poor, they may have little recourse but to extract what they can from the resources available to them. The high fertility rates of poor households further strain the natural resource base.[4]

The situation is portrayed as a 'vicious cycle' or a downward 'spiral' that must be stopped. Some recent studies critiquing this interpretation from a local perspective have pointed out its oversimplicity and, in many cases, its inaccuracy.[5] These works are extremely important in helping to understand the complexities of local forces in environmental degradation in Africa.

Local aspects of environmental stress in Africa, however, are only part of the story. Conspicuously absent from most mainstream accounts of Africa's environmental crisis are the global factors that also contribute, directly and indirectly, to environmental change. It is widely recognized that most of today's environmental problems can be traced to economic activity of one sort or another. And because African economies are profoundly affected not only by internal economic forces but also by global economic conditions, analyses of Africa's environmental crisis should take these global factors into account. The increasingly global economy, characterized by the growth in global finance, trade, and foreign direct investment, has a significant impact on Africa's environment, and so should not be left out of the analysis. In this chapter I argue that the weak position of Africa in the international political economy has made it particularly vulnerable to a number of the environmental side-effects of global economic relationships. While Africa's share of global economic activity is small, the global economy looms large within Africa's economies and sets the context within which environmental change takes place.

## Global Financing: Debt, Aid, and Adjustment

External debt has been a defining feature of African economies over the past 20 years. Africa's debt is small in absolute terms when compared to total developing country debt. But African countries' debt as a proportion of GNP and exports is crippling. Debt service obligations for African countries in the late 1980s averaged just under 50 per cent of export revenues. Total African debt in the early 1990s was equivalent to over 150 per cent of the value of its exports and just under 50 per cent of GNP. The bulk of Africa's debt has been owed to official creditors, that is, debt to governments and multilateral institutions such as the IMF and World Bank. A number of northern creditor governments have rescheduled, and in some cases cancelled, African debt in recent years through institutions such as the Paris Club. But IMF and World Bank loans cannot be rescheduled. Multilateral debt is an increasing problem for Africa, currently accounting for some 24.5 per cent of total African debt.[6] This severe indebtedness has made African economies particularly vulnerable to conditions placed on external financing by lending agencies. These loans have had many direct and indirect effects on the natural environment, as can be seen through both lending for specific projects and lending in support of structural adjustment programs.

### Project Assistance

Bilateral and multilateral project lending to African countries has had significant environmental impact over the past three decades. Most aid agencies did not have any sort of environmental assessment of their projects until the late 1980s and early 1990s. The World Bank in the 1960s and 1970s, for example, had the view that environmental costs were a necessary side-effect of development, and felt that economic growth would eventually produce the revenue to allow countries to undertake measures to clean up and protect the environment. Moreover, the Bank did not have the staff to assess every project on environmental criteria, let alone to incorporate principles of environmental sustainability directly into project planning. Other lending agencies and governments similarly neglected the impact on the environment of the projects they financed in Africa.

The result of this lack of concern was that many externally funded projects have had a negative environmental impact. These include forestry, dam, and agricultural projects. Lending for forestry sector projects often set out to increase the exports of timber or included plans to clear forested lands for more 'productive' purposes. For example, project loans from the World Bank to Cameroon in the 1970s and early 1980s focused on ways to exploit the forest further, rather than to conserve it.[7] Dam projects financed by outside agencies in conjunction with African governments have contributed to a rise in health problems. An increased rate of incidence of water-borne diseases such as shistomiasis was seen following a number of dam and irrigation projects in Egypt, Ghana, Mali, and Sudan.[8] These dam projects have also displaced large numbers of people and forced them onto fragile lands, which often results in environmental degradation. For example, in Nigeria, the World Bank-funded Talata-Mafara irrigation project displaced 60,000 people in a three-year period.[9] Similar displacement from such projects has taken place in other African countries that embarked on dam projects, such as Mali, Côte d'Ivoire, Republic of Congo (formerly Zaire), Ethiopia, Ghana, and Sudan.

Externally funded agricultural projects, prevalent across Africa, have focused on the adoption of 'modern' or 'green revolution' agricultural techniques, including the use of pesticides, fertilizers, and the cultivation of both food and cash crops in a monoculture fashion with new hybrid or high-yielding varieties of seeds. These projects have often been undertaken in conjunction with land-clearing and dam projects. Such techniques have been associated with environmental damage, which has been as problematic as that associated with traditional slash-and-burn agriculture and forest clearing. These include diminished soil fertility and the poisoning of land from the overuse of pesticides and fertilizers, deforestation and desertification through agricultural clearing, and the loss of local biodiversity through the introduction of monocropping.

Only recently have aid agencies such as the World Bank begun to look at the environmental impact of their project lending. In 1987, for example, the World Bank created a central environment department and increased its environment staff. At the same time it pledged to fund more projects designed to bring positive environmental benefits and to consult with affected peoples and environmental groups before embarking on projects that might displace them or cause environmental harm. By 1991 the Bank began to require environmental impact assessments on all of its projects, as did many other donor governments and lending agencies. But African countries continued to receive loans for projects for which the environmental impact had not been carefully thought through, despite claims by the World Bank and other donors to the contrary. A prime example of this is the creation of the Tropical Forestry Action Plan (TFAP) funded by the World Bank, UN Food and Agriculture Organization (FAO), United Nations Development Program (UNDP), and the World Resources Institute (WRI). On paper, TFAP was intended to stem the causes of deforestation in developing countries through the financing of forestry sector aid projects in countries with tropical forests. In practice, the outcome was often quite the opposite in African countries that had national forest action plans financed by the scheme. In Cameroon, for example, an openly declared objective of the national forest action plan was to make that country the largest forest product exporter in Africa. But while this case and others across the developing world soon discredited the TFAP, other forestry sector loans from the World Bank were being funded despite their environmentally dubious measures. For instance, according to Rich, Guinea and Côte d'Ivoire were both lent money in 1990 by the World Bank for forestry projects that created conditions for even more rapid deforestation.[10]

## Structural Adjustment

IMF- and World Bank-sponsored structural adjustment programs (SAPs) were introduced in the 1980s in an attempt to alleviate the severe debt problem in developing countries. By the early 1990s, most sub-Saharan African countries had adopted SAPs. The purpose of structural adjustment loans was to give balance-of-payments support to help countries to repay their debts in exchange for macroeconomic policy reforms such as the liberalization of domestic price, trade, exchange rate, and investment policies and a curtailment of government spending. The basic idea behind these policy reforms was to reorient the economy to bring in much-needed foreign exchange by encouraging exports and attracting foreign direct investment. The World Bank did not foresee any environmental side-effects of adjustment before it went ahead with the promotion of these policies across Africa, and no measures were put into place to protect the adjusting countries' natural resource base. It was largely assumed that the market-based adjustment policies would be best for the environment.

Debates have emerged on the effects of adjustment on the natural environment. Some studies have pointed out that adjustment appears to help the environmental situation in some cases by reducing policy distortions that may have previously underpriced natural resources (which encourages their extraction) and subsidized imported chemicals used in agriculture and industrial production (which encourages their overuse).[11] Others argue that while there are some potential positive environmental impacts of economic reform, adjustment has had definite harmful effects in many cases, and that on balance the outcome appears to be negative as far as the environment is concerned.[12] This is especially true when their is a lack of complementary policies designed to protect the environment during adjustment. While there are no clear-cut conclusions regarding whether adjustment policies have had uniformly positive or negative effects on the environment, in the African case there have been a number of instances where the effects have been less than positive.

The massive devaluation of currencies and liberalization of trade policies across sub-Saharan African countries undergoing adjustment have tended in some cases to encourage the export of natural resources, which is not always carried out in a sustainable manner. The implementation of these policies has meant that African agricultural, mineral, and timber products have become quite attractive on world markets. Ghana is a case in point. According to Toye, deforestation in Ghana rose dramatically after it adopted a SAP. Between 1983 and 1986, exports of tropical timber rose by 42 per cent, while the volume of timber production tripled in that period.[13] In this case it is clear that deforestation cannot be blamed entirely on the use of fuelwood by the poor or on population pressures to clear land for agriculture. Similarly, deforestation has increased in Cameroon, Tanzania, and Zambia following the adoption of adjustment reforms.[14] These cases may not be reflective of all African countries undergoing adjustment, but they do point out that adjustment policies promoting increased exports have the potential to increase unsustainable resource extraction.

Adjustment policies have also had an indirect effect on the environment through the increased overall hardship faced by the poorest segments of African societies, especially in the early years of adjustment before the World Bank began to implement programs to protect the poor. It is very difficult to measure precisely the environmental impact, but one can say that increased poverty has placed growing pressures on the environment by the poor. The elimination of food and fuel subsidies, combined with the rise in prices of imported agricultural inputs, has led to increased hardship for many in Africa. The result has been that under adjustment the poor have continued and in some cases increased the felling of trees for fuelwood or for the expansion of agricultural production, the overcultivation and overgrazing of land, and the use of environmentally unsound technologies. It is not clear whether these negative effects are outweighed by the positive environmental impact of the reduction in the use of imported fuel and pesticides.

A third general effect of adjustment policies on the environment has been the impact of cuts in government spending called for by the international financial institutions. Cuts have negatively affected not only spending on anti-poverty measures, particularly in the early years of adjustment, but also have reduced funding to government programs for environmental protection and conservation.[15] Again, this is difficult to measure. It is true that African governments did not in general spend a great deal of their budgets on the protection of the environment before SAPs were adopted, so cuts to environmental spending may not have led directly to a large-scale increase in environmental harm. But it is the case that now, with international pressure on them to protect the environment, many African governments are unable to spend much at all on improving protection of the environment because of severe budget cuts under SAPs.

## The Global Trade Regime

The globalization of trade over the past 50 years in particular has had important ramifications around the world that have affected the natural environment in the North and South alike. The phenomenal growth in the volume and value of global trade has been linked to trade liberalization under the GATT and the growing importance of regional free trade agreements. Debates have emerged in recent years over whether the promotion of freer international trade policies and protection of the environment are compatible. Free trade advocates argue that freer international trade enables countries to make better use of their comparative advantage and in the end all trading countries benefit economically. This increased income, free trade advocates contend, can be spent on environmental protection. Critics of this view note that this expected economic growth from global trade is itself harmful to the environment and that there is no guarantee that increased income will be spent on environmental protection. They also argue that unfettered free trade can lead to unsustainable exports of natural resources or to imports of potentially dangerous products or wastes, particularly in countries that rely primarily on those resources as their main source of foreign exchange.

Although Africa's share of global trade is approximately 2 per cent, trade is the continent's most important source of foreign exchange.[16] African countries' exports are made up mostly of primary products. Part of the reason for this is the practice of developed countries to charge higher tariffs on manufactured goods imported from developing countries than they do for raw materials. This encourages the export of raw products, which are then manufactured in the North. Moreover, a high percentage of the goods that Africa exports are controlled by very few multinational corporations (MNCs), which often operate price-fixing cartels with the result that producers usually get no more than 20 per cent of the market price for these products. For example, 90 per cent of forest products exports globally are controlled by between three and six of the largest timber corporations.[17] Commodity prices on global markets also tend to fluctuate widely, leaving Africa vulnerable to swings in world market prices, which have on the whole remained depressed since the mid-1980s. And the small percentage of already low world prices that producers generally receive only encourages them to sell even more raw materials in order to earn a decent income. The result has been a steady decline in the continent's natural resource base.

Africa is the second largest exporting region in the world market for tropical timber. About 18 African countries are timber exporters, and 10 of those are net exporters. These net exporters of tropical timber include the West and Central African countries of Cameroon, Central African Republic,

Congo, Côte d'Ivoire, Equatorial Guinea, Gabon, Ghana, Guinea-Bissau, Liberia, and Republic of Congo.[18] Barbier et al. have pointed out the difficulties in drawing clear and direct causal linkages between involvement in the tropical timber trade and increased rates of deforestation. In the African case, for example, only 10 per cent of timber production is exported. They do argue, however, that the linkages, often complex and both direct and indirect, do exist.[19] For example, logging companies, most of them in Africa being foreign-owned, invariably cut new roads to access trees. These roads contribute to further deforestation, as they open up the forest to the poor, who seek fuelwood or land to clear for agricultural expansion. Indeed, most of the West and Central African countries listed above currently face some of the highest rates of deforestation in Africa. Most of the exports of tropical timber find their way to northern industrialized markets, with Africa's exports going primarily to Europe.

Another type of export associated with environmental harm has been Africa's involvement in the international ivory trade. Africa is the principal source of nearly all ivory traded internationally. This trade increased by some 10 per cent per year from the 1940s to the 1980s, when trading in ivory was discouraged through international regulation. The ivory trade has had a devastating effect on the continent's elephant population, which went from 1.2 million to about 600,000 from 1981 to 1989 alone.[20] Nearly all of this ivory ends up in East Asian and northern industrialized countries. African countries have remained involved in the trade precisely because of the foreign exchange it brings in and because prices for internationally traded ivory have increased dramatically over the past decade. Following widespread concern over the declining elephant populations, both within and outside of the continent, African elephants were listed in Appendix 1 of the Convention on International Trade in Endangered Species (CITES) in 1989. This effectively banned the international ivory trade. The debate on the ivory trade was reopened, however, in June 1997 at the 10th Conference of Parties of CITES, when it was decided to allow limited trade in ivory from Zimbabwe, Botswana, and Namibia, as these countries had complained that their elephant populations were no longer endangered and that the trade ban did not put a halt to poaching. Whether this move will cease poaching in these countries remains to be seen.

Africa's environment has been affected not only by exports of natural resources sold on today's globalized markets, but also by certain imports. Africa was a popular target for waste exporters, who during the mid- to late 1980s shipped their toxic waste to many unsuspecting African countries through clandestine deals, usually involving dubious private parties and in some cases corrupt government officials.[21] Africa was a favourite place for waste dealers as it was much cheaper to dump wastes there than in the northern industrialized countries where the waste originated. Africa thus became the dumping ground for the North. The well-known and highly publicized cases of the Italian PCB and asbestos-laced waste dumped in the village of Koko in Nigeria, the toxic incinerator ash from the United States dumped on Kassa Island in Guinea, and, more recently, toxic and medical waste reportedly sent from Europe to Somalia stand out as cases in point. By 1989, well over 50 incidents of waste dumping or attempted dumping on the continent were recorded, with 30 more cases recorded by 1994.[22] This foreign hazardous waste has had a devastating effect on Africa's environment, as it was delivered in leaking containers or in no containers at all. It has killed trees, leached into soils, and made its way into groundwater, streams, and rivers.

Since the waste trade to Africa was made public in the late 1980s and early 1990s, efforts have been taken both within Africa and in the international community to regulate, if not halt, this trade. The Basel Convention on the Transboundary Movement of Hazardous Wastes and Their Disposal, established in 1989, set out to regulate the trade and required exporting countries to give prior informed consent, as a measure of protection for poor countries, providing them with an opportunity to 'just say no'. But the African countries were outraged at being targeted as the North's garbage bin and held out for a ban on the trade. The African countries agreed in 1991 to adopt the Bamako Convention, which does impose an outright ban on the import of waste into Africa. Following several years of campaigning the African and other Third World countries, in collaboration with environmental groups, were successful in 1995 in convincing the parties to the Basel Convention to ban the trade in hazardous wastes to non-OECD countries. Whether this ban will drive the trade underground, like that of the ivory trade, remains to be seen.

## Foreign Direct Investment

The past 40 years have seen a globalization of production linked to the growth in international trade and finance. The rise in the number of multinational corporations involved in industrial production has been evident across the globe, including Africa. Though in the mid-1990s sub-Saharan Africa received only about 3 per cent of the total of foreign direct investment globally, the foreign investment it does receive is very important as it is a vital source of foreign exchange.[23] But at the same time that MNCs may help bring in income, their environmental impact is the subject of debate. While some argue that MNCs tend to bring cleaner and more environmentally sound technologies to developing countries, others point out that there are some clear cases of environmentally harmful practices carried out by MNCs, especially when they import technologies inappropriate for Africa's economic or ecological situation.[24] With most African countries pursuing structural adjustment programs over the course of the 1980s and 1990s, the continent has seen regulation dramatically liberalized in an attempt to attract foreign direct investment. In the African case, there has not been a great deal of research on the environmental impact of FDI to date, signalling a need for more detailed empirical work. It can be said, however, that the MNCs to which Africa is host have been based primarily in sectors traditionally associated with environmental harm.

MNCs have long been involved in extractive industries across Africa, most notably mining of diamonds, gold, bauxite, and copper, as well as oil extraction. It is well known that the process of extracting these minerals is highly polluting, no matter where it is carried out. A significant number of African countries depend on just one or two minerals for the bulk of their income from abroad. At the same time they rely on affiliates of large global corporations to undertake the process of mineral extraction. Namibia, for example, has one of the world's largest open cast uranium mines in the world, owned by RTZ, a British firm. This mining operation has polluted the land and harmed the health of mine workers exposed to the radioactive materials on a daily basis.[25] Most African countries place only weak environmental regulations on mining operations, as many fear that it would raise costs and discourage investment by the MNCs.

Similar environmental problems have arisen in connection with oil drilling. Shell Oil's operations in Nigeria are a prime example. Shell's oil wells in the Ogoni region have attracted much attention in recent years, as the pollution generated by the company's operations have been cited as a factor in the execution of Ogoni human rights activist, Ken Saro-Wiwa, a vocal critic of Shell's poor environmental and human rights record. Shell's oil pipelines in Ogoniland frequently leaked, water supplies were contaminated, soils were polluted from oil spilling onto farmers' fields, and air was fouled by continually burning gas flares.[26] In the mid-1990s, violent conflict broke out in the region as the government tried to suppress the Ogoni people's protests against Shell. This raised international concern over the abuse of human rights by the military regime. In November 1995, Ken Saro Wiwa and eight other Ogoni human rights activists were hanged despite international protests that sought their release from prison. Shell denied that its operations have been the principal cause of environmental harm in Ogoniland. It has also argued that it could not have, nor should it have, interfered with the government's actions against the activists. Shell has since been accused of collusion with the government in suppressing the Ogoni protests.[27]

African countries have also been approached to host other environmentally dubious operations of foreign-owned firms. For example, when the Basel and Bamako waste trade conventions were agreed upon, some global firms sought to 'recycle' their hazardous waste in Africa. A particularly striking case of this is that of British-owned Thor Chemicals, located in Cato Ridge, South Africa. The firm began reprocessing imported mercury-laden waste, just as environmental regulations in Britain no longer allowed that practice. The plant, however, was found to be emitting extremely high levels of mercury, polluting the air and a nearby stream used by the local population for washing clothes and dishes and for bathing.[28] A number of the plant's workers became seriously ill and several died as a result of exposure to mercury. The plant has since been shut down. As the main recipient of FDI in Africa, particularly after the end of apartheid, South Africa is likely to continue to be affected by hazardous industries from abroad.

## Conclusion

Much of the recent literature on Africa's environmental crisis focuses almost exclusively on internal dimensions, primarily on the self-perpetuating cycle between environmental degradation and factors such as domestic policies, population growth, and poverty. While this angle may give some important insights into Africa's environmental predicament, it only tells part of the story. Without trying to downplay the significance of internal factors, this chapter has argued that global economic relationships not only have profoundly affected African economies, but also have had both direct and indirect effects on its natural environment. Debt and external financing for project assistance and for structural adjustment programs, international trade, and foreign direct investment have contributed to environmental stress in Africa.

The impact these global economic factors have on the African economy and environment are largely determined by the continent's status in the global political economy, which has been characterized by extremes of both marginalization and incorporation.[29] Africa accounts for a small fraction of world trade, has a small proportion of global debt and finance, and receives only a tiny amount of foreign direct investment as a percentage of the global total. But at the same time that Africa is largely marginalized in the world economy, these finance, trade, and investment relationships carry significant weight within African economies and environments. Each of these aspects of the global economy is intricately linked not only with one another, but also with domestic factors.

With the acceleration of economic globalization in recent years and its likely continuation, the effect that global economic factors have on Africa's natural environment will only grow in importance. Hence, there is a need for further detailed empirical research on the effects of globalization on the natural environment in Africa. It is also imperative that powerful global economic institutions such as the World Bank recognize the impact of economic globalization, as well as their own activities, on the environmental crisis in Africa and adjust not only their analyses of the situation but also their policies.

## Notes

1  This is a shortened and revised version of the author's 'Global Economic Factors in Africa's Environmental Crisis', in Sola Akinrinade and Amadu Sesay, eds, *Africa in the Post-Cold War International System* (London: Pinter, 1998). On the severity of the environmental crisis, see, for example, Lloyd Timberlake, *Africa in Crisis* (London: Earthscan, 1985); Valentine Udoh James, *Africa's Ecology* (London: Macfarland, 1993); François Falloux and Lee Talbot, *Crisis and Opportunity: Environment and Development in Africa* (London: Earthscan, 1992).

2  See World Commission on Environment and Development, *Our Common Future* (Oxford: Oxford University Press, 1987); Kevin Cleaver and Gotz Schreiber, *Reversing the Spiral: The Population, Agriculture and Environment Nexus in Sub-Saharan Africa* (Washington: World Bank, 1994); Stephen Mink, *Poverty, Population and the Environment* (Washington: World Bank, 1993).

3  World Bank, *Adjustment in Africa* (Washington: World Bank, 1994), 1.

4  Ibid., 161–2.

5  Melissa Leach and Robin Mearns, eds, *The Lie of the Land: Challenging Received Wisdom on the African Environment* (London: International African Institute, 1996); Gavin Williams, 'Modernizing Malthus: The World Bank, Population Control and the African Environment', in Jonathan Crush, ed., *Power of Development* (London: Routledge, 1995).

6  World Bank, *World Development Report 1995* (Washington: World Bank, 1995).

7  Bruce Rich, *Mortgaging the Earth* (London: Earthscan, 1994), 95.

8  Michael Burayidi, 'Environmental Impact Assessment of Aid-Assisted Projects in Africa: Problems and Prospects', in Valentine Udoh James, ed., *Environmental and Economic Dilemmas of Developing Countries: Africa in the 21st Century* (Westport, Conn.: Praeger, 1994), 16; Timberlake, *Africa in Crisis*, 84–5.

9  Fantu Cheru, 'Structural Adjustment, Primary Resource Trade and Sustainable Development in Sub-Saharan Africa', *World Development* 20, 4 (1992): 500; Timberlake, *Africa in Crisis*, 82.

10  Bruce Rich, *Mortgaging the Earth* (London: Earthscan, 1994), 163–5. See also Korinna Horta, 'The Last Big Rush for the Green Gold: The Plundering of Cameroon's Rainforests', *The Ecologist* 21, 3 (1991).

11  David Glover, 'Structural Adjustment and the Environment', *Journal of International Development* 7, 2 (1995): 285–9.

12  See, for example, Korinna Horta in *Environmental Policies for Sustainable Growth in Africa* (Upper Montclair, NJ: Center for Economic Research on Africa, 1991); Dominic Hogg, *The SAP in the Forest* (London: Friends of the Earth, 1994); Cheru, 'Structural Adjustment'.

13  John Toye, 'Ghana', in Paul Mosley, Jane Harrigan, and John Toye, eds, *Aid and Power*, vol. 2 (London: Routledge, 1991), 192.

14  David Reed, ed., *Structural Adjustment, the Environment and Sustainable Development* (London: Earthscan, 1996), 311.

15  David Reed, 'Conclusions', ibid., 151.

16  *UNCTAD Handbook of International Trade and Development Statistics* (Geneva: United Nations, 1993), 28.

17  Neil Middleton, Phil O'Keefe, and Sam Moyo, *Tears of the Crocodile: From Rio to Reality in the Developing World* (London: Pluto Press, 1993), 99.

18  Edward Barbier et al., *The Economics of the Tropical Timber Trade* (London: Earthscan, 1994), 11–12; World Resources Institute, *World Resources 1994–95* (Washington: WRI, 1994), 310.

19  Barbier et al., *The Economics of the Tropical Timber Trade*, 14, 33.

20  Edward Barbier et al., *Elephants, Economics and Ivory* (London: Earthscan, 1990), 2–3. See also Edward Barbier, 'Elephant Ivory and Tropical Timber: The Role of Trade Interventions in Sustainable Management', *Journal of Environment and Development* 4, 2 (1995).

21  Jennifer Clapp, 'Africa, NGOs, and the International Toxic Waste Trade', *Journal of Environment and Development* 3, 2 (1994).

22  Jim Vallette and Heather Spalding, eds, *The International Trade in Wastes: A Greenpeace Inventory* (Washington: Greenpeace, 1990); Paul Heller, ed., *Database of Known Hazardous Waste Exports from OECD to non-OECD Countries* (Amsterdam: Greenpeace, 1994).

23  World Bank, *World Debt Tables 1994–95* (Washington: World Bank, 1994), 4.

24  Felix Edoho, 'Third World Resource Base and Technology Transfer: Environmental Dilemmas of African Extractive Economy', in James, ed., *Environmental and Economic Dilemmas*.

25  Wilfred Asombang, 'The Environment, Optimum Use of Resources and the Dynamics of Sustainable Development in a Mineral-led Economy: The Case of Namibia', in Mohamed Suliman, ed., *Alternative Strategies for Africa Vol. 2: Environment, Women* (London: IFAA, 1991), 58.

26  John Vidal, 'Black Gold Claims a High Price', *Guardian Weekly*, 15 Jan. 1995.

27  Andy Rowell, 'Oil, Shell, and Nigeria', *The Ecologist* 2, 6 (1995): 210–13.

28  See Fred Kockott, *Wasted Lives* (Amsterdam: Earthlife Africa/Greenpeace, 1994).

29  Thomas Callaghy, 'Africa and the World Economy: Caught Between a Rock and a Hard Place', in John Harbeson and Donald Rothchild, eds, *Africa in World Politics* (Boulder, Colo.: Westview Press, 1991).

## Suggested Readings

Barbier, Edward. 'Elephant Ivory and Tropical Timber: The Role of Trade Interventions in Sustainable Management', *Journal of Environment and Development* 4, 2 (1995).

Cheru, Fantu. 'Structural Adjustment, Primary Resource Trade and Sustainable Development in Sub-Saharan Africa', *World Development* 20, 4 (1992).

Clapp, Jennifer. 'Africa, NGOs, and the International Toxic Waste Trade', *Journal of Environment and Development* 3, 2 (1994).

James, Valentine Udoh, ed. *Environmental and Economic Dilemmas of Developing Countries: Africa in the 21st Century*. Westport, Conn.: Praeger, 1994.

Leach, Melissa, and Robin Mearns, eds. *The Lie of the Land: Challenging Received Wisdom on the African Environment*. London: International African Institute, 1996.

Reed, David, ed. *Structural Adjustment, the Environment and Sustainable Development*. London: Earthscan, 1996.

Rich, Bruce. *Mortgaging the Earth*. London: Earthscan, 1994.

Suliman, Mohamed, ed. *Alternative Strategies for Africa Vol. 2: Environment, Women*. London: IFAA, 1991.

Timberlake, Lloyd. *Africa in Crisis*. London: Earthscan, 1985.

## Web Sites

United Nations Environment Program: http://www.unep.ch

World Bank: http://www.worldbank.org/

International Institute for Sustainable Development: http://www.iisd.ca/

Envirolink: http://www.envirolink.org

The Rainforest Action Network, Africa Campaign: http://www.ran.org/ran_campaigns/africa

Greenpeace International: http://www.greenpeace.org

Corporate Watch: http://www.corpwatch.org

Southern Africa Environment Page: http://www.oneworld.org/saep/

Econews Africa: http://www.web.apc.org/~econews/

Basel Action Network: http://www.ban.org

## Chapter 17

# Gendered Representations of the 'Global':
## Reading/Writing Globalization

### Marianne H. Marchand

## Introduction

These days much has already been said about glob-alization.[1] And, although many disagreements exist about the effects, impact, scope, and future of glob-alization, there is a general sense that we are living in times of profound change. Whenever such change occurs, it tends to produce feelings of uncertainty and being adrift. Moreover, as social and political analysis has taught us, major changes or transformations never take place on a level play-ing field. Instead, such changes involve the exercise of power and are superimposed on, as well as medi-ated through, already existing unequal relations of class, ethnicity, gender, race, and so forth. There is no reason to believe that this should be different in the case of globalization or global restructuring.

Feminist and other critical approaches to IPE have already done much to identify some of glob-alization's power dimensions.[2] A first step in reveal-ing these power dimensions has been to dispense with a number of the persistent myths surrounding globalization. This is an important strategy because the language in which globalization is often couched tends to depoliticize public discussions. As one author remarks on the replacement of ear-lier developmentalist ideologies by the new ideol-ogy of globalism:

> The agenda of globalism shows its continuities with earlier discourses of development. If globalism is more efficient as a developmen-talist ideology, it is because it seeks to *conceal*, with some success, that this agenda is set still within the old locations of power. But now it

is with the complicity of Third World states, corporations, intellectuals and experts, who are allowed increasingly to participate in the discourse and processes of development.[3]

A second step in the process of revealing the power dimensions of globalization has been to develop a gender analysis of the current transformations. In this context it is important to note that gender oper-ates on at least three interconnected levels: the individual, the collective, and the ideational/ ideological.[4] As a consequence, developing a gen-der analysis allows us not only to introduce subjects or 'people' and subjectivity into an otherwise rather abstract discussion about processes, structures, markets, states, and so forth; it also sensitizes us to the specifically gendered representations and val-orizations of global restructuring: for instance, is the market becoming increasingly masculinized and (civil) society feminized (and what are the con-sequences of this)?

In the remainder of this chapter I will, first of all, explore how feminist and other critical IPE analyses have been able to explode some of the myths surrounding globalization. Based on these insights I will further address the issue of global-ization's inherent 'genderedness' through which certain inequalities are, on the one hand, being fos-tered, reified, and perpetuated, while, on the other, they may be challenged, eroded, and reversed. For the second part of the analysis I will look primarily at how gender operates ideationally. This is not to say that the individual and collective dimensions are less important; rather, this vantage point will allow us to explore whether certain new or dominant spheres and practices of globalization are discursively constructed and associated with 'masculine' values as opposed to other more 'feminized domains'.[5] What this means is that particular processes, spheres, and practices of globalization tend to produce differential constraints and opportunities for men and women. Yet, this is not as straightforward or banal as it may seem at first sight, because notions of masculinity and femininity are embedded in other social practices and subject to change over time and across space. Moreover, although highly masculinized spheres of the global economy may be predominantly occupied by men, women are not entirely absent in these spheres. The spaces and practices associated with so-called masculine values, however, not only may be more easily accessible to certain types of men, but they are also likely to project a certain image of power and to be associated with the exercise of power.

Alternatively, feminized spaces and practices may provide relatively easy access for women and subordinated groups of men, including working-class, minority, and migrant men; the association with these spaces and practices is mostly one of lack of power and disempowerment. Interestingly, however, these same feminized spaces on occasion can become an alternative source of power: it is often within these spaces that alternatives, oppositional strategies, challenges, and resistances are being articulated, thus undermining dominant forces of globalization.

## Globalization and Its Myths

At least three persistent myths can be identified in the current discussions about globalization.[6] Most of them stem from the rather indiscriminate use of the term in the media and by policy-makers. Often the term is used as a blanket statement, covering a variety of changes and transformations. At other times globalization is used to legitimize certain painful socio-economic policies, such as budget cuts or a more general reorientation of the foundations of the (European) welfare state.[7] Over the last decade or so, there have been various efforts to define and even to distinguish different forms of

globalization. While some analysts provide a very narrow economic definition of globalization, others emphasize its more comprehensive nature and reach rather different conclusions about its repercussions. Trying to distinguish between its positive and negative aspects has been another way of approaching globalization: neo-liberal globalization or 'globalization from above' is seen as negative while 'globalization from below' is positively associated with such efforts as improving human rights, the environment, and labour conditions. Finally, it is possible to discern various distinct 'global' discourses with each emphasizing a particular dimension, ranging from a process (globalization), to an ideology (globalism), to a state of being (globality). Despite these efforts, a few persistent myths about globalization still linger. Some of the most pervasive include the following.

### Myth 1: Globalization Is First and Foremost an Economic Process

Many analyses assume that globalization almost exclusively concerns economics and the economy. They tend to discuss globalization in terms of the market, trade, and finance. However, a fuller understanding of globalization should recognize that, although economic processes play an important role, they are part of a larger complex set of processes encompassing the market, state, and civil society.[8] A much more fruitful approach is the notion that the market, state, and civil society are interdependent or contingent spheres of interaction and that all three are undergoing profound restructuring. These restructuring processes are complex and tend sometimes to reinforce and sometimes to contradict each other. In short, the entire process of global restructuring involves a reassessment of the relations among the state, the market, and civil society.

### Myth 2: Globalization Is a Process Generated Outside Our Own (Immediate) Environment

Often, globalization is portrayed as a 'major league' game, designed for such players as large international banks and transnational corporations, in which ordinary citizens do not really play a role. This image of globalization sometimes leads to a situation where people at the grassroots but also within NGOs feel alienated, overwhelmed, and disempowered. However, if there is one myth that we need to dispense with, it is this one. A closer look at globalization reveals that we are all involved in the process, although obviously not in the same ways. For instance, subsistence farmers in sub-Saharan Africa may be affected by the decision of large-scale agro-businesses to expand their production in the region or to introduce a new seed variety. As a consequence, some of the local women farmers may lose their land or experience a dramatic change in their access to seeds, while other local people may find work with one of these agro-business companies and thus be involved in producing directly for the world market. Although research on cash-crop agriculture in sub-Saharan Africa has shown that many of these changes are negatively affecting local farming communities, it is important to recognize that even among these communities there are differences among individuals in terms of their involvement in globalization. Moreover, these farmers' future survival will also depend on their (personal) perceptions of the changing situation.

Likewise, teenagers in Western Europe are influenced by globalized marketing strategies and the globalization of the media to buy a certain type of jeans, watch particular videos and television programs, and buy a specific kind of music—all of which means that they are also participants in globalization. While local youth subcultures define what is cool and what isn't, European teenagers are also heavily influenced by global advertising campaigns by, for example, running shoe companies and clothing manufacturers.

Needless to say, there are considerable differences among the CEOs in the boardrooms of the agro-businesses, the subsistence farmers, and the Western European teenagers in terms of their capacity to structure the direction of globalization processes. However, it is important to recognize that they are all involved in, and affected by, globalization.

## Myth 3: Globalization Is a Universalizing Process and Has a Similar Effect on Everyone

One of the fears often voiced is that globalization will lead to the 'McDonaldization' of the world, leaving little room for distinct local cultural expressions. It is true that globalization's universalizing force should not be underestimated, especially since many large companies are involved in global marketing strategies for their products. However, the mistake often made is to assume that this universalizing force will affect everyone in much the same way. To recognize certain commonalities in processes of globalization does not imply that their effects are the same. Processes of globalization are mediated through local economic, political, and social structures and, consequently, the outcomes vary considerably, resulting in specific local or regional expressions of globalization.

## Gendered Representations of Globalization/Global Restructuring

I prefer the term 'global restructuring' over 'globalization' since 'it explicitly refers to a process of (partially) breaking down an old order and attempting to construct a new one.'[9] In addition, the concept of global restructuring allows us to analyse how the market, the state, and civil society are simultaneously undergoing some kind of global restructuring. In Janine Brodie's words:

> The current round of restructuring represents a fundamental shift in regimes of accumulation and with it a change in institutional practices, regulatory regimes, norms and behaviours—in other words, the simultaneous realignment of the economic, social and political. A feminist analysis must begin with the premise that restructuring represents a struggle over the appropriate boundaries of the public and private, the constitution of gendered subjects within these spheres and, ultimately, the object of feminist political struggles.[10]

For Brodie, the boundaries that need to be renegotiated are primarily those between the public and private, the state and market as well as the national and international spheres. I would argue that these are not the only 'shifting' boundaries and that globalization involves renegotiating an intricate complex of boundaries including those pertaining to the state/market/civil society complex, the global/local, global/regional, and so forth.[11] Despite this difference with Brodie over which spheres and boundaries are the subject of restructuring, her insights are very helpful for the second part of our chapter. For instance, she recognizes that global restructuring simultaneously involves the economic, social, and political. In other words, changing gender relations, such as the backlash against feminism and the neo-conservative agenda on family values, are, for her, clearly part of this restructuring process. She also notes that the 'gendered subjects' who are inhabiting the spheres under transformation are being reconstituted in the process.

Although Brodie's analysis is helpful in understanding the inherent gendered nature of globalization, it does not, however, directly address our concern with the gendered representations of globalization. For this, we need to turn to recent scholarship on the social construction of gender and gender identities in the context of the global political economy.[12] In his work on masculinity, Bob Connell identifies and traces a hegemonic (Western) masculinity being articulated, through various social practices, in relation to other masculinities as well as femininities.[13] According to Connell it is important to recognize that the construction of gender is dynamic and historical. In other words, he agrees with Brodie that periods of transformation are also characterized by changes in the social organization of gender.

Connell's notion of hegemonic masculinity brings us one step closer to understanding the connections between gendered representations of globalization and its dynamics of power. In Connell's words:

> The concept of 'hegemony', deriving from Antonio Gramsci's analysis of class relations, refers to the cultural dynamic by which a group claims and sustains a leading position in social life. At any given time, one form of masculinity rather than others is culturally exalted. Hegemonic masculinity can be defined as the configuration of gender practice which embodies the currently accepted answer to the problem of legitimacy of patriarchy, which guarantees (or is taken to guarantee) the dominant position of men and the subordinate position of women. . . .
>
> Nevertheless, hegemony is likely to be established only if there is some correspondence between cultural ideal and institutional power, collective if not individual. So, the top levels of business, the military and government provide a fairly convincing corporate display of masculinity, still very little shaken by feminist women or dissenting men. It is the successful claim to authority, more than direct violence, that is the mark of hegemony (though violence often underpins or supports authority).[14]

Brodie's and Connell's observations lead us to two related questions. What characteristics make up contemporary hegemonic masculinity (and are these changing)? What spheres of the global political economy are associated with this hegemonic masculinity (and are these changing)?

Connell himself only provides a partial answer to the first question. For him, the foundation of contemporary hegemonic masculinity has been laid by the accumulation and concentration of wealth during colonial times. This accumulation and concentration of wealth in the past, as well as its continuation today, have been beneficial to men in core countries because it has bestowed on them power over natural resources and other people's labour and services. In addition, the use of technology, especially in the context of the rationalization of the production process and the emergence of a knowledge-based society, has modified contemporary hegemonic masculinity's claim to authority based on 'direct' domination to include claims based on expertise.[15]

Connell does not really address whether hegemonic masculinity is also undergoing changes as part of the larger process of global restructuring. Charlotte Hooper suggests that this is precisely what is happening. Based on her analysis of *The Economist*, she suggests that globalization is evoking images of a new 'entrepreneurial frontier masculinity' combining science, technology, and business.[16] In other words, the global arena is still relatively uncharted terrain that needs to be explored and discovered, not on horseback this time but through the use of new means of communication and information technologies. The most interesting feature of this new global arena, where markets are waiting to be discovered and conquered,[17] is that it is both real and virtual. In fact, to discover the virtual global arena one does not need to move physically; a laptop with Internet connection, mobile phone, fax, and a thermos of coffee are all the gear the explorer needs.

Hooper's analysis also enables us to address our second question about which spaces and practices are associated with contemporary hegemonic masculinity. From her account it is clear that contemporary hegemonic masculinity is being redefined in conjunction with those sectors that have become of central importance to the new global economy. Two examples provide support for this claim. The first shows the primacy of the international or global economy over domestic economic concerns. The example is taken from an article in a prominent Dutch newspaper by Rick van der Ploeg, professor of economics at the University of Amsterdam and currently undersecretary of cultural affairs in the Dutch government. He argues that the Dutch economy (and by extension, other national economies) can be divided into 'hard' and 'soft' sectors. According to van der Ploeg, the 'hard' sector is exposed to international competition and encompasses horticulture, agriculture, mining, heavy industry, international transportation, business and commercial services, trade, and communication. In contrast, the 'soft' sector is relatively insulated from the vagaries of the global economy and is made up of areas dealing with social security and 'welfare'—public health care, culture, education, safety, fighting crime,

housing, and the domestic service sector.[18] Van der Ploeg notes that the gap between the 'hard' and 'soft' sectors is increasing, whereby the former is characterized by export orientation, self-sufficiency (receiving few state subsidies), high growth rates of labour productivity, and pollution of the environment. The 'soft' sector, in contrast, displays the opposite characteristics. Van der Ploeg's conclusion is that the gap between these two sectors needs to be closed by exposing the 'soft' sector to market forces, while the state remains in charge of providing a (reduced) safety net.[19]

This account is an almost classic example of the construction of gendered representations and dichotomies. First, it clearly prioritizes the internationally oriented sectors of the economy over more 'domestic' concerns. Second, statistics tell us that these internationally oriented sectors generally tend to attract more men than women, while the reverse is true for the domestic sectors. Third, the description of the 'hard' sector evokes elements associated with contemporary hegemonic masculinity: facing tough competition, taking on responsibilities and the use of new technologies. The sector's masculinity is further stressed by the frequent use of the term 'hard'. In other words, van der Ploeg's message is not only that the Dutch economy needs to be restructured, but also that this is the new frontier of the Dutch economy and one needs to be a participant in order to gain the authority and power associated with it.

For the second example of entrepreneurial new frontier masculinity at work we need to turn to the financial community. In the aftermath of the collapse of the Bretton Woods system in the early 1970s, the international financial sector took on a much larger role in international economic affairs than before. As some authors have suggested, a gravitational shift took place through which sectors associated with financial capital assumed a central position in the global political economy and gained a certain degree of structural power previously identified with sectors linked to productive capital.[20] Aided by new communication and information technologies, the international financial sector became truly 'globalized' by the mid-1980s. This makes it one of the true new frontiers of the global economy.

Concurrent with these changes, the image of the international (now global) financial sector has also changed dramatically. Nowadays the image of the 'global financial community', inhabited by people like George Soros and Nick Leeson, is a far cry from the stuffy, reliable, almost boring, long-gone world of banking in the City, which was symbolized by middle-aged bankers dressed in pin-stripe suits and sporting bowler hats and umbrellas. As Susan Strange put it so eloquently:

> The Western financial system is rapidly coming to resemble nothing as much as a vast casino. Every day games are played in this casino that involve sums of money so large that they cannot be imagined. At night the games go on at the other side of the world. In the towering blocks that dominate all the great cities of the world, rooms are full of chain-smoking young men all playing these games. Their eyes are fixed on computer screens flickering with changing prices. They play by intercontinental telephone or by tapping electronic machines. They are just like gamblers in casinos watching the clicking spin of a silver ball on a roulette wheel and putting their chips on red or black, odd numbers or even ones.[21]

From this depiction it is clear that contemporary hegemonic masculinity at the new frontier of the global financial community is (re)constructed on the basis of risk-taking (i.e., gambling), expertise as exemplified by the use of new information technologies, the idea that one needs to communicate 24 hours a day about the latest developments in the market, the idea that one is able to survive in a fast-paced environment, and, finally, age—being young is virtually a prerequisite.

This brief description illustrates that the global financial community is much more than a network of integrated computer systems and worldwide financial flows; it is inhabited by real people. Yet, the kind of people associated with the sphere of global finance evokes images of adventurous, risk-taking,

fast-paced, globetrotting young men. Collectively, they are one of the groups embodying contemporary hegemonic masculinity.

What is often overlooked, however, is that this same global financial community cannot function without the existence of an internationalized service economy in both the private and public spheres: for instance, large groups of migrant women (and men) are employed in the global financial centres of London, New York, and Hong Kong as domestic help, nannies, gardeners, etc.; alternatively, migrant women (and men) may find themselves cleaning the offices of Chase Manhattan and similar banks at night; and increasingly, it is also possible for women to find work in the Philippines or India as data-entry clerks for large companies abroad.[22] This suggests that the activities of the global financial community encompass much more than trading in stocks, options, and futures; they also involve the emergence of a feminized 'internationalized' service economy in which male and female migrant labour play a significant role. Yet these groups are notoriously absent in representations of the masculinized sphere of global finance. In other words, representations of the global economy tap into and help to structure existing power inequalities based on class, ethnicity, gender, race, and so forth.

In addition to the export-oriented sectors of the domestic economy and the global financial community, many other spheres and practices of global restructuring can be analysed from a gender perspective. For instance, national and international labour markets have been restructured in such a way that they are increasingly segmented and hierarchically organized along the lines of class, race, ethnicity, gender, and age. The increasing flexibility of labour policies in the OECD countries is leading to a shrinking group of masculinized core labour with relative job security and a growing group of feminized flexible labour[23] with little job security. In the South we find increasingly a feminization and casualization of labour in the rapidly expanding export industries.

Likewise, the changing role and make-up of the state can also be read in terms of gendered representations. Within the state apparatus the balance of power has shifted towards those sectors whose functions are directly related to the global economy (finance, economic affairs, etc.) at the expense of the bureaucracies dealing with such issues as health, education, and social welfare. In other words, patterns of gender representation in the market are being replicated within the state apparatus. The state sectors involved with the global economy are associated with notions of contemporary hegemonic masculinity while departments dealing with, in van der Ploeg's terms, the 'soft' sector of the economy are linked to notions of femininity.

Obviously, it would go beyond the scope of this analysis to discuss these transformations in depth. However, in this last part of the chapter I would like to turn to one other example to illustrate how gendered representations work and how global restructuring also involves the reconstruction of masculinity and femininity. As we have focused thus far on 'globalization from above', I would like to turn now to 'globalization from below'.[24] Loosely defined, globalization from below refers to the mounting opposition to and resistance against neo-liberal global restructuring. What is significant and new about this resistance is that it can take many forms, that it tends to be grounded locally but almost always has a transnational dimension, and that it tries to combine knowledge with politics.[25] As such, globalization from below constitutes an important part of the emerging civil society.[26] Because of its more diffuse and unstructured character, associating globalization from below with certain gendered representations is challenging. One thing is clear, though: it is not a high-powered space inhabited by chain-smoking, risk-taking, and globetrotting young men. And, whereas it would be difficult to come up with names of women who are key players in globalization from above, it is much easier to devise a list of prominent women who have entered the global arena in opposition to this globalization from above. The names of Hannah Asrawi, Cory Aquino, Gro Harlem Brundtland, Aung San Suu Kyi, Rigoberta Menchú, and Jody Williams come to mind. And their names are associated with such social causes as justice, democracy, human rights, peace, the ban on anti-personnel landmines, and the environment. Why is this? Is it just a coincidence that women in leadership positions are more clearly identified with globalization from below than from above? Does this have anything to do with the different gendered representations of globalization from above and globalization from below?

One plausible answer to these questions builds on Connell's notion that hegemonic masculinity is being constructed in opposition to all femininities and subordinate masculinities.[27] Following this line of reasoning, globalization from above, being associated with contemporary hegemonic masculinity, is constructed in opposition to globalization from below, which then almost automatically comes to be linked to notions of reconstructed contemporary femininity and alternative masculinities. At first sight this appears to be a familiar replay of a gendered division of labour: the more powerful spheres and practices are linked to a new-frontier hegemonic masculinity while the 'soft' spheres of the global arena are the terrain of feminized subjects.

Yet, this interpretation hides the fact that global civil society is a somewhat ambiguous and unstructured space, which is not entirely devoid of power or authority. For one, the fact that three of the women mentioned above have received the Nobel Peace Prize based on their activities within the context of globalization from below forces us to take this part of the global arena seriously, as it is hard to deny the (moral) authority and power attached to the Nobel Prize. Moreover, some scholars go so far as to argue that this global civil society actually provides the site and starting point for the construction of a new world order.[28] This view is shared by the Commission on Global Governance, which was created as a follow-up to the Brandt, Olaf Palme, and Gro Harlem Brundtland commissions to report on the challenges facing the world community at the end of the Cold War in terms of global security and global governance.[29] In its report the Commission on Global Governance likens global civil society to a global neighbourhood. The image of a neighbourhood is used to underscore the interconnectedness of the world today: whether we like it or not, we are all neighbours and have to adjust to this new reality and learn to live together. In the Commission's opinion, this can only be done by strengthening certain neighbourhood values (respect for life; liberty; justice and equity; mutual respect; caring; and integrity) and developing a global civic ethic.[30] In other words, global civil society is being actively promoted and upgraded by dominant actors in the global political economy in terms of its projection of (moral) power and authority. Moreover, it is perceived as the site where 'people-centred' alternatives to ongoing neo-liberal global restructuring are being articulated and developed.

This positive reinforcement of globalization from below has an interesting parallel in the fact that notions of dominant femininity have been undergoing some changes as well. As a result of several factors—the emergence of second-wave feminism, the United Nations Decade for Women (including the four UN women's conferences)—women have entered the public sphere of politics and work in large numbers. This transformation has been accompanied by a reconstruction of middle-class, Western femininity, which is now based on the pursuit of such ideals as autonomy, independence, and a career.[31] More generally, it is clear that women's movements worldwide have been actively pursuing a rearticulation of various forms of femininity in their struggle for empowerment. The message conveyed is that empowerment is now part of contemporary, reconstructed expressions of femininity. Yet, this same contemporary, empowered femininity is regularly juxtaposed with hegemonic masculinity, whereby the latter stands for ruthless, individualistic, risk-taking, and competitive behaviour and the former is associated with teamwork, social concerns, and co-operation. Needless to say, individual men and women rarely, if ever, fit any of these stereotypical categories and most often combine characteristics from both, some of which may become more pronounced depending on the environment in which an individual happens to be active.

We can tentatively infer from the previous discussion that the sectors attached to globalization from below appear to be more receptive to women's leadership aspirations than, for instance, the global financial community. For one, in the higher echelons of the corporate world the glass ceiling is still very much present and creates a barrier for many women to further their careers and assume leadership positions in their professions. In addition, there still may be an implicit assumption, based on constructed stereotypes of femininity, that women are better suited to deal with social issues than men (self-selection may also be the result of this assumption). Finally, over the years women have collectively built up a large expertise not only in social causes, but also in oppositional politics. The experiences gained from participating in the women's movement and other social movements in challenging the established order from the margins have created an important legacy. It has shown that power and authority are not only to be found in the boardrooms and halls of government, but that other sites need to be empowered in order to effect the necessary changes. Therefore, the activities connected to globalization from below are familiar terrain to women, as well as among the most interesting if women want to be involved and try to effect changes.

## Conclusion

This chapter has presented a brief glimpse into the gendered nature of globalization. As gender operates at the individual, collective, and ideational levels it is important to dissect globalization with these three levels in mind. In this particular instance I have focused primarily on the ideational and collective levels. As such, the chapter should, therefore, be read in the context of other significant work on gender and globalization or global restructuring. An important starting point for developing a feminist analysis of globalization is to reveal how processes of global restructuring are gendered. This can be done by explicitly bringing subject and subjectivity (that is, people) into the analysis of global restructuring and by focusing on its gendered representations.

To accomplish this, various myths need to be dispelled before we can look at the gendered representations of globalization. The overview of such gendered representations illustrates that a rather paradoxical situation is being created. On the one hand, there are clear signs that contemporary hegemonic masculinity is being rearticulated and linked to the high-powered spheres of global finance and the export sector of the domestic economy. On the other hand, a more diffuse and unstructured part of the global arena, global civil society, has been constructed in such a way that it seems to be associated with notions of reconstructed femininity and subordinate masculinities. This gender division of labour between globalization from above and globalization from below loosely reflects the structural inequalities between women and men. Yet, the feminized part of the global arena is not to be interpreted as a space entirely devoid of power and authority. Rather, it

appears that it is increasingly perceived as a site open to alternative expressions of power and authority as well as a site where people-centred alternatives and strategies to neo-liberal globalization are being formulated.

In sum, students of international political economy are very much interested in analysing its materialist underpinnings in the form of production and circulation of goods. This chapter argues that IPE's relative neglect of the circulation of meaning and the power of representation prevents us from establishing a fuller understanding of the global political economy. Through using gendered images and assigning meanings to spheres of the global economy, existing inequalities may be reinforced or new ones created. Yet, these meanings and representations are also subject to change, thus creating opportunities for counteracting these inequalities.

## Notes

This article is based on some of my earlier work, in particular: 'The New Challenge: The Gender and Development Community Goes "Global"', *Connections* 1, 3 (Sept. 1996): 16–19; 'Reconceptualising "Gender and Development" in an Era of Globalization', *Millennium* 25, 3 (1996): 566–604; 'Globalization versus Global Restructuring', *Connections* 2, 7 (Sept. 1997): 25–8. In addition, I am relying on some of the insights in Marianne H. Marchand and Anne Sisson Runyan, eds, *Gender and Global Restructuring: Sightings, Sites, and Resistances* (London: Routledge, 2000).

1    See, for example, Underhill's Introduction to Part I and the chapters by Cox and O'Brien in this volume.

2    See Robert Cox, 'Making Sense of the Changing International Political Economy', in Richard Stubbs and Geoffrey R.D. Underhill, eds, *Political Economy and the Changing Global Order* (Toronto: McClelland & Stewart, 1994), 45–59; Stephen Gill, 'The Global Panopticon? The Neoliberal State, Economic Life and Democratic Surveillance', *Alternatives* 2 (1995): 1–49; Susan Strange, *The Retreat of the State: The Diffusion of Power in the World Economy* (Cambridge: Cambridge University Press, 1996); Timothy J. Sinclair, 'Passing

Judgement: Credit Rating Processes as Regulatory Mechanisms of Governance in the Emerging World Order', *Review of International Political Economy* 1, 1 (Spring 1994): 133–60; Sandra Whitworth, 'Theory as Exclusion: Gender and International Political Economy', in Stubbs and Underhill, eds, *Political Economy and the Changing Global Order*, 116–29; Jill Steans, *Gender and International Relations* (Cambridge: Polity Press, 1998); Marchand and Runyan, eds, *Gender and Global Restructuring*.

3    Arif Dirlik, 'Globalism and the Politics of Place', *Development* 41, 2 (June 1998): 11; emphasis added.

4    At the individual level, gender operates through the social construction of (physical) male and female bodies; at the (collective) level of social relations gender structures the interactions among men and women in terms of (gender) roles and expectations; the ideational or ideological dimension involves the gendered representations and valorizations of social spheres, processes, and practices. See Marianne H. Marchand and Anne Sisson Runyan, 'Introduction: Feminist Sightings of Globalization: Conceptualizations and

Reconceptualizations', in Marchand and Runyan, eds, *Gender and Global Restructuring*.

5  On the power of representation and international political economy, see Craig N. Murphy and Crisitina Rojas de Ferro, special eds, Theme Section: 'The Power of Representation in International Political Economy', *Review of International Political Economy* 2, 1 (Winter 1995): 63–183.

6  This section is taken from Marchand, 'Globalisation versus Global Restructuring'. For other accounts about globalization myths, see Marchand and Runyan, 'Introduction'; James H. Mittelman, 'How Does Globalization Really Work?', in Mittelman, ed., *Globalization: Critical Reflections*, International Political Economy Yearbook, vol. 9 (Boulder, Colo.: Lynne Rienner, 1997), 229–41.

7  A case in point is the current effort by EU governments to meet the EMU criteria of fiscal restraint: low inflation and low foreign debt.

8  For more details, see Marchand, 'The New Challenge'; Marchand, 'Reconceptualising "Gender and Development"'.

9  Marchand, 'Reconceptualising "Gender and Development"', 577.

10  Janine Brodie, 'Shifting Boundaries: Gender and the Politics of Restructuring', in Isabella Bakker, ed., *The Strategic Silence: Gender and Economic Policy* (London: Zed Books, in association with The North-South Institute, Ottawa, 1994), 51–2.

11  Marchand, 'Reconceptualising "Gender and Development"'.

12  See R.W. Connell, *Masculinities* (Berkeley: University of California Press, 1995); Kimberly Chang and Lily Ling, 'Globalization and Its Intimate Other: Filipino Domestic Workers in Hong Kong', in Marchand and Runyan, eds, *Gender and Global Restructuring*; Charlotte Hooper, 'Masculinities in Transition: The Case of Globalization', ibid.

13  Connell argues that the dominant (and possibly hegemonic) position for Western masculinity finds its roots in colonialism and has more recently been sustained by the spread of 'Western values' through cinema, pop culture, mass media, etc. Obviously, Western masculinity's hegemonic position is being challenged by Asian constructions of masculinity (as embedded in the 'Asian values' debate) and by various religious fundamentalist notions of masculinity. See Connell, *Masculinities*, 185–203.

14  Ibid., 77.

15  Ibid., 164–5, 201.

16  Hooper, 'Masculinities in Transition'.

17  In a distasteful choice of language, *The Economist* referred to this conquering of new 'virgin territories' or markets in an article on Myanmar (Burma), which it titled 'Ripe for Rape'. *The Economist*, 15 Jan. 1994, 65. For a further analysis of this article, see Hooper, 'Masculinities in Transition'.

18  Rick van der Ploeg, 'Zachte Sector van de Economie Moet naar Markt Worden Overgeheveld', *NRC Handelsblad*, 9 Apr. 1994. It is important to realize that the Dutch agricultural and horticultural sectors are very export-oriented and high-tech.

19  Ibid.

20  See Cox, 'Making Sense'; Gill, 'The Global Panopticon?'; Mittelman, 'How Does Globalization Really Work?'.

21  Susan Strange, *Casino Capitalism* (Oxford: Basil Blackwell, 1986), 1.

22  Chang and Ling, 'Globalization and Its Intimate Other'.

23  This includes contract work, part-time work, subcontracted work, homework, and so forth.

24  Richard Falk uses this terminology in 'Resisting "Globalisation-from-above" Through "Globalisation-from-below"', *New Political Economy* 2, 1 (Mar. 1997): 17–24.

25  Ibid., 19. See also Marchand and Runyan, 'Introduction'.

26  Paul Ekins, *A New World Order: Grassroots Movements for Global Change* (London: Routledge, 1992).

27  Connell, *Masculinities*.

28  Ekins, *A New World Order*. See also the discussion on cosmopolitan democracy in David Held, *Democracy and the Global Order* (Cambridge: Polity Press, 1995).

29  Commission on Global Governance, *Our Global Neighbourhood* (Oxford: Oxford University Press, 1995).

30  Ibid., 41–75.
31  For an account of the backlash against this new notion of femininity, see Susan Faludi, *Backlash: The Undeclared War Against American Women* (New York: Crown Publishers, 1991). More recently there have been some suggestions that neo-liberal ideas have influenced feminist thought and that so-called 'power feminism' and 'girl power' are expressions of this.

## Suggested Readings

Connell, R.W. *Masculinities*. Berkeley: University of California Press, 1995.

Kofman, Eleonore, and Gillian Youngs, eds. *Globalization: Theory and Practice*. London: Pinter, 1996.

Marchand, Marianne H., and Anne Sisson Runyan, eds. *Gender and Global Restructuring: Sightings, Sites and Resistances*. London: Routledge, 2000.

Steans, Jill. *Gender and International Relations: An Introduction*. Cambridge: Polity Press, 1998.

Zalewski, Marysia, and Jane Parpart. *The 'Man' Question in International Relations*. Boulder, Colo.: Westview Press, 1998.

## Web Sites

WomenWatch: http://www.un.org/womenwatch

Womensnet: http://www.igc.org/igc/labornet

Corporate Watch:
    http://corpwatch.org/trac/globalization

World Bank Group: GenderNet:
    http://www.worldbank.org./gender/index.htm

# Regional Dynamics

## Introduction

# Regionalization and Globalization

## Richard Stubbs

The previous chapters have reviewed various theoretical approaches to the changing global order and the key global issues that these changes are shaping. Part III examines the increasing regionalization of the international political economy and explores some of the main questions prompted by the rise of a number of specific economic regions, including the issue of the relationship between regionalization and globalization.

The study of regionalism has waxed and waned over the years since World War II. Analyses flourished in the 1950s and 1960s with the growth of European regional organizations but then faded in the 1970s as European integration slowed markedly. Indeed, with the publication in 1975 of *The Obsolescence of Regional Integration Theory* by Ernst Haas analyses of regional integration and regionalism virtually dried up.[1] From the mid-1980s onward, however, regionalism once again became the subject of increasing interest. There were at least three reasons for this. First, with the end of the Cold War and the breakdown of the overarching Cold War structure that underpinned and ordered international relations, each state became aware of its need to re-evaluate its place in the international system. Stripped of the predictability that the Cold War brought to the conduct of international relations, individual states sought out new relations with the emerging constellation of major powers and with their own immediate neighbours. Many states quickly appreciated how much their own welfare was dependent on the stability and well-being of the region in which they were located.

Second, regionalization was seen by governments both as a defence against globalization and as a way of taking advantage of some of the forces set in train by the process of globalization (see Hveem, Chapter 5). Of particular significance was the need to deal with the new non-state sources of global capital, the pressures from the globalization of production, and the influence of intergovernmental organizations such as the IMF and the GATT/WTO.[2] For example, regional organizations could help to attract foreign direct investment and at the same time ensure that a group of states had a voice in the increasing number of international negotiations over the future of the international political economy. And, finally, when the European Community (EC), later to become the European Union, started to expand its activities in the 1980s other regional organizations emerged, some in response to the demonstration effect of the EU, others as a way of countering what was perceived to be the increasing collective economic power of the Western European states.

The wide variety of regional organizations formed from the mid-1980s onward belong to what has been termed the 'new regionalism'.[3] What distinguishes this new regionalism from the regionalism of the 1950s and 1960s is that, rather than stressing regional self-sufficiency and independence from global economy, the emphasis has been on positioning a region so as to strengthen its participation in the global economy in terms of both trade and capital flows.[4] Other distinguishing characteristics include the growing number of regions containing countries from both the North and the

South; the rise of a regional consciousness, even a regional identity, in various parts of the world; the fact that any one country may belong to a number of regional organizations at any one time; and the many different institutional forms that have been developed within which regional co-operation has been organized.[5]

Although defined in various ways, regionalism is most usefully thought of as having three dimensions. The first concerns the extent to which countries in a definable geographic area have significant historical experiences in common and find themselves facing the same general problems. With the world divided into two camps, one dominated by the United States and the other by the Soviet Union, for much of the Cold War, common regional experiences and problems tended to be masked by the need to confront the common enemy. However, as the Cold War ended and the old international order began to break down, each state had to begin to work towards new sets of relationships both with the emerging global powers and with surrounding states. Common historical experiences and problems, for instance, in Western Europe the need to rebuild after World War II and the perceived threat from Soviet communism, became increasingly important as states began to re-evaluate their place in the international system. Moreover, as the globalization process began to gather speed, states quickly realized that their neighbours, who often had similar economies to their own, faced many of the same economic problems. Regional economic co-operation became one way of attempting to come to grips with these common problems.

The second dimension emphasizes the extent to which countries in a definable geographic area have developed sociocultural, political, and/or economic linkages that distinguish them from the rest of the global community. For example, long-standing sociocultural ties, reinforced by common political and security interests and rapidly increasing economic integration, have been important in fostering close connections between the US and Canada. In East Asia the flood of Japanese FDI into Southeast Asia—especially Thailand, Malaysia, Singapore, and Indonesia—following the appreciation of the yen in

the wake of the Plaza Accord of 1985, and the subsequent flow of investment from the newly industrialized economies—Hong Kong, Singapore, South Korea, and Taiwan—into all parts of East and Southeast Asia, as well as the increased trade linkages that have ensued, have combined to produce a growing sense of regional identity. Whether this notion of an 'Asian consciousness and identity' is referred to as 'neo-Asianism' or the 'Pacific Way', it has gained considerable currency.[6] It may even be that, contrary to some expectations in the West, the common experience of having to deal with the fallout from the Asian economic crisis will reinforce this growing regional consciousness.

The third dimension focuses on the extent to which the relations among particular groupings of geographically proximate countries have developed organizations to manage crucial aspects of their collective affairs. The degree of formal institutionalization among regional organizations varies considerably. Obviously, the European Union is the most advanced, with NAFTA much less institutionalized and the East Asian Economic Caucus still in an embryonic form.[7] The degree and form of institutionalization tend to be influenced both by state interests and by regional norms regarding the willingness of states to cede power to a central secretariat or other form of organization.

Regions, then, may be relatively well developed along all three dimensions, as is the case with the EU, or they may be in a relatively early stage of integration with limited progress along one or more of the three dimensions, as is the case with the ASEAN Free Trade Area (AFTA).[8] Moreover, the three dimensions are interrelated. Common historical experiences and increased sociocultural, political, and economic links can lead to the development of organizations to manage the region's collective affairs. In turn, of course, the creation of a regional organization can further multiply the linkages that bind the region together. It is also important to note that while the core countries of any particular region may be easily identified, the actual boundaries are often fluid and debatable. For example, there is considerable debate about the eastern boundaries of the Europe Union and which countries ought to be allowed into the Asia-Pacific Co-operation (APEC) forum.

However regions are defined, the one major question that appears to preoccupy students of international political economy is the extent to which regionalization promotes or obstructs globalization. Can regional patterns of market integration be considered a step down the road towards the rapid globalization of an open international economy, or will the major economic powers and the increasingly economically and politically integrated regions they lead compete with one another in an unprecedented battle of economic giants?

Analysts have attempted to answer this question in a number of ways. A good many studies have been undertaken of the changing patterns of intraregional as opposed to interregional trade to determine the rate of regionalization of economic relations. Analysts have also examined flows of foreign direct investment, portfolio investment, and short-term loans in order to map out the degrees of economic cohesion in various regional groupings. The increased use of the yen and the introduction of the Euro have prompted discussions of competing currency blocs. Similarly, the rise of production networks in Asia has meant that regional economic integration has been viewed from the perspective of competing production arrangements in the three major economic regions—Western Europe, North America, and East Asia. Other analysts have reviewed the activities of multinational corporations and assessed the extent to which they operate regionally as opposed to globally. And finally, studies have been undertaken of the lack of labour market integration, especially in Europe, and the impact this might have on regionalization.

Although these measurements of regional economic co-operation and integration into the global economy can be illuminating, a fundamental point should not be missed. Regional economic activity is heavily influenced by increasingly regionalized forms of capitalism. In some instances these forms of capitalism, which are essentially rooted in regional cultures as well as in common economic, social, and political institutions and similar recent historical experiences, are underwritten by regional

agreements. For example, the Economic and Monetary Union, the Single European Act, and the Maastricht Treaty provide the foundations for capitalism in Europe, and the North American Free Trade Agreement provides the blueprint for capitalism in North America.[9] Although there are still important differences among EU members and NAFTA members in the way they conduct economic activities, there are even greater differences between the economic policies and practices of the two regions. In Western Europe, labour still has a role to play in many aspects of economic policy-making, government intervention in the economy to redress problems created by the market is sanctioned, and the social dimension of economic activities, although under attack, is still important. In North America, NAFTA discourages government intervention in the economy, encourages the unfettered operation of rule-based markets, and underwrites Anglo-American individualistic consumer economics that stresses the importance of the maximization of short-term profits and a return for shareholders.

By contrast, economic policies and practices in East Asia are based on a third form of capitalism. The emphasis here is on economic relations reflecting a harmonious social order and stressing production rather than consumption. Economic transactions are seen as part of the general social intercourse rather than governed by the rule of law. For both Chinese and Japanese businessmen, then, the emphasis is on social obligations rather than legal contracts.[10] East Asian 'collective capitalism' also highlights the synergy of business networks; government intervention to produce a competitive advantage for certain sectors and industries or to strengthen key industries, such as machine tool suppliers and semiconductor chip manufacturers, which helps to build up other industrial sectors; and capturing market share even at the expense of profits.[11] Some see the Asian crisis as a consequence of this Asian form of capitalism and expect to see it change quite radically as the region works its way back to economic health. Others, however, argue that because capitalism is rooted in a combination of regional culture, recent historical experiences, and unique institutions, changes to this form of capitalism will be slow and may not automatically be in the direction of North American neo-liberalism.

Each of the following chapters looks at a different aspect of regionalism and regionalization. Overall, the aim here is to give the reader an appreciation of the emerging political economies of key regions of the world. The analyses can then be set alongside the global changes highlighted in the first two parts of the book. These chapters also give readers a chance to decide for themselves how the relationship between regionalization and globalization might unfold. Will the emergence of regional economic organizations give a boost to globalization or do they indicate the rise of mercantilist blocs that will frustrate the drive to a truly global economy?

## Notes

1  Ernst B. Haas, *The Obsolescence of Regional Integration Theory* (Berkeley: Institute for International Studies, 1975).

2  See Anthony Payne and Andrew Gamble, 'Introduction: The Political Economy of Regionalism and World Order', in Gamble and Payne, eds, *Regionalism and World Order* (Basingstoke: Macmillan, 1996), 15–18; Stephan Haggard, 'Regionalism in Asia and the Americas', in Edward D. Mansfield and Helen V. Milner, *The Political Economy of Regionalism* (New York: Columbia University Press, 1997), 25–31.

3  See Norman D. Palmer, *The New Regionalism in Asia and the Pacific* (Lexington, Mass.: Lexington Books, 1991); J. de Melo and A. Panagariya, 'The New Regionalism', *Finance and Development* 29, 4 (1992).

4  See Paul Bowles, 'ASEAN, AFTA, and the "New Regionalism"', *Pacific Affairs* 70 (Summer 1997): 224–5.

5  See Andrew Hurrell, 'Explaining the Resurgence of Regionalism in World Politics', *Review of International Studies* 21 (Oct. 1995): 331–2; Palmer, *The New Regionalism in Asia and the Pacific*, 1–6.

6  See Yoshi Funabashi, 'The Asianization of Asia', *Foreign Affairs* 72 (Nov.-Dec. 1993): 75; *Nikkei Weekly*, 17 Jan. 1994; Kishore Mahbubani, 'The Pacific Way', *Foreign Affairs* 74 (Jan.-Feb. 1995): 100–11.

7  Richard Higgott and Richard Stubbs, 'Competing Conceptions of Economic Regionalism', *Review of International Political Economy* 2 (Summer 1995).

8  On AFTA, see John Ravenhill, 'Economic Cooperation in Southeast Asia: Changing Incentives', *Asian Survey* 35 (Sept. 1995).

9  See the discussion of this point in Stephen Clarkson, 'Fearful Asymmetries: The Challenge of Analyzing Continental Systems in a Globalizing World', *Canadian-American Public Policy* no. 35 (Sept. 1998).

10  See Richard Stubbs, 'Asia-Pacific Regionalism versus Globalization: Competing Forms of Capitalism', in William D. Coleman and Geoffrey Underhill, eds, *Regionalism and Global Economic Integration: Europe, Asia and the Americas* (London: Routledge, 1998).

11  Stephen Bell, 'The Collective Capitalism of Northeast Asia and the Limits of Orthodox Economics', *Australian Journal of Political Science* 30 (July 1995).

## Chapter 18

# The Political Economy of European Integration:
## Transnational Social Forces in the Making of Europe's Socio-Economic Order

*Bastiaan van Apeldoorn*

The past two decades have witnessed a significant transformation of the European political economy. On both sides of the East-West divide of the Cold War we have seen a resurgence of the free market and its social and political values. The result has been a fundamental restructuring—of which we still have not seen the end—of the prevailing socio-economic order. In Western Europe, this has involved the tendential 'disembedding' of the market from the institutions that had made up the post-war socio-economic order of the Keynesian welfare state. This transformation of Western European capitalism is also reflected in the process of European integration, which experienced a renaissance from the mid-1980s onward with the Single European Act (SEA) and the Maastricht Treaty laying the basis for a single market and a single currency, respectively. The European economic system and concomitant supranational regime of socio-economic governance evolving out of this relaunching of the integration process have increasingly favoured deregulation and the free play of market forces, establishing the primacy of negative integration (market liberalization) over positive integration (providing public goods at a European level). At the same time that Western Europe's national economies were thus further integrated along free-market lines, the economies and societies of Eastern Europe experienced an opening up not only to liberal democracy but, also, willingly or not, to the globalizing capitalist market.

Within this broader context, this chapter focuses on the current transformation of the European political economy and the wider European integration process. Its main purpose is to analyse the social forces involved in the making of the emergent European socio-economic order within a global context. This analysis goes beyond established approaches to the study of European integration inasmuch as these approaches focus largely on the institutional *form* of the integration process and ignore the question of its socio-economic *content*, or the 'social purpose' underlying the European order.[1] Moreover, as conventional theories tend to take the European integration process as a process *internal* to the European Union (EU), these theories often fail to acknowledge the wider global context in which European integration is embedded. The process of European integration extends beyond the present geographical boundaries of the EU, not only because those boundaries are not fixed, with the EU currently preparing to enlarge towards the East (see the chapter by Jeanne Kirk Laux in this volume), but also because European integration is in fact part of wider *global* integration processes. The European countries outside the EU are also part of the European socio-economic order that emerges out of this inasmuch as these countries are also affected by these same global processes, while the impact of these processes may be reinforced by the European integration process more narrowly conceived as these countries have to adopt the rules and policies of the EU in order to qualify for membership.

The central argument of this chapter is that the social purpose underlying the emergent European order is the outcome not so much of bargaining among states or national governments as in the dominant intergovernmentalist (realist) perspective but rather of political and ideological struggles between rival social forces acting through the structures of the member states, but also directly at the European level within an emerging European polity.[2] These social forces are not necessarily internal to the EU or its member states but must rather be located within a global political economy and seen as operating within an increasingly transnational setting. Capitalist production and finance are witnessing a sustained transnationalization, reflected *inter alia* in the increasing dominance of the transnational corporation as an actor in the world economy and the concomitant growing structural power of transnational capital.[3] As the transnationalization of global capitalism deepens, we witness in particular the rise of transnational capitalist élites—forming what Stopford and Strange have called a 'privileged transnational business civilisation'—as key actors in global politics, seeking to set the agenda and to shape policies at both national and international/supranational levels of governance.[4]

The following analysis thus focuses on the role of transnational *agency* in effecting structural change. At the same time, though, the structural forces that shape the actors and their actions in the first place must also be emphasized. Here, it is particularly important not to analyse (Western) Europe as a self-contained entity but rather as a macro-region of a global political and economic order. The process of European regionalization cannot be understood outside the context of the process of globalization. As we shall see, the global and, indeed, globalizing context of a changing world economy has very much shaped the strategic choices (on the part of key élite actors) that have led to the recent renaissance of the integration process. By integrating structure and agency (see Underhill in Part I) we can see that how global change translated into European change depends on the way actors respond to their changing structural environment and on how the struggle between these contending responses evolves.

Below I will identify three such responses as they have developed in the context of a changing global political economy. These responses derive from rival ideological and strategic orientations on

the part of different transnational social forces involved in the struggle over European order. In the 1980s these contending orientations crystallized as rival 'projects' for a relaunched and broadened European integration process. I will then analyse how this struggle evolved from the internal market project to the Maastricht Treaty and beyond, focusing in particular on the role of Europe's transnational business élite. I will argue that the European order—encompassing the wider European region consisting of the EU, the European Economic Area countries, and the new applicant countries—emerging out of this struggle expresses a new social purpose that we may denote with the term 'embedded neo-liberalism', reflecting the interests of Europe's most global transnational corporations (TNCs) but at the same time seeking to accommodate the ideological orientations of other social forces.

## Rival Projects for the Relaunching of Europe

In Western Europe, the 1970s and early 1980s became the period of 'Europessimism' as the integration process stagnated and the postwar 'golden age' of consistent high growth and full employment ended with the world economic crisis of 1973, which was soon perceived by many as revealing structural weaknesses of the European economy that made it lag behind the competing blocs of Japan and the US.

It was within this context that the European integration process was relaunched through the Europe 1992 program for the completion of the internal market (incorporated into the EC treaty by the SEA of 1987). Here, different visions and different projects came to compete with one another. In the analysis below, three such rival projects are identified: 'neo-liberalism', 'neo-mercantilism', and 'pan-European social democracy'. All three projects favoured a relaunching of Europe through the completion of the internal market, but they differed fundamentally on the question of *what kind* of European market it was to be.

Neo-liberalism and neo-mercantilism can be interpreted as contending strategies on the part of rival groups or 'fractions' within the ranks of

Europe's transnational business élite. Throughout the 1980s and into the 1990s, the main dividing line within this élite was between a 'globalist' fraction consisting of Europe's most globalized firms (including global financial institutions) and a 'Europeanist' fraction made up of large industrial enterprises primarily serving the European market and competing against the often cheaper imports from outside Europe (East Asia in particular).[5] The perspective of the former has tended towards neo-liberalism, whereas the latter came to promote the neo-mercantilist project.

## The Neo-Liberal Project

In the context of European integration, the rising power of neo-liberal ideology became first of all manifest in the 'Eurosclerosis' discourse according to which the stagflation of the European economy was the result of institutional rigidities—engendered by excessive government intervention, too powerful trade unions, an overburdened welfare state, etc.—hindering the efficient allocation of resources through the market mechanism and thus impeding the necessary adjustments to the changing global environment.

In the neo-liberal conception of European integration, then, the process should be restricted to negative integration, resulting in more market and less state at all levels of governance. The benefits of the internal market project were thus seen as principally deriving from the freer market it would create—emphasizing its deregulatory effects and expected efficiency gains. In the neo-liberal view, European integration should subordinate Europe's socio-economic and industrial space to what are seen as the beneficial forces of globalization: Europe as an advanced free trade zone within a free trading world.

## The Neo-Mercantilist Project

Whereas the neo-liberal ideology was primarily propagated by global financial capital and industrial TNCs with a truly global reach, most of continental Europe was still dominated by firms that,

although maybe no longer domestic, had yet to develop into 'global players'. As in the wake of the world economic crisis, a global restructuring race ensued—with the rise of Japan further intensifying global competition. These former national champions and 'would-be European champions' perceived the forces of globalization more as a threat to their market shares and competitive position than as an opportunity to force a structural transformation of Europe's 'sclerotic' socio-economic system.

From the perspective of this 'Europeanist' fraction the loss of international competitiveness was blamed less on labour market rigidity, trade union power, or the welfare state and more on the fragmentation of the European market, the (resulting) insufficient economies of scale, and the perceived technology gap *vis-à-vis* the US and Japan. Thus, these forces promoted the creation of a European home market as the centrepiece of their strategy for a relaunching of Europe. As Grahl and Teague note, in the neo-mercantilist interpretation of the internal market project, 'national rivalries and the fragmentation of Community market, have . . . deprived European companies of a key element in competitive success, which the 1992 program will correct.'[6] The neo-mercantilist project therefore constituted a defensive regionalization strategy oriented towards the creation of a strong regional economy, not only through the completion of the internal market, but also through an industrial policy aimed at the promotion of 'European champions', if necessary protected by European tariff walls.[7]

## The Social Democratic Project

The social democratic project for Europe's socio-economic order developed within the context of the initial success of the internal market program, as social democrats came to see European federalism as the answer to the dilemmas of the European left in the era of globalization. This project was partly reflected in the strategy pursued by Jacques Delors (as president of the European Commission), for whom, as for other social democrats, a united Europe offered an opportunity to protect the 'European model of society', and its traditions of the mixed economy and high levels of social protection, against the potentially destructive forces of unbridled globalization. Delors had accepted the creation of a competitive home market (and the market liberalization that went with it) as both an economic and political *sine qua non* for a successful relaunching of the European integration process, but at the same time warned the neo-liberals that '[t]he Community is not and will not be, a free trade zone. It is up to us to make a *European organized space*.'8 And it was '[f]or this reason [that] the backbone of Delors's strategy was to promote state-building programs on the back of market-building successes.'9

## The Transnational Business Élite and the Struggle over Europe's Socio-Economic Order

In the struggle over European order the role of Europe's transnational business élite, as bound up with the growing structural power of transnational capital, is of particular importance. The initiatives and ideas promoted by this business élite have helped both to relaunch the integration process and to shape its socio-economic content. When integration was at its low point in the early 1980s and growing global competition threatened the position of large sections of European industry, leading members of this élite perceived the need for a political initiative as yet lacking from Europe's politicians. These business leaders—coming mainly from what was then the neo-mercantilist wing of European big business—thus founded in 1983 the European Round Table of Industrialists (ERT), with the self-proclaimed aim 'to revitalise European industry and make it competitive again, and to speed up the process of unification of the European market'.10 Today, the ERT consists of close to 50 chief executives and chairmen of Europe's most transnational and biggest industrial corporations, from both the different member states as well as from several non-EU European countries (thus constituting a transnational business coalition wider than the EU itself). The ERT is not a traditional business lobby or an interest association but rather an élite forum for Europe's emergent transnational capitalist class from within which its leaders can

work out a common and cohesive strategy that is then propagated *vis-à-vis* the European institutions, in particular the European Commission. The ERT is generally recognized to be one of the most powerful business groups in Europe, and is acknowledged to have played a major agenda-setting role with regard to the relaunching of Europe, in particular by bringing the completion of the internal market back onto the agenda.11

### From Europe 1992 to Maastricht

Although they aspired to become more global, in the 1980s many of Europe's large industrial firms were still principally *regional* TNCs. The ERT in this period was also dominated by this Europeanist fraction, and its strategic orientation thus tended towards a defensive regionalism, the heart of which was the promotion of a big (and if necessary, protected) European home market.

On the basis of this strategic orientation the Round Table played an active role in setting the agenda for Europe's relaunching by campaigning, right from its founding, for the completion of the internal market. The basis here became a plan (from November 1984) presented by the then CEO of Philips (and prominent ERT member), Wisse Dekker, which laid out a detailed program (including a timetable) that according to several sources formed an important inspiration for the Commission White Paper of June 1985. One former commissioner (of the first Delors team), for instance, stated that 'one can argue that the whole completion of the internal market project was initiated not by governments but by the Round Table, and by members of it, Dekker in particular, and Philips, playing a significant role.'12 In spite of this testimony to its success, the internal market created on the basis of the White Paper in many ways did not turn out to be the kind of home market that many of the early Round Table members (of the Europeanist fraction) had envisaged, that is, a relatively protected home market in which Euro-champions could prosper in order to confront global competition.

The internal market did favour the creation of further economies of scale and did make the

European market a home market more comparable to those of the US and Japan (even though those markets are still more unified). In the end, however, the internal market program was hardly supported by the kind of 'flanking' policies that the neo-mercantilists had hoped would nurture the growth of European champions and protect them against US and (above all) Japanese competition. Responding to the demands of members of the Round Table, among others, the Commission launched intra-European co-operation programs in research and development, such as ESPRIT, and also later started to promote the development of trans-European infrastructure networks (so-called TENs). Such policies, however, fell far short of the kind of neo-mercantilist industrial *relance* of Europe envisaged by some sections of European business.

The fears of a protectionist Europe also turned out to be unfounded. Although those sectors of European industry—cars and electronics—that lobbied the hardest for protectionist measures had their demands partially met, these limited protectionist policies (such as anti-dumping duties and import quotas) have gradually been ended. Both within the ranks of Europe's transnational business élite and at the interstate level where liberal, pro-free trade member states such as the UK, Germany, and the Netherlands blocked the more outright protectionist proposals of France and Italy, the neo-mercantilists were losing the political battle. It was thus that as the internal barriers came down, no external barriers were erected and the internal market provided as much an opportunity for US and Japanese as for European firms.[13] The internal market program—by giving the same opportunities to outside competitors—hence only led to a further opening up of Europe's national economies to the global economy. The regionalization of the European economy, in the sense of the further integration of its national economic systems, therefore went hand in hand with a further globalization of the European region. The external liberalization of the new European market was later completed by the signing of the Uruguay Round of the GATT in 1993, which effectively sealed the fate of the neo-mercantilist project. Of course, on a pan-European

scale, the transition to capitalism on the part of the former command economies of Central and Eastern Europe constituted an even more significant moment in Europe's integration into a globalizing world economy.

The internal market program also had a number of inherent characteristics that, given the prevailing political and ideological power balance, favoured the neo-liberal project. Whereas trade liberalization within the EC had hitherto been limited to the abolition of tariffs, the 1985 White Paper focused explicitly on the removal—through the principle of *mutual recognition*—of non-tariff barriers (NTBs) resulting from national regulations. Moreover, the internal market program, for the first time, also aimed at the complete liberalization of capital flows (concomitant to global developments), further undermining member states' autonomy in managing their own economies. It was thus that, as Loukas Tsoukalis notes, with Europe '92 the process of European integration entered a qualitatively new phase in which for the first time the integration process came to intervene directly into the existing socio-economic order in the different member states.[14] As it turned out, this intervention became bound up with an intensifying process of neo-liberal restructuring.

In the transnational struggle over Europe's relaunching, neo-liberal social forces, strengthened by the ongoing and deepening globalization process, were gaining the upper hand over those that had favoured a neo-mercantilist interpretation of the internal market program. This struggle had also been fought out within the ranks of Europe's transnational business élite in which the Europeanist fraction was slowly losing its dominant position and gradually abandoned its earlier neo-mercantilist perspective. This neo-liberal shift on the part of Europe's business élite was also reflected in the changing strategic orientation of the Round Table, as at the end of the 1980s and into the early 1990s ERT's membership witnessed a significant change in the balance of power between its globalist and Europeanist fractions. This shifting balance must be understood within the context of the accelerated globalization of European industry in this period and the concomitant rising dominance of neo-liberal ideology within the European political economy.[15]

Within the ERT, this neo-liberal reorientation thus enabled a transcendence of the earlier opposition between Europeanists and globalists. This occurred in a context in which global competition further intensified and the old world order experienced a major upheaval with the collapse of 'real' socialism, creating a whole new set of challenges to and market opportunities for Western European business. The latter developments also renewed the old debate of deepening versus widening. It was also in this context that the intergovernmental bargaining that led to the Maastricht Treaty took place. The focus of the treaty negotiations, however, was clearly limited to the question of deepening, ignoring, or at least postponing the question of how to prepare for a possible enlargement to the East. Indeed, the heart of the treaty was formed by the provisions for an Economic and Monetary Union (EMU), the project that has become the linchpin of the current integration process, enhancing its neo-liberal content through its strict convergence criteria.

The socio-economic content of Maastricht can be interpreted as reflecting the transnational configuration of social and political forces within the European political economy at the end of the 1980s. Here, Europe's transnational business élite again played an important agenda-setting role. Many factors may account for the decision of why member states decided to relinquish their monetary sovereignty, including (in line with the new monetarist orthodoxy) the wish to institutionalize the commitment to low inflation, the French desire to further tie Germany into a united Europe and challenge the hegemony of the Deutschmark, as well as the 'spillover' effect of the success of Europe '92.[16] The lobbying efforts of big business must, however, also enter the equation. One important business lobby (with many of Europe's largest firms represented) was formed by the Association for Monetary Union in Europe (AMUE), founded in 1987. The ERT, in the run-up to Maastricht, also called for a single currency and a 'clear and unambiguous timetable' to achieve this goal.[17]

But, next to the business élite, transnational social democratic forces, which, under the leadership of Delors, temporarily gained momentum around the end of the 1980s, also played a role in the Maastricht process. Next to the social chapter, EMU in fact became an equally important centrepiece of the social democratic project, seen as serving the double function of regaining some democratic control of the global financial markets as well as paving the way to a federal political union that could then further advance the cause of organizing European space.

The social democratic interpretation of Maastricht, however, has largely failed so far to materialize. The social chapter has not gone much beyond mere symbolic politics, thanks in large part to the lobbying efforts of big business. Political union, for all intents and purposes, has been postponed indefinitely after the Treaty of Amsterdam of 1997 also failed to deliver on this score, whereas the hope that EMU might restore democratic control over policy-making also continues to be contradicted by the reality of the convergence criteria and the stability pact.

A triumph neither for Thatcherite hyperliberalism nor for the social democratic vision, nor, for that matter, for the neo-mercantilist strategy, Maastricht in fact contained elements of all three rival projects, even though it was biased in favour of the neo-liberal project, given the neo-liberal orthodoxy underpinning EMU. At the same time, however, chapters on 'Trans-European [infrastructure] Networks' and 'Research and Technological Development' did provide a basis for some form of European industrial policy or *Ordnungspolitik* clearly more in tune with the German model of Rhineland capitalism than with the British neo-liberal model. These policies did not amount to a neo-mercantilist strategy, but they did speak to the interests of that part of European industry that—in its dependence on a strong European home base—in the past had propagated a more mercantilist conception of the European project. Finally, the rather weak social chapter nevertheless succeeded in incorporating European social democracy and the trade union movement into the 'New Europe'.

# The Emergent New European Order: Embedded Neo-Liberalism

In retrospect, the Maastricht compromise reflected the gradual emergence of what we here identify as an 'embedded neo-liberal' synthesis, in which the neo-liberal project stops short of fully disembedding the European market economy from its postwar social and political institutions. On the one hand, the primacy lies with freedom of capital and markets, implying that the postwar European model needs to be fundamentally restructured. On the other hand, it is recognized that this restructuring process cannot take place overnight, that it will have to be a gradual process in which a high degree of social consensus is maintained. Finally, and crucially, a pure neo-liberal strategy would also undermine the long-term accumulation prospects of industrial capital, which still needs the state to educate the workforce, to provide the infrastructure, to pursue macroeconomic policies that favour growth and investment, to maintain social and political stability, etc. Embedded neo-liberalism, I would argue, is the dominant strategic and ideological outlook of Europe's transnational business élite as it has moved away from neo-mercantilism and towards neo-liberalism, but without adopting the pure *laissez-faire* model, and this ideology is also underpinning the emergent European socio-economic order.

## The Neo-Liberal Competitiveness Discourse

In the construction of an embedded neo-liberal European order we can once more observe the political and ideological agency of the transnational business élite in shaping the discourse of European public policy-making. This transnational discourse has come to centre around the word 'competitiveness', appealing equally to neo-liberals, neo-mercantilists, and social democrats. But what competitiveness actually means, and how it has to be achieved, is an open question decided in concrete struggles. Here we can observe that competitiveness is increasingly being defined in neo-liberal terms.

Competitiveness, like globalization, has become a keyword in European socio-economic discourse. From the Delors White Paper on 'Growth, Competitiveness and Employment' onward it has become the unofficial central policy objective of the EU.[18] In 1995, following an initiative of the ERT, a Competitiveness Advisory Group (CAG) was set up by the Commission, which since then has helped in 'keeping competitiveness in the forefront of the policy debates'.[19] As can be read from both Round Table and Commission publications, where competitiveness in the past had sometimes been defined more in neo-mercantilist terms, as in the case of the ERT, or in more social democratic terms (that is, mixed with Keynesian and other 'progressive' elements), as in the case of the (Delors) Commission, the meaning of competitiveness has now come to be tied to the neo-liberal project. Invoking the concept 'benchmarking', now also part of the vocabulary of European policy-making, the ERT leaves no doubt as to how competitiveness must be measured: the country or region that is most competitive is that which is most successful in attracting mobile capital: 'Governments must recognise today that every economic and social system in the world is competing with all the others to attract the footloose businesses.'[20] The neo-liberal restructuring this implies, for instance, of the labour market, is also clearly acknowledged by the Commission, which in a recent document identifies labour market reform as a 'vital factor for the competitiveness of European industry', calling for 'a radical rethink of all relevant labour market systems—employment protection, working time, social protection, and health and safety—to adapt them to a world of work which will be organised differently.'[21]

The principal benchmark for government is thus the ability to attract transnational capital by offering it maximum freedom and the best supply conditions. To the extent that these supply conditions require public policies (such as investment in infrastructure and education) that go beyond the neo-liberal ideal of 'leaving things to the market', we can speak of 'embedded neo-liberalism'. It is also embedded neo-liberalism because, in the continental European context, with a tradition of 'social partnership' and the persistent ideology of a

'European social model', there are limits to the extent to which employers can or indeed want to adopt a full-fledged Anglo-Saxon neo-liberal model within industrial relations. Inasmuch as some form of corporatism, and the social consensus it tends to produce, can be combined with more flexible labour markets—think of the celebrated 'Dutch model'—employers are unlikely to want to dismantle fully these market-embedding institutions. However, it is partly through these corporatist institutions that neo-liberal reform of the labour market is implemented within continental Europe ('negotiated neo-liberalism'). While the traditional redistributive and market-correcting role of the state has been redefined towards ensuring what the ERT calls the 'conditions for competitiveness', the embeddedness of the emergent neo-liberal order seems to be geared more to serve the interests of transnational and globalizing capital than those of other social groups.

## Conclusions

Everywhere, globalization is generating pressure (including ideological pressure) for change: for the state to adapt to the exigencies of globalizing markets and transnational capital. At the same time, within this transformation process, political compromises also have to be made with socio-economic groups, such as organized labour, whose interests are hurt by globalization. Moreover, capital, especially industrial capital, cannot live by the logic of what Karl Polanyi called the self-regulating market alone, but needs supporting government policies and social institutions in order to accumulate wealth.[22] The compromises between these different requirements work themselves out in different ways (depending on historical circumstances). This chapter has suggested that within the European region this compromise (to be sure, a very asymmetrical one) is taking the shape of embedded neo-liberalism, which in turn reflects the wider process in which neo-liberal globalization transforms established state-society relations across the different regions of the global political economy.

Embedded neo-liberalism as the underpinning of the currently emerging European order is the outcome of the transnational struggle between the three rival projects of neo-liberalism, neo-mercantilism, and social democracy. The 'embedded' component of embedded neo-liberalism addresses the concerns both of the former neo-mercantilists and of the European labour and social democratic political forces, but this incorporation is done in such a way that these concerns are in the end subordinated to the overriding objective of neo-liberal competitiveness. Indeed, the latter increasingly seems to become the primary goal of European socio-economic governance. This is apparent, first of all, in the competitiveness discourse now central to the Commission's strategy with regard to industrial policy and macroeconomic management. Second, it transpires from the relative failure of the social dimension. Third, it follows from the way the EU has fully committed itself to global free trade. Finally, it is apparent from the neo-liberal character of the EMU, at the heart of the current integration project. Indeed, in many respects, EMU can be seen as a supranational institutionalization of neo-liberal discipline.

The European socio-economic order being constructed thus subordinates the European region (including Eastern Europe) to the exigencies of the global economy and global competition and hence to the interests of global transnational capital. Under the banner of 'competitiveness' the EU pursues the by now familiar neo-liberal policies of budget austerity, deregulation ('freeing' the market), and labour market flexibility (even if wanting to preserve the social consensus model still prevalent in many European countries). While these policies may make Europe attractive in the eyes of transnational capital, other social groups may suffer from this form of competitiveness because these policies shift the burden of adjustment onto labour and society at large, leading to rising inequality and social insecurity. With regard to a renewed opposition on the part of social democratic forces, the problem continues to be how to organize the social base of labour and other social groups that bear the cost of neo-liberal competitiveness at a European level. The project of EMU, however, still harbours a dialectic potential. As the social costs of the neo-liberal discipline, such as persistently high unemployment, provoke further social unrest, a more substantive embeddedness of the European project might still be called for. The struggle therefore is still open.

## Notes

1  Borrowing the words of John Ruggie, 'International Regimes, Transactions and Change: Embedded Liberalism in the Postwar Economic Order', *International Organization* 36, 2 (1982): 379–416, esp. 382.

2  The focus on social forces follows the neo-Gramscian approach as pioneered by Robert Cox and others. See, for example, Robert W. Cox, 'Social Forces, States, and World Orders: Beyond International Relations Theory', in Robert O. Keohane, ed., *Neorealism and Its Critics* (New York: Columbia University Press, 1986), 204–55.

3  There are now about 45,000 TNCs in the world (up from 7,000 in 1970), together controlling US$3.2 trillion in foreign direct investment (FDI) stock (up from US$282 million in 1975). The present centrality of TNCs in the world economy is indicated by the estimate that the 600 largest TNCs are producing more than a fifth of the world's real net output of industrial production, whereas about 40 per cent of employment in the industrialized world depends directly or indirectly on all TNCs. See *World Investment Report 1997: Transnational Corporations, Market Structure and Competition Policy* (New York: United Nations, 1997).

4  John Stopford and Susan Strange, *Rival States, Rival Firms: Competition for World Market Shares* (Cambridge: Cambridge University Press, 1991), 37. My understanding of the rise and role of transnational capitalist élites has been heavily influenced by the work of the so-called Amsterdam School of IPE on what they have termed processes of *transnational class formation*. See, for example, Kees van der Pijl, *Transnational Classes and International Relations* (London: Routledge, 1998).

5  This division of European capital is an adaptation from one proposed by Otto Holman, 'Transnational Class Strategy and the New Europe',

*International Journal of Political Economy* 22, 1 (1992): 3–22.

6  John Grahl and Paul Teague, *The Big Market: The Future of the European Community* (London: Lawrence and Wishart, 1990), 172.

7  For an account of this strategy, see Joan Pearce and John Sutton, *Protection and Industrial Policy in Europe* (London: Routledge & Kegan Paul, 1986).

8  Delors quoted in Alex Krause, *Inside the New Europe* (New York: HarperCollins, 1991).

9  George Ross, *Jacques Delors and European Integration* (Cambridge: Polity Press, 1995), 109.

10  In the words of co-founder Wisse Dekker, quoted in 'Industrialists Drive for a Stronger Europe: Interview with Prof. Dr. Wisse Dekker', *Europe 2000* 2, 2 (1990): 17–19.

11  See especially Maria Green Cowles, 'The Politics of Big Business in the European Community: Setting the Agenda for a New Europe', Ph.D. thesis (American University, 1994). See also Maria Green Cowles, 'Setting the Agenda for a New Europe: The ERT and EC 1992', *Journal of Common Market Studies* 33, 4 (1995): 501–26; Holman, 'Transnational Class Strategy'.

12  Telephone interview by author, Florence, 27 Jan. 1998.

13  See Brian T. Hanson, 'What Happened to Fortress Europe?: External Trade Policy Liberalisation in the European Union', *International Organization* 52, 1 (1998): 55–85.

14  See Loukas Tsoukalis, *The New European Economy* (Oxford: Oxford University Press, 1993), 99, 335.

15  For empirical evidence on the globalization of Europe's élite TNCs, see Bastiaan van Apeldoorn, 'Transnational Capitalism and the Struggle over the European Order', Ph.D. thesis (Florence: European University Institute, 1998).

16  For a detailed analysis of these and other factors, see Wayne Sandholtz, 'Choosing Union: Monetary

Politics and Maastricht', *International Organization* 47, 1 (Winter 1993): 1–39.

17  ERT, *Reshaping Europe* (Brussels: European Round Table of Industrialists, 1991), 46.

18  See European Commission, *Growth, Competitiveness, and Employment* (Luxembourg: Office for the Official Publications of the European Union, 1994).

19  See ERT, *Beating the Crisis* (Brussels: European Round Table of Industrialists, 1993), 27.

20  ERT, *Benchmarking for Policy-Makers* (Brussels: European Round Table of Industrialists, 1996), 15.

21  European Commission, *Benchmarking the Competitiveness of European Industry*, (Brussels, 9 Oct. 1996), 11.

22  Karl Polanyi, *The Great Transformation: The Political and Economic Origins of Our Time* (Boston: Beacon Press, 1957).

## Suggested Readings

Cowles, Maria Green. 'Setting the Agenda for a New Europe: The ERT and EC 1992', *Journal of Common Market Studies* 33, 4 (1995): 501–26.

Crouch, Colin, and Wolfgang Streeck, eds. *Political Economy of Modern Capitalism: Mapping Convergence and Diversity*. London: Sage, 1998.

Gill, Stephen. 'European Governance and New Constitutionalism: Economic and Monetary Union and Alternatives to Disciplinary Neoliberalism in Europe', *New Political Economy* 3, 1 (1998): 5–26.

Hanson, Brian T. 'What Happened to Fortress Europe?: External Trade Policy Liberalisation in the European Union', *International Organization* 52, 1 (1998): 55–85.

Hayward, Jack, ed. *Industrial Enterprise and European Integration*. Oxford: Oxford University Press, 1995.

Holman, Otto. 'Integrating Eastern Europe. EU-Expansion and the Double Transformation in Poland, The Czech Republic and Hungary', *International Journal of Political Economy* 29, 1 (1999).

Nelson, B.F., and A.C.-G. Stubb, eds. *The European Union: Readings on the Theory and Practice of European Integration*. Boulder, Colo.: Lynne Rienner, 1994.

Rhodes, Martin. '"Subversive Liberalism": Market Integration, Globalization and the European Welfare State', *Journal of European Public Policy* 2–3, (1995): 384–406.

Rhodes, Martin, and Bastiaan van Apeldoorn. 'Capitalism versus Capitalism in Western Europe', in Rhodes, Paul Heywood, and Vincent Wright, eds, *Developments in West European Politics*. London: Macmillan, 1997, 171–89.

Streeck, Wolfgang. 'From Market-Making to State-Building? Reflections on the Political Economy of European Social Policy', in Stephan Leibfried and Paul Pierson, eds, *European Social Policy*. Washington: Brookings Institution, 1995.

Tsoukalis, Loukas. *The New European Economy Revisited: The Politics and Economics of Integration*. Oxford: Oxford University Press, 1997.

Wyat-Walker, A. 'Globalization, Corporate Identity and European Union Technology Policy', in William D. Coleman and Geoffrey R.D. Underhill, eds, *Regionalism and Global Economic Integration: Europe, Asia and the Americas*. London: Routledge, 1998, 140–57.

## Web Sites

European Economic and Social Committee: http:\\www.ces.eu.int/en/default.htm

European Round Table of Industrialists: http:\\www.ert.be

World Trade Organization: http://www.wto.org

European Union Central: http:\\www.europa.eu.int

## Chapter 19

# The North American Free Trade Agreement

Tony Porter

On 1 January 1994, the North American Free Trade Agreement (NAFTA) came into effect, tying together to an unprecedented degree the 363 million people and $6.3 trillion in economic activity in Mexico, the United States, and Canada. The new agreement cemented dramatic reversals in attitudes in the respective countries with regard to the costs and benefits of integration. This chapter will discuss, in turn, the reasons for NAFTA, its key features, its effects, and its significance. Although NAFTA was often portrayed by its supporters as primarily an economic arrangement, this chapter will stress, consistent with this book overall, that politics has played a key role in its negotiation and implementation.

## Reasons for NAFTA

For much of the post-World War II period few people would have imagined that Canada, Mexico, and the United States would sign an agreement such as NAFTA. A growing Canadian nationalism, associated with fears about the negative consequences of Canada's increasing dependence on US investment and trade, reached a high point during the 1970s with new government initiatives, such as the Foreign Investment Review Agency, that sought to shape incoming investment in ways that were more beneficial to Canadians, and with efforts to establish closer economic links with Europe and Japan. The Canada-US Free Trade Agreement (FTA), which came into effect in 1989, and NAFTA, which went beyond that agreement by including Mexico and by adding new issues, marked a remarkable turn away from the earlier more nationalist period.

Mexican nationalism had even stronger roots than did the Canadian variety. Anger at foreign influence had helped fuel the Mexican Revolution of 1910 and had contributed to the strongly nationalist constitution of 1917. In the post-World War II period Mexico had been a leading advocate of the right and duty of governments to build economic sovereignty through such measures as nationalization of major industries and controls over cross-border capital and trade flows.[1] Government spending as a share of GNP increased from 13.1 per cent in 1970 to 39.6 per cent in 1976. In 1973 Mexico enacted two major laws to regulate foreign investment and the transfer of technology.[2] Even in 1982, the Mexican government's response to the debt crisis was to take over the privately owned banks, adding them to more than a thousand other state-run enterprises.[3] Yet by 1986 Mexico had signalled its commitment to free trade by joining the General Agreement on Tariffs and Trade, and then, in 1990 by initiating talks with the United States on NAFTA.

While the turn towards regional free trade could be traced through domestic political factors that appear to be unique to each of the three countries, the simultaneous upsurge in enthusiasm in all three countries suggests that systemic factors are at work. It is these factors that this chapter will stress.

One frequently cited systemic factor, especially by supporters of NAFTA, is the worldwide expansion of markets and the opportunities and constraints this expansion presents to policy-makers. Opportunities reside in the capacity of market exchanges to generate growth through allowing people to specialize in the economic activities they can do best, in allowing capital to flow to the activity in which it is most productive as measured by the highest rate of return, and in forcing uncompetitive firms and individuals to modify their behaviour if they wish to survive, a point that also highlights the constraints imposed by markets. These considerations might suggest that NAFTA is simply an expression of the recognition by governments and citizens of these opportunities and constraints, perhaps stimulated by technological advances that have increased the fluidity of international trade and capital flows.

There are three clues, however, that such an explanation is inadequate. First, these countries' earlier policies, for most of the post-World War II period, were associated not with stagnation but rather with unprecedented growth—indeed, with higher growth rates than those that have followed NAFTA. Second, the advantages of market exchange cannot alone explain the regional character of NAFTA. Third, the timing of NAFTA is difficult to explain on the basis of an ongoing expansion of market exchanges alone.

To provide an explanation that can take into account these issues it is necessary to highlight the impact of historically specific international political structures on the three countries, and most particularly the changing fortunes of the United States as the hegemonic leader of the West during the Cold War. In the aftermath of World War II the United States was unrivalled, in part due to the damage inflicted on its major competitors, including the division of Europe, as a result of the war and in part due to the superiority of its productive capacity. In constructing a postwar order with itself at the centre, the United States found it was willing and able to support the arrangements within which international markets flourished, including the trade and monetary regimes, as well as bilateral arrangements with key allies in which political and ideological allegiance was exchanged for relatively free access to US markets. These political arrangements were accompanied by a particular set of production arrangements: the rapidly expanding manufacturing industries upon which the Americans had built their ascendancy were organized by US-based multinational corporations and spread to other countries through those corporations' branch plants and subsidiaries.

Canada's and Mexico's integration into these arrangements, given their proximity to the United States, was a particularly distinctive feature of their postwar political economies. In Canada, US direct foreign investment poured in during the 1950s and 1960s, dominating both the extraction of natural resources destined for the US market and manufacturing industries catering to the Canadian market. These economic ties were facilitated by close and informal political ties, symbolized by phrases such as 'special relationship' and 'quiet diplomacy': as a trusted ally Canada had privileged access for its diplomats in Washington, allowing it to manage tensions and promote integration in the economic relationship. Close economic ties were also associated with a strengthening of the Canadian state, allowing it to cushion its citizens from the negative effects of economic dependence through tariffs and social welfare spending. Similarly, Mexico experienced huge inflows of US capital during the 1960s, and by the end of the 1970s 70 per cent of direct foreign investment and foreign debt originated from the United States and 70 per cent of Mexican exports were to the United States.[4] Beginning in World War II, when hundreds of thousands of Mexicans were recruited into the US army and brought into the country to replace mobilized US workers, close official relations facilitated close economic ties.[5] Like Canada, Mexico tried to offset the negative effects of this close economic relationship by strengthening state intervention.

During the 1970s these arrangements began to change. In response to US fears about its diminishing economic lead over the rest of the world, US indulgence began to be replaced by a more aggressive unilateralism, evident for instance in the ending of its support of the Bretton Woods monetary regime and its surprise imposition of a new duty on imports in August 1971. There were direct negative effects for Canada and Mexico, such as increased trade frictions, but indirect effects as well. For instance, the United States took measures with regard to global finance that, due to the size and centrality of its financial markets, enhanced its own position but left smaller countries, including Canada and Mexico, vulnerable. This was evident in the early 1980s in the contribution to the Mexican crisis of high US interest rates and government deficits and massive inflows of capital to the United States, and the related contribution of the overvalued US dollar to raising the Canadian dollar and making Canadian exports to the rest of the world less competitive.

Given the constraints facing Canada and Mexico during the 1980s the political balance in both countries began to shift towards support for free trade with the United States. Washington was in favour of negotiations on free trade as well, but this was far from a passive recognition of the mutual benefits that could be obtained by allowing markets freer play. The United States had key goals related to its competitive position in the world as a whole and it saw the creation of strong new rules with Canada and Mexico as part of this larger campaign. These included establishing extensive rights for investors, strong intellectual property provisions, and rules compelling Canada and Mexico to open their financial sectors to US firms. Improved access to Mexican and Canadian oil was a way to offset the negative effects on the United States of the high oil prices of the 1970s.[6] There were, in addition, goals specific to Mexico. The Americans aimed to obtain a nearby low-wage location in which the labour costs of US corporations could be reduced (and their competitiveness thereby enhanced) by shifting parts of production to Mexico. Allowing freer access for products made in Mexico to US markets was also seen as a way to stem the tide of illegal immigration from Mexico to the United States as the work done by these immigrants could be shifted back south of the border.

While economic arguments can be made for strengthening rules governing investment, intellectual property, and financial services, these arguments lack decisive empirical confirmation and tend to obscure the political factors contributing to the American enthusiasm for them. In each case such rules facilitated internationalization in areas in which the US saw itself as having a competitive advantage that would offset its diminished lead in

manufacturing. This would be accomplished by establishing new rights that were traceable more directly to the political process of threat and negotiation than to a generalized recognition of their economic or ethical merits. In the case of investment many countries, including Canada and Mexico, had, at various times, argued that the state had a legitimate and useful role to play in seeking to offset the economic and organizational capacity of multinational corporations and that the state should monitor and regulate incoming investment in an effort to enhance benefits and minimize costs for its own citizens. Intellectual property rights establish a temporary monopoly in knowledge, and it is far from clear that the resulting benefits of the increased incentives to produce new knowledge outweigh the costs from the barriers to the free flow of knowledge that this monopoly creates.[7] The financial sector, because of its centrality to the economy as a whole and the intangible and interdependent nature of the transactions upon which it is based, is filled with externalities—social costs and benefits not captured by the prices of particular transactions that have traditionally been a reason for strong state regulation—and it is not clear that the efficiency gains from greater international competition in financial services outweigh the losses from a diminished capacity for regulation. These three areas were ones for which the United States had been campaigning in bilateral negotiations and at the Uruguay Round of trade negotiations and their inclusion in NAFTA would enshrine previous efforts more comprehensively and boldly in a major trade agreement, as well as prod the negotiations at the GATT with an implicit US threat to withdraw into a hemispheric alternative.

In short, NAFTA did not simply come about as a result of a sudden recognition by the three governments of the mutual benefits they would enjoy from a generalized expansion of market exchange. Each government came to the table influenced by constraints and power associated with its particular role in the evolving structure of the international political economy. For the United States, NAFTA was merely one element in a larger effort to promote, in a restructured form, the continuation of the leadership role it had played since World War II. Its key goals were ones it perceived as important for its position relative to other countries, and these goals were in the interest of powerful US business constituencies. Canada and Mexico, by contrast, constrained by the restructuring of the international political economy, had to focus more narrowly on obtaining more secure access to the US market and to substitute negotiated rules governing their relationship with the US for previous informal understandings and independent deployment of their states' capacity.

## Key Features of NAFTA

While the final NAFTA text runs to more than 2,000 pages and is impossible to review comprehensively here, it is useful to discuss its most significant provisions. These include greater market access in a variety of sectors, investment rules, intellectual property rights, dispute settlement, and side agreements on environmental and labour rights. These will be examined in turn.

Market access provisions varied by sector. NAFTA rules were not generally applied to some sensitive industries, including Mexican oil and railways and Canadian culture. On energy, NAFTA reproduced the controversial measures agreed between Canada and the US in the FTA—a prohibition, except under specified unusual circumstances such as national security reasons, on restrictions on energy trade, foreclosing export taxes and other measures used in the past to support nationalist economic policies. The Mexican government did not go that far, but did agree to open up procurement by Pemex, its oil company, to foreign participation, although it retained control of Pemex in Mexican hands. On automobiles NAFTA included provisions for the elimination, over a 10-year period, of tariffs between the three countries for vehicles meeting requirements for substantial regional content. Mexico agreed to phase out its rule that foreign auto manufacturers in Mexico export twice as much as they import, to eliminate restrictions on imports of new vehicles, and to end required levels of local content in auto parts. These

renounced measures had all been designed to get US firms to produce in Mexico rather than simply exporting to it. The goal of the auto provisions were to expand US and Canadian access to Mexico's rapidly growing market, to rationalize and thereby enhance the competitiveness of the continent's auto industry, and to restrict the ability of non-North American firms to produce within the continent for the continent as a whole. In textiles and clothing it was agreed to eliminate tariffs over 10 years for products that satisfied strict regional content rules. On agriculture, the provisions called for the immediate elimination of tariffs on 57 per cent of US-Mexican agricultural trade and the phasing out of other tariffs and quotas over 15 years. As in other sectors, products that do not meet strict requirements for regional content are not covered. In financial services US and Canadian firms obtained greatly expanded rights to operate within the Mexican market, which at the time was expected to grow phenomenally as a result of its lack of basic services such as chequing. US access to Canadian financial services markets had already been expanded under the FTA, although this earlier agreement had had little effect given the traditional size, strength, and competitiveness of Canadian banks.[8]

NAFTA investment rules are the most dramatic in the agreement as a whole. Investors from the other NAFTA parties must be treated in the same way as domestic investors (national treatment) and at least as well as investors from any other country (the most-favoured-nation principle). These provisions apply to both long-term direct foreign investments and portfolio investments (where there is no direct control by the investor of the enterprise). Many governments have been reluctant to eliminate controls on portfolio investments because they are more likely to be short-term and speculative. The rules prohibit virtually all trade-related techniques used by governments, such as those of Mexico and Canada that seek to persuade foreign firms to satisfy domestic public policy goals such as increased employment, research and development, or exports. Such prohibited techniques include requirements to source domestically, to produce unique products that would be sold worldwide (product mandating), to meet export targets, and to transfer technology. NAFTA rules prohibit interference, except under certain restricted circumstances, with investors' transfer of capital or profits across borders. Nationalization of foreign enterprises on economic grounds is prohibited and all nationalizations must be compensated promptly at market value. Previously, Mexico had been a prominent proponent of the view that nationalization was the prerogative of a sovereign state and a useful economic tool, and that compensation could legitimately be less than current market value to make up for past excessive exploitation. Perhaps the most remarkable feature of the agreement is the right of private investors to take a case against a host government to a process of binding international arbitration at the World Bank or the UN. This overturns an enduring principle that holds that only states are recognized actors under international law. Overall, the investment provisions of NAFTA went well beyond any other multilateral agreements, including those that were being negotiated through the GATT.

The intellectual property provisions are also striking. Governments are obligated to protect copyrights on computer programs, to prosecute decoding of encrypted satellite transmissions (such as television programs), and to protect new sound recordings for 50 years, new trademarks for 10 years, and new patents for 20 years. Such levels of protection are controversial because they are seen by critics as giving producers of new technologies excessive profits as a result of the monopoly they are given and because they are seen as interfering with the flow of knowledge to places where it is needed. Supporters argue that the increased profits are a justified incentive that is needed if new knowledge is to be produced. Compulsory licensing was a technique used by governments to force multinational corporations to transfer knowledge to domestic firms, and this was prohibited under NAFTA. Canada, in a political process that generated a great deal of domestic political conflict, reworked its patent regulations for pharmaceuticals to bring them in line with NAFTA obligations. A thriving Canadian generic drug industry had developed as a result of compulsory licensing provisions and many

Canadians felt that this should be preserved on public policy and economic grounds. Multinational pharmaceutical companies, however, were determined to overturn these provisions, in part due to the increased revenues that could be obtained from the Canadian market and in part to eliminate Canada as a negative example for other countries. NAFTA's consolidation of previous American efforts to strengthen Mexico's rules on intellectual property was also seen by the US as an important precedent for future negotiations with developing countries.

Strong dispute resolution procedures are particularly important for smaller partners in trade agreements because they can offset the ability of the stronger partner to use its political power to disregard or interpret the agreement as it pleases. For Canada and Mexico it was important, if their increased access to the US market was to be meaningful, that there be a way to address the long tradition of US firms using US anti-dumping and countervailing duty measures to gain protection from foreign competition. The FTA had put in place a dispute resolution mechanism that, in its first five years, had led to two-thirds of Canadian appeals of US decisions being successful, twice the success rate of appeals by other countries using the non-FTA procedures provided by the US.[9] NAFTA essentially adopted the FTA process, with some further strengthening, and extended it to Mexico. The process, however, 'yields leeway to the reality of the Parties' power asymmetry' by its reliance on self-help in enforcement, and by the fact that it is restricted to reviews of the implementation of each country's own laws.[10] This deficiency would become apparent in the softwood lumber dispute in which, despite favourable panel decisions, Canada was successfully pressured by American threats to impose restrictions on its exports to the United States.

Faced with strong concerns on the part of US citizens that NAFTA would allow US firms to avoid US standards by moving production to a lightly regulated location in Mexico, and then to export manufactured goods freely back into the United States, US President Bill Clinton decided to negotiate two side accords, one on environmental standards and one on labour standards. These established a Commission for Environmental Co-operation and a Commission for Labour Co-operation, each with a council composed of the relevant ministers from the respective countries, who would meet once a year, and a secretariat, the members of which are expected to remain independent of their governments and which is responsible for ongoing administrative and technical support for the commission. The Commission on Environmental Co-operation, reflecting the greater participation of non-governmental organizations in its negotiation, has, in addition, a 15-member Joint Public Advisory Committee that can be composed of scientific experts or others active on environmental issues.[11] The labour agreement establishes national administrative offices in each country that play an important role in receiving and initially considering complaints lodged by either individuals or NGOs.

The agreements both focus on monitoring and enforcing national standards rather than establishing and enforcing common international standards. There are, however, general statements regarding the desirability of standards, the making of joint recommendations, and, in the case of the labour agreement, the parties commit themselves to promoting 10 'labour principles', including, for example, the right to organize and to be compensated for injury. Most complaints are envisioned as being resolved by consultation and arbitration without the use of sanctions. However, in some restricted cases monetary penalties (set initially at a maximum of $20 million, to be spent in the penalized country on environmental or labour issues) can be imposed, and if these fail, there can be a suspension of equivalent NAFTA benefits. With the labour agreement, fines can only be imposed for a failure to enforce health and safety, child labour, or minimum wage standards, and cannot be applied to the right to organize or to strike. Opinion was sharply divided on the significance of the environmental and labour side agreements. Some felt they were precedent-setting in being the first significant attempt to integrate environmental and labour issues into a trade agreement. Others, especially in the labour movement, dismissed them as unenforceable window-dressing.

The provisions of NAFTA, in sum, were very significant, not just because three countries that might otherwise not have been expected to conclude a trade agreement did so, but also because the commitments went well beyond other trade agreements in the range of activities covered and in the strictness of the procedures for enforcement. The US goals concerning investment, intellectual property rights, and financial services were met or exceeded. Canada and Mexico received improved access to the US market for a variety of products. However, the letter of trade agreements, as with any law, is sometimes not as important as their implementation and broader significance. We turn to assess these in the next section.

## The Effects and Significance of NAFTA

Anyone seeking to evaluate NAFTA faces four serious challenges: separating its economic effects from the effects of unrelated factors; gauging what might have happened if NAFTA had not been signed (the counterfactuals); assessing processes, like dispute resolution procedures, which take time to generate a performance record; and coping with criteria for what constitutes a successful agreement that are sharply contradictory because they are based in different perspectives on the way the international political economy more generally does and should work. Nevertheless, it is useful to review some of the main points of debate before turning to a concluding assessment of the significance of politics in NAFTA overall.

A key question in evaluating NAFTA is whether it has improved or diminished the standards of living of the citizens in the countries involved. There is sharp disagreement about this. For instance, President Clinton, in his required 1997 report to Congress on NAFTA, claimed that exports to Canada and Mexico had supported an increase of 311,000 jobs between 1993 and 1996 and cited research indicating that, controlling for the catastrophic aftermath of Mexico's peso crisis, Mexico's worst depression since the 1930s, NAFTA had added $13 billion to US real income in 1996.[12] Critics pointed out that it is meaningless to cite jobs added by exports without noting jobs lost through increased imports and that the peso crisis itself, as discussed below, was linked to NAFTA. Some studies focus only on job losses and downward pressure on wages. For instance, the US Department of Labor's Transitional Adjustment Assistance Program had recorded, by the end of 1997, 151,256 NAFTA-related job losses, undoubtedly an underestimate of total losses give the stringency of the criteria for receiving such assistance.[13] An Economic Policy Institute study, taking exports and imports into account, estimates a net loss of 394,835 US jobs as a result of NAFTA.[14] Debate about the comparative quality and wage levels of jobs lost and jobs gained is ongoing.

There is little disagreement that the economic performance of Canada and Mexico was disappointing in the aftermath of NAFTA. Mexico's experience was the most negative: unemployment doubled between 1993 and 1995 and real hourly wages in 1996 were 37 per cent below 1980 levels. Unemployment levels in Canada were down from 11.3 per cent in 1992, but still high by historical standards in 1997 at 9.6 per cent.[15] There is, however, sharp disagreement about the relationship of this performance to NAFTA. Clinton's 1997 report notes that the recovery of Mexican exports was much faster following the peso crisis than had been the case following the 1982 debt crisis, and argues that this was due to NAFTA. Yet there are strong reasons to think that the peso crisis, with its negative consequences for people's daily lives, would not have occurred at all had excessively large and volatile flows of capital not been encouraged by NAFTA.[16] In the Canadian case, some argue that Canada's economic performance would have been far worse had it been less able to rely on exports to the United States. Persistently higher unemployment rates in Canada as compared to the US, however, might suggest that its relative position in the continent had been weakened rather than strengthened by NAFTA.[17]

Debate is ongoing as well about the effect of NAFTA on labour and environmental standards. A post-NAFTA study by Bronfenbrenner found that half of US firms facing unionization drives countered with the threat to relocate to Mexico, and when forced to negotiate with a union, 15 per cent actually did close all or part of a plant (three times the rate before NAFTA), confirming the fears of NAFTA critics.[18] On the other hand, supporters note dramatically increased Mexican spending on the enforcement of labour and environmental standards since NAFTA.[19] The commissions put in place by the side agreements had, by the end of 1997, handled a small number of cases, 13 environmental and nine labour. Seven of the environmental cases were either rejected by the secretariat or withdrawn by the submitter, five were in process, and one, against Mexico, had resulted in a factual report. Nevertheless, the commissions have had some modest positive impact in publicizing complaints about violations and, in the case of labour, affecting the treatment of some of the workers concerned.[20]

## Conclusion

While sharp disagreement on the effects of NAFTA will continue, it is possible to draw some general conclusions. First, the provisions of most concern to important interests in the United States and to the long-range strategy of the US government—the investment, intellectual property rights, and financial services provisions—are the ones that were most innovatively and strongly developed in the agreement. The dispute resolution mechanism for investment, with the role it permits for private parties, is unprecedented in addressing this new issue and in its strengthening of international legal constraints on sovereignty. The dispute resolution mechanism for other matters, by contrast, remains subject to power politics, even compared to the mechanism in place at the World Trade Organization, and the mechanisms in the labour and environmental agreements are especially weak. Second, and relatedly, NAFTA helps consolidate a strongly market-oriented regime for North America, weakening pre-existing national political instruments that had been developed to offset the negative effects of markets without developing alternative international instruments. In contrast to the European Union, for instance, where a great deal of effort has been devoted to developing an institutional solution to exchange rate problems, such problems in North America are dealt with by individual government initiatives on an ad hoc basis, as was especially apparent in the Mexican peso bailout. This market-oriented regime poses more challenges for Canada and Mexico than for the United States, in part because of the latter's size and in part because it matches more closely the traditional relationship between state and market in the United States than it does in the other countries. Yet the decision of the Clinton administration to pursue labour and environmental side agreements shows that even in the United States there is a limit to the willingness of citizens to increase their exposure to international markets without new ways to safeguard themselves from negative effects. In short, NAFTA, as with other issues in international political economy, reveals the intensely political nature of the evolving international economy.

## Notes

1   Mexico originated the initiative that culminated in the Charter of the Economic Rights and Duties of States, approved by the UN General Assembly in 1974. See Bernardo Sepúlveda Amor, 'International Law and National Sovereignty: The NAFTA and the Claims of Mexico Jurisdiction', *Houston Journal of International Law* 19 (1997): 565–93, esp. 568.

2   Richard S. Weinert, 'Foreign Capital in Mexico', in Susan Kaufman Purcell, ed., *Mexico-United States Relations*, Proceedings of the Academy of Political Science, 34, 1 (New York, 1981), 115–24.

3   The figures in this and the previous sentence are from George W. Grayson, *The North American Free Trade Agreement: Regional Community and the New World Order* (Lanham, Md: University Press of America, 1995), 36.

4   Maria Del Rosario Green, 'Mexico's Economic Dependence', in Purcell, ed., *Mexico-United States Relations*, 104–14, esp. 110.

5   See George W. Grayson, *The United States and Mexico: Patterns of Influence* (New York: Praeger, 1984), 27–31. Mexico's criticisms of excessive US influence in Latin America were tolerated by the United States, which was grateful for its anti-communism, evident, for instance, in Mexico's support of the US blockade during the Cuban missile crisis.

6   Stephen J. Randall, 'NAFTA in Transition: The United States and Mexico', *Canadian Review of American Studies* 27, 3 (1997): 1–18.

7   Bhagwati, a leading economist in favour of free trade, has commented with regard to intellectual property: 'As is now widely conceded among economists . . . there is no presumption of mutual gain, world welfare itself may be reduced by any or more IP [intellectual property] protection, and there is little empirical support for the view that "inadequate" IP protection impedes the creation of new technical knowledge significantly.' Jagdish Bhagwati, 'Regionalism versus Multilateralism', *World Economy* 15, 5 (Sept. 1992): 553.

8   For a useful summary of NAFTA provisions, from which this summary has drawn, see Gary Clyde Hufbauer and Jeffrey J. Schott, *NAFTA: An Assessment*, revised edn (Washington: Institute for International Economics, 1993). On the financial services provisions, see Tony Porter, 'NAFTA, North American Financial Integration, and Regulatory Cooperation in Banking and Securities', in Geoffrey Underhill, ed., *The New World Order in International Finance* (Basingstoke: Macmillan, 1997), 174–92.

9   Alan M. Rugman and Andrew D.M. Anderson, 'NAFTA and the Dispute Settlement Mechanisms: A Transaction Costs Approach', *Journal of World Trade* 20, 7 (Nov. 1997): 935–50, esp. 942.

10  Michael Reisman and Mark Wiedman, 'Contextual Imperatives of Dispute Resolution Mechanisms', *Journal of World Trade* 29, 3 (June 1995): 34.

11  NAFTA also set up the Border Environmental Cooperation Commission, designed to address problems along the US-Mexican border, and the North American Development Bank, designed to fund environmental infrastructure and clean-up

projects. For a critical account, see Andrew Wheat, 'Troubled NAFTA Waters', *Multinational Monitor* (Apr. 1996): 23–5.

12  President Bill Clinton, *Study on the Operation and Effects of the North American Free Trade Agreement*, Report to Congress, July 1997, available at: www.ustr.gov

13  Bill Medaille and Andrew Wheat, 'Faded Denim NAFTA Blues', *Multinational Monitor* (Dec. 1997): 23.

14  Jesse Rothstein and Robert E. Scott, 'NAFTA's Casualties', Issue Brief #20, 19 Sept. 1997, Economic Policy Institute, available at: epinet.org/ib120.html

15  Economic Policy Institute, 'The Failed Experiment: NAFTA at Three Years', Executive Summary, available at: epinet.org/nafta_es.html

16  Porter, 'NAFTA, North American Financial Integration, and Regulatory Cooperation'.

17  Assessing the relative performance of the two countries is difficult because of the range of potentially relevant variables involved. One could argue that in the early 1990s unusually high Canadian interest rates relative to those in the United States, to which the Bank of Canada contributed by its tight monetary policy, also reflected a risk premium demanded by investors in response to their pessimistic assessment of the future performance of the Canadian economy relative to the American economy, and were sufficient to keep the Canadian dollar from dropping, but at considerable cost to the real Canadian economy. Once the interest differential declined and even reversed at the end of decade, the Canadian dollar began declining, a sign of the reduced wealth of Canadians relative to those in the US. For an interesting discussion that stresses other factors, see Kevin Clinton, 'Canada-U.S. Long-Term Interest Differentials in the 1990s', *Bank of Canada Review* (Spring 1998): 17–38.

18  Kate Bronfenbrenner, 'We'll Close! Plant Closings, Plant Closing Threats, Union Organizing, and NAFTA', *Multinational Monitor* (Mar. 1997): 8.

19  Clinton, *Study on the Operation and Effects*.

20  Roy J. Adams and Parbudyal Singh, 'Early Experience with NAFTA's Labour Side Accord', *Comparative Labor Law Journal* 18, 2 (Winter 1997): 161–81. Information on the side accords is available from the commissions' Web sites: www.cec.org and www.naalc.org

## Suggested Readings

Grinspun, Ricardo, and Maxwell A. Cameron, eds. *The Political Economy of North American Free Trade*. Ottawa: Canadian Centre for Policy Alternatives and Montreal and Kingston: McGill-Queen's University Press, 1993.

Randall, Stephen J., and Herman W. Konrad, eds. *NAFTA in Transition*. Calgary: University of Calgary Press, 1995.

## Web Sites

Canadian Embassy in Mexico: www.canada.org.mx/trade/english/nafta0.htm

Institute for Agricultural and Trade Policy, which publishes *NAFTA and Interamerican Trade Monitor*: www.iatp.org

Mexico Online NAFTA/Mexico Resource Directory: www.mexonline.com/nafta.htm

NAFTA Secretariat: www.nafta-sec-alena.org

Texas A&M International University's Office for the Study of US-Mexico Trade Relations and the North American Free Trade Agreement Information Center: www.tamiu.edu/coba/usmtr

Chapter 20

# Regionalism in the Asia-Pacific:
## Two Steps Forward, One Step Back?

Richard Higgott

## Introduction

The early 1990s witnessed largely uncontained optimism in the Asia-Pacific. While the Cold War was not over in the region in the way that it was in Europe, it was a period of lessened tension. Potential sources of conflict remained (indeed, still remain), but for most of the public- and private-sector policy-making élites the principal task was to maximize the economic opportunities present in an era offering abundant supplies of capital and a belief in the benefits of enhanced economic interdependence of a de facto, market-led kind. This increasing interdependence was supported by evolving institutional co-operation, largely state-led and *de jure* in nature. Indeed, the international relations of the region were typified by the proliferation of initiatives, in both the economic and security domains, meant to rapidly enhance collaborative policy co-ordination.

The 1990s were thus a period of exciting, indeed, almost charmingly naïve optimism for greater regional co-operation. This was especially the case in the scholarly and policy-oriented economics community that saw the evolution of APEC and its agenda for securing regional free trade by 2020—through concerted unilateral liberalization following the 1994 Bogor summit—as the only game in town. Accompanying the theoretical interest in the development of open regionalism was a more East Asian focus on the emerging importance of East Asia as an actor in global and regional affairs. At times this was accompanied by what came to be known as the ascendancy of the 'Asian Way' towards international diplomacy. The principal

manifestation of this process was the development of a regional security dialogue via the introduction of the ASEAN Regional Forum (ARF) and the development of the Asia-Europe Meetings process (ASEM) following the first Asia-Europe summit in Bangkok in 1996. The Asian membership of ASEM exactly mirrored those states that constituted the East Asian Economic Caucus (EAEC) within the APEC process.

But in 1997, an 'economic crisis'[1] of unparalleled proportions hit East Asia and spread to other parts of the global economy. This crisis has called forth an explanatory and accusatory industry in both the scholarly and popular press that leaves few facets of this process unexplored. The present chapter isolates out but one aspect of the overall process for location in a wider and longer-term perspective. The chapter asks what has been, and what might be, the effect of the Asian economic crisis of 1997–8 on the continued prospects for regionalism in East Asia? This is a policy question of immediate importance, but it is also a broader analytical and theoretical question for scholars of international political economy in general and scholars of the international relations of the Asia-Pacific in particular. In essence, the answer offered here is twofold.

First, like many analyses of a realist persuasion, the chapter argues that the short-term effects of the crisis have been to expose the limitations of Asian regional institutions to date. Nowhere is this better illustrated than in the demonstrable inefficacy of ASEAN and APEC to make any serious input into the policy process in the wake of the crisis. Second, and by way of a longer-term contrast, the crisis may prove to be a spur to new forms of regional dialogue and policy co-ordination for the institutions for which the groundwork was laid in the late 1980s and early 1990s. These new forms of co-ordination may differ from current forms to the extent that they give rise to a more solidly 'East Asian' orientation in regional policy interaction and co-operation. As such, the arguments advanced in this chapter are theoretically speculative; in several years they will provide a template against which to judge how the regional imperative in East Asia has, or has not, reasserted itself in the wake of the crisis. In so doing, the chapter offers what we might call a hybrid combination of liberal institutionalist co-operative theory fused with some constructivist insights into how region-building in East Asia may, or may not, represent an exercise in intersubjective identity-building.

To posit such an analysis at the height of the economic crisis is not a 'safe' scholarly exercise. It does, however, provide a set of lenses—different from those currently on offer in the mainstream literature—through which to look at regionalism in Asia. Most mainstream literature fails to see events in the region in their necessary wider context—as but part of the first crisis of post-Cold War globalization. This crisis is twofold in its manifestations. At an obvious first level has been a series of economic crises that have altered the economic and sociopolitical fortunes of several hitherto rapidly developing states. At a more abstract though no less significant level, the East Asian economic crisis represents a setback for the inexorable process of international economic liberalization that has come to be known as 'globalization'.

On the eve of the twenty-first century we are experiencing the first serious challenges to the hegemony of neo-liberalism. This resistance is not uniform, nor is it restricted to one site or group of actors. Moreover, in many instances, resistance is as often to practice as much as to principle. Contrary to much Western-style hubris of the 'coming of the second American century' variety,[2] events in Asia represent less the final ideological triumph of liberalism than a context for rethinking significant aspects of the neo-liberal project.

Asian responses to the intervention of the international financial institutions in the context of the debate between protagonists of continued global economic liberalization, on the one hand, and advocates of some form of international capital re-regulation, on the other, demonstrate the tension between dominant Anglo-American understandings of global liberalization and the emergence of East Asian sites of resistance to aspects of it. Asian interests may well test the viability of the 'APEC consensus' as an element in the wider neo-liberal enterprise in the early stages of the twenty-first century.

If the United States and the International Monetary Fund (IMF) have their way, then a Western model of liberalization, replacing the Asian 'high debt model',[3] may come into place over time. Alternatively, there could also be a hardening nationalist resistance to neo-liberalism, for what has been challenged in the crisis of the East Asian newly industrialized economies (NIEs) at the end of the twentieth century is the very model on which they have built their success. It should be seen not only as an economic crisis, but as an 'ideas battle'. The long-standing critique of statism inherent in the neoclassical economic literature and language of the established policy community is seen to be vindicated by the crisis. The speeches of senior US policy-makers and opinion-shapers have been peppered with references to the need to jettison the remaining vestiges of the developmental statist model. This does not play well in East Asia in the short run. It will not play well in the long run either.

The Asian model would have to have changed after the end of the Cold War anyway. But this does not undermine the prospects for growing resentment in the region. During the Cold War, US willingness to supply official capital and to open its markets for an initial one-way flow of exports was predicated heavily on the security consideration of containing communism.[4] In a more benign security environment, with American concerns that it was becoming a 'normal country', or that many of its former junior partners in the Pacific alliance were continuing to free-ride when no longer necessary, there has been an increasing clamour in the US policy community for change in the region. Thus, regional economic trade liberalization and financial deregulation were the pay-off for a continued US security presence in the region. Those sociopolitical practices of the so-called Asian model that were acceptable for security reasons during the Cold War—exclusionary politics, nepotism, and the blurred lines of authority between political and economic power—now clash more violently with the interests of private capital in search of greater market share and profits in an era of deregulation.

At a more specific regional level, a major implication of the experience of Asian states in the crisis, and especially at the hands of the IMF doctors, could be the enhanced development of an 'East Asian' as opposed to 'Asia-Pacific' understanding of region. The desire for national decision-making autonomy in the face of economic crisis and the enhancement of a greater collective regional understanding in the wake of the crisis are not incompatible. Thus, regional social learning from the crisis may well consolidate the trend towards enhanced economic policy co-ordination. The next section looks at a range of circumstantial evidence that has emerged throughout the crisis—especially the debate over an Asian Monetary Fund—that points towards a need for a 'regionalization of thinking' on how to mitigate the kinds of economic problems visited on Asia since 1997.

## The Limits of Regional Co-operation: The United States and the Aborted Asian Monetary Fund

The abortive exercise, in the wake of the Thai and Korean currency crises, to set up an Asian Monetary Fund (AMF) is instructive. While it drew material and rhetorical support from a range of regional states, the United States refused to support it. To be capitalized initially at $100 billion, the AMF was to provide emergency regional support and avoid what many leaders saw as the humiliation of the IMF telling them how to readjust to the new circumstance. A proposal for an AMF made up only of East Asian states was in many ways an exercise in 'thinking East Asian' not dissimilar to the setting up of the East Asian Economic Caucus (EAEC) within APEC.[5]

Interestingly, and in contrast to the development of the EAEC proposal, Japan was willing to lead the proposal for an AMF. It took the initiative in trying to persuade the United States that it was additional to, not incompatible with, the IMF. But the proposal was insufficiently thought out and, with the benefit of hindsight, destined to fail. It was underwritten by, and verbally accompanied by, a large dose of 'Asian Way' hubris among its ASEAN supporters. Regional leaders had still not understood the power of the global financial markets, but the proposal's most naïve failing was to underestimate the strength of the opposition from the United States and the IMF, which felt it would not only undermine their ability to impose tough conditionality on loans but also act as a veritable threat to American interests and influence in Asia. Of course, other factors were salient, but the US desire for the IMF to control adjustment funding prevailed and its dominant role in the process was endorsed at the Vancouver APEC summit in November 1997.

This may, however, be a turning point for APEC. By opposing the proposal (more) seeds of polarization in the relationship between the Asian and Caucasian members of APEC were sown. The exhortatory liberalization rhetoric of the Vancouver APEC meeting only superficially concealed a deeper schism between the two edges of the Pacific. The economic turmoil reinforced the notion that the Asia-Pacific is an artificial construction of region, the long-term salience of which may well have been affected by the economic downturn and regional resentment at the US- and IMF-led responses to the crisis.

The euphoric expectation of the 1993–6 period—that APEC would provide firm institutional ties to mitigate interregional tensions between Asia and the United States—was clearly wishful thinking of a high order. Advocates of APEC championed 'open liberalism' in the region, assuming that it was benign and its enhancement uncontested. Much of the discussion on APEC throughout the first half of the 1990s saw only the benefits of free trade and none of the pitfalls of dramatic increases in deregulated, unrestricted capital mobility. APEC always found its strongest intellectual and political support among the American, Australian, and Canadian members. During the heyday of Asia-Pacific growth, the Asian members were willing to go along with its emerging program, although not necessarily at the pace the Caucasian members wished. In the post-crisis era things have changed. Thus, APEC—rather than being a potential instrument for trade liberalization at the Asia-Pacific level in which a harmony of interest developed between the member states—is seen in some policy communities of East Asia as but another forum in which the United States can hammer home its claim for further capital market liberalization.

Added to the problems now facing APEC, the failure of the AMF leaves us with an open question. Is it more or less likely that there will be further initiatives to provide some kind of regional economic co-operation, in general, and financial policy co-ordination, in particular? The answer is twofold. In the short run, no grand regional strategies are likely to be proposed. In the longer term, however, the international responses to the Asian crises may make the prospect for the increased management of East Asian (as opposed to Asia-Pacific) economic affairs all the more likely.

Indeed, both short-term practical and longer-term conceptual avenues of regional financial co-operation are being explored. Even the AMF idea has not died. At the practical level, ASEAN finance ministers (meeting in Manila in December 1997) inspired and agreed to a framework whereby member states would engage in the mutual surveillance of each other's economies. Such an agreement, unthinkable prior to the crisis, demonstrates a desire to enhance regional policy-making capabilities—especially in a period in which regional states will provide financial aid to each other's reform processes. This is an exercise in the recognition of the 'East Asianness' of the region. The crisis has been a spur to it. While it is anchored within the existing international financial institutional context, the Manila Agreement, as its full title indicates, is intended to 'Enhance Asian Regional Co-operation to Promote Financial Stability'.

The framework will offer a process of enhanced mutual IMF-style surveillance and Asian-style 'peer pressure'. In short, it represents a contribution to the regional institutional economic architecture that does not currently fit with any existing model. The Manila Agreement is very much part of the wider exercise of soul-searching now taking place both within ASEAN and between ASEAN and its other East Asian partners. ASEAN, especially, is facing an identity crisis so that it might be necessary to reconsider some aspects of the ASEAN way of 'non-interference' in the affairs of member states.

At a more exploratory and conceptual level, the idea of an AMF continues to resurface, as do other ideas, as regional states seek ways to stabilize their currencies. For example, there is the Malaysian proposal for local currency-based settlement of trade within ASEAN. In April 1998 a South Korean delegate to the Asian Neighbours Forum in Tokyo raised again the idea that Asian countries needed to think about an AMF, led by Japan, to maintain currency stability in the region. Similarly, the head of the Asian Development Bank Institute, Jesus Estanislao, has suggested that a system not unlike the European monetary system—in which Asian currencies would move against a currency basket consisting of the dollar, the yen, and the Euro—is not impossible in Asia.[6] The crucial point of these avenues of exploration is not their immediate significance. Nor is the point to underestimate the difficulties of such regional policy co-ordination. Rather, it is to suggest that we would be naïve to ignore the possibility that at some stage Asians will introduce greater regional institutional mechanisms for the common management of financial questions.

Those willing to deny the possibility of a common currency in Asia would do well to remember the fate of those similar analyses, emanating from the United States in the 1980s, that ridiculed the idea of a common European currency. The status of regional co-operation in Asia and Europe is, of course, very different. Interregional trade in Asia (at about 40 per cent) is not as concentrated as in Europe (at over 60 per cent); there is no free movement of peoples in Asia as there is within the European Union, and levels of institutionalization are not comparable. But there is a growing recognition in the region that Asian currency fluctuations do

not accurately, or fairly, reflect economic fundamentals. Asian policy communities are now fully
sensitized—in a way that they were not prior to
1997—to the degree to which small open
economies are vulnerable to the global financial
markets and the need to guard against this vulnerability. This, of course, is one of the reasons why the
Malaysian government introduced exchange controls in September 1998.

Whether endeavours to secure greater regional
financial policy co-ordination are contested or supported by the global financial markets will depend
on the nature of the institutional architecture envisaged. It will require a major Japanese leadership
role, both intellectually and by the internationalization of the yen. This, in turn, will depend on the
successful restructuring of the Japanese financial
system. It will also need support from the United
States, which is not currently forthcoming, and
from Europe, which, while less important, is more
likely if the Asia-Europe Meeting Process can
develop and the Euro becomes an important international currency. These discussions are for the
realm of future policy analysis. But whether the
Asians will be successful or not in their endeavours,
there can be little doubt that the exploration of
some form of AMF-style co-operation as a way to
combat vulnerability will be an item on the regional
policy agenda in the twenty-first century.

Given Asian desires to enhance regional surveillance and co-ordinating capacity, it might be
worth considering the nature of US objections to the
AMF. They offer insights into not only US policy but
also the wider relationship between global liberalization and regionalization. US policy towards an
incipient AMF reflects a private-sector desire for
continued financial liberalization, on the one hand,
and, on the other, domestic and international polit-
ical/bureaucratic institutional desire not to cede the
power of the international financial institutions—in
which the United States is dominant—to regional
institutions over which they would certainly have
less ideological/philosophical and practical control.
This two-prong rationale emanates from a wider
policy context—what Jagdish Bhagwati calls the
'Wall Street-Treasury Complex'.[7]

Bhagwati provides a compelling demonstration
of how the actors, values, and interest of the group
he identifies have been at the heart of the US and
IMF policy response to the recent crises in East Asia
in general and in opposition to an AMF in particular. This should comes as little surprise to the student of modern policy analysis. In the application
of values to policy, the Wall Street-Treasury complex, as with many other issue-oriented policy networks, exhibits the now well-understood epistemic
characteristics of a public- and private-sector policy community with strong shared normative values
and common causal, problem-solving methodolo-
gies. The Asian crisis, more than any other recent
example, demonstrates the influence of Washington over the international financial institutions.
Wall Street's concern was that an AMF-style organization would slow down the liberalization of Asian
financial markets.

The US response to the crises, inherent in IMF
policy, has been to liberalize trade, deregulate financial markets, and enhance disclosure rules. All, by
happy coincidence, coincide with the broader
aims—both before and after the crises—of US economic diplomacy in the region. As President Bill
Clinton's first Secretary of Commerce, Jeffrey
Garten, noted, the 'worsening financial flu will
lower Asian immunity to US business'.[8] There were
also more general foreign policy reasons for the
United States not wishing to see an AMF realized.
Most importantly, notwithstanding the declining
share of its quota in the organization, the United
States is still the dominant actor in the IMF. The
development of viable alternative organizations
would diminish its influence.

Moreover, US policy towards Asia over the last
decade, in both the economic and security domains,
has seen a gradual shift from a hub-and-spoke pattern of relations towards a greater multilateralism.
These evolving regional relationships were initially
resisted by the United States but gradually came to
be accepted in the context of a broad definition of
region as the Asia-Pacific, as opposed to the nar-
rower definition of East Asia. APEC, in the economic
domain, became acceptable as a vehicle for US
interests. Similarly, the ASEAN forum was acceptable

in the security domain because it was always secondary to the still dominant bilateral security structure. Viewed through American eyes, then, a successful AMF was not consistent with overall American interests. For many in the US foreign economic policy-making community the AMF seemed like a potential first step towards a yen zone.

With hindsight, US fears that an AMF would have weakened the American hold over the policy process in Asia, especially *vis-à-vis* the Japanese, appear grossly overstated. The AMF was never viewed by the Japanese as a competitor to the IMF, although it may have been by others such as Malaysian Prime Minister Dr Mahathir Mohamad. Japanese unwillingness to push the AMF in the face of US opposition represented a failure to break the 'occupation psychology'[9] in its relationship with the United States and, as a consequence, left other, more desperate regional élites no alternative but to acquiesce to the conditions imposed by the IMF programs. However, such is the perversity of international politics that US opposition to the proposal may well make a further attempt to initiate such a body—in less frenetic times—all the more inevitable.

## Regionalism and Globalism in Contest: The Myth of Convergence?

The economic troubles have caused many Asian political leaders to rediscover the rhetoric of popular nationalism as a way of deflecting domestic criticism. Across the most affected states a discourse of 'robbery' or of a 'new imperialism'—not heard since the years of the immediate post-colonial era—is very strong. This is not only in Malaysia, where Prime Minister Mahathir Mohamad has gone so far as to argue that Western governments and financiers have deliberately punished Asia for its arrogance and refusal to converge more quickly on an Anglo-American, liberal, approach to democracy, market opening, labour standards, and human rights. Similar themes could also be heard in Thailand, the Philippines, South Korea, and Indonesia. The implications of this for the global economy are precisely the opposite of what liberal(izer)s would wish.

Western political élites have underestimated the influence of scapegoat explanations of the crisis within the region. Asians were coming to understand and accept the workings of markets, but this understanding is less than one generation deep. Most Asians have only an instrumental feeling for the market, and there is no strongly socialized or cognitive belief in it. The treatment of East Asia by the financial markets in 1997–8 will have ambiguous longer-term results. While it may make Asian states more responsive to 'market disciplines' in the short run, it may also in the longer run make them more suspicious of them and it will certainly lead Asians to prefer tighter, rather than looser, market regulation. It might be all well and good for Western analysts to say that this is a partial reading of these processes, but perceptions count, and this perception has prevailed in East Asia since the 1997–8 crisis.

In this regard, the Asian crisis is a contest of ideology between Asian and Anglo-American ways of organizing capitalist production. Alan Greenspan, of the US Federal Reserve Bank, has publicly argued that the crisis in East Asia's currency markets will have the effect of moving East Asian economic practice closer to that associated with the US model.[10] In this regard, for many Western analysts, the crisis is a weapon in what they see as the normatively laudable process of convergence. Only time will tell if Greenspan is correct or not. One does not have to accept the cruder versions of this analysis—which suggest that the IMF is merely an instrument of US policy doing Treasury Secretary Robert Rubin's bidding in attempting to bring Asian economic policy-making into line with the dominant approach of the United States—to recognize an important test of intellectual will is in train.

What is questioned by regional leaders—of all political stripes—is the role of the IMF as an instrument of ideological change. Many of the adjustment packages are thought to have gone beyond traditional structural reform strategies, designed not only to restore stability to the regional financial markets and to reform banking sectors, but actually to contest the nature of the political process and the power base of the political élites of the region.

Whether this was normatively a good thing is of little concern to the argument presented here. It is more important to note that the policy communities in most affected states of East Asia believe that the IMF and its major members have taken a more intrusive role in their economic affairs than at any time since the beginning of the post-colonial era. It is a role that Asian leaders—from Jakarta to Tokyo—resent. It is seen as part of an attempt to secure a convergence towards the dominant Anglo-American form of economic development at a time of Asian weakness.

Asians appreciate that there are flaws in their economic system that do not serve it well. But uncontrollable movements of money are deemed to be as responsible for their current problems as are the idiosyncrasies of Asian political and social systems. In the first wave of the crises, it was easier to target the problems of crony capitalism and accept that these needed to be addressed. But continued violent movements of capital caused more and more members of the Asian public- and private-sector policy-making élite to resent the ineffectiveness and the inability of any existing international institutions to offer solutions other than to demand dramatic domestic structural adjustment within Asia.

Liberal economic internationalism is on trial in Asia at the end of the twentieth century. There appears to be little or no recognition of this in US policy circles. Nor is it always fully appreciated that its interventions may not always be fruitful or welcome. The crises, and Western responses to them, demonstrate the danger of interpreting Asian political and economic practice through Western-élite images. These kinds of analysis represent the unthinking assumption that the dynamics of globalization—defined as economic liberalization and political liberalism—will prove as attractive to Asian policy élites as they have to Western policy élites. In so doing, the likelihood of 'convergence' around an idealized Western system of economic management and political practice or an understanding of the culture of modernization as a homogenizing category is always going to be overstated. While there is some evidence of liberal influences finding their way into the élites of states such as Thailand, Korea, and Taiwan, clearly the actions of the Malaysian government in introducing capital controls in September 1998 indicate that other approaches to finding a way out of the crisis had some sway. Moreover, Malaysia's actions have been viewed favourably by government spokesmen in Beijing and Tokyo. The often wholesale generalized assumptions of Western policy élites—that a convergence embodying universal interests will create an Asia more like the liberal stereotypes—lack sound empirical foundations.

If this chapter is a correct reading of Asian élite opinion, it should act as a moderating influence on some analyses that have come from Western scholars and analysts since late 1997. It is a reading that suggests longer-term implications for the international relations of the Asia-Pacific region. The regional economic meltdown has shown Asian observers what they believe to be the darker side of globalization. This has both broader intellectual-cum-ideological implications and more specific policy implications for the relationship between Asia and the wider global economic order.

At the wider level, the crucial lesson is that the Asian crisis, contrary to triumphalist arguments, is not the vindication of the convergence hypothesis that much neoclassical economic analysis would like to assume. The crisis confirms the differences in systemic capitalist organization rather than refutes them. Asian leaders may parrot the language of neo-liberalism within the context of APEC gatherings, but much of it is still opposed in practice. Unlike those non-governmental members of the transnational political community within the regional organizations such as PECC (Pacific Economic Co-operation Conference)—especially Caucasian members—Asian political leaders have always been more instrumental than cognitive in their commitment to neo-liberalism. This general assertion has specific political implications.

For many Asians the feeling that there was an exploitative element in the Pacific economic relationship was never eradicated from fora such as APEC throughout the 1990s. The nature of the IMF crisis reform packages and the overt 'power politics' manner in which they were imposed have brought a North-South divide back into the open in the relationship between the Caucasian and East Asian members of APEC. Indeed, the downsizing of the economic status of the Asian states has rendered redundant the discourse of the 'miracle NICs' and reconstituted a 'Third World', 'us-them', 'haves-have-nots' dependency discourse not too dissimilar to that which prevailed in the 1970s when a call for a New International Economic Order dominated North-South relations.

Such feelings give rise to resentment and resistance not only within the domestic polities and societies of the region but also at the level of the transregional policy-making communities, such as APEC, that had supposedly been making strides towards greater economic dialogue and harmonization of economic policy across the Asia-Pacific. The crisis demonstrated the limits of APEC. As a body capable of making decisions of regional utility it was paralysed by the crisis. The United States drove through the IMF reform packages at the Vancouver summit. In so doing, the crisis has made the gap across the Pacific greater rather than smaller and the inherent tensions more transparent. As a consequence, putative regional economic co-operation—through groupings like the EAEC and the exploration of regional monetary co-operation—may prove more conducive to the longer-term interests of regional policy élites than APEC. Unlike APEC, the EAEC is unambiguously 'regional' and may prove a more comfortable ideological venue for East Asia's political leaders in the era of the new economic reality.

Competing IMF and Asian views of how to manage the regional economic order are delicately balanced. For many of the region's policy communities the crisis confirms the dangers of too much economic liberalization. Asian policy élites may not have solutions, but it is clear to them that there is a problem with the management of the international economic system. We do not have a functioning system of multilevel governance, nor do we have any longer a hegemonic one. The role of the United States is vital, but it is not still hegemonic in the manner envisaged by hegemonic stability theory. Indeed, we need to reassess the role of the United States. Certainly, it is in the Asian region that this reassessment will be most acute in the twenty-first century.

## Conclusion

What the Asian crisis tells us is that there is no consensus on how to manage international capitalism at the end of the twentieth century. The major financial institutions are caught between nationalists and liberals with competing views of how the world should work. These institutions have proved to be lead-footed by comparison with the speed at which markets operate. The international financial institutions (IFIs) have been found wanting in both theory and practice by the events in East Asia. Thus, the desire to enhance supervision of private cross-border flows, especially foreign direct investment in emerging markets, can be expected to grow in the wake of the recent experiences in East Asia.

Nothing is likely to shake the view—held in many Asian capitals—that the markets' punishment of the weaknesses in Asia's financial systems, real as they are, far exceeded the crime. We must expect not only Asians but others to ask what good openness to global capital markets might serve? If the economic crisis in East Asia is to provide a positive learning experience at the multilateral level—as opposed to a negative, resentment-generating learning experience at the regional level—it must trigger a discussion of how to combat the knee-jerk assumption that the unfettered movement of capital (especially short-term lending) is axiomatically a good thing. This is no radical question. As even the *Financial Times* noted, 'the wisdom of over-hasty integration of emerging economies into global financial markets must be reconsidered.'[11]

Thus the events of 1997–8—the most traumatic experienced in Asia since decolonization and the Cold War confrontations of the 1950s and 1960s—also have spawned lessons for Asian regionalism. The crises have sidetracked policy élites from the regional dialogue activities—trade liberalization and security—popular throughout the first half of the 1990s. In this context, ASEAN, as the activist leader of wider Asian regional dialogues, has lost its way since 1997. As the immediate crisis recedes and policy élites begin to think again more constructively about the regional cooperative agenda, the events of 1997–8 will need to be put into clearer analytical perspective.

We can expect the development of multilevel regionalism to continue. In one way or another, East Asia will be a pillar of it. In addition to the role of the United States, the future of the region after the crisis is also now more firmly tied to the role of the two indigenous Asian superpowers than at any time in the past. Specifically, the future of the region depends not only on Japanese economic reform, but also on a willingness of China to continue the new-found regional economic role that it has been so keen to consolidate since the return of Hong Kong and advent of the economic crisis in 1997.

The first few years of the twenty-first century may represent something of a hiatus for Asian regionalism, and other forms of economic and security institutional diplomacy may come to the fore—concerted bilateralism on a range of issues, for example—but governments always operate with a portfolio of bilateral, regional, and multilateral interests and instruments. Regionalism will

continue to be an important level of activity, probably less as an arena of dramatic initiative and more as a meso-level expression of the desire to optimize sovereign decision-making within states in the face of globalization.

The Asia-Pacific, as constituted by the membership of APEC, may continue to form an outer regional shell. Broad economic philosophies, principally liberal in nature, will continue to underpin both the rhetoric of inner core and outer shell—especially a commitment to a broadly defined multilateral trading system. The economic crisis will continue to ensure reform of a market-opening nature in the trade arena. But there will be a different regional spin towards these global issues in East Asia that will reflect more strongly Asian political, cultural, and economic experiences, and this distinctly Asian view may lead to enhanced Asian policy responses to the major global economic questions of our time. East Asian policy-makers may be less willing in the early stages of the next century to subscribe as unreflectively to the tenets of neo-liberalism—especially in the financial sector—than they have been in the closing stages of this century.

## Notes

1  'Crisis' is used here as a generic term to cover a range of currency and financial crises that began in Thailand and spread to other Asian countries throughout 1997 and 1998.

2  Mortimer Zucherman, 'A Second American Century', *Foreign Affairs* 77, 3 (1998).

3  Robert Wade and Frank Venerose, 'The Asian Crisis: The High Debt Model versus the Wall Street-Treasury-IMF Complex', *New Left Review* 228 (Mar.-Apr. 1998).

4  Richard Stubbs, 'War and Economic Development: Export-Oriented Industrialization in East and Southeast Asia', *Comparative Politics* (31 Apr. 1999).

5  See Richard Higgott and Richard Stubbs, 'Competing Conceptions of East Asian Regionalism:

APEC versus the EAEC in the Asia Pacific', *Review of International Political Economy* 2, 3 (1995).

6  *Nikkei Weekly*, 23 Mar. 1998, 12; 25 May 1998, 23.

7  Jagdish Bhagwati, 'The Capital Myth: The Difference Between Trade in Widgets and Trade in Dollars', *Foreign Affairs* 77, 3 (1998): 11.

8  *New York Times*, 14 Jan. 1998.

9  Walden Bello, 'East Asia: On the Eve of the Great Transformation', *Review of International Political Economy* 5, 3 (1998).

10  Annual Convention of the Independent Bankers Association of America, 3 Mar. 1998. http://bog.frb.fed.us/board/docs/speeches/19980 303.htm.

11  *Financial Times*, 16 Jan. 1998, 18.

## Suggested Readings

Kwan, C.H., Donna Vandenbrink, and Chia Siow Yue, eds. *Coping with Capital Flow in East Asia*. Singapore: Institute of Southeast Asian Studies and Nomura Research Institute, 1998.

*Review of International Political Economy* 5, 3 (1998).

Woo-Cumings, Meredith, ed. *The Developmental State*. Ithaca, NY: Cornell University Press, 1999.

## Web Sites

South China Morning Post: http:\\www.scmp.com\

Ministry of Foreign Affairs of Japan, Japan-Asia-Pacific Relations: http:\\www.mofa. go.jp/region/asia-paci/index.html

Far Eastern Economic Review Interactive Edition: http:\\www.feer.com\

Trade and Development Report, 1998: http:\\www.unicc.org\unctad\en\pub\ps1tdr98.htm

*Chapter 21*

# The Return to Europe:
## The Future Political Economy of Eastern Europe

*Jeanne Kirk Laux*

The question of whether and how to integrate Eastern Europe into the political economy, civilization, and security nexus of Western Europe has troubled European and transatlantic debate for a very long time. The end of the Cold War brought with it the promise of the fulfilment of two post-World War II dreams—the European dream of building a regional security order based on common social and economic interests; and the American dream of extending market economics and democratic institutions into a worldwide liberal order. To realize these dreams, in 1989 after the elections in Poland and Hungary, all the wealthy industrial countries responded positively to the G–7 invitation to co-ordinate aid. The member states of the Organization for Economic Co-operation and Development (OECD) pledged to give assistance 'conditional upon political stability in the country concerned, and a continuing commitment to democratic ideals and free market principles'.[1] Country after country in Eastern Europe renounced its Communist past and turned for support to Western governments or the international institutions sponsored by them—from Bretton Woods to Brussels. And they found it. Western governments mobilized assistance and reoriented international institutions to offer funds, tutelage, and, in some instances, membership to ensure the end of official communism and Soviet hegemony.

Now, a decade after the collapse of communism and the breakup of the Soviet Union, the *post-*Cold War era is over. It is clear that there is no such thing as an Eastern European region. Instead, there has been a 'return to Europe'. In the East, most governments pushed to be accepted into the established institutions of market economics and Western security. Once Poland, Hungary, and the Czech Republic were invited in 1997 into that Western bastion, the NATO alliance, the possibility was proven. In the West, new regimes of regional governance have been put in place. These are centred in the European Union (EU) and NATO, both of which assume the right to set the agenda for the new European order based on Western liberal norms. There are no longer any serious alternative regional arrangements in the area once known as Eastern Europe.

In this new Europe-in-the-making, autonomous policy-making is not possible for the former Communist countries. All the 'countries in transition' (CIT) are reconstructing states, institutions, and civil societies within a well-articulated process of regional governance. Many speak of the 'internationalization of foreign policy' to signify the worldwide limits on state autonomy set by interlocking processes of globalization, multilateralism, and regionalism. All the more is this true for the CIT, where both foreign policy and domestic politics are intermediated by those Western governments and transnational élites that act as gatekeepers to liberal/Western international institutions. They oversee what I will call *enabling regimes*, such as the European Union's 'Europe Agreements' and the OECD's 'Partners in Transition', intended to encourage democratization and market opening. Even those CIT, such as Ukraine, which herald their new nationalism, do so defensively, by reference to the norms or sanctions originating elsewhere.

Is everything then settled? Not so fast. Even with the return to Europe and an interlocking set of regional governance regimes to assist the transition, there are risks for the future political economy and security order in Europe. The challenge now is how to accommodate those CIT (mainly Central European and Baltic states) that have fully embraced the return to Europe in their institutional practices without constellating new 'others' (mainly former Soviet republics) that are excluded, whether by Western sanctions or by opting out. How, in other words, is Europe to be redefined through remaking institutions without redividing it along new fault lines?

Before previewing this chapter's agenda, I should say a word about exactly what is, or was, 'Eastern Europe'? The answer is elusive. On a map it is easy to find Russia, Ukraine, or those 12 former republics of the Soviet Union now loosely reconnected as the Commonwealth of Independent States (CIS). From the territory of what was the USSR, we can regroup countries into Central Asia at one geographical and cultural extreme or the Baltic states at the other. There's more. European history won't let us forget the Balkans, otherwise known as Southeastern Europe, nor traditional *mitteleuropa* or Central Europe, where many governments claim resident status and Poland, Hungary, and the Czech Republic certainly have it. Students of international political economy are better off using the term employed by many international organizations: 'countries in transition'. This term refers to all countries that (1) were formerly Marxist-Leninist party-states, (2) adopted some version of a planned economy (even if only to reject it later, as did Yugoslavia), and (3) now renounce that heritage. In all the CIT, elections have established post-Communist governments that (even when composed of former Communists!) officially espouse market economics and/or liberal democracy. Although everyone knows the script, the transition stage presents a changing cast of actors. In the first stage of transition (1989–91), there were a possible nine emerging market democracies, whereas today there are 27 CIT (after the breakup of the USSR and Yugoslavia, the division of Czechoslovakia, and the unification of the Germany). The Czech Republic, invaded by Soviet troops in 1968, now

has two sovereign states between itself and the Russian border! The implosion/explosion of sovereignty makes the very notion of a region volatile and turns the mind back to the dissolution of the Austro-Hungarian and Ottoman Empires after World War I.

This chapter will now present the case for the end of the post-Cold War period by showing how liberal/Western institutions in Europe have reconfigured to shape the transition away from communism and planned economies and how many CIT seek a 'return to Europe', thereby invalidating any other regional alternatives. I will then demonstrate how regional governance, centred on the European Union and NATO, makes policy autonomy obsolete as some CIT are co-opted into membership and others scramble to reduce uncertainty over future access. The risks of regional governance based on liberalism as a right to exclusion are indicated in the concluding section.

## The End of the Post-Cold War: The Return to Europe

In Europe the fall of the Berlin Wall raised hopes of erasing an ideological divide, rethinking the bipolar set of security institutions, and opening markets to create a single pan-European geopolitical and civilizational space. Just before the twentieth century bows out, these three hopes have been realized. This means the post-Cold War era is over. It has ended thanks to a threefold process of (1) reconfiguring institutions by the West, once Soviet institutions collapsed; (2) reorienting foreign policy in the East by governments keen to return to Europe; and, in consequence, (3) marginalizing alternative organizations that might rival those underpinned by Western/liberal norms.

How has the end of the post-Cold War come about? Once the euphoria at the collapse of communism dissolved into concern about the disintegration of the Soviet Union, civil war in Yugoslavia, and precarious economic reforms in Central Europe, the Western governments that had been mobilizing financial and technical assistance to the CIT recognized the need for longer-term strategies to salvage the transition. Not reforms alone, but democratization consistent with Western liberal norms and market opening compatible with the liberalizing global political economy were required. And the driving force would be international institutions. The leading Western economic powers, the G–7, were clear: the priority must be 'to further the integration of these countries in the open international economic system'. To do so, 'governments, the European Community and international institutions should concentrate on helping this essential, market-based transformation.'[2]

A panoply of multilateral organizations moved into the breach left by the collapse of Soviet regional hegemony. As well, a brand new international financial institution, the European Bank for Reconstruction and Development (EBRD), was created, at French initiative, specifically to finance the transition economies. Many examples—from the Council of Europe to the Bank for International Settlements (BIS)—could illustrate the institutional reconfiguration in Europe that has successfully reoriented the policy-making expectations and possibilities for the countries in transition. Here I will look quickly at one universal Bretton Woods organization, the World Bank, and one Euro-Atlantic organization, the OECD, originally set up to co-ordinate the reconstruction of Western Europe after World War II. (A more detailed examination of the role of the European Union comes below.)

The World Bank jumped into the transition process early, moving out from its near-exclusive Third World focus. Even before the former USSR applied for membership, the Bank, along with other organizations such as the International Monetary Fund (IMF) and the OECD, took part in a 'needs assessment' mission to Moscow as requested by the G–7. By 1991, the Bank had signed structural adjustment loans (which support stabilization or economic liberalization programs rather than a specific project) with five CIT. Its board of governors voted an extra US$5 billion designated for the CIT. The breakup of the USSR prompted exceptional funding—for example, a $30-million technical co-operation facility. The former planned economies moved quickly to join the Bank. During

the Cold War, only four Eastern European countries had been active members, whereas the Bank's current membership includes 25 countries in transition. New members justified the creation of a new regional vice-presidency for Europe and Central Asia and a division devoted to 'Transition Economies'. Twelve new field offices were established in Hungary, Albania, and the former USSR. Overall Bank lending to the CIT, just 3 per cent in 1989, now hovers around 16 per cent—for example, in 1997, US$4.3 billion went to 12 transition countries.[3] The Bank's chief economist for the region considered its support to market opening in Eastern Europe as 'surely one of the World Bank's most difficult challenges', which 'rivals even the post-World War II rebuilding of Western Europe'.[4]

The OECD, which regroups Western industrial countries (including Japan), assiduously expanded activities in support of the transition to market economies in the 1990s. Although not a bank or an operational aid agency with funds to transfer, the OECD could offer tutelage in market economics and eventually validation of a CIT's conformity with liberal norms. Here the initiative came from the East when five Central European countries asked for membership over 1989–90 and the USSR sent delegates looking for advisers to prepare its privatization program. Following an investigative mission by its secretary-general, the Executive Council of the OECD set up a new unit, the Centre for Co-operation with Economies in Transition, to channel requests for assistance from the East to the operational directorates and to co-ordinate the resulting projects. Thirty new posts were created for work on the transition and a new Central Europe division was established in the key Economics and Statistics directorate. A flurry of study missions, workshops, and publications followed—e.g., the Group on Privatization met twice a year to permit consultation between OECD experts and officials from Poland, Hungary, and Czechoslovakia. By 1996 the Centre had policy-oriented assistance strategies under way for another eight CIT in Central and Eastern Europe and in 12 former Soviet republics. Most importantly, the OECD put three countries on a fast track to membership by creating a Partners in Transition program that allowed the select (Hungary, Poland, and later the Czech Republic) to participate in OECD committee work.[5]

Such institutional outreach by dozens of organizations has had an enormous impact, drawing all CIT into membership or associative status in Western/liberal institutions. The reconfiguring of institutions was, however, only possible because of the reorientation by post-Communist governments ready to espouse liberal, even neo-liberal, norms and to spurn co-operation among formerly fraternal allies. What I am calling the *return to Europe* signifies the common thrust of transition foreign policy that seeks full access to global markets and Western security regimes and full recognition as being Europeans in the liberal tradition. Their particular interpretation of what liberalism means in practice is another story, of course. None the less, all CIT formally accept the principles and articulate the ambition. Already in 1991, when the EBRD opened its doors in London every post-Communist government, including the USSR, signed Articles of Agreement that formally committed them to 'the fundamental principles of multiparty democracy, the rule of law, respect for human rights and market economics'.[6] This oath both qualified the CIT for assistance and helped consolidate power at home by demarcating new governments from their discredited Marxist-Leninist past. With the collapse of Soviet-sponsored economic and security institutions, it became imperative for all CIT to find new institutional homes—especially the Central Europeans anxious to avoid any renewed Russian sphere of influence.

Once Hungary, Poland, and the Czech Republic were invited into the OECD, NATO, and (with Estonia and Slovenia) the European Union, it became clear that different patterns of reform or styles of parliamentary politics could lead to the same end—reintegration into the heartland institutions of Western liberalism. Beyond immediate security or economic needs the return to Europe projects a desire to rediscover civilizational identity (most overtly in Central Europe). Trying to erase history, the Czech Prime Minister stated at the OECD admission ceremony that he was 'sure that

had it not been for communism the Czech Republic would have been a founding father of the OECD together with other developed nations'.[7] The European Union more than mirrors these civilizational yearnings when it proclaims that the CIT had been cut off from 'the mainstream of European development' and 'now desire to resume their central place in Europe's culture and civilisation.'[8]

Farther east, in the Commonwealth of Independent States, attitudes towards Western liberal conditionality and the return to Europe are more convoluted. These are the countries probably consigned to permanent 'partnership' status with NATO and not welcomed at the EU table. None the less, it would appear that all now recognize the inevitability of the return to Europe and are trying to bargain for a more inclusive definition of the region. For example, the European Union links its assistance to the CIS to Partnership and Co-operation Agreements (PCAs) it signs with each state.[9] These are based on 'shared principles and objectives' such as 'respect for the rule of law and human rights', 'free and democratic elections', and 'a functioning market economy'.[10] Belarus signed a PCA with the EU in March 1995, despite its President's determined sabotage of parliamentary procedure and preference for an administered economy. The European Commission felt obliged within the year to postpone its promised balance-of-payments lending 'due to unsatisfactory progress in reforming the economy'.[11] The Partnership and Co-operation Agreement remains, however, and Belarus officials claim to be liberalizing in their own way. In sum, the policy reference point remains liberal Europe.

The return to Europe also indicates the end of 'Eastern Europe' in that there are no viable region-wide alternative institutions in the zone once covered by Soviet hegemony. In the security realm, Russia clearly preferred to see NATO dissolved and to rely on the pan-European Organization for Security and Co-operation in Europe (OSCE), with its 57 members and consensus decision-making.[12] A compromise to maintain NATO while minimizing the threat to Russia—the Partnerships for Peace program—was founded by the United States in 1994.[13] Despite continuing Russian objections,

NATO has 'enhanced' the Partnership for Peace program and expanded the tasks assigned its 44-member Euro-Atlantic Partnership Council. Although in each 'Distinctive Partnership Charter' with associated states NATO tips its hat to promoting security 'in co-operation with other international organisations such as the OSCE',[14] once the Western military alliance invited in three former Warsaw Pact members at the Madrid summit in 1997, the marginalization of any other security regime was confirmed.

In the economics realm, subregional economic co-operation groupings among CIT have emerged—notably the Central European Free Trade Agreement (CEFTA), which has expanded to become a useful waiting room for those not yet entering the European Single Market. There is also an inclusive policy consultative body, known as the Eastern and European Economic Summit, which brings together heads of state, central bankers, and company officials to discuss economic options, thereby creating a space for complaint if not co-operation.[15] All such fora are helpful, but finally marginal. Regionalism for the CIT fundamentally means access to European and international institutions grounded in traditions of liberalism and guided by the leading Western powers. Eastern Europe no longer exists as a geopolitical option. It is in this sense that the post-Cold War period is truly over. Now the parameters of policy-making are set by new regional governance regimes, centred in NATO and the European Union. A close-up look at the European Union's enlargement agenda will show how regional dynamics for the CIT are being shaped by Western, liberal governance.

## Regional Governance and Euroconformity

Once the initial transfer of political power was secured in Central and Eastern Europe, the overarching purpose of all Western assistance to the CIT has been to ensure a normative and institutional compatibility between post-Communist transition and global political economy. This objective involves two components: extending globalization to the region and applying global governance to particular post-Communist political economies. *Globalization*

refers, in my definition, to three ongoing processes of political economy: (1) the worldwide competitive practices of transnational capital; (2) the global extension of liberal values as the premise for policy-making; and (3) the global regulation of unequal exchange no longer undertaken by a single hegemonic state but by a transnational élite network working through a set of interlinked international institutions. *Global governance* creates the explicit superstructure needed to anchor the second and third processes of globalization in each national setting. It refers to those norms, rules, and procedures articulated by globalizing élites and intended to constrain national policy-making and harmonize practices across states and/or international institutions in the absence of formal legal authority.[16] In Europe, between globalization and the practices of national governments lies regional governance. The regional face of global governance now centres on the European Union's enlargement agenda (with its counterpart in the security sphere being the NATO enlargement strategy). The EU, like NATO and the OECD, has set up intermediate arrangements, or *enabling regimes*, between outsiders and insiders. These normative and regulatory frameworks permit and often oblige harmonization of national policies. Galvanized by their ambition to return to Europe, policy-makers in the CIT must now prove their *Euroconformity* or face the ultimate sanction—exclusion.

The European Union is not shy about its ambitions. At the Luxembourg European Council in December 1997, where the first former Communist countries were invited to begin negotiations for membership, the 15 EU heads of state and government declared that 'With the launch of the enlargement process we see the dawn of a new era, finally putting an end to the divisions of the past. Extending the European integration model to encompass the whole of the continent is a pledge of future stability and prosperity.'[17] The brief history of the EU Europe Agreements—signed with three, four, six, then finally 10 CIT between 1991 and 1996—is a prime example of the way regional governance shapes the expectations and possibilities for policy-making in the countries in transition. At the Copenhagen European Council (June 1993) the EU's agreements with the CIT took on the critical normative and geopolitical functions that now transcend, all the while defining, their trade policy content. After the Council approved a White Paper on preparing for membership, virtually all EU assistance (the Phare programs) has become linked to 'pre-accession', a process centred on the approximation of laws and institutional adaptation. This is the crux of Euroconformity.

Having refused for some years to entertain the notion that former Communist countries could ever join, the 1993 European summit in Copenhagen issued a stunning statement:

> The European Council today agreed that associated countries in Central and Eastern Europe that so desire shall become members of the European Union. Accession will take place as soon as an associated country is able to assume the obligations of membership by satisfying the economic and political conditions required. . . . [including] stability of institutions guaranteeing democracy, the rule of law, human rights and respect for and protection of minorities, the existence of a functioning market economy. . . .[18]

At the Essen Council a year later, after much internal wrangling, ministers finally announced that they had 'decided on a comprehensive strategy' to prepare the post-Communist countries for accession by using two approaches—political and economic.[19] The political component would be implemented by so-called 'structured dialogue' or regularly scheduled meetings between EU and Central European officials. This component, now known as the Association Council, has been embellished to create a wider European Conference where all aspirants meet with member states on a regular basis at the level of heads of state or ministers of foreign affairs. Those left out of the serious process of accession, like Turkey, none the less are invited to attend. The economic component of association aimed at integration into the internal market of the European Community (now Union). Here the focus has been on what Eurotalk calls the

'acquis' or the cumulative regime of European regulations, laws, and so forth. To facilitate integration, two policy instruments were created in 1995 that have since served to frame policy-making in the aspirant CIT. First, a White Paper detailed requirements that candidates for membership must meet and backed them up by obliging the European Commission to submit an annual report to the General Affairs Council on progress towards adoption of the community's internal market rules. Second, the Phare program was revised to prepare the associated CIT for accession.

With the White Paper, the EU moved from being an external actor negotiating assistance with recipient governments to become a participant in policy formation working through transnational élite networks. The paper 'identifies the key measures in each sector and suggests the sequence in which approximation of legislation could be tackled.' Legislation cannot, however, suffice, 'for without the necessary institutional changes, the adoption of internal market legislation could result in a merely formal transposition of rules.'[20] To carry out its new governance responsibilities, the EU directed Phare to narrow its focus and concentrate on the associated CIT. To do so, Phare delegations expanded their advisory function within the administration of those recipient governments. The consolidation of reform, in the Commission's view, required Phare to focus on 'the development of new institutions within government and also non-governmental organisations which have a role to play in the operation and regulation of a democratic, market-oriented system'.[21]

In the Central and Eastern European countries, which of course had not before been recipients of Western foreign assistance, the EU put in place aid co-ordination units and other Project Management Units (PMUs) to facilitate project implementation and thereby build a complex of élite networks. The crucial PMU is the Phare co-ordination office in every recipient country capital that interfaces with Brussels. In Poland, for example, the Office for Assistance was set up by the cabinet alongside the Office for European Integration. The PMU for Phare's pre-accession program was also located in this office. By mid-1995 Phare had put in place in Poland some 40 PMUs with 800 experts on the Phare payroll, of which 80 were EU country citizens. One EU adviser in another CIT capital explained to me that he had spent five years in the PMU, first representing the EU—teaching CIT officials Phare procedures to facilitate getting project funding—and then turning around officially to represent the recipient government in its negotiations with Brussels!

Euroconformity now galvanizes policy-makers in 10 associated countries to align along European standards. This policy conditionality is consensual but unavoidable if the rendezvous with Europe is to be met. The communiqué after the 1997 Luxembourg summit clearly described the process: 'The task in the years ahead will be to prepare the applicant States for accession . . . [in an] ongoing process, which will take place in stages; each of the applicant States will proceed at its own rate, depending on its degree of preparedness.' The carrot is followed by the stick: financial assistance will 'be linked to the applicants' progress and, more specifically, to compliance with the program for adoption of the acquis.' Some CIT showed others how to be fast off the mark. The Hungarian government announced its own two-stage timetable for harmonizing legislation in line with the Europe Agreements and began to draft legislation on patent rights, foreign exchange, environmental protection, and so forth even before the EU White Paper went into effect. This policy agenda was submitted to the EU presidency and, following public and parliamentary debate in Hungary, the program for approximation of legislation was approved.[22] The Hungarian government made it clear that its modernization program derived from its acceptance of the agenda set in Brussels, in that it entails 'efficient restructuring of the economy and transformation of the domestic institutional system in line with current European norms and with regard to the long-term development trends in the EU'.[23]

Regional governance elaborated by the EU will continue to shape policy-making in the CIT even now that the first five candidate countries have been accepted as future members and promises

have been made to the second five (Romania, Lithuania, Latvia, Slovakia, and Bulgaria). The invitation to membership issued at the Luxembourg summit came only after the European Parliament approved the Commission's report specifying the main reforms required of each CIT.[24] New institutions and legislation are expected to correspond to both the norms and specific practices of the European communities. The conditionality of other international institutions reinforces this approach. For example, when Hungary started admission talks with the OECD, it was obliged to approve over 200 OECD resolutions or recommendations and to allow OECD experts to examine Hungarian legislation. Non-conformity with Western standards meant rejection: 'This is why Parliament amended the law on financial institutions . . . enabling foreign tax authorities to look into the accounts of their taxpayers in Hungary.'[25] The World Bank and the EBRD now defer to the EU's central role in governance. They decided 'to join forces in supporting the EU accession of Central and Eastern European countries' and co-finance projects that 'foster the adoption of EU legislation, including the implementation of EU norms and standards in the public and private sectors'.[26]

The European Union has thus created an extraordinary enabling regime through the Europe Agreements and in the process confirmed its central role in redefining the wider European political economy. The European Council in no way pulled back from its tutelary governance role following the opening of formal negotiations for membership in March 1998. Conflicted by its own inability to settle the institutional reforms and budgetary commitments needed for enlargement, the Council, in June 1998, emphasized that eventual accession would require even closer ties to the EU with 'political dialogue and tailored strategies to help them prepare for accession'. The European 15 needed (once again) to resolve their own debates over institutional restructuring by ratifying the Amsterdam Treaty. Even then, the President of the European Parliament was frank regarding continuing tutelage for the CIT: 'I don't think it's possible to do everything by 2001–2006.'[27]

## Redefining Europe: Why Draw New Lines?

The current challenge is this: can regional governance based on Euroconformity define Europe without redividing it? Insiders, outsiders, and in-between—increasingly there is a three-tier Europe in the making. With the NATO enlargement process there are three new members, 26 partners, and 'distinctive' charters for some of these partners. Russia tolerates the new NATO, but barely. It called the Madrid summit that brought in the new members the 'worst mistake' since World War II! And, of course, Austria, Sweden, Finland, and Switzerland hold to their traditions by being observers only. In the EU enlargement process five CIT can be admitted 'if'; five other CIT signed agreements but are consigned to a long-term waiting room; and many CIS countries are not even admitted to that room. Living with the ultimate power of exclusion means constant policy uncertainty for the CIT, and increasingly this is begrudged. At the 1998 Eastern and European Economic Summit, one of those left in the waiting room, Bulgaria's Prime Minister, invoked the risk of more Serbian dictators to underscore that 'We have no alternative to rapid integration' and asked the EU for 'a clear schedule of the accession rather than generalities and promises in principle'.[28]

Less obvious but worrisome is the dividing line between richer and poorer, which sometimes corresponds to a cultural dividing line between Christian and Muslim. The OECD, more specifically its Development Assistance Committee (DAC) composed of all the world's official aid donor countries, has redefined some former Communist countries as developing countries. In 1993, the five Central Asian republics were made eligible for official development assistance, as was Albania. Georgia, Armenia, and Azerbaijan have since been added to the list. This designation may be helpful in increasing their concessional aid, but it also may have the effect of separating out those 'less European' states from those more readily able to be co-opted into the regional governance regimes.

In conclusion, the post-Cold War era is over and the dynamics of regionalism for what was Eastern Europe now centre on reintegration through liberal/Western international institutions—in particular, the European Union and NATO. Both foreign policy and domestic politics in the CIT are intermediated by regional governance—the liberal norms and rules set by transnational élites acting as gatekeepers for international institutions. Most post-Communist governments are committed to a return to Europe and no serious institutional alternatives exist. The end of the post-Cold War and the elaboration of European regional governance are promising. Despite Bosnia and Kosovo, there is, overall, a surprising stability and, in most countries, a welcome democratization. Yet the end of the post-Cold War is also worrying. Governance predicated on the possibility of exclusion draws dividing lines among the former Communist countries. The challenge of redefining without redividing Europe is not yet met. Should it fail, the risk is not another world war, but of creating a three-tier Europe where the values of regionalism over classical sovereignty may be squandered—values of enhanced welfare (wealth and well-being) and security (stability and identity) for all.

## Notes

1   European Community, *Phare–1992*, 2 (this is the annual report on assistance to Central and Eastern Europe and the Baltics). At the Paris summit (July 1989) the G–7 charged the European Community with co-ordinating assistance to the transition. Once the (then) 24 members of the OECD approved their senior experts' report on needs, the Directorate General of External Relations in Brussels set up a task force known as the G–24. This assistance regime mobilized some $70 billion (US) in bilateral and multilateral financing before fading out over 1995–6 in favour of institutionalized co-operation with the countries in transition.

2   Group of Seven, 'Economic Declaration: Building World Partnership', London, 17 July 1991, 5–6.

3   World Bank newsletter, *Transition* (Aug. 1997): 28.

4   Christine I. Wallich, 'What's Right and Wrong with World Bank Involvement in Eastern Europe', paper presented to the conference on The Role of International Financial Institutions in Eastern Europe, Munich, 12–14 Apr. 1994, 34.

5   OECD, *CCET Activities Report 1993* (Paris, 1994) and *Transition Brief* (CCET Newsletter) no. 2 (Winter 1996). The articles governing OECD membership require a unanimous invitation from the member states conditional upon respect for the norms and practices of liberal democracy and market economy.

6   Agreement Establishing the European Bank for Reconstruction and Development, 29 May 1990.

7   *Transition Brief* no. 2 (Winter 1996).

8   This typical Phare (European assistance to the CIT) program rhetoric is cited from Phare's Web page: www.europa.eu.int/dg1a/phare

9   Unlike the European Agreements to be discussed below, these Partnership and Co-operation Agreements do no involve associative status or potential membership in the EU.

10   European Commission, The Tacis Programme, *Annual Report*, 1995 (Brussels, 22 July 1996), Com (96) 345 final. Tacis: Technical Assistance to the Commonwealth of Independent States.

11   Ibid.

12   The OSCE is a vestige of détente politics in the 1970s when negotiation of the Helsinki Accords created an ongoing review process among the 35 signatory states, known then as the Conference for Security and Co-operation in Europe (CSCE).

13   These partnerships gave some operational component to the political consultations with the CIT in the North Atlantic Co-operation Council (NACC—now renamed the Euro-Atlantic Partnership Council) set up in 1991.

14   NATO Basic Texts, 'Charter on a Distinctive Partnership between NATO and Ukraine (9 July 1997), Internet: www.nato.org

15   CEFTA, created in 1991, promotes regional trade among Hungary, the Czech Republic, Poland, Slovakia, Romania, and Slovenia. Six other CIT have asked to join and are admitted as observers to CEFTA meetings: Bulgaria, Croatia, Macedonia, Latvia, Lithuania, and Ukraine.

16   My definition is an amalgam of concepts put forward by Cox, Keohane, Gill, and Rosenau. For example, the third globalization process is what Robert Cox calls 'the internationalization of the state' in his major theoretical work, *Production, Power and World Order: Social Forces in the Making of History* (New York: Columbia University Press, 1987). Also, I am considering governance 'from above', as Richard Falk puts it, rather than the global ambitions and actions of social movements or non-governmental organizations that may be forming a global civil society.

17   European Council, 'Conclusions of the Presidency', Luxembourg European Council (12–13 Dec. 1997), 1. Available on the EU Web site: www.europa.eu.int

18   European Council, 'Conclusions of the Presidency', SN 180/93 Copenhagen (21–22 June 1993), 13.

19   'Report from the Council to the Essen European Council on a strategy to prepare for the accession of the associated countries of Central and Eastern Europe', Annex IV to Conclusions of the Presidency, Essen European Council, Bull. EU 12–1994, 21.

20   Commission of the European Communities, White Paper, *Preparation of the Associated Countries of Central and Eastern Europe for Integration into the Internal Market of the Union* (Brussels, 3 May 1995), Com (95) 163 final.

21   European Commission, *Phare 1994 Annual Report* (Brussels, 1995), 5.

22   Edith Oltay, 'Hungary Sets Schedule for Legal Harmony with EU', Open Media Research Institute (OMRI) nr 11 (16 Jan. 1995); Ministry of Foreign Affairs, Budapest, *Fact Sheets on Hungary*, 'Relations between Hungary and the European Union', no. 4 (1995).

23   Ministry of Foreign Affairs, Budapest, *Fact Sheets on Hungary*.

24   A helpful summary of the issues debated at the Luxembourg European Council is found in *The Economist*, 'Unsafe at Many Speeds', 20 Dec. 1997, 73–4.

25  Embassy of the Republic of Hungary, Ottawa, Communiqué, 28 Mar. 1996, 'Hungary: Interview, Finance Minister Peter Medgyessy', *Transition Brief* (OECD) no. 8 (Autumn 1997): 6.

26  Excerpt from the joint press release, Brussels, 30 Mar. 1998, published in World Bank newsletter *Transition* (Apr. 1998): 11. The OECD, recognizing that the return to Europe is now a foregone conclusion, has merged its Centre for Co-operation with Economies in Transition back into a general Centre for Co-operation with Non-members (worldwide). OECD, *Outreach News* (Summer 1998): 1.

27  Presidency Conclusions, Cardiff European Council, 'Enlargement', and 'EU Reform Delay May Hold Up Enlargement—European Parliament', 15 June 1998 (Reuters Internet).

28  Anatoly Verbin, 'Rift over EU Emerges at Central European Summit', Internet Reuters World Report, 24 June 1998.

## Suggested Readings

Amsden, Alice H., Jacek Kochanowicz, and Lance Taylor. *The Market Meets Its Match: Restructuring the Economies of Eastern Europe.* Cambridge, Mass.: Harvard University Press, 1994.

Haglund, David, ed. *Will NATO Go East? The Debate over Enlarging the Atlantic Alliance.* Kingston: Queen's University Centre for International Relations, 1996.

Kaldor, Mary, and Ivan Vejvoda. 'Democratization in Central and East European Countries', *International Affairs* 73, 1 (1997): 59–82.

Mayhew, Alan. *Recreating Europe: The European Union's Policy Towards Central and Eastern Europe.* Cambridge: Cambridge University Press, 1998.

Preston, Christopher. *Enlargement and Integration in the European Union.* London: Routledge, 1997.

Teunissen, Jan Joost, ed. *Regionalism and the Global Economy: The Case of Central and Eastern Europe.* The Hague: Fondad, 1997.

## Web Sites

European Bank for Reconstruction and Development: www.ebrd.com

European Union assistance programs to Central Europe and Russia: www.europa.eu.int/comm/dg1a/phare or /tacis

Hungarian government: www.meh.hu

NATO's Partnerships for Peace: www.nato.int/pfp

Open Media Research Institute and its journal *Transitions*: www.omri.cz

News updates for Russia: www.russia.today.com

## Chapter 22

# African Renaissance in the New Millennium? From Anarchy to Emerging Markets?

Timothy M. Shaw and Julius E. Nyang'oro

Globalization offers African countries opportunities for accelerating the process of economic recovery.[1]

Slowly and painfully, the era of Africa's Big Men is grinding to a halt. As the Big Men leave the stage, they are being harried by a loose alliance known as the 'New Africans', comprising Ethiopia, Eritrea, Uganda, Rwanda, Angola and Congo-Kinshasa (ex-Zaire,) while South Africa looks on approvingly.[2]

Sub-Saharan Africa is undergoing its most profound changes since the early years of independence. . . . Africa's postcolonial despotic order is finally breaking down. . . . Africa's new leaders have begun to fill the vacuum left by the end of the Cold War. . . . Africa's new bloc . . . is led by market-oriented men who earned their mandates through protracted struggle. . . . Together they comprise a new political-military alliance that is engaged in joint campaigns from the Great Lakes to the Sahara. However imperfect, the bloc changes Africa's balance of power.[3]

As the new millennium approaches the whole of the African continent—including states, regimes, communities, and companies—is at a crossroads in terms of both development performances and policies. After almost two decades of problematic reforms—political and social as well as economic—its stereotypical image of marginalization compounded by anarchy may be yielding to a more positive status of emerging markets. Ironically, just as the negative consequences of globalization become apparent everywhere, symbolized by the intense crisis in the Asian newly industrialized countries (NICs), prospects for an authentic and sustainable 'African renaissance' improve.[4] The contrast between the emerging 'African renaissance' and the hitherto unassailable 'Asian values' is particularly noteworthy, posing challenges for both policy and analysis.

This chapter seeks to understand the apparent turnaround in the continent's fortunes on the eve of the next century. Its resilience—in the face of Afro-pessimism[5]—stands in marked contrast to the ravages produced around the Pacific Rim by the contagious Asian economic flu as well as to the highly detrimental, unanticipated costs of 'big bangs' in the former Soviet Union and Eastern Europe.[6] As one report recently put it, 'After a period of unprecedented decline, Africa's development prospects now appear brighter than at any time since the decade of independence.'[7] This somewhat unexpected, yet welcome, combination of events is a function of changing 'triangular' relations among states, economies, and societies at three interrelated levels: internal, regional, and global. Sustainable development has always required change in the triangular sets of relations at all levels. Yet analyses and policies have all too often tended to focus on the rise and fall of national regimes to the exclusion of other actors operating at each of the other levels. In the first edition of this book, Susan Strange correctly and persuasively argued that 'international relations' at the end of this century involves not just state-state but also state-firm and firm-firm relations.[8] Given the rise in both the practice and analysis of 'civil society' under the 'new' world order, such antidotes to state-centred analysis need now to embrace society as well as governments and companies. In other words, we need to bring civil society into our purview. Nowhere is this more of an imperative today than in the South, especially Africa.

## Contemporary Continent: Changing Perspectives and Policies

The World Bank's *World Development Report 1997* marked the end of the era of neo-liberal triumphalism and the inauguration of a new consensus among the key Washington-based institutions that control development policy throughout the world—the International Monetary Fund (IMF), the World Bank, and the American government. This new consensus revolves around the imperative of partnerships. Many types of partnership are being formed in different parts of Africa. The increasing variety of private-sector corporations and non-governmental organizations (NGOs) and the differing ways in which states, multinational corporations (MNCs), and NGOs interact are seen as having a major influence on how civil societies are emerging across the continent. Together, companies and civil societies have begun to complement the state as major actors in the continent's international or transnational relations. So many local and global issues require the active involvement of a range of heterogeneous actors, leading to complex yet more representative debates and outcomes. This is a result of three phenomena: economic liberalization in the form of structural adjustment programs (SAPs); political liberalization, caused by the relentless demands for participation, accountability, and transparency; and the strengthening of civil society as local communities seek basic human needs and in some areas respond to the decay of the state and the rise of new security issues, including the privatization of security and the introduction of peacekeeping operations.

After almost two decades of proliferating (in terms of numbers of programs as well as states and sectors affected) SAPs, the continent's governments are quite diminished and in some cases have totally collapsed. On the other hand, corporations and

Africa's civil societies are becoming more powerful. The initial generation of SAP conditionalities, which centred on economic liberalization, encouraged the expansion into the continent of the international private sector. This was done through policies such as deregulation, devaluation, and privatization. In practice, this typically encouraged the expansion of the informal sectors as coping mechanisms in response to the shrinkage of the formal domestic private sector. At the same time, the post-Cold War political liberalization advanced formal, multiparty democracy through new constitutions and elections. Economic and political liberalizations have produced both external and structural 'interventions'. This advances what Christopher Clapham calls 'the externalisation of economic management'[9] and leads to what he further characterizes as 'the externalisation of political accountability'.[10] Both can be seen particularly in the implementation of SAPs, which, along with the general trend of globalization, create the conditions for external economic management and external political accountability. Indeed, the latter puts in jeopardy apparent moves towards democratization. As some, if not all, African polities appear to be moving towards greater degrees of openness, so their authority is being undermined by external conditionalities and competitiveness. Hence, any effective recapture of internal sovereignty requires determined and innovative foreign as well as domestic policies.

States are also being challenged by increasingly complex civil societies, some of which are beset by conflict while others are reasonably coherent. Conflicts often occur when economic and political liberalizations produce incompatible consequences. Most particularly, economic liberalization creates increased economic inequalities that can have an adverse impact on political liberalization. In some instances this may generate the very social conflicts to which diverse peacekeeping operations seek to respond. Indeed, the expansion of civil society is caused by two contradictory responses to neo-liberalism: resistance to declines in expenditures on basic human needs, on the one hand, and opportunities and demands for increased services via international NGOs, on the other. Hence, the contradictory character of civil society, which is especially evident within national and international NGOs. Some NGOs essentially act as subcontractors for international agencies while others are in the vanguard of resistance to the effects of SAPs and neo-liberalism. Moreover, there is added tension within the NGO community as some NGOs serve as crucial adjuncts to state peacekeeping forces.

Thus, by the end of the century, Africa's internal and international political economies are characterized by the active roles of not just states but also companies and civil societies. However, the balance among these varies between countries and periods. Moreover, as each of these three is quite heterogeneous, numerous typologies have been generated for each set of actors. However, the most understudied of the three types has been civil societies. This is a grave error, for without due attention to the development of civil societies, which have emerged as a function of both new spaces and opportunities as well as of demands for policy changes and service provision, we cannot begin to account for the continent's apparent revival under the dictates of neo-liberal conditionalities.

This is not an uncontested view. Some analysts have begun a revisionist debate about the utility of the notion of 'civil society' in Africa as elsewhere: is it too broad a concept, as well as a creature of current hegemonic discourses? Certainly, it needs to be subject to critical scrutiny, and diversities among NGOs, media, religions, ethnicities, and so forth should also be considered. But surely there are dangers in throwing the baby out with the bath water, especially when many Africans welcome its potential for keeping state administrations at all levels a little more honest. Moreover, the concept comes under attack from a somewhat unlikely set of allies, such as old-fashioned leftists, who see civil society undermining 'class' forces, and equally old-fashioned pluralists, who fear its erosion of formal party politics![11]

We have also one other caveat. At the outset it is important to note that not all African(ist) scholars would share our relative optimism. In many ways the debate has been hijacked by two competing approaches: rational choice and global studies,

on the one hand, and black 'Africanist' exclusivism, on the other. The middle ground of the mainstream has been eroded by this pincer movement, which may continue to beset analyses into the new millennium, whatever the accomplishments of the 'new African' alliance. However, despite these cautions we still maintain that any prospect of renaissance is due not so much to formal economic or political or other liberalizations as to the tradition of adaptability African communities have built up in the face of droughts, floods, civil strife, and impoverishment. And, importantly, such dynamism occurs not only internally but also regionally.

After more than 15 years of structural adjustment 'reforms', with their relentless and proliferating conditionalities, Africa's political economies are quite transformed from their post-independence state-centrism even if their debt burdens have yet to be fully lifted. In the 1970s, African regimes competed with each other to see who could be the most 'African socialist' or interventionist. By the 1990s, however, they were competing in terms of who offered the most investor-friendly environment. During the first half of the 1990s, private investment jumped tenfold, from less than $1 billion a year in the early 1990s to almost $12 billion in 1996. Furthermore, several of the continent's 20-odd stock markets were in the vanguard of emerging markets: rates of return in Africa averaged 24 per cent between 1990 and 1994 compared with 18 per cent for all emerging markets. This has led to the observation that 'Africa is the Cinderella of emerging markets, better known for war and famine than booming stock markets. But a growing band of investors is being attracted to the continent's nascent stock markets after some spectacular gains in the past two years.'[12] And in the second half of the 1990s, they declined less precipitously than those in the NICs.

However, there have been profound social costs and consequences from almost two decades of structural adjustments, as political economies and political cultures responded to exponential shocks. Once again, as in the era of modernization, the continent served as something of a laboratory, this time for the former Second World as well as for the rest of the

Third. Happily, because of the unacceptable social costs the World Bank has finally begun to reconsider at least some of its theological espousal of SAPs.[13] And the Jubilee 2000 and related pressures for significant debt relief continue to gather momentum, in part because a reduced debt burden is seen as necessary to ensure sustainable human development.

Overall, then, the transformation in Africa's macroeconomics has been quite profound. This is indicated, for example, in the burgeoning of its stock markets. Those in Harare, Johannesburg, Lagos, and Nairobi have a considerable vintage, but they have expanded their listings and turnover in the 1990s, in part because of foreign investor interest, some of it from foreign mutual and pension funds, some of whom sanctioned settler states' race relations before majority rule. Moreover, these pioneers have been joined by new exchanges in Botswana, Cote d'Ivoire, Ghana, Malawi, Mauritius, Namibia, and Swaziland, with others in places like Dakar, Dar es Salaam, and Kampala to follow.[14] Fifteen of the continent's 53 countries now have them, just over half of these in the Southern African Development Community (SADC) region. Such stock markets symbolize and facilitate the privatization of the economy, as former state enterprises can be floated and traded and building societies demutualized. Moreover, private mutual and pension funds, as well as mortgage and finance companies, can invest their holdings more readily, while conglomerates can be more easily unbundled. And in the case of hitherto settler states, especially South Africa, Black empowerment/redistribution can thereby be advanced. The Johannesburg Stock Exchange is the continent's oldest, biggest, and most sophisticated. It has weathered not only sanctions and unrest in the previous quarter-century, but also the transition in the early 1990s along with the drop in the price of gold. Yet in mid-1998, it reached record levels of stock prices and attracted record numbers of listings. African markets led all other emerging markets in 1994, partially because of the 'discovery' of the continent by global mutual funds.

At the other end of the spectrum, micro-credit has also been growing, partially through not-for-profit associations. Yet most informal credit in

Africa remains private, expensive, and open to mafia-style manipulation because it is in scarce supply. Further, in terms of post-industrial niches, Africa has begun to play an important role not only in terms of green tourism, ozone replenishment, and biodiversity, but also in the telecommunications revolution, especially the Internet/World Wide Web and satellite television. This is particularly true for South Africa, which is host to M-Net/DStv and other organizations that now stretch throughout Common Market for Eastern and Southern Africa (COMESA) states. Africa Telecom '98 was held in Johannesburg, where a continent-wide plan was agreed among states, international agencies, and private sectors to spend some US$750 billion over the next five years to almost double the number of phones from 14 million to 23 million. South Africa is by far the largest host country in terms of servers and has over 125,000 Internet host computers. Aside from Egypt and Morocco in North Africa, the other major hosts are in Southern and Eastern Africa. Africa Online now serves seven cities, including Johannesburg, Nairobi, Mombasa, Accra, and Abidjan. The continent has made something of a virtue out of necessity by leapfrogging technologies, going straight to cordless, cellular phones, especially in the regions with the least established infrastructure, most notably in West and Central Africa, or the so-called 'collapsed' or 'failed' countries recovering from sustained civil conflict such as Angola and Somalia. And its larger cities are beginning to host call centres based on the new high-tech infrastructure as well as relatively cheap English- or French-speaking labour, typically trained in private technology colleges such as Damelin and Varsity College in Southern Africa.

Yet, the transition from developmental crises to emerging markets is not without its dark side. Africa still reveals much about the other sides of globalization, in particular the results of social inequalities and the costs of ecological degradation. This is underscored by several new phenomena on the continent, such as street children, child soldiers, the proliferation of landmines and other so-called small arms, and the emergence of private and vigilante policing arrangements. In addition, under SAP reforms and market pressures there has been an endless downward pressure to the bottom produced by the assumed dictates of competitiveness. Several African states have moved to establish Export Processing Zones (EPZs). These have been built mainly along the coast and on islands like Mauritius, but also inland at such places as Athi River outside Nairobi on the Masai plains. They enable the continent to be part of post-Fordist, flexible global-production chains in which only some parts are manufactured in any one location.

Sometimes missed, however, is the intrinsic and organic connection between emerging markets, on the one hand, and social stability and security, on the other. Direct foreign investment and tourists, for example, cannot be attracted without the confidence of economic and social security and stability, which degrees of redistribution and confidence-building measures can ensure or enhance. Thus, risk assessments and credit ratings are endless and crucial, given the pressures of competitiveness. But they are undertaken by non-African agencies, using universal, economistic criteria. For example, because of cheap air travel and a declining shilling, Kenya may have attracted significant numbers of tourists to its game parks and coastal beaches in the 1980s, but once it became somewhat notorious for insecurity as well as growing infrastructural deficiencies such flows declined. Furthermore, while it may have successfully diversified into non-traditional exports, such as horticultural products, which are now Kenya's third most valuable export after tea and coffee, the ecological and basic human needs costs of these crops must be reckoned with.

In other parts of Africa, such as Liberia, Somalia, Angola, and Sierra Leone, the continent's hopes for emerging market status have been undermined by the fact that threats to human security have multiplied at a seemingly exponential rate as new security issues have arisen. For example, in addition to the various state and international peacekeeping operations across the continent, Africa has been in the vanguard of the privatization of security. This turn of events is evident in the ubiquitous armed guards provided by transnational companies,

community-supported vigilante groups, and the 'new' mercenary operations conducted by such companies as Executive Outcomes, DSL, and Sandline. Other human security issues are tied to ecological degradation, the activities of drug gangs, the spread of deadly viruses, and the treatment of women and children.[15] Overall, security problems remain acute in parts of Africa. As the United Nations Secretary-General, Kofi Annan, has argued, 'Despite the devastation that armed conflicts bring, there are many who profit from chaos and the lack of accountability, and who have little interest in stoppping a conflict and much interest in prolonging it.'[16]

Thus, on one hand, Africa is displaying signs of a transition to 'emerging markets' status with all its positive benefits. On the other hand, however, it is still continuing to suffer both from the lingering effects of previous ills (such as debt and SAPs) that produced major economic, social, and political problems and from the new hardships brought on by this newly emerging market status.

## New Regionalisms

Africa in the late twentieth century has become a site of several innovative and problematic experiments in micro- through meso- to macro-level regional organizations. These are not just of the formal variety but also of less formal type. They vary considerably from de facto informal regional economic arrangements and emerging regional civil societies to embryonic regional security communities. In addition, there are ecological and corporate definitions of regions. However, these are not all necessarily consistent or compatible. Indeed, these regions are open to various definitions and differing interpretations as to their goals and purposes.[17]

Such creative regionalisms suggest the desirability of revisiting and revising Samir Amin's pioneering schema for the continent's real regional political economies in the early 1970s. Amin envisioned a trio of Africas: 'colonial trade economy' states, economies dominated by 'concession-owning companies', and states that were essentially 'labour reserves'.[18] Given contemporary global and local political economies (all under the hegemony of neo-liberalism), as the new millennium approaches there are now more than three Africas. These have emerged over the last 20 years or so. In the initial SAP era of the early 1980s, there was a division between reformers and non-reformers, in other words, between those states that adopted IMF reforms and those that did not. As the conditions imposed by the IMF on indebted states proliferated in the early 1990s, there were distinct differences between states in terms of degree of formal multi-party democratization that was adopted in various forms of consolidating and fragile democracies.[19] And by the late 1990s, as the divergencies of (incompatible?) liberalizations compounded, there appeared an Africa made up of the failed or collapsed states,[20] an Africa of states dominated by peacemaking operations, and an Africa of emerging markets.

In addition to these macro typologies, however, 'new' meso-level or mid-level interstate regionalisms have emerged in response to the new international division of labour and new international division of power, as well as to competitive regional proposals made from inside and outside the continent. These range from an expansive SADC to a preoccupied Economic Community of West African States (ECOWAS) and on to a revived and redirected Intergovernmental Authority on Development (IGAD) and the innovative East African Co-operation (EAC) group. Typically, these less exclusive, more open, and often asymmetric regionalisms have increasingly gone beyond interstate economic agreements to anticipate interstate security arrangements. These have also included the involvement of private sectors. The economic agreements were increasingly cast in terms of peace-keeping capacities (for example, ECOWAS Ceasefire Monitoring Group [ECOMOG]) and confidence-building measures, often of a 'track-two' or semi-official variety involving non-state actors such as think-tanks. And the latter typically incorporated larger corporations and chambers of commerce and occasionally labour and more informal sectors.

Well-established intra- and extra-African multi-national corporations (MNCs), especially private South African companies like AAC and South African Breweries (SAB) but also Zimbabwean companies like Delta and South African state enterprises like Eskom, South African Airways (SAA), and Transnet, are defining their own regions through direct foreign investment and regional-scale hub facilities for both production and distribution. And major African cities and tourist destinations, increasingly connected through regional circuits, are linked into continental and global hotel chains, such as Intercontinental, Holiday Inn, and Southern Sun in Southern Africa and Serena in East Africa.

Furthermore, the continent's private sector is developing its own set of Asian-style transnational corridors and triangles. They may be formally connected to established regional structures. These include the Maputo Corridor linking Gauteng to the Indian Ocean and the Trans-Kalahari Corridor linking it to the Atlantic Ocean. Somewhat more distant dreams include spatial development initiatives (SDIs) along the Benguela, Nacala, and Tazara corridors as well as the Kwazulu-Natal/Mozambique/Swaziland Lubombo SDI and Kgalagadi Peace Park between Northern Cape and southwest Botswana. The corridor from Mombasa to Mbarara is crucial for the Great Lakes, and potentially could be traversed by a Rift Valley community from Addis Ababa down to Gauteng.

Moreover, in association with such embryonic regional corridors, triangles, and SDIs, typically involving the private sector if not always local communities, the continent could yet advance some novel regional arrangements such as the Kagera River Basin, Great Lakes, and Nile Valley as well as the macro-level Rift Valley 'communities' based on transnational ecological linkages rather than simply interstate relations. Potentially, these could become the basis for de facto realignments of official international borders. Already, the Maputo Corridor Company constitutes a novel form of extra-, sub-, or non-state governance. Such contemporary non-governmental arrangements present profound implications for old-fashioned interstate regionalisms.

Unfortunately, relatively few regionalist structures on the continent to date embrace or reflect the dynamics of civil societies, even if they build on shared cultures, ethnicities, identities, music, sporting interests, and so forth. Moreover, they rarely include ecological factors, such as common water or energy resources, which will increasingly become new security issues in the coming century; hence the crisis character of droughts and floods in el niño and other years. IGAD has had a greater concern for desertification, as has the Club du Sahel, but these have been donor-driven by NGOs and non-African states rather than indigenous initiatives. Similarly, except in a formal way in ECOWAS and in an informal way in the SADC, nowhere are issues of migration treated, even though the continent has in recent decades experienced large and growing numbers of economic, ecological, and conflict refugees.

In short, civil societies at regional levels are dynamic. They are driven in part by regional NGO groupings like the Forum for African Voluntary Development Organization, Mwelekeo wa NGO (NGO Visions), and the African Network for Development (Réseau African pour le Développement), as well as by de facto regional media like M-Net/DStv and the *Weekly Mail and Guardian*. However, they have yet to be recognized in emerging regionalist arrangements and this has important implications for the possibilities of enhanced and sustained levels of human development and security into the next millennium. Nevertheless, there is a new spirit of openness apparent in some African regional groupings, such as the new Centre for Civil Society Organization in the Economic Commission for Africa (ECA). And the imperative of effectiveness means that this UN commission has closed or amalgamated some moribund agencies. It also has redesignated and diverted resources to its subregional offices as subregional development centres to facilitate their role as building blocks with established groupings for the anticipated African Economic Community.

## Rise (and Demise?) of the African Renaissance

Reflective of the post-Afro-pessimism era, by the mid-1990s a new debate, characterized as the 'African renaissance', was beginning to emerge. It reflected a renewed confidence and optimism that some if not all of the continent could begin to transcend its inherited problems and define its own path. For example, it was felt that indigenous definitions of human development and security could be generated. Such claims have been articulated by the trio of international and transnational actors identified at the start of this chapter—that is, states, companies, and civil societies, particularly states. This notion of an African renaissance has been most notably advanced by the new set of latecomer, post-insurgent states in Eritrea, South Africa, and Uganda. This is the 'alliance of New Africans' noted in the second quotation at the beginning of this chapter. Just as earlier eras of post-nationalist/liberation movement regimes generated first the early 1970s Mulungushi Club trio of Central African presidents and then the Frontline States group against apartheid, so the latest set of 'new states' in the mid-1990s led to notions of an African renaissance.

This renaissance has been defined in a variety of not always compatible ways by different groups of analysts. These include orthodox economists from the World Bank and leading corporations, external government officials, such as those in the US government, non-state donors, such as Oxfam, and the new generation of national leaders on the continent, such as Isaias Afwerki, Thabo Mbeki, and Yoweri Museveni.[21] The issue of who defines the concept of African renaissance and identifies with it is extremely important, for its proponents determine its authenticity and legitimacy. Is it a Machiavellian disguise for renewed US or South African dominance? Does it serve to justify regime changes in, say, Rwanda, Congo, and Brazzaville, which may yet prove to be a set of dominoes influencing the southern Sudan and Kenya? Is it a timely counter to the fraying of 'Asian values' in East Asia? Or does it merely constitute the latest version of post-independence aspirations, which include aspects of culture as well as political and economic liberalization and so may serve to camouflage difficult policy choices and directions, even incumbent governments' intolerance or arrogance?

Ambiguities about the genesis of the African renaissance and the intentions of its advocates have already generated a new debate. But the concept remains symbolic of a new spirit that has not been credible since the heady days of the first round of new, albeit weak, states in the era of Africa's independence in the early 1960s. It may also lead to new forms of realism on the continent as state forces are mobilized to advance regime change in neighbouring countries, as in Congo and Brazzaville in the mid-1990s. In turn, such forcible changes may generate a new, revisionist debate about the continent's inherited borders a century after the Treaty of Berlin first designated these borders.

## The Continent in the Twenty-First Century: Less Marginal and More Integrated?

According to our cautiously optimistic perspective, which reflects current analyses and discourses on the continent itself, African countries and communities at the start of the new millennium may be more or less integrated or marginalized depending on their geographic location and the relationships within any particular country among the trio of state, corporations, and civil societies. In turn, this may lead towards a revived and redirected Organization of African Unity and EAC, especially given their novel peace operations and civil society mechanisms. Indeed, these organizations are increasingly reaching beyond states towards the pair of non-state actors in a search for strategic non-state partners because of the financial and often intellectual impoverishment of their official membership. The hope would be to create mixed-actor coalitions over a series of issues, including currency speculation, debt burdens, development corridors and triangles, droughts, oceans development, and so forth.

One symbolic anniversary, but of decreasingly substantive importance, that coincides with the end of the century is the renewal and redirection, if not revival, of the Lomé Convention between the expanding European Union (EU) and the growing number of African, Caribbean, and Pacific countries associated with the EU. While its economic and financial centrality has long since past, even for the Francophone states, its potential in terms of new multilateral conditionalities, such as human rights and democratic practices, remains. This is especially so for Africa, given new security, peacekeeping, and related issues such as ecology and migration. Yet the continent is already divided, given the associated Mediterranean countries and the special case of South Africa. Nevertheless, even if of residual salience, some version of Lomé will be extended into the twenty-first century, hopefully with some North-South version of the Maastricht Treaty on social agendas.[22]

## Conclusion

Compared to the analysis presented in the Africa chapter in the first edition of this book, the present revisionist perspective incorporates a number of crucial issues hardly raised just five years ago. These include the growing importance of civil societies and the development of emerging markets. In addition, our mid-1990s analysis placed less emphasis on the new regionalisms, despite their genesis in earlier periods. The interrelatedness of many of these newly emerging factors is indicated, for example, in the variety of international NGOs participating in peacekeeping operations and by the roles of MNCs in new regional corridors or triangles. Such novel dimensions give rise to considerable optimism that the notion of an African renaissance is no longer fanciful.

But the longevity of the 'new African' alliance cannot be assured, given the intimidating range of development challenges confronting the continent. External intervention and poor leadership over the last quarter-century have left a legacy of problems and crises. Crucial to Africa's future, especially in terms of attracting foreign direct investment to the continent and developing emerging markets, is economic and political as well as ecological and policy stability. As became all too apparent in the last half of the 1990s, even in the supposed success stories of the Asian NICs, stability and security, whether defined by local communities or currency speculators, cannot be taken for granted.

## Notes

1 African Development Bank, 'Fostering Private Sector Development in Africa', *African Development Report 1997* (Oxford: Oxford University Press, 1997), 6.

2 Patrick Smith, 'The Big Men Go', *The World in 1998* (London: The Economist, 1997), 85–6.

3 Dan Connell and Frank Smyth, 'Africa's New Bloc', *Foreign Affairs* 77, 2 (Mar.-Apr. 1998): 80, 93–4.

4 See Peter Vale and Sipho Maseko, 'South Africa and the African Renaissance', *International Affairs* 74, 2 (Apr. 1998): 271–87.

5 See David F. Gordon and Howard Wolpe, 'The Other Africa: An End to Afro-pessimism', *World Policy Journal* 15, 1 (Spring 1998): 49–59.

6 See also our 'Conclusion: African Foreign Policies and the Next Millennium—Alternative Perspectives', in Stephen Wright, ed., *African Foreign Policies* (Boulder, Colo.: Westview Press, 1999).

7 ECA, 'Proposed Programme of Work and Priorities for Biennium 1998–1999' (Addis Ababa, Mar. 1997, E/ECA/CM.23/10), 10.

8 See Susan Strange, 'Rethinking Structural Change in the International Political Economy: States, Firms, and Diplomacy', in Richard Stubbs and Geoffrey R.D. Underhill, eds, *Political Economy and the Changing Global Order* (Toronto: McClelland & Stewart, 1994), 103–15.

9 Christopher Clapham, *Africa and the International System* (Cambridge: Cambridge University Press, 1996), 169.

10 Ibid., 187.

11 See Chris Allen, 'Who Needs Civil Society?', *Review of African Political Economy* 24, 73 (Sept. 1997): 329–37.

12 *Sunday Morning Post* (Hong Kong), 14 Sept. 1997.

13 World Bank, *World Development Report 1997* (New York: Oxford University Press, 1997).

14 See IFC, *Emerging Stock Markets Factbook 1996* (Washington, 1996).

15 United Nations Development Program, *Human Development Report 1994* (New York: Oxford University Press, 1994).

16 United Nations, 'Report of the UN Secretary-General to the Security Council on Africa' (New York: United Nations, Apr. 1998), 3–4.

17 See the five-volume series edited by Bjorn Hettne, Andras Inotai, and Osvaldo Sunkel on 'new regionalisms' for UNU/WIDER. The first title in the series is *Globalism and the New Regionalism* (London: Macmillan, 1998).

18 Samir Amin, 'Underdevelopment and Dependence in Black Africa—Origins and Contemporary Forms', *Journal of Modern African Studies* 10, 4 (Dec. 1972): 503–24.

19 See Michael Bratton and Nicholas van de Walle, *Democratic Experiments in Africa: Regime Transitions in Comparative Perspective* (New York: Columbia University Press, 1997).

20 See I. William Zartman, *Collapsed States: The Disintegration and Restoration of Legitimate Authority* (Boulder, Colo.: Lynne Rienner, 1998).

21 See Connell and Smyth, 'Africa's New Bloc', 88; Vale and Maseko, 'South Africa and the African Renaissance'.

22 See Gordon Crawford, 'Whither Lomé? The Midterm Review and the Decline of Partnership', *Journal of Modern African Studies* 34, 3 (Sept. 1996): 503–18; Kaye Whiteman, 'Africa, the ACP and Europe: The Lessons of 25 Years', *Development Policy Review* 16, 1 (Mar. 1998): 29–37.

## Suggested Readings

Brown, Michael Barratt. *Africa's Choices: After Thirty Years of the World Bank*. Harmondsworth: Penguin, 1995.

Chazan, Naomi, et al. *Politics and Society in Contemporary Africa*, 3rd edn. London: Macmillan, 1998.

Ellis, Stephen, ed. *Africa Now: People, Policies and Institutions*. London: James Currey, 1996.

Gordon, April A. and Donald L., eds. *Understanding Contemporary Africa*, 2nd edn. Boulder, Colo.: Lynne Rienner, 1996.

Polman, Katrien. 'Review Article: Evaluation of Africa-related Internet Resources', *African Affairs* 97 (July 1998): 401–8.

Stein, Howard, ed. *Asian Industrialization and Africa: Studies in Policy Alternatives to Structural Adjustment.* London: Macmillan, 1995.

Villalon, Leonardo A., and Phillip A. Huxtable, eds. *The African State at a Critical Juncture: Between Disintegration and Reconfiguration.* Boulder, Colo.: Lynne Rienner, 1998.

## Web Sites

African Development Bank Group: http://afdb.org/

African Development Institute: http://africainstitute.com/

Program for Development Research: http://www.prodder.co.za/

University of Pennsylvania, African Studies: http://www.sas.upenn.edu.African_Studies/AS.html

University of South Africa: http://unisa.org/

## Chapter 23

# The Future of the Political Economy of Latin America

Nicola Phillips

One of the most notable features of the globalization of economic activity is the incorporation of previously marginalized developing countries into the mainstream of international production and finance. Latin American countries are some of the most significant of these new participants. The neo-liberal 'revolution' since the mid-1980s transformed the region into one of the fastest growing in the world economy. Virtually without exception, countries have been engaged in extensive processes of unilateral liberalization and structural reform at the domestic level, reinforced by the policy trajectory set in motion by the processes of globalization and regionalization.

The major thesis of this chapter is that there is a qualitatively new situation in Latin America in which the interests of the state are seen to coincide with the 'interests' of the international economy and policy environment. As such, the chapter is concerned with the dynamics of globalization, regionalization, and reform in Latin American political economy. Processes of recent change act on three interconnected levels: domestic (unilateral liberalization), regional (integration initiatives), and global (participation in the globalizing world economy). Policies pursued at each of these levels have interacted to reinforce the new economic model in the region and also, by implication, to consolidate an exclusionary political orientation characterized by high levels of presidentialism and centralization. The consolidation phase of the reform process has coincided with the Mexican, Asian, and Brazilian crises and is characterized by resurgent debate on the management of globalization and on prevalent political models.

## Policy Change and Globalization

The processes of neo-liberal reform at the national level were not prompted initially by external influences. The implementation phase can be traced to conditions of economic and political crisis that affected most parts of the region in the mid- to late 1980s. Neither the timing nor the underlying causes or manifestations of these crises were uniform: while the Mexican crisis was predominantly defined by the 1982 debt crisis, for example, the turning point in Argentina came in 1988–9 with hyperinflation. The common thread is the perception created by economic and political collapse of a real and pressing need for change. By the early 1990s, models of inward-looking development had been entirely discredited, leading to a generalized belief that neo-liberalism was the only available option to governments faced with the task of economic and political reconstitution after the 'lost decade' of the 1980s. Furthermore, there was a widespread perception, reinforced by the European monetary crisis of 1992, of the increasing inability of states to control markets, global or domestic. In this way, the abandonment of the state's regulatory role as part of neo-liberal reform was seen as essential for the recovery of economic and political coherence.

Crucially, neo-liberal reform processes (such as in Mexico under De la Madrid and Salinas, Argentina under Menem, and Peru under Fujimori) were initiated *at the domestic level*, and major involvement from the international financial institutions (Ifis) tended to feature only after their initial implementation. Throughout the 1980s Latin

American countries were the focus of the structural adjustment efforts of the Ifis, but these did not succeed in eliciting complete or lasting compliance, largely as a result of their failure to take into account the domestic political realities of the countries with which they interacted. As a result, the story of the 1980s is one of faltering or half-hearted attempts at reform, during which the International Monetary Fund (IMF) was called in only at moments of crisis to put out the immediate fire. The heterodox experiments under Alfonsín in Argentina and García in Peru were largely homespun attempts to resolve the economic and political bottlenecks in the national arena, which frequently dispensed with the conditions of structural adjustment loans except when the finance became absolutely necessary.

A more explicit connection between international and domestic processes of change exists in the second, consolidation phase of reform from the mid-1990s. Until the end of the 1980s Latin America for the most part was mired in a spiral of economic and political instability, despite which (and the problems associated with transitions to democracy) the bulk of Latin American countries have successfully maintained neo-liberal reform. What is notable, therefore, is not only the sort of reform pursued but also the way governments were able to consolidate it to the extent that there are now relatively few ideas about a radical overhaul of the economic model. Despite increasing concern about fiscal deficits and pressure for greater attention to social policy and the democratization of the state, as well as to the so-called 'second generation' structural reforms, even serious opposition parties do not seriously question the overall orientation. In the case of Argentina, for example, the opposition UCR/FREPASO Alliance has stated that a victory in the 1999 presidential elections would mean a change only of faces, not of policies.[1]

This shift in policy preferences can be traced to the impact of globalization and the new policy consensus surrounding it. Development is now seen to be dependent on the attraction of foreign capital, which in turn requires the establishment and maintenance of the 'right' policy framework. As such, this new policy consensus is linked directly to a changing structure of rewards and punishments in the globalized international economy, which increasingly has constrained the feasible policy options available to national policy-makers. The rewards linked to conformity with the neo-liberal agenda of globalization have become inestimable. Between 1991 and 1996, the Latin American region received 31 per cent of total investment flows directed to developing countries.[2] Financial liberalization and reform of the banking sectors were particularly important in establishing the new investment profile, as well as the opportunities associated with privatization processes. Foreign direct investment (FDI) flows reached a peak in 1997 of around US$80 billion in the first six months of the year (before the Asian crises), two-thirds of which were long-term capital.[3]

The inflows of foreign capital have provided an important cushion for the consolidation of reform. Conversely, these inflows are conditional on a demonstrated commitment to consolidating liberalization and on the maintenance of stability. Given the importance of risk assessment and credit rating in the international investment environment, credibility and confidence are paramount. In Argentina, for example, the 1991 Convertibility Plan established 1:1 parity with the dollar and required the full dollar backing of the monetary base in an attempt to eliminate the persistence of inflation and to stabilize the exchange rate, along with an extensive package of structural reforms. Following its success, by 1994 Argentina had become the third largest recipient worldwide of FDI.

Perhaps more crucially, the costs of nonconformity, especially in terms of failing to maintain the 'right' policy environment, have been amply demonstrated by the Mexican, Asian, and Brazilian crises. The major lesson of the last few years is that capital can flow out quite as easily as it can flow in. Policy measures in the aftermath of the Asian crises of 1997 indicate that governments have preferred to lose a few percentage points on GDP growth in the interests of re-establishing international confidence and putting in place safeguards against future crises. Brazil, Colombia, and Paraguay suffered the most damaging consequences in the area of short-term capital flows, while Chile and Mexico suffered most in the trade sphere as a result of a drop in export prices. All of these countries used monetary policies to address these difficulties.[4] The fiscal lessons from Asia have become particularly important, leading to the elaboration of what has been called a new 'fiscal covenant', involving fiscal consolidation, measures to improve the efficiency of public expenditure, increased transparency, and the promotion of social equity.[5] Reactions in the trade policy sphere have been concentrated in an increased emphasis on anti-dumping and safeguard measures to protect domestic producers threatened by the increased competitiveness resulting from the Asian devaluations.

There is a danger, however, in assuming that responses to globalization are uniform across countries. Huge differences in the competitive strategies pursued by governments often do not correspond entirely with a 'pure' neo-liberal approach. Chile, for example, retains controls on capital inflows and its central bank has intervened on occasions (as in February 1998) to shore up the currency in view of the worsening trade deficit. In Argentina up to 1994, several ad hoc measures were implemented, such as the imposition of compensatory rights against footwear and clothing imports and other temporary adjustments to non-tariff barriers (such as the statistical tax). Similarly, in 1994 the National Commission for External Trade (CNCE) was established as a mechanism for dealing with unfair trade practices. Complaints to date have been directed mainly at Brazilian and Chinese dumping practices.[6]

Globalization has created a situation of crises happening more mechanistically and in far more devastating fashion than previously, given the interconnectedness of national economies. As a result of the Mexican and Asian fallouts (and more recently the Brazilian devaluation), the debate about the management of the costs of globalization, as well as its advantages, took root throughout Latin America. Interestingly, though, in the two countries most affected by the 'Tequila' crisis, the responses diverged. In Argentina, the atmosphere was one of increased caution, reflected in the numerous safeguards put in place, such as increased reserve requirements in banking. In Mexico, on the other hand, the response was to deepen neo-liberalism, including promises for further financial deregulation and a more vigorous approach to privatization.

It is clear from the above that the new rules of the global financial game and the policy bases of participation in global economic activity constrain the options of states, particularly in those countries concerned with constructing a functioning market economy and establishing a viable development strategy. However, this should not be misconstrued to mean that the state has lost control over the national economy. First, the state remains responsible for the design of policies at the national level that are thought to best serve a range of priorities, as the above examples demonstrate. Second, and most importantly, the interests of contemporary Latin American states are for the first time in the postwar period consistent with the 'interests' of the international political economy. In other words, engagement with the forces and agents of the global political economy is seen to be in the interests of the state and, significantly, a means by which reform, for once, could be consolidated. Globalization created a powerful incentive for reform and provided an element of external compulsion and external legitimacy with which the reform agenda could be sold to the national electorates. Thus, the perception of policy change as having been foisted on reluctant governments is exaggerated and misplaced.

## Regionalization as Meso-Globalization

Regional integration in Latin America has become an important answer to the challenges of the management of globalization as well as the consolidation of the neo-liberal reform trajectory. Both of the principal economic blocs—NAFTA (Mexico, the US, and Canada) and MERCOSUR (Argentina, Brazil, Uruguay, and Paraguay, with Chile and Bolivia as associate members)—are examples of what we can call 'meso-globalization'.[7] Latin American countries not only support a system of regionalism that allows trade with the rest of the world (open regionalism) but also are using regionalism as a sort of 'bottom-up' process of integration consistent with the objective of increasingly deep engagement with the process of globalization.[8] This type of regionalization offers clear advantages in terms of domestic economic and political priorities. The most obvious economic dividend was to assist the process of stabilization and structural reform. This in turn contributed to the resolution of the political crises in Latin American countries during the mid- to late 1980s through the bolstering of economic performance. In Mexico, for example, the ailing authoritarian system was seen to require a revitalization of the economy in order to recover from breakdown. In countries like Argentina and Peru, the recovery of political stability depended on the elimination of persistent hyperinflation.

Regional integration is seen at the national level not only as an end in itself but also as an important way in which the policy requirements generated by globalization can be met. Regionalism both reflects and reinforces processes of endogenously rooted change in member countries, acting to 'lock in' a specific economic policy paradigm and to consolidate the results of economic restructuring. On a simple level, liberalization is accomplished most easily at the regional level, where the extent of co-ordination and negotiation necessary for multilateral liberalization is sharply reduced. Most importantly, though, Latin American countries that sought regional integration did so for reasons of domestic discipline. In this sense, integration provides a cushion for the post-implementation difficulties of reform by creating an interstate emphasis on the processes of liberalization and reform. Thus, the locking in of policy measures through a network of regional agreements and commitments accords an element of irreversibility to the reform process at the national level. In this way, regional integration is important in demonstrating that countries are committed to liberalization and globalization.

NAFTA was closely linked with the Mexican liberalization process from about 1984 onward, and was a means of consolidating access to the US and Canadian export markets (see Chapter 19 by Tony Porter). Similarly, the signing of the Treaty of Asunción, which established MERCOSUR in March 1991,

was an important part of consolidating economic change in the Southern Cone. Article 5 of the treaty set out an ambitious schedule of tariff reductions to 1994, which was implemented as planned. The common external tariff (CET) was agreed at the Montevideo summit in December 1992, under which most products were subject to a maximum tariff of 20 per cent. The customs union that took effect on 1 January 1995 was seen as 'almost' full: it was agreed that 5–10 per cent of total trade would remain protected by national tariffs until 1999 to lessen the initial impact on uncompetitive industries. In addition, a further 10 per cent of total trade composed of 'sensitive' or 'strategic' products would only adopt the CET in 2001 (or 2006 for telecommunications and information technology products). A brief analysis of the effects in Argentina demonstrates how domestic reform efforts were locked in at the regional level. The average tariff rate in mid-1994, before the implementation of the CET, was 18.98 per cent (including the statistical surcharge) and the average rate a year later was 12.1 per cent.[9] Trade volumes increased significantly: between 1990 and 1995, exports increased by an annual average of 28.4 per cent and imports by 27.8 per cent. Between 1990 and 1996, MERCOSUR's share of total regional exports increased from 8.9 to 22.6 per cent.[10]

The other side of the meso-globalization coin refers to the impact of regionalization on the development of the global system itself. Although globalization is far from being a homogenizing force, it depends for its survival on a degree of policy convergence between regions and countries. Regionalization is one of the mechanisms by which this can be achieved, at least as long as it maintains its broadly positive engagement with globalization. If regionalization, as demonstrated above, serves to lock in the neo-liberal policies pursued by governments in the region, then it becomes pivotal in creating the national policy conditions on which the sustenance of the globalization process depends. In this sense, regionalization can be seen as the nexus or interface between the national and the global, and the mechanism by which coherence at both levels can be established and maintained.

This argument, clearly, depends on a conception of regionalization here called meso-globalization. Nevertheless, in recent years (perhaps since the Mexican crisis) regional integration has in some ways expanded in importance as a way of shoring up the national economies against the crisis-generating impact of globalization. Regionalization may be seen as the intermediary stage in the relationship between the globalized international economy and states, and is favoured as a mechanism by which states can recover a degree of the policy autonomy lost (or sacrificed) to globalization.[11] This goes back to the argument that globalization cannot be associated with the disintegration of the state. Especially given the highly intergovernmental nature of integration initiatives in Latin America, the state remains central to the construction of policy conditions conducive both to national development and to the maintenance of the globalized international order. In this way, regional integration can in some ways double as a defensive mechanism or contingency plan against the vagaries of globalization.

The question, therefore, is whether the compatibility between regional and global strategies in Latin America will be maintained, especially following the Mexican, Asian, and Brazilian crises. There is no persuasive evidence yet that regionalism is becoming any more or less defensive than previously. MERCOSUR continues to make expansion a priority, and countries throughout the region continue to negotiate bilateral deals with increasing enthusiasm. Similarly, the pattern of membership of MERCOSUR remains on an 'associate' basis pioneered by Chile's accession. This arrangement allows considerable flexibility and was preferred by Chile as a means of maintaining the full range of multilateral trade possibilities while hedging its bets on the stalled NAFTA option. In addition, MERCOSUR has actively pursued links with the EU, and talks with the Asian blocs are gaining ground. These trends demonstrate the inherently 'open' nature of Latin American regionalism and the intention of the countries concerned to pursue regional and global trade and investment strategies simultaneously.

The most recent development is the possibility of a Free Trade Area of the Americas (FTAA), projected to take effect from 2005. Despite the intention for a single hemispheric bloc, however, the most likely scenario at the present time appears to be an alliance between blocs: NAFTA in the north and MERCOSUR in the south (possibly expanded into a South American Free Trade Area or SAFTA). It seems increasingly likely that the other older blocs in the region—such as the Andean Pact and the Central American and Caribbean units—will be subsumed into these two dominant arrangements. The expansion of MERCOSUR has gained significant extra impetus in the light of these hemispheric negotiations. One motive is the perceived need to counteract the negotiating strength of the US, which for obvious reasons prefers to negotiate on a country-by-country basis while MERCOSUR prefers to negotiate as a bloc. The other motivation may be that a SAFTA could function as a contingency plan in the event that the FTAA collapses or never comes to fruition.

Mexico and Brazil appear at present to be the most reticent about the FTAA.[12] Mexico's reservations are also based on a defence of its preferential access to the North American market, which would be compromised by the negotiation of hemispheric integration along the proposed lines. While most other Latin American countries continue to conduct trade relations with the rest of the world as well as North and South American partners, Mexico's trade structure is almost exclusively dominated by trade through NAFTA.[13] Therefore, Mexican objectives in both regional and hemispheric trade negotiations diverge significantly from the rest.

Although it has avoided being cast as the villain of the piece, Brazil is the principal counterweight to the US and has voiced differences of opinion regarding tariff reduction schedules as well as doubts concerning the scope of the negotiations. From a Brazilian perspective the US is seen to be promoting provisions beyond those agreed to during the Uruguay Round, while Brazil's preference in the short term is to consolidate the measures agreed to in the World Trade Organization. Similarly, Brazil and most other South American countries are concerned principally with trade issues, while the American objectives are more focused on newer issues such as services, intellectual property rights, competition policy, and government procurement.[14]

## State vs Society? The Development of Politics

The processes of globalization and regionalization have had significant influence on political as well as economic trends in Latin America. Here we return to our basic thesis: that there is a genuine coincidence between the (perceived) interests of Latin American states and the interests of the globalizing international financial and economic system. This basic proposition generates a number of observations concerning recent political development in the region.

The first concerns the development (or perhaps reinforcement) of an exclusionary style of politics that features highly presidentialist and centralized government. It is now commonplace to identify shifting accountability structures at both the national and international levels as a result of contemporary international change, to the effect that we are seeing a 'marginalization of democracy'.[15] What has been less theorized is the connection between specific types of political change and contemporary currents of international change. In part these linkages derive from the connection between the latter and neo-liberal economic reform, and there is a clear connection between high levels of presidentialism or centralization and the nature of both the reform process and the policy agenda itself. It has been argued that the success of government élites in implementing neo-liberal restructuring is directly linked to the strength of the president.[16] The contrast between the fate of reform efforts in Brazil and Uruguay, on the one hand, and in Argentina, Bolivia, and Peru, on the other, appears to corroborate this contention. In this sense, if we draw a connection between globalization, the new policy and development consensus it brings with it, and neo-liberal reform in Latin America, then the combination of these contributes to the generation of this particular political orientation.

There is some debate, however, as to whether neo-populist personalist government is inimical to democracy. These systems feature extensive use of presidential decree and veto powers, as well as ad hoc constitutional reform usually in the political interests of the president in question. The other salient characteristic is the persistence of corruption, traditionally a reliable indicator of low levels of accountability and transparency. These trends certainly go against the grain of democracy if defined in participatory or representative terms. The counter-argument holds that these traits have assisted the consolidation of political stability and the survival of democratic government in a region formerly characterized by frequent political collapse and democratic breakdown.[17]

The other less commonly analysed dimension of the linkages between globalization and political change relates to what we can call the 'internationalization of the state', which, according to Cox, involves 'the global process whereby national policies and practices have been adjusted to the exigencies of the world economy of international production'.[18] This process is seen to give 'precedence to certain state agencies—notably ministries of finance and prime ministers' offices—which are key points in the adjustment of domestic to international economic policy'.[19] Along with the consolidation of the centrality of the private sector discussed below, these trends have increasingly located policy-making responsibility (1) in the hands of unaccountable actors such as international financial agents, central bankers, and technocratic élites, and (2) outside the boundaries of the national state. In important ways this has contributed to the recomposition of the state and of political legitimacy in Latin America, as well as to the solidity of state institutions, but the linkages between states and societies they theoretically represent have been fundamentally altered so that, at least in the early 1990s, societal input into the political process was minimal. In sum, the exclusionary political model can be traced to the internationalization of the state and to the highly intergovernmental nature of regionalization, as well as the political economy of neo-liberal reform.

The second and related dimension of political change, then, fleshes out the above proposition. It concerns the reconfiguration of political interests in the region that, in the same way as most other countries of the world, features most notably a shift of power away from labour and towards business and financial interests. The changes associated with globalization significantly increase the influence and importance of pro-liberalization forces at both the domestic and the international levels.[20] One of the ways this works is that globalization acts to increase the mobility of capital, and therefore the 'exit option' of capital holders in the domestic economy, making the political management of these interests pivotal to economic stability and continued development.[21] The upshot of this is that the construction of a support coalition based on a nexus between the state and business is essential to the stability and survival of neo-liberal democracy in Latin American countries.[22] The implementation of economic restructuring depends not only on the co-operation of the private sector but also on its role as the powerhouse behind economic development. As a result of the reform of the state and public sector, the private sector in Latin America has assumed responsibility for economic growth, replacing the state-led model of development pursued previously. In this way, business sectors have come to form the backbone of political support for reforming governments and have also become central to the maintenance of their legitimacy.

At the same time as business groups were incorporated into the mainstream of policy-making throughout the region, other societal groups were marginalized. The most obvious of these is the labour sector, which had previously exercised, to a greater or lesser extent, a veto power over the political process in many countries. Argentina, for example, had the most militant trade unions, which exerted a stranglehold over the policy-making agenda throughout the postwar period. Here the unions were systematically disarticulated by the Menem government through a combination of purposive policies and the effects of the reform of the state: on the one hand, privatization and the reform of the public sector eliminated the arena in which these interests had been active and able to press their demands; on the other hand, the government played on the economic weaknesses and the internal fragmentation of the union movement to eliminate its veto power. Similar processes took place in countries like Mexico and Peru.

The political coalition constructed to maintain support for the new direction of economic policy, therefore, remains élite-dominated. The state is still the site of a significant centralization of power, and linkages between the state and most sectors of civil society have become particularly tenuous as a result of economic reform and the internationalization of the state. The early 1990s were characterized by a clear demobilization of societal actors as a result of economic crisis and hyperinflation in such countries as Argentina, Venezuela, Peru, and Brazil. Since the mid-1990s, however, the region has seen something of a resurgence of popular mobilization in the form of strike action, student riots, and provincial unrest (such as in Argentina), as well as the emergence of new and serious forms of political opposition. An example can be found in the FREPASO party in Argentina formed to fight the 1994 presidential elections and the alliance between FREPASO and the Radical Party (UCR) to fight the 1999 elections. In Mexico the opposition parties have won significant electoral victories in a formerly one-party system. The trend towards independent candidates of various colours remains strong—the line-up for the December 1998 Venezuelan presidential elections is a case in point.

Together with this, previously marginalized groups such as labour and public opinion can be seen to be taking a more meaningful role in political and economic debate: the 1996 IMF negotiations in Argentina, for example, were characterized by an unprecedented level of participation from the unions and other interested groups in society, as well as by extensive public debate through the media. Non-state actors such as non-governmental organizations have not been especially visible until quite recently, partly as a result of the exclusionary process of decision-making outlined above. Generally, the development of significant activities on the part of NGOs has lagged behind that in some other areas of the world, although transnational groups concentrating on such issues as human rights, the environment, and women's rights have been increasingly active. 'Native' civil society, however, is starting to flourish through linkages with more established transnational networks, and increasingly vociferous demands for the democratization of the state are likely to provide greater possibilities for participation, input, and influence.

For the most part, these new forms of mobilization are predicated on growing demands for participation in hitherto exclusionary political processes. It can be hoped that the initial marginalization of democracy was linked to the short-term political economy of reform and that exclusionary government has started to give way to a revitalization of demands for participatory democracy that can be accommodated within the existing political framework. The question, however, is whether this will have any significant impact. Latin America is perhaps different from some other regions, notably Asia, in that the consensus surrounding neoliberalism and engagement with the globalization of economic activity does not appear to be fragmenting, at either the élite level or the popular level: even the most visible and violent instances of mobilization, such as in the Mexican state of Chiapas, involve demands for inclusion rather than an opt-out type of radical opposition. None of the mainstream opposition groupings, new or old, has questioned the fundamentals of the economic strategy. The internationalization of the state and the network of international and regional commitments constructed by government élites similarly throw doubt on the possibilities for genuine change. It seems that the possibilities for participation are vast, but that its capacities are significantly limited.

## Conclusion: Looking Forward

The political economy of Latin America continues to be bound up with contemporary processes of globalization and regionalization. This is entirely intentional on the part of national government élites and is unlikely to unravel in the short or medium term. The story of the 1990s is one of the construction of increasingly close linkages among the national, regional, and global levels. The internationalization of the state in this respect has given a fundamentally new colour to the political economy of the region, as politics and economics become increasingly defined by external linkages. The debate is about the management of these linkages and about ways to escape the more deleterious effects of future crises: in other words, the debate is about how to optimize participation in the international political economy rather than about whether to participate at all.

The future trajectory of the region is characterized at present by a handful of unknowns. The Asian crisis has been a mixed blessing for Latin America. The loss of confidence in the Asian markets has led to a renewed focus on the alternatives, the most attractive of which are found in Latin America. But at the same time the Asian crisis, and the subsequent collapse in Russia, led to an increased caution with respect to emerging markets generally. From the time that the currency crises first broke in July 1997, the risk premiums for many such economies shot suddenly upward.[23] The collapse of the Brazilian currency (the real) in early 1999 was undoubtedly due in part to these patterns of market behaviour, but also had been widely predicted in view of the overvaluation of the real and the high levels of fiscal deficit maintained principally for political and electoral reasons. The possible contagion effects in other South American countries are only just emerging (at the time of writing), but it is clear that both the macroeconomic environment and the regional project are under considerable pressure.

Politics in Latin America is also in a state of flux. The consolidation of democratic rule has made room for an increasing questioning of the nature of the democratic systems themselves. This has generated demands for more inclusionary, representative, and participatory forms of political organization throughout the region, and in turn this has brought into play a host of new actors such as NGOs and grassroots movements. At the start of the decade authoritarian styles of democracy were thought to be the most suited to neo-liberal economic policies. At the end of the decade the consensus has shifted: neo-liberal economic policies are here to stay, but they cannot ensure continued development without adaptation to social and political realities. Even if this does not amount to the politicization of the market, it certainly looks like the revitalization of politics in Latin America.

## Notes

1  *El Cronista*, 24 June 1998.
2  ECLAC, *1997 Report—Foreign Investment in Latin America and the Caribbean* (Santiago, 1997).
3  ECLAC, *The Impact of the Asian Crisis on Latin America* (Santiago, 25 May 1998), 19.
4  Ibid.
5  ECLAC, *The Fiscal Covenant: Strengths, Weaknesses, Challenges* (Santiago, 1998).
6  CNCE, *Informe Anual* (Buenos Aires, 1995).
7  I am grateful to Richard Higgott for first suggesting this idea.
8  Diana Tussie, 'In the Whirlwind of Globalisation and Multilateralism: The Case of Emerging Regionalism in Latin America', in William D. Coleman and Geoffrey R.D. Underhill, eds, *Regionalism and Global Economic Integration* (London: Routledge, 1998), 92.
9  Roberto Bouzas, 'Mercosur and Preferential Trade Liberalisation in South America: Record, Issues and Prospects', Serie de Documentos e Informes de Investigación no. 176, FLACSO/Buenos Aires, Feb. 1995, 17.
10  IDB/INTAL, *Informe Mercosur*, no. 2 (Jan.-June 1997), ii.
11  Richard Higgott, 'Globalisation, Regionalisation and Identity in East Asia: Lessons from Recent Economic Experience', in Peter Dicken et al., eds, *The Logic(s) of Globalisation in the Asia Pacific* (London: Routledge, 1999).
12  Paulo S. Wrobel, 'A Free Trade Area of the Americas in 2005?', *International Affairs* 74, 3 (July 1998): 557.
13  Diana Tussie, 'Multilateralism Revisited in a Globalizing World Economy', *Mershon International Studies Review* 42 (May 1998): 192.
14  Pedro Da Motta Veiga, 'Brazil's Strategy for Trade Liberalization and Economic Integration in the Western Hemisphere', mimeo, Inter-American Dialogue, June 1996, 6–7.
15  For example, Jan Aarte Scholte, 'Global Capitalism and the State', *International Affairs* 73, 3 (1997).
16  George Philip,'The New Economic Liberalism and Democracy in Latin America: Friends or Enemies?', *Third World Quarterly* 14, 3 (1993); Stephan Haggard and Robert R. Kaufman, 'Estado y Reforma Económica: La Iniciación y Consolidación de las Políticas de Mercado', *Desarrollo Económico* 35, 139 (Oct.-Dec. 1995): 358.
17  George Philip, 'The New Populism in Spanish South America', *Government and Opposition* 33, 1 (Winter 1998).
18  Robert W. Cox, *Production, Power and World Order: Social Forces in the Making of History* (New York: Columbia University Press, 1987), 253.
19  Robert W. Cox, 'Social Forces, States and World Orders: Beyond International Relations Theory', *Millennium: Journal of International Studies* 10, 2 (Summer 1981).
20  Stephan Haggard and Sylvia Maxfield, 'The Political Economy of Financial Liberalization in the Developing World', in Robert O. Keohane and Helen V. Milner, eds, *Internationalization and Domestic Politics* (Cambridge: Cambridge University Press, 1996), 156.
21  Helen V. Milner and Robert O. Keohane, 'Internationalization and Domestic Politics: A Conclusion', in Keohane and Milner, eds, *Internationalization and Domestic Politics*, 245.
22  Jean Grugel, 'State and Business in Neo-liberal Democracies in Latin America', *Global Society* 12, 2 (May 1998).
23  ECLAC, *The Impact of the Asian Crisis.*

## Suggested Readings

Keohane, Robert O., and Helen V. Milner, eds. *Internationalization and Domestic Politics*. Cambridge: Cambridge University Press, 1996.

Mansfield, Edward D., and Helen V. Milner, eds. *The Political Economy of Regionalism*. New York: Columbia University Press, 1997.

Tussie, Diana. *The Policy Harmonization Debate: What Can Developing Countries Gain from Multilateral Negotiations?* Buenos Aires: FLACSO, 1994.

Coleman, William D., and Geoffrey R.D. Underhill, eds. *Regionalism and Global Economic Integration: Europe, Asia and the Americas*. London: Routledge, 1998.

## Web Sites

MERCOSUR:
http://www.americasnet.com/mauritz/mercosur

Institute for International Economics:
http://www.iie.com

World Trade Organization: http://www.wto.org

Part IV

---

# Responses

# to

# Globalization

# Introduction

# Globalization and State Policies

## Richard Stubbs

The chapters here complement those in previous sections by examining responses to globalization and their effect on the changing global order. In particular, the chapters pick up some of the themes suggested in Geoffrey Underhill's introduction to this volume and examine a number of key states and how they have responded to the forces generated by globalization. In addition, Part IV explores how the European Union has attempted to develop a coherent foreign policy in the context of globalization and how firms have had to adapt their strategies to the changing global order.

It is important to review the ways in which states have responded to globalization because the state has long been considered the primary actor in international affairs and, therefore, pivotal to the study of international relations and the international political economy. Even though interest in the state has waxed and waned among students of international relations in recent years, it is still crucial to our understanding of the workings of the international political economy.

Yet, despite its centrality to the discipline, there is currently little consensus over how the 'state' should be defined. The traditional view of the state, found in realist and neo-realist international relations texts, emphasizes the state's comprehensive control, through coercive and administrative means, over its territory and population, as well as its capacity to operate as a unitary, autonomous actor in an anarchic international system. The assumption is that the state pursues policies in the international arena in the name of its people and territory. There is much to be said for this approach; it is central to international law and, moreover,

nearly everyone uses it as a convenient shorthand for talking about various actions in the international arena. For example, we are accustomed to media references to the 'American policy' on trade liberalization or the 'Japanese position' at deliberations of the World Bank.

But scholars who approach the study of IPE with a background in comparative politics view the state in a very different way. They see the state in domestic institutional, or Weberian, terms as 'a set of administrative, policing and military organizations headed, and more or less well coordinated by, an executive authority'.[1] Such a view of the state paves the way for analyses of the impact of competing domestic pressures on the state and recognition that the state itself may be divided on a particular foreign economic policy issue. These two views of the state, while not the only ones used in analysing the international political economy, demonstrate the lack of agreement over how this core concept should be defined.

Not only is the very definition of the state in doubt, but its role in the global economy is also being hotly debated. One set of analysts argues that the state's power is in decline or, as Susan Strange asserts, that what we are experiencing is the 'retreat of the state'.[2] The power of the state, so this argument goes, is being undermined by an array of factors, including the rapid mobility of capital and the increasing integration of capital markets; the rising power of the major multinational corporations; the revolution in communications; and the expanding authority of international organizations. Globalization is thus depicted as a process that subverts the state's capacity to act in the interests of its citizens.

In addition, it should be noted that one of the key reasons for the formation and development of states—to fight wars—has been removed in many areas of the world with the end of the Cold War. If we take seriously Charles Tilly's aphorism, that 'wars make states',[3] then the relative peace of the post-Cold War years of the 1990s means that some of the rationale for state intervention in the economy has been eroded. Certainly, citizens are not so willing to cede power to state institutions in order to increase their security against military threats. Moreover, the lack of any external threat may also mean the rise of subnational groups that were hitherto kept in check by the need for a united front against a common enemy. States, then, are depicted as either distracted by internal problems or incapable of wielding the economic power they once held. States are viewed as being marginalized as other actors direct the global economy.

Yet there are those who would refute this view of the role of the state. Some argue that globalization and, therefore, its effects have been greatly exaggerated.[4] As a consequence, of course, globalization is viewed as not nearly as detrimental to the power of the state as the 'retreatists' would have us believe. Others argue that the state is not so much in decline as in the process of being transformed.[5] Globalization, it is argued, has required that the institutional state must reconcile the domestic interests it represents and the pressures that emanate from the international political economy. In mediating between domestic interests and the international political economy, states are being forced to transform themselves and the economies they regulate in such a way as to ride out, or even take advantage of, the changes to the international political economy brought about by globalization. Hence, the argument that the transformation of the state should not be confused with the decline of the state.

Analyses of state responses to globalization have also centred on the extent to which there has been convergence in economic structures and economic policies. In terms of economic structures it is clear that the central economic agencies of the state, such as finance departments and the central banks, have become increasingly important in state

decision-making. Moreover, these central economic agencies have also developed greater links not just with each other but with key international financial institutions such as the IMF and the World Bank. A constant round of meetings ensures that key finance ministers and central bankers are well informed as to the current thinking of international experts on how to resolve any particular problem, for example, inflation or unemployment. As a consequence, governments around the world have been encouraged, and in some cases forced, to adopt policies that reflect international rather than domestic imperatives. Some analysts would also see the growing links between international capital, particularly banks and other financial institutions, and governments as indicative of the changes that globalization has brought to economic structures within states.

At the same time, there has been a great deal of discussion of the way globalization has produced policy convergence among states. It is argued that this policy convergence has been brought about by a number of factors.[6] These include direct intervention by external authorities, such as the IMF or WTO; the influence of epistemic communities or transnational groups that share information and expertise about how to solve common problems; copying what are seen as 'best practices' of other states in particular policy areas and emulating the policies of those states that are competitors for foreign direct investment or even international portfolio capital; and harmonizing policies so that there is as little 'friction', or conflict, over policies as possible with trading partners. Each of these approaches, it is argued, produces some degree of policy convergence among states. In combination they are said to have created a situation in which there is a good deal of convergence in a number of policy areas, especially in economic policies.

But just as there are analysts who question the extent to which the state has been undermined by the advance of globalization, so, too, others question the degree to which state policies have converged. While it is accepted that some minimal level of convergence has taken place, it is argued that policies are said to be the product of particular sets of governing institutions that have arisen out of the unique cultures and the different recent historical experiences of individual states. As one analysis of public policy in Canada and the United States argues, 'the primary forces that contribute to distinctive national choices are rooted in the culture and political traditions' of the two countries.[7] As a result, then, of the wide variety of political cultures and political values and the very diverse political institutions to be found around the world, responses to globalization vary quite significantly. Moreover, because current policies are often heavily influenced by past policies, previous differences in the way governments have responded to crises have an effect on the way the current wave of globalization is managed. States, which may appear on the surface to be similar and to be in similar situations, can, therefore, enact very different policies as they attempt to deal with comparable pressures

produced by the forces of globalization.[8] The very different ways that Thailand, which accepted IMF advice, and Malaysia, which adopted policies exactly contrary to the IMF's prescription, have responded to pressure from international financial institutions in attempting to recover from the Asian economic crisis provide clear evidence that the convergence thesis has its limitations.

The following chapters give an indication of the way in which some of the key states around the world have attempted to deal with the globalization process and the consequences of the policies they have adopted. Readers will be able to judge for themselves the validity of the various views of the role of the state in the international political economy, and the extent to which globalization has affected state policies, in the rapidly changing global order.

## Notes

1 Theda Skocpol, *States and Social Revolutions* (Cambridge: Cambridge University Press, 1979), 29.

2 Susan Strange, *The Retreat of the State: The Diffusion of Power in the World Economy* (Cambridge: Cambridge University Press, 1996). One of the first to make this argument was Kenichi Ohmae in *The Borderless World* (New York: Collins, 1990).

3 Charles Tilly, 'War Making and State Making as Organized Crime', in Peter B. Evans, Dietrich Rueschemeyer, and Theda Skocpol, eds, *Bringing the State Back In* (Cambridge: Cambridge University Press, 1985), 170.

4 Paul Hirst and Grahame Thompson, *Globalization in Question* (Cambridge: Polity Press, 1996); Paul Hirst, 'The Global Economy—Myths and Realities', *International Affairs* 73 (July 1997).

5 See, for example, Linda Weiss, *The Myth of the Powerless State: Governing the Economy in a Global Era* (Cambridge: Polity Press, 1998).

6 See, for example, Colin J. Bennet, 'Review Article: What Is Policy Convergence and What Causes It?', *British Journal of Political Science* 21 (1991); Suzanne Berger, 'Introduction', in Berger and Ronald Dore, eds, *National Diversity and Global Capitalism* (Ithaca, NY: Cornell University Press, 1996).

7 Richard Simeon, George Hoberg, and Keith Banting, 'Globalization, Fragmentation and the Social Contract', in Banting, Hoberg, and Simeon, eds, *Degrees of Freedom: Canada and the United States in a Changing World* (Montreal and Kingston: McGill-Queen's University Press, 1997), 400.

8 See Weiss, *The Myth of the Powerless State*, 194–6.

Chapter 24

# Political Globalization and the Competition State

Philip G. Cerny

## Introduction: Three Paradoxes

Economic globalization does not translate automatically into political globalization.[1] Indeed, the latter requires a transformation of politics itself, i.e., the metamorphosis of the nation-state into what is called here a 'competition state'. This process is profoundly paradoxical in at least three ways. In the first place, globalization can *both* undermine the domestic autonomy and political effectiveness of the state *and* at the same time lead to the actual expansion of de facto state intervention and regulation in the name of competitiveness and marketization. Second, states and state actors are themselves among the greatest promoters of further globalization as they attempt to cope more effectively with 'global realities'. In undermining the autonomy of their own 'national models'—embedded state forms, contrasting modes of state interventionism, and differing state/society arrangements—by chasing international competitiveness, they disarm themselves. And finally, states seem to be getting more and more socially fragile—thereby further undermining the capacity of political and social forces within the state to resist globalization. This political globalization, in turn, forces the pace of globalization in economic, social, and cultural spheres, too.

## Globalization as a Political Process

Economic explanations of globalization are well known. The first is the interpenetration of national markets by various goods and assets, from money to industrial products to labour. The second is the

advent of new technology that, in contrast to the hierarchical technological forms of the Second Industrial Revolution—the age of the industrial state and the welfare state—is structurally amorphous and rapidly diffused. The third involves private and public economic institutions, from multinational enterprises to strategic alliances to private and even public regulatory regimes. Sociological explanations focus on two levels. On the one hand, people's perceptions of themselves as subjects or citizens of a particular nation-state are challenged from above by the crystallization and dissemination of global images and identities from above—the 'global village'. At another level, however, for postmodernists, what is emerging is an intensely speeded-up world where cultural fragmentation is seen as undermining all grand narratives and sociopolitical projects from underneath rather than from above. But from both economic and sociological perspectives, political institutions and practices are seen as epiphenomenal, dependent variables.

In contrast, globalization as a *political* phenomenon basically means that the shape of the playing field of politics itself—the possibilities of effective collective action internally and the capacity of states to make credible commitments externally—is increasingly determined not within insulated units, i.e., relatively autonomous and hierarchically organized structures called states. Rather, it derives from a complex aggregation of multilevel games played on multilayered institutional playing fields, *above* and *across*, as well as *within*, state boundaries. These three-level games are played out by state actors and other political forces, as well as by market actors and cultural actors. Political globalization derives first and foremost from a reshaping of political practices and institutional structures in order to adjust and adapt to the growing deficiencies of nation-states as perceived and *experienced* by such actors. The very idea of what constitutes a society—and therefore a political community—in the modern world has crystallized in the territorial nation-state, looking both outward to the system of states and inward to those ties of justice and friendship that Aristotle saw as distinguishing the *politeia* from the other. It involves attributing to the state a holistic character, a sense of organic solidarity that is more than any simple social contract or set of pragmatic affiliations. If there is an increasingly paradigmatic crisis of the state today, it concerns the erosion of this posited underlying bond.

Globalization itself has all too frequently been assumed to be a process of convergence, a homogenizing force; increasingly, however, analysts are arguing that globalization is fundamentally complex and 'heterogenizing'—even polarizing—in its nature and consequences. Complexity means the presence of many intricate component parts. It can mean a sophisticated and elegantly co-ordinated structure, but it can also mean that the different parts mesh poorly, leading to friction and even entropy. A globalizing world is intricately structured at many levels, developing within an already complex social, economic, and political context.[2] As a consequence, the globalization process does not involve some sort of linear withering away of the state as a bureaucratic power structure; paradoxically, in a globalizing world, states play a crucial role as stabilizers and enforcers of the rules and practices of *global* society. Indeed, state actors are the primary source of the state's own transformation into a competition state.

## The Slow Erosion of the Industrial Welfare State

The essence of the postwar national industrial and welfare state lay in the capacity that state actors and institutions had gained, especially since the Great Depression, in insulating certain key elements of economic life from market forces while promoting other aspects of the market.[3] These mechanisms did not merely mean protecting the poor and helpless and pursuing welfare goals like full employment or public health, but also regulating business in the public interest, 'fine-tuning' business cycles to promote economic growth, nurturing 'strategic industries' and 'national champions', integrating labour movements into corporatist processes to promote wage stability and labour discipline, reducing barriers to international trade, imposing controls on 'speculative' international movements of capital, and the like. The notion of national citizenship widened to include such issues, too. Following World War II, the expansion of these economic and social functions of the state came to be seen as crucial for the 'modernization' and 'development' of any country, rich or poor.[4]

But this compromise of domestic regulation and international opening was eroded by increasing domestic structural costs (the 'fiscal crisis of the state'[5]) as well as the structural consequences of growing external trade and, perhaps most importantly, of international financial transactions.[6] The crisis of the industrial welfare state lay in its decreasing capacity to insulate national economies from the global economy—and from the combination of stagnation and inflation that resulted when they tried. Today, rather than attempt to take certain economic activities *out* of the market—to 'decommodify' them as the welfare state was organized to do—the competition state has pursued *increased* marketization to make economic activities located within the national territory, or that otherwise contribute to national wealth, more competitive in international and transnational terms.[7]

The modern industrial welfare state was seen by neoclassical economists to combine a series of specific types of economic intervention to prevent 'market failure', including welfare spending, macroeconomic fine-tuning, and market-enforcing regulation such as anti-monopoly legislation or stock market regulation and labour market regulation; even indicative planning was rationalized as a market-clearing exercise.[8] More direct, non-market control or regulation was legitimized by reference to the need to organize production by natural monopolies, the provision of public goods and services, or the need to maintain basic or strategic industries. In this view, then, the industrial welfare state was based on a paradox. It might save the market from its own dysfunctional tendencies, but it carried within itself the potential to undermine the market in turn.

From a market perspective, then, the industrial welfare state had to be both (a) restrained in its application and (b) regularly *deconstructed*—deregulated and privatized—in order to avoid the 'ratchet effect' that leads to stagflation, fiscal crisis, and the declining effectiveness of each new increment of demand reflation and functional expansion. Failure to do this would result in a lumbering, muddling, 'overloaded' state. The international recession of the 1970s and early 1980s was widely perceived in this light; as a result, political decision-makers have undergone a fundamental learning process that has altered the norms according to which they operate. The result was the rise of what has been called *neo-liberalism*, or a revival of purist versions of neoclassical economic policy nostrums associated primarily with the Thatcher government in the United Kingdom and the Reagan administration in the United States. Nevertheless, the resulting competition state took on a variety of forms.

## Forms of the Competition State

The key to making the state more efficient, in the neo-liberal view, is to open it up—in terms of both its internal organizational structure and the regulatory and policy constraints it imposed on the market—to wider, i.e., global, market forces. The challenge for state actors today, as viewed through the contemporary neo-liberal discourse of globalization (in both its economic and political versions), is mainly to juggle four kinds of policy approaches: (1) a shift from macroeconomic to microeconomic interventionism, as reflected in both deregulation and industrial policy; (2) a shift in the focus of that interventionism from the development and maintenance of a range of 'strategic' or 'basic' economic activities in order to retain minimal economic self-sufficiency in key sectors to a focus on flexible response to competitive conditions in a range of diversified and rapidly evolving international marketplaces, i.e., the pursuit of 'competitive advantage' as distinct from 'comparative advantage';[9] (3) an emphasis on the control of inflation and general neo-liberal monetarism—supposedly translating into non-inflationary growth—as the touchstone of state economic management and interventionism; and (4) a shift in the focal point of party and governmental politics away from the general maximization of welfare within a nation (full employment, redistributive transfer payments, and social service provision) to the promotion of enterprise, innovation, and profitability in both private and public sectors.

In this context, there have been some striking similarities as well as major differences among leading capitalist countries. Within the competition state model, national policy-makers have a range of potential responses, old and new, with which to work. The challenge is said to be one of getting the state to do both *more* and *less* at the same time. Getting more for less has been the core concept, for example, of the so-called 'reinventing government' or 'New Public Management' movement, itself a major manifestation and dimension of the competition state approach.[10] The competition state involves both a transformation of the policy roles of the state, on the one hand, and a multiplication of specific responses to change, on the other. The essence of these changes lies in the differential capacity of the state to promote distinct types of economic development.

On the one hand, traditional kinds of strong state intervention have often been extremely effective at promoting what is called *extensive development*. Extensive development means finding and bringing in new *exogenous* resources and factors of capital (land, labour, physical capital such as factories and infrastructure, and financial capital) to new (and old) economic activities. Governments can help undermine feudal and peasant structures and use taxes, spending, regulation—and physical force—to channel investment (and other factors of production such as labour) away from non- or pre-industrial uses into capitalist industry and finance.

That's how Germany developed at the end of the nineteenth century and how Russia developed under both Tsarist and Communist regimes. But the potential drawbacks are the increasing tendency to produce costly and technologically outdated goods produced more cheaply elsewhere, featherbedding of labour and management, and corruption and overbureaucratization—leading to a vicious circle of inefficiency, hyperinflation, and state authoritarianism to keep the system going.

On the other hand, state intervention has been notably poor at promoting *intensive development*. Intensive development occurs mainly *after* extensive development (although they can occur simultaneously), and it means improving the *endogenous* efficiency of production, investment, and market structures and processes. As Adam Smith wrote, 'to improve land, like all other commercial projects, requires exact attention to small savings and small gains'. Intensive development means continually improving the microeconomic efficiency, competitiveness, and profitability of industry—even to the extent of regularly engaging in what Joseph Schumpeter called 'creative destruction' of old capital and technology to make way for the latest cutting-edge production, financing, and marketing methods. It means giving individual owners, managers, and workers market-based incentives to involve themselves in a day-to-day process of improvement of the competitiveness of the firm. In today's world of the competition state, fundamental changes in how states and economies interact have forced several types of policy change to the top of the political agenda, and these changes are intended to shift economic development from its extensive to its intensive form.

Among more traditional policy issue-areas is, of course, trade policy, including a wider range of non-tariff barriers and targeted strategic trade policies. The core issue in the trade issue-area is to avoid reinforcing through protection the existing rigidity of the industrial sector or sectors in question, while fostering or even imposing adaptation to global competitive conditions in return for temporary protection. Transnational constraints are growing rapidly in trade policy, however, as can be seen

in the establishment of the North American Free Trade Agreement, the proposed North Atlantic Free Trade Area, the Asia-Pacific Economic Co-operation group, and the World Trade Organization. Two other traditional categories, monetary and fiscal policy, are perhaps even more crucial today, and the key change is that relative priorities between the two have been reversed; tighter monetary policy is often pursued alongside a looser fiscal policy consisting of tax cuts and public deficits, though rising fiscal debt eventually forces fiscal retrenchment. And exchange rate policy, difficult to manage in the era of floating exchange rates and massive international capital flows, is none the less still essential; however, it is increasingly intertwined with monetary and fiscal policy.[11]

Potentially more innovative, combining old and new measures, is the area of industrial policy and related strategic trade policy. By targeting particular sectors, supporting the development of both more flexible manufacturing systems and transnationally viable economies of scale, and assuming certain costs of adjustment, governments can alter some of the conditions that determine competitive advantage: encouraging mergers and restructuring; promoting research and development; encouraging private investment and venture capital, while providing or guaranteeing credit-based investment where capital markets fail, often through joint public/private ventures; developing new forms of infrastructure; pursuing a more active labour market policy while removing barriers to mobility. The examples of Japanese, Swedish, and Austrian industrial policy have been widely analysed in this context.

A third category of measures, and potentially the most explosive, is, of course, deregulation. The deregulation approach is based partly on the assumption that national regulations, especially the traditional sort of regulations designed to protect national market actors from market failure, are insufficiently flexible to take into account the rapid shifts in transnational competitive conditions characteristic of the interpenetrated world economy of the late twentieth century. However, deregulation must not be seen just as the lifting of old regulations, but also as the formulation of new regulatory structures designed to cope with, and even to anticipate, shifts in competitive advantage. Furthermore, these new regulatory structures are often designed to *enforce* global market-rational economic and political behaviour on rigid and inflexible private-sector actors as well as on state actors and agencies. The institutions and practices of the state itself are increasingly marketized or 'commodified', and the state becomes the spearhead of structural transformation to international market norms both at home and abroad.[12]

Although each of these processes can be observed across a wide range of states, however, there are significant variations in how different competition states cope with the pressures of adaptation and transformation. There is a dialectic of divergence and convergence at work, rather than a single road to competitiveness. The original model of the competition state was the strategic or *developmental state*, which writers like John Zysman and Chalmers Johnson associated with France and Japan.[13] This perspective, which identifies the competition state with strong-state technocratic *dirigisme*, lives on in the analysis of newly industrializing countries (NICs) in Asia and other parts of the Third World. However, the difficulty with this approach has been that the scope of control that the technocratic patron-state and its client firms can exercise over market outcomes diminishes as the integration of these economies into global markets proceeds, with the resulting challenges this interdependence poses to policy-makers in different countries.

Essentially, the developmental state, like traditional forms of state intervention, works best when it pursues extensive development. It can play a crucial role in nurturing new industries and reorienting economic structures and actors to the world marketplace, but beyond a certain threshold even the most tightly bound firms and sectors will act in a more autonomous fashion when presented with the exogenous opportunities and constraints of international markets. And as more firms and sectors become linked into new patterns of production, financing, and market access, often moving operations offshore, their willingness to follow the script

declines. However, there are distinctions even here. Within this category, for example, Japanese administrative guidance and the ties of the *keiretsu* system have remained relatively strong despite a certain amount of liberalization, deregulation, and privatization, whereas in France the forces of neo-liberalism have penetrated a range of significant bastions, from the main political parties to major sectors of the bureaucracy itself.[14] The recent Asian economic crisis, however, is essentially a crisis of the developmental state.

In contrast, the orthodox model of the competition state today is not the developmental state but the neo-liberal state (in the European sense of the word 'liberal', i.e., orthodox free-market economic liberalism, or what is called 'nineteenth-century liberalism' in the United States). Thatcherism and Reaganism in the 1980s provided both a political rationale and a power base for the revival of free-market ideology generally—not just in the United Kingdom and the United States but throughout the world. The flexibility and openness of Anglo-Saxon capital markets, the experience of Anglo-American élites with international and transnational business and their willingness to go multinational, the corporate structure of American and British firms and their (relative) concern with profitability and shareholder returns rather than traditional relationships and market share, the enthusiasm with which American managers have embraced lean management and downsizing, and the relative flexibility of the US and UK labour forces, combined with an arm's-length state tradition in both countries—all of these factors are widely thought to have fought off the strategic state challenge and to have led eventually to more competitive states today.

Nevertheless, liberalization, deregulation, and privatization have not reduced the role of state intervention overall, just shifted it from decommodifying bureaucracies to marketizing ones. 'Reinventing government', for example, means the replacement of bureaucracies that directly produce public services by ones that closely monitor and supervise contracted-out and privatized services according to complex financial criteria and performance indicators. And industrial policy is alive and well, too, secreted in the interstices of a decentralized, patchwork bureaucracy, which is the American tradition and the new British obsession.

Throughout the debate between the Japanese model and the Anglo-American model, however, another model was widely canvassed. The European neocorporatist model, rooted in the postwar settlement and given another dimension through the consolidation of the European Union, has been presented by many European commentators as a middle way (although Britain has always been on its margins). In bringing labour into institutionalized settings, not only for wage bargaining but for other aspects of the social market, in doggedly pursuing conservative monetary policies, in promoting extensive training policies, and in possessing a universal banking system that nurtured and stabilized industry without strategic state interventionism, the European neocorporatist approach (as practised in varying ways in Germany, Austria, and Sweden in particular) has seemed to its proponents to embody the best aspects of both the Japanese and the Anglo-American models. However, despite the completion of the Single European Market and the signing of the Maastricht Treaty, the signs of what in the early 1980s was called 'Eurosclerosis' have reappeared; the European Monetary Union project is widely regarded as deflationary in a context where costs are unevenly spread; and the liberalizing, deregulatory option is increasingly on the political cards again (as it was, for a while, in the 1980s), especially in the context of high French and German unemployment.

On one level, then, the competition *among* different kinds of putative 'competition states' has been central to political globalization. 'National developments'—i.e., differences in models of state/economy relations or state/societal arrangements—as Zysman writes, have 'driven changes in the global economy'.[15] At another level, however, states and state actors seek to convince, or pressure, other states—and transnational actors such as multinational corporations or international institutions—to adopt measures that shift the balance of competitive advantage. The search for competitive advantage adds further layers and cross-cutting cleavages to the world economy, and these layers and cleavages increase the complexity and density of networks of interdependence and interpenetration. Finally, genuinely transnational pressures can develop—whether from multinational corporations or from nationally or locally based firms and other interests (such as trade unions) caught in the crossfire of the search for international competitiveness—for the establishment or expansion of transnational regimes, transnational neocorporatist structures of policy bargaining, transgovernmental linkages among bureaucrats, policy-makers and policy communities, and the like. In this context, the neo-liberal, Anglo-American variant of the competition state appears dominant in the late 1990s.

In all of these settings, then, the state is no longer able to act as a decommodifying hierarchy (i.e., taking economic activities out of the market). It must act more and more as a collective commodifying agent (i.e., putting activities *into* the market) and even as *a market actor itself*. It is financier, middleman, advocate, and even entrepreneur in a complex economic web where not only do the frontiers between state and market become blurred, but also where their cross-cutting structures become closely intertwined and their behavioural modes become less and less easy to distinguish. In such complex conditions, the state is sometimes structurally fragmented, sometimes capable of strategic action—but increasingly it is caught up in and constrained by cross-cutting global/transnational/domestic structural and conjunctural conditions. Thus, although the problems faced by all capitalist industrial states have given rise to certain similarities of response, significant divergences remain. Different states have different sets of advantages and disadvantages in the search for international competitiveness. They differ in endogenous structural capacity for strategic action both domestically and internationally. They differ in the extent to which their existing economic structures, with or without government intervention, can easily adapt to international conditions. And they differ in their vulnerability to international and transnational trends and pressures.

## The Scope and Limits of the Competition State

One element of convergence is that states and state actors—seemingly voluntarily—have given up a range of crucial policy instruments. In this context, states are less able to act as 'strategic' or 'developmental' states and increasingly become 'splintered states'.[16] One result is that state actors and different agencies are more intertwined with 'transgovernmental networks'—systematic linkages between state actors and agencies overseeing particular jurisdictions and sectors, but cutting across different countries and including a heterogeneous collection of private actors and groups in interlocking, unevenly developed cross-border policy communities. These transgovernmental policy networks can also help to set actors and agencies within the *same* state into increased policy competition *with each other*, further reinforcing wider transnational linkages. The functions of the state, although central in structural terms because the state seeks to maintain domestic and global stability alike, are increasingly residual in terms of the range of policy instruments and outcomes they entail.

In international terms, states—in pursuing the goal of competitiveness—are becoming more involved in what John Stopford and Susan Strange have called 'triangular diplomacy', consisting of the complex interaction of state-state, state-firm, and firm-firm negotiations.[17] But this concept must be widened further. Interdependence analysis has focused too exclusively on two-level games. Although this is an oversimplification, complex globalization has to be seen as a structure involving (at least) *three*-level games, with third-level (transnational) games including not only 'firm-firm diplomacy' but also transgovernmental networks and policy communities, internationalized market structures, transnational cause groups, and many other linked and interpenetrated markets, hierarchies, and networks. Thus, the actual amount of government involvement in social life can increase while the power of the state to control specific activities and market outcomes continues to diminish.

On the one hand, financial globalization and deregulation have intensified pressures for governments to increase monitoring of financial markets, criminalize insider trading, stabilize failing banks, combat money laundering, and the like. The growth of competing authorities with overlapping jurisdictions does not reduce interventionism; it merely expands the range of possibilities for splintered governments and special interests to carve out new fiefdoms, both domestically and transnationally, while undermining their overall strategic and developmental capacity—what has been called 'neomedievalism'.[18] On the other hand, while some countries, because of their infrastructure, education systems, workforce skills, and quality-of-life amenities, are able to attract mobile, footloose capital of a highly sophisticated kind, others may increasingly have to depend on low-wage, low-cost manufacturing or agricultural production. Indeed, such changes may well destabilize less favoured states, whose already fragile governmental systems will be torn by the ascendancy of religious, ethnic, or other grassroots loyalties. Today's revival of nationalism is not of the state-bound, nineteenth-century variety; it is more elemental, and leads to the breakup of states rather than to their maintenance.

If we want to look for an alternative way of understanding the competition state, probably the best place to look is at American state governments. These governments can claim only a partial loyalty from their inhabitants, and their power over internal economic and social structures and forces has been limited indeed. They have been required to operate over the course of the past two centuries in an increasingly open continental market. Their taxing and regulating power has been seriously constrained in many spheres by the expansion of the weight and the legal prerogatives of the federal government. At the same time, however, their ability to control development planning, to collect and use the tax revenues they do impose (as well as offering tax incentives and subsidies), to build infrastructure, to run education and training systems, and to enforce law and order gives these subnational states a capacity to influence the provision of immobile factors of capital in significant ways—indeed, more than many governments in Third World countries.

The attempt to make the state more 'flexible' has moved a long way over the past decade or so, not only in the United States and Britain—where deregulation, privatization, and liberalization have evolved furthest—but also in a wide range of other countries in the First and Third Worlds (and more recently in the Second World, too). The 'ratchet effect'—the term used by Mrs Thatcher's guru, Sir Keith Joseph, for what was once called 'creeping socialism', i.e., that each attempt to use the state to achieve a new discrete policy goal ratchets up the size and unwieldiness of the state as a whole—has been turned on its head. In a globalizing world, the competition state is more likely to be involved in a process of competitive deregulation and *creeping liberalization*.

## Conclusion: Globalization and the Competition State as Paradoxes

The central paradox of globalization itself—of the displacement of a crucial range of economic, social, and political activities from the national arena to a cross-cutting global/transnational/domestic structured field of action—is that rather than creating one big economy or one big polity, it also divides, fragments, and polarizes. Convergence and divergence are two sides of the same coin. Whether the forces of convergence will lead a complex but stable pluralistic world based on liberal capitalism and the vestiges of liberal democracy[19] or the forces of divergence and inequality are creating a more volatile and fragmented world remains to be seen. Whatever direction the future takes, however, political strategies and projects will increasingly become multilayered and globally oriented—whether on the right ('globalization' in the sense of pursuing economic efficiency in a liberalized world marketplace) or on the left (a regeneration of genuinely internationalist socialism). The post-modern irony of the competition state is that rather than simply being undermined by inexorable forces of economic globalization, politics is becoming not only the engine room but also the steering mechanism of a political globalization process that will increasingly drive and shape the context—and the substance—of economic, social, and cultural globalization.

## Notes

1  For an intelligent (if overstated) critique of the concept of globalization, see Paul Hirst and Grahame Thompson, *Globalization in Question: The International Economy and the Possibilities of Governance* (Oxford: Polity Press, 1996).

2  P.G. Cerny, 'Globalization, Governance, and Complexity', in Aseem Prakash and Jeffrey A. Hart, eds, *Globalization and Governance* (London: Routledge, 1999).

3  Karl Polanyi, *The Great Transformation: The Political and Economic Origins of Our Time* (New York: Rinehart, 1944).

4  Reinhard Bendix, *Nation-Building and Citizenship: Studies of Our Changing Social Order* (New York: Wiley, 1964).

5  James O'Connor, *The Fiscal Crisis of the State* (New York: St Martin's Press, 1973).

6  Susan Strange, *Casino Capitalism* (Oxford: Basil Blackwell, 1986).

7  P.G. Cerny, *The Changing Architecture of Politics: Structure, Agency, and the Future of the State* (Newbury Park, Calif.: Sage, 1990).

8  Saul Estrin and Peter Holmes, *French Planning in Theory and Practice* (London: Allen & Unwin, 1982).

9  The distinction between comparative advantage and competitive advantage is a central theme in John Zysman and Laura d'Andrea Tyson, eds, *American Industry in International Competition* (Ithaca, NY: Cornell University Press, 1983).

10  David Osborne and Ted Gaebler, *Reinventing Government: How the Entrepreneurial Spirit is Transforming the Public Sector, From Schoolhouse to Statehouse, City Hall to the Pentagon* (Reading,

Mass.: Addison-Wesley, 1992); Patrick Dunleavy, 'The Globalisation of Public Services Production: Can Government Be "Best in World"?', *Public Policy and Administration* 9, 2 (Summer 1994): 36–64.

11   Jeffry A. Frieden, 'Invested Interests: The Politics of National Economic Policies in a World of Global Finance', *International Organization* 45, 4 (Autumn 1991): 425–51.

12   P.G. Cerny, 'The Limits of Deregulation: Transnational Interpenetration and Policy Change', *European Journal of Political Research* 19, 2–3 (Mar./Apr. 1991): 173–96.

13   John Zysman, *Governments, Markets, and Growth: Financial Systems and the Politics of Industrial Change* (Ithaca, NY: Cornell University Press, 1983); Chalmers Johnson, *M.I.T.I. and the Japanese Miracle: The Growth of Industrial Policy, 1925–1975* (Stanford, Calif., Stanford University Press, 1982).

14   Steven K. Vogel, *Freer Markets, More Rules: Regulatory Reform in Advanced Industrial Countries* (Ithaca, NY: Cornell University Press, 1996);

Vivien A. Schmidt, *From State to Market? The Transformation of French Business and Government* (Cambridge: Cambridge University Press, 1996).

15   John Zysman, 'The Myth of a "Global" Economy: Enduring National Foundations and Emerging Regional Realities', *New Political Economy* 1, 1 (1996): 157–84; cf. Louis W. Pauly and Simon Reich, 'Enduring Differences in the Era of Globalization: National Structures and Multinational Corporate Behavior', *International Organization* 51, 1 (1997): 1–30.

16   Howard Machin and Vincent Wright, eds, *Economic Policy and Policy-Making Under the Mitterrand Presidency, 1981–84* (London: Pinter, 1985).

17   John Stopford and Susan Strange, *Rival States, Rival Firms: Competition for World Market Shares* (Cambridge: Cambridge University Press, 1991).

18   P.G. Cerny, 'Neomedievalism, Civil War and the New Security Dilemma: Globalisation as Durable Disorder', *Civil Wars* 1, 1 (Spring 1998): 36–64.

19   Francis Fukuyama, *The End of History and the Last Man* (New York: Free Press, 1992).

## Suggested Readings

Cerny, P.G. *The Changing Architecture of Politics: Structure, Agency, and the Future of the State.* Newbury Park, Calif.: Sage, 1990.

Frieden, Jeffry A. 'Invested Interests: The Politics of National Economic Policies in a World of Global Finance', *International Organization* 45, 4 (Autumn 1991): 425–51.

Hirst, Paul, and Grahame Thompson. *Globalization in Question: The International Economy and the Possibilities of Governance.* Oxford: Polity Press, 1996.

Osborne, David, and Ted Gaebler. *Reinventing Government: How the Entrepreneurial Spirit is Transforming the Public Sector, From Schoolhouse to Statehouse, City Hall to the Pentagon.* Reading, Mass., Addison-Wesley, 1992.

Polanyi, Karl. *The Great Transformation: The Political and Economic Origins of Our Time.* New York: Rinehart, 1944.

Prakash, Aseem, and Jeffrey A. Hart, eds. *Globalization and Governance.* London: Routledge, 1999.

Reich, Robert B. *The Work of Nations: Preparing Ourselves for 21st-Century Capitalism.* New York: Knopf, 1991.

Rhodes, Martin, and Yves Mény. *The Future of European Welfare: A New Social Contract?* London: Macmillan, 1998.

Vogel, Steven K. *Freer Markets, More Rules: Regulatory Reform in Advanced Industrial Countries.* Ithaca, NY: Cornell University Press, 1996.

Zysman, John. *Governments, Markets, and Growth: Financial Systems and the Politics of Industrial Change.* Ithaca, NY: Cornell University Press, 1983.

## Web Sites

OECD's Policy Brief on the Multilaterial Agreement on Investment: http:\\www.oecd.org/publications/pol_brief/9702_pol.htm

European Central Bank: http:\\www.ecb.int

European Union Central: http:\\www.europa.eu.int

## Chapter 25

# Agricultural Policy: Regionalization and Internationalization

## William D. Coleman and Grace D. Skogstad

In the past 30 years, trade in agricultural commodities and in processed food products has grown significantly. This increase in the internationalization of the agri-food sector has not resulted, however, in the globalization of agriculture. Rather, the increased cross-border activity has led to the development of integrated regional markets more than to the creation of a totally global market. None the less, the rise in cross-border trading in a sector where various protectionist domestic policies and border measures have long been in place created new situations inviting conflict between states over agricultural trade. This intensification of conflict in the 1980s fuelled international and regional trade agreements based on market-liberalizing premises.

The most important of these agreements were the multilateral Uruguay Round of the General Agreement on Tariffs and Trade (GATT) of 1986–93 and the North American Free Trade Agreement (NAFTA) implemented in 1994. Alongside domestic fiscal pressures, these trade agreements have promoted liberalizing domestic agricultural policy reforms in the world's most important agricultural nations. The further liberalization of agricultural policies will continue into the next century, as agricultural markets become more economically integrated on a regional basis. Despite this liberalization, conflict in the agricultural trading system can be expected to continue as disputes erupt over non-tariff trade barriers linked to food safety and agro-biotechnology. Rooted in cultural differences between North American and European farmers and consumers, such disputes will be characterized by a broader public debate than has marked agricultural trade disputes in the past.

This chapter develops these arguments in four steps. First, we examine the concepts of globalization, internationalization, and regionalization as applied to the agri-food sector, highlighting the market dynamic in favour of increased regionalization. Second, we review the liberalizing aspects of the GATT Uruguay Round and NAFTA as well as the internal liberalization sparked by the Common Agricultural Policy in Europe. Third, the chapter examines the impacts of these supranational agreements on domestic policy change in the European Union, the United States, Canada, and Australia. The chapter concludes with an examination of emerging issues in the sector by reviewing the increasing disputes arising from biotechnological innovations leading to genetically modified products.

## Internationalization, Globalization, or Regionalization?

To assess the character of recent economic changes in agriculture, it is useful to distinguish between internationalization and globalization as processes. Internationalization refers to the growth of cross-border trade and investment relations between national economies leading to the increased integration of more and more nations and economic actors into world market relationships.[1] In this process, national economies remain the principal organizing entities, with multinational firms engaging in foreign direct investment through branch plants and subsidiaries. In contrast, globalization refers to the development of economic relationships that transcend borders; they extend across widely dispersed locations at the same time, and capital can move anywhere in the globe virtually instantaneously.[2] Distinct national economies become subsumed and 'rearticulated' into a global economy by these transnational processes and transactions.[3] The global economy becomes a single entity in its own right, with competition manifesting itself often in worldwide *intra-firm* divisions of labour or in co-operative inter-firm networks organized in multiple locations.[4]

The distinction between crossing and transcending borders may also be applied in a regional context. *Market* regionalization will refer to a process where national economies remain the primary actors in the regional system, but the growth of cross-border trade and investment integrates those economies into a single regional market. Multinational corporations organize foreign direct investment through branch plants in the various economies in the region. In contrast, *transcendent* regionalization denotes a process where national economies dissolve into a regional economy, with corporations and networks of firms organizing production region-wide, taking no account of national borders.

The agri-food sector has clearly internationalized over the past quarter-century. The total value of international agri-food trade increased from $65 billion in 1972 to $381 billion in 1993.[5] Growth in trade in processed food products was more rapid than in agricultural commodities, with the former's share in world agricultural trade rising from 58 per cent in 1972 to 67 per cent in 1993.[6] This growth was facilitated by advances in transportation technology, management strategies using information technology, and storage and handling facilities. The application of these technologies, however, has not led to the globalization of the sector; multinational firms remain the dominant organizational form, with processing facilities being located close to production areas.[7]

The increase in cross-border trade and investment has been most pronounced within regions. Trade within the European Community increased more than sixfold between 1960 and 1993.[8] Dell'Aquila's more comprehensive and recent research shows that intraregional trade flows in North America and Europe have increased further since the beginning of the 1980s.[9] Since 1980, this market regionalization has also included raw commodities, for which markets have traditionally been more international than regional. In the European Union, where market regionalization has been institutionalized since the 1960s, trans-European agrifood corporations like Unilever, Danone, and Montedison have emerged. And with the prospect of an economic and monetary union at hand, transcendent regionalization may receive still another push in Europe.

Agricultural producers have also been integrated into transnational economic relations over the past 30 years as a result of their changing relations with input suppliers and buyers. Family ownership of the production unit remains dominant in all countries. However, food processors have come to manufacture food products rather than simply process food commodities, and they place more stringent demands on producers, sometimes using production or marketing contracts to secure a steady supply of farm products of known quality and specifications. In the United States, contracting and vertical integration have become dominant business practice in the broiler, turkey, egg, milk, and specialty crop markets, and increasingly common in hog operations.[10] Whether the US model will extend to Canada and the EU as market regionalization and internationalization proceed is an important empirical question.

Agricultural producers also experience transnational economic relations through the input side of their operations. Most farmers rely on borrowed capital to finance the purchase of land, the modernization of equipment and facilities, and the short-term expenses incurred in production. Historically, access to and the cost of financing were somewhat sheltered from broader banking markets in most OECD countries through specialized credit facilities. Over the past 20 years, however, most of these facilities have been either privatized or integrated into regular financial services markets where they compete with private firms.[11] Remaining state-owned facilities now prefer to guarantee loans provided by private firms rather than to sell their loans directly. Consequently, farm enterprises now face the same risk assessment as other firms served by the highly internationalized banking systems in the OECD.

Many other input sectors—agricultural machinery, agrochemicals, fertilizer, seeds—have come to be dominated by relatively small numbers of multinational firms. The effects of this internationalization have intensified as biotechnology expands in agriculture. To name but a few examples, biotechnology firms have developed herbicide- and pesticide-resistant plants, genetically modified soya beans, canola, and maize with properties particularly valued by processing firms, and hormones to increase the productivity of dairy cows and the growth of beef cattle.[12] These developments, in turn, have encouraged consolidation among agricultural input suppliers. For example, agrochemical companies such as Monsanto enter the seed business to sell packages of herbicide and their herbicide-resistant seeds. They also furnish producers with advice and assistance in planting and cultivating crops.[13] Genetically modified products (GMPs) have expanded rapidly in North America, with estimates, for example, of one acre in seven of the US soya bean harvest being grown from genetically modified seed in 1997.[14] The European Union has resisted accepting imports of GMPs, an act, in turn, that has brought large US multinational corporations engaged in biotechnology into the political struggle for liberalized international trade in agriculture.

Milner and Keohane propose that as internationalization (and we would add market regionalization) makes domestic economies more vulnerable to externally generated shocks, pressures will increase for governments for major reforms of policy and institutional arrangements.[15] Without further systematic analysis, it is difficult to say whether increased internationalization and regionalization are direct causes of policy change. The following two sections of the chapter provide some justification for investigating the Milner/Keohane proposition further. They describe how regional and international trade agreements and domestic policy change have yielded liberalized agricultural policies.

## Agriculture in Regional and International Trade Agreements

The recent inclusion of agriculture in a number of regional trade agreements[16] and in the multilateral GATT/WTO is a sharp historical departure. Agriculture was not an integral part of the postwar liberalizing world trade regime. Exempted by various provisions of the GATT, agriculture's exclusion was further completed when the United States obtained a waiver from most of its GATT obligations concerning agriculture in 1955. Other countries followed suit, most particularly the European Economic Community, with the implementation of the Common Agricultural Policy (CAP) in the 1960s.

The CAP marked an important exception to agriculture's remaining outside liberalizing trade agreements. It instituted free trade in agricultural commodities among the original six (and today, 15) members of the European Community/Union (EC/EU). Designed to remove tariff and non-tariff barriers to agricultural trade within the region and the EC, the policy also protected European agriculture from foreign competition by using price supports above world market levels and variable import levies. Export subsidies ensured European agricultural products could be sold abroad at competitive prices. The CAP goal of intraregional liberalization while maintaining protection against commodities outside the region was consistent with the general postwar trend for national governments to afford substantial expenditure and regulatory assistance to their agricultural sectors.

At its inception and with successive enlargements, the regional integration of agricultural markets in the EC/EU has been driven by political and strategic motivations. A common market was central to the political process of European integration as a means to ensure peace in Western Europe. Economic factors were initially of secondary importance but gained significance over time. In contrast, the incorporation of agriculture in more recent regional trade agreements, including the 1989 Canada-US Free Trade Agreement (FTA) and NAFTA in 1994, is principally a response to increased market interdependence. Canada's dependence on the American market and its desire to maintain secure access to this market are primary factors explaining both the FTA and NAFTA.[17] Economic concerns were similarly key to Mexico's entry into NAFTA. Geopolitical considerations were most important for the US: NAFTA was a means to secure the political and economic stability of Mexico and to prod the multilateral trade negotiations, which were floundering over the impasse on agriculture.

The FTA and, to a lesser extent, NAFTA deviate from the EC/EU in not seeking regional free trade. Neither Canada nor the United States was interested in making the liberalization of its agricultural policies a focal point of the bilateral trade discussions. As a result, the FTA imposed limited obligations on the two countries in terms of removing protectionist policies. Eventually, NAFTA left in place the Canada-US FTA provisions for agriculture, while providing for new agreements between Canada and Mexico, and Mexico and the United States. It further extended the creation of a free trade area in grains and grain products, and provided timetables for the removal of most agricultural tariffs and non-tariff barriers among the three countries over a 10–15-year period. Again, however, the most heavily protected, supply management sectors were exempted from the liberalization initiative.

The unprecedented inclusion of agriculture since 1994 in the World Trade Organization, as a result of the Uruguay Round negotiation, was in response to interdependent international markets. Global trade in agricultural products grew modestly in the postwar period, but rose sharply between 1975 and 1980.[18] The EC shifted from being a net importer of grains, dairy products, and beef to being a significant exporter of these commodities in the 1970s. With its agricultural exports declining in the early 1980s[19] and frustrated by its previous failures to bring agriculture under the discipline of the GATT, the United States promoted the Uruguay Round. It was supported by the Cairns Group[20] and the

intellectual weight of the OECD and agricultural trade policy specialists. The result was strong pressure for the multilateral liberalization of agricultural markets. In sharp contrast to previous GATT practice of opening international markets by reducing border protection, the Uruguay Round targeted not only tariff and non-tariff border measures, but also domestic policies, including export subsidies and internal policies and practices that distorted trade.

The 1994 Marrakesh Agreement ending the Uruguay Round created the World Trade Organization and signalled a new era in the internationalization of agriculture. For the first time, domestic and agricultural trade policies become subject to international rules as laid out in the Agreement on Agriculture and the Sanitary and Phytosanitary Agreement, and as enforced by strengthened dispute settlement procedures and institutions. Two WTO bodies ensure the promotion of liberal norms: the Trade Policy Review Body, entrusted with analysing WTO members' policy changes; and the Committee on Agriculture, which meets four or five times a year to review countries' implementation of their WTO commitments.

The international institutionalization of agricultural trade policy should lead to a modest liberalization of agricultural markets. In all three areas—market access, domestic support measures, and the use of export subsidies—the Agreement on Agriculture fell well short of free trade in raw commodities and processed products. First, existing export subsidies (the area of highest priority for the United States and the Cairns Group) were to be reduced only 21 per cent by volume and 36 per cent by expenditure as calculated on a 1986–90 base. New agricultural export subsidies were prohibited. Second, all border protection measures (import controls, variable import levies, import licences) were to be converted to tariffs and then reduced by 36 per cent in aggregate over the six-year implementation period of the WTO (1995–2000). As well, market access was promoted by requiring countries to allow imports equal to 3 per cent and rising to 5 per cent of domestic consumption at minimal tariffs. However, special safeguard provisions allow countries to impose additional duties if the volume or price of imports causes domestic prices for specified commodities subject to tariffs to fall below a given level.

And third, the Agreement on Agriculture required total internal support to be reduced by 20 per cent from a 1986–8 base over the period 1995–2000. Not subject to this discipline were minimally trade-distorting domestic supports, which include 'green box' measures divorced from both production decisions and market prices.[21] Examples are expenditures for market promotion, crop insurance, disaster relief, conservation, research and extension, and rural and regional development. Also exempt from the aggregate measure of support (AMS) calculations were partially divorced payments, that is, those not related to market prices but designed to limit production. These measures included then existing US deficiency payments and the European Union compensation payments introduced in 1992.[22]

Certainly, the direct and short-term effect of the Uruguay Round Agreement on Agriculture in leveraging domestic liberalizing reforms is modest. The new tariffs were usually set at such high levels for both basic and 'sensitive' processed products that they resulted in higher average rates of protection than provided by the import barriers they replaced.[23] The low level of AMS reduction and the decision to exclude some key subsidies enabled most GATT signatories to meet the AMS requirement without changing their internal support programs. Indeed, the Agreement did not necessarily reduce overall financial support for farmers.

The indirect and medium-term effects of the Agreement on Agriculture are noteworthy and can be expected to be greater in the future. During the Uruguay Round, the pressure on the EU to reform the CAP in order to salvage the Round itself was an important catalyst to CAP reforms and affected the configuration of these reforms. The template of decoupled programs has been used by other countries redesigning their domestic support measures, including Canada and the United States. And the limits on export subsidies will likely necessitate further liberalizing reforms to the CAP.[24]

## The Liberalization of Domestic Agricultural Policy

Over the past decade or more, most of the major Western industrialized countries, including those of the EU, have reformed their agricultural policies to expose producers more to market price signals. In many countries, this increased reliance on market prices has been accompanied by reduced government trade-distorting transfers to the agricultural sector. Such transfers have declined over the past decade in Canada, the United States, and New Zealand and in OECD countries as a whole. The decline in distorting subsidies does not mean necessarily that total financial transfers to agriculture have diminished. The more market-liberal instruments introduced in the United States in 1996 and the European Union in 1992 actually increased government expenditures over previous, more trade-distorting programs.

A second liberalizing pattern is discernible. Although market price support remains the dominant form of assistance, OECD countries are moving away from commodity-specific programs supporting market prices to direct payments, fully or partially decoupled from market prices and production decisions. Deemed less trade-distorting than market price supports, direct payments reduce the insulation of consumers and producers from world markets. The shift to direct payments is fully evident in the EC/EU. The 1992 MacSharry reforms introduced compensatory payments that break 'the direct link between price support levels and farm receipts'.[25] Payments based on the yield of arable crops were replaced with direct payments based on acreage, with payments to large producers contingent on production controls. A similar partial decoupling occurred in the European beef sector. In Canada, commodity-specific programs were replaced with a joint government/producer-funded income stabilization program (the National Income Stabilization Act). The 1996 US farm bill replaced deficiency payments tied to market prices or planting restrictions with fixed transfers to cereal, oilseeds, and cotton producers for the 1995–2002 period.

Consistent with the move to non-trade-distorting policy instruments is evidence that government fiscal support for agriculture appears to be concentrated in the 'green box' category. This is particularly true in the two countries where government transfers are lowest: Australia and New Zealand. Even in countries, like Canada, that continue to invest significant (albeit declining) sums in their agricultural sectors, government support is shifting away from income support to research, food product safety, training, and general services—all found in the green box.

The liberalizing pattern is not, however, uniform. Japanese and European agriculture continue to receive substantial state support. Across countries, markets for politically important commodities, like rice in Japan, peanuts and sugar in the United States, and dairy and poultry products in Canada, continue to be highly protected as import barriers remain robust. And export subsidies continue to be an instrument of European and American agricultural policy.

Can this pattern of increased, but uneven, liberalization of domestic agricultural policy be attributed to either the international or regional institutionalism of agricultural policy-making? The answer: 'only to a limited extent', and to a greater degree for some countries than for others. First, New Zealand, Australia, and the European Community all reformed their agricultural policies prior to the conclusion of the Uruguay Round. In an important sense, then, the Agreement on Agriculture locked in reforms that were implemented before and during the Uruguay Round in developed countries. Where significant market-liberalizing reforms were implemented after the Round's conclusion, such as in Canada in 1995 and in the United States in 1996, the reforms followed the path of earlier policy modifications and/or were consistent with the debate in the agricultural policy community. The American move to rely more on direct income support through deficiency payments began with the 1985 farm bill and was continued in the 1990 farm bill. The 1996 Federal Agricultural and Improvement Reform (FAIR) Act

accelerated this trend. The Canadian decision to eliminate entirely grain export subsidies and offer a one-time adjustment fund reflected the consensus that had evolved over more than 10 years in the grains and oilseeds sector.

Second, the primary catalysts to market-liberalizing reform in Australia, New Zealand, Canada, and the United States were domestic factors rather than the pressure of international rules. Of these, domestic budgetary pressures were paramount in Canada and highly important in Europe. The removal of agricultural subsidies in New Zealand and the deregulation of Australian agriculture were part of economy-wide reforms, driven largely by the neo-liberal ideological preferences of governing parties. The market-liberalizing orientation of the 1996 US farm bill was independent of multilateral commitments, the result of budgetary pressures and a Republican-controlled Congress determined to reduce the regulatory burden on American farmers and sympathetic to large competitive farmers and agribusiness.[26]

If domestic factors are primary in explaining liberalizing agricultural policy reforms in Western industrialized countries, this is not to deny that internationalization has played some role. The Australian Labour government argued successfully that deregulation of manufactured milk prices was required to meet the anticipated more liberal and more competitive markets that would ensue when the Uruguay Round concluded. The MacSharry reforms to the CAP in Europe were made with an eye to breaking the deadlock in the Uruguay Round negotiations that ensued when the United States and the Cairns Group were unwilling to allow negotiations in other sectors to conclude until EC concessions on agriculture were forthcoming. The reforms themselves were aimed at 'increasing the competitiveness of European agriculture'.[27] The desire to increase the productivity of US agriculture to ensure its international competitiveness also figured in the shift to decoupled payments in the US FAIR Act. The WTO Agreement on Agriculture can be given credit for providing a template for the redesign of Canadian policy instruments, including the shift to direct payments, tariffs, and the reconfiguration of dairy export subsidies. The difficulty of redesigning freight rate subsidies to conform to the new WTO volume limits was a factor in the Canadian government's decision to eliminate them entirely.

The discourse of competitiveness that now shifts domestic agricultural policy debates in a market-liberalizing direction is in large part due to the impact of regionalization. The need to be competitive within regional markets has already affected policy reforms. The predominance of intra-industry trade that results from foreign direct investment in the food-processing industries is linked to regional free trade agreements. Within these more liberal and more competitive blocs, 'business decisions on where to locate become more sensitive to differences in domestic policies and practices.'[28] For example, in NAFTA, the market-led integration that results from increased trade and investment is bringing pressure on the smaller partners, Canada and Mexico, to harmonize their policies with those of their larger partner, the United States. Such pressure to alter significantly domestic policies is difficult to resist, given the asymmetrical trading relationship of the two countries with the United States.

Regionalization as a force for market-liberalizing reforms is also evident in the European Union. Enlargement of the EU to include Central and Eastern European countries at the turn of the century has created strong liberalizing pressures, since the CAP would become prohibitively expensive were it made available in its current form to farmers in the new member states.

## Conclusion

International and regional trade agreements and domestic policy changes have exposed many agricultural commodities and processed food products more fully to market forces. These policy changes have considerable institutional backing, whether through the CAP, NAFTA and its dispute settlement mechanism, or the WTO and its reinforced and binding settlement procedures. If these agreements and policy changes hold, freer markets will likely develop in the agri-food sector, bringing perhaps additional liberalizing pressures on policy. Preliminary assessments of the implementation of the Uruguay Round agreement indicate that the new provisions are being followed without any particular upsurge in agricultural disputes.

It is unlikely, however, that the path will be a straight one to greater internationalization, let alone globalization. Agricultural commodities and processed food products occupy central places in human cultures, and agricultural cultivation practices have deep roots in many cultural systems. The great farms and ranches of the American and Canadian West, the huge pastoral operations in Australia, the highly cultivated, centuries-old rural landscapes of Europe—all are parts of the respective economies to be sure, but also of the cultures of the peoples living in those regions. As the market forces unleashed in agriculture come to threaten or undermine core cultural values and practices, we can expect individuals in these societies to respond politically. As Polanyi notes, 'For if market economy was a threat to the human and natural components of the social fabric, as we insisted, what else would one expect than an urge on the part of a great variety of people to press for some sort of protection?'[29]

An example is the resistance of ecologists, consumers, and some sections of the farm community to the use of genetically modified seed and the importation of genetically modified agricultural commodities or processed products made from these commodities. They argue that these products may be unsafe for European consumers or that they invite the use of pesticides and herbicides that will accentuate the damage to the environment already associated with intensive agriculture. North American trade experts respond that GMPs are not covered by the current Sanitary and Phytosanitary Agreement because they do not contain additives or contaminants harmful to health. They suggest that biotechnology is simply a way of producing a product more reliably and quickly than conventional breeding methods.[30]

In this kind of dispute, culture, whether in the form of consumer preferences or conceptions of the countryside, becomes part of regional (EU) struggles against internationalization and the associated recourse to 'science'. The GMP dispute also illustrates, however, the complexity of the interplay between regionalization and internationalization. The European Commission has challenged the Austrian ban on GMPs in court on the grounds that it interferes with the free regional market in agricultural products. This challenge is supported, in turn, by European biotechnology companies that seek full access not only to the EU market, but also to international markets.[31]

In short, the close links between human culture and agriculture make it very difficult for states and regional organizations to unleash fully the power of market forces in this sector. Liberalization of markets will continue, to be sure, but it will be slow, with every step discussed, debated, and then carefully negotiated. Although international and regional trading rules are now more institutionalized and liberalized than ever before in this century, these remain open to challenge as some farmers, ecologists, and consumers press states to protect health, rural landscapes, and culture.

## Notes

1   Paul Hirst and Grahame Thompson, *Globalization in Question: The International Economy and the Possibilities of Governance* (London: Polity Press, 1995), 8; Jan Aart Scholte, 'Global Capitalism and the State', *International Affairs* 73, 3 (1997): 430.

2   Scholte, 'Global Capitalism and the State', 431.

3   Hirst and Thompson, *Globalization in Question*, 10.

4   David Goodman, 'World-Scale Processes and Agro-Food Systems: Critique and Research Needs', *Review of International Political Economy* 4, 4 (1997): 665.

5   Dennis R. Henderson, Charles R. Handy, and Steven A. Neff, *Globalization of the Processed Food Market* (Washington: USDA-ERS, 1996), 7–8.

6   Ibid., 8.

7   Michael R. Reed and Mary A. Merchant, 'The Behavior of US Food Firms in International Markets', in Alessandro Bonnano, Lawrence Busch, William H. Friedland, Lourdes Gouveia, and Enzo Mingione, eds, *From Columbus to ConAgra: The Globalization of Agriculture and Food* (Lawrence: University Press of Kansas, 1994), 156; Charles R. Handy and Dennis R. Henderson, 'Assessing the Role of Foreign Direct Investment in the Food Manufacturing Industry', in Maury E. Bredahl, Philip C. Abbott, and Michael R. Reed, *Competitiveness in International Food Markets* (Boulder, Colo.: Westview Press, 1994), 212.

8   Albert Cheminot, B. Daviron, and M. Griffon, 'Globalisation des économies agricoles et alimentaires', *Economie rurale* no. 234–5 (1996): 4.

9   Crescenzo Dell'Aquila and Karl D. Meilke, *Regionalism and World Agro-Food Trade: Empirical Evidence and Implications for Regional Integration of Agriculture*, report prepared for Agriculture and Agri-Food Canada (Ottawa, 1997).

10   About 11 per cent of US farms had at least one marketing or production contract in 1993, but these farms tended to be larger than average. They received 34 per cent of gross cash income and accounted for about 40 per cent of production, as measured by gross sales. See Robert A. Hoppe, Robert Green, David Banker, Judith Z. Kalbacher, and Susan E. Bentley, *Structural and Financial Characteristics of U.S. Farms, 1993: 18th Annual Family Farm Report to Congress* (Washington: USDA-ERS, 1996), 10.

11   W.D. Coleman and Wyn P. Grant, 'Policy Convergence and Policy Feedback: Agricultural Finance Policies in a Globalizing Era', *European Journal of Political Research* 34, 2 (1998).

12   David Goodman, Bernard Sorj, and John Wilkinson, *From Farming to Biotechnology* (Oxford: Basil Blackwell, 1987), ch. 3.

13   Elizabeth Hawkins, 'Technological Change in the Regulation of Agriculture', in P. Lowe, T. Marsden, and S. Whatmore, eds, *Regulating Agriculture* (London: David Fulton, 1994), 86.

14   Alison Maitland, 'Genetic feast or famine', *Financial Times*, 9 Jan. 1998, 19.

15   Helen Milner and Robert Keohane, 'Internationalisation and Domestic Politics: An Introduction',

in Milner and Keohane, eds, *Internationalisation and Domestic Politics* (Cambridge: Cambridge University Press, 1996), 18.

16  Besides NAFTA, these agreements include MERCOSUR, the Andean Pact, CARICOM, and the Closer Economic Relations Trade Agreement between Australia and New Zealand. An important regional agreement that does not incorporate agriculture is ASEAN.

17  Other important economic considerations were the desire to benefit from economies of scale and to restructure industries focused on small domestic markets.

18  John Whalley and Colleen Hamilton, *The Trading System After the Uruguay Round* (Washington: Institute for International Economics, 1996), 16.

19  Ronald T. Libby, *Protecting Markets: U.S. Policy and the World Grain Trade* (Ithaca, NY: Cornell University Press, 1992), 51.

20  The Cairns Group was an alliance of developed and developing states with important export-oriented agricultural sectors that sought the end of export subsidies and other liberalizing measures in agriculture. Australia, Canada, and New Zealand were members from the OECD.

21  The negotiators at the GATT used a kind of 'traffic light' metaphor for classifying subsidies. Those that were highly distorting of trade were termed 'red' (and thus had to be ended), those with the potential to cause significant distortion were classified as 'amber' (and were to be reduced), and those that did not distort trade were defined as 'green'. The 'green box' thus refers to the collection of these latter policy instruments.

22  For overviews, see Jeffrey J. Schott, *The Uruguay Round: An Assessment* (Washington: Institute for International Economics, 1994), 47–54; Stefan Tangermann, 'An Assessment of the Agreement on Agriculture', in OECD, *The New World Trading System: Readings* (Paris: OECD, 1994), 143–9.

23  Will Martin and L. Alan Winters, *The Uruguay Round: Widening and Deepening the World Trading System* (Washington: World Bank, 1995), 16.

24  Michael Tracy, *Agricultural Policy in the European Union and Other Market Economies*, 2nd edn (Genappe, Belgium: Agricultural Policy Studies, 1997).

25  Tim Josling, 'The Reformed CAP and the Industrial World', *European Review of Agricultural Economics* 21, 3–4 (1994): 514.

26  Robert Paarlberg, 'Agricultural Policy Reform and the Uruguay Round: Synergistic Linkage in a Two-Level Game?', *International Organization* 51, 3 (1997): 413–44.

27  European Commission, *The Agricultural Situation in the Community 1993 Report* (Luxembourg: Office for Official Publications of the European Communities, 1994), 8.

28  Wayne Jones and David Blandford, 'Trade and Industrial Policies Affecting Processed Foods', in Daniel H. Pick et al., *Global Markets for Processed Foods* (Boulder, Colo.: Westview Press, 1998), 50.

29  Karl Polanyi, *The Great Transformation: The Political and Economic Origins of Our Time* (Boston: Beacon Press, 1944), 150.

30  Frances Williams and Guy de Jonquières, 'Beef rulings give EU food for thought', *Financial Times*, 13 Feb. 1998, 8.

31  *Agra-Europe*, no. 1750, 6 June 1997, E7.

## Suggested Readings

Coleman, W.D., Grace Skogstad, and Michael M. Atkinson. 'Paradigm Shifts and Policy Networks: Cumulative Change in Agriculture', *Journal of Public Policy* 16, 3 (1996): 273–301.

Coleman, W.D., and Grace Skogstad. 'Neo-Liberalism, Policy Networks, and Policy Change: Agricultural Policy Reform in Australia and Canada', *Australian Journal of Political Science* 30 (1995): 242–63.

Friedmann, Harriet, and Philip McMichael. 'Agriculture and the State System: The Rise and Demise of National Agricultures, 1870 to the Present', *Sociologia Ruralis* 29, 2 (1989): 93–117.

Goodman, David. 'World-Scale Processes and Agro-Food Systems: Critique and Research Needs', *Review of International Political Economy* 4, 4 (1997): 663–87.

Josling, Timothy, Stefan Tangermann, and T.K. Warley. *Agriculture in the GATT*. Basingstoke: Macmillan, 1996.

Skogstad, Grace. 'Agricultural Policy', in G. Bruce Doern, Leslie Pal, and Brian Tomlin, eds, *Border Crossings: The Internationalization of Canadian Public Policy*. Toronto: Oxford University Press, 1996.

Swinbank, Alan, and Carolyn Tanner. *Farm Policy and Trade Conflict: The Uruguay Round and CAP Reform*. Ann Arbor: University of Michigan Press, 1996.

## Web Sites

World Trade Organization: www.wto.org

Directorate General for Agriculture, European Commission: europa.eu.int/en/comm/dg06

Economic Research Service, United States Department of Agriculture: www.econ.ag.gov

United States Department of Agriculture: www.usda.gov

Institute for Agriculture and Trade Policy: www.iatp.org

## Chapter 26

# International Corporate Strategies and Restructuring

Winfried Ruigrok

## Introduction: IPE and Management Studies

The field of international political economy (IPE) is interdisciplinary by nature, since no single discipline can provide sufficient explanations for the multidimensional phenomena studied. As can be seen in this book, IPE's main 'supplying disciplines' are political science, international relations, and international economics, although other disciplines also play a role, such as history, international law, and sociology. Each of these disciplines has its own evolution, concepts, and limitations, making communication among them, and hence the development of IPE as a field, rather difficult. Further, interdisciplinary work may run into opposition from well-established members of the 'supplying disciplines' because the questions raised, the methods used, and the literature referred to will often be unfamiliar and the quality of academic work difficult to assess.

In a similar way, with a few notable exceptions in the literature, IPE scholars have long ignored the international management literature and research, even though most IPE scholars readily acknowledge that multinational companies are playing a key role in today's world economy.[1] This chapter seeks to relate the international management literature to the area of IPE. It explains what multinational companies are, identifies major patterns of domestic and international restructuring, and indicates how these restructuring patterns produce rival visions of the preferred state of domestic and international affairs.

## Multinational Companies: An Introduction

Table 1 compares the field of international management with other disciplines relevant to the development of IPE. International management (just as international relations) is an interdisciplinary field, combining inputs from economics, social sciences, and management areas such as marketing, finance, and strategy. From an IPE perspective, the multinational company may be seen in a continuous (manifest or latent) bargaining relationship with (supra)national governments.

Put simply, multinational companies seek to persuade governments to adopt their specific views and interests and advocate these as a general interest. Many though not all MNCs have been important driving forces behind policies of deregulation and liberalization of the global economy so as to increase trade and investment flows and thereby facilitate their strategies. In this sense they have played a crucial role in increasing transborder transactions on both regional and global bases. This, in turn, intensifies competition and the need for restructuring itself. In this sense, the MNC-state bargaining relationship, along with the restructuring efforts of the corporate entities themselves, drives the restructuring and 'globalization' process in the first place. This chapter aims to illustrate multinational companies' *strategic motives* in this bargaining relationship with political and regulatory authorities.

A multinational company controls operations or income-generating assets in more than one country.[2] By definition, every MNC has engaged in foreign direct investments through which it either

## Table 1: International Management Compared with Other IPE Supplying Disciplines

| | **Political Science** | **International Relations** | **International Economics** | **International Management** |
|---|---|---|---|---|
| Type of discipline | Mono discipline | Inter-discipline | Mono discipline | Inter-discipline |
| Paradigm development | Competing paradigms | Weak | Relatively high paradigms | Competing paradigms |
| Central concepts | Power, ideology | Integration, conflict | Scarcity | Efficiency, effectiveness |
| Main phenomena to be explained | Role/composition of governments; state behaviours, ideologies; social and war movements | International regulation and mediation; peace | International trade; foreign direct investments | Organization and strategies of the multinational firm |
| Perception of national governments | Focal actor; arena where rival interests meet | Main actors | Co-regulators of world economy provide statistics | May be ally or foe: always bargaining relation |
| Level of analysis | Meso or macro level | Macro or meta level | Macro or meta level | Micro or meso level |

built new facilities or acquired a majority or minority share in existing operations. Since the second half of the 1980s, foreign direct investment activities have grown dramatically, reflecting a growing importance of MNCs. Some examples:

- General Motors' 1996 revenues of $164 billion outstripped the gross national product of economies such as China, Israel, Poland, and Venezuela. The combined revenue of the world's 10 largest MNCs is greater than that of the entire African continent.
- MNCs control large shares of international trade (partly through intra-firm trade), reducing government's abilities to influence trade flows between countries.
- MNCs are the actors carrying out foreign direct investments, thus affecting the growth perspectives of all world regions.
- MNCs employ tens of millions of people, with a disproportionate share of the most talented,

skilled, determined, and prosperous people in the world.

- MNCs do not have to account for themselves in the same way (Western) governments have to, making it far more difficult to interpret or control their behaviour.
- MNCs will usually be formidable bargaining partners to national governments due to their size, financial muscle, expertise, lack of transparency, and the promise of employment and tax income.

The fate of MNCs, and their political importance, is tied intrinsically to that of their industry. In Western economies, coal and steel producers as well as shipbuilders lost most of their political influence (and thus also state support) after the 1970s, whereas computer and semiconductor producers have seen their political influence increase —in the 1980s, US and European governments supported such industries for defence as well as for

## Figure 1: Four Types of MNC Management Challenges

*inside the MNC*

**1. Restructuring the firm's home base**

*home base*

**2. Managing subsidiaries abroad**

*abroad*

**3. Managing domestic political, social, and economic relations**

**4. Managing international political, social, and economic relations**

*outside the MNC*

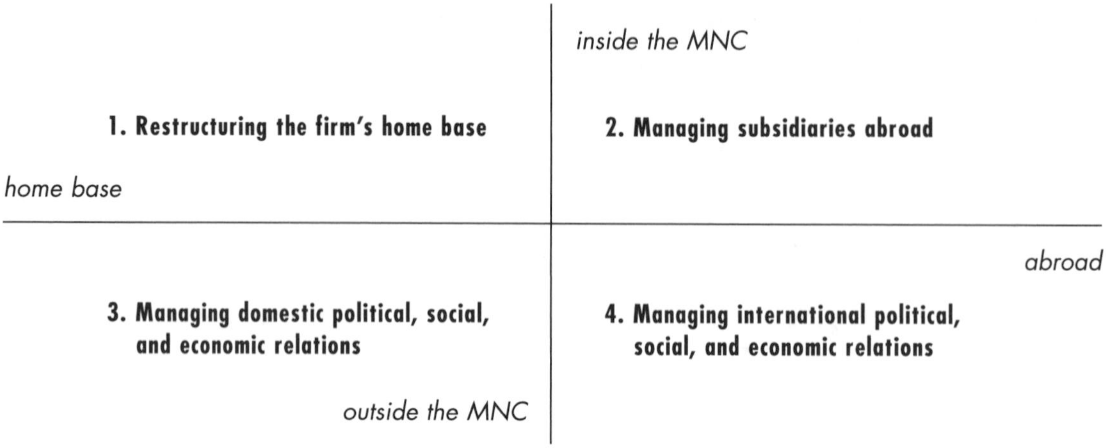

international competition purposes. Only a few industries, such as agriculture, have been able to sustain a politically important role over a long period of time.

MNCs may differ from each other in terms of size, industry, organizational structure, objectives, geographical presence, internal processes, corporate culture, ownership structure, value patterns, management approach, mode of conduct, etc. These differences translate into different strategies *vis-à-vis* their economic, social, and political partners and may even imply very different visions of the preferred international order. Diversity among MNCs may even be greater than that among countries, since many MNCs can only survive by continuously seeking to differentiate themselves from their competitors.

For the purposes of this chapter, it is useful to present a simple categorization of MNC management challenges (Figure 1). The horizontal axis refers to the *geographical boundaries* of countries: home versus abroad. The vertical axis refers to the *boundaries inside or outside the MNC*. Put together, four sets of MNC management challenges emerge. The MNC's influence is highest in the first quadrant and lowest in the fourth. The following sections explore each of these quadrants and their economic, social, and political implications.

## Restructuring the Home Base: Changing Structures, Processes, and Boundaries

A fundamental factor underlies MNC development and corporate restructuring. Since the 1980s, a series of *new technologies* have come up, clustered around information technology and new media, as well as around biotechnology and new materials.[3] These new technologies have led to a series of product (computers, CD-ROMs) and process innovations (e.g., the use of information systems within organizations), as well as to the rise of entirely new companies and industries.

Inevitably, new technologies shake up existing forms of organizing and the power centres associated with them—both within and outside the firm. For instance, the emergence of new transportation and communication technologies (railroads, telegraph, refrigeration, automobiles) enabled the rise of the vertically integrated, divisionalized, and international firm from the 1920s onward and then laid the foundations for the rise of international Fordism.[4] We are currently witnessing a set of *objective* technological changes, leading to a set of *subjective* economic, social, and political choices. Although these technological changes have far from crystallized, it is possible to identify some first patterns of MNC restructuring and to draw some intermediary social and political conclusions.

Referring to the first quadrant of Figure 1, many multinational (as well as domestic) firms across Europe, North America, and elsewhere are going through a series of *structural changes*. These include attempts to de-layer the organization (i.e., remove management levels and shorten the distance between top management and lower-ranking managers), decentralize decision-making (e.g., on changing suppliers), and introduce projects and teams composed of individuals from different functional backgrounds (manufacturing, marketing, finance) and different divisions. Thus, companies are partially seeking to break up existing internal hierarchies and functional divisions in order to exploit the opportunities of technological development and to compete better in the international marketplace.[5]

A second set of first-quadrant restructuring refers to *process changes*. Especially since the beginning of the 1990s, large companies have invested massively into information technology systems and are seeking to enhance company-internal networking (i.e., bypass internal boundaries between divisions and departments) in order to give room to innovative ideas. Furthermore, many firms have, finally, identified human resources as key to their future competitive success. These changes reflect the emergence of what has been termed the knowledge society, in which the technical means and the personal skills to find and interpret information and knowledge have become crucial to a firm's success, and in which top management and senior staff can no longer plan but at best *facilitate* the development and fulfilment of new ideas.

Third, firms are changing their organizational *boundaries*. Companies have begun to focus on their core competencies by outsourcing certain activities (e.g., auto makers procure seats from suppliers rather than produce seats themselves).[6] This has come about with a rapid increase in the number of start-up firms. By reducing levels of vertical integration, large firms are thus removing the very foundations of the old Fordism: the coupling of vertical integration, economies of scale, and trade unions'

abilities to organize employees within one business organization. Likewise, many firms are reducing levels of horizontal integration, i.e., cutting diversification, since it has proven increasingly difficult to manage different activities, each with its own business logic and technological trajectories, in a highly competitive world market. Instead of attaining direct control over such businesses and technologies, many companies are seeking 'new combinations'[7] or cost reductions by establishing strategic alliances with immediate competitors. Examples range from the early 1980s joint development of the CD-ROM technology by Philips and Sony to the late 1990s Star Alliance in the airline industry (consisting of United, Air Canada, Lufthansa, SAS, Thai, and Varig).

These joint restructuring efforts, deemed inescapable by many firms and managers and obviously providing specific individuals with good career chances, also have some less often discussed social and political effects. Our research suggests that the structural and process changes actually *enhance* top managers' control span in the organization. Also, structural and process changes enforce the organizational and business logic onto individual employees, making it easier to identify those employees unwilling or unable to co-operate on top management's terms. The boundary changes effectively undermine trade unions' ability to organize employees and force MNCs to search for new ways to manage their newly created dependence on suppliers or alliance partners. Boundary changes finally pose the challenge to governments of how to deal with 'quasi-cartels' of MNCs that are co-operating with each other. As we shall see below, MNCs have different ways of dealing with these challenges.

## Managing Subsidiaries Abroad

Many MNCs, such as Nestlé, Electrolux, and Philips, have a long history of foreign involvement (quadrant 2). Those firms originally expanded in a world dominated by fragmented markets, diverging standards and regulations, and distinct consumer tastes, and had excellent skills in dealing with different local conditions.[8] Other firms have internationalized production only fairly recently. Toyota, for instance, had long relied on exports from Japan. Toyota's main drive, as of many Japanese auto and electronics producers, became a fear of mounting trade barriers after the establishment of the Canada-US Free Trade Agreement (1987), the North American Free Trade Agreement (NAFTA, 1994), and the European Union (EU, 1992). Consequently, Toyota opened its first US plant in 1988 and its first European plant one year later.

Responding to the integration of regional (NAFTA and EU) markets, many MNCs (especially in autos, food, and pharmaceuticals) have raised a regional organizational structure, integrating development, production, and marketing at a North American or European level. Thus, they aim to reap economies of scale and to be in a better bargaining position to play off countries within one region (e.g., on investment decisions) and to confront NAFTA and EU authorities with one voice.

There has been a heated debate on the extent to which MNCs have become *global* players. A globalization strategy seeks to produce and market *the same product in the same way all over the world*, exploiting countries' comparative advantages.[9] Numerous authors have shown that there are very few such global players, and that even large MNCs usually remain national actors—albeit with significant activities abroad.[10] Thus, few MNCs have also implemented a global organization, i.e., integrated divisions and functions at a global level. Ford, the US auto maker, is a notable exception. It launched a 'world car' concept in the late 1970s, and, after this failed, established a 'global' organizational structure in the 1990s to try again. However, it has proven very difficult to co-ordinate the development, production, and marketing of one auto (which consists of some 40,000 components) in the same way all over the world—even the name of the car is different in North America and Europe.

A more notable consequence of the evolution of MNCs is the gradual emergence of an internationalized managerial élite. MNCs based in the UK, the Netherlands, and Switzerland and those active in pharmaceuticals and chemicals are taking the lead in hiring non-domestic top managers and non-executive (or supervisory) directors. Such foreigners may bring a better appreciation of foreign markets and cultures and may shake up too-cosy relationships in the corporate boardroom. In many MNCs the barriers to hiring foreigners to fill the top jobs are still considerable: when Siemens, the German electronics giant, indicated in 1998 that it wished to recruit a foreign executive director, it was quick to add that this would not happen until five years later. However, the trend is undeniable, and it may further weaken the relationship between MNCs and their home countries.[11]

## Managing Domestic Economic, Social, and Political Relations

Usually, the establishment of subsidiaries abroad implies the export of a specific organizational and management model—and its social and political relations. Crucial here is that every MNC aspires to position itself at the *core* of supply and distribution networks, as well as of political and financial networks, in order to be best able to influence its future and to play a leading role in the creation of value added. A *core firm* aspires to be the spider of a value-creating web, and to be in control of the process of creating value. A core firm can be defined by its direct access to domestic and foreign end markets, and owes its relative independence to a certain financial strength and its control over core technologies or other strategic competencies particular to an industry or activity. Most importantly, a core firm has an explicit vision on (1) the organization of its home base and its foreign activities; and (2) the role that external actors (such as banks, trade unions, and governments) should play in creating value added and in (re)structuring the network or industrial complex.

A useful concept for studying MNC restructuring at home and abroad is the *industrial complex*. An industrial complex is *a bargaining configuration of a core firm and five (groups of) actors: suppliers; workers and trade unions; distributors and dealers; financiers; and governments*. (In principle, the term 'industrial complex' also pertains to 'service industries'.) Below, five broad restructuring strategies contending for hegemony in modern capitalism will be presented, each with notably different appeals to the core firm's bargaining partners.[12]

The first restructuring pattern is based on networks of small and medium-sized firms aimed at industrial craft-oriented production for small to medium-scale markets. This type of industrial organization has been called *'flexible specialization'*.[13] Examples include the networks of small textiles, ceramics, and shoe producers in Italy's Emilia Romagna, the networks of family-owned machinery firms in the German state of Baden-Württemberg, and the Dutch agricultural networks producing tomatoes and flowers. Companies in this category tend to be small and geographically clustered, using specialized banking, insurance, and R&D services. Companies in these networks may easily get tied into outsourcing or alliance networks controlled by large firms, and for this reason they seek to minimize their dependence on other partners. Thus, they prefer government abstention, only generic economic support measures, and a fierce competition policy (to avert concentration) and intellectual property rights enforcement.

The second restructuring pattern can be labelled *industrial democracy*. Industrial democracy emerges as a result of the bargaining power of the core firm's partners, such as governments, banks, and trade unions. MNCs in this restructuring pattern know how to co-operate with external partners (through outsourcing or alliances) and have little problem decentralizing decision-making, innovating internal work practices, and empowering employees. However, they are walking a tightrope: faced with strong bargaining partners, the core firm has to comply with many of its partners' demands. In the 1970s, Swedish core firms such as Saab and Electrolux, faced with a strong bank, influential suppliers, and a powerful trade union and national government, were close to this pattern. Other examples include aerospace and defence companies, which are highly dependent on government expenditures and thus easily turn to their national governments for extra spending or to support cartel-like structures (e.g., Airbus, a venture involving companies from France, Germany, the UK, and Spain). In the 1970s, industries such as steel and shipbuilding, when confronted with tough international competition and trade union pressures, also sought governmental support measures, though with declining success rates. Telecommunication and utility services (formerly considered as a public good) have long been subject to government controls as well. However, partly due to technological developments, governments' influence has decreased dramatically in these industries. As these examples show, industrial democracy as a restructuring strategy has been on the decline for many years now.

The third restructuring pattern has been aimed at creating mass production in *vertically semi-integrated firms* on the basis of formal hierarchies producing for mass markets. In *macro-Fordism*, core firms are confronted with relatively strong bargaining partners, such as national trade union federations and national governments.[14] The difference between the industrial democracy and macro-Fordist restructuring strategy is that, in the latter case, the core firm itself has a stronger bargaining position. Under such conditions, the core firm will be forced to strike deals with other actors that most closely resemble a *coalition*. Macro-Fordist MNCs therefore are more likely than the following two types to engage in partnerships with competitors and suppliers. Macro-Fordism also implies the delegation of interest representation to a national employers' organization that bargains with governments and national employees' organizations in a national or supranational context. Macro-Fordism furthermore implies the existence and occasional use of implicit or explicit central mediation or conflict-resolution institutions. In smaller industrial countries this has led to tripartite corporatist bargaining institutions. Macro-Fordism is characterized by a certain degree of consensus-seeking, and may lead to industrial policies or protectionism aimed at reconciling conflicting domestic interests (at least temporarily). Many German, French, and Italian MNCs have long been operating in a macro-Fordist context, although recently core firms based in these countries have managed to improve their relative bargaining position. The attempts to establish a European social charter and other efforts to improve European social legislation represent campaigns by trade unions and national authorities to re-conquer some of their lost bargaining power.

The fourth restructuring pattern is called *micro-Fordism* and represents the 'ideal typical' Fordism as pioneered by Henry Ford between 1910 and World War II.[15] In micro-Fordism, *large vertically integrated core firms* are aiming at economies of scale through a company-internal division of labour. High levels of vertical integration lead to a concentration of bargaining power at the core firms and relatively adversarial bargaining relations with suppliers, distributors/dealers, and governments. Deals with workers are struck at the level of the firm or the industry at most. Even if micro-Fordist firms outsource production or strike alliances, they will do so hesitantly. Micro-Fordist MNCs are characterized by a concentration of power at the top; hence, they are likely to de-layer (a device to expand top management's control span) and less likely to seek extensive uncontrolled networking with large MNCs. Under micro-Fordism, there are very few mediation mechanisms at a national level. Micro-Fordist firms can be found in the US and, to a lesser extent, in the UK and the Netherlands. More recently, and contrary to their origins, micro-Fordist core firms have sought to renew micro-Fordism by *reducing* their levels of vertical integration (their very power base) while trying to maintain control over their bargaining partners. Chrysler, quite advanced along this trajectory, paid by losing its independence to Daimler in 1998.

The fifth restructuring pattern evolves around *large vertically de-integrated firms* overseeing relatively *informal hierarchies* producing for medium-scale markets at first, but later also for mass markets. These *Toyotist* firms may accomplish faster production runs and higher levels of flexibility than Fordist firms.[16] Over the 1980s and early 1990s, the Toyotist restructuring concept enabled firms to outperform their micro- and macro-Fordist competitors. The name, of course, has been derived from Toyota, which successfully developed an intimate network of dedicated suppliers and subsequently produces a much lower percentage of an auto in-house than do its Western rivals.[17] Thus, Toyotist firms have specific competencies in managing outsourcing practices, and these competencies have been acknowledged and partially copied by firms adhering to the other four patterns. Toyotist firms are not necessarily Japanese, however, and Japanese firms are not necessarily Toyotist. For instance, Japanese companies such as Honda, Canon, and Sony are closer to the micro-Fordist concept of control, since they have been unable to establish structural control over a legally independent supply and distribution base and because they have been relatively isolated on the domestic industrial and political scene (which has been shaped by more established companies such as Toyota, Nissan, and Matsushita).

These five restructuring patterns represent ideal types of how *temporarily* to resolve the five basic control problems of capitalist production and accumulation: control over labour, supplies, technology, capital, and distribution/consumption. Each of these ideal types has been developed in a very specific economic, social, and political setting, and has flourished in a particular international context. Therefore, after it has first appeared, the 'purest' form of a given restructuring strategy will long be found in the country of origin. However, the principles of each restructuring strategy are universally applicable, provided that the proper economic, social, and political environment is available or created at the same time. The latter condition is very difficult to realize. Thus the five restructuring strategies are at the same time *unique* in the sense that they require a specific infrastructure and governance structure to emerge and *general* in their potential as models for capitalist production and accumulation.

Even if one restructuring pattern may temporarily outperform another, history suggests that *no one restructuring pattern is inherently superior or more efficient than another*. Thus far, no one resolution of control problems has triumphed forever: any settlement of the five aforementioned control problems eventually provoked new contradictions and control problems. During the early 1990s, many US and European managers and politicians were convinced of the future Toyotist superiority—only a few years later, opinions have changed drastically in the shadow of Japan's economic difficulties.

Finally, since national economies often contain more than one industrial complex, it is useful to distinguish between an industrial complex and the *national industrial system*.[18] For instance, the German auto system consists of the Volkswagen, Daimler-Chrysler, Ford, GM, and BMW complexes. If a national system contains more than one industrial complex, different types of bargaining and different restructuring concepts may coexist for a transient period, contending for hegemony in the national system. Generally, however, bargaining patterns have tended to converge along the lines of the bargaining rules set by the most cohesive complex, at the expense of the weaker complex(es).

## Domestic and International Political Agendas

A firm's domestic restructuring pattern in turn shapes its internationalization strategy and its social and political agenda. In Figure 1, MNC activities in quadrants 1 and 3 will affect quadrants 2 and 4. The reason is that a core firm's domestic bargaining relations effectively act as *sunk costs* in its internationalization process. A core firm will try to stick to its winning formula by extending bargaining arrangements abroad (especially with suppliers, workers, and governments) that helped it to build up its strong position in its home base. Even if the MNC has to make concessions to foreign bargaining partners, its vision will often be derived from its home base. Table 2 shows how internationalization strategies and, consequently, domestic and international political agendas vary depending on the underlying restructuring strategy.

Firms in flexible specialization networks tend to keep governments at arm's length. At home (quadrant 3), they usually reject government intervention unless such intervention has a generic nature (i.e., does not favour any actor in particular). These small firms desperately seek to avert concentration and situations where large firms, which could eventually overshadow their smaller competitors, may emerge. Hence, such firms usually favour a fierce competition policy and fiscal

## Table 2: The Link between MNC Restructuring, Internationalization, and Political Agendas

| Restructuring Strategy | Internationalization Strategy | Domestic and International Political Agenda |
|---|---|---|
| Flexible specialization | exports, only a few MNCs | no government intervention (unless for generic purposes); fierce competition and intellectual property rights policy; open markets abroad |
| Industrial democracy | country-by-country strategy (fails to exploit integrating markets) | various industrial and trade policies, legitimized by social contract |
| Macro-Fordism | regional division of labour | restructuring may justify temporary industrial, regional, and trade policies |
| Micro-Fordism | either regional organization in various world regions or globalization | minimize government intervention; 'free trade but fair trade' |
| Toyotism | 'global localization': copy Toyotist model, control foreign bargaining partners, and tailor products to regional markets | support core firm's control strategy over other bargaining partners; little opposition to trade barriers after 'insider' position has been secured |

SOURCE: Winfried Ruigrok and Rob van Tulder, *The Logic of International Restructuring* (London: Routledge, 1995).

policies aimed at discouraging 'bigness'. Abroad (quadrant 4), small and specialized firms usually favour a relatively liberal trading regime, although their concern will be much more to have access to markets abroad than to open up domestic markets for foreign competition. Highly specialized firms (such as designers) usually favour a fierce enforcement of intellectual property right laws.

The concept of industrial democracy presupposes that governments have a legitimate role to play in supporting individual firms or entire industries. This may be done through various types of industrial and trade policies, such as providing subsidies or creating national champions or domestic cartels. However, there is a trade-off here: governments will simultaneously seek to enforce a national 'social contract' aimed at spreading wealth over the society and maintaining social cohesion. Yet, in times of stiff competition, rapid technological change, new emerging organizational forms, and integrating markets, governments' ability to support domestic MNCs and help them compete successfully has proven very limited— government officials often do not make good business people (and same is true in reverse). Attempts to engineer an international social contract (quadrant 4) have been unsuccessful so far, especially due to trade unions' lack of international bargaining power.

Macro-Fordism implies a relative balance of power among MNCs, governments, trade unions, and MNCs' business partners. In such a setting, firms, governments, and trade unions may consider various types of industrial and trade policies as legitimate means to solve national conflicts or to raise international competitiveness. Due to ongoing internationalization, MNCs have undeniably tilted the balance in their favour. The establishment of the EU may be seen as an attempt by European governments to stem a further slipping of their relative bargaining position. However, the EU is confronted with 15 industrial systems and dozens of industrial complexes, producing a cacophony of agendas competing for political dominance that poses a truly insurmountable barrier to forging coalition policies at an EU level.[19]

The micro-Fordist domestic and international political agenda is to protect firms from any undesirable government influence and to pursue free trade abroad. The belief in these values may be best illustrated by IBM's former slogan, 'peace through trade'. However, that is not the end of the story. First, to support their competitive position, various micro-Fordist computer, semiconductor, and aerospace companies over the 1980s received huge state subsidies, legitimized by the military relevance of those industries: within the dominant US logic of the 1980s, the Department of Defense was not a regular bargaining partner, and support from that angle could hardly be questioned. Second, micro-Fordist firms over the 1980s and 1990s had become confronted, at least temporarily, with some formidable, seemingly invincible, Toyotist competitors. Claiming that Toyotist firms barred foreign competition in their home bases, many micro-Fordist firms campaigned in favour of 'free trade but fair trade', thus seeking some kind of trade protection.[20]

The Toyotist domestic and international political agenda is to appeal to each possible actor at the local, national, and regional level to help further the core firm's effectiveness. At home, this implies a series of mechanisms to attain the unconditional co-operation of suppliers, workers, and governments, with government frequently sanctioning control mechanisms devised by the core firm.[21] Abroad, Toyotist core firms attempt to extend this line of behaviour by setting up integrated development, production, and distribution systems. After an intermediary phase, Toyotist core firms may subsequently lose their interest in free trade: their aim will be primarily to serve regional markets and tastes, not to use their regional base as an expansion platform for global exports or a global production strategy. Put bluntly: Toyota has no inherent interest in free trade—Ford (with its global vision) does.

## Conclusion

The objective of this chapter has been to illustrate how the area of international management may help explain phenomena that IPE seeks to understand. This has been done by providing a diagram explaining the MNC's management challenges, by analysing recent patterns of MNC internal restructuring, by identifying some patterns and implications of how MNCs are managing their subsidiaries abroad, by assessing how this affects the MNC's external bargaining relations, and by identifying different MNC political agendas.

The framework suggested here helps us to understand how MNC restructuring shapes domestic and international economic, social, and political environments. The framework explains that in times of rapid technological growth and stiff competition, multinational corporations perceive that governments only have a limited role to play in international economic life. In addition, it inter-

prets the emergence of regional trade blocs and the *relative* support for a gradual trade liberalization as MNC strategies to reduce some of the national governments' bargaining power.

While it is possible to identify some broad similarities in the internal and external restructuring strategies of MNCs, it is equally important to appreciate the differences among them. In fact, since the goals and interests of the members of an industrial complex differ and may conflict, and since some of the core firms' partners may have substantial independence and force the core firm to give in to their demands, bargaining in industrial complexes is also a source of diversity in international capitalism. Even if there has been a shift of power from governments to MNCs, there hardly seems to be a trend towards a growing global convergence.[22]

## Notes

1   Exceptions include Jonathan Story in this volume (who relates corporate governance to financial systems); John Stopford and Susan Strange, *Rival States, Rival Firms: Competition for World Market Shares* (Cambridge: Cambridge University Press, 1991); Lee Preston and Duane Windsor, *The Rules of the Game in the Global Economy: Policy Regimes for International Business* (Dordrecht, the Netherlands: Kluwer, 1997); John Zysman, 'How Institutions Create Historically Rooted Trajectories of Growth', *Industrial and Corporate Change* 3, 1 (1994); M. Fennema, *International Networks of Banks and Industry*, Studies in Industrial Organization, vol. 2 (The Hague: Martinus Nijhoff, 1982); Helen Milner and David Yoffie, 'Between Free Trade and Protectionism: Strategic Trade Policy and a Theory of Corporate Trade Demands', *International Organization* 43, 2 (Spring 1989): 239-72.

2   Geoffrey Jones, *The Evolution of International Business* (London: Routledge, 1996), 4.

3   Rob van Tulder and Gerd Junne, *European Multinationals and Core Technologies* (London: Wiley and Sons, 1988).

4   For a fascinating discussion from a business perspective of the interplay between technological development and organizational models, see

Alfred Chandler, *The Visible Hand: The Managerial Revolution in American Business* (Cambridge, Mass.: Harvard University Press, 1980).

5   These organizational changes and their implications are the object of a broad study by the INNFORM (Innovative Forms of Organizing) project, led by Andrew Pettigrew (University of Warwick) and consisting of management researchers at the Universities of Oxford (UK), St Gallen (Switzerland), Jönköping (Sweden), IESE (Spain), Erasmus (Netherlands), Duke (US), and Hitotsubashi (Japan). First publications are expected by 1999.

6   On core competencies, see C.K. Prahalad and Garry Hamel, 'The Core Competence of the Corporation', *Harvard Business Review* (May-June 1990): 79–91.

7   Joseph Schumpeter, *Capitalism, Socialism and Democracy* (London: George Allen & Unwin, 1943).

8   See Winfried Ruigrok and Rob van Tulder, *The Logic of International Restructuring* (London: Routledge, 1995), 160–2.

9   Theodore Levitt, 'The Globalization of Markets', *Harvard Business Review* (May-June 1983): 92–102.

10   Ruigrok and van Tulder, *The Logic of International Restructuring*; Paul Hirst and Grahame Thompson, *Globalization in Question: The International Economy and the Possibilities of Governance* (London: Polity Press, 1996); Yao-Su Hu, 'Global or Stateless Corporations Are National Firms with International Operations', *California Management Review* 34, 2 (Winter 1992): 107–26; Pari Patel and Keith Pavitt, 'Large Firms in the Production of the World's Technology: An Important Case of "Non-Globalisation"', *Journal of International Business Studies* 1, 1 (1991): 1–21.

11   At the Research Institute of International Management, University of St Gallen, we are investigating the internationalization of top management and non-executive directors in the 100 largest firms in 1995 in the US, Japan, Germany, the UK, the Netherlands, and Switzerland. The first publications will be available over the course of 1999.

12   Ruigrok and van Tulder, *The Logic of International Restructuring*.

13   The term has been introduced by Michael Piore, and Charles Sabel, *The Second Industrial Divide: Possibilities for Prosperity* (New York: Basic Books, 1984); see also Michael Best, *The New Competition: Institutions of Industrial Restructuring* (Cambridge: Polity Press, 1990).

14   Lars Mjøset, 'Nordic Economies in the 1970s and 1980s', *International Organization* 41, 3 (Summer 1987): 403–56; Peter Katzenstein, *Small States in World Markets: Industrial Policy in Europe* (Ithaca, NY: Cornell University Press, 1985).

15   Antonio Gramsci, *Selections from the Prison Notebooks*, ed. Q. Hoare and G. Nowell Smith (London: Lawrence and Wishart, 1980).

16   The term was introduced by Knuth Dohse, Ulrich Jürgens, and Thomas Malsch, 'Vom "Fordismus" zum "Toyotismus"? Die Organisation der industriellen Arbeit in der japanischen Automobilindustrie', *Leviathan* 12, 4 (1984). (Published in English in *Politics and Society* 14, 2 (1985): 115–46.) See also H. Jacot, ed., *Du Fordisme au Toyotisme? Les Voies de la Modernisation du Système Automobile en France et au Japon* (Paris: Commissariat General du Plan, La Documentation Française, 1990).

17   For a discussion of Toyotism (here labelled 'lean production') at the heyday of its hegemony, see James Womack, Daniel Jones, and Daniel Roos, *The Machine that Changed the World* (New York: Rawson Associates, 1990).

18   For this term, see Bengt Åke Lundvall, *National Systems of Innovation: Towards a Theory of Innovation and Interactive Learning* (London: Pinter, 1992); Richard Nelson, *National Innovation Systems: A Comparative Analysis* (Oxford: Oxford University Press, 1993).

19   Winfried Ruigrok and Rob van Tulder, 'The Price of Diversity: Rival Concepts of Control as a Barrier to an EU Industrial Strategy', in Pat Devine, Yannis Katsoulacos, and Roger Sugden, eds, *Competitiveness, Subsidiarity and Objectives: Issues for European Industrial Strategy* (London: Routledge, 1996), 79–103.

20   For the relationship between protectionist sentiments in the US auto industry and US trade policies, see Winfried Ruigrok and Rob van Tulder, 'Exploring the Potential for US-EU Trade Cooperation in Asia in the Automobile and Auto Parts Industries', in Richard Steinberg and Bruce Stokes, eds, *Partners or Competitors? The Prospect for U.S.-European Cooperation on Asian Trade* (Denver: Rowman & Little, 1999).

21   For a discussion of how the Japanese government has helped auto makers to enforce test inspections on their suppliers, see Winfried Ruigrok and John Jay Tate, 'Public Testing and Research Centres in Japan: Control and Nurturing of Small and Medium-sized Enterprises in the Automobile Industry', *Technology Analysis and Strategic Management* 8, 4: 381–406.

22   Suzanne Berger and Ronald Dore, eds, *National Diversity and Global Capitalism* (Ithaca, NY: Cornell University Press, 1996).

## Suggested Readings

Jones, Geoffrey. *The Evolution of International Business.* London: Routledge, 1996.

Pfeffer, Jeffrey. *Managing with Power: Politics and Influence in Organizations.* Cambridge, Mass.: Harvard Business School Press, 1992.

Ruigrok, Winfried, and Rob van Tulder. *The Logic of International Restructuring.* London: Routledge, 1995.

Stopford, John, and Susan Strange. *Rival States, Rival Firms: Competition for World Market Shares.* Cambridge: Cambridge University Press, 1991.

## Web Sites

Cultural Factors in Business: An Incomplete Anthropological Bibliography: http://www.gsia.cmu.edu/afs/andrew/gsia/jh38/refs.html

Commission of the European Union: http://europa.eu.int

Virtual International Business and Economic Sources: http://www.uncc.edu/lis/library/reference/intbus/vibehome.htm

Globalization and business practice: Managing across boundaries: http://www.seattleu.edu/~parker/homepage.html

Research Institute of International Management: http://www.fim.unisg.ch

A business researcher's interest: http://www.brint.com/interest.html

Helsinki School of Economics Library, Center for Economics and Business Information: http://helecon.hkkk.fi/helecon/index_eng.html

## Chapter 27

# Negotiating Globalization: The Foreign Economic Policy of the European Union

## Michael Smith

## Introduction

The European Union (EU)[1] represents a paradox in a globalizing political economy. At a time when processes of integration at the global level are both widely noted and felt by policy-makers in the national and global arenas, the EU expresses a strong and highly institutionalized variety of regional integration in both the political and the economic spheres.[2] As a result, it can be seen in at least three ways in relation to globalization processes. First, it can be seen as a barrier against globalization, capable because of its continental scale and strong institutions of resisting the forces of global integration. Second, it can be seen as a site for globalization, providing an integrated continental political economy within which globalizing forces can work untrammelled by national authority. Finally, the EU can be seen as a promoter of globalization, in the sense that it actively encourages the globalizing activities of European corporations and other actors. Each of these tendencies has arguably been intensified during the 1990s. Having moved decisively in the late 1980s and early 1990s towards the creation of a single market for its existing members, during the late 1990s the EU moved further in two directions: on the one hand, 11 of its members agreed in 1998 to initiate a single currency, the Euro, in 1999; on the other hand, 1998 also saw the opening of negotiations with the first half-dozen of what might eventually be at least 10 new member states. At the same time, the moves towards further definition of a Common Foreign and Security Policy for the Union, in the context of the Amsterdam Treaty agreed to in June 1997, held promise of progress in the area not merely of economic security and regulation, but also of 'high politics' and an eventual defence policy. Such developments have raised, in new forms, the globalization/regionalization tension inherent in processes of economic integration and have given new dimensions to the notion of an EU foreign economic policy.

But how valid is the notion of 'foreign economic policy' for the EU and for the EU's role in a globalizing world? After all, the concept of foreign policy itself implies the existence of a central governing authority and, by extension, the existence of a state. While the nature of state structures and authorities can vary widely between national contexts, thereby creating difficulties for the conduct of foreign policy analysis, the EU seems to raise special problems. First, the EU indisputably has international presence and international effects, but are these systematic enough and purposeful enough to constitute a form of foreign economic policy or international economic policy? In the course of exploring this issue, one is led to a second set of questions, about the effectiveness and impact of policy itself. How effective is the process of policy formation and execution within the Union? How, and how well, does the EU translate its economic potential into economic and political effects? The issue is not simply one of the mechanics of policy formation and implementation; rather, it concerns the characteristics of the EU as a governance system and the ways in which it is possible to distinguish between the ability to form relationships and the capacity to carry out policy. As such, it gets to the heart of the EU's status, as a structuring factor or as an active presence, in the global arena.

This area of inquiry thus also holds important implications for the study of responses to globalization. If we assume that the EU needs a foreign economic policy in order to hold at bay or to manipulate the forces of globalization—the 'barrier' function mentioned above—this can lead to a view of the Union as a quasi-statist concentration of material and institutional power competing with other such concentrations on an intercontinental scale. But if we assume that the EU as a regional governance system is part of an emerging system of global economic and political governance, we are led to explore the ways in which, first, the EU's external economic policies reflect its penetration by forces in the global economic order—the 'site' function—and second, how the EU's regional experiences can be diffused or used to exert leverage at the global level—the 'promoter' function. In reality, pure cases of each function are likely to be rare or non-existent. Foreign economic policy in the EU is likely to reflect a continuous and complex negotiation in which aims and interests, and functions and impacts, are intermingled. This chapter sets out to explore how this negotiation process emerges and is managed within the EU and to examine the implications for the global/regional balance.

## Does Statehood Matter? The EU, Foreign Economic Policy, and the Global Arena

As already noted, 'foreign economic policy' carries with it a conventional component of statehood or governmental authority. One of the problems in analysing the EU is therefore the extent to which it measures up to established criteria of statehood and whether this matters in either conceptual or practical terms. Much of the literature on IPE has as a central focus the issue of statehood and the relationship between statehood and processes of production and exchange in the global political economy; the EU thus presents a test of this literature from a distinctive but highly significant angle. To put it crudely, analysis of the EU enables the analyst to ask: Does

statehood matter in a focused and empirically substantial way?[3]

To pursue this question, it is important first to address the issue of statehood in the IPE of the early third millennium. This chapter conceives of statehood as a variable in the international political economy, and also accepts that government often does not take place exclusively through the agency of competitive national states. In consequence, the notions of foreign policy and foreign economic policy also need amendment. Conventionally, these would be seen as the embodiment of national aims and interests, pursued through the mobilization and application of national resources. In the case of foreign economic policy, the aims and the means would be defined as economic, although the ultimate goals would be implicitly political or concerned with security. The contemporary era demands questioning of this rather restrictive and privileging view of the processes. A revised version would focus not so much on the mobilization of national governmental power as on the building of networks for action, which may or may not coincide with purely national boundaries. It would also focus on the role played by regulatory structures and rules at both the subnational and transnational levels, providing a framework for the pursuit of goals by a variety of actors, both public and private. This does not mean that the notion either of foreign policy or of foreign economic policy 'disappears'; rather, it recognizes that actions with meaning and effect can be produced by a range of actors and from a variety of sources, among them revitalized national authorities.

Importantly, within this framework the status and impact of the European Union are most salient, suggesting that the EU is in many ways a reflection of precisely these changed conditions. Many of the established views of the EU, though, tend to subject it to the tests of a traditional model of foreign economic policy and to identify the ways in which the Union falls short of the implied standards of statehood. Thus, there has been a strong focus on the economic 'weight' of the EU and on the undeniable fact that there is no direct translation of economic raw material into economic or political 'muscle'. Other analyses have focused on the extent to which the Community has become 'statelike' in conventional ways, or how it has supplanted state powers in particular domains such as trade. By implication, in areas where this has not happened, the EU cannot provide for its citizens the range of services that can be provided by 'real' states, either at home or abroad. We have just noted, though, that this kind of conventional analysis, both of statehood and of policy, is open to criticism. In the light of the revised analysis proposed above, what can now be said about the EU, its international status, and its policy potential?

The EU is quintessentially a mixed system of participation, regulation, and action, epitomized by its 'three-pillar' institutional structure: the first pillar containing the European Community with its economic powers and procedures, the second containing the Common Foreign and Security Policy (CFSP), and the third containing provisions for Justice and Home Affairs (JHA). Although it can be said that on the one hand the European Commission represents the basis for an eventual European government with supranational powers, and on the other the member states in the Council of Ministers symbolize the continuity or even the dominance of conventional state power, the reality is a complex and multilayered set of networks, which constitute powerful mechanisms of regulation and behaviour modification. The areas of Community activity in which either the Commission or the Council of Ministers has exclusive policy competence are relatively few, and particularly limited in the external domain, where trade policy is always cited as the example of shared competence; this situation was reaffirmed after the conclusion of the Uruguay Round, when the European Court of Justice confirmed that trade in services or matters of intellectual property were subject to shared competence between Commission and Council within the Community framework.[4] The converse of this is that there are also few areas in which the member states themselves can claim unfettered power, either precisely because of their membership in the EU or because of the global spread of interdependence and

interpenetration. In addition, the impact of interpenetration means that the notion of a privileged external or foreign policy domain is itself difficult to maintain. Finally, the increasingly close linkage between security policy and economic policy and the pervasiveness of politicization in the global political economy mean that the supposed limitation of the first pillar to 'low politics' is difficult to argue, although the process of linkage and politicization itself causes undoubted policy problems.

As a result, the EU has much to offer the analyst of foreign economic policy. It combines elements of several layers of action and influence: subnational, intergovernmental, transnational, and in some areas supranational. It possesses a complex set of institutions, which provide a powerful framework for continuous bargaining and for the adjustment of differences between member states and other groupings. In this sense, although the EU can be evaluated in terms of power and the inability to translate economic weight into tangible effects, such analysis is in part misguided; what really demands attention is how and the extent to which the EU facilitates the achievement of joint objectives through predominantly economic and diplomatic means, and how it promotes effective communication and negotiation between member states and other groupings.

Analysis of foreign economic policy in the EU context must also take account of the multilayered and sectorally specific nature of policy determination. There is a continuous competition, with well-established rules, for leverage within the Union, and at the same time an attempt to realize national or sectional objectives through EU means. It is important to recognize that this does not make the EU unique: the above description of the 'pulling and hauling' within the EU could be applied in many respects to the United States and to other federal or fragmented government systems. There is in the case of the EU an important question to be asked about the extent to which it captures or contains the economic or political activities of its members and other groupings, but this is not in principle different from similar questions arising from the permeability of national political and economic systems.

## Power and Process in the EU's Foreign Economic Policy

The argument so far has identified three coexisting characteristics of EU foreign economic policy, each with its echoes in the broader literature of IPE and links to processes of globalization. First, the process is that of a multilevel game played according to distinct but intersecting rules in a number of sectors. Second, one of the key features of the process is the constant adjustment of state policies and the interaction of national preferences with the institutions of the Union itself in a complex bargaining process. Third, the EU operates not only to provide a framework for the expression and adjustment of state and other interests, but also to structure the global political economy and thus to form an institutional expression of major forces within the global system. Whether this makes the EU into either a 'partial state' or 'quasi-state' is an important question. No less important is the empirical issue: What does the EU do and what roles does it perform within the global political economy?

It has already been noted at several points that the conversion of economic weight into economic and political effects is one of the great continuing problems of foreign economic policy at the EU level. One key constraint on the effectiveness of this conversion process is the Union's institutional structure. The division of influence and competence between the member states and EU institutions, particularly the Commission, is a central driving force in the Union as a whole, but it has particular implications for external policy activities. In a formal sense, it is difficult if not impossible for the EU to operate collectively without a consensus in the Council of Ministers and without a convergence of views between the Council and the Commission. This is encapsulated most clearly in the conduct of trade negotiations, such as those under the World Trade Organization (WTO). Here, the Commission can negotiate on behalf of the Community, but only on the basis of a mandate provided by the Council of Ministers under Article 113 of the Treaty of Rome (now Article 133 of the consolidated Treaty on European Union). Not surprisingly, such a mandate

can restrict the capacity of EU negotiators to react flexibly and creatively to events, or to initiatives from other negotiating partners. In the WTO context, things are further complicated by the fact that although the Commission may negotiate on behalf of EU member states, those states themselves are individually represented in the WTO.[5]

There is a further dimension to the constraints exercised by the EU division of powers. Quite apart from the limitations on external policy-making that arise from the Union's constitution, the impact of globalization and interpenetration means that external and internal policies are intimately linked. In agriculture, for example, the EU's negotiating position in the WTO is inseparable from the difficulties of reforming the Common Agricultural Policy (CAP)—an issue that engages national sensitivities and on which national governments have very strong views. Thus, during the mid-1990s, the attempts to find a basis for agreement on agricultural issues in the WTO were fundamentally affected by the national problems faced by the French, the Germans, and others with powerful farm lobbies. In other areas there is a similar if often less dramatic linkage between levels: for instance, the development of EU policies on high technology is decisively influenced by the positions of national authorities with 'national champions', and by the development of cross-national business alliances, and this feeds inexorably into the Community's stance in relation to disputes with the United States and Japan.

The development of European institutions since the Single European Act (SEA) during the mid-1980s, and later the Treaty on European Union (in force since 1993), promised to make decision-making and the 'conversion process' less constrained, through the introduction of majority voting and a clearer specification of the ground rules. They also promised a more effective role for the European Parliament in the conduct of external relations, through the exercise of its powers of assent on international agreements. But even after the Amsterdam Treaty the situation remains one in which the vital treaty-making and negotiating powers lie between the Commission and the Council, for example, on WTO agreements. With the introduction of the Euro as a single currency in 1999, the situation has become further complicated, first, by the fact that not all EU member states will initially be members of 'Euroland', and second, by the need for co-ordination between the different structures and processes set up in commercial and monetary policy. This brings us again to the distinctiveness of the EU. How different is the process of divided decision-making in the EU from that in the United States, for example, where Congress has considerable powers over trade policy and related areas and where the Federal Reserve holds sway over monetary policy? Both the EU and the United States are known to be difficult international negotiation partners, but is there anything distinctive in the fact that the division of powers in the EU is between a supranational and an intergovernmental body, rather than between an executive and legislature?

The decision-making and conversion problems identified here also link with the types of resources mobilized by the EU for external action. From the outset, the Community (the 'first pillar') had certain important powers in trade policy, particularly those relating to market access and the Common Commercial Policy; these have been added to over the years, with such mechanisms as anti-dumping regulations and rules of origin giving the Union a powerful trade policy armoury. Add to this the treaty-making power, which has been exercised to enter into association agreements and other relationships with 'outsiders', and there is the clear basis for a partial but powerful foreign economic policy. Thus, in the case of the Lomé Conventions, the EU has constructed a complex web of links with Third World countries; equally, the development of links with the European Free Trade Area (EFTA) countries led to the conclusion of a major agreement on the European Economic Area in 1991, while the newly democratizing states of Central and Eastern Europe were introduced to the EU network through the so-called 'Europe Agreements' during the early 1990s. In the latter two cases, the deepening of the economic and political links has led to applications for membership in the EU itself, with Sweden, Finland, and Austria entering in 1995 and several Central and Eastern European countries starting entry negotiations.

Alongside these assets and resources, the EU also experiences severe constraints in the area of external policy. Throughout its history, the EU has faced the delicate problems surrounding the transfer of legal, financial, and other resources from the national to the European level, and the limitations to EU autonomy even when such transfers can be agreed upon. For its internal policies, the EU relies on an uneasy blend of transfers from national governments, allocation by the Commission, Council, and Parliament, and implementation by the same national governments as originally transferred the resources; thus, it is not surprising that the claims for a *juste retour* or 'fair return' have affected such areas as regional policy, and that the arguments over 'hard resources' such as money have been accompanied by equally severe tensions over 'soft resources' such as legal powers and institutional rules. This contest intersects with some of the central processes of globalization, such as investment by large corporations and the regulation of service provision across national boundaries, which have local as well as regional, national, and European implications. In external policy, although the Commission can be delegated to negotiate or to implement rules, there are uncertainties about the level of commitment of national authorities, especially when it comes to the political and economic costs of agreement. The mobilization of resources at the EU level is thus always political; while the development of routines or institutional habits may dilute the confrontation, there are always potential barriers to effective action or to the expansion of Commission competence.

A logical consequence of the features already noted is that the Union exercises power predominantly at the 'soft' end of the spectrum, as opposed to the 'hard' or coercive power taken to be the ultimate sanction available to state authorities. But as Joseph Nye has pointed out, states themselves, including the most powerful states of all, depend increasingly on 'soft' power to achieve outcomes in an interdependent and globalizing world. The capacity to co-opt, to enmesh in procedures and institutions, and to influence by contact and example is a growing part of the state's armoury, and it is a part in which the EU is well practised.[6]

It is thus possible to argue that the EU plays a powerful shaping role in the global political economy, both by developing structured commercial ties with its neighbours and competitors and by shaping the expectations of others in negotiation or diplomacy. In an increasingly globalized and increasingly turbulent world political economy, it might be argued that this capacity will become more significant both for the EU and for its partners and targets during the early years of the new millennium. The EU as a 'community of law' has both inherent limitations and attractions, and can offer and deny rewards such as market access or privileged dialogue. The financial crises and related issues of trade and development that characterized large parts of the global political economy in the late 1990s were such as to place a large premium on institutional order, and on precisely the assets in which the EU is richest.

In a turbulent political economy, this can be and has been a powerful magnet for outsiders. The very fact that the EU is not a state like other states has attracted third parties, whether in the Middle East, the Asia-Pacific, or elsewhere, to engage in dialogue and economic institution-building. In the conditions of Europe after the end of the Cold War, the EU appeared as an island of stability and prosperity, and as a source of both economic and political advancement. But this in itself was a potent challenge to the EU's foreign economic policies, since the then European Community had existed for all of its life under the constraints of a divided Europe and prospered on the basis of exclusion and privilege rather than co-optation and inclusion. The ability to 'capture' neighbouring countries is thus an uncomfortable asset: how many, how, and when? It is not at all surprising that the EC response through the 'Europe Agreements' and other channels was initially uncertain, and that suspicions in the new democracies were aroused by the view that Community membership is a privilege to be bought at a high price and over an extended period. When the EU published its *Agenda 2000* document as the basis for policy reform in the context of enlargement during 1997, it was also apparent that the process of negotiation with the candidates for membership would be accompanied by intense negotiation among the existing members themselves.[7] The results of these tensions between the 'EU order' and the demands of the outside world were thus paradoxical, and likely to remain so: increasing attractiveness, demands for access if not membership, and an EU response veering between the acceptance of responsibility as a 'regional superpower' and a form of conservative paralysis.

The implication of the discussion here is that foreign economic policy for the EU revolves as much around process as around substance. The process is one of continuous negotiation at the European level, where policy determination and policy output constitute an almost seamless web and where the feedback between processes of internal bargaining and international action can be extremely difficult to disentangle. Two distinct phenomena can be identified here, each of crucial significance to the international activity of the EU and of interest in the broader analysis of globalization. On the one hand, there is what might be termed a process of externalization, through which the internal bargaining between member states and within institutions spills over or is projected into the global arena. The example of agricultural policy already cited is one of the most salient in this respect, given the direct linkage between the reform of the CAP and the demands not only of global trade negotiations but also of interregional agreements or of the enlargement of the Union itself. This is likely to be a crucial focus of tensions as the EU confronts the logic of its extension during the early years of the third millennium, since it connects closely with the need for budgetary reform and the implications of the single European currency as European Monetary Union (EMU) takes effect.

Other examples are not hard to find: thus, in the case of high-technology policy, the internal effort to reach a consensus on support for the EU semiconductor industry has frequently spilled over into the attempt to regulate access to the European market and thus into relations with the United States and Japan. A key development in the new millennium will be the ways in which such specific high-technology issues have come together in areas such as telecommunications and how the EU can shape the external implications of its newly unified telecommunications markets. In turn, this links with a further area of 'externalization'. During the late 1990s, it also became evident that trade in services posed distinctive problems: 'internal' EU efforts to regulate the growth of electronic commerce, for example, would inexorably lead to tensions with the United States in particular, while successive episodes in the application of EU competition rules to cross-national business alliances demonstrated the complexities of dealing with powerful firms at the same time as powerful governments.[8]

While the process of externalization links the internal affairs of the EU with the global political economy, there is a parallel process of internalization, through which external developments and external actors can become part of the European Agreements bargaining process, and thereby used either by member states or by the Commission and other institutions as a factor in the determination of policy. In the first stages of the Single Market Program (SMP), US officials went so far as to call for a seat at the table for negotiation of EU measures, a rather dramatic way of expressing the need not just to be in the European market but also to be involved in the generation of rules and regulatory regimes crucial to its operation.[9] Although this was a politically charged episode, the SMP also involved intense efforts by US and Japanese multinational corporations to gain access to decision-making, efforts that were arguably more effective because they were less confrontational. The other side of the internalization coin is that the threat of external penetration of the process can be used by EU lobbies and member governments in defence of their own interests. Thus, the origins of the SMP itself lay partly in the perception by European industrial lobbies that international trends threatened the competitive position of the EU, a perception that could be used to drive internal reform in the shape of the Single European Act and to influence the SMP in detail. Perhaps more dramatically, the perceived threat of political and economic collapse in Central and Eastern Europe in the early 1990s fed directly into bargaining over market access, which enabled those

countries and their sponsors to engage with the EU policy process more or less effectively. By the late 1990s it was apparent that such pressures would be affected in the coming century by the combination of external financial turbulence—if not collapse—and the potential held by EMU, both as a safe haven for assets and as a lever of potential political influence. To put it crudely, would the EU be able to operate as a new financial superpower, and what would be the costs and benefits of this status?

The conception of the EU as a continuous—and continuously reshaped—bargain is an important avenue for the analysis of policy, which adds to the evaluation of the Union's power resources and their deployment. The added elements of externalization and internalization are not unique to the EU, but the EU does provide fertile ground for their occurrence, given its multilayered and relatively open policy framework. If for no other reason, these processes are important inasmuch as they express political intervention in the decision-making arena—by insiders (EU member governments, lobbies), by outsiders (governments, multinationals, other international organizations), or by both acting in the context of global networks. In each such case, as Susan Strange has pointed out, the identification of a 'European' interest or line of policy can be put in question by the emergence of complex global alignments and cross-cutting interests.[10]

This discussion leads into consideration of a final element in the EU's foreign economic policy: the distinctive pressures and opportunities created by the Union's development of a complex governance system centred on regulatory and institutional structures. This set of structures, as already noted, plays an important part in shaping policy-making. But it is possible to view it in another light, exploring the ways in which the Community's regulatory and governance structures provide a potential asset for the pursuit of global objectives. There are two dimensions to this issue. In the first place, there is an increasing perception of the Community as an effective model for the management of capitalist societies, based roughly on a modified social market economy as opposed to the free market capitalism of the American model. If this is indeed the case, then it is only a short step to the argument that the EU model can be used to shape developments in the outside world, buttressed by the legal base of the treaties and their impact on growth and stability in Western Europe. Thus, the negotiation of the European Economic Area in 1990–1 demanded of the EFTA countries a reshaping of their economic and regulatory structures so that they could become compatible with the Community. Indeed, the reshaping was so profound that a number of members decided it was better to apply for full membership and, thus, full access to EC decision-making. The Europe Agreements of 1991–2 in regard to Central and Eastern European countries also gave evidence for the argument that the EC model could be used to capture new adherents, with much the same results, although there were also very strong political incentives driving the countries concerned to make their applications for membership. The new model constituted by EMU, as has been argued, could prove a powerful source of leverage—as well as a source of responsibilities—in the new millennium.

Second, the success of market regulation and integration in Western Europe is often seen by EU officials as providing the base for reshaping of global regulatory regimes. The SMP provided such an impetus in areas such as technical standards and public procurement within the context of the GATT. Within the WTO, the EU has acted in major sectoral negotiations such as those on financial services, telecommunications, and information technology to build coalitions on which important agreements could be based (often in juxtaposition to the stance taken by the United States). The 'muscle' available to the Europeans depends by implication on the success of the EU method internally and the effectiveness of its own regulatory structures. A number of analyses have drawn attention to the growth of 'competition among rules' as a central process of the relations between industrial societies; in this process, the existence in a given industry or sector of different regulatory structures gives a basis for attempts to lever open domestic economic activities to the benefit of those whose rules are the most widely adopted or attractive. By this means, the interpenetration of separate national economies can become more intense, and equally clearly, the more successful regulatory structures can create regional or national advantage. The position of the EU in this respect is critical, reinforced by increasing market integration and by the 'capture' of ever-larger parts of the European economic space, and is expressed in the incentives created for outsiders by the unified market. This has been recognized by outsiders such as the American and Japanese governments, but also and at least as significantly by firms and other private organizations; such recognition in the late 1990s has been intensified by the imminence of EMU. Whether the EU is capable through its decision processes of capitalizing on the leverage given by the 'Community model' and of controlling market access or financial resources effectively in an increasingly globalized world is, in the light of the earlier discussion, an open question, but one that will be vital to the global economic order of the twenty-first century.

## Conclusion: The European Union and the Global Political Economy

This chapter has focused on two interrelated aspects of the European Union's external economic policies. First, it has asked the question, can the EU have a foreign economic policy in the conventional sense? Second, how effective are the forms of power and the decision processes within EU foreign economic policy, and what impact does the EU have in a globalizing world? The answers to both these questions are qualified, but no less significant for that. In the first place, the EU cannot be said to possess a foreign economic policy in a traditional state-centric form; but the nature of the Union and of the global political economy has changed in such a way as to cast considerable doubt on the utility of the conventional conception of foreign economic policy. The EU, therefore, is as much a reflection of the new reality as it is of a challenge to an entrenched notion. In the second place, evaluation of the EU's policy effectiveness in terms of its satisfaction of traditional state-centred criteria is misplaced. Just as the European Union reflects new realities in the conception of foreign economic policy, so does it demand new criteria for the evaluation of policy effectiveness based on the mobilization of predominantly soft power, on the attractiveness of its negotiating and regulatory structures, and on the multiple roles played by the EU in the global political economy. Three central roles can be identified for the EU in relation to processes of globalization: those of 'barrier', 'site', and 'promoter'. While conceptually separable, these roles are, in policy terms, often closely interrelated, and they encapsulate many of the tensions between global and regional integration processes; within the EU, as illustrated by many of the examples cited in this chapter, they constitute a major focus for continuous negotiation and renegotiation, both at the level of policy sectors and at the level of institutional understandings.

In this light, the EU is not necessarily the only possible model of a new form of foreign economic policy, but it is a challenge to conventional categories and a phenomenon that should make us look very seriously and critically at prevailing assumptions—not least, those encapsulating notions of order and stability in the global political economy. The EU has often been the object of fears or suspicions on the part of outsiders, as the potential core of a 'fortress Europe' or as the major building block for a world of competing super-regions. This is indeed one possible future direction for the EU, but the Union will not construct that future by its own efforts alone; the roles of the United States and Japan will also be crucial, as will the efforts of transnational groupings and mechanisms of global governance. At least as powerful is the image of the EU as a major contributor to global governance, encouraging the building of transnational networks and providing a model of continuous negotiation that is one way of coping with the emergence of a global political economy.

## Notes

1  In general, this chapter adopts the term 'European Union' for all uses except two: first, those where the reference is clearly to the European Community (the 'first pillar' of the EU); second, where the reference is clearly to the period before 1993 when the Treaty on European Union came into force.

2  For a general discussion of this tension, see William D. Coleman and Geoffrey R.D. Underhill, *Regionalism and Global Economic Integration* (London: Routledge, 1998), Introduction.

3  See Susan Strange, *States and Markets*, 2nd edn (London: Pinter, 1994); Peter Dicken, *Global Shift: The Internationalization of Economic Activity*, 2nd edn (London: Paul Chapman, 1992); Brigid Laffan, Rory O'Donnell, and Michael Smith, *Europe's Experimental Union: Rethinking Integration* (London: Routledge, 1999), ch. 3.

4  See I. Macleod, I.D. Hendry, and Stephen Hyatt, *The External Relations of the European Community* (Oxford: Oxford University Press, 1996), Part 1.

5  A similar though not identical situation exists in other intergovernmental organizations. See Coleman and Underhill, *Globalization and Regional Economic Integration*, Introduction.

6  See Joseph S. Nye Jr, *Bound To Lead: The Changing Nature of American Power* (New York: Basic Books, 1990), ch. 5.

7  See David Allen and Michael Smith, 'External Policy Developments', in Geoffrey Edwards and Georg Wiessala, eds, *The European Union 1997: Annual Review of Activities* (Oxford: Basil Blackwell, 1998).

8  See Michael Smith, 'The European Union', in Brian Hocking and Stephen McGuire, eds, *Trade Politics: Actors, Issues and Processes* (London: Routledge, 1999).

9  See Brian Hocking and Michael Smith, *Beyond Foreign Economic Policy: The United States, the Single European Market and the Changing World Economy* (London: Pinter/Cassell, 1997).

10  Susan Strange, 'Who Are EU? Ambiguities in the Concept of Competitiveness', *Journal of Common Market Studies* 36 (1998): 101–14.

## Suggested Readings

Coleman, William D., and Geoffrey R.D. Underhill. *Regionalism and Global Economic Integration*. London: Routledge, 1998.

Dent, Christopher M. *The European Economy: The Global Context*. London: Routledge, 1997.

Dicken, Peter. *Global Shift: The Internationalization of Economic Activity,* 2nd edn. London: Paul Chapman, 1992.

Hocking, Brian, and Michael Smith. *Beyond Foreign Economic Policy: The United States, the Single European Market and the Changing World Economy*. London: Cassell/Pinter, 1997.

Smith, Michael, and Stephen Woolcock. *The United States and the European Community in a Transformed World*. London: Pinter for the Royal Institute of International Affairs, 1993.

Piening, Christopher. *Global Europe: The European Union in World Affairs*. Boulder, Colo.: Lynne Rienner, 1997.

Tsoukalis, Loukas. *The New European Economy Revisited*. Oxford: Oxford University Press, 1997.

Wallace, William. *Regional Integration: The West European Experience*. Washington: Brookings Institution, 1994.

## Web Sites

Index of European Union Policy Sites by Sector:
http://www.europa.eu.int/pol/index-en.htm

European Union Agenda 2000:
http://www.europa.eu.int/comm/agenda2000/

## Chapter 28

# The United States and Globalization

Bruce E. Moon

## Introduction

Most nations can only react to globalization, but the United States, as the system's dominant economic and political actor, is also able to affect the speed and character of the globalization process itself. By promoting the institutions that integrated national economies after World War II, it appears that the United States acted as predicted by hegemonic stability theory (HST).[1] As American dominance faded, the global system drifted away from the coherence of its original Bretton Woods design to the present chaotic patchwork of inadequate governance, a pattern that also lends credence to HST explanations centred on the relative decline of the hegemonic power. However, America's distinctive foreign policy tradition and peculiar political, economic, and social structure offer a better explanation for the character of the globalization that has emerged.

At the end of World War II, the United States exhibited the two most important characteristics required of a candidate to champion global liberalism.[2] First, it possessed the dominance that affords a hegemon both the greatest incentive and the greatest capacity to advance globalization. As the most productive economy it was the most likely to benefit from open goods markets, and as the largest source of both supply and demand for capital it was the most likely to exploit open capital markets. Its power was used to persuade or co-opt a majority of nations, compel most of the remainder, and isolate the few dissenters. Second, the liberalism of the American domestic economy demonstrated that 'its social purpose and domestic distribution of power [were] favorably disposed toward a liberal inter-

national order.'[3] However, America's dominance is accompanied by a profound isolationism and its liberalism is coloured by its unique circumstances. The effects of these eccentricities were discernible in the Bretton Woods design but eventually became dominant in both American policy and the global regime it sponsored.

## Hegemonic, but Isolationist

No account of American foreign policy can ignore the monumental shadow cast by the deep historical isolationism of the United States. From its colonial period onward, America has displayed hostility to foreign pressures and an abiding antipathy towards multilateral policies and supranational institutions.[4] This isolationism has been overcome only occasionally by extraordinary exigencies, most notably the combination of military, political, and economic challenges to the immediate postwar order in Europe. Even then, its commitment to a global institutional order has been reluctant and sporadic, not at all the attitude expected of a hegemon by HST.

This profound disinterest in foreign affairs has been sustained by a frequently ignored economic reality: the American economy has been and remains relatively unaffected by developments elsewhere in the global economy. The historic insulation of the American economy from the global one stems from the size and physical remoteness of the US market, which relies less on trade than virtually any other in the world.[5] For most nations, of course, a small foreign sector would imply proportionately small external influence, but the overwhelming size of the US market means that even a modest percentage of American GNP constitutes a sizeable share of global economic activity. In the early 1950s, for example, American exports constituted more than a third of industrial country exports, yet less than 5 per cent of US GNP.

This odd pattern of dominance has cross-cutting implications for the ability of the United States to embrace its theoretical role of global hegemon. It had the power to shape the international system's fundamental structure, but little need to do so to protect either the national economy or the interests of subnational groups. This autonomy allowed the United States to be inattentive to systemic issues and left the system vulnerable to the re-emergence of America's natural isolationism whenever external pressures abated. However, when the United States *was* engaged with questions of system design, it could easily afford to indulge the interests of others—as expected of a hegemon —because that seldom required much sacrifice of its own modest stake.

## Liberal, but Myopic

Minimal external reliance also affected the character of American liberalism. With such a small import-competing sector, protectionist pressures were modest, even though theory identifies groups that normally oppose free trade. The Stolper-Samuelson theorem predicts that trade would harm unskilled labour, but that group is notoriously poorly represented by structures of American political power. Unlike the European working class, which has been championed economically by a strong trade union movement and defended politically by resultant social democratic parties, unskilled labour in the United States has been divided by ethnic identification, language, and region, leaving it politically impotent and economically vulnerable. The Heckscher-Ohlin trade theory implies that inefficient sectors of the economy will suffer losses, but the general dominance of American industry in the immediate postwar era made these niches of comparative advantage for foreigners hard to find and, given high transportation costs, difficult to exploit.

As American supremacy has eroded since the 1970s, greater vulnerabilities have produced dislocations in scattered industries, most prominently in textiles, steel, and autos. But no ideological current exists to frame these as the inevitable consequences of globalization, and no organized opposition demands that accommodation be made. Instead, these inroads have been interpreted as reflections of 'cheating' by other nations (especially Japan), triggering a response in the foreign policy arena rather than an acknowledgment of the trade-offs endemic to an open economy. In short, US foreign economic policy has a built-in liberal inclination because its unusually small foreign sector is made up of elements either economically invulnerable to foreign competition or politically powerless to resist it.

As a result, American liberalism, largely unchecked by contrary domestic forces, has become theoretically rigid and ideologically extreme. From Cordell Hull's influential plea for free trade as the key to international peace in the 1940s to American commentary on Russia in the 1990s, US rhetoric has associated free markets with material prosperity, stability, justice, democracy, human rights, international peace, and more. As James Fallows puts it:

> The Anglo-American system of politics and economics, like any system, rests on certain principles and beliefs. But rather than acting as if these are the best principles, or the ones their societies prefer, Britons and Americans often act as if these were the *only possible* principles and no one, except in error, could choose any others. Political economics becomes an essentially religious question, subject to the standard drawback of any religion—the failure to understand why people outside the faith might act as they do.[6]

Herein lies a contradiction. Though a passionate proselytizer, the United States maintains a more shallow commitment to liberalism than nations whose small market size makes trade openness inevitable or those for whom it represents a conscious acceptance of its mixed welfare implications.

Nor is it as stable as in those nations where it has evolved as a strategic compromise among powerful political actors. As a result, American systemic designs are not as attentive to the complex side-effects of globalization as would be expected from a hegemon more deeply affected by the system it created.

## Bretton Woods

Over 50 years ago, the combination of American hegemonic credentials and fortuitous circumstances were sufficient to fashion a system to meet the delicate balance between national and systemic needs. At the system's core lie the multilateral trade negotiations for the General Agreement on Tariffs and Trade/International Trade Organization (GATT/ITO), designed to rekindle economic growth by restoring trade to levels reached before the catastrophic two-thirds decline in trade during the Great Depression. However, the key to the success of Bretton Woods—and the sharpest contrast with the current system—was the recognition that liberalization also brought problems and constraints that not only undermined its benefits but threatened the capacity of individual nations to embrace it.

The Bretton Woods design acknowledged the sacrifices required of nations in order to liberalize and contained various provisions for easing those burdens. The GATT allowed nations to demand access to foreign markets for their exports as compensation for the dislocations caused by imports, thus providing political cover for shaky governments to withstand protectionist pressures and creating domestic constituencies to balance them. The negotiation process enabled nations to liberalize trade at a pace compatible with resolving the domestic political and economic problems it created, and the GATT itself contained a number of escape clauses that recognized the inherent tension between liberalization and other domestic economic goals. The International Monetary Fund (IMF) not only prescribed stable exchange rates but also offered resources to member states to facilitate their co-operation in maintaining them: its lending facilities provided an alternative to exchange rate

devaluation and protectionism for nations feeling balance-of-payments pressures. Finally, the World Bank offered longer-term funding to rebuild war-torn economies that otherwise could not survive international competition, most notably from the United States. American unilateral and bilateral policy towards Europe, especially the Marshall Plan and the temporary tolerance of European protectionism, greatly augmented these arrangements, perhaps dwarfing them in effect.

The system as a whole was coherent and realistic, allowing nations to move towards free capital and goods markets at their own pace. They fashioned arrangements consonant with their own priorities and circumstances but generally reflected 'the compromise of embedded liberalism'.[7] The challenge 'to devise a form of multilateralism compatible with the requirements of domestic stability'[8] was not seen as a lofty aspiration, but rather as an absolutely essential requirement to achieve any kind of workable system at all. Without the flexibility it provided, nations would neither have agreed to the obligations implicit in acceptance of Bretton Woods initially nor would they have been capable of meeting them subsequently. At stake was the very political legitimacy of the state itself, which must not only achieve economic prosperity but also maintain enough control over the domestic political economy that its claim to being responsive to the citizenry is seen as plausible.

Still, Bretton Woods, whose sparse institutional component contained no permanent trade organization, a monetary authority with sharply limited enforcement capacity, and an underfinanced development bank, represented as minimal a core as could be squared with the label of 'system'. If the profound threats of the 1940s made *some* institutional structure absolutely imperative, the American influence was responsible for its minimalist character. Proposals for an IMF and World Bank with a broader charge and expanded powers fell victim to American antipathy towards intrusive supranational institutions that would challenge US policy autonomy. During heated negotiations over the charter for the International Trade Organization, the United States blocked provisions that would give the organization greater authority over domestic economic policies and a larger role in adjudicating trade policy disputes, yet permit nations greater freedom to adopt protectionist measures. Even so, the American Congress refused ratification, the result of a coalition of free trade purists who thought the agreement too illiberal and isolationists who thought it too internationalist. Thus, the tariff reduction negotiations of the skeletal GATT, intended as an interim measure until the ITO could commence operations, became the only instrument for regulating global trade. The result was globalization with relatively little active involvement by either the United States or an international institution. Subsequently, the system was to drift further from the compromises necessary for its founding and closer to the American vision of proper (that is, minimal) economic management.

To the extent that the modestly internationalist position of the United States in Bretton Woods could be reconciled with the role expectations of a hegemon, American policy changes since then make clear that it was a temporary aberration from traditional practice. Motivated since the 1970s by its rising vulnerability to trade competitors and its changing pattern of comparative advantage, American policy has increasingly become narrowly self-interested. The United States has become less attentive to matters of global system structure, instead pursuing its goals through aggressive unilateralism and regionalism. Even when actively engaged, its multilateral agenda is now less likely to champion initiatives justified by global welfare considerations, particularly if they appear to require sacrifice of more immediate national goals or ideological purity. Most telling is the American emphasis on liberalization of capital markets—where the US comparative advantage remains dominant—even though the theoretical case is much stronger for free trade in goods markets and evidence continues to accumulate that excessive capital flows have become injurious to global welfare. The American neglect of systemic concerns has accelerated in recent years because its global leadership had always been sustained by the Cold War image that international architecture was required to maintain its national security. The end of the Cold War allowed the United States to return to its historic propensity to seek a naïve combination of economic benefits but political disengagement, best exemplified by George Washington in his Farewell Address: 'The great rule of conduct for us in regard to foreign nations is, in extending our commercial relations to have with them [the nations of Europe] as little political connection as possible.'

## Aggressive Unilateralism

As the US stake in the global economy has grown—trade levels as a percentage of GDP have nearly tripled since the immediate postwar period, for example—both threats and opportunities have increased. American attempts to minimize the former while maximizing the latter have required a dual strategy. US efforts to promote opportunities for American exporters and foreign investors remain concentrated in its multilateral drive for a global system free of barriers, while its unilateral and bilateral policies have increasingly erected such barriers to protect American firms that compete with imports. The United States justifies its unilateral actions as consistent with its systemic philosophy because they are designed to compensate for the unfair trade practices of others, but other nations have criticized this pattern as hypocritical, especially because the US has resisted the creation of more binding trade dispute resolution mechanisms.

While American tariff rates for most-favoured nations have remained low, non-tariff barriers targeted against particular nations have risen. They have taken several forms, some fully in accord with GATT rules and even consistent with liberal principles. Section 201 of the Trade Reform Act of 1974 implemented the GATT's Article 19 escape clause, permitting nations to suspend tariff reductions for industries suffering from sudden increases in imports, regardless of cause. This escape clause has not been frequently used, no doubt because it undermines the American case for systemic liberalism. The United States has felt more free to employ Section 301 (and its extension in the 1988 Trade Act dubbed 'Super 301') because it is designed to target particular countries found to be engaging in 'unjustifiable, unreasonable or discriminatory' trading practices. It authorizes countervailing duties to offset dumping by foreign manufacturers or subsidies by foreign governments. As such, these actions can be squared with the idea of 'fair trade' even if their consistency with 'free trade' is more dubious.

Competitors object to such an approach for many reasons. They contend that these actions are often invoked for purely protectionist purposes, including the desire to deter sharp competition for the American market by threatening successful competitors with the rigours of the US legal process and potential retaliation. They resent the extension of American domestic principles to the international arena through extraterritoriality and ideological hegemony, especially because 'the Anglo-American view has taken on a moral tone. . . . If a country disagrees with the Anglo-American axioms, it doesn't just disagree—it is a cheater.'[9] Further, it has become common for the United States to threaten use of such 'fair trade' actions in order to require competitors 'voluntarily' to reduce exports through voluntary export restraints, the most prominent of which was the 1980s agreement that restricted the import of Japanese autos (to be phased out under the Uruguay Round accords). Moreover, it is not easy to predict when these actions will be invoked.[10] This has led some to conclude that 'the greatest potential for the erosion of multilateralism lies in the ability of the powerful to heavy-ride rather than in the small and weak to free-ride.'[11] By playing on the ambiguity of free trade and fair trade, these policies have enabled the United States to champion free trade and deny its disruptive impact, yet simultaneously protect the most vulnerable American industries. As a portent, at the time of writing the US steel industry was pushing hard for import quotas.

## The Rise of Regionalism

A second dimension of US trade policy can be seen in a similarly ambivalent light. For the past decade, the United States has displayed a tolerance—perhaps even a preference—for regional trade systems.

The clearest example is the Canada-United States Free Trade Agreement, which quickly evolved into the North America Free Trade Agreement (NAFTA). Many liberal critics saw this as a rejection of multilateralism and a dangerous step towards regional trade blocs eventually bound to compete along mercantilist lines. Adding to these worries was American encouragement of various Pacific Rim initiatives and continuing pressure by the Clinton administration to extend NAFTA throughout the Western Hemisphere as the Free Trade Area of the Americas (FTAA).[12]

In contrast, the United States contends that NAFTA and the FTAA represent an *affirmation* of its hegemonic role of cajoling and bullying others to support multilateral liberalism—because NAFTA was a bargaining ploy to counter regionalism in Europe and thus re-energize the then-languishing Uruguay Round of GATT talks. NAFTA may have had that effect, but it also demonstrated that the US is far more satisfied with regional schemes than with being the mythical hegemon of HST.

In fact, these regional agreements create liberalization structured along the lines favoured by the American vision but blocked at the global level by competing European perspectives. NAFTA, which lacks not only a secretariat but even an identifiable physical location, embodies the American ideal of a regime without institutions.[13] It also contrasts dramatically with the rich tapestry woven of the EU's multiple agencies, which are meant to mitigate the effects of liberalization and thus facilitate its extension and deepening. The United States remains intolerant of extranational constraints, especially if they challenge America's vision of liberalization without side-effects.

## The Multilateral Agenda

As US dominance has eroded, America's willingness to ignore its own interests in fashioning global policies has faded with it. The United States continues to promote liberalism, but mostly in those areas in which American economic interests are directly involved. Only agriculture became a real priority among producer-consumer talks in the Uruguay

Round, in part because the US has become more reliant on financial flows than trade competitiveness. Thus, even while trade barriers of major interest to less developed nations remain unresolved, US energies in the GATT/WTO have been directed to auxiliary issues such as trade-related investment measures (TRIMs), the protection of intellectual property rights, and trade in services.

With its advantages in financial services intact, the United States has been especially active in promoting capital liberalization. One proposal would amend the IMF charter to make the liberalization of capital movements one of the purposes of the Fund and extend its jurisdiction to supervise restrictions on capital flows. Another was the abortive effort to enact a Multilateral Agreement on Investment (MAI), the centerpiece of which was the quintessential American position that foreign investors should be guaranteed national treatment—that is, virtually all national restrictions on foreign direct investment should be prohibited. At least in the short term, such liberalization would no doubt benefit multinational corporations (MNCs), whose political influence, already strong in the US because of its unusual pattern of class relations, has grown further in recent years. Without an institutional locus for working-class solidarity—American labour prefers the moniker of 'middle class'—the interests of multinational capital have seldom been explicitly challenged. Initiatives favourable particularly to finance capital have also been aided by the breathtaking speed of further class transformation in American society, driven by the decline of manufacturing, the rise of the white-collar service sector and high technology, and, especially, the widespread distribution of equity issues through Regulation 401–K and mutual funds. The capitalist class has expanded—more than a third of American households now own stock—while the decline in manufacturing has shrunk the mobilizable working class.

## The American Vision

Even in the face of increasing evidence of its flaws, the United States remains committed to a global system in line with its unique ideological vision—liberalism supported by a very sparse institutional structure to mitigate the adverse consequences of the globalization it produces. The dilemma, faced squarely at Bretton Woods but neglected since, is put most plainly by a leading proponent of globalization: 'the most serious challenge for the world economy in the years ahead lies in making globalization compatible with domestic social and political stability—or to put it even more directly, in ensuring that international economic integration does not contribute to domestic social *disintegration*.'[14] The threat arises from the significant distributional consequences that attend massive trade and capital flows. Immediate dislocations[15] create tensions and contribute strongly to the politically and socially divisive income inequality that has been well documented in recent years. Furthermore, globalization engenders conflict over domestic norms and the social institutions that embody them, including the potential for a 'race to the bottom' in labour standards and environmental protection.

None of these problems need undermine the case for global liberalization, however, because most admit of governmental amelioration. Indeed, that is precisely the direction taken by 'the compromise of embedded liberalism' in the Bretton Woods era: 'societies were asked to embrace the change and dislocation attending international liberalization. In turn, liberalization and its effects were cushioned by the newly acquired domestic economic and social policy roles of governments.'[16] Over the longer term, however, the unencumbered capital mobility of contemporary globalization affords an exit option to capital owners that gives them unprecedented bargaining leverage over nation-bound actors. Workers face declines in wages, benefits, and working conditions and suffer the costs of increasing insecurity. Meanwhile, the difficulty of taxing foot-loose capital severely undermines the capacity of governments to provide social insurance or, indeed, to raise the revenues required to address *any* of the problems exacerbated by globalization. Further, regulation to advance environmental or other social goals becomes increasingly infeasible.

When the ability of national governments to cope with such problems has been sharply reduced, one option is to augment national capacities with international ones. Another is to free governments to balance these pressures as they see fit and even to facilitate their choice. The GATT's escape clause could be reinvigorated and anti-dumping mechanisms more explicitly monitored, for example. If the IMF and World Bank were to encourage social insurance instead of demanding austerity, government pull-backs from the intolerably harsh discipline of the so-called 'Washington consensus' could be avoided. The role of these international financial institutions in dictating policy is widely seen as undemocratic, especially since the privatization urged as part of the Washington consensus moves power from elected and accountable public officials to unelected, unaccountable, foreign actors. Instead, the contemporary system has bound nations even more tightly to liberal orthodoxy and contributed further to the crisis of political legitimacy unleashed when governments are unable to insulate their citizens from the effects of global markets. It is significant that the last attempt to so submerge alternative values to market discipline occurred earlier in this century in the context of much less democratic polities.

The Asian currency crisis demonstrates what may be the most significant weakness of the current system's devotion to capital mobility—the monetary pressures that arise from the Mundell-Fleming constraint that a nation cannot simultaneously achieve the three goals of capital mobility, exchange rate stability, and monetary policy autonomy. Fidelity to the first of these is enforced both by World Bank/IMF policy and by the power of capital markets themselves to demand the freedom to engage in capital flight as a condition for not exercising that right. States forced to choose between the remaining two goals must hope that domestic economic and political needs do not require the exercise of real autonomy and that exchange rate volatility does not escalate beyond the tolerable. When the foreign exchange reserves of even the largest and most powerful economies are inadequate to move appreciably the exchange rate through direct intervention, and where the absence of a central institution to perform that role leaves

domestic economies to adjust very painfully to rapid movements of capital, an attentive hegemon might consider weakening the forces of global finance. The United States, however, cannot empathize with the complex effects of exchange rate movements on other nations because its own small foreign sector transmits so few impacts on price levels or output. Furthermore, capital controls threaten the interests of the MNC, one of the few powerful American actors that relies heavily on the global economy.

Prominent alternatives exist. Provision could be made to exchange information to restrict tax strategies available to MNCs. The Tobin tax proposed by economist James Tobin would tax foreign exchange transactions, both to raise funds to support international efforts and to reduce the appeal of the destabilizing short-term capital flows that have been implicated in economic crises in East Asia and Latin America. The capital controls used successfully in otherwise liberal economies like that of Chile could be countenanced. The EU, with its social charter and a host of other policies and procedures enacted in recognition that such pressures represent possible impediments to future liberalization, demonstrates again that greater regulation can go hand in hand with greater liberalization of trade. The funding available for crisis management could be enhanced.

Instead, the United States has retreated from even its tepid style of leadership. While the global financial system appeared poised on the brink of collapse in the fall of 1998, disappointment with the IMF's management of the Asian crisis led the isolationist American Congress to seek the demise of the IMF rather than to alter either its policies or the liberal system as a whole.[17] Congress refused to fund an extension of the IMF and also refused to make good on more than $1 billion in back dues owed to the UN. Worse yet for the image of a benign hegemon, The US Congress has offered to meet financial obligations to the UN only in return for acquiring veto power with respect to the reproductive health agendas of all UN constituents (e.g., barring any mention of abortion). As Diana Tussie notes, 'The United States has often interpreted a rule-based order to mean the extension of American rules and procedures to the rest of the world.'[18]

It is arguable whether the unresponsiveness of American policy towards the costs implicit in accelerating globalization results more from design or neglect. Two sets of explanations—one centred on isolationism and the other on a striking narrowness of strategic vision—converge. Certainly, the American image of a successful international economic system is decidedly less regulated and institutionalized than that held by others. In line with standard liberal theory, Washington seeks only to decrease national governmental control of cross-border transactions, confident that the resulting flows will increase prosperity. When problems arise (as in Mexico, Southeast Asia, and Russia), it is content with ad hoc responses that maintain hegemonic autonomy rather than advancing global institutional authority.

It is also true that the United States is poorly positioned to design ways of resolving or coping with costs of globalization it does not feel. The US has little experience with ameliorating trade-induced dislocations, unlike Europe, where generous welfare provisions have long complemented protectionism to afford security to the working class and where regionalism has eased the pressures on the national state. Indeed, the division of authority between levels of government makes it difficult for the United States to integrate trade policy, which is enacted by the federal government, and welfare and education policy, which are largely functions of state and local government. On the finance side, the US is even less familiar with the challenges of coping with volatile and uncomfortable capital flows that have lately plagued developing countries.

## Contemporary Globalization: A Patchwork of Inadequate Governance

A regime committed to this neo-liberal brand of globalization has severe limitations, most notably that it is less stable than one built to withstand the predictable economic and political forces that emerge within any underregulated system. This involves not only such 'economic' forces as destabilizing capital flows but 'political' forces that have not been accommodated in system creation (e.g., dissenting nations and subnational interests.) Instead of exploring alternatives, the United States has hoped to silence dissenters by portraying globalism as natural, inevitable, and irreversible. To the contrary, the 1920s demonstrated that when globalization is seen as a source of problems by citizens not convinced of its benefits, it can be reversed with breathtaking speed. Or, as Rodrik notes, 'social disintegration is not a spectator sport—those on the sidelines also get splashed with mud from the field.'[19]

In short, the explanation for the recent evolution of the system lies in the peculiar character of American hegemony. Only an ideological hegemon would fail to see the need for more aggressive action and only an isolationist one would fail to act on it. As a result, it appears that the gravest threat to the globalization goal lies not in diminished American hegemony, but rather in continuing implementation of America's peculiar vision of its hegemonic role.

## Notes

1  Robert Gilpin, *The Political Economy of International Relations* (Princeton, NJ: Princeton University Press, 1987), 72–92.

2  John Ruggie, 'International Regimes, Transactions, and Change: Embedded Liberalism in the Postwar Economic Order', *International Organization* 36 (1982): 382.

3  Ibid. For the generally unregulated character of 'Anglo-Saxon' capitalism, see James Fallows, 'How the World Works', *Atlantic Monthly* (Dec. 1993): 61–87.

4  Evidence that the United States eschewed global leadership for half a century after its economic dominance entitled it to such a role includes the refusal to join the League of Nations and to cooperate at the World Economic Conference in London in 1933. The persistence of this attitude was demonstrated in 1971 when President

Richard Nixon unilaterally dissolved the fixed-rate monetary order that threatened American policy autonomy.

5   Exports account for slightly over 10 per cent of US GNP, roughly a third of the European average. The US has relied on foreign capital to balance perpetual trade deficits but it has not been forced to alter policy to attract it.

6   Fallow, 'How the World Works', 65. His inclusion of Britain is clearly misplaced, except during the Thatcher period.

7   For an elaboration of this noteworthy phrase, see Ruggie, 'International Regimes'.

8   Ibid., 399.

9   Fallows, 'How the World Works'.

10   Indeed, Canadian government and business enthusiasm for the Canada-US FTA owed much to its binational trade dispute resolution panels, which could block arbitrary American actions.

11   Diana Tussie, 'Multilateralism Revisited in a Globalizing World Economy', *Mershon International Studies Review* 42 (1998): 190.

12   Congressional opposition, motivated by nationalist and protectionist sentiment, blocked the latter by refusing to grant 'fast-track' authority to negotiate agreements exempt from legislative amendment.

13   Without a class-based system of political representation, the best-organized American opposition to such agreements has come from such progressive organizations as environmental groups. They have joined with elements of the right to emphasize, rather than distributional consequences, the potential threats to national autonomy represented by the WTO and NAFTA's dispute resolution panels.

14   Dani Rodrik, *Has Globalization Gone Too Far?* (Washington: Institute for International Economics, 1997), 2.

15   For example, 'under typical parameters, lowering of a trade restriction will result in $5 or more of income being shuffled among different groups for every $1 of net gain.' Ibid., 30.

16   John Ruggie, 'At Home Abroad, Abroad at Home: International Liberalization and Domestic Stability in the New World Economy', *Millennium: Journal of International Studies* 24, 3 (1995): 508.

17   Designing a more humane globalization requires a combination of attributes not to be found in Congress, where internationalists are almost exclusively liberal whereas opponents of the market are both protectionist and isolationist.

18   Tussie, 'Multilateralism Revisited', 189.

19   Rodrik, *Has Globalization Gone Too Far?*, 7.

## Suggested Readings

Block, Fred L. *The Origins of International Economic Disorder.* Berkeley: University of California Press, 1977.

Blumenthal, Sidney. 'The Return of the Repressed: Anti-Internationalism and the American Right', *World Policy Journal* 12 (1995): 1–13.

Cline, William R. *Trade and Income Distribution.* Washington: Institute for International Economics, 1997.

Crabb, Cecil. *Policy-Makers and Critics.* New York: Praeger Publishers, 1976.

Goldstein, Judith. 'Ideas, Institutions, and American Trade Policy', *International Organization* 42, 1 (1988): 179–217.

Helleiner, Gerald. 'Transnational Enterprises and the New Political Economy of U.S. Trade Policy', *Oxford Economic Papers* 29, 1 (1977).

Kindleberger, Charles. *The World in Depression 1929–39.* Berkeley: University of California Press, 1973.

Kennedy, Paul. 'The (Relative) Decline of America', *Atlantic Monthly* (Aug. 1987): 29–38.

Pauly, Louis. *Who Elected the Bankers? Surveillance and Control in the World Economy.* Ithaca, NY: Cornell University Press, 1997.

Polanyi, Karl. *The Great Transformation.* New York: Rinehart, 1944.

Rogowski, Ronald. 'Political Cleavages and Changing Exposure to Trade', *American Political Science Review* 81, 4 (1987): 1121–37.

## Web Sites

Free Trade Area of the Americas:
   http://www.alca-ftaa.org

World Trade Organization: http://www.wto.org

OECD Policy Brief on the Multilateral Agreement on
   Investment: http://www.oecd.org/publications/
   pol_brief/9702_pol.htm

International Monetary Fund: http://www.imf.org

## Chapter 29

# The Political Economy of East Asia at a Time of Crisis

## Mark Beeson

The economic and political dislocation that began to engulf East Asia[1] in the latter part of 1997 may prove to be one of the defining events of the post-Cold War era. At the very least, it dramatically illustrated the way an increasingly internationalized and interlinked global economy operates and the impact associated flows of financial capital can have not just on individual nation-states, but on entire regions. At another, less immediate level, the East Asian crisis drew renewed attention to important questions about the autonomy of national governments, the possibility of pursuing policies of which markets disapprove, and the viability of a distinctively 'Asian way' of managing political and economic relationships. In the longer term, the crisis and the attempts of institutions like the International Monetary Fund (IMF) to manage it may presage a more enduring struggle to define the rules that govern the global economy—an issue of particular significance given the IMF's close links with the United States and an Anglo-American agenda of market-oriented reform.[2] If recent events in East Asia had one unequivocal lesson it was that the process of crisis management was not simply a question of applying the 'correct' economic remedies for essentially 'technical' problems. On the contrary, attempts to impose a new, market-based order replete with more transparent economic practices were necessarily a highly politicized, direct threat to established distributional coalitions and patterns of economic organization throughout the region.

To understand why the sorts of reforms proposed by intergovernmental agencies like the IMF were so deeply political and potentially destabilizing, it is helpful to look at East Asia before the crisis. By examining the distinctive way in which capitalism developed in East Asia we can see both why its reform was considered to be so desirable by many outsiders and why it has proved so problematic. Consequently, I initially examine the East Asian patterns of capitalist organization, particularly the Japanese and Chinese variants, before considering the styles of policy-making that chartacterize government-business relations in much of East Asia. I illustrate the importance of these relations in the Malaysian case. Finally, I look at East Asia in the context of an increasingly interlinked global economy. The central argument I develop here is that the crisis not only highlighted fundamental differences between East Asian and Anglo-American variants of capitalism, but presented a possibly unique opportunity for the Anglo-American nations to force the adoption of neo-liberal policies in a region that has hitherto shown little enthusiasm for them.

## Capitalism in East Asia

At the outset, it should be borne in mind that regions are necessarily imprecise, arbitrarily defined entities. Not only is it debatable which countries ought to be considered part of 'East Asia', but the very conceptualization of discrete regions suggests a homogeneity that is generally unwarranted. Indeed, in the case of East Asia, the putative region is characterized by a diversity of ethnic, political, and cultural divisions that make generalization difficult and potentially misleading. However, two qualities in particular help to define and demarcate the East Asian region and make such a broad-brush conceptualization meaningful. First, East Asia is distinguished by several highly distinctive forms of capitalist organization that bear little resemblance to either stylized Anglo-American economic theory or corporate activity in North America, Britain, Australia, or New Zealand. In Japan, (South) Korea, and throughout the Chinese diaspora, patterns of economic organization are deeply embedded in the societies of which they are a part and are likely to prove resistant to wholesale reform of the sort proposed by bodies like the IMF. Second, in the more narrowly defined arena of public policy, especially its economic aspects, there are enough commonalities of approach across the region to lend credence to the idea of a distinctively 'Asian way' of economic management. Moreover, it is a tradition of policymaking that has been reinforced by the regional integration of economic activity, in general, and by the consolidation and institutionalization of close relations between business and political élites throughout East Asia, in particular.

Japan has provided both the principal engine of economic integration and an influential model of economic development for the region as a whole. Japan pioneered a model of state-led economic development that not only underpinned its own remarkable resurrection in the aftermath of World War II, but also provided a role model for a number of other countries within the region. At one level Japan's own experience has invited emulation as the region's most successful economy and the only country thus far to have challenged successfully the economic dominance of North America and Europe. At another more fundamental level, however, Japan's influence has been far more direct and—especially in the cases of Taiwan and Korea—is attributable to its role as a colonial power.[3] In both Korea and Taiwan, Japanese colonialism was instrumental in centralizing national power structures and consolidating the role of the state in domestic economic development. Korea used Japan's *keiretsu* system of interlocked, diversified industrial groups as the model for its own *chaebols*. Less obvious, but with potentially equally profound long-term consequences, has been the role played by Japanese trade and investment in the region as

Japanese transnational corporations (TNCs) have expanded from their domestic base.

Japanese corporations have provided one of the key forces propelling regional integration. Successive waves of investment and expansion have initially seen labour-intensive industries like textiles, and subsequently more sophisticated industries like electronics and car manufacturers, shift all or parts of their operations into the East Asian region to take advantage of lower production costs and access potentially important new markets. Two points are worth emphasizing about this process because they are central to this distinctive form of capitalism. First, the *keiretsu* structure means that Japanese companies are less reliant on markets to mediate or determine economic outcomes,[4] especially within the borders of individual nation-states. The relatively autonomous structure of the *keiretsu* groups, particularly their financial and marketing capacities, combined with a proclivity for intra-firm as opposed to intra-industry trade, means that they enjoy a degree of insulation from the actions of host governments. Even more significantly—and this is the second key point—Japanese corporations have entrenched their position within the region by establishing close connections with domestic political élites. Japanese companies, often with the direct assistance of the Japanese government, have spun a complex web of governmental and business relationships throughout the region, cementing their privileged position through the strategic use of aid and infrastructure packages that effectively lock host governments into symbiotic relationships with Japanese capital.[5] Not only do such relationships and corporate independence militate against wholesale change, but Japanese corporations will remain influential, well-networked, and competitive in whatever economic order ultimately emerges.

The highly distinctive, government-assisted strategies that underpinned the industrial expansion of Japanese corporations are especially significant in the context of an international political economy characterized by more than one form of capitalist organization. Simply put, Japanese transnational corporations have generally proved to be formidable competitors in an ostensibly liberal and 'open' international trading environment. Companies that originate in the Anglo-American economies, however, which enjoy neither the benefit of being part of an integrated co-operative network nor 'insider' status in what are still the potentially important markets of East Asia, may not compete as successfully as the Japanese in a region that both considers government involvement in economic development to be legitimate and makes contingent economic 'distortions' and market imperfections a source of potential competitive advantage.[6] Seen in this context, the East Asian crisis has provided a possibly unique window of opportunity for countries like the United States to impose a new market order on the region that could—theoretically, at least—encourage the sort of competition in which American companies might be expected to succeed.

The other major form of capitalist organization in East Asia that is unlikely to be swept aside by neo-liberal reform is that of the Chinese. Principally associated with the estimated 50 million ethnic overseas Chinese who live outside China in East Asia, Chinese capitalism is centred on familial relations and complex networks of personal obligation. Whereas in Japan economic control and authority depend on elaborate structures of interlocking shareholdings, Chinese capitalism revolves around more informal interpersonal relationships (*guanxi*). In all the variants of Asian capitalism—Japanese, Korean, and Chinese—the key point to recognize is that each one is principally a socially embedded and institutionalized *network*.[7] The distinctive network form, whether it is reinforced through personal connections or corporate structures, provides the systemic dynamism of each variety of capitalism in East Asia and simultaneously imparts a degree of path-dependency to overall economic development. In other words, capitalist organization and expansion are not simply reflective of an identical universal dynamic but mediated by the social setting in which they are embedded. This is especially important in the case of Chinese capitalism and its consolidation in the region's social and political structures.

Chinese business people have achieved a disproportionately significant position in the region's economic infrastructure, and not just in the more obvious areas such as China itself and Taiwan. Throughout Southeast Asia in particular, Chinese capitalists have been central to the economic development of individual countries. In Indonesia, for example, although less than 4 per cent of the population, ethnic Chinese business people control more than 70 per cent of listed firms by market capitalization.[8] Chinese capitalists consolidated their economic position by establishing close relationships with the ruling political élite in Indonesia, especially the Suharto family. True, this has not insulated them from Indonesia's general collapse or saved small-scale Chinese capitalists from racially motivated attacks as the economy collapsed. However, this does not invalidate the general point that the conventional 'Western' distinction made between the public and private sectors is a good deal less meaningful in Southeast Asia. The significance of this institutional fusion is most apparent in the distinctive patterns of public policy-making that characterize the region.

## Policy-Making in East Asia

The distinctive political economies of East Asia have been subjected to increased scrutiny in the wake of the recent economic crisis. Particular attention has been paid to regional policy-making practices and the close relations between governments that are associated with them. It should be remembered, however, that until very recently even prominent champions of the prevailing market-centred economic orthodoxy, such as the World Bank, were prepared to concede that government intervention in economic processes could play an important role in facilitating industrial development.[9] Similarly, the massive inflows of foreign direct and portfolio investment that helped fuel East Asia's remarkable economic rise were attracted to the region *despite* the relationships that have of late apparently engendered such concern in the minds of potential investors. Indeed, in the authoritarian regimes of Southeast Asia in particular, the cronyism and collusion now routinely depicted as the source of East Asia's problems[10] hitherto appeared to be an integral component of the region's dynamism, stability, and profitability.

If it is possible to talk of an 'Asian way' of policy-making, once again Japan has been the principal role model and exemplar. Not only has what Chalmers Johnson famously described as Japan's 'developmental state' become the prototype for a model of accelerated industrial development, but the close relationships between the private and public sectors that permitted government policy to be effectively implemented in Japan have been reproduced in one form or another throughout the region.[11] At its most benign, co-operation between the public and private sectors of the type that has underpinned Japan's remarkable postwar renaissance is an essential prerequisite for the effective application of various 'industry policies'. Government-sponsored industry policies, in which the state encourages specific economic activities in pursuit of an overarching vision of national industrial development, have been one of the hallmarks of East Asia's rapid industrialization. Until very recently there was little doubt as to the apparent effectiveness of such policies. Indeed, so successful have the countries of East Asia been in exporting to the established industrialized powers of Europe and North America that trade disputes—especially between the United States and the Northeast Asian giants, Japan and China—have become a fixture in the international trading system. Again, many of the potential benefits and drawbacks of Asian variants of political and economic organization are exemplified in the Japanese case.

The close relations that exist between Japan's corporate sector and bureaucracy have been central to the latter's ability to co-ordinate and direct Japanese economic policies. Japan developed a governmental infrastructure that permitted the implementation of policies through a range of institutionalized consultative mechanisms in which key bureaucratic, political, and business figures co-ordinated their activities in pursuit of collective goals. Japan's bureaucracy is famously powerful, and for a long period its ability to construct and implement policy—in apparently selfless devotion to the national interest—provided a model for other

regional states. However, the opaque, unaccountable nature of the policy-making process and the nexus that developed between powerful political and corporate interests led, particularly in the construction industry, to outright corruption and the misallocation of public money. Not only have a number of scandals undermined domestic public confidence in the hitherto unimpeachable bureaucracy, but these scandals have made it more difficult for the Japanese government to resist international calls for further reform.

A couple of general points are worth making here, however. First, many of Japan's—and by implication, the region's—problems stem from an earlier general loosening of government controls and, in particular, from moves towards financial deregulation. Many of the problems associated with the so-called 'bubble economy' that developed in Japan during the late 1980s flowed directly from financial sector liberalization. The controls over credit allocation, which had been such an integral part of directing the development of domestic industry, were gradually relaxed in response to US pressure and the growth of increasingly accessible international financial markets.[12] Second, even in the event that a combination of foreign pressure and the increased power of financial markets forces a wholesale reconfiguration of business-government relations in Japan and brings about more transparent policy-making processes, this will not necessarily unravel the integrated *keiretsu* system. Where international market pressures and transitional regulatory bodies have a more immediate impact is over the smaller economies of Southeast Asia.

## East Asian Political Economies: The Malaysian Exemplar

The smaller countries of Southeast Asia have been particularly hard hit by the crisis, and not just economically. For Malaysia in particular, the crisis was an especially humbling experience as its Prime Minister, Mahathir Bin Mohamad, played a prominent role in attempting to develop a critique of neo-liberalism, the role of pro-market regulatory authorities, and the influence of 'the West' more generally. Malaysia also highlights an important contrast between Northeast Asian state-led development and the 'crony capitalism' associated with a number of Southeast Asian countries. As such, it is an important exemplar of many of the issues central to the clash of capitalisms between 'Asia' and 'the West'.

At the outset, it is important to recognize that the Malaysian political economy is distinguished by a number of ethnic, political, and economic relationships that make it very different from the general Anglo-American experience. As in the rest of East Asia, economic policy-making in Malaysia has had a critically important and overtly political dimension. Indeed, in East Asia, national sovereignty is much more closely bound up with economic security than it is in North America or Western Europe.[13] In East Asia nation-building is a comparatively recent experience and often a less completely realized project. Consequently, the legitimacy of ruling élites is often fragile, not endorsed by genuinely democratic elections, and dependent on the ability of governments to deliver continuing economic growth. In such a context, threats to economic stability are potentially threats to the existing political order.

Malaysia is a good example of the way business structures, ethnic divisions, and political allegiances intersect to form a distinctive, yet characteristically East Asian political economy. A key influence on Malaysia's contemporary evolution has been the desire to promote an indigenous Bumiputera capitalist class. Although initially intended as a counter to the dominance of local Chinese capitalists, of late it has given way to an ethnic *rapprochement* leavened by money.[14] In short, networks of personal relationships have helped embed an economic order in which Chinese capitalism is a central part. These relationships have been further cemented by Malaysia's political system, in which the ruling United Malays' National Organization (UMNO) has used its position to centralize political power and create holding companies that control key areas of the economy. The mutually rewarding symbiosis developed by the ruling political and economic élites has been further entrenched as politics has become a vehicle for achieving and consolidating economic power, and Chinese business leaders have provided financial support for UMNO political leaders.

Mahathir's anti-market fulminations become more comprehensible in the context of a country in which political and economic interests are tightly fused. At one level Mahathir's attacks on international financial markets and 'the West' more generally can be read as self-serving rhetoric designed to shift the blame for the crisis elsewhere.[15] Clearly, much about this discourse and the notion of distinctively 'Asian values' is designed to legitimize and insulate from criticism political and economic practices that are grossly inequitable. And yet Mahathir makes several points that not only have the potential to find a sympathetic resonance within the region, but also raise important questions about economic organization and management more generally. This is especially true in the case of Mahathir's attempts to use currency controls to insulate the Malaysian economy from the destabilizing impact of massive, highly liquid, and essentially speculative flows of capital. The outcome of this experiment is likely to be affected by Malaysia's domestic political crisis, but if it is only moderately successful it may well be copied by other regional governments that despair of orthodox, neo-liberal remedies ever working.

Many of Mahathir's most compelling claims revolve around the threat to national policy autonomy posed by massive, unregulated capital flows and an international economic regime that facilitates them. Significantly, his speeches often explicitly and approvingly invoke Japan as a model of state-led industrialization. Mahathir also recognizes that such a developmental path will be difficult to emulate in an international economic order in which, on the one hand, markets can punish policies of which they disapprove, while, on the other, a range of agreements reached under the international auspices of bodies such as the World Trade Organization and the Asia-Pacific Economic Cooperation (APEC) forum outlaw discriminatory industry policies.[16] As Mahathir, among others, has pointed out, the gross disparity in economic weight between countries like the United States and smaller countries like Malaysia and the potential benefits of scope and scale that accrue to multinational corporations from the early industrializing nations mean that it is very difficult for companies in smaller countries to compete, or for the countries themselves to play anything but a peripheral role in the global economy. Even in the unlikely event that it were possible to establish an international 'level-playing field', it would advantage those countries—or more precisely, the companies that emanate from such countries—currently prominent in the world economy; and the advantaged positions of those companies, without exception, were achieved with the active assistance of states.[17] In other words, the 'inherent inequity' of the international liberal market order means that the economic security of late industrializing nations is systematically threatened and constrained by the dominance of the established industrial powers.[18]

Thoroughgoing neo-liberal reform therefore presents a dual threat to regional political élites. Calls for greater openness and transparency are necessarily a challenge to the close business relations that characterize regional political economies. Yet, the outlawing of discriminatory trade and investment practices means that not only is the glue that binds such relationships together weakened, but the chances of intervening to hasten and direct the process of industrialization are diminished. It is hardly surprising, then, that Mahathir has attempted to promote institutional forums that potentially reflect and legitimize regional, East Asian-style economic and political practices. The East Asian Economic Caucus (EAEC), which Mahathir has tirelessly championed as, at the least, an Asian caucus within, if not an alternative to, the wider APEC forum, is an example of and potential vehicle for an alternative model of crisis management.[19]

## East Asia in a Global Economy

If the crisis in East Asia unambiguously confirmed one thing, it is quite how integrated and interdependent the world economy has become. Justifiable

scepticism about some of the more uncritical conceptualizations of 'globalization' notwithstanding,[20] recent events highlight just how powerful so-called 'contagion effects' can be, and how quickly systemic shocks can be transmitted throughout regions, if not within the entire world economy. In other words, the way the global economy is currently configured encourages the movement of massive, often speculative and short-term flows of capital with potentially deeply destabilizing effects on individual countries.[21] Yet the conventional wisdom among orthodox economists is that the region's problems stem from the opaque nature of business-government relationships in particular and the inscrutable, unaccountable nature of East Asian economic practices more generally. It is worth briefly revisiting the origins of the crisis to gain a clearer picture of its dynamics and the key structures that continue to shape regional and transregional relations.

The initial trigger for East Asia's difficulties was a currency crisis in Thailand, which flowed from an ill-conceived attempt to peg and then defend the baht's value against the US dollar. The escalating crisis and the rapid, concomitant loss of investor confidence drew attention to the structure of the Thai political economy and the apparent importance of 'money-politics' in bringing about its downfall.[22] However, it should be noted that Thailand's long-established political structures had not been previously proved either a disincentive to international investment or a constraint on profitability. On the contrary, the chance of making rapid profits led to large inflows of capital, which ultimately found expression in a speculative property bubble. As Mexico discovered to its cost several years ago, massive, unregulated inflows of highly liquid capital can seriously destabilize and distort domestic economic activity.[23] While access to mobile international capital for domestic investment is clearly one way of promoting rapid economic development, it leaves the host nation potentially vulnerable to sudden withdrawal and a range of external institutional and economic pressures.

As the crisis spread outward from East Asia it highlighted how interconnected the world economy had become, suggesting that the crisis might have more to do with the contradictions of capitalism in general than with some uniquely East Asian problems. A key potential transmission mechanism of Asian contagion was what Robert Gilpin called the 'Nichibei economy', or the structural interdependence between the United States and Japan.[24] Not only was this relationship central to the well-being of the international economic system in general, but it had allowed both countries to pursue policies that would otherwise have been problematic. Japan's access to North American markets was the cornerstone of its high-growth, export-oriented developmental model, while the United States was able to run substantial budget deficits despite being the world's largest debtor—largely thanks to the willingness of Japanese investors to buy US Treasury bonds. But as the hitherto formidably competitive Japanese economy sank into recession it raised questions both about the continuance of Japanese outflows in the face of a domestic banking crisis and about more enduring and widespread problems of declining profitability and massive manufacturing overcapacity throughout the industrialized world.[25]

In short, the East Asian crisis highlighted potential systemic fault lines that tended to be obscured beneath the euphoria and hyperbole associated with the region's 'miraculous' growth era and the seemingly unstoppable ascendancy of capitalism—albeit with decidedly East Asian characteristics. Moreover, the crisis provided a forceful reminder that while all countries may be affected by widespread changes in the international political economy, especially the growing power of financial markets, some countries were more susceptible to shifts in market sentiment than others. US indebtedness and past profligacy do not appear to have diminished its moral authority or practical input in shaping the global economic order. Revealingly, the impact of the crisis in East Asia stands in stark contrast to the United States' own financial catastrophe—the Savings and Loan scandal of the late 1980s—during which there was no suggestion that dismembering Anglo-American-style capitalism might be an appropriate way of dealing with that crisis. For all the talk of an 'Asian century', therefore, the international response to the crisis suggested

that the contemporary balance of global power remained firmly with the United States.

## Conclusion

The intention of this chapter has not been to defend East Asian forms of capitalism, capitalists, or political élites. Rather, I have sought to highlight some of the factors that will continue to shape political and economic outcomes in the region, and to suggest that attempts to manage the crisis involved much more than simply the appropriateness of public policy choices or the possible desirability of transparent business practices. On the contrary, the crisis stands as a watershed in transregional relations, which has helped to consolidate not only the international rules, norms, and institutional frameworks within which capitalism of any variety is managed, but the possible future trajectory of capitalist development more generally.

If different forms of capitalism are to converge on some common end-point, then it will necessitate the removal or transformation of embedded patterns of political authority, business practice, and social relationships.[26] Yet the hostility with which the IMF's strictures were greeted in countries like China and the connection made with a wider Anglo-American reform agenda[27] suggest that their ultimate impact may be to provide a mechanism with which to foster regional solidarity and resistance. Much depends on the constellations of domestic political forces within the nations of East Asia and their relative influence on the overall direction of policy-making.[28] The more general and crucial point to re-emphasize here is that, whether successfully realized or not, *the crisis presented a possibly unique opportunity for the Anglo-American nations in general and the United States in particular to force the East Asian nations to converge on their own, possibly less competitive form of capitalism.*[29]

Despite the apparent success of external forces in imposing neo-liberal, market-oriented reforms on a number of countries in East Asia, the more important and enduring questions raised by the crisis may be about the durability of capitalism itself in its contemporary global configuration. When seen as a part of long-term global capitalist development, one of the most striking aspects of the East Asian crisis is the disjuncture between what might be broadly described as industrial or productive capital and financial capital, something that has characterized earlier systemic crises of capitalism.[30] What distinguishes the contemporary period, however, is the *globalized* nature of economic activity. Massive, potentially destabilizing flows of highly liquid financial capital are able to transmit systemic shocks or imbalances with unprecedented rapidity and force—a development from which no nation is immune. Thus, IMF attempts to enhance the influence of market mechanisms within East Asia may ultimately exacerbate the potentially destructive and destabilizing power of capital itself. In such a situation disagreements about economic policy threaten to assume an urgency and intensity that may generate wider, unpredictable forms of inter-regional contestation.

## Notes

1  By 'East Asia' I mean Japan, China, South Korea, Taiwan, and the countries of the Association of Southeast Asian Nations (ASEAN)—Brunei, Indonesia, Malaysia, Philippines, Singapore, Thailand, Myanmar (Burma), Vietnam, Laos, Cambodia.

2  As *The Economist* (13 Dec. 1997, 78) noted, many of the measures being imposed on the region by the IMF 'have Washington's finger-prints all over them'. For a more detailed examination of the US-IMF relationship, see Louis W. Pauly, *Who Elected the Bankers? Surveillance and Control in the World Economy* (Ithaca, NY: Cornell University Press, 1997).

3  Bruce Cumings, 'The Origins and Development of the Northeast Asian Political Economy: Industrial Sectors, Product Cycles, and Political Consequences', *International Organization* 38 (1984): 1–40.

4  Rob Steven, *Japan and the New World Order: Global Investments, Trade and Finance* (New York: St Martin's Press, 1996), 54.

5  Walter Hatch and Kozo Yamamura, *Asia in Japan's Embrace: Building a Regional Production Alliance* (Cambridge: Cambridge University Press, 1996).

6  Winfried Ruigrok and Rob van Tulder, *The Logic of International Restructuring* (London: Routledge, 1995), 200.

7  Gary Hamilton et al., 'The Network Structures of East Asian Economies', in Stewart R. Clegg et al., eds, *Capitalism in Contrasting Cultures* (Berlin: de Gruyter, 1990), 105–29. Network-based forms of capitalism are not simply more deeply embedded in social systems and therefore resistant to change, but they may enjoy distinct competitive advantages as far as the development of new technologies and patterns of flexible production are concerned. See Manuel Castells, *The Rise of the Network Society* (Cambridge, Mass.: Blackwell, 1996), 172–200.

8  East Asia Analytical Unit, *Overseas Chinese Business Networks in Asia* (Canberra: DFAT, 1995), 40–1.

9  World Bank, *World Development Report 1997: The State in a Changing World* (Oxford: Oxford University Press, 1997), 61.

10  See, for example, 'Frozen Miracle: A Survey of the East Asian Economies', *The Economist*, 7 Mar. 1998.

11  Chalmers Johnson, *MITI and the Japanese Miracle: The Growth of Industry Policy 1925–1975* (Stanford, Calif.: Stanford University Press, 1982). It is important to emphasize that the states of Southeast Asia generally have a good deal less technocratic competence and bureaucratic insulation than do the states of Northeast Asia. See Linda Weiss, *The Myth of the Powerless State* (Ithaca, NY: Cornell University Press, 1998).

12  Michael Moran, *The Politics of the Financial Services Revolution: The USA, UK and Japan* (London: Macmillan, 1991).

13  Mark Beeson and Kanishka Jayasuriya, 'The Political Rationalities of Regionalism: APEC and the EU in Comparative Perspective', *Pacific Review* 11, 3 (1998): 311–36.

14  Edmund T. Gomez and Jomo K.S., *Malaysia's Political Economy: Politics, Patronage and Profits*

(Cambridge: Cambridge University Press, 1997), 137.

15  Richard McGregor, 'Mahathir Blames Manipulative West', *The Australian*, 22 Sept. 1997, 17.

16  See, for example, Mahathir Bin Mohamad, 'Asian Economies: Challenges and Opportunities', speech to the World Bank-IMF annual meeting, 20 Sept. 1997, Hong Kong: http://www.world bank.org/html/exdr/am97/amsp_001.htm

17  David S. Landes, *The Wealth and Poverty of Nations: Why Some Are So Rich and Some So Poor* (New York: W.W. Norton, 1998), 265.

18  Barry Buzan, *People, States and Fear*, 2nd edn (Boulder, Colo.: Lynne Rienner, 1991), 246.

19  For a discussion of the competing conceptions of economic co-operation and regionalism implicit in APEC and EAEC, see Richard Higgott and Richard Stubbs, 'Competing Conceptions of Economic Regionalism: APEC versus EAEC in the Asia Pacific', *Review of International Political Economy* 2 (1995): 516–35.

20  Paul Hirst and Grahame Thompson, *Globalization in Question: The International Economy and the Possibility of Governance* (Cambridge: Polity Press, 1996).

21  For an examination of the impact of new financial flows and structures on Indonesia, see Mark Beeson, 'Indonesia, the East Asian Crisis, and the Commodification of the Nation-State', *New Political Economy* 3, 3 (1998): 357–74.

22  Pasuk Phongpaichit and Chris Baker, *Thailand's Boom and Bust* (Chiang Mai: Silkworm Books, 1998).

23  It should also be noted that the principal beneficiaries of the Mexican rescue package were not ordinary Mexicans but the large institutional investors that had poured massive destabilizing flows of speculative capital into Mexico in the first place. See Hans-Peter Martin and Harald Schumann, *The Global Trap: Globalization and the Assault on Democracy and Prosperity* (Leichhardt: Pluto Press, 1997).

24  Robert Gilpin, *The Political Economy of International Relations* (Princeton, NJ: Princeton University Press, 1987), 336–9.

25  Robert Brenner, 'The Economics of Global Turbulence: A Special Report on the World Economy, 1950–98', *New Left Review* no. 229 (May-June 1998).

26  Mark Beeson, 'Asia's Disparate Political Economies and the Prospects for Transnational "Convergence"', *Asian Journal of Public Administration* 18 (1996): 141–67.

27  Michael Richardson, 'Uncle Sam Risks Virulent Nationalist Backlash', *The Australian*, 13 Jan. 1998, 9.

28  In countries like Indonesia, for example, a group of technocrats has provided domestic support for the pro-market policy prescriptions of such organizations as the World Bank and the IMF. Significantly, the influence of these Western-trained economic advisers has risen and fallen in line with the overall position of the Indonesian economy. See John Bresnan, *Managing Indonesia: The Modern Political Economy* (New York: Columbia University Press, 1993).

29  Barbara Stallings and Wolfgang Streeck, 'Capitalisms in Conflict? The United States, Europe, and Japan in the Post-Cold War World', in Barbara Stallings, ed., *Global Change, Regional Response: The New International Context of Development* (Cambridge: Cambridge University Press, 1995), 94.

30  Giovanni Arrighi, *The Long Twentieth Century: Money, Power and the Origins of Our Times* (London: Verso, 1994).

## Suggested Readings

Berger, Mark T., and Douglas A. Borer, eds. *The Rise of East Asia: Critical Visions of the Pacific Century*. London: Routledge, 1997.

Berger, Suzanne, and Ronald Dore, eds. *National Diversity and Global Capitalism*. Ithaca, NY: Cornell University Press, 1996.

Hamilton, Gary, ed. *Asian Business Networks*. Berlin: de Gruyter, 1996.

Katzenstein, Peter J., and Takashi Shiraishi, eds. *Network Power: Japan and Asia*. Ithaca, NY: Cornell University Press, 1997.

Lazonick, William. *Business Organization and the Myth of the Market Economy*. Cambridge: Cambridge University Press, 1993.

Rodan, Garry, et al., eds. *The Political Economy of South-East Asia*. Melbourne: Oxford University Press, 1997.

Weiss, L., and J.M. Hobson. *States and Economic Development: A Comparative Historical Analysis*. Cambridge: Polity Press, 1995.

## Web Sites

ASEAN Secretariat: http://www.asean.or.id

Asian Development Bank: http://www.adb.org

Far Eastern Economic Review: http://www.feer.com/restricted/index.html

## Chapter 30

# Globalization and the British 'Residual State'

## Andrew Baker

In his introduction to this volume, Geoffrey Underhill posits that '[u]nderstanding the state—what it is and where it fits into Cox's state-society complex—is in a way *the* problem of international political economy.' Accordingly, this chapter approaches the study of the various social, political, and economic relationships that comprise the global order by focusing on changing patterns of British state-society relationships and the changing social basis of the British state. This chapter is directly concerned with the interaction between global systemic change and national policy. In this respect the British state has simultaneously initiated, promoted, and responded to a worldwide process of market liberalization and an evolving global discourse of sound money policies and open markets. Consequently, the British state has a complex, reciprocal, and mutually reinforcing relationship with changes in the global system, and an inherent circularity to this makes it difficult to identify cause and effect. Particular emphasis is given here to the changing social basis of the British state to illustrate that the emerging global economy is not something that exists exclusively above the contemporary state system; rather, the global economy is intimately interconnected to and interwoven with the state system.

Salient contemporary processes of market liberalization, transnationalization (increased cross-border socio-economic activity), state transformation, and discourse configuration are ongoing and far from complete. Moreover, the British state continues to promote these processes and increasingly concentrates on the provision of the appropriate institutional and legal foundations for world

markets. However, this can only be understood in terms of the social basis of the state, the series of social and institutional relationships that comprise this, and the process through which the British state has been transformed from a Keynesian welfare state to what might be termed a 'neo-liberal competition or residual state'.[1] The first section of this chapter looks at both the cause and the effect of this transformation. The next section looks at the current dominant global neo-liberal consensus, its social and institutional foundations, and its impact on policy change in Britain. The final section considers future processes, challenges, and contradictions that are likely to characterize the politics of the British state in the next millennium.

## The Transformation of the British State

In the second half of the 1970s British governments abandoned the Keynesian approach to policy-making that had prevailed since the end of World War II and progressively dismantled the structures of the welfare state. The Keynesian welfare state involved the management of aggregate demand through fiscal and monetary policies to approximate full employment. This was accompanied by an active social policy, including redistributive transfer payments and public services. In part, this was facilitated by a restrictive international monetary system and a comprehensive system of national capital controls under the Bretton Woods order that gave the government access to the financial resources required for investment in national infrastructural projects.[2] In Britain such policies took place within the constraints of a commitment to maintaining the parity of sterling against the American dollar in the fixed exchange rate system.[3] This was most actively promoted within the state by a Bank of England-Treasury overseas financial axis. Both big business and organized labour were also integrated into the policy-making process. The Keynesian welfare state therefore embodied a compromise among the interests of domestic industrial capital, financial capital, and organized labour as well as between domestic and international objectives.

In the second half of the 1970s, however, the British state was transformed by a paradigm shift. The Keynesian approach to policy was abandoned and a monetarist approach, which rested on the assumptions of neoclassical economists, was adopted. The principal reason for the demise of Keynesianism in Britain was its inability to respond to acute economic problems in the 1970s. The traditional reflationary response to recession failed to address rising inflation, economic stagnation, major payments imbalances, and repeated sterling crises. The British economy began to function differently in the 1970s and it became increasingly difficult for domestic industrial capital and labour to extract concessions from the government. In contrast, financial markets were virtually able to force certain policy actions on the government. This was evident in the increased cohesion of national bond markets following liberalization measures in 1971.[4] Bond markets were able to refrain from buying 'gilts' (UK government bonds) in the 1970s, effectively forcing the government to pursue more restrictive monetarist-style policies involving interest rate rises or public expenditure cuts. Second, these pressures were reinforced by the effects of the breakdown of the fixed exchange rate system and the decision to let sterling float in June 1972. The traditional postwar policy of protecting the status of sterling in the fixed exchange rate system had effectively produced an overvalued pound. Once sterling's rate was determined by the market, its artificially high level made it especially vulnerable to speculative pressures, particularly in the context of large public-sector deficits, a declining manufacturing sector and spiralling inflation. This was compounded by the British and US governments initiation of the

Euro markets, which allowed funds to be moved from one currency to another with increasing ease, facilitating larger outflows from sterling.[5] A recourse to the International Monetary Fund (IMF) in 1976 in the face of a sterling and a balance-of-payments crisis led to further public expenditure cuts. The conditionality in that IMF loan had the effect of accentuating policy changes already under way rather than instigating any fundamental state transformation.

In this context there was a growing base of popular support for monetarist ideas and a discontent with the prevailing approach, which spanned the social spectrum. Wages among white-collar corporate sector workers had been tightly controlled by the income policies of the 1970s, tax levels were punitive, and the trade unions had become unpopular, even with much of their own constituency, following the winter of discontent of 1978–9. Proposals for tax cuts, restrictions on trade unions, and the end of state support for uncompetitive nationalized industries became increasingly popular. Moreover, a growing number of research institutes, private-sector pamphlets, and increased amounts of financial coverage in the national press constituted an outside marketplace in economic ideas in Britain that were sympathetic to monetarist policies.[6] By contrast, the predominant international consensus remained broadly Keynesian, as the co-ordinated international locomotive growth strategy of 1978 indicated.[7] For these reasons the demise of Keynesianism and the adoption of monetarism in the UK should primarily be understood in terms of historical changes in the social basis of the state, specific national economic problems, and a national climate of ideas that reflected these trends. This was reinforced by the problems posed by the demise of the fixed exchange rate system and the emergence of international capital mobility.

## Thatcherism, Internationalization, and the Changing Socio-Economic Context

In the context described above, Margaret Thatcher was able to come to power and implement a radical free market agenda, shifting the social basis of the

British state even further in the direction of finance capital and other mobile factors of production. This involved a reordering of the objectives and priorities of policy-making. Most especially, macroeconomic policy has involved a growing focus on the control of inflation rather than economic growth or full employment. One element of this has consisted of attempts to reduce public expenditure and the size of the state sector by privatizing unprofitable nationalized industries. There have also been attempts to increase efficiency in the public sector by introducing the market mechanism into the delivery of public services, with the so-called 'new public management' resulting in contracting out of services and a growing commodification of the state. Finance has been liberalized and internationalized as a consequence of the decision to abolish foreign exchange controls in 1979 and to remove restrictions on bank lending in 1980. Deregulation and the removal of restrictions on business were a further aspect of the Thatcher agenda, particularly in the financial services sector following the 'big bang' reform in the City of London in 1986. More generally, business has been given a freer hand in the field of employment practices. Labour market deregulation has been designed to reduce labour costs, and this has been accompanied by sustained attacks on the power of trade unions. Finally, there has been what amounts to an outward-looking competitive strategy, designed to expose British business to international competition and to attract inward foreign direct investment. This has consisted of tax cuts, a uniform business rate, and the removal of burdensome red tape.

Partly as a consequence of the implementation of this radical agenda the institutional form of the British state has changed, resulting in a 'hollowed-out state' or a 'competition state' that focuses on making economic activities more competitive in international or transnational terms, rather than on promoting national welfare.[8] In particular, the British central state consists of a dwindling number of core officials who provide policy advice. Its institutional arrangements increasingly concentrate on the residual function of providing the most appropriate institutional and legal foundations for the operations of efficient markets. Moreover, this form of state exists in an entirely different world context from the postwar Bretton Woods era. It involves huge international capital flows such as those in the 24-hour globally connected foreign exchange markets. By 1996 over a trillion dollars a day were traded in currencies, an exponential increase of nearly 32 times a year since 1989. Furthermore, a dominant globalization discourse or belief system often referred to as the 'Washington Consensus', emphasizing the value and benefits of open markets and sound money policies, has emerged.

In Britain one of the effects of the Thatcher agenda has been the blurring of national patterns of production and ownership, resulting in growing interdependencies with other economies. This presents challenges for the way the disciplines of international relations and international political economy conceive of the international system and the role assigned to the state in that system, because the social basis of states, particularly the British state, is increasingly transnationalized. Britain is now more heavily integrated into a global circuit of capital than any other country in the world. London is home to more foreign banks than anywhere else and is the only financial centre on the planet that offers free trade in all types of international securities and banking markets to both commercial and investment banks. In contrast to Tokyo and New York, which have a more domestic orientation, the City of London specializes in servicing international capital. European, Japanese, and US institutions dominate the City. The UK's flagship industry is not British, but largely foreign owned. Likewise, the British economy has become dependent on foreign inward investment, particularly in the modernization of its manufacturing infrastructure. The total stock of inward direct investment in Britain, taken as a percentage of GDP, is higher than in any other G–7 country. Furthermore, the UK manufacturing sector has often deployed plant, equipment, and capital abroad simply to protect the profit levels of its owners. Overseas investment from the UK is higher as a percentage of GDP than it is for any other G–7 country, and Britain is home to more multinationals than any country except the US. For some, this has constituted a process of deindustrialization, in which there is a growing disjuncture between British capital and the British economy.[9] Certainly, high levels of outward investment have meant that instead of producing manufactured goods and exporting them, British investors have increasingly consumed rewards from overseas investments resulting in a more active service sector.

In the manufacturing sector only the most internationally competitive have survived and mergers and takeovers involving foreign conglomerates have become commonplace. To encourage more competitive foreign multinationals to locate in the UK, successive governments have employed a competitive cost-cutting strategy that has relied on downward flexibility in wage levels, particularly in the public and small-to-medium business sectors, which has fed financial and manufacturing sectors.[10] This has been achieved by allowing nationalized industries to downsize in preparation for privatization. Much UK-based industry, particularly coalmining and shipbuilding, has largely disappeared or has been replaced by other more mobile factors of production. In a climate of rising unemployment, labour costs have been kept low by Western standards. In European terms at least, Britain has assumed a particular niche role in a global system of production as a relatively 'low-cost' branch plant for foreign multinationals.[11] A comparatively low skills base means that Japanese firms locate their assembly plants in the UK but their research and development facilities in Germany. The other major dimension to this strategy has involved the provision of an investor-friendly tax environment.

These developments, taken together, constitute a politically engineered shift in the social basis of the state and a discernible 'internationalization' in the most important economic sectors. Union power has been crushed as the British economy has been opened up to the world economy, while predominantly domestic industrial capital no longer exists to any great extent in the UK. Not only is the state less involved in the economy and the provision and distribution of material resources, the British economy is also increasingly internationalized. Consequently, for both the major political parties, a

continued ability to attract foreign direct investment and to protect British investments abroad has become synonymous with successful economic performance. Accordingly, the interests of the financial services sector, British multinationals operating abroad, and foreign multinationals in the UK now provide the principal social basis of the British state. Their interests have progressively penetrated the state apparatus and they have been given privileged status in accordance with this. Low inflation is prioritized in public policy because 'Britain's competitive position on the world market depends on a policy of financial stability to maintain and improve conditions of exchange on the world market itself.'[12]

## The British Residual State in the 1990s: A Transnationalized State

Internationally mobile capital increasingly provides the social basis of the British state. At the same time, the policies pursued by the Thatcher governments have contributed to increasingly integrated global markets. This has resulted in the emergence of a prevailing globalization discourse, the so-called 'Washington Consensus'. This belief system has provided the intellectual rationale for both British domestic and foreign economic policies in the 1990s. However, this also has to be understood in terms of the social basis of the British state and the patterns of social relations the state represents. In this respect certain sections of the state, acting on behalf of certain transnationalized social interests, are contributing to the generation of this dominant discourse.

For some authors the most explicit manifestation of the transformation of the state from a Keynesian welfare state to a neo-liberal form of state has been the increased status of those state agencies closely connected to the global economy, such as finance ministries and central banks. On the other hand, agencies, such as ministries of welfare, labour, and industry, with domestic constituents are increasingly subordinated.[13] Certainly there is evidence that the British Treasury's capacity to exert controls on spending departments has increased as a consequence of the introduction of cash limits

(1976), cash planning (1982), a planning total (1988), a new control total (1993), and, most recently and crucially, new fiscal rules that prohibit government borrowing on current expenditures. Furthermore, the Bank of England has increased its role in monetary policy, while financial regulation has become a public-private affair with a bigger role for market actors. This has been part of the process of institutionalizing market-based criteria in the policy process.

However, these institutions have also restructured themselves, notably the Treasury. In the postwar period the functional divisions within the Treasury were effectively a microcosm of the broader political struggles and balance of power that characterized British society. Both Keynesian and neoclassical positions were represented, by the domestic economy and overseas finance sections, respectively. The domestic economy section was concerned with domestic industrial productivity, economic growth, and full employment. It provided analysis that informed fiscal policy, which remained largely insulated from international pressures. The overseas finance section had responsibility for the exchange rate and was concerned with balance-of-payments questions. It sought to protect the status of sterling through the use of exchange reserves and by pushing the case for disciplined monetary policies. In the 1980s this balance of power changed as the domestic economy section lost its representation at senior levels and generally lost its status within the department. Furthermore, throughout the postwar period the exchange rate acted as proxy for the views of overseas investors and those of the City. In the 1980s responsibility for the exchange rate was moved to a domestic monetary team from the overseas finance section, which had always been viewed as the team that played away. Consequently, the views of the City and those of overseas investors were effectively represented at the heart of the Treasury in core domestic policy debates, as the British state reoriented itself to reflect its increasingly transnationalized social basis and to ensure that disciplined financial policies were prioritized over other economic objectives. This trend has continued into the 1990s. Those

parts of the state apparatus associated with the planning aspects of Keynesianism, such as the National Economic Development Council and its various working parties, have generally been abolished. In addition, there has been a restructuring in government departments such as the Department of Trade and Industry, where market divisions have replaced sponsorship sections.

These changes have been representative of a reorientation at the heart of government, which has involved the prioritization of the interests and concerns of internationally mobile capital over those of domestic capital and labour. Transnationalized interests have effectively penetrated the very core of central state agencies. Rather than being merely one sectoral interest represented in the debates and analysis generated by a core executive agency such as the Treasury, they have become the principal interest, as a narrow anti-inflationary goal has been progressively institutionalized at the heart of the British state. It is therefore possible to identify an internationalization or transnationalization process in which the British state restructures itself to reflect the extent of Britain's integration into the global economy. In accordance with this, the emerging global economy is not something that exists independently of the state. It is developing because certain state agencies have acted on behalf of certain social forces and actively promoted it. The crucial relationships are those that exist on a national level between a transnationalized City and the Treasury and the Bank of England. The global economy is not, therefore, something that exclusively overlays or exists above the state. The mobility of global economic actors means that they do exist outside of and beyond the state, but as they increasingly provide the social basis of the British state, they also simultaneously exist beneath it and within it.

Globalization is not a process that involves the 'retreat of the state' because the state remains a strategic contested terrain, control of which is pivotal to world order. It is a process involving increased cross-border socio-economic activity, making it enormously difficult to distinguish between global and national—in fact, the global becomes the national and vice versa. This renders the excessively vertical view of the world found in mainstream international relations theory in the form of traditional levels of analysis and dichotomous external-internal approaches, increasingly meaningless.

## New Labour, the Washington Consensus, and the Social Basis of the State

The prevailing globalization discourse or Washington consensus, which stresses the principles of open markets and sound money, has a reciprocal and mutually reinforcing relationship with the social basis of the British state, and is characterized by some degree of circularity. This is perhaps best illustrated by recent British domestic and foreign economic policies, which have served further to institutionalize, both domestically and internationally, the objectives of low inflation and balanced budgets so favoured by financial markets. The conversion of the British Labour Party to the broad principles of sound money and open markets as a recognition of a new global reality is one example of this.

Since its election in May 1997 the new Labour government has introduced a new monetary framework and rules for the conduct of fiscal policy. The Bank of England now has responsibility for setting interest rates to meet a preordained national inflation target set by the government. In particular, the decision was heavily influenced by one of the 'commandments' of the Washington consensus—that fiscal and monetary policy should be separated and that central banks should be functionally independent and should focus on national price stability as the most effective route to low inflation. This practice has been increasingly implemented throughout the industrialized world. The principal architect of the framework, Ed Balls, the personal economic adviser to Gordon Brown, the Chancellor of the Exchequer, was clearly influenced by this international intellectual consensus as a consequence of long-standing intellectual connections with key members of the Washington establishment.

While emphasizing the debt he owed to this broad international intellectual consensus, Balls has pointed to a more significant motivation behind the new framework—the importance of macroeconomic credibility in a world of global capital markets, 'primarily because markets immediately punish any government which strays from the macroeconomic straight and narrow.'[14] The framework is based on the assumption that the markets themselves are most concerned with monitoring current and projected inflation rates and fiscal deficits.[15] For reasons of market guidance and confidence, the framework therefore precommits the Bank of England's Monetary Policy Committee to a national inflation target. Likewise in the area of fiscal policy, the government is currently in the process of introducing a series of fiscal rules to impose legal restrictions on government borrowing. The Labour government has adopted these commitments to macroeconomic discipline to establish its credibility with the international business community and, in particular, the City of London.

Another interpretation of the British government's recent decisions is that they should be understood as part of preparations for British entry into a single European currency. However, the current status of the Bank of England does not comply entirely with the provisions of the Maastricht Treaty, which emphasizes that central banks should be completely independent rather than operationally autonomous. Furthermore, the government's current wait-and-see stance on European Monetary Union (EMU) suggests the motivation for recent reforms may result more from a commitment to macroeconomic discipline for intellectual and political reasons, including the perceived need for credibility with global capital markets, than from any specific attachment to the European project.

These recent Labour reforms resemble what has been referred to as the 'new constitutionalism'—'a legal and political strategy for separating economic forces and policies from broad political accountability and securing management of the economy in the hands of central bankers and technocrats responsive to transnational capital'.[16] The reforms have constituted an implicit attempt to depoliticize macroeconomic policy-making by insulating decision-making from popular pressures, by removing notions of societal winners and losers, and by asserting that a particular approach to policy is technically correct. The Bank's mandate means that interest rate adjustments only have one objective, the inflation target, rather than a broad range of objectives and the cyclical requirements of the British economy. Consequently, there is an inherent bias in the new framework towards interest rate rises. Such a bias clearly benefits the holders or lenders of capital rather than the recipients. In effect, the moves have been indicative of a shift in accountability away from the national electorate towards a financial and business sector that is increasingly internationalized and has benefited from the reforms of the 1980s and 1990s. In this sense the framework not only institutionalizes an anti-inflationary approach to macroeconomic policy but also is an expression of these changing patterns of social relations.

In the 1990s both the Treasury and the Bank of England have promoted City interests through the propagation of open global markets within a framework[17] and, indirectly, via their increased capacity to exert financial discipline within the national policy process in accordance with global financial and monetary imperatives. Domestically, they focus on the residual objectives of low inflation and sound public finances to create investor confidence and prevent the financial volatility seen to beset countries that fail to pursue such prudent policies. They effectively police the new world financial order on the local terrain. Internationally, these agencies seek to maintain the momentum of the globalization process and strengthen and reinforce the Washington consensus of sound money and open markets advocated in a range of international and transnational fora such as the IMF/World Bank, the OECD, the Basel Committee, the World Trade Organization and the European Union (EU).

According to one American official the British government retains some influence internationally because 'the City is one of the world's leading financial centres, it operates in a context set by Whitehall and therefore what London thinks matters.'[18] Following successive financial crises in a number of emerging market economies in the second half of the 1990s, investment banks in the City feared that many countries affected by speculative financial flows might well attempt to reintroduce capital controls or seek to prevent their initial removal, thereby denying investors access to their markets. Working on the basis of the simple calculation that what would be bad for the City would be bad for Britain, Treasury and Bank of England officials have sought to prevent this and to consolidate the progress towards liberalization made in the first half of the 1990s. Britain has proposed a major reform of the official articles of the IMF to encourage further capital account liberalization. The measure is designed to signal the direction in which all IMF members are expected to proceed if they are to retain the benefits of membership, to discourage backsliding in the light of successive financial crises, and to give the Fund a legitimate role in supervising an orderly process of capital account liberalization worldwide. Other recent British initiatives have included Chancellor Gordon Brown's proposals for the IMF to adopt a code of practice for fiscal transparency. The code is intended to emphasize the desirability of fiscal balance and of reductions in the level of public-sector debt, while stressing the need for clear standards on the release of data and information that have informed fiscal policy decisions. In another British initiative the Fund is currently drawing up a code of practice for monetary policy. This is a form of transparency designed to inform market operations and discipline national policy.

All three efforts to influence the mandate of the IMF have been an attempt to 'lock in' the principles of sound money and open markets in the global institutional architecture and so create international institutional as well as market imperatives for such policies. In a more formal manner the British government under John Major accomplished something similar within the EU through the Maastricht Treaty's convergence criteria on budget deficits, public debt, and levels of inflation, which reflected the ideas of neoclassical economists.[19] The criteria were negotiated by the influential Monetary Committee, with Treasury's leading international official, Sir Nigel Wicks, playing a prominent role.[20]

## The British Residual State: Prospects, Problems, and Contradictions

The British state has sought to establish firmly the Washington consensus of open markets and stable money in a diffuse international institutional architecture and thus to maintain the momentum of the liberalization of the world economy. This has been done under the guise of the promotion of British or, more precisely, City interests, on whose behalf officials have acted. In this respect the transnationalized interests that provide the social basis of the British state have acted through certain sections of the state apparatus to promote their interests in a whole range of international fora and to generate an international system and interstate consensus favourable to their interests. This has been evident in the continued promotion of the single European market, trade liberalization, particularly in the area of financial services, and attempts to influence the mandate of the IMF in the direction of further capital account liberalization and disciplined national economic policies. In the immediate future the British state seems likely to continue to execute the residual function of policing the new world order of global finance on the local terrain, while promoting further liberalization and market integration in a range of international fora. The two are intimately connected because open global capital markets provide the rationale for sound money policies, while the transnationalized social basis of the state provides the impetus for both.

Projecting further into the future, the possibility of Britain joining the single European currency does not appear to pose a fundamental challenge to the current orientation of policy because the EMU process has been dominated by the ideas of sound money. Most significantly, the hawkish policies of a prospective European central bank and the austere fiscal rules associated with a single currency are likely to find favour with the British state's transnationalized constituency. Moreover, the current

global consensus and its mutually reinforcing relationship with the British state are unlikely to change unless there is a drastic politically engineered shift in the social basis of the state. For the time being the *laissez-faire* doctrine of open markets and sound money and the progression towards an integrated global market society continue, as these core principles are strategically embedded in the social and institutional relationships that comprise the contemporary world order.

This does not mean, however, that the residual state does not face a series of problems and contradictions, not least of which is resistance from those who have suffered as a consequence of the neo-liberal agenda. This is a broad-ranging group encompassing public-sector workers, pensioners, the long-term unemployed, a growing underclass, workers in traditional manufacturing industries, some British-based manufacturing exporters, and trade unionists, among others. In short, the emergence of the globalizing neo-liberal agenda has been to the detriment of the broad welfare state coalitions that provided the backbone of demand in the post-war period. Ultimately, this might lead to a shortfall in aggregate demand and possibly contribute to a global deflationary situation. In the short term this has manifested itself in a widening income differential between high and low wage-earners, increased inequality, and reduced social cohesion evident in rising crime rates. For Philip Cerny, the state's focus on an increasingly narrow set of residual objectives based on market criteria has undermined the capacity of the state to embody a kind of communal solidarity or *Gemeinshaft*, which has been its principal source of legitimacy.[21]

The current Labour government is attempting to tackle inequality through a series of initiatives it has termed the 'third way'. The biggest obstacle to the success of this agenda is the problem of scarce resources. Moreover, whether the logic of the residual state form and its focus on a stable macroeconomic framework are at all compatible with such initiatives is far from clear. For example, whether the fiscal consolidation strategy can be reconciled with increased investment in public services and improved vocational training is an issue that is yet to be resolved. Furthermore, the abolition of state pensions may yet fatally undermine the fragile legitimacy of the British residual state. After years of public expenditure squeezes there are no easy targets to ensure that the government keeps to its golden fiscal rule. Political conflicts over nurses' pay, teachers' pay, and health service waiting lists are the first indications of the sort of future problems the 'residual state' is likely to encounter.

Perhaps the best indication of what the Blair agenda can achieve is provided by the experience of the Clinton administration. The Blair government has looked to the United States as an example of how a left-of-centre government can govern in the modern world. Here the progressive elements of that agenda, such as Robert Reich's pledges to invest in human capital and reduce inequality, remain largely unfulfilled, while the most notable achievement of President Clinton's two terms in office appears to be the successful budget deficit reduction program. Health and education systems in the United States remain in need of reform and the gap between rich and poor shows no signs of narrowing.

## Conclusion

The current British state is a considerably different creature from the postwar Keynesian welfare state. Its transformation has been bound up with the ongoing processes of market liberalization, integration, and transnationalization that have shifted the social basis of the British state. The British state has promoted open global markets and a discourse of globalization that advocates disciplined macroeconomic policies, and at the same time has responded to this discourse by adjusting its own policy frameworks in accordance with the conventional wisdom in a form of 'new constitutionalism'. The contemporary state system is therefore intimately interconnected and interwoven with the emerging process of globalization. In large part this can be explained with reference to the increasingly transnationalized social basis of the British state, most evident in relationships among the Treasury, the Bank of England, and the City. However, a concentration on the promotion of market forces worldwide and a focus on the residual function of providing the appropriate institutional and legal foundations for global markets have produced challenges for the residual state concerning democratic legitimacy and a sustainable popular base of support. The ability to tackle inequality and to 'square the circle' in public spending remains integral to its survival and that of the current global order.[22] It is likely that political struggles over the diminishing state sector and the need to arrive at an appropriate balance between financial discipline and national social solidarity will increasingly characterize the British residual state in the years ahead.

## Notes

1   P. Cerny, 'Paradoxes of the Competition State: The Dynamics of Political Globalization', *Government and Opposition* (Spring 1997): 251–74. Also see Cerny's contribution to this volume.

2   E. Helleiner, *States and the Re-emergence of Global Finance: From Bretton Woods to the 1990s* (Ithaca, NY: Cornell University Press, 1994). See also Pauly's contribution to this volume.

3   S. Strange, *Sterling and British Policy: A Political Study of an International Currency in Decline* (London: Oxford University Press, RIIA, 1971); S. Blank, 'Britain: The Politics of Foreign Economic Policy, the Domestic Economy and the Problem of Pluralistic Stagnation', in P. Katzenstein, ed., *Between Power and Plenty* (Madison: University of Wisconsin Press, 1978).

4   M. Moran, *The Politics of Banking*, (London: Macmillan, 1988); W. Keegan and R. Pennant-Rae, *Who Runs the Economy? Control and Influence in British Economic Policy* (London: Maurice Temple Smith, 1979).

5   S. Strange, *Casino Capitalism* (Oxford: Basil Blackwell, 1986).

6   P. Hall, 'Policy Paradigms, Social Learning and the State: The Case of Economic Policy Making in Britain', *Comparative Politics* (Apr. 1993): 275–96;

R. Cockett, *Thinking the Unthinkable: Think Tanks and the Economic Counter Revolution, 1931–1983* (London: HarperCollins, 1994).

7 For a coverage of the G–7 economic summits in the late 1970s, see R. Putnam and N. Bayne, *Hanging Together: Co-operation and Conflict in the Seven Power Summits* (London: Sage, 1987).

8 R. Rhodes, 'The Hollowing Out of the State', *Political Quarterly* 65 (1993): 138–51. Also see Cerny's contribution to this volume.

9 D. Coates, *The Question of UK Decline* (Hemel Hempstead: Harvester Wheatsheaf, 1994).

10 Wages in skilled manufacturing have not fallen over the longer term because Japanese multinationals had efficient automated production processes that enabled them to pay premium rates and allowed them to pick up the best of the skilled labour force.

11 B. Jessop, 'Thatcherism and Flexibility: The White Heat of a Post-Fordist Revolution', in B. Jessop, H. Kanstendik, K. Nielsen, and O. Pedersen, eds, *The Politics of Flexibility: Restructuring State and Industry in Britain, Germany and Scandinavia* (Aldershot: Edward Elgar, 1991), 146–7.

12 W. Bonefield, A. Brown, and P. Burnham, *A Major Crisis? The Politics of Economics Policy in Britain in the 1990s* (Aldershot: Dartmouth, 1995), 187.

13 R. Cox, 'Global Peristroika', in R. Miliband and L. Panitch, eds, *The Socialist Register* (London: Merlin Press, 1992).

14 E. Balls, 'Open Macroeconomics in an Open Economy', *Scottish Journal of Political Economy* 45, 2 (May 1998): 122.

15 Ibid. See also L. Mosely, 'International Financial Markets and Government Economic Policy: The Importance of Financial Market Operations', paper presented to the 1997 annual meeting of the American Political Science Association, Duke University.

16 S. Gill, 'Analysing New Forms of Authority: New Constitutionalism, Panopticism and Market Civilisation', paper presented at 'Non-State Actors and Authority in the Global System' conference at ESRC Centre for the Study of Globalisation and Regionalisation, University of Warwick, 31 Oct.-1 Nov. 1997, 1.

17 The Treasury has even established a City Promotional Panel within its Financial Regulation and Industry Directorate to ensure that debates within the Treasury are aware of the latest thinking in the City, particularly on the issue of EMU, and to ensure that City interests are promoted in dealings with foreign governments.

18 Confidential interview with US official, Jan. 1998.

19 K. Dyson, *Elusive Union: The Process of Economic and Monetary Union in Europe* (London: Longman, 1994).

20 S. Hogg and J. Hill, *Too Close to Call* (London: Little, Brown, 1995).

21 Cerny, 'Paradoxes of the Competition State'.

22 C. Thain, 'Squaring the Circle in Public Spending', *Parliamentary Brief* 5, 3 (1998): 23–5.

## Suggested Readings

Baker, A. 'Nébuleuse and the "Internationalization of the State" in the UK? The Case of HM Treasury and the Bank of England', *Review of International Political Economy* 6, 1 (1999): 79–100.

Cerny, P. 'Paradoxes of the Competition State: The Dynamics of Political Globalization', *Government and Opposition* (Spring 1997): 251–74.

Coates, D. *The Question of UK Decline*. Hemel Hempstead: Harvester Wheatsheaf, 1994.

Hall, P. 'The Movement from Keynesianism to Monetarism: Institutional Analysis and British Economic Policy in the 1970s', in K. Thelen, S. Steinmo, and F. Longstreth, eds, *Structuring Politics: Historical Institutionalism in Comparative Perspective*. Cambridge: Cambridge University Press, 1992.

Jessop, B. 'Thatcherism and Flexibility: The White Heat of a Post Fordist Revolution', in B. Jessop, H. Kastendik, K. Nielsen, and O. Pedersen, eds, *The Politics of Flexibility: Restructuring State and Industry in Britain, Germany and Scandinavia*. Aldershot: Edward Elgar, 1991.

## Web Sites

The European Union Central:
    http://www.europa.eu.int

Foreign and Commonwealth Office, UK:
    http://www.fco.gov.uk

Department of Trade and Industry, UK:
    http://www.dti.gov.uk

Bank of England: http://www.BankofEngland.co.uk

World Trade Organization: http://www.wto.org

Organization for Economic Co-operation and Development: http://www.oecd.org

HM Treasury, UK: http://www.hm-treasury.gov.uk

## Chapter 31

# Globalization:
## A Fundamental Challenge to the German Model?

Sigurt Vitols

## Introduction

In the 1970s and 1980s West Germany was widely seen as an attractive national model for other advanced capitalist economies seeking responses to the problems posed by the emerging global economy. These problems included slower growth, greater financial instability, and increasing competition from developing countries. The 'German model' was based on a co-operative (or 'corporatist') approach among the state, business, and labour to industrial modernization. This model performed impressively on a number of indicators, including low unemployment, a high export surplus, and low income inequality.

In the mid-1990s, however, a marked increase in unemployment and a setback in company profitability and export performance initiated a debate on whether these corporatist institutions were flexible enough to deal with the growing challenges of the future. This chapter reviews the major features of the German model and the new challenges it is facing: German unification, the continued transformation of global production patterns and product markets, changing social norms of household behaviour, and European integration. Increasing criticism of German institutions and the call for a more deregulated system along Anglo-Saxon lines could be heard from the business community and the Christian Democrat (conservative)-Free Democrat (liberal) government in the mid-1990s. However, the successful restructuring of business in the second half of the 1990s and the victory of a red-green coalition in the October 1998 national elections are likely to lead to a reaffirmation of the corporatist approach in Germany. The presence of left-leaning governments in almost all European Union member states may lead to a strengthening of corporatist approaches at the European level as well.

## Characteristics of the German Model

The deep oil crisis recession of 1973–4 ushered in the end of the postwar 'golden age' of high-growth, low-unemployment capitalism. While all economies were affected by this recession, the policy response and subsequent economic performance differed greatly among the advanced industrialized countries. West Germany in particular received widespread attention as an attractive alternative to market-oriented (neo-liberal) and state-directed (dirigiste) models of adjustment to slower worldwide growth, greater competition from developing countries, and financial instability. The term *Modell Deutschland*, originally coined by the German Social Democratic Party in its 1978 re-election campaign, came to symbolize adaptation to these new conditions through a strategy of export-oriented industrial modernization.[1] While OECD countries, including the United States, the United Kingdom, and France, generally had trade deficits between 1980 and 1990, Germany ran an annual trade surplus equivalent to 1.7 per cent of gross domestic product (GDP) (see Table 1). On the basis of this export success, Germany had an average rate of unemployment of 5.8 per cent during the 1980s, lower than those three countries and the OECD average. Germany was also able to avoid the sharp trend towards wage and income inequality experienced in

## Table 1: Comparative Economic Performance, 1980–1990, Germany, US, UK, France, and OECD Average

|                      | Germany | US   | UK   | France | OECD |
|----------------------|---------|------|------|--------|------|
| Unemployment rate    | 5.8     | 7.0  | 9.7  | 9.0    | 7.2  |
| Trade surplus/GDP    | 1.7     | −1.6 | −0.1 | −1.1   | −0.7 |
| GDP growth per capita| 1.8     | 1.9  | 2.4  | 2.0    | 2.2  |

SOURCE: OECD, Historical Statistics and National Accounts, various years.

most other industrialized countries.[2] Interestingly enough, this superior performance was not based on a faster rate of GDP growth per capita, which averaged only 1.8 per cent per annum in the 1980s.[3]

At the heart of this German model of adjustment was the upgrading of a broad spectrum of industrial sectors to concentrate production on higher-quality, specialized goods targeted towards premium domestic and world markets. This strategy—variously named diversified quality production (Sorge and Streeck), new production concepts (Kern and Schumann), and flexible specialization (Piore and Sabel)—is based on a combination of building on traditional strengths, such as the technical ability and flexibility of skilled manual workers, and the rapid incorporation of new machinery and production methods. This capacity, visible as early as the end of the last century when Germany became an industrial leader in Europe, was strengthened after the first oil shock of 1973–4 through a mass upgrading of the skill base and the rapid diffusion of a number of innovations, most notably the microchip.[4]

In his landmark study of the industrial profiles of 10 countries, Michael Porter notes the exceptional breadth of Germany's competitive advantage across a wide range of industrial sectors.[5] The most visible sector among these 'success stories' is the automobile industry, which for millions of consumers worldwide has come to symbolize the craftsmanship and performance embodied in goods 'made in Germany'. The great expansion of production of traditionally low-volume luxury producers Mercedes-Benz and BMW to increase sales at the high end of the market is a significant story in

and of itself. However, Germany's capacity to change has been most clearly demonstrated in the dramatic transformation of Volkswagen, which had been established expressly to mass-produce a low-cost car accessible to every household ('the Beetle'). After the first oil shock, Volkswagen radically changed its product market strategy by terminating production of the Beetle in Germany, introducing a range of new models aimed at significantly higher market segments, and purchasing the niche producer Audi.[6] This example was repeated again and again, not only in sectors familiar in the literature in English, such as industrial machinery and chemicals, but also in such sectors as steel, food processing, textiles, and wooden furniture.[7]

The joint contributions of business, labour, and the state were crucial for the success of the German model. At the danger of some oversimplification, these contributions occurred within an institutional framework that can be characterized as 'corporatist'. Unlike the neo-liberal state, the German state has supported a co-ordinated and proactive response to market forces. Unlike the dirigiste state in countries such as France and Japan, the level of targeting of resources to specific sectors and companies ('national winners') in Germany has been low and initiatives have come mainly from the private sector.

Perhaps the most important contribution of the corporatist state is to support the collective organization of interest groups such as business and labour. The state provides these private associations with special privileges, such as access to policy-making processes and assists them with representation vis-à-vis other associations. Furthermore, the state provides these associations with resources either directly through state funding or through the levying of membership fees. The strength of corporatism in Germany can be attributed both to cultural traditions and to a strong federalist system, which often leads to political conflict.

As a result of this support, business has a high capacity to co-ordinate and co-operate through a dense network of industry associations and local chambers of commerce and industry. This co-ordination capacity has helped business to pursue its collective interests in the political arena, to participate in the provision of collective goods important for restructuring, such as skill formation, and to help avoid the kind of destructive price competition that has plagued adjustment in other countries. This capacity has been key in creating an 'institutional infrastructure' for competitiveness that includes research institutes and day-release schools for the dual training system.[8]

The corporatist approach extends into the industrial relations system. Approximately 90 per cent of employees are covered by collective bargaining between unions and employers' associations at the sectoral level. Most workers in larger companies are also represented at the plant level by works councils and at the firm level by employee representation on company boards. Perhaps best captured in the phrase 'conflictual partnership', labour has co-operated in the often drastic measures involved in adjustment without losing its capacity to pressure employers to take the 'high road' and to mobilize the rank and file when the integrity of the industrial relations system is threatened. The state has also reduced conflict by providing extensive early retirement subsidies to support restructuring in declining industries.[9]

Although each of these three actors is potentially powerful enough to disrupt the system, their co-operation has been rewarded throughout the 1970s and 1980s. Business enjoyed export success and reasonable profits, labour received high wages and a high level of income equality, and the state experienced a strong balance of payments, moderate expenditures for labour market programs, and thus relatively low debt levels.

## The German Model: Overwhelmed by New Challenges?

In the 1990s, however, the German model came under increasing stress in dealing with challenges, including (1) the 'post-Communist' political order, particularly German unification; (2) continuing shifts in the global production system; (3) changes in demographic patterns and in social norms of household behaviour; and (4) a qualitative leap forward in European integration. Perhaps the most obvious indicator of this stress is deteriorating economic performance. The large export surpluses enjoyed in the 1980s disappeared in 1991 and the unemployment rate has increased to over 10 per cent (see Table 2). Yet, the sense of crisis in the German model goes beyond economic performance and has initiated a debate on whether the German system of corporatist institutions is capable of handling new social and political problems.

While the current crisis has multiple causes, the trigger was undoubtedly German unification, which took place in October 1990. Unification originally created a boom in economic activity due to great demand for consumer goods in East Germany. Industrial production and GDP growth in West Germany increased by more than 5 per cent in 1990. This boom was financed in large part through large fiscal transfers from the West.

At the same time, however, much of the rest of the world was slipping into recession, and in 1992–3 Germany finally followed. The recession was quite sharp, with real GDP in the first quarter of 1993 at 2 per cent below the previous year's level. Business profitability in 1993 reached a postwar low of 1.9 per cent of sales before taxes. East Germany was particularly affected because of the collapse of demand from its traditional markets, the former Soviet bloc countries. Of greater concern to the public at large has been the dramatic deterioration in the employment situation; registered unemployment has risen to more than 4 million persons, or well over 10 per cent of the labour force, the 'highest levels seen since 1933', as ominously reported by the *Financial Times*. When the so-called 'hidden' unemployed are included (those on training and

## Table 2: German Economic Performance, 1988–1997 (in per cent)

|  | 1988 | 1989 | 1990 | 1991 | 1992 | 1993 | 1994 | 1995 | 1996 | 1997 |
|---|---|---|---|---|---|---|---|---|---|---|
| GDP | 3.7 | 3.6 | 5.7 | 13.2 | 2.2 | –1.2 | 2.7 | 1.8 | 1.4 | 2.2 |
| Industrial production | 3.6 | 4.7 | 5.2 | 3 | –2.6 | –7.2 | 3.6 | 2 | 0.5 | 4 |
| Unit labour cost | 0.2 | 0.8 | 2 | 8.1 | 5.7 | 3.3 | –0.1 | 1.4 | –0.3 | –1.9 |
| Export surplus/GDP | 4.4 | 5.1 | 5.5 | –0.1 | –0.7 | –0.4 | –0.4 | –0.6 | 0.0 | 1.0 |
| Unemployment | 7.6 | 6.8 | 6.2 | 6.6 | 7.7 | 8.9 | 9.6 | 9.4 | 10.3 | 11.5 |

NOTE: GDP, industrial production, and unit labour cost are annual growth figures. Figures starting in 1991 are for unified Germany.

SOURCE: OECD Economic Surveys: Germany, Aug. 1998.

make-work programs), the unemployment rate in East Germany is more than twice this figure.

The unification-related problems pointed to the difficulties of the German model in dealing with diversity within interest groups. Productivity in East Germany was only one-third of the West German level at the time of unification. However, the replacement of the East German currency with the Deutschmark—and thus the imposition of a single currency on all of Germany—removed the possibility of compensating for productivity differences through adjustments in the exchange rate. Since the wage-bargaining system and company operations were predicated on a high level of unity and equal conditions, the unions felt obliged to demand the rapid equalization of wages and working conditions.

The sense of crisis was not limited to East Germany, however. World market shares of Germany's core 'medium-tech' industries—autos, chemicals, industrial machinery, and electronics—were slipping throughout the first half of the 1990s, particularly relative to the Japanese competition. Production and employment in high-tech areas such as information technology and biotechnology also remained underdeveloped relative to the United States and United Kingdom.[10]

Compounding the shrinkage of employment in the manufacturing sector were changes in households. The 'male breadwinner/full-time housewife' pattern of household organization has been particularly strong in Germany, as reflected in one of the lowest rates of female labour force participation

among OECD countries. This model is being challenged by an increasing number of women searching for full- or part-time work. However, unlike in the US and UK, the German economy has not been able to compensate for declines in manufacturing through massive increases in service-sector employment. This problem has been exacerbated by the growing number of students seeking part-time employment to help finance their education; the average duration of university studies is extremely high in Germany in comparative perspective.

The fourth major challenge is European integration. The European Single Market initiative and European Monetary Union (EMU) are European responses to the globalizing economy. This process is at the same time constraining Germany's ability to respond to its domestic economic problems, particularly unemployment. At one level this constraint is financial. The European Union budget has increased dramatically with the accession of less wealthy 'peripheral' countries such as Portugal, Spain, Ireland, and Greece. These countries have demanded the establishment of structural and regional funds to help deal with the changes caused by the removal of trade and other barriers. As the 'paymaster' or largest net contributor, Germany's financial commitment to the EU has thus increased dramatically. At the same time, the Maastricht Treaty, which lays the groundwork for the EMU and the single European currency (the Euro), imposes strict criteria for fiscal and monetary discipline as prerequisites for countries participating in the EMU.

While intended to encourage convergence among member countries and confidence in the stability of the new currency, these criteria have restricted Germany's ability to use deficit spending and loose monetary policy to encourage economic growth and employment creation.

Perhaps more significant, however, are the institutional changes involved in the process of deregulation and harmonization of legislation in the EU. Large sectors of the economy, such as telecommunications and transport, are being deregulated in order to encourage more competition within the European Union. In Germany both sectors are areas where the public sector provided large amounts of employment and where equal service to all citizens and regions—not ability to pay—has been the guiding principle for service provision. Draft legislation attempting to harmonize company law and hostile takeovers has threatened important characteristics of the German model, including representation of employees on company boards (co-determination) and the dense co-operative network of cross-shareholdings and interlocking directorships between large companies and banks. Since EU decision-making is mainly based on negotiations between member governments, the shift of power to the European level has also called into question the role of interest groups in Germany's traditionally corporatist policy-making processes. The way the EU evolves has important implications for whether the institutional core of the German model will survive.

## The Response to New Challenges

One response within Germany to these challenges, which has been strongest among the business community and in the liberal-conservative coalition in power until October 1998, is to demand the reform of German institutions more along the lines of the Anglo-Saxon liberal or market model. These critics blamed strong unions, high labour costs, extensive regulations, and the government bureaucracy for the increasing unattractiveness of 'Standort Deutschland' (production location Germany). Companies claim that they face a major cost disadvantage relative to other countries due to high wages, social security contributions, and business taxes. Labour costs are exacerbated by a generous system of entitlements, including requirements that employers' provide 100 per cent sick pay for six weeks and unemployment benefits with a net replacement rate of around 70 per cent of pay. Strong unions, works councils, and dismissal protection legislation have constrained flexibility in the use of labour. Because wage levels are set through industry-level bargaining, employers complain that they cannot design firm-level incentive systems needed to motivate employees. Finally, the business community argues that the state bureaucracy has imposed unnecessary barriers on innovation, most notoriously in strict regulations on genetic research in the biotechnology industry.

These critics eye the 'American model' with envy. In 1996, then Chancellor Helmut Kohl announced an initiative to cut unemployment in half by the year 2000. To achieve this goal he pushed through legislation to weaken dismissal protection, to lower the statutory minimum requirement on employers for sick pay from 100 per cent to 80 per cent of normal pay, to reduce unemployment and income assistance benefit rates and eligibility for early retirement pensions, and to deregulate financial markets and increase the supply of venture capital. In addition, government commissions were established to develop proposals to reduce the cost burden on employers through the fundamental reform of the tax and social security systems.

In the collective bargaining arena, the increasing desire of large companies to offer incentives to highly skilled workers and lower the wages of the unskilled led to proposals to weaken significantly the cornerstone of the German system of co-ordinated bargaining, the sectoral-level collective agreement (Flächentarifvertrag).[11] Impatient with the pace of reform, record numbers of companies left or threatened to leave employers' associations in order to negotiate company-level agreements. This phenomenon of Verbandsflucht, which has been particularly strong in East Germany and during the 1992–3 recession, has raised the spectre of the loss of the co-ordinating capacity of capital, one of the cornerstones of the German model.

With the resumption of a reasonable level of economic growth and the recovery of business profitability and market shares in 1997, criticisms from industry became more muted. German businesses have made remarkable progress in restructuring. More efficient 'lean production' methods of manufacturing developed by the Japanese have been adopted on a widespread basis in sectors such as automobiles and electronics. Some of the most effective experiments with lean production have taken place in East Germany, such as in the new Volkswagen and Opel plants, which provide the basis for regional industrial revitalization. A number of larger companies have also partially adopted Anglo-Saxon organizational and strategic concepts, such as 'shareholder value' to boost profitability— within, however, the framework of consultation with employee representatives over the implementation of these principles.

German companies are also proving adept at turning globalization to their advantage. While Eastern Europe was originally seen as a low-cost threat to German employment and production, a new division of labour is emerging between Germany and this region. German companies are transferring technology and know-how, particularly for the efficient production of less complex production (e.g., auto components), through a variety of mechanisms, including the purchase of privatized enterprises, joint ventures, and informal co-operation with indigenous companies. Germany is benefiting from lower-cost production in this region and from the sale of more complex products, such as industrial machinery. A take-off in growth in Eastern Europe would be an important source of demand for Germany's capital goods manufacturers.[12]

Finally, German companies are also increasingly exploiting the comparative advantages of advanced industrialized countries through their global research and development and production strategies. One good example of this is the purchase of innovative American biotechnology companies and the establishment of research facilities in the United States by the chemical/pharmaceutical conglomerates Bayer and Hoechst. The US institutional framework, where employees can be rewarded with more pay incentives and career structures that are less rigid, is more hospitable to such highly innovative activities. At the same time, these companies are maintaining traditional areas of strength in production and research in less rapidly developing fields, for example, specialty chemicals in Germany. While the chemical/pharmaceutical industry is the most prominent example of this global division of labour, other examples can be found, as in the shift of operations in the rapidly changing investment banking field to London and New York.[13]

Criticism of German institutions from the government coalition also became more muted as the 1998 national elections approached. The governing centre-right parties had an interest in claiming that economic conditions were improving as a result of their policies. Furthermore, these parties ran into a credibility problem with the electorate when making the case for another term in office after relatively little progress in reform in the 16 years since they started the coalition.

A final rejection of the neo-liberal model was provided by the electorate in the October 1998 elections. Instead, majority support was given to the German Social Democratic Party (SPD) and the Green Party (Bündnis 90/Die Grünen). These parties support a more activist approach to economic modernization than their centre-right predecessors. One key proposal is an 'ecology tax' on non-renewable energy sources to reduce harm to the environment and dependence on expensive imports. A second proposal is to modernize the dual apprenticeship system and to increase the number of apprenticeships. Perhaps the most significant initiative, however, is to put corporatist institutions at the centre of tackling the employment problem. The proposed Alliance for Jobs (Bündnis für Arbeit) is based on a co-operative approach of business, labour, and the state to discuss, develop, and implement solutions to economic and employment problems. This alliance rests on the hope that Germany can repeat the positive experiences with a corporatist solution developed in the Netherlands.

Within a tripartite context, the unions agreed to wage moderation, the state agreed to make labour market institutions more flexible, and employers agreed to increase employment, particularly part-time employment in the service sector. The result of this approach for the Netherlands has been a significantly lower unemployment rate and a higher level of employment generation in the service sector than in Germany. The first meetings of the Alliance for Jobs in Germany have made good progress in identifying areas for discussion and agreement on reforms, including youth employment, the system of collective bargaining, and the social security system.

Support for corporatist solutions to fundamental economic problems is increasing not only domestically but also at the European level. Left-wing or left-leaning governments, as noted earlier, have been elected in almost all of the EU member states. These governments are likely to support more active labour market policies at the European level and to put more emphasis on employment effects in fiscal and monetary decisions than has been the case under predominantly conservative regimes. To co-ordinate these policies governments will need to consult with both unions (one of the core constituencies of left-wing parties) and business, whose support is needed for success.

## Conclusion

The German national model of adjustment to new global challenges came to prominence in the 1970s and 1980s. This corporatist model—based on co-operation between the state and highly organized business and labour interests—was able to contribute successfully to the modernization of a wide variety of traditional medium-technology industries. In the 1990s, however, the ability of this model to deal with four challenges—German unification, continued shifts in global production and consumption systems, changes in social norms of household behaviour, and European integration—was increasingly questioned. Segments of the business community and the ruling centre-right coalition suggested that Germany should reject its corporatist institutions in favour of a more market-oriented Anglo-Saxon approach to problem-solving.

Since the peak of the economic crisis was reached in the mid-1990s, however, support for such a neo-liberal model has decreased. Businesses, particularly large multinationals, have managed to regain profitability by implementing more efficient means of production and by increasing their presence in the Americas and Asia. The liberal-conservative coalition, which was able to implement a deregulatory approach only in part, was resoundingly defeated in national elections in October 1998. The new red-green coalition has put an Alliance for Jobs at the centre of its proposals for dealing with the problem of mass unemployment. This reaffirmation of the corporatist tradition in Germany is also likely to be reflected in stronger support for corporatist approaches to problem-solving at the European level.

## Notes

1   A. Markovits, *The Political Economy of West Germany: Modell Deutschland* (New York: Praeger, 1982).

2   OECD, *Employment Outlook 1993* and *Employment Outlook 1994* (Paris: OECD).

3   The divergence between this stellar export performance and less impressive GDP and productivity growth may be explained by the absence of an indicator taking into account quality, especially important for a country whose manufacturers have focused on the higher end of the market. See Wendy Carlin and David Soskice, 'Shocks to the System: The German Political Economy under Stress', *National Institute Economic Review* 159 (1997): 57–76.

4   On diversified quality production, see A. Sorge and W. Streeck, 'Industrial Relations and Technical Change: The Case for an Extended Perspective', in R. Hyman and W. Streeck, eds, *New Technology and Industrial Relations* (Oxford: Basil

Blackwell, 1988). On new production concepts, see Horst Kern and Michael Schumann, *Das Ende der Arbeitsteilung?* (Munich: Verlag C.H. Beck, 1986). On flexible specialization, see Michael Piore and Charles Sabel, *The Second Industrial Divide: Possibilities for Prosperity* (New York: Basic Books, 1984). For the historical origins of the German model, see Alfred Chandler, *Scale and Scope: The Dynamics of Industrial Capitalism* (Cambridge, Mass.: Belknap, 1990); Gary Herrigel, *Industrial Constructions: The Sources of German Industrial Power* (Cambridge: Cambridge University Press, 1995).

5 Michael E. Porter, *The Competitive Advantage of Nations* (New York: Free Press, 1990).

6 Wolfgang Streeck, *Industrial Relations in West Germany: A Case Study of the Car Industry* (London: Heinemann, 1984).

7 For an excellent collection of institutional and sectoral studies on changes in the 1980s, see Peter J. Katzenstein, *Industry and Politics in West Germany* (Ithaca, NY: Cornell University Press, 1989).

8 Josef Esser, Wolfgang Fach, and Kenneth Dyson, 'Social Market and Modernization Policy: West Germany', in Dyson and Stephen Wilks, eds, *Industrial Crisis* (New York: St Martins Press, 1983); David Soskice, 'The Institutional Infrastructure for International Competitiveness: A Comparative Analysis of the UK and Germany', in A.B. Atkinson and R. Brunetta, eds, *The Economics of the New Europe* (London: Macmillan, 1992).

9 The term 'conflictual partnership' is described in Walther Müller-Jentsch, 'Germany: From Collective Voice to Co-Management', in Joel Rogers and Wolfgang Streeck, eds, *Works Councils: Consultation, Representation, and Cooperation in Industrial Relations* (Chicago: University of Chicago Press, 1995), 53–78. For the beneficial effect of institutional constraints on economic performance, see Wolfgang Streeck, *Social Institutions and Economic Performance: Studies of Industrial Relations in Advanced Industrialized Countries* (Beverly Hills, Calif.: Sage, 1992). For the concept of negotiated adjustment, see Kirsten S. Wever, *Negotiating Competitiveness: Employment Relations and Organizational Innovation in Germany and the United States* (Cambridge, Mass.: Harvard Business School Press, 1995).

10 Deutsches Institut für Wirschaftsforschung, *FuE-Aktivitäten, Außenhandel und Wirtschaftsstrukturen: Die technologische Leistungsfähigkeit der deutschen Wirtschaft im internationalen Vergleich* (Berlin: Duncker & Humblot, 1996).

11 Carlin and Soskice, 'Shocks to the System'.

12 Dieter Schumacher, 'Mehr Beschäftigung in der EU durch Außenhandel mit Transformationsländern', *DIW Wochenbericht* 63 (1996): 557–65.

13 Sigurt Vitols, Steven Casper, David Soskice, and Stephen Woolcock, *Corporate Governance in Large British and German Companies: Comparative Institutional Advantage or Competing for Best Practice* (London: Anglo-German Foundation, 1997).

## Suggested Readings

Carlin, Wendy, and David Soskice. 'Shocks to the System: The German Political Economy under Stress', *National Institute Economic Review* 159 (1997): 57–76.

Casper, Steven, and Sigurt Vitols. 'The German Model in the 1990s: Problems and Prospects', *Industry and Innovation* 4, 1 (June 1997).

Herrigel, Gary. *Industrial Constructions: The Sources of German Industrial Power*. Cambridge: Cambridge University Press, 1995.

Katzenstein, Peter J. *Industry and Politics in West Germany*. Ithaca, NY: Cornell University Press, 1989.

Müller-Jentsch, Walther. 'Germany: From Collective Voice to Co-Management', in Joel Rogers and Wolfgang Streeck, eds, *Works Councils: Consultation, Representation, and Cooperation in Industrial Relations*. Chicago: University of Chicago Press, 1995.

Streeck, Wolfgang. *Social Institutions and Economic Performance: Studies of Industrial Relations in Advanced Industrialized Countries*. Beverly Hills, Calif.: Sage, 1992.

Vitols, Sigurt, Steven Casper, David Soskice, and Stephen Woolcock. *Corporate Governance in Large British and German Companies: Comparative Institutional Advantage or Competing for Best Practice.* London: Anglo-German Foundation, 1997.

Wever, Kirsten S. *Negotiating Competitiveness: Employment Relations and Organizational Innovation in Germany and the United States.* Cambridge, Mass.: Harvard Business School Press, 1995.

## Web Sites

German parliament:
http://www.bundestag.de/btengver/e-index.htm

DIW (German Institute for Economic Research):
http://www.diw-berlin.de

HWWA (Economic Research Institute—Hamburg):
http://www.hwwa.uni-hamburg.de/english/
index-engl-overview.htm

German Bundesbank: http://www.bundesbank.de

Social Sciences Center Berlin (WZB):
http://www.medea.wz-berlin.de

Max Planck Institute for the Study of Societies:
http://www.mpi-fg-koeln.mpg.de

## Chapter 32

# Regionalization Trumps Globalization:
## Japanese Production Networks in Asia

### Walter Hatch

In the apocalyptic but increasingly orthodox vision of many observers, globalization—the flow of capital, goods, and technology across borders—is wiping out distinctive institutions, including the nation-state, creating everywhere a uniform if somewhat bland McCapitalist System that obeys only the principles of the almighty market. Globalization, according to these observers, is an irrepressibly powerful force that has 'swallowed most consumers and corporations, made traditional borders disappear, and pushed bureaucrats, politicians, and the military toward the status of declining industries.'[1]

This chapter uses the case of Japan to evaluate the globalization/convergence thesis, which reflects liberal or neoclassical economic analysis. Japan serves as a 'critical case' because it is the industrialized economy that most defies the Anglo-American standard of modern capitalism, the market-oriented standard to which all economies are said to be conforming. Indeed, in Japan, where a different model of coalition capitalism exists, government bureaucrats, acting in collaboration with business executives, use informal means ('administrative guidance') to organize markets. Independent firms maintain long-standing, mutually reinforcing ties with one another, manifested by cross-shareholdings, personnel transfers, and interfirm transactions. Workers in many of the largest firms remain with one employer for most of their lives, acquiring new work opportunities and higher wages inside rather than beyond the firm.

One need only glance at the newspaper headlines to recognize that Japan is facing enormous pressure to change. This pressure comes in the form of political browbeating from Western, particularly US, policy-makers and opinion-leaders, who say Japan must pursue deregulation and other so-called liberalization measures. And it comes in the form of quieter but no less powerful market forces such as rising input costs, lagging labour productivity, and heavy government debt. Thus, if the globalization/convergence thesis is correct, one would certainly expect Japan to be undergoing structural change.

I argue that it is not. Contrary to the globalization/convergence thesis, my hypothesis is that Japan's system of coalition capitalism, characterized by a high level of what I call 'relationalism', has experienced a great deal of distributional change, but very little structural change in the 1990s. I test this hypothesis by examining evidence collected across the three nexus of co-operation that stand at the centre of Japan's highly relational political economy: (1) collaboration between state and industry; (2) interfirm ties (including *keiretsu*); and (3) management-labour relations.

Assuming this hypothesis is correct, how does one explain such continuity? The existing literature in political economy presents at least two possible answers. One, which represents the 'historical institutionalist' approach, suggests that established institutions constrain the options and even the preferences that actors otherwise might have.[2] In this case, then, Japanese policy-makers and opinion-leaders are stuck in a rut of 'path dependence' in which, barring some jolt, they continue to act as they have in the past.[3] A second explanation, drawn from rational choice theory, is that actors seek to maximize their own narrow, short-term interests at the expense of the larger, longer-term interest of society.[4] Japanese politicians, according to this perspective, are eager to win re-election and thus curry favour with farmers, small business owners, and other conservative constituents who supply necessary votes by opposing proposals for economic reform.[5]

These approaches offer valuable insights but ultimately fall short because they (1) rely on a unit of analysis that is, as Granovetter has noted, either undersocialized (the atomistic, individual utility maximizer of rational choice theory) or oversocialized (the Leviathan of hierarchy in historical institutionalism); and (2) ignore the critical variable of power.[6] I propose a third answer, which represents a political economy application of network theory as used by some sociologists. When exchange is highly 'relational', and thus carried out in relatively dense networks, actors who occupy central positions within such networks enjoy what I call 'positional power', a privileged access to network resources such as information. They are therefore unlikely to sever voluntarily the relationships that have afforded them such power.

Using this framework to summarize the results of our case study, we find that Japanese business and bureaucratic élites, who enjoy positional power in the domestic political economy of Japan, are buying themselves time, cutting themselves slack in part by regionalizing the production and administrative networks that stand at the core of Japan's system of coalition capitalism, or relationalism. That is, they are forestalling change by expanding these networks into Asia, where they also enjoy a measure of positional power.[7] What this suggests is that regionalization, under certain conditions, can trump globalization, or at least cushion its impact.

## Relationalism and Positional Power

If we hope to use these concepts as explanatory tools, we must first define and operationalize them more carefully. 'Relationalism' refers to the extent to which pre-existing social connections guide exchange decisions. To some degree, all transactions—even those carried out in modern, highly marketized economies—are relational and thus embedded in and constrained by ongoing social relations.[8] But some are indeed more relational than others. The least relational transactions are spot market deals in which buyer and seller meet only at the point of sale and communicate merely on the basis of price. At the opposite end of the spectrum, the most relational transactions take place within a single institution, such as the vertically integrated firm, and thus bypass the market altogether. Most transactions, however, take place somewhere between these two extremes in quasi-markets or quasi-hierarchies; in fact, they often take place in a large grey area that includes various forms of networking.

This microanalysis of relationalism can be easily extended to the macro level, and political economies can be evaluated along a continuum. Some political economies are thus only thinly relational not only because they operate more on the basis of spot market transactions, but also—more fundamentally—because individual actors in those economies, responding to structural incentives created by institutions of their own making, are less inclined to forge long-lasting social ties. In the United States, for example, people now move relatively freely from job to job, from city to city, and often do not plant themselves deeply in a community. They often seem to eschew long-standing relationships. Other political economies, meanwhile, are quite heavily relational. In Japan, for example, people tend to stay put for longer periods of time in both employment and residence; long-term, reciprocal relations or coalitions form the foundation of business and politics.

Relationalism works best in the context of development, when firms are able to defy the law of gravity as outlined in neoclassical economy theory and achieve declining long-run average costs by adopting successively more sophisticated technology.[9] Indeed, Japan's system of coalition capitalism functioned quite well in the early part of the postwar period, when the nation was still trying to catch up with the industrialized West. Government officials, working in consultation with trade associations, channelled scarce capital to strategic industries and authorized temporary cartels to cope with periodic bouts of production overcapacity. Manufacturers, meanwhile, used interfirm linkages to overcome bottlenecks in a developing industrial structure and forged long-term ties with their own workers to protect investments in human capital, particularly on-the-job training. In other words, Japanese élites spun a web of co-operative networks in the 1950–73 period to move to the edge of the global technological frontier; once they got there, however, they found themselves unable to push aggressively beyond it.

In the slower growth phase of a mature economy, relationalism is likely to produce collusion between government and business, and higher costs for manufacturers. Indeed, by the 1990s, the Japanese political economy experienced a severe crisis, as evidenced by declining total factor productivity, a rising deficit in intellectual property royalty payments, lagging sales growth in key industries such as computers, and rising unemployment and underemployment. Élites faced a choice: they could either dismantle the system of relationalism they had constructed, paving the way for structural reform; or they could try to export this system to a still-developing economy or economies, where such production and administrative networks might still be effective.

Japanese élites chose to export relationalism to developing Asia because they did not want to abandon the relationships that have afforded them such a high degree of 'positional power' in Japan's political economy. Positional power is a kind of structural power determined by relative *access* to resources embedded in a network of relationships rather than actual *possession* of such resources. Insiders, those who are centrally positioned in the network and thus able to tap its embedded resources with relative ease, gain leverage or power over outsiders who must 'pass through' or 'turn to' those insiders to achieve similar access to resources. In this way, power

> emerges from [an actor's] prominence in networks where valued information and scarce resources are transferred from one actor to

another. Positions are stratified according to the dependence of other positions on them for these essential resources. Not only the direct connections are important in determining positional power, but the indirect connections are critical because they comprise limits and opportunities for obtaining desired ends.[10]

This approach relies heavily on Emerson, who sees power as the inverse of dependence.[11] That is, a particular actor's power is measured by the extent to which others in a social exchange network rely on that actor to achieve outcomes, or, conversely, by the extent to which that actor can achieve outcomes without relying on others. This is similar to the concept of 'substitutes' in consumer economics: one's power ('elasticity of demand') increases as the number of equally accessible but alternative paths ('substitutes') to a goal ('utility') increase. Marsden has refined this model further to show that centrally positioned actors may act as discriminating monopolists, as price-makers, restricting the flow of resources (information) and thereby increasing the value of resources under their control by 'capitalizing on the fact that their trading partners lack valuable alternatives to an exchange relationship'.[12]

Japanese élites clearly enjoy a great deal of positional power within Japan's highly relational political economy. Ordinary individuals, for example, play a marginal role in the ownership and control of large Japanese firms, which tend to invest heavily in one another and sometimes even employ shady underworld figures known as *sokaiya* to muzzle independent stockholders at annual meetings. Likewise, ordinary individuals exercise very little influence over the rule-making that occurs in the Japanese bureaucracy, where outside views are solicited less often via public hearings and more often via *shingikai* or deliberation councils made up of academics, business people, and other invited élites. Given the power and the prestige associated with occupying such central positions in Japan's dense production and administrative networks, one cannot expect Japanese élites to dismantle this system voluntarily.

# Retaining Relationalism

For non-élites, Japan's system of coalition capitalism has come to produce far fewer benefits than it used to. This is evident in statistics on bankruptcies and unemployment, which recently have increased to record levels for Japan. But the system itself has changed very little in the 1990s, the decade in which the forces of globalization supposedly have pounded Japan the hardest. In other words, Japanese relationalism—characterized by co-operative bonds between state and industry, between firms, and between management and labour—has undergone distributional but not structural change. Let us examine the evidence in each of these three nexus of co-operation.

## State and Industry

One way to measure the relationship between state and industry is to examine the amount of government regulations imposed on business. Although much has been made of Japan's drive to deregulate industry, statistics collected by the Japanese government itself indicate that the volume of regulatory activity has been remarkably stable in recent years. In 1986, when the Management and Co-ordination Agency began collecting statistics, Japanese government agencies enforced a total of 10,054 regulations—from licensing and permitting requirements to quality standards. A decade later, in 1996, that number had increased by almost 10 per cent to 10,983. One of the leading producers of new regulations was the Ministry of Finance, which contributed a net additional 344 regulations during a period when Japanese financial markets were being exposed to heavier and heavier doses of globalization.

A strong commitment to rule-making, however, is hardly unique to Japan, or to highly relational political economies in general. To measure change accurately in this nexus of co-operation, we would do better to probe *inside* the regulatory regime and examine the reciprocal ties that bind the regulators and the regulated. In Japan, such linkages traditionally have been solidified through the practice of *amakudari* ('descent from heaven'), whereby government officials leave their public posts at age 55 and take up private posts in firms they once regulated. This practice helps the Japanese state intervene unobtrusively in the marketplace, using the velvet glove of 'administrative guidance' rather than the iron fist of regulation. But it also allows private industry to convey its desires effectively to policy-makers. Both sides thus benefit from this 'hostage-taking' practice, which keeps information flowing in both directions.[13] Statistics on government officials who have 'descended' from the bureaucracy show remarkably little change in the use of this practice since the late 1970s.

## Business and Business

Volumes have been written about the 'collapse' of *keiretsu*, or interfirm groups, in Japan. In fact, however, this institutional characteristic of relationalism is alive and well—albeit in a reconstituted form. What is happening is not so much the 'unravelling' as the 're-ravelling' of *keiretsu* ties. While the bonds between some firms have loosened, those between others have tightened.

One measure of these ties is mutual or cross-shareholding, a practice whereby firms hold stock in one another. This practice serves several functions; it is, for example, a hedge against hostile takeover, an insurance mechanism to cope with risk, and a means of reducing transaction costs, particularly the cost of negotiating and enforcing contracts. Japanese firms today engage in cross-shareholding nearly as much as they did a decade ago.

But we are more interested here in the vertical ties between large manufacturers, operating as assemblers, and smaller suppliers. Subcontractors, who traditionally have supplied a relatively high proportion of the value-added in production, continue to make up more than half of all small and medium-sized manufacturing firms in Japan. And while many are trying to expand their ties with a larger number of customers, or parents, these subcontractors also generally seek to maintain or strengthen the traditional bonds with their primary customer.[14] Neither of these goals is easy to achieve, particularly for the smallest suppliers. One finds overwhelming evidence of polarization (*nikyoku bunka*) in the ranks of Japanese subcontractors; some, primarily the smaller third-tier suppliers, are being squeezed or simply jettisoned by their main customers while others, primarily the larger first-tier suppliers, are being drawn into even closer, mutually reinforcing relations.[15] Even some formerly independent suppliers have joined *keiretsu*.[16] In general, parents are not engaging in transactions outside their supply groups but are instead becoming increasingly selective as they tend to rely more and more on just one highly trusted subcontractor, rather than a set of subcontractors, for every kind of part.[17] In other words, subcontracting orders are being concentrated in the hands of a smaller and smaller group of élite suppliers who maintain extremely close relations with their customers.

### Management and Labour

For years, journalists have forecast the demise of the Japanese employment system, a system of long-term if not lifetime tenure in large firms that is buttressed by the use of seniority pay. Most recently, this prediction has been accompanied by reports of rising numbers of part-time workers, including contract workers dispatched by temporary employment agencies on a daily or monthly basis. It is true, of course, that the use of part-timers and 'temps', predominantly women, has expanded rapidly in Japan. Indeed, they now make up as much as 20 per cent of the workforce.[18] It is also true that the use of *shukko*, or the seconding of employees to related firms, has increased dramatically.[19]

Both of these practices, however, are serving to *consolidate* rather than dissolve the system of long-term employment—at least for core (male) employees. A two-tiered system has thus evolved in which, as Higuchi suggests, 'the main regular employees can expect to continue to enjoy the long-term employment relations that had always occurred in the past', while 'outside workers and subcontractors' are used increasingly to add flexibility to an otherwise rigid employment system that no longer supplies a developing or rapidly growing economy.[20]

Indeed, tenure rates for employees in manufacturing firms with over 1,000 workers have actually grown over the past 20 years.[21] And recent studies show that Japan's employment system continues to be far more stable than those in other industrialized countries. One such study, published in 1998, indicated that managers in large Japanese manufacturing firms still spend almost twice as long with the same company as their counterparts in the United States and Germany.[22] Indeed, the Japanese government has marvelled at how manufacturing firms in that country have managed to preserve the upward sloping wage gradient and to retain core employees in the midst of hard economic times.[23]

## Regionalization to the Rescue

In 1990, the speculative bubble that had driven Japan's economy for five years finally popped, prompting cost-conscious Japanese manufacturers to run for cover. Many of them ended up in Asia, which received as much as 79 per cent of the cases and 43 per cent of the money associated with their foreign direct investment (FDI).[24] One company alone, Matsushita, built 54 factories in Asia (more than 60 per cent of all its regional facilities) during the 1990s.

Asia turned out to be a safe haven for Japanese manufacturers (and, as we shall see, for other government and labour élites as well)—at least until 1997, when the region descended into a deepening economic crisis. For one thing, they found they could earn twice as much profit, on average, than they earned in North America or Europe, and significantly more than they earned inside Japan. In addition, they could use their new Asian production bases to continue supplying US and European export markets; in some industries, such as electronics, they managed to do so far more cheaply, and with fewer political repercussions, than they could from home. But most importantly, they found they could revive on a regional level the embattled networks that had afforded them positional power in Japan. In the process, they came to enjoy positional power in the region as a whole, dominating key manufacturing industries particularly in Southeast Asia.[25]

By the late 1990s, Asia was an extension of Japan's highly relational political economy. Japanese political and business élites viewed the entire region, including the home base, as one organic unit, or what the Ministry of International Trade and Industry (MITI) began to call 'a soft co-operation network'. Automotive and electronics manufacturers led this initiative, allocating production facilities to different economies in the region based on their technological level and then swapping the fruits of production. Tightly tethered to the parent company in Japan, these regional production networks lured their most trusted suppliers from Japan, replicated fundamental elements of their home-grown employment systems, and relied—to an extent they had not done at home for years—on Japanese government assistance. In a nutshell, regionalization reinforced relationalism at its most desperate moment. Let us examine the evidence across the three nexus of co-operation we considered earlier.

### State and Industry

Facing the prospect of declining jurisdictional authority at home, Japanese bureaucrats have eagerly promoted the expansion and regionalization of Japan-centred production networks. In an interview, an MITI official confided that his agency had seized on this concept as a way of protecting its otherwise threatened *nawabari* (turf). The government has set up offices in Bangkok, Jakarta, Manila, Kuala Lumpur, and other regional nodes to provide what it calls 'regional guidance' to overseas investors, primarily manufacturers, from Japan. In addition, it now offers 'regional guidance' to host governments and private industry representatives in Asia on a broad range of industrial policies—from measures to attract foreign, particularly Japanese, investment to initiatives designed to nurture supporting industries. To that end, MITI has created the so-called 'CLM-WG' (Cambodia-Laos-Myanmar Working Group), which originally was intended to promote policies to encourage the economic development of

those prospective members of ASEAN but now is pursuing a more ambitious goal of achieving an industrial division of labour throughout the region. The Japanese government staffs and finances this program, and uses official development assistance (ODA) to pursue other forms of 'regional guidance'. As of late 1997, the Japan International Co-operation Agency (or JICA, which administers Japanese grants to foreign governments) had 260 Japanese bureaucrats in Indonesia and 160 in Thailand, all working inside those governments as loaned 'experts'.

In Japan, government officials work closely with Japanese investors, particularly small and medium-sized enterprises, providing information on destinations and matching them with possible joint-venture partners. In December 1996, MITI published a 63-page manual outlining forms of assistance the government could provide to small and medium-sized firms thinking about setting up a factory overseas. The agency continued, as of late 1998, to have two ongoing *shingikai* (deliberation councils) to consider ways to promote the regionalization of both production networks and industrial policies.

Citing a credit squeeze for small and medium-sized firms, the Japanese state has given a new mandate to several government-affiliated banks that had been slated for closure, merger, or simply a slow-down in lending activities.[26] Much of the new financing is intended for ventures in new fields, including manufacturing investment in Asia. For example, the Export-Import Bank of Japan used $331 billion in 1996 to subsidize private investment in Asia—double what it lent in 1993 and 28 times what it lent in 1986. Loans for private investment in Asia now account for nearly a quarter of the bank's annual lending activity.

### Business and Business

Japanese manufacturing investment in Asia has come to be called 'convoy-style' (*sendan-gata*) FDI because it typically is carried out by an assembler followed closely by his most trusted suppliers.[27] In the mid-1990s, as many as 32.5 per cent of all firms investing in the ASEAN-4 and as many as 21.3 per cent of those investing in China indicated they had decided to make the move to 'supply parts to an assembly manufacturer', meaning in nearly all cases a Japanese transplant.[28] In effect, the Japanese *keiretsu* system is steadily becoming regionalized. This seems particularly evident in the case of the automobile industry in Southeast Asia, where Japanese assemblers have recreated the core of their home-based supply *keiretsu*. In Thailand, for example, Toyota has a local version of its Kyoho-kai, dominated by the local affiliates of its leading subcontractors in Japan; Nissan has its Thai Takara-kai; Mitsubishi Motors has its Thai Kashiwa-kai; and so on.

This trend serves to foster the kind of polarization in the ranks of Japanese subcontractors described earlier. Indeed, it is the large, first-tier supplier with sufficient capital and technological capacity—not the small subcontractor—that is making the move to Asia. These suppliers are using regionalization strategies to reinforce their already close ties with their parent firms/primary customers, while the latter are being left behind. Consider the case of Nisshin, a Honda brake parts supplier. In the 1990s it reorganized its operations, shutting down its second- and third-tier subcontracting plants and spreading its remaining, higher-tech production capacity among Asian countries in which Honda has established assembly plants. It has, in the process, become an important member of Honda's emerging production network in Asia.[29]

It is undeniable that vertical *keiretsu* between Japanese assemblers and their suppliers in Asia have been more 'open' (less exclusionary) than those in Japan. But this is driven by a simple fact: most Japanese assemblers in Asia are not big enough customers to allow suppliers in the region to achieve economies of scale by relying solely on them. In the mid-1990s, as host-country markets expanded and Japanese assemblers in the region developed global export strategies, this constraint weakened and traditional ties began to re-emerge. Furthermore, Japanese manufacturing affiliates in Asia themselves now operate much like first-tier subcontractors of their parents in Japan. They are

tightly controlled by the home office, which co-ordinates the swapping of parts among various regional operations. As a result, complex Japanese production networks are forming across the region on the basis of long-standing, mutually reinforcing relations, rather than merely price.

## Management and Labour

Although they generally have been slow to transfer some of the more 'democratic' characteristics of their domestic production and employment systems, Japanese multinational enterprises (MNEs) in Asia have moved more quickly to replicate essential features emphasizing 'companyism' and encouraging long-term employment.[30] More importantly, they have incorporated their Asian operations into region-wide personnel systems that allow them to better protect the job security of core employees in Japan.

At a time when employment is contracting at home, Asian affiliates provide a place to park rather than lay off surplus white-collar workers in Japan. Hitachi Ltd, for example, has reduced its domestic employment by more than 10,000 since the early 1990s. It has done so without resorting to lay-offs, relying instead on natural attrition, an early retirement program, and *shukko* (seconding), including what I call 'cross-border *shukko*'. In 1991, the electronics giant had 450 Japanese managers stationed overseas, including Asia; by 1996, that number had nearly doubled to 830. Hitachi's experience is typical: the total number of Japanese employees at private firms in Asia increased almost twofold over that period, reaching 103,688 by 1996.[31]

Japanese MNEs, heavily criticized by host government officials for employing relatively large numbers of Japanese staff at their affiliates in Asia, have for years made promises to 'localize' their management. But as long as the domestic economy remains sour, they may find it difficult to fulfil this pledge. Indeed, in a recent survey, about 60 per cent of Japanese affiliates in Thailand, Malaysia, and Singapore indicated that they expected to maintain or increase their Japanese staff in the coming years.[32] In interviews, Japanese officials concede that the parent company in Japan uses its Asian affiliates as a kind of buffer, a temporary holding pen for employees made redundant by hard times in Japan.

## Implications

The regionalization of Japanese production and administrative networks is extending the shelf life of a domestic political economic system of relationalism that faces enormous pressure from the forces of globalization. In the process, it is forestalling structural change that would invigorate the Japanese economy by loosening ties that did, one must concede, serve a productive function when that economy was still developing but that now, when that economy has matured, tend to foster collusion, rigidity, and exclusivity. In lieu of structural change, distributional change is shifting the increasing costs of relationalism onto outsiders (non-élites)—those without positional power in the Japanese political economy, such as the owners and employees of small manufacturing firms.

This sector is bearing a disproportionate share of the burden of Japan's post-bubble recession. Suppliers, squeezed ferociously by major assemblers, have been prodded to slash their prices nearly every year during the 1990s. Many, particularly the smaller second- to fourth-tier subcontractors, have simply gone bankrupt. At the same time, relationalism is blocking the growth of new entrepeneurs in their place. Japan still lacks a forward-looking venture capital market that could feed small, unknown, and thus high-risk enterprises in new industries such as software and biotechnology. Increasingly, new enterprises are created by existing parent firms seeking, among other things, to reduce skyrocketing payroll expenses without laying off core employees. In the early postwar period, 47.3 per cent of start-up enterprises in Japan were created by truly independent entrepreneurs; in the 1990s, only 8.7 per cent were.[33]

As they regionalize their production and administrative networks, then, Japanese élites wield a double-edged sword. With one blade, they are cutting themselves slack, preserving a system of relationalism that affords them positional power in Japan and now, increasingly, in Asia as well. With the other blade, however, they weaken the Japanese economy and thus jeopardize their own long-run interests and that of the region as a whole.

## Notes

1   Ken'ichi Ohmae, *The Borderless World: Power and Strategy in the Interlinked Economy* (New York: Harper Perennial, 1991), x.

2   See Sven Steinmo, Kathleen Thelen, and Frank Longstreth, eds, *Structuring Politics: Historical Institutionalism in Comparative Analysis* (Cambridge: Cambridge University Press, 1992).

3   See, for example, Steven K. Vogel, *Freer Markets, More Rules: Regulatory Reform in Advanced Industrial Countries* (Ithaca, NY: Cornell University Press, 1996).

4   See, for example, Robert Bates, *Markets and States in Tropical Africa: The Political Basis of Agricultural Policies* (Berkeley: University of California Press, 1981).

5   Frances McCall Rosenbluth and J. Mark Ramseyer, *Japan's Political Marketplace* (Cambridge, Mass.: Harvard University Press, 1993).

6   Mark Granovetter, 'Economic Action and Social Structure: The Problem of Embeddedness', *American Journal of Sociology* 19, 3 (Nov. 1985).

7   Unless defined otherwise, Asia here means China, the four Asian NIEs (the newly industrializing economies of South Korea, Taiwan, Singapore, and Hong Kong), and the ASEAN-4 (the four core members of the Association of Southeast Asian Nations: Thailand, Indonesia, Malaysia, and the Philippines).

8   See Granovetter, 'Economic Action and Social Structure'.

9   Neoclassical economic theory assumes that all firms, in developing as well as developed economies, eventually face increasing long-run average costs and thus declining returns. This is because the marginal gain of adding a new worker or an additional machine will, it is

assumed, bump into critical resource constraints.

10 David Knoke, *Political Networks: The Structural Perspective* (Cambridge: Cambridge University Press, 1990), 9.

11 Richard M. Emerson, 'Power-dependence Relations', *American Sociological Review* 27 (1962): 31–41.

12 Peter V. Marsden, 'Restricted Access in Networks and Models of Power', *American Journal of Sociology* 88 (1983): 714.

13 See Ulrike Schaede, 'The "Old Boy Network" and Government-Business Relationships in Japan', *Journal of Japanese Studies* 21, 2 (Summer 1995): 293–317.

14 Ministry of International Trade and Industry (MITI), *Heisei Kyunenban: Chusho kigyo hakusho* (White Paper on Small and Medium-Sized Enterprises) (Tokyo, 1997), 149.

15 See MITI, *Heisei hachi-nen: Chusho kigyo hakusho* (White Paper on Small and Medium-Sized Enterprises) (Tokyo, 1996), 199–203. Also see Chusho kigyo kinyu koko, 'Jidosha, kadenkigyo ni miru shitauke bungyo kozo no henka: kozo hendo ni tsuyoi shitauke kigyo no shutsugen', *Chushokoko repoto* no. 97–2 (May 1997): 16–18.

16 See D.H. Whittaker, *Small Firms in the Japanese Economy* (Cambridge: Cambridge University Press, 1997), 103.

17 See, for example, Shoko Chukin, 'Chusho kikai kinzoku kogyo bungyo kozo jittai chosa hokukusho: Dai-go kai' (Fifth Survey Report on the Division of Labour Among Small and Medium-Sized Machinery and Metalworking Industries), 1995, 22–3; MITI, *Heisei hachi-nen*, 188–9.

18 Management and Co-ordination Agency, *Shugyo kozo kihon chosa* (Employment Status Survey), various years.

19 Hiroki Sato, 'Keeping Employees Employed: Shukko and Tenseki Job Transfers—Formation of a Labour Market within Corporate Groups', *Japan Labour Bulletin*, 1 Dec. 1996.

20 Yoshio Higuchi, 'Trends in Japanese Labour Markets', in Mari Sako and Hiroki Sato, *Japanese Labour and Management in Transition: Diversity,* *Flexibility and Participation* (London: Routledge, 1997), 48–9.

21 Ministry of Labour, *Chingin Kozo Kiban Tokei Chosa* (Basic Survey of the Wage Structure), various years. Okazaki confirms these results in her own survey work. See Keiko Okazaki, 'A Measurement of the Japanese Lifetime Employment System', *Keio Business Review* 33 (1996): 105–15.

22 Takao Kato, 'Preliminary Findings on the Nature and Scope of Career Development of Managers in Japan, the U.S., and Germany: Evidence from a Cross-National Survey', in Japan Institute of Labour, *Kokusai Hikaku: Daisotsu Howaitokaraa no Jinsai Kaihatsu/koyo Shistemu: Nichi, Bei, Doku no Daikigyo* (Personnel Development and Employment Systems for White-Collar College Graduates: An International Comparison of Large Firms in Japan, the U.S., and Germany) (Tokyo: JIL, 1998).

23 Economic Planning Agency, *Economic Survey of Japan, 1995–96*, 329.

24 Ministry of Finance data for 1995. Small and medium-sized firms drove this trend, concentrating 92 per cent of their overall FDI in Asia that year.

25 Japanese affiliates in Thailand and Indonesia, for example, control more than 90 per cent of local production in the automobile industry. Consequently, they also dominate auto parts manufacturing, owning 46 of the 53 major joint ventures in Indonesia.

26 MITI oversees three banks for small and medium-sized firms. In addition, the Ministry of Finance oversees the Japan Development Bank and the Export-Import Bank.

27 Fumihiko Adachi, 'Kyuseicho Suru Ajia to Nihon Chusho Kigyo' (A Rapidly Growing Asia and Japanese Small and Medium-Sized Firms), in Nobuharu Tatsumi and Yoshio Sato, eds, *Shinchushokigyo-ron wo manabu* (Towards A New Analysis of Small and Medium-Sized Firms) (Tokyo: Yuhikaku, 1996), 182.

28 Export-Import Bank of Japan, 1995 survey. See also MITI, *Heisei Kyunenban*, 204, which shows the results of its own survey of small and medium-sized enterprises. The reason most often

mentioned for investing in the ASEAN-4 was 'to follow one's parent firm, or main customer'.

29  Author interviews.

30  See, for example, Mitchell W. Sedgwick, 'Does Japanese Management Travel in Asia? Managerial Technology Transfer at Japanese Multinationals in Thailand', MITI Japan Project Working Paper 96–04, 1996; S. Yamashita, J. Takeuchi, N. Kawabe, and S. Takehana, 'ASEAN shokoku ni okeru nihonteki keiei to gijutsu iten ni kansuru keieisha no ishiki chosa' (Survey of Japanese Managers on Japanese-style Management and Technology Transfer to ASEAN Countries), *Hiroshima Economic Studies* (1989): 10.

31  Ministry of Foreign Affairs, *Kaigai Zairyu Hojinsu Chosa Tokei*, various years.

32  Mamoru Kitajima, 'ASEAN shokoku no kogyo-ka to nihon-gata shisutemu no item' (Industrialization in ASEAN Countries and the Transfer of the Japanese System), an unpublished report by the Kikai Shinko Kyokai Keizai Kenyujo (Economic Research Institute of the Association for the Promotion of Machine Industries).

33  MITI, *Heisei Kyunenban*, 320.

## Suggested Readings

Ernst, Dieter. 'Partners for the China Circle? The Asian Production Networks of Japanese Electronic Firms', BRIE Working Paper 91, Jan. 1997. (BRIE Web page)

Guyton, Lynne E. 'Japanese Investments and Technology Transfer to Malaysia', in John Borrego, Alejandro Alvarez Bejar, and Jomo K.S., eds, *Capital, the State and Late Industrialization: Comparative Perspectives on the Pacific Rim*. Boulder, Colo.: Westview Press, 1996.

Hatch, Walter, and Kozo Yamamura. *Asia in Japan's Embrace: Building a Regional Production Alliance*. Cambridge: Cambridge University Press, 1996.

Katz, Richard. *Japan: The System that Soured*. Armonk, NY: M.E. Sharpe, 1998.

Katzenstein, Peter, and Takashi Shiraishi. *Network Power: Japan and Asia*. Ithaca, NY: Cornell University Press, 1997.

Knoke, David. *Political Networks: The Structural Perspective*. Cambridge: Cambridge University Press, 1990.

Yasusuke, Murakami. *An Anti-Classical Political Economic Analysis: A Vision for the Next Century*. Stanford, Calif.: Stanford University Press, 1996.

## Web Sites

Berkeley Roundtable on the International Economy:
http://brie.berkeley.edu/BRIE

Government of Japan, Ministry of International Trade and Industry:
http://www.miti.go.jp/index-e.html

Massachusetts Institute of Technology, MIT Japan Program:
http://www-japan.mit.edu/mitjapanprogram

Japan Information Access Project:
http://www.nmjc.org/jiap/text.html

## Chapter 33

# China: Geopolitics and the Political Economy of Hesitant Integration

Shaun Breslin

When analysing China's global role and the impact of globalization on China, we should remember that it is still a relatively new international actor. While the Chinese economy was never totally closed,[1] international economic relations during the Maoist period were strictly limited. Although Deng Xiaoping's assumption of de facto control of the Chinese Communist Party (CCP) in 1978 marked the start of the reform process, it was not until 1984 that the Chinese economy began to engage with the global economy in a meaningful way. Even then, international economic contacts were geographically focused on four Special Economic Zones,[2] and it was only at the end of the 1980s that most areas of China were free to seek foreign investment and to engage with the global economy.

Economic reform was never intended to reduce the CCP's grip on power. On the contrary, it was an attempt to strengthen party rule by creating a new basis of legitimacy. With the population thoroughly disenchanted with political campaigns and ideological indoctrination, the post-Mao leadership looked to economic success as a means of regaining popular support, or at least, of minimizing opposition to one-party rule. The logic, pace, and scope of reform were also influenced by external affairs. The end of the Cold War reduced military tensions and allowed the radical Maoist denunciation of all things capitalist to slide into obscurity, while the collapse of Communist control in the Soviet Union and Eastern Europe provided a concrete example of the potential dangers of reforming a socialist system.

Nevertheless, domestic political issues have been the major determinants of the trajectory of China's reform experience in general and China's relationship with the global economy in particular. One-party rule does not mean that political conflict and popular pressures are irrelevant in policy-making—they just take on a different form. The battle lines may have changed over the years, but understanding the nature of inter-élite conflict remains the key to understanding Chinese leaders' perceptions of China's position in the global economy. Perhaps most important of all, understanding the importance of employment creation for Chinese leaders' perceptions of the strength of their own grip on power is the key to understanding the political constraints on economic reform.

## Re-engaging the Global Economy

Given the lateness of China's entry into the global economy, the speed at which it has developed a global economic profile and impact has been remarkable. Two decades of high growth have been accompanied by, and in no small part achieved by, a huge expansion in trade (see Tables 1 and 2). And if this were not enough in itself to raise international attention, the opening of the world's largest population to the international economy has attracted the interest of many foreign businessmen. Indeed, the sheer size of the Chinese population does much to increase China's importance for the global economy. Over one billion people do not have to generate much national product per capita for China to have one of the biggest gross national products in the world.

The dominant vision of China in the West is that of a vibrant, developing, and modern society that has grasped capitalism and has made the most

## Table 1: The Growth of Chinese Trade, 1978–1997 (US$ billions)

| Year | Exports | | Imports | | Total | | Deficit/Surplus | |
|------|---------|------|---------|------|---------|------|---------|------|
| | Nominal | Real | Nominal | Real | Nominal | Real | Nominal | Real |
| 1978 | 9.8 | 23.1 | 10.9 | 25.7 | 20.7 | 48.9 | −1.1 | −2.6 |
| 1979 | 13.7 | 29.0 | 15.7 | 33.3 | 29.4 | 62.3 | −2.0 | −4.3 |
| 1980 | 18.1 | 33.8 | 19.5 | 36.4 | 37.6 | 70.3 | −1.4 | −2.6 |
| 1981 | 21.5 | 36.4 | 21.6 | 36.6 | 43.1 | 73.0 | −0.1 | −0.2 |
| 1982 | 21.9 | 34.9 | 18.9 | 30.2 | 40.8 | 65.1 | +3.0 | +4.7 |
| 1983 | 22.1 | 34.2 | 21.3 | 32.9 | 43.4 | 67.1 | +0.8 | +1.3 |
| 1984 | 24.8 | 36.8 | 25.9 | 38.4 | 54.5 | 80.8 | −1.1 | −1.6 |
| 1985 | 27.3 | 39.1 | 42.5 | 60.8 | 69.8 | 99.9 | −15.2 | −21.7 |
| 1986 | 31.4 | 44.1 | 43.3 | 60.8 | 74.7 | 104.9 | −11.9 | −16.7 |
| 1987 | 39.5 | 53.4 | 43.2 | 58.6 | 82.7 | 112.2 | −3.7 | −8.9 |
| 1988 | 47.5 | 61.8 | 55.3 | 72.0 | 102.8 | 133.8 | −7.8 | −10.2 |
| 1989 | 52.5 | 65.2 | 59.1 | 73.4 | 111.7 | 138.8 | −6.6 | −8.2 |
| 1990 | 64.5 | 76.0 | 54.5 | 64.2 | 119.0 | 147.8 | +10.1 | +11.8 |
| 1991 | 71.9 | 81.3 | 63.8 | 72.2 | 135.7 | 153.5 | +8.1 | +9.1 |
| 1992 | 84.9 | 93.2 | 80.6 | 88.5 | 165.5 | 181.7 | +4.4 | +4.7 |
| 1994 | 91.7 | 98.1 | 104.0 | 111.2 | 195.7 | 209.3 | −12.2 | −13.1 |
| 1994 | 121.0 | 125.8 | 115.6 | 120.2 | 236.6 | 245.9 | +5.4 | +5.6 |
| 1995 | 148.8 | 150.9 | 132.1 | 134.0 | 280.9 | 284.9 | +16.7 | +16.9 |
| 1996 | 151.1 | 151.1 | 138.8 | 138.8 | 289.9 | 289.9 | +12.2 | +12.2 |

Nominal = figures for that year.
Real = adjusted to common 1996US$.

SOURCES: *Zhongguo Tongni Nianjian (China Statistical Yearbook)* (Beijing: China Statistical Information and Consultancy Service Centre, various years); *Direction of Trade Statistics Yearbook* (Washington: International Monetary Fund, various years).

of integration with the global economy. We see images of the dramatic transformation of cities like Beijing and Shanghai; the gradual merging of Hong Kong and southern China into a new megalopolis; the growth of Chinese consumerism. Yet despite the growth rates, China remains a poor developing state still grappling with the problems of transforming the old state-planned economy.[3] For every urban dweller, at least another three live in the countryside. Notwithstanding the fact that most in the countryside are much wealthier than they were before the reform process started, one does not have to travel too far out of Beijing to witness the growing gap between urban and rural dwellers in China, indeed, to witness not just relative but absolute

poverty. Furthermore, reform and liberalization have hurt the provision of health, education, and welfare services as the collective has given way to the individual.[4] The drive for efficiency has driven many off the land, with perhaps as many as 140 million rural labourers without a job for most of the year,[5] many flocking to the cities as rural unemployment becomes an urban problem.

In urban China, too, there are many examples of the economic problems that remain to be overcome. The state-planned economy created thousands of large state-owned enterprises (SOEs) that became the backbone of the socialist economy. With SOEs so inefficient and unproductive, they could not compete (for the time being at least) and

## Table 2: Real Growth in Chinese Trade, 1978–1996

| Period | Category | % Growth Rate | Average Annual % Growth Rate |
|--------|----------|---------------|------------------------------|
| 1978-96 | Exports | 554.1 | 11.37 |
| 1978–96 | Imports | 440.1 | 11.02 |
| 1978–96 | Total Trade | 492.8 | 10.80 |
| 1987–96 | Exports | 183.0 | 14.00 |
| 1987–96 | Imports | 136.9 | 9.25 |
| 1987–96 | Total Trade | 158.4 | 10.89 |
| 1992–6 | Exports | 62.1 | 13.64 |
| 1992–6 | Imports | 56.8 | 14.07 |
| 1992–6 | Total Trade | 59.5 | 13.72 |

NOTE: Prices adjusted 1996 US$.

SOURCES: *Zhongguo Tongji Nianjian (China Statistical Yearbook)* (Beijing: China Statistical Information and Consultancy Service Centre, various years); *Director of Trade Statistics Yearbook* (Washington: International Monetary Fund, various years).

so had to be protected. In addition to their economic function, these SOEs undertook important social functions, providing health, education, and welfare for employees and the families of employees. But in the new world of post-socialist China, these SOEs have become a massive economic burden on the Chinese state.

The decision to re-engage with the global economy was in large part inspired by the problems of reforming the residual socialist economy—it was seen as a means of jump-starting development in China. Rather than spend years developing finance and technology through domestic internal development, it was deemed quicker to allow the global economy to fill the gap and bring China to what many in China believe to be its true and rightful position as a leading world power. But while emotional or ideological perceptions of China's place in the world should not be discounted (and will be discussed in more detail below), the bottom line for perhaps all economic policy is maintaining employment, particularly in the urban sectors, a bottom line drawn by fear of social instability that would result from large-scale urban unemployment.

The Chinese leadership did not resist globalization—they embraced it and welcomed it to China. This warm reception was even warmer among local leaders, particularly in southern and coastal China, who saw international contacts as the best way of gaining access to investment capital and new jobs. Indeed, the importance and role of local governments as agents of China's global economic role cannot be overstated.

But the Chinese leadership did resist those elements of globalization deemed dangerous to China's economic interests and that could jeopardize employment and therefore social stability. The Chinese approach was to accept and encourage globalization where it benefits China and resist it where it does not. In their attempt to attain this objective (an objective perhaps shared by state élites across the globe), the Chinese authorities developed a three-pronged policy towards the global economy. First, they supported and promoted export-oriented industries and attracted those foreign interests looking to locate export industries in China. Second, they attracted foreign interests that could provide technology, expertise, goods, and services that the Chinese economy was lacking. Third, they provided protection from market forces and international competition to those enterprises and economic sectors that were unable to compete.

In addition to sheltering domestic producers from competition, the Chinese authorities also decided to maintain a relatively closed financial system, and in particular to minimize the importance of international capital flows. The development of stock markets in Shanghai and Shenzhen provides a good example here. While over 700 companies are quoted on the A-share list of the markets, which only Chinese citizens are permitted to trade in, a mere 101 are quoted on the B-list, which is open to international traders. Stock markets might appear at first sight to be characteristic of liberalization and capitalism, but the actual working of the markets is a good example of how liberalization and capitalism in China have been regulated, restricted, and only partially integrated with the wider global economy.

In pursuing a relatively protectionist re-engagement with the global economy, China has been aided by its position as a late developer—perhaps we should say an even later developer. Chinese leaders can point to the gradual liberalization of the Chinese economy as a sign to the international community of things to come, and that real progress is being made to fit into the international order. But what is important here is that the Chinese economy is less open and more protected than those of its major trading partners. It is also less open and more protected than many of those now crisis-ridden competitor states, particularly in Southeast Asia, that are searching for lucrative export markets in Japan, North America, and Europe as an engine of growth.

## Selected Integration

### Promoting Exports

The rapid expansion of Chinese exports is closely related to the growth of foreign investment in China. Since 1993, China has been the largest recipient of foreign direct investment in the developing world, the vast majority of it from the rest of Asia. It is notable that economic flows have flourished despite considerable political and diplomatic friction. For example, trade with South Korea developed in the 1980s despite the fact that Beijing did not recognize the regime in Seoul, regarding Communist North Korea as the sole legitimate government on the Korean peninsula. The growing importance of South Korea as a trade and investment partner did much to pave the way for the establishment of full and formal diplomatic relations in 1992. Historical Cold War antagonisms were put aside for the sake of economic gain.

Economic relations with Taiwan have also increased, despite the fact that the Beijing and Taipei governments are officially rival regimes that both claim authority over all of China. Political problems clearly obstruct the emergence of 'normal' economic relations, but the expansion of cross-strait ties says much about the flexibility and pragmatism on both sides of the Formosa Strait when it comes to generating growth. It also highlights the increasing role of external non-state actors, particularly the overseas Chinese investment community, and domestic local-state actors in the evolution of China's external economic relations.

In overcoming these political obstacles, China has been aided by the special role of Hong Kong in China's international economic relations. Where direct bilateral contracts are not possible, then routing trade and investment through Hong Kong can overcome political barriers. Hong Kong has become the hub of a network of relationships linking China (and southern China in particular) to the global economy. And it is not just Taiwanese capital that uses Hong Kong as an entry point to China. For example, the proportion of Chinese exports to Hong Kong that are re-exported to the United States increased from 4.86 per cent in 1979 to 41.6 per cent in 1994, while just over half of all Hong Kong exports to China in 1994 were goods of US origin.[6]

Encouraging inward investment has thus become an important tool in promoting export-led industrialization and growth. The Chinese government has also deployed a number of other policies and mechanisms to promote Chinese trade in the recent era, and these have had repercussions for economies in Asia. Not least among these policies was a competitive currency devaluation in 1994. The Chinese currency, the Yuan or renminbi (RMB), is not fully convertible on international markets, and exchange rates remain under central government management and control. However, in the early 1990s, a market rate of sorts appeared as the government relaxed regulations on currency exchanges. To facilitate increased international economic contacts, a number of 'swap shops' were established[7] where individuals could exchange the RMB for foreign currency.[8] Although the official exchange rate at the time was RMB5.7 to the dollar, the swap-shop rate was influenced by supply and demand, and was closer to RMB9 to the dollar.

Faced with this disparity and a record trade deficit in 1993, the government essentially moved to the swap-shop rate in 1994, with the new exchange rate of RMB8.7 to the dollar. On the face of it, this represented a 50 per cent devaluation. However, in reality, most Chinese traders were already using the swap-shop rates in their overseas activities, meaning that the real impact on the price of Chinese exports was variable and below the 50 per cent headline figure. Never the less, the devaluation did increase the relative competitiveness of Chinese exports—notably, relative to the cost of exports from other states in Southeast Asia following export-led growth strategies. While difficult to quantify, this strategic devaluation at least contributed to the financial crises that beset Southeast Asia in 1997—crises that in some respects resulted in belated and drastic currency realignment in response to China's 1994 reforms.

Furthermore, there are other forms of support for Chinese exporters. Partial price reform in China obscures hidden state subsidies for the state sector and even for private enterprises with close links to the state. The price of land, labour, and key industrial inputs such as energy and steel are not solely or in some cases primarily set by market forces. While market forces are an increasingly important presence in the Chinese economy, the state sets prices much lower than the prevailing market price,

and the retention of state control entails a hidden subsidy to favoured producers.[9]

### Protecting the Domestic Market

This state support for exporters is accompanied by significant protection from global competition, with partial economic reform playing an important role. For example, incomplete currency convertibility restricts access to foreign currency to either the chosen few or those operating within the designated production zones—and it also means that converting and repatriating profits is difficult if not impossible for foreign firms. Access to the Chinese market is also restricted by the retention of import tariffs and quotas. Not surprisingly, the biggest restrictions here are on iron and steel, textile yarns, and machinery—the critical sectors where inefficient domestic producers in the state sector are most vulnerable to international competition and where exports from the state sector are strongest.

Chinese import tariffs remain among the highest in the world. Average tariff rates have been falling in response to international pressure. From a high point of 43 per cent in 1992, they have been progressively lowered to around 17 per cent, with a promise for further reductions to 15 per cent by the year 2000. However, foreign exporters argue that the real tariff rate is nearer 40 per cent, as value-added tax is always added to imports, while domestic producers are typically granted exemptions by local authorities.

Those foreign companies that try to gain access to the Chinese market by locating their operations in China also find themselves subject to different charges and rules of the game than domestic producers in the same sector. For example, while Chinese producers, particularly in the state sector, will benefit from cheaper state-set prices for key inputs, foreign companies usually have to pay the higher market rate for the same commodities. Chinese enterprises are also supported through massive subsidies, which often take the form of loans from government or the banking system that will never be repaid. For example, the World Bank calculates that such non-performing loans account for 20 per cent of the assests of Chinese banks,[10] and the Chinese State Statistical Bureau announced that unpaid loans to various levels of government accounted for 10 per cent of Chinese GNP in 1995.[11]

Finally, foreign actors claim that two other issues create an uneven playing field. The first is the wide-scale infringement of intellectual and property rights in China, where the production of counterfeit and fake products is commonplace. The second is the lack of transparency in China's policy-making process. For example, the state news agency, Xinhua, has an official monopoly in the dissemination of economic information and ensures that this information serves the interests of the Chinese state rather than the interests of the international community.

## Pressures to Liberalize

The Chinese approach to controlling integration with the global economy has, on the face of it, been a great success. Wealth and jobs have been created through the promotion of exporting industries; new and better-quality consumer goods are readily available in most of China; and the inefficient SOEs have largely stayed in business providing jobs and welfare facilities in the cities.

But the policy of protecting domestic producers and supporting exporters has not been cost-free, and the long-term viability of the policy became increasingly questioned in the second half of the 1990s, with pressures to liberalize coming from both internal and external sources. Yet, while the economic logic of liberalization is largely accepted by the current Chinese leadership, domestic political pressures to resist further liberalization remain an important consideration for China's leaders.

### *To Liberalize or Conserve?*
### *The Domestic Debate*

When the Chinese first embarked on the process of reintegration, considerable domestic opposition and scepticism existed. For some, the argument was quite straightforward—China was meant to be a socialist state laying the foundations for the creation of a classless communist society. Using capitalist forms and co-operating with the capitalist global economy were simply ideologically wrong. Others accepted the need to try to sponsor economic growth by the eclectic and limited use of capitalist forms, but were concerned over the potential political and social side-effects. They feared that re-engagement with the global economy would lead to 'spiritual pollution' and a growth of interest in Western political ideas that could loosen the party's grip on power. These sceptical leaders could invoke the strong popular nationalist sentiments against former colonialist powers that the party had harnessed to help bring it to power during the revolution.

The intensity of the opposition to reintegration was one of the reasons why initial international economic contacts were limited to the Special Economic Zones (SEZs), and then only gradually extended to other parts of the country. Never the less, resistance to China's participation in the global economy was not totally silenced. Over the years, more conservative elements used any signs of economic downturn or political unrest to reassert their misgivings and reservations. The reform process in the 1980s was punctuated by a number of campaigns to combat the unwanted growth of Western political ideas that, it was argued, were an inevitable consequence of embracing Western economic ideas. The most notable case here was the dismissal of party leader Zhao Ziyang in the wake of the suppression of the 1989 Tiananmen Square demonstrations. And Zhao was the second head of the party to lose his position in less than three years. Hu Yaobang had also been dismissed after student demonstrations calling for more democracy in 1986 were taken as a signal of the spiritual pollution that more conservative leaders had warned would inevitably follow economic reform.[12]

But despite these victories for the resisters, the conservatives had essentially lost the argument by the middle of the 1990s. This is partly a consequence of the passage of time. The old guard of leaders who fought over liberalization in the 1980s had been replaced by a younger generation of leaders[13] with different backgrounds, experiences, and attitudes. This generational and attitudinal shift is, if anything, more apparent at lower levels of the administrative hierarchy in China. Young Chinese scholars have been flocking abroad to be educated in Western ways and methods. These younger, better-educated, and often foreign-educated (or at least foreign-influenced) generations may not yet hold the top positions in China, but they are influencing policy and polity, and their influence is likely only to increase with the passage of time and the passing of the old guard.

A second major reason for the decline in opposition to integration with the global economy was the success of early experiments in the SEZs. It was difficult for sceptics to oppose the process because it was seen to be generating rapid growth. Once the ideological question of whether it benefited socialism was discounted, then opposing a successful policy became increasingly difficult.

The ideological conundrum was resolved by emphasizing the low level of development in China. China was in the 'primary stage of socialism'. It had a poor, backward, underdeveloped, and primarily agrarian economy. The primary task of the CCP was to strengthen and build that economy to the point, at some vague and distant time in the future, where the creation of a communist society was feasible. The main goal in the short and medium term was 'expanding the productive forces', and anything that helped expand the economy was therefore compatible with the long-term goal of building communism.[14] This approach conveniently meant that using capitalist mechanisms and collaborating with international capital were in keeping with socialism and building communism—though whether anybody either inside the party or without really thought that this was the case is another question altogether.

Furthermore, through the decentralization of power during the 1980s, the locus of economic decision-making power was shifted from the central authorities to local leaders. Inspired by the success of open areas, local leaders lobbied to be allowed the same privileges and access to the global market. Once these privileges were gained, they established their own economic projects and objectives—objectives that at times ran counter to official government policy.[15]

With the ideological debate more or less dead, the focus of attention has moved to the viability of maintaining the existing structure and keeping SOEs out of competition. More liberal Chinese economists, such as Zhou Shulian, point to the distorting impact on the allocation of resources that results from maintaining production in SOEs irrespective of their efficiency.[16] On one level, the 'top-slicing' of scarce raw material resources, and particularly energy, to the state sector has denied resources to more efficient producers. On another, the quality and reliability of supplies from the state sector are so low that the World Bank estimates that 17 per cent of China's GDP consists of 'unsaleable' SOE-manufactured goods.[17] A second, more pressing concern is that many SOEs are losing money hand over fist. Maintaining production in the state sector was initially achieved by running budgetary deficits. More recently, deficits have been largely replaced by the government and bank loans that the lenders know will never be repaid.

In 1992 the state sector accounted for 51.5 per cent of total manufacturing production, but this figure had fallen to 28.5 per cent by 1996. Despite this falling market share, the state sector still accounted for 58.6 per cent of total assets in manufacturing and 65.2 per cent of employment. While much of the employment in the state sector is essentially a hidden form of state provision of social welfare, the productivity of the state sector is still very low.

### External Pressures to Reform

These internal pressures for liberalization have been compounded by external criticism of China's trade regime. Given the residual and sizeable barriers to penetrating the Chinese market, it was perhaps inevitable that China would face international pressure to create a more level playing field for external actors. The fact that China runs large trade surpluses with the United States, Europe, and Japan has only served to bring the question of China's trade regime into even sharper focus (see Tables 3–5).[18]

## Table 3: China's Major Trade Partners, 1978–1996

| Country/Region | 1978 | 1981 | 1984 | 1987 | 1990 | 1993 | 1996 |
|---|---|---|---|---|---|---|---|
| US | 641 (1,699) | 2,551 (7,936) | 3,432 (5,693) | 4,111 (6,562) | 6,259 (97,763) | 18,079 (11,323) | 26,731 (16,179) |
| Canada | 224 (1,352) | 308 (1,985) | 383 (1,576) | 555 (1,904) | 522 (1,748) | 1,275 (1,459) | 1,616 (2,559) |
| Australia | 278 (1,685) | 295 (947) | 323 (1,331) | 404 (1,798) | 551 (1,603) | 1,139 (2,081) | 1,637 (3,438) |
| France | 419 (582) | 483 (669) | 343 (530) | 592 (1,220) | 770 (1,972) | 1,377 (1,752) | 1,908 (2,240) |
| Germany | 778 (2,427) | 1,415 (2,266) | 1,133 (1,868) | 1,659 (4,246) | 2,340 (3,415) | 4,229 (6,449) | 5,852 (7,325) |
| Italy | 391 (450) | 437 (583) | 449 (642) | 773 (1,693) | 1,029 (1,280) | 1,391 (2,916) | 1,838 (3,247) |
| UK | 872 (697) | 700 (397) | 488 (754) | 772 (1,221) | 859 (1,629) | 2,053 (1,772) | 3,199 (1,892) |
| Japan | 4,051 (7,316) | 8,046 (10,480) | 7,648 (11,954) | 8,673 (13,687) | 10,848 (9,018) | 16,750 (24,817) | 30,888 (29,190) |
| Hong Kong | 5,969 (177) | 8,920 (2,095) | 9,771 (4,199) | 18,676 (11,448) | 31,994 (17,155) | 23,500 (11,183) | 32,904 (7,839) |
| South Korea | na | na | na | na | 510 (278) | 3,046 (5,708) | 7,527 (12,484) |
| Malaysia | 384 (262) | 324 (203) | 291 (286) | 346 (410) | 436 (1,003) | 750 (1,154) | 1,374 (2,246) |
| Singapore | 584 (108) | 1,115 (191) | 1,794 (209) | 1,795 (838) | 2,375 (1,000) | 2,391 (2,848) | 3,753 (3,613) |
| Thailand | 167 (174) | 386 (261) | 372 (279) | 408 (549) | 1,006 (455) | 799 (640) | 1,259 (1,890) |
| Taiwan | na | na | na | na | 377 (2,655) | 2,388 (13,774) | 2,804 (16,186) |
| Africa | 271 (259) | 1,147 (385) | 806 (460) | 1,669 (209) | 1,399 (420) | 1,281 (788) | 2,077 (1,405) |
| Middle East | 801 (485) | 3,593 (376) | 3,613 (415) | 3,585 (379) | 1,684 (562) | 2,721 (1,785) | 3,484 (3,062) |

NOTES: Values in millions of US$ adjusted to common 1996 US$.
First figure represents Chinese exports to; figure in parentheses is imports from.

SOURCES: *Zhongguo Tongji Nianjian (China Statistical Yearbook)* [Beijing: China Statistical Information and Consultancy Service Centre, various years]; *Direction of Trade Statistics Yearbook* [Washington: International Monetary Fund, various years].

## Table 4: Changing Distribution of Chinese Trade, 1978–1996

| Country/Region | Exports to | | | | | Imports From | | | | |
|---|---|---|---|---|---|---|---|---|---|---|
| | 1978 | 1984 | 1989 | 1993 | 1996 | 1978 | 1984 | 1989 | 1993 | 1996 |
| US | 2.8 | 9.3 | 8.34 | 18.5 | 17.7 | 6.5 | 14.8 | 13.2 | 10.3 | 11.7 |
| Canada | 1.0 | 1.0 | 0.8 | 1.3 | 1.1 | 5.1 | 4.1 | 1.8 | 1.3 | 1.8 |
| Australia | 1.2 | 0.9 | 0.8 | 1.2 | 1.1 | 6.4 | 3.5 | 2.5 | 1.9 | 2.5 |
| France | 1.9 | 0.9 | 1.0 | 1.4 | 1.3 | 2.2 | 1.4 | 2.4 | 1.6 | 2.5 |
| Germany | 3.5 | 3.1 | 3.0 | 4.3 | 3.9 | 9.3 | 4.9 | 5.7 | 5.9 | 5.3 |
| Italy | 1.7 | 1.2 | 1.4 | 1.4 | 1.2 | 1.2 | 1.7 | 3.1 | 2.6 | 2.3 |
| UK | 3.9 | 1.3 | 1.2 | 2.1 | 2.1 | 2.7 | 2.0 | 1.8 | 1.6 | 1.4 |
| Japan | 18.0 | 20.8 | 15.9 | 17.2 | 20.4 | 27.9 | 31.0 | 17.8 | 22.5 | 21.0 |
| Hong Kong | 26.5 | 26.5 | 41.4 | 24.1 | 21.8 | 0.7 | 10.9 | 21.2 | 10.1 | 5.7 |
| South Korea | na | na | na | 3.1 | 4.5 | na | na | na | 5.2 | 9.0 |
| Malaysia | 1.6 | 0.8 | 0.7 | 0.8 | 0.9 | 1.0 | 0.7 | 1.2 | 1.0 | 1.6 |
| Singapore | 2.6 | 4.9 | 3.2 | 2.5 | 2.5 | 0.4 | 0.5 | 2.5 | 2.6 | 2.6 |
| Thailand | 0.7 | 1.0 | 0.9 | 0.8 | 0.8 | 0.7 | 0.7 | 1.3 | 0.6 | 1.4 |
| Taiwan | na | na | na | 1.6 | 1.9 | na | na | na | 12.6 | 11.7 |
| Africa | 1.2 | 2.2 | 1.1 | 1.3 | 1.4 | 1.0 | 1.2 | 0.7 | 0.7 | 1.0 |
| Middle East | 3.6 | 9.8 | 2.7 | 2.8 | 2.3 | 1.9 | 1.1 | 1.0 | 1.6 | 2.2 |

1978 = status quo ante of pre-reform era.
1984 = open-door policy effectively takes off.
1989 = anti-inflationary policy and Tiananmen incident.
1993 = explosion of FDI after Deng's southern tour.

China can ill afford to ignore these external pressures for change. If exports to Hong Kong that are subsequently re-exported to other countries are factored into China's direction of trade statistics, then we see that around 26 per cent of all exports go to the United States, around 17 per cent to the European Union countries, and 21 per cent to Japan. The major export markets in the rest of Asia are South Korea and Taiwan, with exports to all the ASEAN states roughly equal to the figure for South Korea alone. When the domestic Chinese economy is booming, then the growth of exports (and therefore access to export markets) is only one component in the government's job-creation strategy. But when growth slows in the domestic economy, then export-led growth becomes ever more important as a means, perhaps even the only means, of generating the jobs that the Chinese leadership perceives need to be created to maintain social stability.

It is no coincidence that the Chinese leadership was most committed to joining the GATT/World Trade Organization as a means of stabilizing and normalizing access for foreign markets (particularly the US market) in 1989–90, when the Chinese domestic economy was undergoing a period of slow growth. This was a period when China was also fearful that problems in negotiating international free trade might see the creation of closed trading blocs in Europe and North America that would obstruct job creation through export-led growth.

### Balancing Conflicting Considerations

Thus, China's leaders face a contradiction between the economic case for liberalization and further

## Table 5: Alternative Views of Chinese Trade, 1996 (millions of US$)

| Country/Region | Chinese exports to | imports from | Chinese deficit/surplus |
|---|---|---|---|
| US | 26,731 | 16,179 | +10,552 |
|  | 54,409 | 11,978 | +42,431 |
| Canada | 1,616 | 2,559 | –943 |
|  | 3,610 | 2,067 | +1,543 |
| Australia | 1,637 | 3,438 | –1,801 |
|  | 3,227 | 3,029 | +198 |
| France | 1,908 | 2,240 | –332 |
|  | 6,029 | 2,423 | +3,596 |
| Germany | 5,852 | 7,325 | –1,473 |
|  | 11,915 | 7,225 | +4,690 |
| Italy | 1,838 | 3,247 | –1,409 |
|  | 4,035 | 2,868 | +1,167 |
| UK | 3,199 | 1,892 | +1,307 |
|  | 3,443 | 1,155 | +2,288 |
| Japan | 30,888 | 29,190 | +1,698 |
|  | 40,405 | 21,827 | +18,578 |
| Hong Kong | 32,904 | 7,839 | +25,069 |
|  | 73,757 | 61,980 | +11,777 |
| South Korea | 7,527 | 12,484 | –4,957 |
|  | 8,533 | 11,486 | –2,953 |
| Malaysia | 1,374 | 2,246 | –872 |
|  | 1,875 | 1,882 | –7 |
| Singapore | 3,753 | 3,613 | +140 |
|  | 4,441 | 3,394 | +1,047 |
| Thailand | 1,259 | 1,890 | –631 |
|  | 1,953 | 1,868 | +85 |

NOTE: The first horizontal column for each country represents Chinese figures; the second line represents that country's figures.

SOURCES: *Zhongguo Tongji Nianjian (China Statistical Yearbook)* (Beijing: China Statistical Information and Consultancy Service Centre, 1997); *Direction of Trade Statistics Yearbook* (Washington: International Monetary Fund, 1997).

reform, on the one hand, and the political logic of maintaining social stability through guaranteeing jobs, on the other. This contradiction is reflected, and indeed complicated, by the different political constituencies making conflicting demands on the central leadership. In addition to the international pressures to liberalize noted above, there is a strong domestic constituency for reform, particularly within the central leadership itself.

Chief among these leaders is China's Premier, Zhu Rongji, who previously served as vice-premier with special responsibility for reorganizing China's financial system and institutions. Whether inspired by his awareness of the perilous state of the financial drain on state and bank coffers of maintaining support for ailing SOEs or by his previous experiences as local leader in Shanghai, or perhaps simply by his ideological approach, the liberal voice is represented at the very apex of the Chinese political system.

But in many ways, top-level support for liberalization is unrepresentative of the feeling within the party-state as a whole and within the broader Chinese population. Practical and pragmatic considerations are the major cause of resistance, not ideology. For example, representatives of those industrial ministries that fear they have most to lose from international competition are, not surprisingly, reluctant to push ahead with reform. They are supported by leaders from geographic areas where the state-owned enterprises are most heavily concentrated. For many local leaders, it is not so much a question of potential instability if liberalization proceeds, but of dealing with existing problems as announcements of impending redundancies and unpaid welfare payments to retired and laid-off workers have become a common phenomenon in recent years.

On a popular level, there is considerable suspicion of the actions and motives of foreign actors, which at times is manifest in a strongly nationalistic, almost xenophobic, rejection of the international system. This suspicion is fired by memories of China's treatment at the hands of foreign imperial powers in the nineteenth and early twentieth centuries. And there is no shortage of people

prepared to evoke historical precedent as a warning of China's potential future subservience to foreign powers and interests if the path of liberalization and integration is continued. The party must take some responsibility itself for this popular resistance and the re-emergence of Chinese nationalism. While the party has primarily tried to build legitimacy on the back of economic success, it has also played the nationalist card and promoted itself as the defender of China's national interests in the face of a hostile Western world. For example, when Western powers or NGOs criticize China's human rights record the party responds by vilifying the critics for trying to impose unfair and inappropriate Western standards on China.

In essence, the Chinese leadership wants the outside world to perceive China as a trustworthy partner making every possible effort to conform to international standards, and its own people to see the party as the stout defender of China's national interests.[19] Party stalwarts should not be surprised that their own nationalist message is sometimes taken further than originally intended, or that this nationalist stance might make the process of liberalization more difficult to justify to a domestic audience.

## Resistance or Liberalization: The Unfinished Debate

Despite the existence of considerable opposition to reform, the central party leadership appeared to come down on the side of liberalization at the 1997 national party congress. In what some took at the time to be a decisive and final victory for the liberalizers, the central leadership announced that the residual state sector was to be restructured. Where possible, enterprises would be subjected to market disciplines in an attempt to break the chain of debt shackling government finances. If this meant closing those factories that were unable to compete, then so be it. But this move immediately generated new—or exacerbated existing—problems for the leadership. The only way to maintain employment while restructuring the domestic economy was through an even greater reliance on promoting exports as an engine of growth. This, in turn, made Chinese growth more contingent on the vagaries of the international economy.

China had re-entered the global economy at a period of great growth in East Asia, but this was to change. The Chinese were, of course, far from alone in failing to foresee the economic crises that hit many regional states in 1997. Had they been blessed with such foresight, they might not have chosen the same year to try to restructure their own domestic economy and place an even greater reliance on export-led growth. And notwithstanding the fact that China escaped the worst ravages of the regional crises in 1997, the crises have never the less had an important impact on Chinese perceptions of globalization.

China shares many of the structural weaknesses that contributed to the crises in Malaysia, Thailand, and Indonesia. It, too, has massive bank debts caused largely by the provision of non-performing loans to the state sector. It has invested millions of dollars in construction projects that people do not want.[20] It also has an economy characterized by both oversupply and undercapacity. For example, in 1996 half of China's industry operated at below 60 per cent capacity, while the official *Jingji Ribao* (Economics Daily) indicated that stockpiles of goods that cannot be sold exceeded RMB500 billion.[21]

Indeed, one of the reasons China did not suffer the same fate as its regional neighbours was its relative *lack* of liberalization and openness compared to other regional states. With a managed exchange rate underpinned by strict limitations and controls on currency convertibility, the renminbi was safe from attack by international speculators. In addtion, the 'hot money' that foreign investors had ploughed into capital markets meant that the vast majority of—indeed, almost all—foreign capital inflows into China were in long-term investment projects; it had built many more factories than it had purchased share certificates.

But in the aftermath of the crises, China's export-led growth strategy began to encounter new challenges. On one level, the problems in Japan, the region's most developed state, raised the prospect of a shrinking market for Chinese exports. On another level, the collapse of currencies in Southeast Asia meant that China lost it competitive advantage in export prices that it had gained from its own strategic and managed devaluation in 1994. As China's relative lack of liberalization had provided protection from the regional economic crises, the case for abandoning such protection and moving towards a more liberalized economy lost much of its force. It also provided those sceptics within the party the ammunition they needed to call for a rethinking and postponement, if not abandonment, of liberalization reforms.

Indeed, the course of opening up the economy was affected throughout 1998 as the leadership postponed some promised reforms and even reversed earlier policy. For example, the long promised move towards full currency convertibility was postponed until an indeterminate future date. The authorities also restructured the futures markets in response to excessive speculation, reducing the number of markets from 14 to just three and the number of goods traded on the markets from 35 to 12.

It is notable that some of the measures aimed at reversing liberalization policies did not come from the top party leadership but were directly imposed at lower levels. For example, some industrial ministries have reintroduced price controls to guarantee income for vulnerable producers, while many local governments have pressured local banks to loan more money to support exporters. The central government responded to these initiatives by criticizing the ministries for hampering reform and by taking the drastic step of abolishing local branches of the People's Bank of China.[22] It also refused to cover those credits arranged by the collapsed Guangdong International Trade and Investment Corporation that had not been approved and registered by China's central bank. What we see here is a manifestation of a battle between the central leadership and local governments and ministries for control of China's reform process—a battle that has been ongoing for much of the reform period[23] and that is unlikely to be settled decisively for some time to come.

# Conclusion

The Chinese economy has changed dramatically since the late 1970s, but the process of economic reform is far from complete.[24] The transition to communism has been replaced by a transition from socialism, but residual elements of the old socialist system remain in place. In this respect, Chinese perceptions of globalization, and China's place in the global economy, are very much shaped by considerations of domestic economic change and domestic political and social stability. The path of promoting exports appeared to provide the way out of the conundrum. But it also made growth and therefore social stability more reliant on external economic actors and forces than ever before. China needs access to global markets to maintain its export momentum, but it can ill afford to reciprocate by granting equal access to the Chinese market for external actors. And while external pressures to liberalize are unlikely to diminish, internal voices of dissent and caution have grown ever louder in the wake of the Asian financial crises. In short, leaders are thus caught, like many other state élites, between conflicting demands and conflicting requirements, both external and internal.

# Notes

1  For example, Chinese trade with the West doubled between 1970 and 1974, and total trade increased fivefold between 1971 and 1978, reaching US$20.6 billion in 1978.

2  Shenzhen, Shantou, Zhuhai, and Xiamen. Hainan Island later became the fifth SEZ.

3  It is worth noting that after two decades of near double-digit growth rates, Chinese per capita GNP in 1997 was still less than that of Russia.

4  See World Bank, *China 2020* (Washington, 1997).

5  Unemployment drops during the harvest season.

6  Y.Y. Kueh, 'China and the Prospects for Economic Integration within APEC', in J. Chai, Y.Y. Kueh, and C. Tisdell, eds, *China and the Asia Pacific Economy* (Commack, NY: Nova Science 1997), 40.

7  Others emerged outside the official structure.

8  The situation was also complicated by the existence of foreign exchange certificates. When foreigners in China changed currency, they were given FECs rather than normal Chinese renminbi. As these FECs could be used to purchase imported goods not available using renminbi, they acted as quasi-foreign currency and a wide-scale black market in RMB-FEC transfers emerged.

9  Other mechanisms deployed to promote exports include loans through the creation of specialist banks and a number of tax exemptions and other incentives for exporters.

10  J. Harding, 'Jitters in Beijing', *Financial Times*, 10 Nov. 1997, 3.

11  State Statistical Bureau via *China News Digest*, 15 Dec. 1996.

12  It was Hu Yaobang's death from natural causes during a heated meeting of CCP leaders debating the future of economic reform that sparked the 1989 demonstrations.

13  Not least, because many of those leaders have died.

14  The ideas here have much in common with Deng Xiaoping's commitment to building a strong economy in the 1960s and not worrying too greatly about the political correctness of economic development strategies. The main difference was that the party was now sanctioning a much greater acceptance of market forces and a greater role in the international economy than was envisaged in the 1960s.

15  The best example here is the way that local governments ignored the central government's deflationary strategy implemented in 1989 and continued to expand their local economies through international collaboration.

16  *China News Digest*, 10 Mar. 1996.

17  *China Business Review*, Mar.-Apr. 1997.

18  Note that Chinese customs officials calculate their data in different ways from the norm in the West. This acts to deflate the size of the trade surplus and, in the case of trade with Germany, turns what the Germans claim is a US$4.6 billion surplus on the Chinese side to a US$1.5 billion

surplus on the German side. See Table 5 for an idea of the scale of the disparity.

19 For a detailed analysis of this issue, see C. Hughes, 'Globalisation and Nationalism: Squaring the Circle in Chinese International Relations Theory', *Millennium* 26, 1 (1997): 103–26.

20 For example, less than half of the offices in the new Pudong development zone in Shanghai had been occupied by the end of 1998.

21 T. Walker, 'Stockpiles disguise China's slowdown: Consumer industry growth leading to inventory build-up in factory warehouses', *Financial Times*, 21 Mar. 1997.

22 The local branches were replaced by nine regional offices under the direct control of the bank's central authorities.

23 See S. Breslin, *China in the 1980s: Centre-Province Relations in a Reforming Socialist State* (New York: St Martins Press, 1996).

24 See N. Lardy, *China's Unfinished Economic Revolution* (Washington: Brookings Institution, 1998).

## Suggested Readings

Gungwu, Wang, and John Wu, eds. *China's Political Economy*. Singapore: Singapore University Press, 1998.

Lardy, N. *China's Unfinished Economic Revolution*. Washington: Brookings Institution, 1998.

MacFarquhar, Roderick, ed. *The Politics of China: The Eras of Mao and Deng*. Cambridge: Cambridge University Press, 1997.

Nathan, Andrew J., Tianjian Shi, and Helena V.S. Ho. *China's Transition*. New York: Columbia University Press, 1998.

Overholt, William. *China: The Next Economic Superpower*. London: Weidenfeld Nicolson, 1998.

Zhang, Yongjin. *China in International Society Since 1949: Alienation and Beyond*. Basingstoke: Macmillan, 1998.

## Web Sites

*China News Digest*: www.cnd.org

China News Service: www.chinanews.com

Chinese newspapers:
www.dds.nl/~kidon/medialink/aspapers.shtml

Institute of Chinese Studies, Heidelberg University: sun.sino.uni-heidelberg.de/igcs

# Contributors

**Bastiaan van Apeldoorn** Research Fellow, Max Planck Institute, Cologne (Germany)

**Andrew Baker** Lecturer, Queen's University, Belfast (UK)

**Mitchell Bernard** Lecturer and Associate Director, Joint Centre for Asia Pacific Studies, Department of Political Science, York University (Canada)

**Mark Beeson** Lecturer, School of Modern Asian Studies, Griffith University (Australia)

**Shaun Breslin** Research Fellow, Centre for the Study of Globalization and Regionalization, University of Warwick (UK)

**Philip G. Cerny** Professor of International Political Economy, University of Leeds (UK)

**Jennifer Clapp** Assistant Professor, Comparative Development Studies and Environmental Studies, Trent University (Canada)

**William D. Coleman** Professor, Department of Political Science, McMaster University (Canada)

**Robert W. Cox** Emeritus Professor, Department of Political Science, York University (Canada)

**Ronald J. Deibert** Assistant Professor, Department of Political Science, University of Toronto (Canada)

**Daniel Drache** Director, Robarts Centre for Canadian Studies, York University (Canada)

**Stephen Gill** Professor, Department of Political Science, York University (Canada)

**Walter Hatch** Lecturer, Jackson School of International Studies, University of Washington (US)

**Eric Helleiner** Associate Professor, Department of Political Science, Trent University (Canada)

**Richard Higgott** Professor of International Political Economy and Director, Centre for the Study of Globalization and Regionalization, University of Warwick (UK)

**Helge Hveem** Professor, Department of Political Science, University of Oslo (Norway)

**Jeanne Kirk Laux** Professor, Department of Political Science, University of Ottawa (Canada)

**Marianne H. Marchand** Senior Lecturer, Department of Political Science and Research Center for International Political Economy, University of Amsterdam (Netherlands)

**Bruce E. Moon** Associate Professor, Department of International Relations, Lehigh University (US)

**Julius E. Nyang'aro** Chair, Department of African and Afro-American Studies, University of North Carolina (US)

**Robert O'Brien** Assistant Professor, Department of Political Science, McMaster University (Canada)

**Louis W. Pauly** Professor, Department of Political Science and Director, Center for International Studies, University of Toronto (Canada)

**Nicola Phillips** Lecturer, Department of Politics and International Studies, University of Warwick (UK)

**Tony Porter** Associate Professor, Department of Political Science, McMaster University (Canada)

**Winfried Ruigrok** Professor, Faculty of Business, University of St Gallen (Switzerland)

**Susan K. Sell** Associate Professor of International Relations, George Washington University (US)

**Timothy M. Shaw** Professor, Department of Political Science and Director, Centre for Foreign Policy Studies, Dalhousie University (Canada)

**Grace D. Skogstad** Professor, Department of Political Science, University of Toronto (Canada)

**Michael Smith** Professor of European Studies, University of Loughborough (UK)

**Jonathan Story** Professor of Political Economy, INSEAD (France)

**Susan Strange** Late Professor, Department of Politics and International Studies, University of Warwick (UK)

**Richard Stubbs** Professor and Chair, Department of Political Science, McMaster University (Canada)

**Geoffrey R.D. Underhill** Chair of International Governance, Department of Political Science, University of Amsterdam (Netherlands)

**Sigurt Vitols** Wissenschaftszentrun Berlin fur Sozialforschung (Germany)

**Michael C. Webb** Associate Professor, Department of Political Science, University of Victoria (Canada)

**Sandra Whitworth** Associate Professor and Research Associate at the Centre for International and Security Studies, Department of Political Science, York University (Canada)

**Gilbert R. Winham** Professor, Department of Political Science, Dalhousie University (Canada)

# Index